Lecture Notes in Computer Science 4206

Commenced Publication in 1973
Founding and Former Series Editors:
Gerhard Goos, Juris Hartmanis, and Jan

Paul Dourish   Adrian Friday (Eds.)

UbiComp 2006: Ubiquitous Computing

8th International Conference, UbiComp 2006
Orange County, CA, USA, September 17-21, 2006
Proceedings

 Springer

Volume Editors

Paul Dourish
University of California, Irvine
Donald Bren School of Information & Computer Sciences
Irvine, CA 92697-3440, USA
E-mail: jpd@ics.uci.edu

Adrian Friday
Computing Department
Lancaster University
InfoLab 2, South Drive, Lancaster LA1 4WA, UK
E-mail: Adrian@comp.lancs.ac.uk

Library of Congress Control Number: 2006932025

CR Subject Classification (1998): C.2, C.3, D.2, D.4, H.4, H.5, K.4

LNCS Sublibrary: SL 3 – Information Systems and Application, incl. Internet/Web
and HCI

ISSN   0302-9743
ISBN-10   3-540-39634-9 Springer Berlin Heidelberg New York
ISBN-13   978-3-540-39634-5 Springer Berlin Heidelberg New York

Springer is a part of Springer Science+Business Media

springer.com

© Springer-Verlag Berlin Heidelberg 2006
Printed in Germany

Typesetting: Camera-ready by author, data conversion by Scientific Publishing Services, Chennai, India
Printed on acid-free paper   SPIN: 11853565   06/3142   5 4 3 2 1 0

Preface

Fifteen years after the publication of Weiser's seminal paper in *Scientific American*, ubiquitous computing is a large, thriving field of academic research and commercial innovation. The proceedings of the 8th International Conference on Ubiquitous Computing reflect the strength, diversity and vigor of the research program that Weiser initiated. We hope that you will find much in the papers contained herein to stimulate new and exciting work as we reach forward toward ubiquitous computing together.

The location of the conference, in Orange County, California, was particularly apposite given recent directions in the field. A Pacific Rim location linked the conference to last year's venue in Tokyo, Japan, and provided an appropriate space to reflect on the different implementations and visions of ubiquitous computing in different parts of the world. Two significant elements of local industry – the software industry and the entertainment industry – reflect concerns heavily represented in recent research in ubiquitous computing, with mobile and ubiquitous gaming, for instance, an obvious link. The unique metropolitan setting of the Los Angeles region provided a useful setting in which to develop research agendas in urban computing. Finally, while there are no papers in the proceedings on surfing-based Ubicomp, the cultural focus on healthy lifestyles in Southern California relates to concerns with aging and health as important application areas for ubiquitous computing technologies and solutions.

This year, the conference received a total of 232 paper submissions. These reflected contributions from 31 countries, drawn almost equally from Europe (38%), the USA (32%), and Asia (26%). From these, the Program Committee selected 30 papers for inclusion in the conference, on the basis of a rigorous double-blind review process. Every paper received at least three independent reviews; most received four, and some more. Reviewers were selected as experts in the field, reflecting a range of specific expertise for the content of each paper as well as a general Ubicomp readership.

Our primary concern in the review process was to form a program that reflects the diversity of research activity in ubiquitous computing. The field gains much of its strength from the breadth of interdisciplinary work that it engenders, encompassing computer science, engineering, social science, humanities, arts, and more. As it reflects a maturing discipline, we are as concerned with studies of real-world practice and the realities of ubiquitous computing today as we are with future directions and the potential for ubiquitous computing tomorrow. We are concerned, too, with critical reflection upon our own intellectual and practical histories and research practices. Accordingly, we sought to form a Program Committee that drew broadly from the larger ubiquitous computing community, and the result, we believe, is a vigorously interdisciplinary program that reflects a wide range of contemporary research and intellectual inquiry.

Like many conferences in computer-related fields, the Ubicomp series has seen its submission rate rise significantly over the last few years, from 117 papers in 2003 to 144 in 2004, 230 in 2005, and 232 this year. This trend marks the increasing interest in ubiquitous computing as a topic, the growing reputation of the Ubicomp conference as a forum, and the growing relevance of ubiquitous computing topics to other areas of research endeavor. On the other hand, it poses its own challenges. In order to remain vibrant and in order to grow, it is important that the conference have space for new ideas and for challenges to received wisdom. The inherently normalizing tendency of peer review creates a tension between innovation and assessment.

Reflecting the record submission rate, this year's roster of 30 accepted papers is also a new record, and we have worked with Conference Chair Cristina Lopes to create space in the conference format for an enlarged program. At the same time, with an acceptance rate of just 13%, Ubicomp remains an extremely competitive venue, making it clear that a commitment to openness and innovation does not come at the expense of quality and rigor in the reviewing process.

Given the large number of submissions and the broad nature of their content, the reviewing process was a challenging one. The members of the Program Committee and the reviewers worked extremely hard under severe time pressure to evaluate papers and deliberate on their merits. The Program Committee members were responsible for finding, assigning, and monitoring reviewers for each paper, as well as for writing reviews themselves and for representing papers at the Program Committee meeting in Irvine in early June. The feedback from reviewers enabled us to make balanced assessments of papers' contributions as well, we hope, as providing useful feedback to authors that will assist in the revision of those papers that could not be included in the program. We are immensely grateful to all who volunteered significant amounts of time and energy to helping us create a strong program for Ubicomp 2006. Conferences of this sort depend entirely on volunteer labor, and we owe a huge debt of thanks to the committee members and reviewers.

Even more, we are grateful to the 639 authors who submitted papers to the conference. Although space restrictions limit the number of papers that can be accepted, this represents a tremendous amount of effort, and the conference depends crucially on the outstanding strength of the submitted work.

Finally, we would like to extend our gratitude to Conference Chair Cristina Lopes and to Local Arrangements Chair Don Patterson for their contributions both to the papers review process and, more generally, to making Ubicomp 2006 an exciting and enjoyable event.

We hope that you find in the program much to inspire and support your own research efforts.

Paul Dourish
Adrian Friday

Conference Organization

Organizers

General Chair and Treasurer
Cristina Videira Lopes   University of California, Irvine, USA

Program Chairs
Paul Dourish   University of California, Irvine, USA
Adrian Friday   Lancaster University, UK

Demonstrations Chairs
Julian Bleecker   University of Southern California / Techkwondo, USA
Khai Truong   University of Toronto, Canada

Posters Chairs
Itiro Shiio   Tamagawa University, Japan
Beverly Harrison   Intel Research, USA

Videos Chairs
Marc Langheinrich   ETH Zurich, Switzerland
Louise Barkhuus   University of Glasgow, UK

Doctoral Colloquium Chairs
Beki Grinter   Georgia Institute of Technology, USA
Gregory Abowd   Georgia Institute of Technology, USA

Workshops Chairs
John Krumm   Microsoft Research, USA
Ken Anderson   Intel Research, USA

Student Volunteers Chairs
Amir Haghighat   University of California, Irvine, USA
Gillian Hayes   Georgia Institute of Technology, USA

Publications Chair
Florian Michahelles   ETH Zurich, Switzerland

Publicity Chairs
Timothy Sohn   University of California, San Diego, USA
Matthias Kranz   University of Munich, Germany
Takashi Matsumoto   Keio University, Japan

Webmaster
Amanda Williams   University of California, Irvine, USA

Local Arrangements
Don Patterson   University of California, Irvine, USA

Sponsors

Silver Sponsor: Intel
Bronze Sponsors: Microsoft
                               Google
                               IBM
                               Nokia
                               Samsung

Supporting Societies

UbiComp 2006 enjoys in-cooperation status with the following special interest groups of the Association for Computing Machinery (ACM):
SIGBED (Embedded Systems)
SIGCHI (Computer-Human Interaction)
SIGSOFT (Software Engineering)
SIGMOBILE (Mobile Computing)

Program Committee

Elizabeth Belding-Royer	University of California, Santa Barbara, USA
Genevieve Bell	Intel, USA
A.J. Brush	Microsoft Research, USA
Vinny Cahill	Trinity College Dublin, Ireland
Matthew Chalmers	University of Glasgow, UK
Sunny Consolvo	Intel Research Seattle, USA
Joelle Coutaz	IMAG, France
Gregory Abowd	Georgia Tech, USA
Boriana Koleva	Nottingham University, UK
John Krumm	Microsoft Research, USA
Anthony LaMarca	Intel Research Seattle, USA
Eyal de Lara	University of Toronto, Canada
Rainer Malaka	European Media Laboratory, Ireland
Henk Muller	University of Bristol, UK
Moira Norrie	ETH Zurich, Switzerland
Naohito Okude	Keio University, Japan
Jun Rekimoto	Sony Computer Science Laboratory, Japan
Yvonne Rogers	Indiana University, USA
Albrecht Schmidt	University of Munich (LMU), Germany
Mirjana Spasojevic	Yahoo! Research Berkeley, USA
Beatriz da Costa	University of California, Irvine, USA
Khai Truong	University of Toronto, Canada

Reviewers

Karl Aberer	EPFL, Switzerland
Mark Ackerman	University of Michigan, USA
Luis von Ahn	Carnegie Mellon University, USA
Fahd Albinali	University of Arizona, USA
Brian Amento	AT&T, USA
Ken Anderson	Intel Research, USA
Ian Anderson	University of Bristol, UK
Paul Aoki	Intel Research, USA
Trevor Armstrong	University of Toronto, Canada
Yuji Ayatsuka	Sony Computer Science Laboratories, Japan
Chris Baber	University of Birmingham, UK
Maribeth Back	Fuji Xerox Palo Alto Laboratory, USA
Jean Bacon	University of Cambridge, UK
Ravin Balakrishnan	University of Toronto, Canada
Rajesh Balan	Carnegie Mellon University, USA
Rafael Ballagas	RWTH Aachen University, Germany
Luciano Baresi	Politecnico di Milano, Italy
Louise Barkhuus	University of Glasgow, UK
John Barton	IBM Research, USA
Agathe Battestini	Nokia Research Center, Finland
Martin Bauer	NEC Europe Ltd., Germany
Christian Becker	Universität Stuttgart, Germany
Richard Beckwith	Intel Research, USA
Ashweeni Beeharee	University College London, UK
Michael Beigl	University of Karlsruhe, Germany
Marek Bell	University of Glasgow, UK
Steve Benford	University of Nottingham, UK
Abraham Bernstein	University of Zurich, Switzerland
Jan Beutel	ETH Zurich, Switzerland
Nina Bhatti	HP Laboratories, USA
Nilton Bila	University of Toronto, Canada
Alan Blackwell	University of Cambridge, UK
Julian Bleecker	University of Southern California, USA
Sara Bly	Sara Bly Consulting, USA
Marc Bohlen	University at Buffalo, USA
Gaetano Borriello	University of Washington, USA
Andrew Boucher	Goldsmiths University of London, UK
Michael Boyle	Smart Technologies, Canada
Patrick Brezillon	Université Pierre et Marie Curie, France
Harry Brignull	Amber Light, UK
Barry Brown	University of Glasgow, UK
Ciarán Bryce	University of Geneva, Switzerland
Tilo Burghardt	University of Bristol, UK
Gary Burnett	University of Nottingham, UK
Andreas Butz	University of Munich, Germany

Masaaki Fukumoto	NTT DoCoMo Multimedia Laboratories, Japan
Krzysztof Gajos	University of Washington, USA
Areti Galani	University of Newcastle, UK
Eric Garcia	University of Washington, USA
Anurag Garg	University of Trento, Italy
William Gaver	Goldsmiths College, UK
Erik Geelhoed	HP Labs, UK
Hans Gellersen	Lancaster University, UK
Andreas Girgensohn	FX Palo Alto Laboratory, USA
Patrick Goddi	HP Labs, USA
Elizabeth Goodman	Intel Corporation, USA
Paul Grace	Lancaster University, UK
Tom Gross	Bauhaus-University Weimar, Germany
Michael Grossniklaus	ETH Zurich, Switzerland
Dennis Groth	Indiana University, USA
Dirk Haehnel	Intel Research Seattle, USA
Joseph Hall	University of California Berkeley, USA
Paul David Hankes Drielsma	ETH Zurich, Switzerland
Vicki Hanson	IBM, USA
Robert Harle	University of Cambridge, UK
Eric Harris	University of Sussex, UK
Beverly Harrison	Intel Research Seattle, USA
William Harrison	Trinity College Dublin, Ireland
Michael Harrison	University of Newcastle upon Tyne, UK
Lonnie Harvel	Georgia Gwinnett College, USA
Gillian Hayes	Georgia Institute of Technology, USA
Mike Hazas	Lancaster University, UK
Cina Hazegh	University of California, Irvine, USA
William Hazlewood	Indiana University, USA
Jong Hee Kang	University of Washington, USA
Urs Hengartner	University of Waterloo, Canada
Jeffrey Hightower	Intel Research Seattle, USA
Tad Hirsch	Massachusetts Institute of Technology, USA
Larissa Hjorth	RMIT, Australia
Paul Holleis	University of Munich, Germany
Jason Hong	Carnegie Mellon University, USA
Yih-Chun Hu	University of Illinois at Urbana-Champaign, USA
Elaine Huang	Georgia Institute of Technology, USA
Richard Hull	Hewlett-Packard Laboratories, UK
Giovanni Iachello	Georgia Institute of Technology, USA
Liviu Iftode	Rutgers University, USA
Takeo Igarashi	University of Tokyo/JST PRESTO, Japan
Masahiko Inakage	Keio University, Japan
Stephen Intille	Massachusetts Institute of Technology, USA
Jun Ito	Sony, Japan
Shahram Izadi	Microsoft Research, UK
Amit Jardosh	University of California, Santa Barbara, USA

Jay Lundell	Intel Corporation, USA
Evan Magill	University of Stirling, UK
Scott Mainwaring	Intel Research, USA
Lena Mamykina	Siemens Corporate Research and Georgia Institute of Technology, USA
Jennifer Mankoff	Carnegie Mellon University, USA
Panos Markopoulos	Eindhoven University of Technology, The Netherlands
Natalia Marmasse	IBM Research, Israel
Herve Martin	Université Joseph Fourier, France
Kenji Mase	Nagoya University, Japan
Maristella Matera	Politecnico di Milano, Italy
Friedemann Mattern	ETH Zurich, Switzerland
Walterio Mayol-Cuevas	University of Bristol, UK
Rene Mayrhofer	Lancaster University, UK
Michael McCarthy	University of Bristol, UK
David McDonald	University of Washington, USA
René Meier	Trinity College Dublin, Ireland
Brian Meyers	Microsoft Research, USA
Danius Michaelides	University of Southampton, UK
Masateru Minami	Shibaura Institute of Technology, Japan
April Mitchell	Hewlett-Packard, USA
Kimaya Mittal	University of California Santa Barbara, USA
Jun Miyazaki	Fuji Xerox, Japan
Michael Mock	Fraunhofer Institute for Autonomous Intelligent Systems, Germany
Iqbal Mohomed	University of Toronto, Canada
Margaret Morris	Intel Corporation, USA
Mor Naaman	Yahoo! Research Berkeley, USA
Kris Nagel	Georgia Institute of Technology, USA
Yasuto Nakanishi	Keio University, Japan
Junya Nakata	Japan Advanced Institute of Science and Technology, Japan
Andronikos Nedos	Trinity College Dublin, Ireland
Steve Neely	UCD Dublin, Ireland
Carman Neustaedter	University of Calgary, Canada
Mark W. Newman	Palo Alto Research Center (PARC), USA
Jeff Nichols	Carnegie Mellon, USA
Robert Nideffer	University of California, Irvine, USA
Chris Nippert-Eng	IIT, USA
Yoshifumi Nishida	Sony Computer Science Laboratories, Japan
Toyoaki Nishida	Kyoto University, Japan
Paddy Nixon	University College Dublin, Ireland
Kenton O'Hara	HP Laboratories, UK
Yoosoo Oh	GIST, Korea
Gérald Oster	ETH Zurich, Switzerland
Veljo Otsason	University of Tartu, Estonia

Raju Pandey	University of California, Davis, USA
Joseph Paradiso	Massachusetts Institute of Technology, USA
Shwetak Patel	Georgia Institute of Technology, USA
Sameer Patil	University of California, Irvine, USA
Donald Patterson	University of California, Irvine, USA
Simon Penny	University of California, Irvine, USA
Trevor Pering	Intel Research, USA
Matthai Philipose	Intel Research Seattle, USA
Claudio Pinhanez	IBM T.J. Watson Research Center, USA
Kevin Ponto	University of California, Irvine, USA
Robert Porzel	University of Bremen, Germany
Ivan Poupyrev	Sony CSL, Japan
Aaron Quigley	University College Dublin, Ireland
Rakhi Rajani	Central Saint Martins College of Art and Design, UK
Krishna Ramachandran	University of California, Santa Barbara, USA
Umakishore Ramachandran	Georgia Institute of Technology, USA
Cliff Randell	University of Bristol, UK
Pierre-Guillaume Raverdy	INRIA, France
Madhu Reddy	Penn State University, USA
Stuart Reeves	University of Nottingham, UK
Josephine Reid	HP Labs, UK
Patrick Reignier	University Joseph Fourier/INRIA, France
Derek Reilly	Dalhousie University, Canada
Heather Richter	University of North Carolina at Charlotte, USA
Thomas Rist	FH Augsburg, Germany
Toni Robertson	University of Technology Sydney, Australia
Tom Rodden	University of Nottingham, UK
Jennifer Rode	University of California, Irvine, USA
Manuel Roman	NTT DoCoMo Labs USA, USA
Troy Ronda	University of Toronto, Canada
Åsa Rudström	Swedish Institute of Computer Science, Sweden
Enrico Rukzio	University of Munich, Germany
Lee Sanggoog	SAIT, Korea
Bernt Schiele	TU Darmstadt, Germany
Bill Schilit	Intel Research, USA
Chris Schmandt	Massachusetts Institute of Technolgy, USA
Holger Schnädelbach	University of Nottingham, UK
Odilo Schoch	Architect, Switzerland
Jean Scholtz	NIST, USA
Heiko Schuldt	University of Basel, Switzerland
Jamie Schulte	Stanford University, USA
Jamieson Schulte	Stanford University, USA
Gerrhard Schwabe	University of Zurich, Switzerland
James Scott	Intel Research Cambridge, UK
Jean-Marc Seigneur	University of Geneva, Switzerland
Abigail Sellen	Microsoft Research, UK

Shondip Sen	CSIRO, Australia
Aline Senart	Trinity College Dublin, Ireland
Phoebe Sengers	Cornell University, USA
Steven Shafer	Microsoft Research, USA
Irfan Sheriff	UC Santa Barbara, USA
John Sherry	Intel Corporation, USA
Beat Signer	ETH Zurich, Switzerland
Itiro Siio	Ochanomizu University, Japan
Brooke Singer	SUNY Purchase, USA
Morris Sloman	Imperial College London, UK
Alan Smeaton	Dublin City University, Ireland
Ian Smith	Intel Research Seattle, USA
Joshua Smith	Intel Research Seattle, USA
Timothy Sohn	University of California, San Diego, USA
Xiang Song	Georgia Institute of Technology, USA
João Pedro Sousa	Carnegie Mellon University, USA
Flavia Sparacino	Sensing Places/MIT, USA
Alexandre de Spindler	ETH Zurich, Switzerland
Cormac Sreenan	University College Cork, Ireland
Danäe Stanton Fraser	University of Bath, UK
Thad Starner	Georgia Institute of Technology, USA
John Stasko	Georgia Institute of Technology, USA
Anthony Steed	University College London, UK
Kilian Stoffel	University of Neuchatel, Switzerland
Erik Stolterman	Indiana University, USA
Thomas Strang	DLR, Germany
Mark Stringer	University of Sussex, UK
Jing Su	University of Toronto, Canada
Yasuyuki Sumi	Kyoto University, Japan
Jay Summet	Georgia Institute of Technology, USA
Yan Sun	University of Rhode Island, USA
Martin Svensson	Swedish Institute of Computer Science, Sweden
Shigeru Tajima	Sony CSL, Japan
Kaz Takashio	Keio University, Japan
Desney Tan	Microsoft Research, USA
Hiroya Tanaka	Keio University, Japan
Karen Tang	Carnegie Mellon University, USA
Alex Taylor	Microsoft Research Cambridge, UK
Lucia Terrenghi	Microsoft Research Cambridge, UK
Michael Terry	University of Waterloo, Canada
Sotirios Terzis	University of Strathclyde, UK
Hiroaki Tobita	Sony CSL, Japan
Hideyuki Tokuda	Keio University, Japan
Niraj Tolia	Carnegie Mellon University, USA
Kentaro Toyama	Microsoft Research, India
Quan Tran	Georgia Institute of Technology, USA
Mike Twidale	University of Illinois, USA

Table of Contents

A Quantitative Method for Revealing and Comparing
Places in the Home.. 1
    Ryan Aipperspach, Tye Rattenbury, Allison Woodruff, John Canny

Principles of Smart Home Control 19
    Scott Davidoff, Min Kyung Lee, Charles Yiu, John Zimmerman,
    Anind K. Dey

Historical Analysis: Using the Past to Design the Future 35
    Susan Wyche, Phoebe Sengers, Rebecca E. Grinter

Extending Authoring Tools for Location-Aware Applications with
an Infrastructure Visualization Layer 52
    Leif Oppermann, Gregor Broll, Mauricio Capra, Steve Benford

Automated Generation of Basic Custom Sensor-Based Embedded
Computing Systems Guided by End-User Optimization Criteria......... 69
    Susan Lysecky, Frank Vahid

An Experimental Comparison of Physical Mobile Interaction
Techniques: Touching, Pointing and Scanning....................... 87
    Enrico Rukzio, Karin Leichtenstern, Vic Callaghan, Paul Holleis,
    Albrecht Schmidt, Jeannette Chin

An Exploratory Study of How Older Women Use Mobile Phones 105
    Sri Kurniawan

Farther Than You May Think: An Empirical Investigation of the
Proximity of Users to Their Mobile Phones......................... 123
    Shwetak N. Patel, Julie A. Kientz, Gillian R. Hayes, Sooraj Bhat,
    Gregory D. Abowd

No More SMS from Jesus: Ubicomp, Religion and Techno-spiritual
Practices 141
    Genevieve Bell

Scribe4Me: Evaluating a Mobile Sound Transcription
Tool for the Deaf 159
    Tara Matthews, Scott Carter, Carol Pai, Janette Fong,
    Jennifer Mankoff

SenseCam: A Retrospective Memory Aid.......................... 177
Steve Hodges, Lyndsay Williams, Emma Berry, Shahram Izadi,
James Srinivasan, Alex Butler, Gavin Smyth, Narinder Kapur,
Ken Wood

Development of a Privacy Addendum for Open Source Licenses: Value
Sensitive Design in Industry 194
Batya Friedman, Ian Smith, Peter H. Kahn Jr., Sunny Consolvo,
Jaina Selawski

Mobility Detection Using Everyday GSM Traces 212
Timothy Sohn, Alex Varshavsky, Anthony LaMarca, Mike Y. Chen,
Tanzeem Choudhury, Ian Smith, Sunny Consolvo, Jeffrey Hightower,
William G. Griswold, Eyal de Lara

Practical Metropolitan-Scale Positioning for GSM Phones 225
Mike Y. Chen, Timothy Sohn, Dmitri Chmelev, Dirk Haehnel,
Jeffrey Hightower, Jeff Hughes, Anthony LaMarca, Fred Potter,
Ian Smith, Alex Varshavsky

Predestination: Inferring Destinations from Partial Trajectories 243
John Krumm, Eric Horvitz

Fish'n'Steps: Encouraging Physical Activity with an Interactive
Computer Game 261
James J. Lin, Lena Mamykina, Silvia Lindtner, Gregory Delajoux,
Henry B. Strub

Hitchers: Designing for Cellular Positioning 279
Adam Drozd, Steve Benford, Nick Tandavanitj, Michael Wright,
Alan Chamberlain

Embedding Behavior Modification Strategies into a Consumer
Electronic Device: A Case Study 297
Jason Nawyn, Stephen S. Intille, Kent Larson

Instrumenting the City: Developing Methods for Observing and
Understanding the Digital Cityscape 315
Eamonn O'Neill, Vassilis Kostakos, Tim Kindberg,
Ava Fatah gen. Schiek, Alan Penn, Danaë Stanton Fraser,
Tim Jones

Voting with Your Feet: An Investigative Study of the Relationship
Between Place Visit Behavior and Preference 333
Jon Froehlich, Mike Y. Chen, Ian E. Smith, Fred Potter

Lo-Fi Matchmaking: A Study of Social Pairing for Backpackers 351
  Jeff Axup, Stephen Viller, Ian MacColl, Roslyn Cooper

Experiences from Real-World Deployment of Context-Aware
Technologies in a Hospital Environment 369
  Jakob E. Bardram, Thomas R. Hansen, Martin Mogensen,
  Mads Soegaard

Doing Community: Co-construction of Meaning and Use with
Interactive Information Kiosks 387
  Tom Hope, Masahiro Hamasaki, Yutaka Matsuo,
  Yoshiyuki Nakamura, Noriyuki Fujimura, Takuichi Nishimura

Moving on from Weiser's Vision of Calm Computing: Engaging
UbiComp Experiences 404
  Yvonne Rogers

Ferret: RFID Localization for Pervasive Multimedia 422
  Xiaotao Liu, Mark D. Corner, Prashant Shenoy

PowerLine Positioning: A Practical Sub-Room-Level Indoor Location
System for Domestic Use 441
  Shwetak N. Patel, Khai N. Truong, Gregory D. Abowd

UbiREAL: Realistic Smartspace Simulator for Systematic Testing 459
  Hiroshi Nishikawa, Shinya Yamamoto, Morihiko Tamai,
  Kouji Nishigaki, Tomoya Kitani, Naoki Shibata, Keiichi Yasumoto,
  Minoru Ito

Instant Matchmaking: Simple and Secure Integrated Ubiquitous
Computing Environments 477
  D.K. Smetters, Dirk Balfanz, Glenn Durfee, Trevor F. Smith,
  Kyung-Hee Lee

A Wirelessly-Powered Platform for Sensing and Computation 495
  Joshua R. Smith, Alanson P. Sample, Pauline S. Powledge,
  Sumit Roy, Alexander Mamishev

Automated Application-Specific Tuning of Parameterized Sensor-Based
Embedded System Building Blocks 507
  Susan Lysecky, Frank Vahid

Author Index 525

A Quantitative Method for Revealing and Comparing Places in the Home

Ryan Aipperspach[1,2], Tye Rattenbury[1], Allison Woodruff[2], and John Canny[1]

[1] Berkeley Institute of Design, Computer Science Division,
University of California, Berkeley, USA
{ryanaip, rattenbt, jfc}@cs.berkeley.edu
[2] Intel Research Berkeley, USA
woodruff@acm.org

Abstract. Increasing availability of sensor-based location traces for individuals, combined with the goal of better understanding user context, has resulted in a recent emphasis on algorithms for automatically extracting users' significant places from location data. Place-finding can be characterized by two sub-problems, (1) finding significant locations, and (2) assigning semantic labels to those locations (the problem of "moving from location to place") [8]. Existing algorithms focus on the first sub-problem and on finding city-level locations. We use a principled approach in adapting Gaussian Mixture Models (GMMs) to provide a first solution for finding significant places within the home, based on the first set of long-term, precise location data collected from several homes. We also present a novel metric for quantifying the similarity between places, which has the potential to assign semantic labels to places by comparing them to a library of known places. We discuss several implications of these new techniques for the design of Ubicomp systems.

1 Introduction

The importance of understanding users' contexts is widely accepted in the Ubicomp community. Understanding context can help systems behave appropriately in a variety of situations and integrate more seamlessly into everyday life. Recently, the increased availability of position sensing technologies has resulted in a focus on finding significant places based on traces of a user's position [3,8,9,10,12,13,23]. Places are stable contexts within which social practices are situated [7], playing a significant role in broader definitions of context.

Hightower et al. [8] list two problems in developing algorithms for finding significant places for individual users: (1) finding significant locations and (2) assigning semantics or names to those significant locations ("moving from location to place"). The primary contributions of this work are a solution to the first problem in the domain of the home and the introduction of a novel method for addressing the second problem, based on a measure for comparing the similarity between places. Most existing algorithms for finding significant locations target building-sized locations within city-scale areas, since most available location data sets exist at a building-scale resolution. We have collected the first

P. Dourish and A. Friday (Eds.): Ubicomp 2006, LNCS 4206, pp. 1–18, 2006.

long-term, high-precision home location traces [2], enabling us to begin developing place-finding algorithms for the home. The distribution of places within the home differs markedly from the distribution at city-scale, motivating the development of new techniques for finding places in the home. To validate our algorithm choice, we discuss the places it finds in several homes.

Most existing place-finding algorithms focus on the problem of finding significant locations rather than on assigning semantic labels to the places they find. Instead, they rely on *geocoding* repositories (e.g. Microsoft MapPoint) or on hand-labeling by people [26] to apply labels. Hightower et al. [8] also note that geocoded information, like raw coordinates, "does not correspond to someone's mental model of their personal routine nor to the terminology they use when discussing the places they go." We provide a step toward solving this problem.

Concretely, we describe a method for measuring the similarity between different places that should enable automatic labeling of new places. By measuring the similarity between places, it is possible to find recurring structures that reveal the shared types of place within a particular culture (e.g., bedrooms in one home should be similar to bedrooms in other homes within the same culture). While it is difficult to learn the specific details of a place, we claim that the shared attributes of places can be automatically detected. Using these attributes, new places can be compared to a library of known places resulting in an (indirect) understanding of the new place. The limited availability of location traces from homes makes it difficult to build and test a library of similar places. In this work, we make use of the largest high-precision home location data set currently available to highlight the potential of such techniques. Our similarity metric is based on emergent properties of places resulting from people's patterns of behavior. Consequently, we claim that it satisfies some of the notions of context constructed through actions, rather than imposed via a fixed structure.

In section 2 we describe existing definitions of place and argue for the importance of measuring the similarity between different places. In section 3 we discuss related work. Section 4 describes our algorithm and the results of applying it to a set of location data collected in several homes. Finally, section 5 describes potential design implications and section 6 concludes and provides directions for future work.

2 A Definition of Place

2.1 Existing Definitions of Place

The definition of place that we use in this paper is most aligned with the work of Harrison and Dourish [7]. They observe that designers of interactive systems and virtual environments often build notions of "space" – the three dimensional environment in which objects interact and events occur – into their systems with the goal of facilitating interaction by framing users' behavior in the same way that it is framed in the physical world (i.e., by relying on spatial metaphors). However, they argue that behavior in the physical world is framed not only by space but also by the actions normally performed in that space.

Harrison and Dourish define place as "a space which is *invested with under-standings* of behavioral appropriateness, cultural expectations, and so forth," saying that "we are *located* in space, but we *act* in place". That is, a place is useful for framing behavior because a user can make use of culturally embedded knowledge to determine what activities are appropriate for particular places. Whether walking into a church, a post office, a living room, or a kitchen, people use cues based both on both the architecture and configuration of the space and on the observable behaviors of others to understand what kind of place they are entering and how they should act. According to this definition, a place's meaning is jointly constructed by the physical structure of a location and the activities that regularly occur there.

This definition of place is a useful definition for designers of Ubicomp systems. Many recognize the need for determining users' context to better support their activities through appropriate and relevant actions [4]. They look for cues that determine appropriate behavior in particular situations, which is exactly what Harrison and Dourish suggest that "place" encodes. Interestingly, Harrison and Dourish's definition of place is similar to definitions in other fields, such as *place settings* in environmental society [27]. However, a discussion of these similarities is beyond the scope of this paper.

2.2   Working Definition of Place

From the existing definitions of place, we highlight six attributes of place along two different dimensions:

- *Attributes relating to time-invariant physical configuration*
  - **Position**, a bounded region in three-dimensional, physical space
  - **Physical structure**, the architectural components of a space
  - **Object co-presence**, the consistently present artifacts in a space (e.g. furniture)
- *Attributes relating to the historical behavior within a place*
  - **Time**, the distribution of time spent in a particular place
  - **Stable patterns of behavior**, the set of activities that occur in a place
  - **Person co-presence**, the patterns of presence of other people within a place

Drawing on activity theory [11], we argue that common patterns of interaction between people, objects, and locations (as captured in the six attributes above) embody the set of common behaviors characteristic to each place as suggested by Harrison and Dourish. The categorization of these attributes into two dimensions is a matter of conceptual convenience. In general, the physical configuration attributes and the historical behavior attributes are deeply intertwined. (Notions like "affordance" attempt to capture this connection.) In fact, their interconnection can be considered both a consequence of and a generator of social culture [7]. Practically, however, the distinction between physical and behavioral attributes prescribes a basis for the algorithms we present later.

Shared Notions of Place. Because places are intertwined with culture, there exist common notions of place within specific cultures (e.g., "kitchen", "meeting room", "bedroom"). This fact is captured in the following argument: because strangers can enter spaces and, at a glance, assess both the names of the places and the activities likely to occur there, there must exist a shared notion of types of places and the appropriate actions for each of those types. (Of course, strangers may miss more idiosyncratic activities, e.g. eating cereal for breakfast while standing in the kitchen).

As a result of these shared cultural definitions of place, it should be possible to measure the similarity between particular "instantiations" of those places in individual homes – e.g., bedrooms should appear similar to other bedrooms, and kitchens should appear similar to other kitchens. In this work, we present an initial metric for comparing places in the home. We utilize the fact that different types of places tend to support different typical activities, basing our comparison metric on the patterns of use in the spaces we compare. The correlation between types of place and typical activity patterns is supported by previous work. For example, in a study of 100 Brazilian homes, Monteiro [15] found a correlation between the types of activities carried out in different places and the relative distance of each place from the entrance of the home. In section 5 we discuss several implications of a system for measuring shared notions of place.

3   Previous Work

Recently, a number of authors within the ubiquitous computing community have considered the problem of finding significant locations based on a person's location history. We describe some of the existing methods below. Most algorithms focus on finding significant locations at the city-scale. In agreement with previous studies of place within the home [18,28], we argue that places in the home are significantly different from larger-scale places. Consequently, different methods are required for finding places in the home.

3.1   Existing Place-Finding Algorithms

Existing place-finding algorithms can be divided into two classes, *geometry-based* and *fingerprint-based* [8]. Examples of geometry-based algorithms include those by Marmasse et al. [13], Ashbrook and Starner [3], Liao et al. [12], and Kang et al. [9]. Each of these algorithms takes a history of locations from a single person (e.g. from GPS readers) and finds locations where the person spends significant periods of time. The algorithms vary based on the type of sensor data they use and on the specific clustering algorithm they use. For example, Ashbrook and Starner search GPS data for locations where position changed slowly or readings dropped out completely, indicating times when the user was not moving or was inside a building. They apply a hierarchical variant of k-means to cluster the candidate locations. Kang et al. use sensor-agnostic location traces to determine when users remained within a (specified radius) "space-sized" region for at least some minimum amount of time to find significant locations.

Examples of fingerprint-based algorithms include those by Trevisani and Vitaletti [23], Laasonen et al. [10], and Hightower et al. [8]. These algorithms calculate the "fingerprint" of a person's location (e.g., a vector of currently visible cell towers and wireless access points), find recurring fingerprints where the person spends a significant amount of time, and return a list of places based on significant fingerprints. These algorithms make the assumption that there exists a stable mapping between the fingerprints they find and the three-dimensional physical space that humans inhabit.

Existing place-finding algorithms find significant locations for different individuals, but they do not attempt to label types of places or to compare places across different people. For example, existing algorithms do not address the problem of automatically labeling places as belonging to the class "work" or "home" or of determining that two people's "work" places are similar unless those places are in the same physical location. Without knowledge of these distinctions, it is more appropriate to treat these methods as finding significant locations, not places.

3.2   Place in the Home

There has been little work done in determining significant places in the home based on location histories, primarily because high-resolution (sub-meter accuracy) location traces for residents within the home have not been available. However, several observational studies have explored the concept of place in the home. Oswald et al. [18] found that elders tend to spend much of their time in *favored places*. These centralized locations, which often provide easy access to essential (e.g., medication and food) and important objects (e.g., pictures and diaries) are crucial in allowing elders to remain autonomous as moving about their homes becomes more difficult. Based on qualitative studies in a range of homes, we found similar use of favored places within a more general population (see [28]). Like Oswald, we found that study participants spent the majority of their time in favored places. However, we found that participants also visited a range of *kinetic places*, or places used for shorter duration activities often involving physical manipulations, such as the bathroom, a mirror for doing one's hair in the morning, or a kitchen counter used to make sandwiches for lunch.

The work cited above suggests that places in the home exist at a variety of levels, ranging from small places like a single mirror to entire rooms. In this work, we are interested in finding places that are large enough to capture generic usage patterns across people and homes (e.g. cooking, sleeping), yet small enough to reveal differences in these patterns. Places satisfying these constraints should be comparable between people and be semantically meaningful. Often, different sized places exist even at the same semantic level (e.g., living rooms and bathrooms). The range of place sizes makes it difficult for existing algorithms that assume places at a single level have similar sizes (e.g. [9,13]).

Additionally, places in the home are much closer together in relation to their size than are places at the building scale (consider the distance between work and home, compared to the difference between two rooms in a home). The small size and close proximity of places in the home means that the separation between places is close to the scale of errors in location sensor readings, even when using very accurate sensors. (The size of places and typical error bounds for our sensor data are both on the order of meters.) As a result, a more probabilistic view of places is necessary than is taken in many existing place-finding algorithms. For example, we applied Kang et al.'s place-finding algorithm to the data for each participant (with a place-size of 2 meters and a time window of 2 minutes). Because place sizes and noise in the home are at similar scales, readings taken while a user remains in a single place frequently fall outside the bounds of that place. Of data while users where home and awake, the Kang algorithm labeled an average of 45% of points as "moving between places" and 55% as belonging to a specific place. However, qualitative data analysis and interviews based on our data found that most people spend the majority of their time in a small number of favored places and little time moving around [2], suggesting this large portion of unlabeled data is an undesired artifact of the algorithm.

Consequently, we developed a new geometry-based algorithm for finding significant places in the home. This algorithm must work for environments where the ratio of place size to inter-place distance is high. Therefore, the algorithm must be capable of finding places without relying on the detection, either explicitly or implicitly, of movement paths between places.

4   Finding Place in the Home

As discussed earlier, we treat place as an emergent quality of the physical structure of a location and of the routine activities that people carry out there. Instead of directly processing the rich details intrinsic to both of these dimensions, we use simple proxies. For physical structure we use the set of locations that people have occupied. For action and activity we use the first-order temporal patterns in each person's position data. Both proxies are common input features for existing place-finding algorithms (e.g. [8,9]), and the tunable parameters used by our algorithm are similar to those used by other algorithms. However, while these algorithms are reliable and accurate in their intended domains (city-scale areas), they do not work at the scale of places within a home (see section 3.2).

Like other place-finding algorithms, our main algorithm described in section 4.2 identifies significant locations rather than places. However, the similarity metric described in section 4.3 considers the activity patterns that differentiate places from locations, helping to address the problem of moving from location to place. While the location data in our data set does not capture the full range of attributes of place described in section 2.2, the spatial and temporal patterns provide a good starting place for such analysis. As richer data sets become available, the algorithm can be expanded to include additional attributes of place.

4.1   Data Set

There are currently few data sets providing accurate in-home location information. Typical examples are Rowan and Mynatt [20], who collected one year of data from a single woman using in-floor pressure sensors, providing meter-level accurate location traces, and Tapia et al. [22], who collected 2 weeks of data from 2 single-person apartments using ~80 binary state-change sensors with known locations, providing sub-room level accuracy.

In this study, we make use of highly-precise (sub-meter) sensor data which we collected from 3 homes using ultra wideband (UWB) sensors from Ubisense, Ltd. [25]. To our knowledge, this is the first long-term, high-precision set of location data collected in the home. The data set includes location traces for each person (7 total) in the study, over a time period ranging from three weeks to several months in each home. Each data point is a 4-tuple containing: (1) x position, (2) y position, (3) time, and (4) the duration of time that the measurement covers. For more information about the data collection process, see [2]. The participants from each home are described below:

1. *Home 1: Brad and Jacqueline.* A one-bedroom apartment occupied by Brad and Jacqueline, two graduate students from Australia.
2. *Home 2: Jack and Margaret.* A one-bedroom apartment occupied by Jack and Margaret, a recently married couple from England.
3. *Home 3: Sierra, Gaby, and Cathy.* A three-bedroom, single story home occupied by Sierra and Gaby, a female couple, and their roommate, Cathy.

4.2   An Algorithm for Detecting Significant Locations in the Home

Before describing the details of our algorithm, we introduce the following terminology as a matter of convenience:

candidate place: a bounded region proposed as a likely place
merge: the process of combining two candidate places into one candidate place

Candidate places are the primary data element that our algorithm uses. Merging is the primary action performed on these elements.

Algorithm Description. The algorithm we use in this work is an agglomerative clustering version of the standard Gaussian Mixture Model (GMM). Our choice was influenced by the fact that we needed to find robust clusters with respect to noisy position readings (which led us toward GMMs) and the fact that we did not want to hand-code the number of places to find (which led us toward an agglomerative process).

To ground our discussion, we first describe the standard GMM algorithm. The GMM algorithm is an iterative process for fitting Gaussian probability distributions to data, consisting of two sub-steps. The pseudo-code is as follows:

1. choose a fixed number of clusters, M
2. initialize these clusters to cover different portions of the data
3. loop until convergence

   (a) for each data point and each cluster, calculate the probability that the cluster generated the data point
   (b) for each cluster, calculate the best Gaussian parameters to explain the data that is strongly associated with it

Usually, the initialization is performed using k-means. We refer to the Gaussian clusters in our algorithm as candidate places. Each candidate place is a three dimensional Gaussian distribution. Two of the dimensions correspond to position and one to time.[1]

Our algorithm augments the basic iterative architecture of the standard GMM with one additional sub-step: an agglomerative step that merges clusters meeting various merging criterion. This additional step occurs after step 3 in the pseudo-code above. We employ three different merging criteria during three phases of our algorithm. At a high level, these phases are (1) merge data points adjacent in space and time into "visits", (2) merge temporally adjacent visits that do not individually meet a minimum duration, (3) merge spatially similar visits into significant locations. Each of these merging steps has an associated parameter that relies on a measure of closeness between candidate places. In describing the algorithm below, we will introduce these parameters, the values we used for the parameters, and the measure of closeness that they rely on.

The algorithm starts by creating one candidate place for each data point. Because each candidate place is initially generated from one data point, the associated Gaussian distribution will have zero variance in the two position dimensions. To combat this issue, we require all candidate places to have a minimum variance along each dimension. Although our position data has sub-meter accuracy, the sensors can give sporadic noise readings that are several meters away. Consequently, we set the minimum variance to be 1.0 for each dimension of the Gaussian distribution.

The choice of minimum variance determines the minimum size of a candidate place. For our choice of parameters, this means that no candidate place can be smaller than about 1 meter in radius. For our data, this is a reasonable constraint. Obviously, the minimum variance values will have to be adjusted for data covering different temporal and spatial scales.

Now, we discuss the three phases of the algorithm and their associated merging steps. In the first phase, we use the following heuristic for merging candidate places: *if two candidate places are temporally adjacent and cover similar positions, they are likely covering data from the same place and should be merged into one visit.* "Similar spaces" is captured in a parameter, λ_1. λ_1 is a thresholdon the

---

[1] To simplify the calculation performed by our algorithm, we treat each dimension in the Gaussian distribution as independent.

joint KL-divergence[2] between the two candidate place probability distributions. This heuristic is utilized in most existing place-finding algorithms, used to determine when two location readings come from the same place, and is similarly enforced using a threshold on some distance metric between candidate places.

In the second phase, we continue to apply the heuristic used in phase one and also apply the following heuristic: *a place visit should explain a minimum duration of data*. We encode this heuristic in the parameter τ. Again, many place-finding algorithms encode this heuristic in a parameter as well. Generally, it is described as the minimum time that a person must spend in a candidate place before it is treated as a true place.

Finally, in the third phase we apply the following merging heuristic: *if two candidate place visits cover similar spaces but are not temporally adjacent, they are likely encoding two different visits to the same place and should be merged*. This heuristic is captured in the parameter λ_2, which, like λ_1 from phase 1, is a threshold on the joint KL-divergence between candidate places. Many existing place-finding algorithms also utilize this heuristic, and there has even been discussion on different metrics for capturing it numerically [8]. There is an important distinction between this merging step and the previous two. When merging two candidate places, instead of averaging the distributions for each place in the time dimension, we create a new candidate place whose distribution is the union of the two candidate place's distributions. As a result, candidate places take on a slightly new form during phase three: they have a single two-dimensional Gaussian distribution of x and y positions but potentially many Gaussian distributions over time. This allows each candidate place to account for many disjoint visits to the same place.

The space and time complexity of this algorithm depends on both the parameter values and the input data. In the best case, the algorithm will use $O(Nlog(N))$ time and space, where N is the initial number of data points. In the worst case, it will require $O(N^2)$. We implemented the algorithm in Matlab and ran it on a Pentium 4 with 1GB of RAM. The algorithm took between 30 minutes and 2.5 hours to run (we had between 38K and 110K points for each person).

Setting Parameter Values. The algorithm has three parameters: λ_1, τ, and λ_2 corresponding to the three different phases of merging. λ_1 encodes the conditions for merging time-adjacent points into candidate places and is constrained by the geometry of the data and the minimum variance values that are chosen for the initial candidate places. We could treat the minimum variance values as additional parameters; however, we found the following steps for adjusting λ_1 provide sufficient control over phase one of the algorithm. The first step is to set the minimum variance values based on the geometry of the data and a common-sense idea of minimum place size. We used 1.0 meter for both position

---

[2] KL-divergence, or Kullback-Leibler divergence, is a calculation of the similarity between two probability distributions. It is written $D_{KL}(P||Q)$, where P and Q are probability distributions over the same space. Since KL-divergence is not symmetric in its arguments, we calculate $D_{KL}(P||Q) + D_{KL}(Q||P)$, the joint KL-divergence.

dimensions and 1.0 millisecond for the temporal dimension. The second step is to consider the distribution of joint KL-divergences between the initial candidate places. Although not strictly bi-modal, this distribution exhibited a strong peak of values such that choosing $\lambda_1 = 1.0$ merged most of the candidate places that covered similar positions and avoided merging candidates from different places. We fixed $\lambda_1 = 1.0$ for the remainder of this discussion and for all the results presented in section 4.4.

To set the second parameter, τ, which encodes the minimum duration of a visit to a place, we tested many possible values ranging from 30 seconds up to 10 minutes. As discussed in [8], this parameter needs to satisfy conflicting constraints. First, it needs to be short enough that good candidate places are not discarded for not having been visited long enough. Second, it needs to be long enough so that spurious places, created by noisy sensor readings or by brief pauses in an insignificant location, are discarded. Since we are interested in finding places with relatively short visits, like bathrooms, a short minimum duration seemed appropriate. For our data, we found that a τ value of 1 or 2 minutes worked well for most participants.

Finally, λ_2, which encodes the conditions for merging spatially overlapping places during phase three, needs to be set so that candidate places covering approximately the same place are merged while candidate places covering different places are not. The value of this parameter depends on the ratio between the size of single place to the distance between places. Unlike at the city scale, where sensor readings rarely exhibit noise that makes a point intended for one place, e.g. "work", appear near a different place, e.g. "grocery store", our sensor data at the scale of a single home often exhibits noise characteristics that make readings ambiguous as to which place a person is in. Although not a rigorous test, we used two out of the three houses to observe the effects of this parameter (treating the third house as a held-out test set). $\lambda_2 = 2.0$ works well for the data used in this study.

4.3   Measuring the Similarity Between Places

The similarity score that we calculate is derived from the output of our place-finding algorithm. We calculate the score as follows. First, we use each data point's posterior distribution (over candidate places) to label it with its most likely candidate place. In general, the posterior distributions for data points are very peaked, so taking the maximum value is appropriate. Next, using the sequence of data point labels, we calculate the duration of each visit made to each place. For example, if ten successive data points covering 45 seconds all received the same place label, and the preceding and succeeding data points received different labels, then these ten data points constitute a single visit lasting 45 seconds. We also record the time of day that this visit covers. From these visit segments, we calculate a joint distribution over durations (discretized into exponentially growing bins, e.g. 1-2min, 2-4min, 4-8min) and times-of-day (discretized into twenty-four overlapping 5 hour windows) for each place. We claim that these joint distributions roughly characterize the shared attributes of a place, based

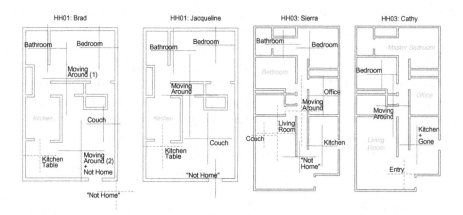

Fig. 1. Places found for several study participants. Each place is centered on the Gaussian distribution found for that place; the length of the cross lines shows one standard deviation in the X and Y directions. Places plotted with dashed lines account for less than 5% of the data, and italic labels show regions not labeled as a place for each person.

on the notion that activity patterns follow regularities in terms of their duration and the time-of-day during which they occur. The logical measurement to make between distributions is the joint KL-divergence. Although the KL-divergence between the complete joint probability distributions (over durations and time-of-day) provided reasonable results, we found that using only the distribution over durations resulted in better matchings between the places we found in our data set, and we use this distribution in calculating the similarity scores reported below.

4.4   Results

We ran our place-finding algorithm on the data from each study participant, throwing out places accounting for less than 1% of all data. This resulted in an average of 6.6 places per person (ranging from 4 to 9). In general, each person had one place accounting for "not home" data (participants placed their sensors at a predetermined location, typically by the front door, when they were away from home) and one place accounting for sleeping. The remaining places accounted for activity patterns while participants were at home during the day. Sample places from Households 1 and 3 are shown in figure 1. The fit of these places to the true place in the home, based on experiences in interviews with participants, is discussed in section 4.5.

The similarity measures between all pairs of places were also calculated as described previously. We used these measures to find the optimal many-to-one bipartite matching between the places for each pair of people (matching each place from one person to the "closest" place from each other person). Sample matchings are shown in table 1.

Table 1. Similarity-based place mappings. Italic place-names indicate unexpected mappings.

Within household

Brad	Table	Living	Gone	*Moving(1)*	Bath	Couch	Bed
Jacqueline	Table	Living	Gone	*Bath*	Bath	Living	Bed
Margaret	Table	*Kitchen*	Couch	Bath	*Gone*	Spare room	
Jack	Table	*Gone*	Couch	Bath	*Kitchen*	Spare room	

Between households

Sierra	Office	*Bed*	*Living*	Moving	Bath	Couch	*Gone*
Brad	Table	*Moving(2)*	*Gone*	Moving(1)	Bath	Couch	*Bed*

4.5   Evaluation

Evaluation of Place-Finding Algorithm. Quantitatively evaluating the "correctness" of places in the home is a particularly difficult process. Systems designed to operate at the city scale are often evaluated based on the percentage of places in the data that they correctly identify. However, this evaluation metric requires that it is possible to identify each important place by hand. For a city, this is straightforward (Hightower et al. [8] had participants carry around a clipboard and write down every place they visited), but places in the home are less well defined, depending on subtle patterns of use. We argue that the "correct" places in the home should not be identified to match a set of *a priori* hand-labeled locations but rather allowed to emerge from the behavior of users, constrained only by the limitations of the characteristics of place that we defined and built into our algorithm. We evaluate the found places by considering how well they match places that would be expected from a taxonomic labeling of people's places (e.g. bedrooms, living rooms, etc.) and by looking for the presence of interesting places that emerge from unexpected patterns of use. We base these evaluations on the qualitative interviews we conducted in each household [2,28].

Figure 1 illustrates examples of typical and atypical places in Households 1 and 3. For each person, typical places such as couch, kitchen table, bedroom and bathroom often appear. Because these places emerge only when there are significant lengths of time spent in them, the set of labeled places is different for each individual. This is best shown an example from Household 3, where Sierra and Gaby live together and rent their spare room to Cathy. The sets of places for Sierra and Cathy reflect the partitioning of the house between the different people: Sierra's places include the master bedroom, office, living room, and kitchen; and Cathy's places include her bedroom and the kitchen. This distribution of places highlights the difference in space use for the different people, as well as highlighting the kitchen as the primary shared space in the house.

The benefit of allowing other, unexpected, places to emerge, rather than evaluating them with respect to an *a priori* metric can be seen in an example from Household 1. In the main living area of the house, both Brad and Jacqueline reported that there were two significant places: the living room couch and the kitchen table. However, for both Brad and Jacqueline, our algorithm found three places covering portions of the main living area: the living room, the kitchen table, and a third "moving around" area that included both places.[3] Looking at the periods when this larger space was used, we found that it was used during the night of Brad's birthday party. During that time, the two were moving around in the entire main living area of the house *as if it were a single place*. In this case, our place-finding algorithm revealed a significant pattern of place use that would not have been identified in a hand labeling of places and that was not apparent from our interviews. Looking more closely at the sequence of places visited by Jacqueline during the party, we discovered that she began the party in the "moving around place" and as the end approached began to spend more time in the "kitchen table" and "couch" places, suggesting that her use of space became much more localized at the end of the party.

Similar unexpected places are revealed in data from the other households. During the study period, Jack and Margaret in Household 2 had just moved into their apartment and had not yet purchased a bed, sleeping instead on the futon in the main living room of the house each night. As a result, neither labeled the bedroom as a significant place during the study. However, the spare bedroom did show up as a significant place for both Jack and Margaret. In Margaret's case, this was because she used the room to do exercises. In Jack's case, this was because he had an ant farm in the spare bedroom that he would visit periodically throughout the day to take pictures of the ants. (He was creating a time-lapse video of their behavior.) Again, our algorithm revealed patterns of activity and place use that were not immediately apparent upon examination of the architectural space or reported by participants but instead arose from activity.

Evaluation of Similarity Measure. The limited amount of in-home location data available makes it difficult to rigorously test our similarity measure. Our goal here is to highlight the potential usefulness of comparing the similarity between places. We evaluate our measure by showing that the resulting mappings between the places of different people are semantically appropriate (e.g., bedrooms are mapped to bedrooms). We also discuss instances where this mapping is unintuitive. Finally, we consider the usefulness of the mappings in capturing common structures by using them to improve predictive models of people's movement patterns in their home.

Table 1 shows the optimal bipartite mappings between the places of different participants. In general, the mappings between the places of two people from the same household are good. For example, a comparison between Brad and Jacqueline fits the expected semantic mapping between places except for mapping "Moving" to "Bathroom" (the couch to living room mapping is reasonable because Jacqueline does not have a separate couch place). Similarly, the

---

[3] Brad's moving around place was split and partially merged with a "not home" place because his sensor frequently produced readings in the main living room when it was actually near the front door (where he hung his tag while away).

mapping between Margaret and Jack is as expected, except for mapping between "Kitchen" and "Gone". This incorrect mapping can be attributed to sensor noise – Jack and Margaret's kitchen and door (where they hung their tags) were so close together that readings often bounced between them.

Mappings between participants from different households fit with expected mappings in most instances but show more unexpected mappings than within household comparisons. In the mapping between Sierra and Brad, bedrooms are incorrectly matched. However, this mapping also reveals an interesting behavior pattern: Sierra's office and Brad's kitchen table appear to be incorrectly mapped together. But, interviews with both participants revealed that Sierra tended to work in the office and Brad tended to work at the kitchen table more often than eating there. Because our similarity score compares patterns of behavior between places, it captures the fact that, while Sierra's office and Brad's table appear on the surface to be different, the two in fact function as similar places.

The similarity measures between places can also be used to capture and share common patterns of behavior between different people. Many researchers have attempted to predict movement patterns of people between places. For example, Ashbrook and Starner [3] use a second-order Markov model to predict transitions between significant places, Aipperspach et al. [1] use higher-order Markov models to predict transitions, and Liao et al. [12] use a hierarchical activity model to predict transitions. We suggest that good measures of the similarity between places will help to capture "typical" transition patterns between different types of places (e.g., the pattern "people often go from sleeping to the bathroom").

As a method of evaluating the benefit that can be gained by using typical patterns of movement between places to aid in learning movement patterns for an individual in the home, we have built a 3rd-order Markov model over the sequence of place-visits for each individual, as in [1] and [3]. We then build a model that is "bootstrapped" with data from other individuals, using the mappings between places generated based on our similarity measure. This model is built using the Bayesian mixture method implemented in the SRI Language Modeling Toolkit (SRILM) [21].

In evaluating the performance of each model, we use cross-validated perplexity as reported by the SRI toolkit. (A model that perfectly matches the data has a perplexity of 1; models with less than perfect matches have higher perplexity.) Following Mehta et al. [14], we define F_0 to be the area between the learning curve for the first (single person) model and its optimal value (e.g., the area below each dotted line in figure 2). We then define $F_{0|H}$ as the area between the learning curve for the second (multi-person) model and its optimal value (e.g., the area below each solid line in figure 2). Each F measures the performance of its model based on rate of learning and maximum performance, and the *transfer ratio*, $\frac{F_0}{F_{0|H}}$, measures the performance gained when using information about typical movement patterns between different genres of place.

Figure 2 shows the results of running the predictive models on the data from Brad in Household 1, showing the performance when the model is bootstrapped with data from Jacqueline (in-household transfer). The bootstrapped model has

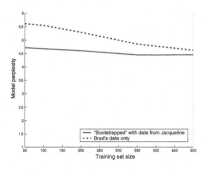

Fig. 2. Learning curves showing transfer between Brad and Jacqueline in Household 1. The dashed line shows the model performance for a model trained only on data from Brad, and the solid line shows the model performance of the same model initialized with data from Jacqueline. The model has a transfer ratio of 1.20.

a transfer ratio of 1.197 when compared with the model using only Brad's data, indicating successful transfer of shared movement patterns when using the similarity-based mappings between places.

When evaluating transfer between other study participants, we discovered that our mappings resulted in significantly lower transfer ratios. The primary reason for this is that two people's places do not always have an isomorphic mapping. Hence, requiring a single set of place names to function for two people is a strong assumption to make. In our data set, only Brad and Jacqueline had isomorphic place mappings. We identify two potential solutions to this. First, one could increase the library of known places to include enough cases that an isomorphism is likely to exist between two sets of places. Second, we could allow for probabilistic place name mappings.

5 Design Implications

5.1 Predicting Activities

Several projects are focusing on building models of human activity, which is a difficult process involving the collection and labeling of large histories of data from different types of sensors [6,19,22]. However, the shared context of culture can significantly simplify this problem. For example "common sense" repositories (like the Internet) can be automatically mined for information about common tasks [29]. Similarly, since culturally shared notions of place encourage certain activities and not others, an algorithm which can determine how similar a place is to "typical" places of various types could enable context-aware applications to determine the activities most likely to occur in that place. Given a broad enough sample of places from different homes, applications could potentially learn common types of places and then learn typical behaviors for each. Additionally, Ubicomp systems that reference places by name (e.g. [24]) could use names derived from similarity to places with known names to replace hand-labeled names for locations. Currently, the limited availability of accurate location and activity data from multiple homes makes it impossible to fully validate the possibility of learning typical places and associated activities from sensor data. As more data becomes available, we intend to explore more fully the improved activity prediction that can be carried out using shared notions of place.

5.2   Place, Similarity, and Context

An understanding of a user's context is an important aspect of Ubiquitous computing. Dourish [5] describes several problematic assumptions made by traditional views of context. He argues that context is not a stable object, definable separately from the activities of an individual. Rather, he suggests that context is a dynamically defined phenomenon, emerging from and maintained by the patterns of activity collectively carried out by individuals. According to Dourish, our goal as technologists is not "to support particular forms of practice, but to support the evolution of practice."

Our notions of place in the home are in part an attempt to distill meaningful information encoded in people's patterns of movement in a manner compatible with the goals described by Dourish. In particular, both the places that we find and the relationships between them are allowed to emerge entirely from activity. We make few assumptions about the structure of those patterns and instead look for an emergent structure based on people's actions.

The ability to find and compare emergent contextual structures suggests several design possibilities. We consider an example in elder care. One common task in elder care applications is to detect changes in behavior that provide early warning of changes in a person's health [16]. Our similarity metric could be applied to monitor how a single person's place usage changes over time (e.g., by calculating the similarity between the same person's places over two time periods). A low similarity between the sets of places found for an elderly individual may show changes in sleeping patterns or activity levels. These changes in place use could be used to highlight potential health issues. The changes could also be visualized as part of more reflective technologies, such as the ambient health feedback displays developed by Morris [17].

6   Conclusions and Future Work

In this paper, we have presented the first (to our knowledge) algorithm for finding significant places in the home based on location sensor data, and have explored the novel technique of calculating the similarity between places as an aid in understanding the places found by our algorithm. This work is based on the first sub-meter accuracy location traces collected in the home. In order to more fully validate our techniques, particularly in light of the relative uncertainty in the boundaries and definition of place in the home, it will be necessary to continue collecting accurate location traces from a larger set of homes. This will allow us to explore the range of places that exist in the home and to begin to categorize and understand the different types of places that exist across homes, quantifying the work done in [28]. We also plan on collecting and analyzing more diverse types of sensor data. By deploying a broader range of sensors to detect both location and activity, we will be better able to explore the relationship between place and activity and to determine if culturally shared notions of place and appropriate activities can be used to improve activity recognition algorithms.

Currently, the only long-term high-precision location data from the home is in the form of (X,Y) location traces. With current location technology, this data is difficult to collect, requiring a lengthy sensor installation and calibration process. We expect that in-home location traces will become more readily available as location-tracking technologies improve. Another possibility is to explore fingerprint-based place-finding algorithms for the home. Because fingerprint algorithms rely only on recurring patterns of sensor readings, not on detecting the absolute position of each person, the sensor installation process would be greatly simplified. For example, a typical installation may involve only the placement of radio beacons throughout a home instead of the careful installation and calibration of sensors in known positions. Given such fingerprint data for the home, it would be possible to find significant locations and compare their similarity to each other using a variant of our algorithms, at the expense of losing the mapping between the places found and absolute position within the home.

Finally, while we developed our current metric for comparing the similarity between places based on the types of patterns we saw in place usage in the home, we are interested in trying these similarity metrics on place usage at other scales. We plan on applying our similarity measures to existing place data available at the city scale.

References

1. Aipperspach R., Cohen, E., Canny J.: Analysis and Prediction of Sensor Data Collected from Smart Homes. In: Proc. Pervasive '06 (2006)
2. Aipperspach, R., Woodruff, A., Anderson, K., Hooker, B.: Maps of Our Lives: Sensing People and Objects Together in the Home. Tech. Report EECS-2005-22, EECS Department, UC Berkeley (2005)
3. Ashbrook, D., Starner, T.: Using GPS to Learn Significant Locations and Predict Movement Across Multiple Users. In: Personal and Ubiquitous Comp., Vol. 7 (2003)
4. Dey, A., et al.: A Conceptual Framework and a Toolkit for Supporting the Rapid Prototyping of Context-Aware Applications. In: Human-Computer Interaction, Vol. 16 (2001)
5. Dourish, P.: What We Talk About When We Talk About Context. In: Personal and Ubiquitous Computing, Vol. 8 (2004) 19-30
6. Dragunov, A.N., et al.: TaskTracer: A Desktop Environment to Support Multitasking Knowledge Workers. In: Int'l. Conf. on Intelligent User Interfaces (2005)
7. Harrison, S., Dourish, P.: Re-Place-ing Space: The Roles of Place and Space in Collaborative Systems. In: Proc. CSCW '96 (1996)
8. Hightower, J., et al.: Learning and Recognizing the Places We Go. In: Proc. Ubicomp '05 (2005)
9. Kang, J.H., Welbourne, W., Stewart, B., Borriello, G.: Extracting Places from Traces of Locations. In: Proc. Workshop on Wireless Mobile Applications and Services on WLAN Hotspots, WMASH (2004)

10. Laasonenm K., Raento, M., Toivonen, H.: Adaptive On-Device Location Recognition. In Proc. Pervasive '04 (2004)
11. Leont'ev, A. N.: Activity, Consciousness, and Personality. Prentice-Hall, Englewood Cliffs, NJ (1978)
12. Liao, L., Fox, D., Kautz, H.: Learning and Inferring Transportation Routines. In: Proc. AAAI '04 (2004)
13. Marmasse, N., Schmandt, C.: Location-Aware Information Delivery with Commotion. In: Proc. Symposium on Handheld and Ubiquitous Computing, HUC (2000)
14. Mehta, N., Natarajan, S., Tadepalli, P., Fern, A.: Transfer in Variable-Reward Hierarchical Reinforcement Learning. In: Proc. of the Inductive Transfer workshop at NIPS 2005 (2005)
15. Monteiro, C.: Activity Analysis in Houses of Recife, Brazil. In: Proc. First Int'l. Space Syntax Conf (1997) 20.1-20.13
16. Morris, M., Intille, S.S., Beaudin, J.S.: Embedded Assessment: Overcoming Barriers to Early Detection with Pervasive Computing. In: Proc. Pervasive '05 (2005)
17. Morris, M.: Social Networks as Health Feedback Displays. In: IEEE Internet Computing, Vol. 9(5) (2005) 29-37
18. Oswald, F., et al.: The Role of the Home Environment in Middle and Late Adulthood. In: Wahl, H.-W., et al. (eds.): The Many Faces of Health, Competence and Well-being in Old Age: Integrating Epidemiological, Psychological and Social Perspectives. Springer, Heidelberg (2006)
19. Philipose, M., et al.: Inferring Activities from Interactions with Objects. In: IEEE Pervasive Computing (October 2004) 50-57
20. Rowan, J., Mynatt, E.D.: Digital Family Portraits: Providing Peace of Mind for Extended Family Members. In: Proc. CHI '01 (2001)
21. Stolcke, A.: SRILM - An Extensible Language Modeling Toolkit. In: Proc. of the Int'l. Conf. on Spoken Language Processing (2002)
22. Munguia Tapia, E., Intille, S.S., Larson, K.: Activity Recognition in the Home Setting Using Simple and Ubiquitous Sensors. In: Proc. Pervasive '04 (2004)
23. Trevisani, E., Vitaletti, A.: Cell-Id Location Technique, Limits and Benefits: An Experimental Study. In: Proc. IEEE Workshop on Mobile Computing Systems and Applications, WMCSA (2004)
24. Truong, E., et al.: CAMP: A Magnetic Poetry Interface for End-User Programming of Capture Applications for the Home. In: Proc. Ubicomp '04 (2004)
25. Ubisense, Ltd. Website, http://www.ubisense.net.
26. Wang, J., Canny, J.: End-User Place Annotation on Mobile Devices : A Comparative Study. In: Extended Abstracts, CHI '06 (2006)
27. Wicker, A.: An Introduction to Ecological Psychology. Brooks/Cole Publishing Company, Monterey, California (1979)
28. Woodruff, A., Anderson, A., Mainwaring, S.D., Aipperspach, R.: Portable, But Not Mobile: A Study of Wireless Laptops in the Home. Tech. Report EECS-2006-88, EECS Department, UC Berkeley (2006)
29. Wyatt, D., Philipose, M., Choudhury, T.: Unsupervised Activity Recognition Using Automatically Mined Common Sense. In: Proc. of AAAI '05 (2005)

Principles of Smart Home Control

Scott Davidoff, Min Kyung Lee, Charles Yiu, John Zimmerman, and Anind K. Dey

Human-Computer Interaction Institute + School of Design
Carnegie Mellon University
{scott.davidoff, mklee, cmyiu, johnz, anind}@cmu.edu
http://smarthome.cs.cmu.edu

Abstract. Seeking to be sensitive to users, smart home researchers have focused on the concept of control. They attempt to allow users to gain control over their lives by framing the problem as one of end-user programming. But families are not *users* as we typically conceive them, and a large body of ethnographic research shows how their activities and routines do not map well to programming tasks. End-user programming ultimately provides control of devices. But families want more control *of their lives*. In this paper, we explore this disconnect. Using grounded contextual fieldwork with dual-income families, we describe the control that families want, and suggest seven design principles that will help end-user programming systems deliver that control.

1 Introduction

In order for smart homes to achieve their promise of significantly improving the lives of families through socially appropriate and timely assistance, they will need to sense, anticipate and respond to activities in the home. Interestingly, expanding system capabilities can easily overstep some invisible boundary, making families feel at the mercy of, instead of in control of that technology [1][5][6][21][30]. An important goal of smart home research then becomes how to appropriately expand system capabilities to produce more control – both perceived and actual.

Researchers often frame the problem of control as one of end-user programming [13][21][27][34]. However, end-user programming as it is typically conceived requires *a priori* specificity and rigidity that conflict with a large body of ethnographic research on the organic, opportunistic, and improvisational ways that families construct, maintain, and modify their routines and plans, *e.g.* [3][14][15][16][17][25][26][38][42][45].

In exploring the issue of control and the smart home, we have chosen to focus on dual-income families, a large and growing segment of the population of the United States. These families often feel out of control due to the complex and rapidly changing logistics that result from integrating and prioritizing work [41], school, family [10], and enrichment activities [3][15][17][25].

While end-user programming returns some measure of control to the user over pre-programmed or learning-only systems [1][21], ultimately, framing the problem as end-user programming leads researchers to view the research and evaluation in terms

P. Dourish and A. Friday (Eds.): Ubicomp 2006, LNCS 4206, pp. 19 – 34, 2006.

of *control of devices*. Our fieldwork on dual-income families, however, shows that more than control of their devices, families desire more *control of their lives*. We suggest that the problem of home control should be widened to include not just control of artifacts and tasks, but control of the things families most value – their time, their activities, and their relationships. We argue that the way to do this is to enable end-user programming systems to more flexibly and appropriately reflect the complex nature of observed human interaction.

In this paper, we discuss how a smart home might provide dual-income families with more control over their lives. We describe the approach current end-user programming systems take to the problem of control. We then describe an ethnography we conducted with this population, and then situate our findings within the existing body of social research to outline a rich description of the kind of control families value, and the flexibility they utilize to manage their daily lives. Finally, based on these findings, we define seven principles to help researchers operationalize this concept of families being in control of their lives, as applied to end-user programming systems.

2 Related Work

As research in ubiquitous [48] and context-aware [18] computing moves into the home, and systems begin to take action on behalf of users [22] either in a proactive or reactive sense, researchers are finding that users feel unexpectedly challenged by these systems [30].

In traditional desktop models of human-computer interaction, systems are slaves to human input. But advanced context-aware systems can break this interaction model [6], and, in doing so, they challenge or even invert the user's sense of who is actually in control. Expanding system capabilities while maintaining users' sense of control then becomes one of the central concerns of context-aware computing.

One approach views the problem of smart home control in terms of end-user programming (in this paper we use the terms end-user programming and smart home control interchangeably). These end-user programming systems explore various interfaces to provide end-users control of home devices, including natural language [27], interlocking puzzle pieces [34], visual programming [35], programming by demonstration [19], and magnetic refrigerator poetry [46]. The end-user programming approach has several benefits. It provides users control over an unpredictable confederation of interoperating devices [40], and allows users to customize services as they might see fit [34], even inventing new services [46].

Existing end-user programming systems, however, also face certain limitations, especially in relation to how they might apply to dual-income families. First, families resist categorization as users. The user tends to be singular, while families are, by definition, plural. Unlike users, families both individually and collectively resist clearly-defined goals [15][17][38]. Also, family relationships are complex and evolve organically over time [10][16], whereas conceptions of the user tend to be static.

In addition, programming requires definition, formality, and specification which conflict with a large body of ethnographic research on how families operate. Responsibility or ownership of tasks in a family is rarely clearly-defined [3][16], while the majority of programming tasks connote clear lines of ownership. Also, various individuals have multiple [26] (often competing [25]) methods of completing tasks and metrics for the quality of their performance [16], while programming requires clear boundaries for task completion. Lastly, most programming tasks assume complete access to relevant information, and the focused attention of the programmer. But rapid context switching between home and work oblige families to make decisions with incomplete information [2] and marginal attention [41].

But most importantly, end-user programming studies define success in terms of usability, and overlook other core metrics contained in the human value proposition [43]. Systems are designed to facilitate the successful completion of tasks that often involve configuration of and complex interaction with multiple devices. But we suggest that usability measures should be contained within the larger discussion of value, which include utility and likeability [43].

We are suggesting that end-user programming consider not just the usability of the system, and how the users manage the artifacts that constitute it, but what utility the system is ultimately responsible for delivering. Existing end-user programming systems that focus on artifacts cannot repair the diminished sense of control that dual-income families already experience. But by expanding their evaluation metric to include the utility smart home systems provide, end-user programming systems might be able to help families regain a sense of control over their lives.

To understand how to appropriately support families in making that transition, we undertook an ethnography of dual income families. Here, our work builds upon the comprehensive studies of Darrah [14][15][16] and Beech et al [3]. While our work focuses on issues of routines, planning and control, other studies of family life have focused on household communication [13] and its relationship to locations [24], time management [25], communication technology [26], use of refrigerator magnets [44], knowledge specialization [42], routines [45], overall technology use [47], or calendaring [7].

3 Ethnography of Dual-Income Families

3.1 Participants

Our study began with an exploration of the needs of 12 dual-income families with school age children. These families represent an interesting population for several reasons. First, at 43% of the population of the United States and growing [32], dual-income families represent a significant demographic whose sheer magnitude merits attention.

In addition, dual-income families show a particular need for support. By moving away from the single-income model, these families are exposed to a surprising variety of stressors [14][15][32]. Taxing schedules and no anchor presence at home impose particularly high coordination costs. Parents are also exposed to role strain, where they feel pressures in trying to comply with the expectations attached to their roles as parents [2][12], which adds to an already stressful existence.

Lastly, we believe dual-income families are realistically poised to receive the benefits of smart home advances. The challenges dual-income families face often drive them to aggressively adopt and experimentally use new communication and coordination technologies [26]. Their demonstrated desire for increased flexibility and control over their own lives, and this historical precedent of using technology to satisfy those needs, we believe places dual-income families as prime candidates to become smart home early adopters.

Our families were solicited through bulletin board advertisement, and in person at shopping malls. We pre-screened families in order to include a wide range of professions, ages of parents and children, and economic class. Since our interest includes end-user programming, we also disqualified families where one of the parents had a job involving programming. Table 1 contains information about each of the families we recruited.

Table 1. Detailed description of participating families

Family	Mother	Father	Children
A	Not provided, Administrative assistant	Not provided, Carpenter	15, son 18, son
B	47, Department manager	48, Art gallery director	9, daughter 15, daughter
C	41, Professor	39, Teacher	1, son 5, daughter
D	38, Business manager	41, Marketing manager	5, son 8, daughter 10, son
E	Not provided, Professor	Not provided, Carpenter	15, son
F	45, Secretary	46, Truck driver	15, daughter
G	32, Surgeon	31, Graduate student	5, son
H	36, Project manager	34, Graduate student	1, daughter 5, daughter
I	52, Nurse	53, Steam fitter	15, son 19, daughter
J	49, Administrative assistant	50, Manager	15, daughter 20, son
K	54, Events coordinator	55, Salesman	21, son
L	43, Legal secretary	46, Landscaper	11, daughter 15, daughter 17, daughter 19, daughter

Participant homes averaged 2.3 bedrooms, and 6.6 rooms in total. Five homes had two floors, while the remaining seven had one floor. A typical footprint would include a modest family space near the front door connected to a small dining area. The kitchen area would form the hub of the home, while bedrooms were situated on the periphery or on the second floor.

3.2 Method

Fieldwork began with three-hour contextual interviews in the homes of the families. Time was organized to include directed storytelling, artifact walkthrough [8], and role-playing activities. The entire family was asked to participate in all the research activities.

Fieldwork pilots identified the "wake up" and "arrive home" times as key opportunity areas for smart home assistance, so we focused our investigation on those time windows. During directed storytelling we solicited personal accounts of waking up or arriving home from particular family members. In addition, we asked them to act out the scenes so we could better understand the relationship between their routine and its context. During the artifact walkthrough, we asked families to demonstrate the use of their main coordination artifacts, often a large kitchen calendar, and their various personal calendars. During role-playing, we asked families to pretend to coordinate for a fictitious school field trip, for which we provided simulated school paperwork. The interviews covered both predictable days, like weekdays and weekends, predictable exceptions like business trips and holidays, and unpredictable exceptions such as sick days or miss-the-bus days.

To gain additional insight into the wake-up and arrive-home activities, we left families with a cultural probe package [29]. The package explored the stressors and pleasures of waking up and arriving home. We also asked parents to comment on the parts of their lives that make them feel like good moms and dads. The package included a book of stimuli questions, free response text space, and a camera to photograph related vignettes.

Finally, we asked each family to log their wake-up and arrive-home activities for one week. We captured stress and rush levels, principal activities, immediate needs, and preoccupations.

3.3 Data Analysis

To analyze our data, we mapped each home, photographed objects and locations of interest, and recorded photo locations on our maps. We coded our interview notes for emergent themes. We also evaluated our photographic record, grouping images to provide both visual support for themes identified during interviews, and themes that contained uniquely visual information, often place- or object-related.

We created individual schedules for each family member, including typical days (often weekdays), and regular exceptional days (like weekends), and occasional exceptional days (e.g. snow days, holidays). Schedules included both an order of activity and, if available, a corresponding time. Multiple timelines allowed us to compare order of operations both within and between families.

The cultural probes helped us identify emotional connections between families and their homes, and how families define themselves through their products and their uses with them.

Finally, the activity logs allowed us to identify specific stress triggers and compare stress levels between weekdays and weekend days. They also provided rich description of family priorities when faced with competing needs.

4 Findings

Many of the logistical challenges that produce this feeling of "life out of control" can be traced to the enrichment activities that children participate in. While work and school add to the complexity of daily living, they tend to present predictable logistical needs. But many qualities of enrichment activities make them resistant to simple logistical management.

Enrichment activities present rapid seasonal changes. They also require constantly evolving transportation needs. And they often present both anticipated and unanticipated attendant responsibilities. These factors make them much more resistant to the development of a consistent routine and much more likely to cause a breakdown requiring improvisation to the underlying logistical plan.

Other sources of loss of control can be attributed to unpredictable events and breakdowns, like sick children, or missing the school bus.

Generally our families address this loss of control by increasing their *flexibility*. We consider this situation in more detail.

4.1 Less Than Ideal Control

Enrichment activities frame the day. Dual-income families fill their children's lives with enrichment activities. These activities benefit the children in many ways such as teaching values, providing physical fitness, teaching competition and teamwork, supporting existing social structure and providing supplemental education. Families often select activities based on long-term goals such as preparing their kids for a successful career or increasing the chance of college admission to selective schools [15]. In addition, the activities often serve as *de facto* "babysitting" to help cover the time parents are at work. Every child in every family we interviewed participated in at least one (and on average two) enrichment activities.

While children form the principal participants, enrichment activities affect every member of the household. In addition to the management of their households and the completion of whatever work they might have brought home, parents are charged with the successful logistical management of their children as they relate to these activities.

Even the simple is complex. Family J's soccer practice shows how much logistical complexity can be contained within a single event. First, getting the kids wherever they need to be represents a challenge. Practices are held in one of two locations. Games are held in any number of locations. Locations are printed on the team schedule, which is kept on the family refrigerator. This sheet has no directions. Parents who carpool have to coordinate who picks up and who drops off. Practices start at consistent times, but games start at one of three times.

Kids also have to come prepared. If the event is on turf, kids will need to bring their flat shoes. If the event is on grass, they will need to bring their cleats. Kids always need to bring their shin guards and knee pads. Games require either the home or away uniform. Practices require practice jerseys. All clothes need to be laundered, which often means washing them the night before so that they are clean for the day of use.

Even parents have homework for soccer games. Three families bring refreshments to each game – juice for thirsty players during the game, juice for after the game, and oranges for halftime. This information is also encoded on the schedule on the fridge. Forgetting comes with a high social cost. Either the team goes thirsty, and the child is embarrassed, or the parent has to face the panic and stress of racing to get kids to the field on time while running to the store to buy drinks and fruit.

A simple activity, like leaving the house, is rarely "simple." To get the kids to school, parents need to make sure children are awake, washed, dressed, fed, and ready for their rides. These activities depend on the (sometimes unwilling) participation of the child(ren), the coordinated use of (or competition for) scarce resources (e.g., bathroom time) with other family members, and the presence of these and other resources (e.g., school bag) along with the knowledge of their whereabouts. Our Family H's Dad described a successful morning as one where "we all get out the door, and there are no major disasters."

Activities resist routinization. Routines allow families to function without having to carefully consider every option at every moment [45]. However, routines for enrichment activities prove difficult to construct. And even when possible, these routines provide many opportunities to break down. Their high variability in both detail and responsibility make construction of a "normal" routine difficult. In addition, most of these activities do not run for an entire year. Instead they are "seasonal," forcing families to constantly re-adjust schedules as seasons end and new seasons begin.

Transportation to activities such as team sports almost always involves variability in the routine. Most dual-income parents needed to rely on others to provide some transportation due to other commitments in their complex schedules and due to the different locations and times of the events. In addition, most activities required inconsistent use of special equipment such as the types of shoes and uniforms mentioned above.

Responsibilities bleed past fixed boundaries. Timing and order also play major roles in the capable execution of enrichment activities, adding further to their logistical complexity. Many activities, like musical groups, require special equipment. And since children often go to their activities directly from school, children must take this equipment with them in the morning, extending the time window of responsibility to the morning of the event. For Family H, washing soccer uniforms extended responsibility to the night before the event.

Responsibility can even extend significantly further than a single day. Family H, for example, has to bring in snacks for the entire class one day each month. Parents have to remember this day, and make sure to have enough snacks for the entire class in the house on the morning of the day on which the snack is their responsibility. This extends the time window for the event as far back as the weekend before the event, when Family H would go food shopping for the week.

Breakdowns cause cascade effects. Because children and parents are so interdependent, their schedules are united by a chain of dependency. Small failures that affect one individual can extend individual failures into multiple, shared coordination failures. We found this scenario to be common among our participant families: Mom might be running behind for a business meeting, so she needs the bathroom first. Her Son is forced to shower second, and misses his bus. Dad then has to drive him to school, which makes him late for his morning meeting.

The chain of dependency can also become more complex when parents, out of necessity, divide the jobs surrounding certain tasks. For example, in Family H, it is Dad's job to get their Daughter ready for ballet, and it is Mom's job to take their Daughter to ballet as part of a carpool. When Mom goes away on a business trip, and the carpool parent providing the ride calls with a cancellation, Dad lacks the resources to easily arrange a new ride. He does not know which other parents he can lean on, as this task is not part of his regular responsibilities.

Not enough gas in the car, traffic, a forgotten briefcase, an extra trip to the grocery store – all simple events that might delay one person – cascade into the schedules of other family members, who all depend on one another.

"Busyness" is a moral good. It would seem that if enrichment activities caused so much distress and made families feel "out of control", then a simple strategy to regain control would be to do less. However, this strategy is conspicuously absent in dual-income families. The parents in our ethnography value the enrichment their children receive through participation in these activities. In addition, participation allows them to demonstrate their mastery of "busyness", and the ability to master busyness is one of the values these families who have generally self-selected to be dual-income wish to pass on to their children [14][16].

4.2 Flexibility as Coping Strategy

Families exhibited many behaviors that allow them to manage this hyper-busyness. Some families imposed simple rules. Family L, for example, limited their four children to no more than three activities each. Many families assigned responsibilities for specific events to particular parents, liberating the other parent from dealing with those details. All our families leveraged some technological infrastructure [26] and had routines surrounding its use.

In general, we observed across almost all coping strategies, a quality of flexibility. We explain in more detail by example.

Detail is acquired when necessary. One flexibility strategy involved incrementally adding details to plans as they became necessary. This tendency causes long-term plans to differ substantially from short-term plans.

Long-term plans tend to resemble rough sketches. When Family H learns their day for snacks is weeks away, Mom puts the snack calendar on the fridge. She does not consider what snack to get at that time because what she buys will depend in part on what her daughter wants and what other families have provided that week. She doesn't know if she will purchase the snack when food shopping the weekend before or if Dad will have time to pick it up on his way home the night before. Only summary knowledge is either known or even possible to be known.

But on the day of certain activities every logistical detail has to be covered. The night before a soccer game, just before dinner, for example, Family H consults the various media that include information relevant to that game: the location, home or away, who is dropping off, and who is picking up. Mom knows it is her job to pick up, so she confirms with her Daughter where to wait for her. Mom also confirms who else she will be taking in the carpool. Mom confirms all the details and places just to be sure that nothing had changed since its codification on the central artifacts.

Improvise. Many events never acquire any *a priori* detail at all. Sometimes, this was due to constraints of memory. Family H, for example, reported keeping "only two or three [plans] in our head at one time." And so on days when there were multiple events after school, Mom and Dad would speak on their cell phone multiple times and watch many plans evolve without preplanned conception of their ultimate order of operations. In fact, we observed that many plans started out as successful improvisations, and then were adopted as routines because of that success.

Frissen [26] and Darrah [16] also describe parents adopting new communication technology so that they could become more available and ultimately increase their flexibility. Because they could be reached by their families at a moment's notice, plans were able to evolve and be improvised even closer to their target times.

Work and home blend. Mom and Dad also tend to bring their work life home, and arrange their home life at work [41]. By bringing the two contexts together, parents don't have to constrain all their home planning to the house, or all their work planning to the office. This ability to seamlessly move between contexts allows for plans to dynamically evolve, and allows for more flexibility in how time is used. In Family F the Mother worked at home in the evenings close to her daughter to allow her to focus both on work and her family simultaneously.

This flexible changing between home and work also extends to artifacts. Parents would seamlessly shift between whatever media was most immediately available [3] [13][26]. We found that our families stored work information on their home calendar, and home information on their work calendar [25]. This opportunistic use of media helps parents master their busyness while, at the same time, complicates their lives by requiring synchronization between the many artifacts that impact the different aspects of their lives.

Lifestyle choices. We observed families making deliberate choices about highly important parts of their lives so that they could have more flexible routines.

Family J chose to live close to Dad's work so that Dad could be available in emergencies. In [15], Darrah found families who would consolidate their children into one school so as to simplify logistics. Family L staggered their work schedules so that one parent could be more available for unexpected events, like children being sick.

5 Design Principles

The homes that we observed were inhabited by complex families full of contradictory human beings in need of support. To help these families regain control of their lives, researchers might try to help them make better lifestyle choices, including simply reducing the number of activities in which they are actively involved. But our findings suggest that these activities play a central role in the social identity of families and modifying them would damage this fundamental aspect of family life. Instead of proposing a social engineering solution, we approach the problem by exploring the role of technology in supporting families' existing lifestyles and identities.

Currently, we observe a disconnect between the nuanced lifestyles our study demonstrates, and the smart homes that many technologists envision. This suggests that for technology to help families regain control over their lives, we refocus the end-user programming of smart home systems to more appropriately reflect that complexity.

To begin this investigation into a new kind of end-user programming, we provide a list of principles that such a system would need to adhere to. The principles include the following:

1. Allow for the organic evolution of routines and plans
2. Easily construct new behaviors and modify existing behaviors
3. Understand periodic changes, exceptions and improvisation
4. Design for breakdowns
5. Account for multiple, overlapping and occasionally conflicting goals
6. The home is more than a location
7. Participate in the construction of family identity

We address each principle in turn.

5.1 Allow for the Organic Evolution of Routines and Plans

Routines form the basis of normalcy in many domestic situations, and allow family members to focus their attention on other, more demanding activities [3][15][25][45]. Plans allow families to coordinate the substantial number of activities they carry out during an average day. Plans and routines represent an important and powerful way families manage to resist entropy and regain elements of control over their lives. Thus a smart home system that intends to provide families some measure of control over their lives must account for the concept of the routine. But routines, as we and others [45] have observed, contain many subtle inflections that resist the simple models of computation imposed by many end-user programming systems.

First of all, describing all the routines of a family would constitute an enormous undertaking. Next, our families would likely not recall all their routine behaviors, as some have simply become so routine that they have passed below consciousness [15]. But even known routines rarely conform to the notion that they might be able to be completely specified *a priori*. Many routines themselves were once successful improvisations that have been incorporated into a family's daily activities. Other plans begin with only cursory detail, and gain in precision as the day of their enacting encroaches.

On the surface, existing smart home control systems attempt to provide support for routines. But, their concept of routines is too rigid, requiring *a priori* specification of all the routines that the user can remember.

To give families a sense of control over their lives, a smart home system will have to both support the concept of routine, but not bind families to that notion. Such a system will need to allow plans and routines to evolve organically. Systems that enforce rigidity in routines, including most end-user programming systems built for the home, do not match our observations of how people behave and will not be successful at helping families take control of their lives. This inflexibility will lead to families losing control to the technology itself, replacing control with an inflexible algorithmic tyranny.

While an extreme case, evidence from the MavHome, a smart home research environment [11] illustrates this point well. The MavHome had a lighting model that turned off its lights late at night because its occupant did not have visitors late at night and was asleep. When the occupant did have visitors, they literally had to "remain in the dark" because of the difficulty in controlling and changing the home's behavior. Systems that support this design principle would have to incorporate the flexible, organic nature of routines that people adhere to themselves.

5.2 Easily Construct New Plans and Routines, and Modify Existing Ones

Many of our families engaged in planning and coordination tasks daily. We fully expect that families would interact just as frequently with a smart home system that supported the concepts of plans and routines. Such a smart home system would need to offer a low-cost way for families to describe plans and routines.

Additionally, given the need to support the organic evolution of routines, including occasional improvisation, and breakdowns and exceptions in those routines, this system will also need to provide a low-cost way to modify existing behaviors.

5.3 Understand Periodic Changes, Exceptions and Improvisation

Even if routines could be specified entirely beforehand, people both intentionally and necessarily deviate from routines. Some deviation is seasonally mandated, such as children participating in soccer in the fall, and in basketball in the winter. Some deviation occurs due to exceptions – Mom wants to get a surprise gift for her daughter. Many routines are substantially improvisational, representing constantly shifting targets.

A smart home system that enforced a single, rigid correct model of routines would find that few routines were ever capably executed according to that model, and would be constantly interrupting and misinterpreting what was actually happening.

Once again, smart home technology that reflected observed behavior would have to understand that exceptions to routines are actually not exceptional, and be prepared to interpret them correctly. This means that a representation of a routine or plan cannot be rigid, and the system has to understand concepts like periodicity, what an exception is and how to recover from or adapt to it, and how to deal with improvisation. Simply put, any computational model that is expected to take action on behalf of families would be confronted with the fact that routines can prove to be anything but.

5.4 Design for Breakdowns

Even when routines are capably carried out by family members, and the family machine marches forward like clockwork, we found many instances where the surrounding world simply did not cooperate. Family I's Dad gets the kids ready for school on time, but his Son's shoes have gone mysteriously missing. The carpool stops while Dad scours the house for the delinquent footwear. Family J's Dad has to bring his Daughter to physical therapy after school. But she forgets, and goes to her friends' house. Mom has to drive out of her way to pick her Daughter up. Plans just don't always work. Routines sometimes fail. A smart home system will need to expect, account for, understand, and appropriately respond to these eventualities.

Also, a smart home would need to recognize when a breakdown is occurring and understand the kind of cascading failures that can occur and learn or know how to react to them and ideally avoid as many of the attendant failures as possible.

5.5 Account for Multiple, Overlapping and Occasionally Conflicting Goals

Sometimes it is not the world, but the family structure itself that causes complexity or breakdowns in plans or routines. Laundry may be Mom's job on Monday, but it is Dad's job on Tuesday. These collaborative tasks suggest another aspect of the flexibility that a smart home system would have to reflect.

Many tasks simply do not fit a simple model of ownership. Family F's Daughter's is responsible for walking the dog every morning, except when she's running behind. In these circumstances, Mom was happy to help out. Other tasks resist the concept of ownership all together. Everybody in Family L shares in the laundry duties. Other tasks move between individuals on particular days of the week, muddling the notion that responsibility is owned by any single individual.

We also might find open conflict regarding a chore or routine [38]. Preferences vary widely for what constitutes a comfortable temperature, and many families battle over the thermostat. Other conflicts may surround varying methods for task completion, varying tolerances and metrics of quality, or the priority of a particular task. For example, Mom may make a rule that says "don't use the scrubber on the pots." But everybody in the family knows the rule really means "don't use the scrubber on the pots *when Mom's in the room.*"

A smart home system would need to participate in this ambiguous notion of responsibility. A smart home may need to face, interpret and react to a situation where goals conflict and the situation may still be valid. In such a situation, the system would have to provide a way to maintain internal consistency in data structure in the face of external disagreement.

5.6 The House Is More Than a Location

As opportunistic planners, our families did not limit their coordination activities to the physical constraints of any single location within the house, or even the house itself. Planning and coordination also occur at work, at school, at the place of the activities themselves, and during transportation between any of these locations.

The functional boundaries of the smart home will need to extend beyond the physical parameters of the home itself, and be accessible anywhere planning for or activities receiving support occurs. A smart home that participates in a family's planning dialog will have to allow for the family to enter and update information from these various locations as easily as if they were at home.

This specification extends to routines as well. A smart house would need to support planning activities, and also be able to monitor everything else going on outside the home to better understand how routines are changing and whether breakdowns, exceptions and/or organic changes are taking place.

The blending of spaces also extends to information space. Families enter information in calendars at both home and work. Paper school flyers and sports schedules find their way onto refrigerators. Calendars also cross the boundaries of individuals.

A smart home system that allows its inhabitants to feel in control of their information will need to be able to blend elements across contexts, media and individuals and aggregate them into a unified model of what is happening.

A smart home that supports this principle would support planning tasks and maintenance of routines everywhere the family goes, monitor and react to family activity in and out of the house and be able to leverage all available artifacts that the family uses.

5.7 Participate in the Construction of Family Identity

Potential smart home services might also potentially collide with how individual family members derive their identity. Consumption and use of products contribute to how people formulate their social identity [4][23][37]. And since the home represents the largest purchase most people ever make, to many families the home itself makes the largest product-based contribution through which they realize their social identity. By extension, we can expect that the services a smart home provides will in many ways contribute to how individuals formulate their social identity.

Here, grocery list support provides a good example. While cooking dinner every night might be challenging and a source of frustration for Mom, automating the cooking process could also remove an opportunity for Mom to feel like a good Mom [44]. The act of preparing food constitutes an important part of Mom's identity. Instead, automating the creation of a grocery list is an assistive task that aids Mom without challenging her identity.

Existing smart home systems often focus on the usability or efficiency of a particular task, but remove that task from the larger context in which it is so importantly embedded. Many tasks are time-intensive but are vital to our identities as Moms, Dads and Families. As researchers search for new services a smart home can provide, they will have to extend their evaluation metrics to include this important component of the human value proposition.

This understanding of how smart home services contribute to our identity also extends to situations where the smart home may take action on behalf of users. When a smart home system is making a decision about when it is appropriate to take an action, it has to be aware of these invisible value lines, and have some understanding of social protocol, so that it can decide when it is appropriate to cross those lines, and when it is not.

6 Conclusions

In this paper, we have presented seven principles that we believe smart home researchers should address in the systems they build, in order for families to take control of their lives. These principles were derived from an ethnography we conducted with dual-income families that illustrated the loss of control these families feel over their lives. Enrichment, work and school activities and the exceptions and breakdowns that can occur, combined with parents trying to instill their values into children all contribute to families' sense of loss of control.

Much of the smart home research that addresses control, leverages end-user programming. However, in practice, these systems promote control over artifacts and devices, rather than promoting control over the routines, planning and time (in short, the lives) of families. From our ethnography, we found that the key to regaining control over complex lives is to support flexibility.

Our design principles focus on providing flexibility in the planning of activities, construction and modification of routines, through support for organic formation of routines, along with support for exceptions, improvisation and breakdowns in those routines. They also suggest the need to accommodate conflicting goals and responsibilities among family members, to push the boundaries of the home beyond the physical construct of the home itself, and to participate in the construction of a positive family identity.

We acknowledge that it will be difficult to embed these principles into working end-user systems, but our contribution is in pointing out that an end-user control system will likely fail unless it adheres to the principles. Our next step is to build and evaluate a smart home system that adheres to these principles and makes families be and feel more in control of their lives. An important goal in sharing these principles is to initiate a discussion with other smart home researchers about smart home occupants and their feelings of control. In particular, we hope to bring attention to the social and often chaotic nature of family life, the impact it has on smart home technology and the impact smart home technology can have on it.

References

[1] Barkhuus, L., & Dey, A.K. (2003) Is context-aware computing taking control away from the user? Three levels of interactivity examined, *Proceedings of Ubicomp 2003*, 159-166.

[2] Barnett, R.C. (1994). Home-to-work spillover revisited: A study of full-time employed women in dual-earner couples, in *Journal of Marriage and the Family*, 56: 647-656.

[3] Beech, S., Geelhoed, E., Murphy, R., Parker, J., Sellen, A. & Shaw, K. (2004) Lifestyles of working parents: Implications and opportunities for new technologies, *HP Tech report HPL-2003-88 (R.1)*.

[4] Belk, R.W. (1988) Possessions and the extended self, *Journal of Consumer Research*, 15(2): 139-168.

[5] Bellotti, V., Back, M., Edwards, W.K., Grinter, R.E., Henderson, A., & Lopes, C. (2002) Making sense of sensing systems: Five questions for designers and researchers, *Proceedings of CHI 2002*, 415-422.

[6] Bellotti, V. & Edwards, W. K. (2001) Intelligibility and accountability: Human considerations in context-aware systems, *Human-Computer Interaction*, 16(2-4): 193-212.

[7] Bernheim Brush, A.J. & Combs Turner, T. (2005) A Survey of personal and household scheduling, in *Proceedings of Group 2005*, 330-331.

[8] Beyer, H. & Holtzblatt, K. (1998) *Contextual design: Defining customer-centered systems*, San Francisco: Morgan Kaufman Publishers.

[9] Blackwell, A.F., Burnett, M.F. & Peyton Jones, S. (2004) Champagne prototyping: A Research technique for early evaluation of complex end-user programming systems, in *Proceedgings of VLHCC 2004*, 47-54.

[10] Cherlin, A. J. (1988) *The Changing American family and public policy*, Washington, D.C.: Urban Institute Press.

[11] Cook, D.J., Youngblood, M., Heierman, E., Gopalratnam, K., Rao, S., Litvin, A., & Khawaja, F. (2003) MavHome: An agent-based smart home, in *Proceedings of PerCom 2003*, 521-524.

[12] Cowan, R. S. (1989) *More Work for Mother*, London: Free Association Books.

[13] Crabtree, A., Rodden, T., Hemmings, T. & Benford, S. (2003): Finding a place for ubicomp in the home, in *Proceedings of Ubicomp 2003*, 208-226.

[14] Darrah, C.N. & English-Lueck, J.A. (2000) Living in the eye of the storm: controlling the maelstrom in Silicon Valley, in *Proceedings of the 2000 Work and Family: Expanding the Horizons Conference*.

[15] Darrah, C. N., English-Lueck, J. & Freeman, J. (2001) Families at work: An ethnography of dual career families, *Report for the Sloane Foundation* (Grant Number 98-6-21).

[16] Darrah, C.N. (2003) Family models, model families, in *Proceedings of the 2003 American Anthropological Association Annual Conference*.

[17] Davidoff, S., Lee, M.K., Zimmerman, J. & Dey, A.K. (2006) Socially-aware requirements for a smart home, in *Proceedings of the International Symposium on Intelligent Environments*, 41-44.

[18] Dey, A., Abowd, G., & Salber, D. (2001) A conceptual framework and a toolkit for supporting the rapid prototyping of context-aware applications, *Human-Computer Interaction*, 16(2-4).

[19] Dey, A.K., Hamid, R., Beckmann, C., Li, I., & Hsu, D. (2004): a CAPpella: programming by demonstration of context-aware applications, *in Proceedings of CHI 2004*, 33-40.

[20] Dey, A.K., Sohn, T., Streng, S., & Kodama, J. (2006) iCAP: Interactive Prototyping of Context-Aware Applications, *in Proceedings of Pervasive 2006*, 254-271.

[21] Dey, A.K., Newberger, A.N., & Chau, E. (2006) Support for context monitoring and control, in submission.

[22] Dourish, P. (2004) What we talk about when we talk about context, *Personal and Ubiquitous Computing*, 8(1):19-30.

[23] Dittmar, H. (1989) Gender identity-related meanings of personal possessions, in *British Journal of Social Psychology*, 28(6):159-171.

[24] Elliot, K., Neustaedter, C., & Greenberg, S. (2005) Time, Ownership and Awareness: The Value of Contextual Locations in the Home, in *Proceedings of Ubicomp 2005*.

[25] Fleuriot, C. (2001). An Investigation into the management of time in complex lifestyles, Ph.D thesis, University of the West of England.

[26] Frissen, V.A.J. (2000) ICTs in the rush hour of life, *The Information Society*, 16: 65-75

[27] Gajos, K., Fox, H., & Shrobe, H. (2002) End user empowerment in human centered pervasive computing, in *Proceedings of Pervasive 2002*, 1-7.

[28] Garfinkel, H. (1967) *Studies in Ethnomethodology*, Engelwood Cliffs, NJ: Prentice Hall.

[29] Gaver, B., Dunne, T., & Pacenti, E. (1999) Design: Cultural probes, *interactions*, 6(1): 21-29.

[30] Grinter, R.E. & Edwards, W.K. (2001) At Home with ubiquitous computing: Seven challenges, In *Proceedings of Ubicomp 2001*, 256-272.

[31] Harper, R. (2003) Inside the smart home: Ideas, possibilities and methods. in Richard Harper (Ed.) *Inside the smart home*. New York: Springer, 1-14.

[32] Hayghe, H. V. (1989) Children in 2 worker families and real family income, in *Bureau of Labor and Statistics' Monthly Labor Review*, 112(12): 48-52.

[33] Hindus, D. (1999) The importance of homes in technology research, in *Proceedings of CoBuild 1999*, 199-207.

[34] Humble, J., Crabtree, A., Hemmings, T., Åkesson, K., Koleva, B., Rodden, T., &Hansson, P. (2003) "Playing with the bits": User-configuration of ubiquitous domestic environments, in *Proceedings of Ubicomp 2003*, 256–263.

[35] Jahnke, J.H., d'Entremont, M., & Stier, J. (2002) Facilitating the programming of the smart home, *IEEE Wireless Communications*, 9(6): 70-76.

[36] Kidd, C., Orr, R.J., Abowd, G.D., Atkeson, C., Essa, I., MacIntyre, B., Mynatt, E., Starner, T., & Newstetter, W. (1999) The Aware Home: A living laboratory for ubiquitous computing research, in *Proceedings of CoBuild 1999*, 191-198.

[37] Kleine, R.E., Kleine, S.S., & Kernan, J.B. (1993) Mundane consumption and the self: A social identity perspective, in *Journal of Consumer Research*, 2(3): 209-235.

[38] McCalley, L. T., Midden, C. J. H. & Haagdorens, K. (2005) Computing systems for household energy conservation: Consumer response and social ecological considerations, in *Proceedings of CHI 2005 Workshop on Social Implications of Ubiquitous Computing*.

[39] Mozer, M. (1998) The neural network house, in *Proceedings of AAAI Symposium on Intelligent Environments*, 110-114.

[40] Newman, M., Sedivy, J. Z., Neuwirth, C. M., Edwards, W. K., Hong, J. I., Izadi, S., Marcelo, K., & Smith, T. F. (2002) Designing for serendipity: Supporting end-user configuration of ubiquitous computing environments, in *Proceedings of DIS 2002*, 147-156.

[41] Nippert-Eng, C. (1995) *Home and work. Negotiating boundaries through everyday life.* Chicago: University of Chicago Press.

[42] Rode, J.A., Toye, E.F. & Blackwell, A.F. (2005) The domestic economy: A broader unit of analysis for end user programming, in *Proceedings of CHI 2005*, 1757-1760.

[43] Shackel, B. (1991). Usability – context, framework, definition, design and evaluation, in Shackel, B. & Richardson, S. (Eds.) *Human Factors for Informatics Usability*, Cambridge, UK: Cambridge University Press, 21-37.

[44] Taylor, A.S. & Swan, L. (2005) Artful systems in the home, in *Proceedings of CHI 2005*, 641-650.

[45] Tolmie, P., Pycock, J., Diggins, T., MacLean, A. & Karsenty, A. (2002) Unremarkable computing, in *Proceedings of CHI 2002*, 399-406.

[46] Truong, K. N., Huang, E. M., & Abowd, G. D. (2004) CAMP: A magnetic poetry interface for end-user programming of capture applications for the home, in *Proceedings of Ubicomp 2004*, 143-160.

[47] Venkatesh, A., Chuan-Fong E.S. & Stolzoff, N.C. (2000) A Longitudinal analysis of computing in the home based on census data 1984-1997, in *Proceedings of HOIT 2000*, 205-215.

[48] Weiser, M. (1991) The computer for the 21st Century, *Scientific American*, 265(3): 94-104.

Historical Analysis:
Using the Past to Design the Future

Susan Wyche[1], Phoebe Sengers[2], and Rebecca E. Grinter [1]

[1] GVU Center
College of Computing
Georgia Institute of Technology
Atlanta, GA, USA
{spwyche, beki}@cc.gatech.edu
[2] Information Science
Cornell University
Ithaca, NY, USA
sengers@cs.cornell.edu

Abstract. Ubicomp developers are increasingly borrowing from other disciplines, such as anthropology and creative design, to inform their design process. In this paper, we demonstrate that the discipline of history similarly has much to offer ubicomp research. Specifically, we describe a historically-grounded approach to designing ubicomp systems and applications for the home. We present findings from a study examining aging and housework that demonstrate how our approach can be useful to sensitize ubicomp developers to the impact of cultural values on household technology, to reunderstand the home space, and to spur development of new design spaces. Our findings suggest that historically-grounded research approaches may be useful in more deeply understanding and designing for context both in and outside of the home.

1   Introduction

As ubicomp moves beyond the work environment and into a broader social and cultural world, researchers are drawing on an expanding set of disciplinary perspectives to inform design. Ubicomp developers commonly employ anthropological methods, most notably ethnography [e.g., 24,26,27]. Similarly, researchers borrow from art and design to develop novel ways to explore the home, such as cultural probes [13]. In this paper, we describe how ubicomp developers can borrow from another discipline useful for exploring domestic environments: history. Examining the past has previously been used to inspire new form factors and styles such as retro; we suggest that history can be further used to provide strategies that, like anthropology, unpack the culture of the home and, like art-inspired design, defamiliarize the home [2]. In this paper we present a study examining housework by older adults and describe how we integrate historical analysis into the design process. We then present findings from a study of older adults' experiences with housework that suggest history can be beneficial in understanding the culture of the home, in defamiliarizing the home, and in spurring designers' imaginations, thereby opening new design spaces.

P. Dourish and A. Friday (Eds.): Ubicomp 2006, LNCS 4206, pp. 35 – 51, 2006.
© Springer-Verlag Berlin Heidelberg 2006

Specifically, our findings demonstrate that historical analysis sheds new light on recurring cultural themes embedded in domestic technology, and by extension, 'smart homes.' Questioning these themes has the potential to lead designers to rethink assumptions about domestic technology use. For example, rather than using "ease of use" as a guiding principle, elders described difficult, yet enjoyable aspects of housework that technology removed. Older adults fondly recalled products that were durable, contradicting the consumption-driven theme that arguably underlies many of the systems and devices being developed for smart homes. This leads to new heuristics for design; for example, do we assume users will be interested in constant software upgrades and stylistically new gadgets and devices or would it be more appropriate to develop products that last for decades? Historical analysis and elders' personal accounts of their histories revealed the importance of sensual aspects of housework lost with the introduction of new technologies. Participants described the isolating impact of technologies introduced to the home, specifically electric dishwashers and washing machines. Developing technologies to support one person rather than multiple people or families is a historical theme repeating itself in current domestic systems.

In each of these examples, understanding how technology has changed for better or worse in the past suggests new options for contemporary technology design. We believe using historical analysis could benefit other designers by providing an additional way to understand context and by spurring their imaginations.

2 Background

Why study history, if our goal is to design the future? One answer can be found in philosopher George Santayana's famous proclamation, "Those who cannot remember the past are condemned to repeat it" [28]. This quotation is widely used to argue that exploring the past helps us understand who we are today and where we are going. For ubiquitous computing, historical awareness can deepen designers' understanding of the context they are designing for. In addition, history can spur designers' imaginations by revealing the contingency of the present situation, rendering it less obvious and inevitable. As Bell et al. suggest [2], using history to defamiliarize the present supports designers in envisioning future domestic life less constrained by present-day cultural assumptions embedded in technology.

Historical awareness could also prompt ubicomp developers to make design decisions that have more positive social and cultural ramifications. As Bell and Kaye have argued [3], new designs for 'smart homes' often repeat themes from the past that, with reflection, designers may not wish to propagate. Critics of smart home prototypes similarly suggest that technologists' visions of the future tend to look backwards rather than forwards. Spigel [31] describes this as "yesterday's future." She uses surveillance systems to demonstrate how familiar uses of technology persist in past and present visions of the smart home. Systems that give parents the ability to survey their children's activities and to monitor unusual behavior have been touted as "the future" for the past 60 years. Even the architectural styles of smart homes demonstrate such repetition; Spigel describes how Tudor, Spanish, and colonial styles have been consistently used for smart home prototypes since their inception as a marketing tool in the 1920's. Indeed, distinguishing the exterior of older "home of tomorrow concepts" presented at fairs and conventions from today's newer "smart homes" is difficult. If designers recognize such themes at the time of development, they can consciously choose whether they should be repeated or altered [29].

There has been some mention of history's relevance in designing for the future in ubicomp and related literature, the most notable being Blythe et al.'s "technology biographies" [6]. These are a set of questions that ask participants to reflect on their present, past, and future experiences with technologies. One element of the technology biographies, "personal histories," are questions aimed at uncovering users' feelings of loss and nostalgia as they relate to technological change. For instance, a participant may be asked to remember their first home computer or how they communicated at work prior to using e-mail. These historical reflections are integrated into an ethnographic study approach.

In this paper we present a historically grounded approach that complements and reinforces history as an element of ubicomp design. Our goal in this paper is to show how history can be integrated into the early stages of design of ubicomp systems through a case study of early design for housework technology. In the following section, we outline the process by which historical analysis was integrated into early design in our case study. This is followed by findings from our study examining aging and housework. We conclude with a discussion about how historically grounded research approaches can benefit the design process.

3 Using Historically Informed Approaches to Explore the Home

Our case study was motivated by two major goals. Topically, our objective was to examine housework as a dimension of the smart home. Housework is a domestic activity largely absent from current smart home discourse (with a few exceptions [4, 5, 11, 25]). Indeed, housework is often rendered obsolete in visions of the future [4], despite the fact that even after more than a century of automation the number of hours women work in the home has remained remarkably stable [10]. Methodologically, our goal was to integrate existing ubicomp data collection methods with sensitivity to history. We intend for these techniques to supplement commonly used ubicomp data gathering methods, such as interviewing and design ethnography [7, 26].

In this section, we describe our approach. First, we describe the historical analysis we engaged in as background research for our study, which included examining historical texts, first-hand sources of popular culture such as magazines and catalogues, and patents. Then, we describe how this historical research led to the development of a new data collecting tool, the 'memory scrapbook', used to elicit additional historical data from study participants. Finally, we describe how our in-home study was structured to leverage historical awareness.

3.1 Historical Analysis

A history is an account of some past event or combination of events. Historical analysis is, therefore, a method of discovering, from records and accounts, what happened in the past [20]. In historical analysis, researchers consider various sources of historical data such as historical texts, newspaper reports, diaries, and maps. The method is commonly used by historians to gain insights into social phenomena. Designers can similarly use historical analysis to identify themes embedded in their work, avoid re-inventing systems that already exist, and establish background prior to user observation or interviewing. Indeed, leading design firm IDEO recognizes this and includes historical analysis in the early stages of their design process [18]. As we will describe below, in our work, we drew on three particular kinds of sources to establish common themes and design opportunities for housework: we reviewed the **historical literature** to find trends that historians have already identified as relevant to domestic technology; we studied **patents** to identify previously attempted technologies and to spark inspiration for new design, and we immersed ourselves in **primary sources from popular literature** that give an experiential sense of the past and provide design resources.

History is not culturally universal. Because we were interested in domestic design in US contexts, we focused our study on the American history of domestic technology. Our results will hold to some extent for other Western contexts which have a similar history, but different histories would need to be told for other cultural contexts.

3.1.1   Reviewing Historical Texts

We began our work by reviewing relevant literature on the history of housework. Although this step took time, it helped establish a background prior to the project's next phases. We took advantage of historians at our university, who specialize in the history of American homes, to point us to seminal works in the field. Our analysis was limited to historical texts written after 1900, because the decades following the industrial revolution are widely considered a time of dramatic change in American homes [9]. We describe here three themes that emerged from the literature as particularly important to understanding the last 100 years of housework in the US: 1) the "labor saving" debate, 2) domestic technology's gendered character, and 3) loss of sensual and emotional qualities that accompanied housework.

Designers often conceive of products thinking they will make tasks easier or faster to perform. However, domestic technologies which are proposed as labor-saving and efficient historically have had a different impact. Research suggests new technologies have often increased time spent doing housework rather than decreased it [9,34]. In part this was due to the rising cleanliness standards that accompanied electric technology into homes during the twentieth century. This created higher expectations for women to produce spotless and hygienic bathtubs, sinks, and toilets. With the introduction of the electronic washer, laundering increased because there was greater demand for clean clothes. Indeed, novel cleaning approaches often divert time from one task to another, thus creating 'more work for mother' [9].

Today, women remain largely responsible for maintaining a home. The drawbacks of assuming housework is "women's work" are well documented [4,9,19,32]. Sweeping, washing, vacuuming, and tidying-up, arguably confine women to the "domestic sphere," thus making it more difficult for them to participate in the socially influential "public sphere."

Finally, as technology makes its way into our domestic lives, some of the felt qualities embedded in everyday experiences become lost. McCarthy and Wright describe *feltness* as the emotional and sensual aspects that make up humans experiences using technology [22]. For example, before dryers, women hung laundry in their backyards where they would talk and exchange gossip with neighbors. Today, dryers are confined to laundry rooms or basements, isolating those who use them from others and thus diminishing some of laundries' felt qualities. We are careful not to downplay the technologies' contributions to removing much of the drudgery associated with housework, but use this example to suggest there are subtle characteristics that shape users' experiences with technology that we risk losing if efficiency and production drive technology development.

Historical awareness enabled us to consciously choose which of these themes deserved repeating, and which we wanted to resist in our designs. For instance, we understood how housework has arguably contributed to woman's marginalization in society and acknowledged this was not a theme we wanted to perpetuate in the smart home. The final benefit of conducting a historical analysis during the initial design phase was that it helped us develop the protocol for our study's interview stage, to be described later.

3.1.2 Patent Search

In order to better understand the historical design space for domestic technology, we engaged in a patent search. The United States Patent office represents a tremendous body of original knowledge and technological innovation.[1] Online databases such as the one found on the Unites States Patent and Trademark Office's website (www.uspto.gov) and freepatentsonline.com make exploring issued patents, patent applications, and expired patents, dating back to 1790 accessible to anyone with internet access. We searched patents from a variety of years, but focused on those issued between 1940 and 1965, because this is considered the height of America's preoccupation with domestic cleanliness [17]. We broadly looked for issued patents related to cleaning technology such as vacuums, dishwashers, irons, and washing machines.

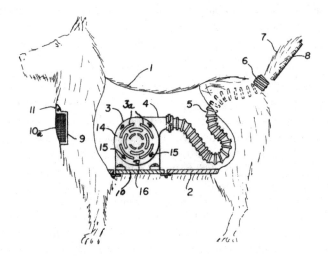

Fig. 1. US Patent no. 3,771,192 Combination Toy Dog and Vacuum Cleaner

---

[1] We chose USPTO because we were interested in designs that had the US market in mind.

Patent searches were useful in tracking the historical roots of many common cleaning technologies used in homes today and making us aware of inventions not mentioned in the history of housework literature. Archived in patent databases were ideas that were never made commercially available, for reasons we did not explore, including a patent for a dinner table that converts into a dishwasher [35], a vacuum cleaner that is disguised to look like a dog [37], and a prototype for a self cleaning house [1]. These forgotten examples spurred us to imagine wildly different ways to think about housework.

3.1.3 Popular Magazines and Catalogues

Recognizing that housework was not only interesting from the standpoint of technological development, but also from the perspective of consumer culture, we examined back issues of magazines and catalogues. This technique, also found in historical accounts of household technology, provides an opportunity to learn about how appliances were sold to and perceived by the public, typically using advertising, problem pages, and articles to elicit that information. We chose to look at *Good Housekeeping, Ladies Home Journal,* and copies of *Sears Roebuck* catalogues because they are considered valid sources for understanding the nature of domestic work in relation to consumer culture in the first half of the twentieth century [8,21].

Wanting to understand housework through the consumer's lens during this time, we looked through randomly selected copies of early magazines. Libraries typically have bound volumes of old magazines shelved chronologically. These primary sources supported a different kind of historical awareness than historical texts, less intellectual and more experiential. We felt like we were traveling back in time, looking at the ads and glancing at the articles in the format in which they originally appeared. Just as with the patent search, there were things to be learned about the history of housework not revealed in historical texts.

It was housework that led, in part, to the creation and rise of these magazines. At the end of the twentieth century, changing attitudes towards cleanliness and the decline of domestic servants led to the proliferation of magazines like *Good Housekeeping* and *Ladies Home Journal.* This was the time of "the great hygienic boom." Breakthroughs in germ theory were taking place and middle-class women were becoming increasingly concerned with germs and their potential to spread disease [17]. The resulting increased standards of cleanliness prompted manufacturers to develop a myriad of products to help homemakers disinfect every room in their homes. The magazines provided a forum for manufacturers to advertise their new products and to offer advice on how to properly maintain a home.

Good Housekeeping and *Ladies Home Journal* have been in continuous publication since the late 1800's and are considered indicators of the social and technical change that have occurred in American, middle-class homes [8]. We had read about the electrification of homes during the 1920's, but observing the transition from laundry tubs to electric washers in catalogues added another dimension to our understanding. The decline in household assistants, or maids, is frequently discussed in historical texts, but viewing advertisements demonstrated the significance of this change. The sharp decline of images picturing maids to ones depicting housewives cheerfully touting various new products was clear. A particular strength of these ads and images was that they provided a rich illustration of changes occurring in the home between the years 1920-1960, in a way that could not be gotten from historical accounts alone.

3.2   Home Studies to Elicit Histories: Elders and the Memory Scrapbook

Reviews of historical literature, patents, and magazines identified a variety of themes and design opportunities for domestic technologies that we decided to explore in an empirical study. Again, we turned to another historically grounded approach to gather empirical evidence: oral histories. Oral histories are verbal testimonies about past events or simply stories from any individual's life [16]. We recognized that, at a time when computer networks are entering homes, much can be learned from those who experienced the past wave in which electricity was introduced into the home. Inspired by Blythe et al.'s technology biographies [6], we decided to integrate oral histories into an ethnographic home study, similar to those already used in ubicomp [7]. There were two core elements to our home study: the selection of appropriate participants and the development of a 'memory scrapbook' to help elicit stories from our informants.

3.2.1   Selection of Project Participants

In order to elicit oral histories, a decisive factor was our selection of participants. We chose to work with older adults who would be able to share their housework experiences from the years 1940 to 1965. Interviews with elders became an important way to breathe life and personal meaning into the historical data we had collected.

Specifically, we did home studies with 11 female homemakers who described themselves as being largely responsible for housework in their homes during the years 1940 to 1965. During these ethnographic-style home studies, we toured their homes and intensively interviewed the homemakers on their housekeeping practices. With the exception of one participant, all had lived in single-family household structures with children, environments similar to what we saw in the advertisements. The age range was 69-84 years old, with a mean age 76 years. Thus, the older participants in our study were approximately 20 to 54 years old during the years we focused on, while younger participants ranged from being children to young adults. Younger participants frequently recalled memories from their adult years as well as their childhoods. We recruited participants by asking colleagues and acquaintances if we could talk to their parents and/or grandparents. Participants were predominantly from the northeastern part of the US. They were compensated for their participation with $50 or a gift certificate to a popular restaurant in their area.

3.2.2   Eliciting Histories Using the Memory Scrapbook

In addition to home tours and intensive interviewing, we developed a research instrument called the 'memory scrapbook' to support collection of historical experiences. In this section, we will explain how the memory scrapbook was designed, then describe its deployment as part of our home studies.

Design of the memory scrapbook

The memory scrapbook design is based on photo elicitation, or the use of photographs to provoke a response. Photo elicitation is based on the simple idea of inserting photographs into a research interview [15]. It is used by anthropologists and historians to stimulate recollection of personal and public memories. The difference between using photos and typical interviewing techniques is that images can evoke deep elements of human consciousness, thus helping uncover richer aspects of a user's experience [20]. In addition, we hoped that photo elicitation might help offset problems with memory that typically occur as people grow older.

We chose to put the images in a scrapbook because it was an attractive and familiar medium for eliciting memories. Scrapbooking is a hobby that emerged in the late 1800s when Americans began pursuing the art of pasting letters, photos, greeting cards and other mementoes in books, as a way of preserving them for future generations [10]. We could expect our participants to be familiar with scrapbooks as a genre for stimulating discussion of the past. Additionally, we hoped the scrapbook's informal and personal nature would be useful in establishing a rich dialogue with our informants while keeping the interview grounded in housework and history.

We drew on our previous historical analysis for design inspiration, returning to the back issues of *Good Housekeeping*, *Ladies Home Journal*, and *Sears Roebuck* catalogues we had looked through earlier. In the magazines we looked for advertisements related to housework. This included products used for doing laundry, washing dishes, polishing silver, and scrubbing toilets, countertops, and floors. We avoided advertisements related to childcare and personal hygiene because we were specifically interested in house cleaning. In the *Sears Roebuck* catalogues we looked for images of cleaning instruments such as brooms, irons, and washing machines. Pictures were selected according to their graphical interest. Selected images were then scanned and catalogued according to their date and what they depicted. Approximately 100 ads and photographs were chosen to potentially be in the scrapbook. They were cropped to take out irrelevant background details so that the focus would be on the advertisement or image.

We purchased an 8.5 x 11 inch, fabric-bound scrapbook at a chain crafts store. There are a variety of scrapbook styles, ranging from ones covered in multi-colored flowers to costly leather bounds ones. Wanting to keep in line with the dated imagery inside the scrapbook, we chose a book covered in a simple black fabric with gold embossed trim. Selected images were color printed on white card stock and arranged on each page with attention to visual composition. There were 12 pages in the book and a total of 52 variously sized images from the years 1940 and 1964 (see Figure 2).

Deployment of the memory scrapbook

The scrapbook was used during our home visits. Following the home tours we returned to the living room or kitchen and asked participants to interact with the scrapbook. It was introduced after the home tour because we were interested in creating a contrast between elders' current housework experiences and their past ones.

We wanted to collect stories rather than facts, which prompted us to develop something more engaging than a typical survey. As with cultural probes [12], the scrapbook was meant to question the preconception of researchers as authorities.

Fig. 2. Page from Memory Scrapbook

Indeed, older adults were the experts in our case because no one on our research team was alive during the time period we were examining. We were also sensitive to the fact that we were using an unfamiliar implementation—the scrapbook—of the oral history research technique. Participants were told that the scrapbook was an experiment on our part:

> *This is a "memory scrapbook," its a way for us to find out more about you and how technology has changed during your lifetime, ignore things you are not familiar with, and discuss things you are. There is no right or wrong answer and I hope it is fun.* –study's principal investigator

We let participants hold the scrapbook and flip through the pages at their own pace. While thumbing through the scrapbook, we stressed that we were interested in memories related to the advertisements and that, if there were images that they were unfamiliar with, not to worry and to go on to the next page.

4   Findings of the Study

In this section, we present findings from our study organized into three topic areas, including issues raised by our study and the resulting design implications. First, we examine the tension between making domestic tasks easier and the challenging aspects that accompanied housework in the past. This suggests that designers should not always make reduction-of-effort a central focus of housework technology, instead retaining some of the challenging and rewarding aspects that elders enjoyed. Second, we discuss the decline in the quality of manufactured cleaning products and suggest that designers should work towards developing systems that are as durable and long-lasting as Fuller brushes. Finally, we analyze the historical tendency of technology to individualize domestic tasks rather than preserving appealing social aspects, and propose ways entertainment and communication devices in the home could bring people together.

4.1 "Hands and Knees"

Using the scrapbook during our interviews, we asked elders to discuss how cleaning had changed over time. Unsurprisingly, many described technology's role in making tasks easier during their lifetimes. Images of wringer washers sparked stories about preferring today's electric washing machines to the earlier manual versions. Wringer washers were commonly used to clean clothes in the 1930's and early 1950's; they were physically demanding and dangerous to use. Advertisements for the laundry soaps like *Bon Ami, Duz,* and *Tide* caused some to recollect when they needed to scrape and boil their own soap; all were pleased that they could buy these items at the store rather than having to make their own.

Despite the positive changes brought by making household tasks easier, many informants described missing difficult aspects of it that became less common with the introduction of efficiency driven domestic technologies. For instance, many participants preferred using their "hands and knees" to clean floors as opposed to using a floor mop.

> *I was a hands-and-knees washer. And I still am basically hands and-knees, if it really has to be done, because just swishing the mop around, you don't get the corners, you really don't do the job.* - 72 year old woman

Prior to the introduction of floor mops and the more recent Swiffer™ cleaners, hands and knees was a common way to clean floors. Though it is physically demanding and time-intensive, some elders preferred this technique because of its thoroughness, the challenge of making a dirtied floor "sparkle," and the sense of satisfaction that followed finishing the job.

> *It's a rather superficial job, using the mop. I would prefer a more thorough job like you get when you get down on the floor yourself.* - 81 year old woman

or

> *I like to have things clean. Like, I enjoy working and cleaning the kitchen floor, you know, making things look good. I feel like I have accomplished something.* - 77 year old woman

Others preferred cleaning on their hands and knees because it was a form of exercise. Indeed, rather than removing the physical effort required to clean a floor, some enjoyed it and considered it a source of physical activity.

When its cold or raining outside I can't go out walking, getting down and cleaning the floors is how I exercise; it's good for me. - 81 year old woman

We have no intention of implying that technology needs to make tasks more difficult and agree that efforts to decrease the amount of time spent on housework are beneficial. However, our findings suggest that by focusing on making tasks effortless, other positive aspects of the experience may be lost.

In addition to developing systems to make tasks easier, perhaps other aspects should be considered. For instance, rather than being a chore, computational systems and devices could be developed that treat housework like a game [5]. Or designers could imagine scrubbing floors as a form of exercise and develop cleaning systems that monitor how many calories users burn, similar to the feedback workout equipment provides. If thoroughness in cleaning is a concern, perhaps that signals a need to develop systems that communicate to users how clean their floors are. If anything, the finding suggests that by exploring how housework was done in the past, designers can consider new ways of envisioning how it can be done in the future.

4.2 Designing Durable Systems and Devices

Included in the scrapbook were images of cleaning supplies taken from *Sears Roebuck* catalogues, like mops, feather dusters, wringer washers, and vacuum cleaners. These images inspired comments about how the quality of cleaning instruments had declined over time. The "Fuller Brush" ads exemplified this trend, because they elicited comments about how durable some products were in the past. The Fuller Brush Company has continuously manufactured cleaning brushes since 1906 and touts itself as creating "the best products of their kind." Indeed the quality and durability described in the brushes' ads proved true. Informants dug into their closets and drawers and eagerly showed us brushes from years ago. Despite frequent use, the participants described how the brushes' bristles always stayed in place.

They were high quality you know . . .very good quality . . . they say bristles don't come out, well they don't. Of course years ago most of our products were well made you know . . . its different today. - 79 year old woman

This sharply contrasted with informants' attitudes regarding products today, which many described as lacking the quality evident in older products.

I remember the Fuller Brush man; his brushes were expensive but wonderful. And they lasted forever. Not like the ones you get at [a chain department store] today. -68 year old woman

And

Oh yes, Fuller Brushes, they were the best brushes ever made, I still have two of them, they are nice, not made out of that cheap plastic you get today. – 71 year old woman

This claim was further supported by elders' comments during our in-home tours. We discovered that participants continued to use some of the same tools to clean that they had used decades earlier. When asked about why they chose to use these older versions, many describe quality as being key.

> *I think back then we care more about things and make them last. Today they don't. You just go buy new ones. I mean I could use this to death [referring to feather duster] and it wouldn't fall apart. Now they throw 'em away. Everything is replaceable today. And back when I was growing up, it wasn't.* - 70 year old woman

One design implication is clear. Rather than designing computational devices and systems that will become outmoded in a limited amount of time, i.e. incorporate planned obsolescence, designers should consider borrowing from Fuller's Brush Company's mantra of making "making things last." Today, computers are becoming almost as disposable as toilet brushes. Monitors fill up landfills and hard drives abound in thrift stores because they no longer work or are out of fashion. The opportunities for new devices in future homes is an opportunity to subvert planned obsolescence and potentially develop ubiquitous computing devices that are sustainable and long-lasting.

4.3   Design to Support Togetherness

Five of the 11 participants had fond memories related to washing dishes when they were growing-up. They described missing the social interaction that accompanied this common household chore. This finding personalizes a theme common in historical accounts, that technology has made housework more isolating. Indeed, as technology made its way into homes, the unplanned interactions that were a common part of housework tended to disappear.

Prior to the electric dryer, garments were dried outside on clotheslines. When electric dryers were introduced, homemakers ceased to go outdoors to hang their washing out, instead going to their own indoor basements or laundry rooms to dry clothes. This led to decreased opportunities to serendipitously interact with neighbors.

> *We lived in a row house. So of course backyards were backyards. . . . but every Sunday, there would be a lot of wash on the line. And I would go and help my grandmother bring it all in. And there would be neighbors there and we would all talk. And my mother, when she would go out and hang wash, we would always talk to our neighbors outside. We always hung wash - we didn't have dryers.* -81 year old woman

Others fondly recalled domestic life prior to electric dishwashers. For many, manual dishwashing was an activity that supported informal conversations among family members.

Well, one of the things I apparently like doing, oddly enough, is washing dishes. I hardly use my dishwasher. Because when I was growing up, the only time I really had a relaxed communication with my mother was when she would be washing dishes, and I would be drying. That became a – and also with my kids, when they were growing up, it became a nice, easy communication – non-threatening communication time. - 69 year old woman

And

I think we have lost something because of the dishwasher that used to be kind of a good time to talk about things and discuss what had been going on in the day and what was bothering you. If you were doing it with your sisters and brothers, or your mother or maid or anybody, it was a nice time. We didn't realize it at the time. We didn't care for doing the dishes, but we have lost that now. - 77 year old woman

Indeed, we see this trend of designing home entertainment and communication technologies for one user rather than multiple ones repeated today. We use *personal* computers at home and TiVo® recording systems note preferences for one user, instead of multiple family members, something which has been empirically seen to cause tension in the group-oriented setting of the home [14]. Rather than having a shared landline, we increasingly see people relying on their personal cell phones when communicating, thus limiting the opportunities for serendipitous interactions with others.

Once again, we are aware that advances in technology have vastly improved how housework is done today, but we also want to draw attention to the sensual qualities of users' experience that have been lost over time. We are arguing that ubicomp developers should design systems and devices to support collective as well as individual activity in order to preserve the social interaction that were an important part of our users' domestic chores.

5   Discussion and Future Work

What became clear from our use of historical methods to understand housework was how different domestic life was 50 years ago. It was effective in helping us understand the subtle changes that have resulted with the introduction of new domestic technologies and in opening new space for design. Although the historical texts already revealed themes pertinent to ubicomp design (i.e. labor-saving debate and technology's gendered character), by drawing on popular texts, patents, and interviews with elders as well, we learned things that could not easily be gleaned from texts alones. For instance, cleaning fluids used to be packaged in glass rather than plastic bottles, the "super sized" packages that detergent are sold in today did not exist, and rather than having dozens of brands of window cleaner to choose from people used to have two or three. Indeed it was primarily the sensual or felt aspects of the domestic experience that appear to have been lost with the introduction of domestic technologies motivated by efficiency. With current interest in restoring felt experience as central to design [22], we believe that historical analysis is an important source for becoming aware of sensual aspects of experiences that have become lost but could be addressed in new forms of technology design. In particular, the multidimensional aspects of our analysis—not only reading historical texts but also looking at patents and images and talking to elders with images as a stimulus—support the development of a rich sense of the felt experience of the activity we are seeking to redesign.

In addition to revealing how felt qualities are altered with the introduction of new technologies, another benefit of our historically grounded approach is its potential to inspire radically novel design concepts. A collection of speculative design proposals resulted from our process [see 30 and 36 for details]. Like ethnography, history forces designers to become more aware of their preconceptions about a topic. Because of its ability to defamiliarize the present, history can be a powerful recourse for inspiring innovative computational devices and systems.

5.1 Broader Implications

Although our study focused on housework, we believe the same strategies would be useful for other aspects of the domestic environment, such as cooking, childcare, or entertainment, as well as for other activities outside the home. For example, during our interviews, many older adults described massive changes in how they shopped for household goods; exploring this changing history of shopping could reveal design opportunities for e-shopping today. Even the design of workplace systems could arguably be inspired by an understanding of how work has changed over the last century.

Central to our techniques for historical analysis is a carefully designed, material artefact which stimulates oral histories. Other than a scrapbook, we believe other mediums have potential for eliciting stories from the past for the purpose of inspiring design. For instance, a view-master with a slide reel from the early games and toys could be an evocative way to elicit stories about how gaming systems have evolved over the last 40 years. Specially-designed recipe books could be deployed to understand how kitchen technologies have changed over time, while researchers exploring urban computing could use old maps and atlases to elicit stories about how urban space has changed. In all these cases, carefully designed artefacts can provide an evocative and engaging focus for conversation with users.

6 Conclusion

In recent years ubicomp researchers and developers have increasingly been influenced by methodologies deployed by designers, sociologists, and anthropologists. In this paper we extend this trend to include methods from the discipline of history and demonstrate how doing so can contribute to understanding the domestic environment for the purpose of design. The process of historical analysis that we developed involved four major steps. First, we analysed historical texts to identify major themes in the development of technologies (often automation) for the activities under investigation, in our case housework. Second, we gained a broader understanding of the existing technological design space through the search of patents. Third, we developed a personal sense of the changing nature of housework through examination of primary sources from popular culture. Finally, as part of broader fieldwork we gathered oral histories from older people, using a designed, material artefact that reflected the popular history of housework to stimulate memories and reflections. Through these steps, we both developed a better understanding of the activities under design and defamiliarized ourselves from the standard technology design process, opening up new spaces for technology design in the home.

Acknowledgments

We would like to thank all of the homemakers who kindly let us into their homes to talk about housework. We would also like to thank Paul Dourish, Giovanni Iachello, Kris Nagel and Amy Voida for their supportive advice on how to structure this paper, and the anonymous reviewers for helpful comments, criticisms, and suggestions. This work was supported by a research grant from the S.C. Johnson and Son Co. and by NSF Grant IIS-0238132.

References

1. Bateson, F.G. (1984) "Self-cleaning Building Constructions." United States Patent and Trademark Office. Patent no. 4,428,085.
2. Bell, G., Blythe, M. and Sengers, P. (2005) "Making by Making Strange: Defamiliarization and the Design of Domestic Technology." *Transactions on Computer-Human Interaction (TOCHI)*, Special issue on Social Issues and HCI, vol. 12, no. 2, pp. 149-173.
3. Bell, G. and Kaye, J. (2002) "Designing Technology for Domestic Spaces: A Kitchen Manifesto." *Gastronomica*, vol. 2, no. 2, pp.46-62.
4. Berg, A.J. (1999) "A gendered socio-technical construction: the smart house," in *The Social Shaping of Technology*, D. MacKenzie and J. Wajcman (eds.), Second ed. Buckingham: Open University Press, pp. 301-313.
5. Blythe, M., and Monk, A. (2002) "Notes Towards an Ethnography of Domestic Technology." *Proc. DIS 2002*, pp. 279-282, London: ACM Press.
6. Blythe, M., Monk, A., and Park, J. (2002) "Technology Biographies: Field Study Techniques for Home Use Product Development." Extended Abstracts *CHI 2002*, pp. 658-659, Minneapolis, MN: ACM Press.
7. Consolvo, S., Arnstein, L., and Franza, B.R. (2002) "User Study Techniques in the design and Evaluation of a Ubicomp Environment." *Proc. UbiComp '02*, pp. 73-30, Göteborg, Sweden: Springer.
8. Cowan, R.S. (1976) "The 'Industrial Revolution' In the Home: Household Technology and Social Change in the 20th Century." *Technology and Culture*, vol. 17. pp.1-23.
9. Cowan, R.S. (1983) *More Work for Mother: The Ironies of Household Technology from the Open Hearth to the Microwave*. Basic Books Inc.
10. Fram, E. (2005) "The Booming Scrapbooking Market in the USA: Despite Phenomenal Growth, the Future's Unclear." *International Journal of Retail & Distribution Management*. vol. 33, no. 3, pp. 215-225.

11. Forlizzi, J., and DiSalvo, C. (2006). "Service Robots in the Domestic Environment: A Study of the Roomba Vacuum in the Home," *Proc. Of Human-Robot Interaction 2006*. Salt Lake City, Utah: ACM Press.

12. Gaver, W. (2001) *The Presence Project*. Computer Related Design Research, RCA London.

13. Gaver, W., Dunne, A., and Pacenti, E. (1999) "Cultural Probes," *Interactions*. vol. 6, no. 1, pp 21-29.

14. Grinter, R.E., Edwards, W.K., Newman, M.W., and Ducheneaut, N. (2005) "The Work to Make a Home Network Work," *Proc. of the Ninth European Conference on Computer-Supported Cooperative Work* (ECSCW'05). Paris, France.

15. Harper, D. (2002) "Talking About Pictures: A Case for Photo Elicitation." *Visual Studies*. vol. 17, no.1. pp. 13-26.

16. Hoopes, J. (1979) *Oral History: An Introduction for Students*. Chapel Hill, NC: The University of North Carolina Press.

17. Hoy, S. (1997) *Chasing Dirt: The American Pursuit of Cleanliness*. Oxford University Press.

18. IDEO (2003) "IDEO Method Cards: 51 Ways to Inspire Design." San Francisco, CA: W. Stout Architectural Books.

19. Lupton, E. (1993) *Mechanical Brides: Women and Machines from Home to Office*. New York, NY: Cooper-Hewitt National Museum of Design.

20. Marshall, C. and Rossman, G.B.(1998) *Designing Qualitative Research*. Newbury Park, CA.: Sage Publications, Inc.

21. Martens, L. and Scott, S. (2005) "The Unbearable Lightness of Cleaning: Representations of Domestic Practice and Products in Good Housekeeping Magazine: 1951-2001." *Consumption, Markets and Culture*, vol. 8, no.4, pp. 379-401.

22. McCarthy P., and Wright, P. (2004) *Technology as Experience*. Cambridge, Mass.: MIT Press.

23. Modell, J. and Brodsky, C. (1994) "Envisioning Homestead: Using Photographs in Interviewing" in *Interactive Oral History Interviewing*, E. McMahan and K.L. Rogers (eds.), Hillsdale, NJ: Erlbaum.

24. Rode, J.A., Toye, E.F. and Blackwell, A.F. (2004) "The Fuzzy Felt Ethnography - Understanding the Programming Patterns of Domestic Appliances." *Personal and Ubiquitous Computing 8* , pp. 161-176

25. Rode, J. (2005) "Appliances for Whom? Considering Place*."   Proc. of the 3rd International Conference on Appliance Design*. Bristol, UK.

26. Salvador, T., Bell, G. and Anderson, K. (1999) "Design Ethnography." *Design Management Journal*, vol. 10, no. 4, pp. 35-41.

27. Salvador, T., and Anderson, K. (2003) "Practical Considerations of Context for Context Based Systems: An Example from an Ethnographic Case Study of a Man Diagnosed with Early Onset Alzheimer's Disease." *Proc. UbiComp '03*, pp.   243-255. Seattle, WA: Springer.

28. Santanaya, G. (1953). "Reason in Common Sense." *The Life Of Reason,* Rev. Ed. New York: Charles Scribner's Sons.

29. Sengers, P. (2004) "Doomed to Repeat? How History Can (and Should!) Inform Home Technology." Position paper presented at CHI 2004 Workshop on "Designing Culturally Situated Technologies for the Home." Available online: www.cemcom.infosci.cornell.edu/papers/doomed-to-repeat.pdf

30. Sengers, P., Kaye, J., Boehner, K., Fairbank, J., Gay, G., Medynskiy, E., Wyche, S. (2004) "Culturally Embedded Computing." *IEEE Pervasive Computing*, vol. 03, no.1, pp. 14-21.

31. Spigel, L. (2001) "Yesterday's Future, Tomorrow's Home." *Emergences*, vol. 11, no. 1., pp. 29-49.
32. Strasser, S. (2000) *Never Done: A History of American Housework*. New York, NY.; Henry Holt.
33. *The Sears Roebuck Catalogues of the Thirties: Selected Pages from the Entire Decade.* (1978) Franklin Square, N.Y.: Nostalgia, Inc.
34. Vanek, J. (1974) "Time Spent in Housework." *Scientific America*, vol. 231, pp. 116-120.
35. Wilson, W. (1961) "Combined Dining Table and Dishwasher." US Patent no. 2,971,519.
36. Wyche, S. (2005) "Designing Speculative Cleaning Products for the Home." Proc. DUX '05. San Francisco, Ca.: ACM Press.
37. Zaleski, A.M. (1973) "Combination Toy Dog and Vacuum Cleaner." United States Patent and trademark Office. Patent no. 3,771,192.

Extending Authoring Tools for Location-Aware Applications with an Infrastructure Visualization Layer

Leif Oppermann[1], Gregor Broll[2], Mauricio Capra[1], and Steve Benford[1]

[1] Mixed Reality Laboratory, University of Nottingham
Wollaton Road, Nottingham, NG8 1BB, UK
{lxo, mxc, sdb}@cs.nott.ac.uk
[2] Embedded Interaction Research Group, University of Munich
Amalienstraße 17, 80333 Munich, Germany
gregor@hcilab.org

Abstract. In current authoring tools for location-aware applications the designer typically places trigger zones onto a map of the target environment and associates these with events and media assets. However, studies of deployed experiences have shown that the characteristics of the usually invisible ubiquitous computing infrastructure, especially limited coverage and accuracy, have a major impact on an experience. We propose a new approach in which designers work with three layers of information: information about the physical world, information about digital media, but also visualizations of ubiquitous infrastructure. We describe the implementation of a prototype authoring tool that embodies this approach and describe how it has been used to author a location-based game for mobile phones called Tycoon. We then outline the key challenges involved in generalizing this approach to more powerful authoring tools including acquiring and visualizing infrastructure data, acquiring map data, and flexibly specifying how digital content relates to both of these.

1 Introduction

As location-aware applications continue to emerge and mature so attention increasingly turns to the question of how best to author and configure them. Applications as diverse as tourism, games, navigation and mobile information retrieval require the creation of content in which digital assets – images, sounds, text, video and graphics – are attached to locations in the physical world to be triggered by participants who enter, leave or dwell in them.

Dedicated authoring tools and techniques for location-aware applications have begun to emerge in response. All of the examples produced to date share a common overarching approach – the idea of taking a map of the physical area in which the experience is to take place and then somehow placing or drawing a series of regions, locales or hotspots on top of this that are triggered according to a set of basic events such as participants entering and leaving them.

The Mediascape tool (see figure 1, left) from the Mobile Bristol project is one such tool in which designers can place different sized and shaped triggers on a map and associate these with a range of events. Mediascape [1] has been used to support a

P. Dourish and A. Friday (Eds.): Ubicomp 2006, LNCS 4206, pp. 52–68, 2006.

variety of location-aware applications including: Scape the Hood [2] in which users explored an area of San Francisco, triggering stories as they entered different city blocks and Riot! [3], an audio experience in which participants triggered spatialized sounds as they explored a large city-centre square.

A variant on this approach is the idea of Colour Maps (figure 1, right), in which artists directly paint location triggers onto a map, affording a high degree of flexibility in terms of their size and shape and also enabling them to use existing and familiar paint tools. This approach was used to support the projects Uncle Roy All Around You in which a group of artists defined a trail of text clues around a city for players to follow as part of an interactive performance [4], and Savannah in which groups of six children at a time role played being lions on a virtual savannah that appeared to be overlaid on their school playing field [5].

As a third example, Caerus [6], enables a designer to administer trigger areas that overlay a digital map. The user can add further maps, points of interest and multimedia streams.

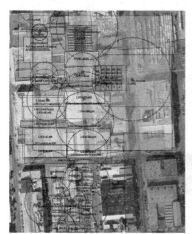 

Fig. 1. The design of Scape the Hood in Mediascape (left), The design of Uncle Roy All Around You using Colour Maps (right)

2 Designing for the Uncertainty of Positioning and Communications

However, published studies of location-aware applications suggesting that there is more to designing them than attaching media assets to a map. Rather – in strong contrast to traditional wired applications – designers need to be aware of the inherent uncertainties in the ubiquitous infrastructure, most notably limited coverage of wireless communications and limited coverage and accuracy of positioning systems.

Studies of Can You See Me Now? (CYSMN), a game of chase in which online participants were chased through a 3D virtual model of a city by performers who, equipped with PDAs and GPS units, had to run through the actual city streets in order to catch them, showed that limited coverage and accuracy had a major impact on the game [7]. Performers, game managers and designers had to understand and account for the local characteristics of the ubiquitous computing infrastructure at each new city that they visited, building up a common stock of knowledge as to coverage and performance blackspots. The extent of the problem can be seen on in figure 2 which visualizes the characteristics of GPS and Wi-Fi over the course of a two hour performance on a peninsula in Rotterdam. The light colored areas correspond to locations where performers acquired a GPS fix and were able to transmit it back to the game server over Wi-Fi (i.e., where both Wi-Fi and GPS were available). Light blue shows high estimated GPS accuracy and light green lower accuracy. The dark areas represent areas where either the performers never ventured or some combination of GPS and/or Wi-Fi were not available. Given that the performers ventured widely, there were clearly many areas that were not playable, especially the central thoroughfares between the main buildings (which are shown as back rectangles – the surrounding black area is water where the performers never went). Furthermore, the availability and performance of GPS and Wi-Fi vary over time as objects move into and out of the environment and GPS satellites move over the sky, so that such pictures can in fact be highly dynamic.

This raises a fundamental question for location-aware authoring tools? What is the point of placing assets at physical locations where there is insufficient coverage or performance to reliably access them? Or put another way, how can we enable designers to taken account of the usually invisible ubiquitous infrastructure as well as the nature of the physical environment when authoring an experience. This is the key challenge addressed by this paper.

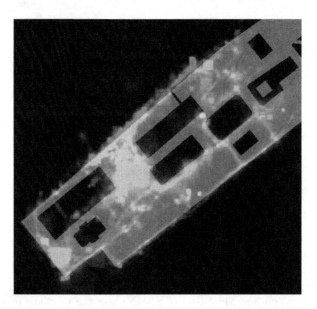

Fig. 2. A visualization of GPS and Wi-Fi coverage and accuracy from CYSMN

3 Extending Authoring Tools to Reveal the Ubiquitous Infrastructure

In our extended approach, we support the designer with knowledge of the physical world and the ubiquitous infrastructure at the same time. The authoring process now involves overlaying information characterizing communications and sensing systems on meaningful backgrounds that facilitate the orientation of the game designer. For geo-coded data this would be a map of the area, for time-stamped data this might be a timeline. For the scope of this paper we will limit the possibilities to interactively visualizing geo-coded data on maps.

Figure 3 summarizes the overall concept behind our authoring tool for location-aware applications. The tool enables designers to work with three layers of information: the *physical environment layer*, with representations of the target physical environment; the *infrastructure layer*, with representations of the ubiquitous computing infrastructure across this environment, and the *content layer*, with representations of digital media. In practice, each layer may consist of a series of sub-layers that reveal different types of information: maps, aerial photographs and GIS data for the physical environment; recorded and predicted information about the coverage and accuracy of communications and sensing systems for the infrastructure layer; and triggers, hotspots, assets and events and the content layer.

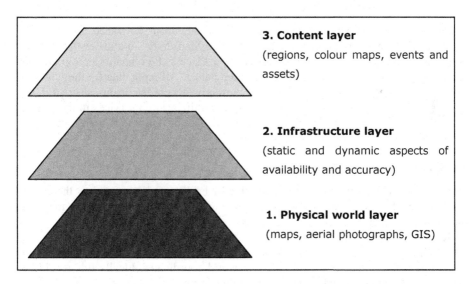

3. Content layer

(regions, colour maps, events and assets)

2. Infrastructure layer

(static and dynamic aspects of availability and accuracy)

1. Physical world layer

(maps, aerial photographs, GIS)

Fig. 3. Authoring Content Triggers based on Infrastructure Visualization

The key innovation here in relation to previous tools is the insertion of the infrastructure layer. This layer helps the designer to understand the spatial spread of otherwise invisible infrastructure (e.g. GSM network, Wi-Fi, GPS) at authoring time.

4   Designing the Authoring Tool

Our new authoring tool is designed to work with a large number of samples that measure the characteristics of the underlying infrastructure. Due to potential screen space constraints we decided to implement the visualizations in an interactive way. We have adopted a 'detail-on-demand' approach to visualization following Ben Shneiderman's Visual Information Seeking Mantra: "Overview first, zoom and filter, then details-on-demand" [8].

wxWidgets[1], OpenGL[2] and SDL[3] are used as a platform independent base-system, providing the necessary user input and output channels for our interactive application as shown in the data-flow diagram in figure 4.

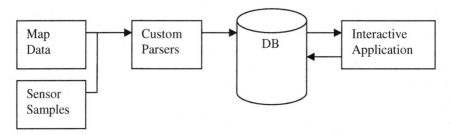

Fig. 4. Data-Flow Diagram

For our maps, we used closed source vector-data from Ordnance Survey[4] and parsed it with FWTools[5] before rendering it with Mapserver[6] to a raster file-format. The sensor samples have been collected using a Place Lab compatible program and parsed from a flat-file storage using our custom parser. All input data for the *physical world layer* and *infrastructure layer* is currently accessible using abstract C++ interfaces. The overall architecture leans towards utilizing web services in the future, which would support the use of different programming languages across different computers for different interaction tasks.

4.1 Physical World Layer

This layer provides the user with a meaningful background in regard to the target environment. For the current prototype we limited the background to 2D maps in Cartesian coordinates.

Reading common file-formats, the tool also allows for using digitized maps or orthophotos. The loaded bitmaps can then be geo-coded by supplying two points, both in the image coordinate-space and the real world coordinates. Ideally this would be the lower-left and upper-right coordinates of the map.

---

[1] http://www.wxwidgets.org/

[2] http://www.opengl.org/

[3] http://www.libsdl.org/

[4] http://edina.ac.uk/digimap/description/

[5] http://fwtools.maptools.org/

[6] http://mapserver.gis.umn.edu/

4.2 Infrastructure Layer

The infrastructure layer contains samples of network information tagged with time and/or position. It is projected in the same way as the background map and thus the samples are put into the right context when the two layers are stacked up. This enables the user to reason about the infrastructural data, e.g. decide about whether an area has been sampled densely enough. Figure 5 (middle) shows a generally well sampled area which could eventually need some more data on the northern and western side of the area. Each of the green dots in the image represents a sample (in this case of GSM cell data that has been geo-referenced using GPS).

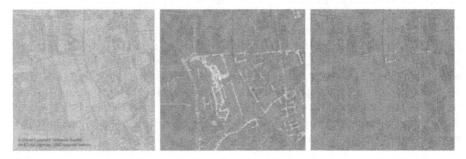

Fig. 5. A map of Nottingham, UK (left), overlaid with GSM sensor-data (middle), view interactively filtered by Cell ID (right)

The samples are referenced by unique ID-strings. If the ID-strings themselves should be used to trigger content in the final experience they will have to be reproducible on the target device by accessing the infrastructure. Examples of sources for such possible ID-strings are given in the following table.

Table 1. Reproducible ID-strings for different infrastructures

GSM	Full Cell ID (MCC_MNC_LAC_CI)
Wi-Fi	BSSID (Mac Address of Access Point)
GPS	Location (latitude/longitude)

4.3 Content Layer

The interactive visualization itself only acts as a hint to the user. The actual content is defined and refined in the content layer. Here the author can make informed decisions about where to place assets, where the experience should take place or which observed sensors could serve as triggers for events. For example the right image in figure 5 shows the infrastructure filtered to show the possible spread of a single GSM cell across a region of space. This cell could arguably be used to trigger events which have a notion of location but do not require exact latitude/longitude coordinates, e.g. traffic info for the surrounding area or virtual locations in a mobile phone game. The following section presents a game design that works using this principle.

5 Authoring Tycoon – A Game for Mobile Phones

In order to demonstrate our proposed approach to authoring ubiquitous experiences we have created Tycoon, a location-based multiplayer trading-game for mobile phones. The gameplay in Tycoon is driven by players entering and leaving different mobile phone cells which are associated with different game resources. Choosing which resources to associate with specific cells is therefore a key aspect of designing the game and in turn, requires an understanding of how the cells are distributed across physical space.

The basic idea behind Tycoon's gameplay is a simple producer-consumer-cycle. Players have to roam a designated gaming area (e.g. a park or the centre of a city), collect resources and trade them for objects that earn them certain amounts of credits. The objective of the game is to collect as many credits as possible in order to win the game. Tycoon uses the different physical GSM-cells of a service-provider network within the gaming area and maps one or several of them to virtual locations in the game that represent producers, consumers or neutral areas (figure 6). The game uses the metaphor of a wild-west scenario to communicate its basic mechanisms of collecting resources from producer-locations which are called "mines" and using them to buy objects from consumer-locations which are called "brokers" and have the names of towns or counties in California, USA.

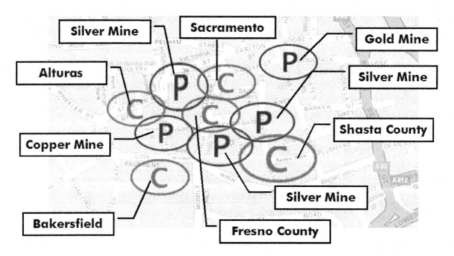

Fig. 6. Example of a Tycoon gaming-area with its mapping of physical locations to consumers (C) and producers (P)

During the game, players have to explore the gaming area and discover the locations of brokers and mines (figure 7, left). After their discovery, players can collect local resources from mines by staying in them for a certain period of time (figure 7, middle). Each mine provides an unlimited amount of one local resource in the game – gold, silver or copper – which differ in their value and the time it takes to collect them. They are called "local resources" since players collect them independently from each other and do not compete for them.

Brokers on the other hand each keep a list of unique global objects, e.g. different buildings in towns or estates in counties (figure 7, right). Players can see these lists after having discovered the location of the corresponding broker. The number of global objects in the game is limited, each one is unique (e.g. there is only one hotel in the city of Bakersfield) and players compete against each other for claiming them. Each object has a certain price in different local resources and a corresponding value of credits. Players can claim global objects from a broker's list after entering his area and earn the objects' credits provided they can afford their price and the desired objects are still available.

Fig. 7. Different screen images from Tycoon's interface: location discovery (left), collecting Resources (middle), claiming objects (right)

5.1 Seams in Mobile Applications

Ubiquitous Computing systems and especially applications for mobile communication and navigation are susceptible to the effects of so-called seams in the underlying technical infrastructure. Seams can be seen as deviations in actual use from a notional ideal of technological continuity or uniformity, including discontinuities in technologies themselves and discontinuity between what actually happens and what the system observes [9]. They are mostly caused by technical limitations and constraints in the heterogeneous infrastructure of a system. They may reveal their effects on the user experience, showing themselves as uncertainties, ambiguities or inconsistencies when users interact with a supposedly seamless system. Common examples for seams in mobile applications are deviations in positioning, unavailability of network services or patchy network coverage. As such, they may come to the users' attention as interruption and loss of services or uncertainty about current position.

Previous research has identified a range of different strategies for dealing with these kinds of seams when designing ubiquitous experiences [10]. These include improving or deploying the underlying technologies so as to *remove* them; carefully designing the experience to *hide* their worst effects from users; carefully *managing* the experience from behind the scenes; *revealing* the presence of seams to users so that they can adapt to them; and even deliberately *exploiting* the seams as part of the design (the approach of 'seamful design' as described in [9]). All of these approaches require that the designer become aware of the presence of seams across their chosen physical environment, which of course is the purpose behind our proposal to add a visualization layer to current authoring tools.

Tycoon follows the approach of exploiting seams that arise from the use of GSM cells as a basis for positioning. Users are normally unaware of their current GSM cell or location while using their mobile phones, as this information is mostly hidden by the system and the handover between adjoining cells is handled seamlessly [11]. While seamless design usually neglects this information, our seamful approach to mobile games reveals the presence of individual mobile phone cells and uses them to drive the overall user experience.

Since location-awareness is crucial for Tycoon's gameplay, we use information from GSM cells for positioning which is sufficient for our approach but also implies several constraints and seams. Figure 8 gives an example of GSM cell propagation and coverage which depends on many factors, is very dynamic and has irregular, fluctuating shapes. Cells do not have fixed boundaries and do not share exact borders with adjoining cells but often overlap with them. These properties can become a problem for mobile applications whose behaviour is dependent on exact positioning.

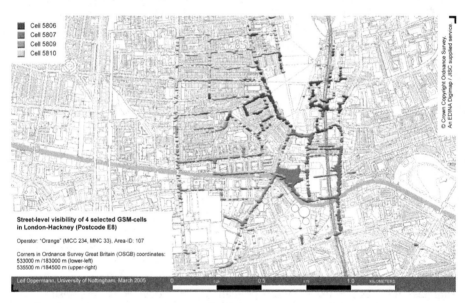

Fig. 8. GSM cell coverage and propagation indicated by samples of cell-IDs and their GPS-position in London

Being a mobile multiplayer game, Tycoon's gameplay is driven by the competition between several players with mobile phones. Tycoon is implemented using a client-server-architecture and players need continuous access to globally shared data on the game-server in order to compete successfully with each other. Therefore mobile Internet-access is most convenient and almost indispensable for accessing the global server and synchronising its shared game-state with mobile clients. A seamless approach would try to guarantee as little inconsistency between the global and all local game-states as possible by frequent updates between the mobile clients and the game-server. Whenever a mobile client locally changes the game-state, e.g. by claiming a globally shared object, the game-server would either have to route this change to all clients or they would periodically have to ask the server for updates on the latest changes. Either way, a considerable volume of expensive GPRS-traffic would be generated. Given the definition of seams in [9], these expenses might also be considered to be self-made, artificial seams, since they are neither caused by technical constraints nor show themselves as uncertainties or ambiguities. But as costly expenses for GPRS-traffic still constrain the uniformity and continuity of mobile applications, we want to treat them as a significant seam.

The frequency of updates between server and mobile clients in order to maintain a globally correct game-state is tightly linked to the probability of data inconsistencies which occur as a consequence of insufficient synchronisation. Inconsistencies emerge when individual clients update data that is shared with other clients through a common server. When a Tycoon client synchronises its locally altered data with the shared server in order to update the globally shared game-state, e.g. after claiming an object, local copies of that data on other clients become inconsistent with the updated game-state and have to be updated accordingly.

5.2 Augmenting Mobile Gameplay with Seamful Design

Tycoon's game-logic and interface are designed to incorporate and exploit the seams of dynamic cell positioning, expensive internet-access and data-inconsistencies in order to enrich its gameplay.

Tycoon's gameplay is location-dependent and applies positioning through the recognition of unique GSM cell identifiers in a gaming area. As mentioned above, this method of positioning is not very accurate and can comprise considerable deviations. In order to improve navigation and orientation for the user, the main screen of Tycoon's interface always displays the name of the current location, along with the amount of collected resources and earned credits (figure 9, left). When a player changes from one cell into another, an alert is triggered and a notification about them entering a new location is displayed (figure 9, middle). Afterwards the name of the new location is shown on the main screen until the next change (figure 9, right).

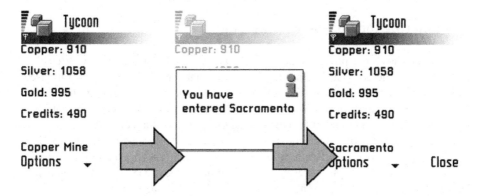

Fig. 9. Tycoon's alert-mechanism for location-visualization

This alert-mechanism is more flexible than a static map of the gaming area, reveals information about fluctuating coverage and propagation of GSM cells, and improves the visualization of locations and their boundaries. Thus the design of Tycoon is intended to decrease players' uncertainties about their position, improve their interaction with the seam of dynamic cell propagation and use it as an important part of game logic.

Instead of providing players with a complete map of the area showing them exactly where to find mines and brokers, we want them to start the game by having to explore the area, gather their own knowledge about it and discover mines, brokers and their locations themselves. This way, players are encouraged to use their spatial knowledge about the gaming-area in order to adopt their own strategies of moving between cells and finding the most efficient tactics of which resources are needed to buy which available objects and where to find them in nearby mines.

During this process of appropriation, players can exploit positioning ambiguities caused by dynamic cell propagation more effectively when they find an area where adjoining cells overlap and easily flip after some time without moving. This issue is especially interesting for designing the gaming-area and assigning mines and brokers to different locations.

5.3 Considering Locations According to the Game-Design

Since the game is running on a mobile phone, it is easy to assume the phone visits different locations given that people move over time. We wanted the game to be playable during the players' daily life without neither interfering too much with what they are doing nor requiring to them to visit special places. We therefore decided that locations in the game should be mapped to places that people come across anyway.

Our game-design defines that Tycoon is going to be played by the inhabitants of a city over a long summer weekend to facilitate discovering places. Assuming that people are doing their shopping at weekends we choose the city-center and shopping malls to be the brokers. Parks and recreational areas are defined to be the mines.

The next section shows how the current prototype tool can be used to author Tycoon for these locations.

6   Authoring for Locations in Tycoon

This section shows our prototype design tool can be used to author Tycoon. We show how the infrastructure visualization layer helps to make a GSM based location based game. Using the tool we define cell ID based regions that serve as triggers for virtual locations in the game. In the following, the presented GSM infrastructure data has been collected over a period of two days using one phone and a GPS receiver.

Figure 10 above shows two screenshots of the authoring tool with a 6 x 6 km view of a city in England overlaid with infrastructure data from the Orange GSM network. Thousands of coloured dots represent where a combination of GSM and GPS data has been sampled. Each dot represents one sample and shows that a particular cell ID has

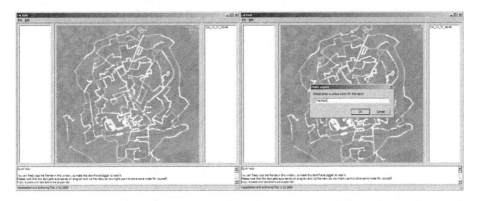

Fig. 10. Initial graphical definition of a region

been seen at this specific position. Dots with the same colour represent the same ID-string (here: cell ID). By hovering the mouse over the visualization the user can see which ID is next to the mouse pointer and where else that ID has been observed. The samples with the current ID are highlighted by jumping yellow dots (bold dots in these screenshots). Having animated features allows the user to easily distinguish between samples that belong to the current selection and those that do not. The current selection of one or more IDs is shown in the listbox to the right of the window. The user can store this selection as a region by giving it a unique name (figure 10, right). The region then appears in the region listbox to the left (see figure 11, left).

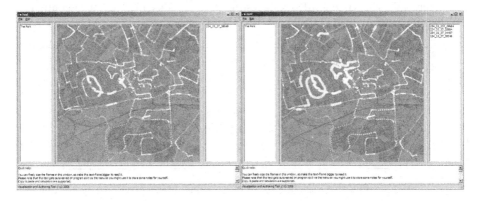

Fig. 11. Close up (left) and refined definition (right)

By zooming the view, the user can look over the details of their selection. Figure 11 shows the same selection as before but with a more close-up view. In this example, the user wanted to select the area around the park in the left part of the image. Although the area seems to be well covered by just one cell, the visualization certainly shows samples with different colours nearby. The user can now modify his selection in the zoomed view and apply any modifications should they be needed.

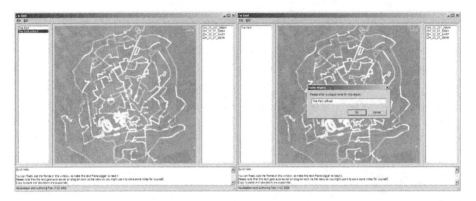

Fig. 12. Zoomed out for overview (left) and save refined region (right)

Figure 12 (left) shows the refined region definition that covers more of the park. There are now 4 Cell IDs in the selection. By zooming out, the selection can be visually verified once again before saving it as a region if satisfied (figure 12, right).

The resulting region definitions (textual ID-strings) can then be post-processed and translated into an application specific format to serve as location triggers in the game.

6.1 Deploying the Game Content to the Clients

The Tycoon game client runs on Symbian phones and uses a client-server architecture. The server uses a standard LAMP[7] software installation. The MySQL database on the server is filled by a PHP script parsing the XML region definitions (see figure 13). The same XML-file is also used by another PHP script to configure the clients when they log into the server.

```
<r>
        <rid>4</rid>
        <n>Sacramento</n>
        <t>broker</t>
        <lid>234_33_237_29678</lid>
        <lid>234_33_37_34457</lid>
        <lid>234_33_37_24949</lid>
</r>
```

Fig. 13. Example XML Content Definition (Excerpt)

Figure 13 shows an excerpt from the content definition. It defines the region number 4 called "Sacramento" to be a broker. The region will be triggered when a player's phone is connected to one of the cells that construct the supplied ID-strings. Figure 14 shows the propagation of the regions from the XML file through the server to the clients.

---

[7] Lamp = Linux, Apache, MySQL, PHP/Perl/Python.

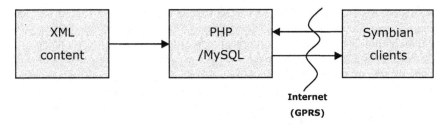

Fig. 14. Propagation of content from server to client

7 Challenges for Further Work

We have presented a prototype authoring tool that supports the designer of location-aware applications with interactive visualizations of ubiquitous infrastructure in addition to the typical map background. The prototype has been used to author a location aware game for mobile phones that does not require a GPS device for positioning. However, if we want to generalize our authoring approach and transform it into something that can be used anywhere in the world we need to address some key issues related to our three underlying layers: the maps, the infrastructure and the visualizations.

7.1 Issues with Maps (Physical World Layer)

Maps form the background of the authoring view. They are not strictly required but do help give an understanding of the physical area in which an experience will take place and will therefore often be used.

There are two important data-sources for this layer: printed maps/photos and online-services/GIS. Existing printed maps or aerial photos can be used if the coordinates are known or can be measured. The image just needs to be digitized in this case and afterwards geo-referenced.

Online services can be used to acquire digital maps. The advantage of digital maps is that they are already precisely measured. This means that the overlay in the authoring tool will be as precise as possible. Unfortunately most of the services on the market are only available after the payment of a fee. Our visualization tool is based on Digimap data from Edina [12] due an existing subscription made by our university. Edina offers several products that could be added to the visualization as additional information layers, e.g. transport networks, boundaries, buildings, contours lines, etc.

Another (free) service we used is Google Earth, especially its KML markup-language [13]. The KML-language allows us to quickly plot the surveyed data onto a virtual globe and thus visually check the data for validity. The real image of buildings, roads or cities for example helps us to understand the context in which the data was collected.

However, one of the main issues for the future of our approach is scalability. This can bring some difficulties in the visualization process, especially in map acquisition across many different countries. We are conscious that our approach needs to be flexible to interoperate with web based services like *Web Map Service* and *Web*

Feature Services as defined by the Open Geospatial Consortium [14]. Both services are Internet operated and return data and/or images of a specific area on request. Also Google Maps and Google Earth will continue to be helpful for what we are doing.

Another important point is to make our tool is able to communicate with GIS packages like the open source GRASS [15] and PostGIS [16] or commercial packages like Erdas Imagine [17] or ArcGIS [18]. More generally, we suggest that authoring tools for location based games are getting closer to Geographical Information Systems (GIS) and will soon begin to merge.

7.2 Issues with Data Collection (Infrastructural Layer)

Our main source of infrastructure data is self-collected. It has been initially obtained using the Placelab [19] stumbler software but we later moved to our own program called Pystumbler. The program takes a snapshot of the supported networks (i.e. GSM on the phone) about every second and also gets a GPS fix about every few seconds. The file-format is a well formed text-file which is compatible across platforms. We wrote a parser to support this file-format.

Pre-mapping an area using a network stumbler is time-consuming. It can take several hours to map an area in a dense city centre and several days to get a rough picture of the observed infrastructure in wider parts of a city. The ultimate goal of the stumble method would be to know how the characteristics of the infrastructure on every street. This is not feasible with only few people doing the data collection. For this reason this approach is not feasible for games that are to be played on a much larger, national or planetary scale without modifications. It is therefore interesting to see how the data collection process can be interwoven with the game-play or how data-collection can be archived as a by-product of other applications, e.g. games.

In addition to the more sophisticated stumbler setup using GPS we also created a less obtrusive long-term data collector that can run as a background task on a phone for a very long time without requiring any attention. It logs the cell ID once per minute and also every cell ID change up to a granularity of ten seconds. We have tested this software to track the movement of ten persons over the period of a month. The generated log-files contain universally valid cell adjacency information as well as subjective (i.e. only valid for the subject) patterns of movement.

Knowing that other people do similar things, it is also interesting to interoperate with projects like Wigle [20], Place Lab [21] or Mobilife [22] to utilize the data which has already been collected. Infrastructural data collection (also known as 'wardriving'), especially for Wi-Fi networks has been done for many years. Some of the data is shared through online-databases. The data presented there is usually the averaged position per network ID which means that the data shows less detail than the self collected trails of stumbler data but is potentially still very useful as it would allow authoring for unknown areas if it can be trusted. A verification and modification (cleaning) process will also be needed later on.

7.3 Issues with the Visualization

Choosing an appropriate visualization style for the data is the key question for any information visualization application. For our current prototype we deliberately decided to not abstract the data in any way (e.g. creating bounded regions from collections of individual sample points) but rather have tried to do as much as we can with the full data in its pure form (i.e. each sample visible on screen). We choose an interactive visualization because it allows the user to make quick visual queries into the data.

The current point visualization is however not enough. Many different views on the same data are possible and the tool should be flexible enough to allow those different views to be set up simultaneously. Not all visualizations will require a high-performance implementation in C++ and it should be possible to access the shared data using other programming languages like Java and Python as well. Also an advanced user should be able to interact with the data through a scripting interface for those occasions where the visualization alone is not sufficient.

Beyond this, we identify two major challenges for visualization. First is representing uncertainty. The collected data will be subject to uncertainties that designers may need to bear in mind. Positioning technologies such as GPS (that underpins the Tycoon data) are subject to error. Furthermore, data sets will be incomplete, requiring designers to interpolate between particular samples. Visualizations may need to convey uncertainty or be able to suggest possible interpolations. A second challenge lies in the time-varying nature of the ubiquitous infrastructure. Visualizations may also need to account for the ways in which coverage and accuracy vary over time as well as over space.

8 Conclusion

The idea that designers can author location-aware experiences by placing locales or hotspots on maps and other representations of physical spaces is already well established and forms the basis of several existing prototype tools. However, studies of previous experiences suggest that designers also need to be able to account for the characteristics of the usually invisible infrastructure of positioning and communication technologies, especially (but not only) their limited coverage.

We are therefore proposing that authoring tools for location-aware experiences be extended to include visualizations of the likely state of the infrastructure across a selected environment so as to guide designers as to how their intended experience might actually be experienced by end users in practice.

Essentially, we propose that future authoring tools should provide access to three broad layers of information (each of which might consist of several sub-layers): a physical world layer that describes the target physical environment; an infrastructure layer that represents the likely state of the infrastructure across this target environment; and a content layer that defines locales or hotspots that associate events or media assets with geographic locations.

We have produced an initial demonstration of how this general approach can assist the design of a location-based game, and have discussed key challenges that need to be met at each layer in order to develop it further. Our future work will of course involve addressing these challenges. It will also involve refining our current prototype authoring tool and working with external designers in order to elicit their more detailed requirements and to evaluate the longer-term potential of our approach through practical experience.

Acknowledgements

We gratefully acknowledge the support of IPerG, the European Project on Pervasive Gaming, project FP6-004457 under the European Commission's IST Programme (www.pervasive-gaming.org). We are also grateful for additional support from the Equator Interdisciplinary Research Collaboration which has been funded by the UK's Engineering and Physical Sciences Research Council (www.equator.ac.uk).

References

1. Hull, R., Clayton, B., Melamed, T.: Rapid Authoring of Mediascapes. In: Proc. Ubicomp (2004) 125-142
2. Mediascape. Scape the Hood.[Online]. Available: http://www.webtales.us/Scape1.html
3. Mediascape. Riot! - An Interactive Play for Voices.[Online]. Available: http://www.mobilebristol.com/QueenSq.html
4. Flintham, M.: Painting the Town Red: Configuring Location-Based Games by Colouring Maps. In: Proc. ACE (2005)
5. Benford, S., et al.: Life on the Edge: Supporting Collaboration in Location-Based Experiences. In: Proc. CHI (2005) 721-730
6. Naismith, L.: CAERUS Overview. The University of Birmingham (2004). [Online]. Available: http://portal.cetadl.bham.ac.uk/caerus/default.aspx
7. Crabtree, A., et al.: Orchestrating a Mixed Reality Game 'On the Ground'. In: Proc. CHI (2004) 391-398
8. Shneiderman, B.: The Eyes Have It: A Task by Data Type Taxonomy for Information Visualization. In: Proc. IEEE Symposium on Visual Languages (1996) 336-343
9. Chalmers, M. And Galani, A. 2004. Seamful Interweaving: Heterogeneity In The Theory And Design Of Interactive Systems. In Proceedings Of The 2004 Acm Symposium On Designing Interactive Systems, August 2004, Cambridge, Massachusetts, Acm Press, 243-252.
10. Benford, S, Crabtree, A., Flintham, M., Drozd, A., Anastasi, R., Paxton, M., Can You See Me Now?, ACM Transactions on CHI, 13 (1), March 2006.
11. Willassen, S. Y.: A method for implementing mobile station location in GSM. Norwegian University (1998)
12. Edina. (2005) Digimap.[Online]. Available: http://edina.ac.uk/digimap/description/
13. Google. Google API.[Online]. Available: http://code.google.com/apis.html
14. Open Geospatial Consortium Adopted Document Baseline.[Online]. Available: http://www.opengeospatial.org/specs/?page=baseline
15. GRASS Development Team. (2005) Welcome to GRASS GIS.[Online]. Available: http://grass.itc.it/
16. Refractions Research. (2005) What is PostGIS?[Online]. Available: http://postgis.refractions.net/
17. Leica Geosystems LLC. (2004) IMAGINE Virtual GIS. Leica [Online]. Available: http://gis.leica-geosystems.com/Products/files/vgis_ds.pdf
18. ESRI. (2006) ArcGIS Family of Products.[Online]. Available: http://www.esri.com/software/arcgis/index.html
19. LaMarca, A., et al.: Place Lab: Device Positioning Using Radio Beacons in the Wild. In: Proc. Pervasive Computing (2005) 116-133
20. Wigle. [Online]. Available: http://www.wigle.net/
21. Placelab. [Online]. Available: http://www.placelab.org/
22. MobiLife. [Online]. Available: http://www.ist-mobilife.org/

Automated Generation of Basic Custom Sensor-Based Embedded Computing Systems Guided by End-User Optimization Criteria

Susan Lysecky[1] and Frank Vahid[2,*]

[1] Department of Electrical and Computer Engineering
University of Arizona
Tucson, AZ 85721
slysecky@ece.arizona.edu
[2] Department of Computer Science and Engineering
University of California, Riverside
Riverside, CA 92521
vahid@cs.ucr.edu

Abstract. We describe a set of fixed-function and programmable blocks, *eBlocks*, previously developed to provide non-programming, non-electronics experts the ability to construct and customize basic embedded computing systems. We present a novel and powerful tool that, combined with these building blocks, enables end-users to automatically generate an optimized physical implementation derived from a virtual system function description. Furthermore, the tool allows the end-user to specify optimization criteria and constraint libraries that guide the tool in generating a suitable physical implementation, without requiring the end-user to have prior programming or electronics experience. We summarize experiments illustrating the ability of the tool to generate physical implementations corresponding to various end-user defined goals. The tool enables end-users having little or no electronics or programming experience to build useful customized basic sensor-based computing systems from existing low-cost building blocks.

1 Introduction

The cost, size, and power consumption of low-end microprocessors in the past decade has dropped tremendously as silicon technology continues to follow Moore's Law. For example, an 8-bit microprocessor chip may cost less than $1, occupy just a few millimeters, and consume just microwatts of power. Such reductions enable integration of microprocessors into domains previously unthinkable, such as RFID tags, ingestible pills, and pen tips.

Meanwhile, a problem in the design of basic sensor-based embedded computing systems is that end-users cannot setup basic custom embedded systems without the assistance of engineers. An end-user is an individual developing a sensor-based computing system who likely does not have programming or electronics expertise,

---

* Also with the Center for Embedded Computer Systems at UC Irvine.

P. Dourish and A. Friday (Eds.): Ubicomp 2006, LNCS 4206, pp. 69–86, 2006.

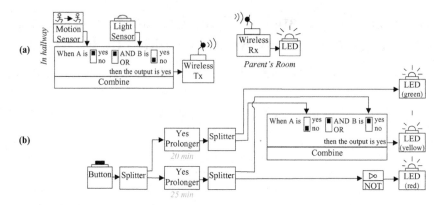

Fig. 1. Example sensor based applications built with fixed-function blocks, (a) Sleepwalking Detector, (b) Presentation Timer

such as a homeowner, teacher, scientist, etc. For example, a homeowner may wish to setup a custom system to indicate that a garage door is open at night, that a child is sleepwalking, or that an ageing parent has yet to get out of bed late in the morning. A scientist may wish to setup an experiment that activates a video camera when an animal approaches a feeding hole, or activates a fan when a temperature exceeds a threshold. Countless other examples exist. Despite the fact that such systems could be built from computing and sensing components whose total cost is only a few dollars, end-users cannot build such systems without knowledge of electronics and programming. Just connecting a button to an LED (light-emitting diode) would require knowledge of voltages, grounding principles, power supplies, etc. Making such a connection wireless requires further knowledge of communications, microcontroller programming, wireless devices, etc. Hiring engineers to build the system immediately exceeds reasonable costs. Off-the-shelf solutions for specific applications are hard to find, costly due to low volumes, and difficult to customize.

Our previous work addressed this problem through development of basic blocks, called *eBlocks*, that enable end-users with no electronics or programming experience to define customized sensor-based systems merely by connecting blocks and performing minor configuration of those blocks [5]. The blocks incorporate small inexpensive microprocessors into previously passive devices like buttons, motion sensors, and beepers. Each device has a fixed function, and can be easily connected to other devices merely by snapping together standard plugs, with the devices communicating using predefined basic networking protocols. Figure 1 illustrates several applications built using eBlocks. A sleepwalking detection application is shown in Figure 1(a), which consists of motion and light sensor outputs combined using a logic block (configured to compute motion and no light), whose output connects to a wireless transmit block. The wireless transmit block is matched with a wireless receiver block (through setting of switches to identical positions), which ultimately activates a beeper block when motion at night is detected. Figure 1(b) illustrates a second example, a presentation timer, which turns on a green light for 20 minutes, followed by a yellow light for 5 minutes, and lastly a red light indicating time has expired. The design splits a button press to two prolonger blocks, one that prolongs the button press for 20 minutes, another for 25 minutes. Additional logic turns on the appropriate lights depending on whether both, one, or neither prolonger block is outputting a true value.

eBlocks represent one of several new research approaches that utilize physical ("tangible") objects to enable end-users to program electronic devices [12]. Other examples include Media Cubes [1], Electronic Blocks [20], and Tangible Programming Bricks [16]. Commercial X10-based devices [18] communicate through household power lines and are complementary to our approach.

This paper describes our recent efforts to develop computer-based tools that an end-user could use to optimize an eBlock system or to map a virtual eBlock system to a limited set of physical blocks. While the work in this paper describes a tool to help end-users to *build* eBlock systems, related work that we have done [15] describes a tool to help end-users to *tune* low-level eBlock parameters, such as microprocessor clock frequency and communication baud rate, in order to achieve goals like maximizing battery lifetime and/or minimizing system latency.

2 eBlocks Overview

The key idea of eBlocks is to enable end-users to build useful customized sensor-based systems merely by connecting blocks, like buttons, motion sensors, logic, beepers, etc. eBlocks' key feature is that they encapsulate previously passive components by an ultra-lightweight compute wrapper. The following sections briefly describe two types of eBlocks, fixed function blocks and programmable blocks. A section also describes the eBlocks simulator, a multifaceted graphical environment that can simulate system functionality, configure programmable blocks, and provide the interface for the technology mapping and optimization tool introduced in this paper. Further details on eBlocks are discussed in [6].

2.1 Fixed-Function Blocks

Fixed-function eBlocks have a specific predefined function. Two types of fixed-function eBlocks are Boolean and integer. Boolean blocks send "yes" or "no" packets, while integer blocks send integer packets. While this paper focuses on Boolean blocks, the methods generally apply to integer blocks, and our future work will address such application. Four categories of Boolean blocks exist: sensor, compute, communication, and output blocks.

Sensor blocks sense events, such as motion, light, sound, button presses, or temperature. When a sensor detects the presence of an event (i.e. a light sensor detects light), the sensor generates a yes output, and otherwise generates a no output.

Compute blocks perform logic or state computations on inputs and generate new outputs. A 2-input "Combine" block (a.k.a. "Logic") computes a 2-input logic function configured by the end-user (e.g., AB, or A'+B). A 3-input Combine block is also available. An inverter block inverts a yes input to no output, or a no input to yes output. A "Yes Prolonger" block prolongs a yes input over the block's output for an end-user-configured duration. A "Toggle" block switches between yes and no outputs on successive yes inputs. A "Pulse Generator" block generates yes and no output

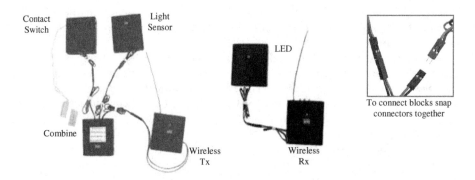

Fig. 2. Garage Door Open At Night Dector is built by snapping various fixed function eBlocks together

pulses for an end-user-configured duration. A "Once-Yes Stays-Yes" (a.k.a. "Tripper") block trips to a yes output state when the main input receives a yes, and stays in that state until a yes appears on a reset input.

Communication blocks include wireless transmit and wireless receive blocks, which must be configured to implement a point-to-point channel by setting the corresponding switches on each block to the same channel value. A splitter block splits a single input into multiple identical outputs.

Output blocks beep, turn on LEDs, control electric relays, or provide data to a PC for logging or other processing. A yes input activates output blocks. For example, a beeper block beeps when its input is yes, and is silent when its input is no. Figure 2 shows our initial physical prototype versions of eBlocks. Each physical block contains a PIC microcontroller for local computation and inter-block communication. The connections among blocks (along with any configurations of each block) define a system's functionality. A unidirectional, packet-based protocol provides the basis for block communication. Each block includes hardware specific to the block's task (e.g., sensors, resistors, voltage regulators, etc.). An end-user connects blocks using wired connectors or can replace a wire by a wireless connection by utilizing wireless transmit and receiver blocks. We have built over 100 prototype physical blocks, successfully used in controlled experiments by over 500 people of various skills levels, mostly end-users with no programming background [5].

2.2   eBlock Simulator

The eBlock simulator, shown in Figure 3, is a Java-based graphical user interface (GUI) for eBlock system entry and simulation and is available online at [6]. End-users can connect, test, and optimize various eBlock systems before interacting with physical blocks. End-users drag a block from a catalog on the right edge of the simulator to the workspace on the left and connect the blocks by drawing lines between the blocks' input and outputs. The user can choose between a "simple mode" in which commonly-blocks appear in the catalog, and an "advanced mode" containing more blocks. eBlocks that sense or interact with their environment include accompanying visual representation to simulate the corresponding environment. For

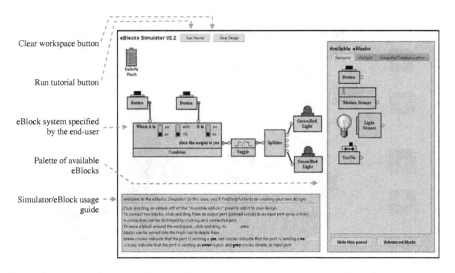

Fig. 3. Capture and synthesis tool illustrating the cafeteria food alert system

example, a "day/night" icon accompanies the light sensor. End-users can alternate the icon between day and night by clicking on the icon, causing the light sensor's output to change accordingly. The gray text box situated in the bottom-left of the simulator displays context-sensitive help such as a block's description and interface when the mouse cursor hovers over the corresponding block.

2.3 Programmable Blocks

In contrast to fixed-function blocks, a programmable block can be programmed to implement arbitrary behavior. Our current programmable block has two inputs and two outputs, as shown in Figure 4. An expert user could write C code that describes the block's behavior, and our tools would then combine that with the eBlock protocol code into a binary, which the user could then download using our serial cable interface.

However, most end-users will not have C-coding expertise. We thus provide a tool for automatically converting internal (non-sensor, non-output blocks) fixed-function blocks into a smaller network of programmable blocks that preserves the system's functionality, automatically generating code for each programmable block. In this context, a programmable block is a means for slightly more advanced users to reduce the block count and hence cost of their systems.

3 Technology Mapping

3.1 Problem Description

A problem with using physical fixed-function blocks is that an end-user may only have a subset of possible blocks readily available, and/or may have limited numbers

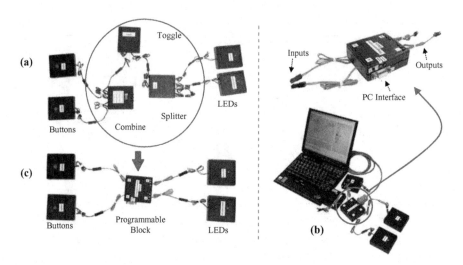

Fig. 4. Programmable blocks: (a) An original system using fixed-function blocks, (b) programming a programmable block to replace the inner fixed-function blocks, (c) the new system using the programmable block

of particular blocks. For example, an end-user may have three types of blocks available – 2-input logic, tripper, and prolonger blocks – of which many instances of each exist. Defining the desired application behavior using just those blocks would be a significant challenge even for an expert end-user. Instead, we provide for the end-user a way to capture the desired behavior in the graphical simulator using any combination of standard fixed-function blocks. The end-user also lists the types and numbers of available physical fixed-function blocks, forming what is essentially a constrained block library. We then define an automation tool that creates a new block network with the same functionality as the desired network, but only using blocks from the constrained library. Sensor and output blocks have specialized circuitry (e.g., light sensors, LEDs, beepers), so the physical counterparts for those blocks must be available – i.e., we cannot build a light sensor out of motion sensors. The mapping problem thus only involves *inner* blocks, namely compute and communication blocks.

The above-described problem is essentially a *technology-mapping* problem, common in chip design, with some differences from traditional problems. Technology mapping is a central part of the chip design process. Chip designers describe a desired circuit's behavior using easy-to-work-with components, such AND, OR, and NOT logic gates, with any number of inputs on each gate. However, a chip's underlying technology may support only 2-input and 3-input NAND gates, requiring that generic AND/OR/NOT circuits be mapped to a circuit consisting only of such NAND gates. Modern technologies consist of far more complex mappings of generic circuits to technology-specific components. Efficient technology mapping has been intensely researched for decades [2,3,4,8,9]. Our technology-mapping problem has some differences from previous technology-mapping problems. In the domain of field programmable gate arrays (FPGAs), technology mapping translates a digital circuit to a physical implementation on lookup tables (LUTs) [7]. A LUT is capable of specifying any logic function with a given number of inputs (defined by the size of the physical LUTs within the FPGA). Because LUTs are general programmable structures, the mapping methods correspond more to the problem of converting to programmable blocks than to that of fixed-function blocks. In application-specific integrated circuit (ASIC) design, technology-mapping implements a hardware circuit using a library of physical cells with fixed functions [7]. However, the final ASIC implementation can use an essentially unlimited number of any physical cells within the library. In contrast, our problem has a fixed numbers of each block, and furthermore does not necessarily have a balanced set of blocks. Nevertheless, our solution approach borrows from existing ASIC techniques.

3.2   Transformation Rule Base

A straightforward but non-optimal ASIC technology mapping method converts every technology independent circuit element into a technology-dependent universal gate element. In circuits, a NAND gate or a NOR gate represents a universal gate. In our problem, we found that we could implement nearly every block using some network of 2-input logic and splitter blocks. Defining a universal mapping heuristic that would replace each unmapped block in a network by an equivalent network consisting of the universal blocks is one possible method to perform technology mapping.

A better optimizing ASIC technology-mapping method involves graph-covering methods [13]. A library is built of mappings from technology independent sub-circuits to technology dependent sub-circuits, and then directed acyclic graph covering methods cover the unmapped circuit. The methods are built on similar graph methods used for instruction coverage generation in compilers. While such methods could be applied to our problem, we found that the state-based functions associated with our fixed-function blocks might introduce significant complexity into the graph cover heuristics. In fact, such traditional methods typically focus on the combinational part of the circuit, whereas state-based (sequential) blocks are a key part of our problem.

Another ASIC technology mapping method involves rule-based technology mapping [10,11]. Those techniques perform local optimizations on a circuit based on a set of transformation rules. We used this method as the basis for our first solution to the problem, which we call the transformation rule method. We developed a transformation rule base as follows. For each standard fixed-function block, we manually built alternative implementations of that block (the source block) using other various subsets of standard fixed-function blocks (target blocks). For example, for a 2-input logic block, we defined a transformation for implementing that block using a 3-input logic block, as shown in Figure 5(a) (*Config.* shows the truth table entries for the block). Figure 5(b) shows a transformation of a tripper block into an equivalent set of blocks involving a logic block and a splitter block, with the required logic configuration shown. Figure 5(c) shows multiple transformation rules for a inverter block. The invert block can be replaced utilizing either a 2-input logic block or a 3-input logic block, configured to implement the invert on the first input.

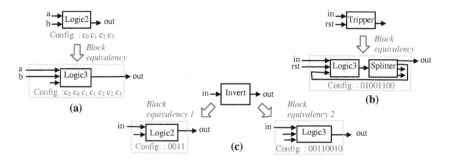

Fig. 5. Sample block equivalencies used in the technology mapping equivalncy library

We point out that we could have treated logic blocks using logic synthesis methods, wherein we would convert every sub-network of logic blocks (2- and 3-input logic blocks and invert blocks) into a Boolean expression, optimize the expression, and then map the expression into logic blocks in the library using traditional circuit technology mapping. However, as this is a first work, we preferred a transformation rule approach for consistency with the other blocks, resulting in a simpler tool but a less optimized mapped network. Nevertheless, incorporating logic synthesis methods is an area of future improvement.

4   Optimization

4.1 Problem Description

Given a network of fixed-function blocks, there may exist more blocks than necessary, arising from two situations. First, an end-user may have created a network of fixed-function blocks that is easy to comprehend, but has more blocks than necessary. Alternatively, technology mapping may have inserted two adjacent sub-networks with perimeter blocks that could be merged into fewer blocks. We thus developed a method to reduce block count while preserving network behavior.

We considered different methods for reducing blocks. A model-based method would utilize a formal understanding of the underlying finite-state machine (FSM) (or combinational) behavior of each block. This method would compose the FSMs into a single network-level FSM, eliminate equivalent and redundant states, and remap the reduced FSM to physical blocks. This approach appeared overly complex and possessed the problem that the reduced FSM might not be mappable to existing physical blocks. Another method builds on peephole optimization, an optimization method commonly found in compilers. This method inspects a local area of code to identify and modify inefficient code [17]. We can similarly inspect sections of the block network to optimize inefficient or redundant sections. The peephole optimization method enables us to preserve the pre-defined block structure because we are operating on the block level and eliminates the need for additional mapping.

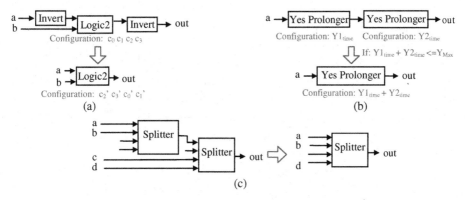

Fig. 6. Sample peephole optimization used in the optimization library

4.2 Peephole Optimizations

We analyzed a variety of networks and identified commonly occurring inefficient block combinations. We added optimization templates to the library that reflect these inefficient block combinations, along with a corresponding optimized block network. The optimizer traverses the network specification searching for subsystems matching any of the corresponding optimization templates and replaces the inefficient block combination by the optimized block network defined by the template.

Figure 6 illustrates several optimization templates defined within the optimization library. Figure 6(a) illustrates inverters located at the input or output of logic blocks that an end-user could have merged into the logic block. The optimizer eliminates the inverters and updates the logic block configuration accordingly. The optimization shown in Figure 6(b) merges chained prolonger blocks into a minimum number of prolonger blocks. If the combined yes time of the chained prolonger blocks is less than the maximum yes time of a single prolonger block, the optimizer can merge the chained prolonger blocks into a single prolonger block. If the combined yes time of the chained prolonger blocks exceeds the maximum yes time of a single prolonger block, then the minimum number of prolonger block are used. Figure 6(c) analyzes the number of unused inputs on chained splitters and attempts to combine splitters. Each peephole optimization is treated independent of others peephole optimizations as well as independent of the technology mapping transformations.

5 Programmable Block Operations

Technology mapping transformation rules and peephole optimizations discussed in previous sections pertain to fixed function blocks. Inclusion of programmable blocks presents further opportunity for technology mapping and optimization. For example, if a fixed function block does not exist in the physical library, a programmable block can by configured to replace the missing fixed function block. Furthermore, multiple fixed-function blocks can be replaced by a single programmable block to reduce block count and/or cost of the system.

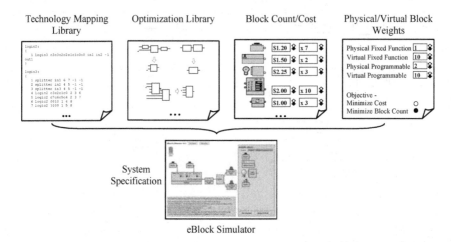

Fig. 7. Technology mapping and optimization environment

Several options exist to deal with the existence of programmable blocks. One option is to develop a separate partitioning algorithm, utilized in a secondary stage, which aims to assign multiple fixed-function blocks to programmable blocks. A simpler method is to define low-level technology mapping transformation rules and peephole optimizations specific to programmable blocks, and to incorporate those rules and optimizations into the main technology mapping and optimization heuristic (discussed in Section 6). The second method follows closely what we have done with fixed-function blocks, thus we defined several programmable block operations and incorporated them into the appropriate libraries.

6   Technology Mapping and Optimization Methodology

Figure 7 illustrates the overall technology mapping and optimization design methodology intended to aid end-users in generating an optimized physical sensor-based system based on end-user defined criteria. Two parties are responsible for the input specification, the node designer and the end user. The node designer is an expert who has an understanding of the underlying details of the various eBlocks and provides the pertinent block information prior to the release of the mapping and optimization tool. The end-user may have no expertise in programming or electronics but wants to construct a customized sensor-based system. The end-user provides input specific to their situation and the application being created.

6.1   Node Designer Input

The node designer defines the technology mapping transformations discussed in Section 3 by creating a text-based technology-mapping library read in by the tool. Furthermore, the node designer defines various peephole optimizations discussed in

Section 4 utilized by the tool. The optimization library is currently a C file that contains various functions to perform each of the peephole optimizations, alternatively these optimizations could be defined in a text file as the technology mapping transformation which is then translated by the technology mapping and optimization tool. These files are provided by the node designer and are independent of the various sensor-based systems constructed by the end-user.

6.2 End-User Input

The end-user needs to specify which fixed-function and programmable blocks are physically available, the functionality of the specific application being built, and the optimization goals.

The end-user first defines the "Block Count/Cost" input, i.e., how many of each type of block is physically available and the cost of each eBlock (regardless of whether they are physically available). The input specification can be done in a graphical environment in which an end-user can manually enter a number in a text box next to the graphical depiction of the block of interest or click on up/down arrows until the appropriate value is displayed (shown in Figure 8 under the "Block Count/Cost" heading). The end-user can similarly define block cost.

The end-user's next task is to define the "Physical/Virtual Block Weights" input. We define physical blocks as blocks that are physically available in the end-user's block set; virtual blocks do not exist in the block set, meaning they would have to be purchased to create the physical system. The end-user specifies four weights:

$$W_{P\_FF} = physical\ fixed\ function\ block\ weight$$
$$W_{V\_FF} = virtual\ fixed\ function\ block\ weight$$
$$W_{P\_PROG} = physical\ programmable\ block\ weight$$
$$W_{V\_PROG} = virtual\ programmable\ block\ weight$$

These values are used within a cost equation to evaluate whether a given system configuration yields an improvement (further discussed in Section 6.3). By simply assigning various weights, with lower weights indicating preferred block types, an end-user can direct the technology mapping and optimization to use preferred block types when possible. For example, an end-user who is uncomfortable with programmable blocks and wants to only utilize fixed function blocks, whether virtual or physical, can set the blocks weights to $W_{P\_FF} = 1$, $W_{V\_FF} = 1$, $W_{P\_PROG} = 10$, and $W_{V\_PROG} = 10$. Selection of a programmable block by the tool yields ten times the cost of a fixed function block, guiding the tool to favor fixed-function blocks. Alternatively, an end-user who wants to utilize blocks already existing in their physical block set, whether fixed or programmable, can set the block weights to $W_{P\_FF} = 1$, $W_{V\_FF} = 25$, $W_{P\_PROG} = 1$, and $W_{V\_PROG} = 25$. Again, virtual blocks yield higher cost, thus the tool is biased to select physically available blocks before utilizing any virtual blocks. The end-user can adjust the four block weights to reflect a variety of situations and to guide the technology mapping and optimization tool in creating an appropriate physical sensor based system.

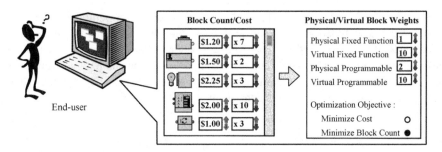

Fig. 8. Using a graphical interface, the end-user specifies, (a) the block count/cost library and, (b) the physical/virtual block weights

Within the "Physical/Virtual Block Weight" input, the end-user must also choose the optimization criteria – either to minimize the number of blocks utilized or to minimize the monetary cost of the resulting system. The end-user selects the optimization goal by selecting the corresponding radio button.

The last task required of the end-user is to create the eBlock system, thus defining the desired system functionality. The end-user creates the eBlock system within the block simulator (Section 2.2) by dragging and connecting blocks in the workspace.

6.3 Design Space Exploration

Once all inputs to the technology mapping and optimization tool are defined, our tool uses simulated annealing to explore the design space and generate the finalized sensor based system. The simulated annealing algorithm [14] is a popular optimization approach modeled after annealing in metallurgy, wherein a material is continuously heated and cooled to increase the material's strength. The algorithm randomly searches the design space by generating random changes, and accepts a change if an objective function value is decreased. Alternatively, a change that increases the objective function value can also be accepted based on a probability linked to a global "temperature" value. Early in the algorithm, changes that increase the objective function cost are more likely to be accepted, to avoid being trapped in a local minimum early on. As the algorithm continues to run, these higher cost changes are less likely to be accepted, thus settling into a minimum cost solution. The rate of decline in which higher cost solutions are accepted is based on a definable cooling schedule. The longer the algorithm runs, the higher a chance of a good solution, thus the key is to define a cooling schedule that balances the solution quality and runtime. We chose simulated annealing due to the heuristic's generality – we can simply define a set of possible changes consisting of the various transformations and optimizations discussed in previous sections, and let the tool search the solution space. While computationally expensive, the power of modern computers coupled with the relatively small sizes of eBlock systems make the use of annealing effective.

Depending on the end-user defined optimization criteria, we use one of two weighted cost functions to determine the system cost. If minimizing block count is the objective, the following cost equation is utilized:

$$\text{block cost} = \left(W_{P\_FF} * \# \text{ of physical fixed function blocks}\right) + \left(W_{V\_FF} * \# \text{ of virtual fixed function blocks}\right) +$$
$$\left(W_{P\_PROG} * \# \text{ of physical programmable blocks}\right) + \left(W_{V\_PROG} * \# \text{ of virtual programmable blocks}\right)$$

If minimizing total system cost is the objective, the following cost equation is utilized:

$$\text{system cost} = W_{P\_FF} * \sum_i \left(\text{price of block}_i * \# \text{ of physical fixed fucntion block}_i\right) +$$
$$W_{V\_FF} * \sum_i \left(\text{price of block}_i * \# \text{ of virtual fixed fucntion block}_i\right) +$$
$$W_{P\_PROG} * \sum_i \left(\text{price of block}_i * \# \text{ of physical programmab le block}_i\right) +$$
$$W_{V\_PROG} * \sum_i \left(\text{price of block}_i * \# \text{ of virtual programmab le block}_i\right)$$

The end-user, as described in Section 5.2, assigns the various block weights. The technology mapping and optimization tool utilizes simulated annealing and performs random changes consisting of an optimization or a transformation from a randomly chosen single technology mapping transformation rule (Section 3, a peephole optimization (Section 4), or a programmable block operation (Section 5).

7   Technology Mapping and Optimization Results

Utilizing the technology mapping and optimization methodology previously discussed, we now consider several eBlock systems and provide the corresponding physical eBlock system implementation determined by the technology mapping and optimization tool taking into consideration user-specified block availability and preferences. We considered six different scenarios in which end-users have varying types and quantities of physical eBlocks already available, as well as differing preferences as to the types of eBlocks the end-user wants to utilize to build the desired eBlock system. Section 7.1 looks at scenarios where the optimization criterion selected is block size reduction and Section 7.2 looks at scenarios where the optimization criterion selected is system cost reduction.

For each scenario, we considered sixteen eBlock system specifications, ranging from a "Night Light Controller" consisting of two internal blocks to a "Digital Hourglass Timer" consisting of over 50 internal blocks. The "Technology Mapping" library and "Optimization" library input files specified by the node developer are consistent across each scenario considered. The "Block Cost" input contains the monetary cost of each block type, derived from [19], are also consistent across each scenario considered. Each scenario defines the "Block Counts" input specifying the number and type of physical blocks already available to the end-user, i.e., the eBlocks that end-user currently has on hand. Each scenario further defines the "Physical/Virtual Block Weight" input specifying the end-user's preference towards available physical blocks or virtual blocks the end-user wants to utilize in constructing the final eBlock system implementation.

7.1   Minimizing Block Count

We first consider a scenario, referred to as Scenario 1, in which an end-user may have just stumbled upon eBlocks online and wants to try to build various systems using the

Table 1. Breakdown of physical block counts and weights for each sceanrio

	Block Count Assignment	W_{P_FF}	$W_{V\_FF,}$	W_{P_PROG}	W_{V_PROG}
Scenario 1 & 7	Block Set A	10	10	100	100
Scenario 2 & 8	Block Set A	10	10	10	10
Scenario 3 & 9	Block Set B	1	10	1	100
Scenario 4 & 10	Block Set B	1	10	1	10
Scenario 5 & 11	Block Set C	1	10	1	100
Scenario 6 & 12	Block Set C	1	10	1	10

Table 2. Breakdown of physical block counts for each block set, all input and output blocks are assumed to contain unlimited corresponding physical block counterparts

	Physical Block Count												
Block Set	2-Input Logic	3-Input Logic	Inverter	Toggle	Prolonger	Tripper	Pulse Generator	Wireless Transmitter	Wireless Receiver	Splitter	Prog_2_2	Prog_4_4	Prog_6_6
Block Set A	0	0	0	0	0	0	0	0	0	0	0	0	0
Block Set B	10	2	2	10	2	2	2	10	10	10	0	0	0
Block Set C	10	2	2	10	2	2	2	10	10	10	2	2	2

eBlock simulator and has no physical eBlocks available. Block Set A, listed in Table 2, reflects that the end-user has no physically available blocks. Furthermore, the Block Set corresponds to the "Block Count" input of the technology mapping and optimization tool. To realize the eBlock system specified within the eBlock simulator, the end-user is willing to purchase fixed function blocks but is weary of utilizing programmable blocks. Thus, the end-user can specify this preference by adjusting the "Physical/Virtual Block Weights" input, setting the fixed function block weights to 10 and programmable block weights to 100, as listed in Table 1. Having no physical eBlocks (as specified by Block Set A) and a desire to utilize only fixed function block (as specified by the block weights listed in Table 1), we then utilized the technology mapping and optimization tool to implement each of the sixteen eBlock systems. Figure 9 illustrates a breakdown of block types for each system, indicating the number of physical fixed function, physical programmable, virtual fixed function, and virtual programmable blocks each eBlock system is composed of. Only a subset of systems is illustrated in Figure 9 due to space limitations. In Scenario 1, programmable blocks are penalized, thus all sixteen final eBlock systems consist solely of fixed function blocks with solutions yielding and average of 12.9 inner blocks.

In the second scenario (Scenario 2), the end-user again has no physical blocks available, but the end-user in this scenario is willing to purchase fixed function and programmable blocks. Again, as the end-user has no available blocks, Block Set A is utilized to specify the "Block Count" input. Furthermore, as the end-user does not have a preference towards fixed function or programmable blocks, all block types are

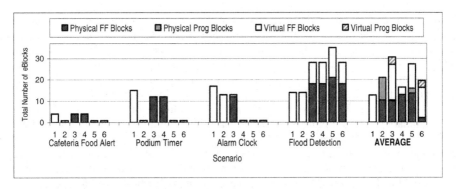

Fig. 9. Resulting number of physical fixed function (FF) blocks, physical programmable (Prog) blocks, virtual fixed function blocks, and virtual programmable blocks for several scenarios and systems

equally weighted in the "Physical/Virtual Block Weight" input. Figure 9 illustrates a breakdown of block types for a subset of the sixteen eBlock systems considered. Overall, five solutions can take advantage of programmable blocks, resulting in solutions that on average require 10.5 inner blocks. By allowing programmable blocks, the final eBlocks systems can be implemented using on average 2.4 fewer inner blocks compared to a system composed of solely fixed function blocks (Scenario 1).

In the next two scenarios considered (Scenario 3 and 4), an end-user has access to some physical fixed-function blocks, perhaps having purchased a initial set eBlocks consisting of only fixed function blocks, with the number and type of physical blocks available listed in Block Set B. In addition, the end-user in Scenario 3 is willing to purchase fixed function blocks if needed but is apprehensive to purchase programmable blocks. Block weights are set to so physical blocks have lower weights, virtual fixed-function blocks are weighted slightly higher, and virtual programmable blocks are heavily weighted, as listed in Table 1. In Scenario 4, an end-user is willing to purchase fixed function and programmable blocks. Virtual blocks have slightly higher weights, but the block weights make no distinction between fixed-function and programmable blocks. In Scenarios 3 and 4, a limited number of physical fixed function blocks exist, thus the tool will bias solutions to utilize physically available blocks before choosing virtual blocks as shown in Figure 9. Scenario 3 further penalizes usage of virtual programmable blocks, thus no solutions include virtual programmable blocks. On average, solutions require 16.44 inner blocks but only require end-users to acquire an additional 3.44 inner blocks. While Scenario 3's final inner block count is higher than in Scenarios 1 and 2, existing blocks are utilized minimizing the number of additional blocks required. Scenario 4 yields solutions with an average inner block count of 13.7, of which an average of 2.3 additional blocks are required. Again, this occurs because the programmable blocks are utilized, enabling reduction of fixed-function blocks.

In Scenarios 5 and 6, an end-user has a slightly larger set of physical fixed function and programmable blocks available as listed in Block Set C. The end-user in Scenario 5 is willing to purchase fixed function blocks, thus the end-user sets W_{V_FF} to 10 while W_{V_PROG} is set to 100. Lastly, in Scenario 6, an end-user is willing to purchase fixed function and programmable blocks. While higher than the physical block weights, both virtual block weights (W_{V_FF} and W_{V_PROG}) are equally weighted. In scenario 5 and 6, a larger physical block library exists, including both fixed function and programmable blocks. Figure 9 shows Scenario 5 yields a further reduction of inner blocks of 14.1, and 2.3 additional blocks because an expanded physical block set is available and specifically because physical programmable blocks are available. Scenario 6 results in further decrease resulting in an inner block count of 12.9 and an additional block count of 2.9 because virtual programmable blocks are not penalized.

7.2 Minimizing Total System Cost

In this section, we consider the same scenarios previously discussed but aim to minimizing the total system cost. Because the end-user is interested in cost reduction, the tool must consider the price of blocks utilized in the final solution. In block count reduction utilizing a 2-input logic block and 3-input logic block made no difference because both had a block count of 1. However, in the system price reduction a 2-input logic block is a better choice at $7.42 than the 3-input logic block at $9.05.

Figure 10 provides a breakdown of system cost based on the block classification - physical fixed-function, physical programmable, virtual fixed-function, or virtual programmable. Figure 11 indicates the cost of blocks not currently available within the physical set that an end-user needs to purchase to implement the physical system indicated by the tool. Scenarios 7 and 8 again consider block libraries in which no physical blocks are available, thus the tool tries to find the lowest cost system implementation. Although Scenario 8 does not penalize use of programmable blocks, there was no cost benefit in utilizing programmable blocks. Both Scenarios 7 and 8 resulted, on average, in an inner block cost of $71.29. Scenarios 9 and 10 include a library of fixed function blocks, where the end-user assigns larger weights to virtual blocks with virtual programmable block receiving an even higher weight.

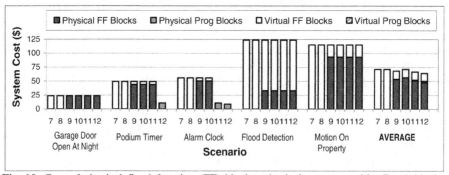

Fig. 10. Cost of physical fixed function (FF) blocks, physical programmable (Prog) blocks, virtual fixed function blocks, and virtual programmable blocks

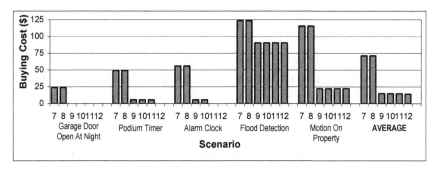

Fig. 11. Additional inner block cost required to implement the corresponding system

Again, there was no cost benefit in utilizing programmable blocks with both scenarios resulting in a total system cost of $71.20, and a cost of $14.80 for virtual blocks. Scenarios 11 and 12 included a library of both fixed function and programmable blocks thus resulting in inner block costs of $58.62 and $64.13 and an additional block cost of $9.31 and $14.12 respectively.

Overall, our technology mapping and optimization enables end-users to successfully design a system with existing blocks or with minimal additional blocks required. Additionally, our optimization tool is effective in reducing the size of end-user designed systems and reducing system cost. On average, our tool is extremely fast, requiring only 6 second per application, executing on a 2.8 GHz Xeon computer. When the end-user selected system cost reduction as the optimization criteria, the tool yielded a 23% reduction of system cost compared to the original implementation. When the end-user selected block count minimization as the optimization criteria, on average the tool yielded system implementations requiring six virtual blocks.

8   Conclusions and Future Work

We described a technology mapping and optimization tool to aid end-users in transforming a virtual eBlock system into an optimized physical block system. The tool requires no programming or electronics experience on the end-user's part, yet provides end-users with the ability to guide the tool in producing a system optimized for size or cost based on a constrained block library. The tool presented in paper is part of a larger framework. We plan to continue to add more blocks to the eBlock set as well as to expand the tools to support customization of the communication protocol and block parameters. The blocks, combined with the tool, help end-users setup useful basic sensor-based embedded computing systems to monitor and control the end-users' environments.

Acknowledgments

This work is supported in part by the National Science Foundation under grant CCR-0311026. Any opinions, findings, and conclusions or recommendations expressed in this material are those of the author(s) and do not necessarily reflect the views of the National Science Foundation.

References

1. Blackwell, A., R. Hague. AutoHAN: An Architecture for Programming the Home. IEEE Symposia on Human-Centric Computing Languages and Environments, 2001.
2. Chen, K., J. Cong, Y. Ding, A. Kahng, P. Trajmar. DAG-Map: graph-based FPGA technology mapping for delay optimization. IEEE Design & Test of Computers, Volume 9, Issue 3, Sept. 1992.
3. Cong, J., Y. Ding. On area/depth trade-off in LUT-based FPGA technology mapping. IEEE TVLSI, Volume 2, Issue 2, June 1994.
4. Cong, J., Y. Ding. FlowMap: an optimal technology mapping algorithm for delay optimization in lookup-table based FPGA designs. IEEE Transactions on Computer-Aided Design of Integrated Circuits and Systems, Volume 13, Issue 1, January 1994.
5. Cotterell, S., F. Vahid. A Logic Block Enabling Logic Configuration by Non-Experts in Sensor Networks. Conference on Human Factors in Computing Systems, April 2005.
6. eBlocks: Embedded Systems Building Blocks. http://www.cs.ucr.edu/~eblock
7. Francis, R. Technology Mapping for Lookup-Table Based Field-Programmable Gate Arrays. PhD Thesis, Department of Electrical Engineering, Univ. of Toronto, 1993.
8. Francis, R., J. Rose, Z. Vranesic. Technology mapping of lookup table-based FPGAs for performance. ICCAD, 1991.
9. Francis, R., J. Rose, K. Chung. Chortle: a technology mapping program for lookup table-based field programmable gate arrays. DAC, 1990.
10. Gregory, D., K. Bartlett, A. de Geus, G. Hachtel. Socrates: A System for Automatically Synthesizing and Optimizing Combinational Logic. DAC, 1986.
11. Joyner, W. H., L.H. Trevillyan, D. Brand, T. A. Nix, S. C. Gundersen. Technology Adaptation in Logic Synthesis. DAC, 1986.
12. Kelleher, C., R. Pausch. Lowering the Barriers to Programming: A taxonomy of programming environments and languages for novice programmers. ACM Computing Surveys (CSUR), Vol. 37 Issue. 2, 2005.
13. Keutzer, K. DAGON: technology binding and local optimization by DAG matching. DAC, 1987.
14. Kirkpatrick, S., C. Gerlatt, M. Vecchi. Optimization by Simulated Annealing, Science 220, 671-680, 1983.
15. Lysecky, S., F. Vahid. Automated Application-Specific Tuning of Parameterized Sensor-Based Embedded System Building Blocks. UbiComp, 2006.
16. McNerney, T. Tangible Programming Bricks: An Approach to Making Programming Accessible to Everyone. S.M. Thesis, MIT Media Lab, 2000.
17. Morgan, R. Building an Optimizing Compiler Butterworth-Heinemann, 1998.
18. Smarthome, http://www.smarthome.com, 2006.
19. Vahid, F., S. Cotterell, S. Bakshi. eBlocks: Embedded Systems Building Blocks. Harvard Business School Business Plan Contest, 2004.
20. Wyeth, P. and H. Purchase. Tangible Programming Elements for Young Children. Extended Abstract CHI, 2002.

An Experimental Comparison of Physical Mobile Interaction Techniques: Touching, Pointing and Scanning

Enrico Rukzio[1], Karin Leichtenstern[2,1], Vic Callaghan[2],
Paul Holleis[1], Albrecht Schmidt[1], and Jeannette Chin[2]

[1] Research Group Embedded Interaction, Media Informatics Group, University of Munich
{enrico, karin, paul, albrecht}@hcilab.org
[2] Intelligent Inhabited Environment Group, University of Essex
{leichten, vic, jschin}@essex.ac.uk

Abstract. This paper presents an analysis, implementation and evaluation of the physical mobile interaction techniques *touching*, *pointing* and *scanning*. Based on this we have formulated guidelines that show in which context which interaction technique is preferred by the user. Our main goal was to identify typical situations and scenarios in which the different techniques might be useful or not. In support of these aims we have developed and evaluated, within a user study, a low-fidelity and a high-fidelity prototype to assess *scanning*, *pointing* and *touching* interaction techniques within different contexts. Other work has shown that mobile devices can act as universal remote controls for interaction with smart objects but, to date, there has been no research which has analyzed when a given mobile interaction technique should be used. In this research we analyze the appropriateness of three interaction techniques as selection techniques in smart environments.

1 Introduction

Mobile devices have become pervasive; most people carry one, have them turned on almost continuously and use them in different contexts. So far they are mostly used for interaction between a user, mobile device and a service. In such situations the context of use, which is one of the focuses of this work, is generally not considered. In the last decade there has been an increasing interest from industry and academia in using mobile devices for interactions with people, places and things in the real world [1]. This paper focuses on mobile interactions between a user, a mobile device, and a smart object in the real world. We call this specific mobile interaction technique *physical mobile interaction*. In this approach the user interacts with the mobile device and the mobile device interacts with the smart object.

The most popular and promising physical mobile interaction techniques are *touching*, *pointing* and *scanning*. As the name suggests, for the first two of these the user has to touch or to point on a smart object to indicate that she is willing to interact with it. For scanning, the user simply uses the mobile device to discover what controllable devices are available. As mentioned earlier, to date, there has been no

P. Dourish and A. Friday (Eds.): Ubicomp 2006, LNCS 4206, pp. 87–104, 2006.

research that has analyzed in which context a given interaction technique is preferred by a user and which interaction techniques should be supported by the smart objects. The location of the object, the distance between object and user, the service related to the object, the capabilities of the mobile device and the preferences of the user are important factors for the selection of an interaction technique.

The primary results of the work described in this paper are findings and guidelines for when to use or to prefer a particular physical mobile interaction technique. In this work we have focused on the usage of mobile devices for interactions with objects in smart environments. There are numerous scenarios in which such an interaction makes sense including additional services such as reading the manual of a microwave after touching it with the mobile device or requesting direct support for a specific device. Other examples are the provision of interaction functionalities for devices without an interface (e.g. power consumption of electronic devices) or remote control of objects (e.g. requesting the current status of the washing machine while watching TV). To address these and other questions, we conducted a comprehensive online survey; developed and evaluated a paper prototype; implemented the interaction techniques *touching*, *pointing* and *scanning*; and evaluated this prototype in a real world setting. This development process was based on user centred design, to set the user at the focus so as to retrieve as much user feedback as possible.

The paper is organized as follows. The next section relates our work to existing approaches whereby the interaction techniques *touching*, *pointing* and *scanning* are discussed in detail. Following this we present the results of our analysis which are based on an online survey with 134 participants. We then discuss a paper prototype which was developed based on the findings of the analysis phase and which was evaluated in a small user study. After that we describe the implementation and evaluation of the three interaction techniques and their usage in a demonstrator. Finally, we discuss the findings and guidelines for physical mobile interaction techniques based on the results of our analysis, the evaluation of the paper prototype and a user study based on the high-fidelity prototype.

2 Related Work

Our research is related to physical mobile interactions in general but focused on the usage of techniques for interaction with objects in smart environments. Therefore, we first discuss smart environments in general before discussing mobile interactions within smart environments. Following this, we conduct an analysis of *touching*, *pointing* and *scanning* interaction techniques.

A smart environment is an environment fitted with a variety of sensors and electronically operated devices which allow the occupants to customize the functionality of their living environment (e.g. a domestic home). Using the system, it is possible to e.g. monitor light level, temperature, window and door status and who is currently in a house [2]. Most research related to smart environments currently focuses on context aware systems which adapt according to contextual information. In [22] the authors describe the Easy Living project providing an overview of interaction modalities in such context-aware smart environments. Such environments are usually equipped with a set of smart objects which are augmented by sensors or actors to interact with their physical environment and which often provide a user interface [3]. One issue is how to interact with and control these objects. One solution is to use mobile devices as remote controls. Examples include the Home Automation System [4] and the Pebbles Research Project [5]. However, so far, the literature reports very little work on the evaluation of physical mobile interaction techniques in general and in particular in smart environments. The only comparable analysis of mobile interaction techniques was done by Ballagas et al. [6]. Unlike our work they focused on the classification of interaction techniques based on previous work and personal experience. Furthermore they did not run a questionnaire or user studies to compare the mobile interaction techniques.

The following subsections analyze the physical mobile interaction techniques *touching*, *pointing* and *scanning* in detail.

2.1 Touching

Touching relates to selecting a smart object by bringing the user's mobile device into contact with the object the user wishes to interact with. For this the user must be nearby the object and aware it is augmented with a touch capability. In the next step the user has to touch the object which results in the related services being presented to the user on their mobile device. Through this, additional services can be accessed that are not provided by the device itself. This interaction technique is seen as natural because it conforms to our everyday physical interactions as we often touch objects with our hand or fingers to support the comprehension of the listener when talking about it. Want et al. [7] were among the first to present a prototype for the *touching* interaction technique which incorporated RFID tags and a short range RFID reader in a mobile device (in this case a tablet computer). They used their prototype to demonstrate the augmentation of books, documents and business cards to establish links to services such as ordering a book or picking up email addresses. Another implementation was described by Välkkynen et al. [8] who developed an interaction technique called *TouchMe* that uses proximity sensors to sense the distance between the augmented object and the mobile device. Common technologies for implementing this interaction technique are Radio Frequency Identification (RFID) and Near Field Communication (NFC) [9] which means objects need not be touched directly, rather circa 0-3 centimetres is sufficient for the selection.

2.2 Pointing

Using the *Pointing* interaction technique the user can select a smart object by aiming at it with a mobile device. This interaction technique is regarded as natural as it reflects one of our everyday physical interactions such as pointing at objects with our finger when we speak to support the comprehension of the listener. This interaction technique can be realized by several technologies such as visual markers, optical beams or image recognition technologies. Fitzmaurice [10] was one of the first who described the concept of using mobile device pointing for interaction with smart objects, which involved getting information from a map augmented with a computer based library. Rekimoto and Nagao were among the first to present an implementation of this interaction technique based on their *NaviCam* [11] system which consisted of a mobile device with an attached camera that interpreted visual codes on physical objects. They used this prototype to obtain additional information about entities such as pictures, an active paper calendar and an interactive door. In the last decade, several projects or standards such as QR code [12], Semacode [13] or visual codes [14] have focused on further development of visual markers and their interpretation on mobile devices. Other projects have used *pointing* based on cameras and object recognition approach rather than visually augmented objects [15]. Välkkynen and Tuomisto [8] for example implemented *pointing* using light sensors on the object which are illuminated using laser or infrared beams attached to the mobile device. IrDA is built-in to many mobile devices and can be seen as an example of interaction via *pointing*. Typical mobile device support distances range from 0 to 60 cm. For example, such system is used by *Mobipoint* [16] which is a commercial installation provided by the *Deutsche Post* to receive codes from a poster. The system can be used to download ring tones for free from a webpage. When the pointing distance is less than 10 cm, IrDA might be seen as one way of realizing *touching* interaction technique.

2.3 Scanning

Scanning allows user to get a list of nearby smart objects by using a wireless mechanism. Selecting one item from the list of discovered smart objects results in the listing of its services. The advantage of this type of interaction technique is that the user does not need to be aware of the augmentation of a smart object nor must this object be visually changed to get the attraction of a person. The idea of using a mobile device for scanning the environment was first seen in the early Star Trek television series (1966-1969) where a *tricorder* [17] was used to scan unknown environments. There exist several implementations of this interaction technique; most are based on radio frequency communication such as Bluetooth phone services.

3 Analysis

The goal of this phase was to analyze the needs of potential users and to deduce which services are useful when interacting via a mobile device with a smart object. The analysis and the prototypes are based on mobile phones because most people own this special kind of a mobile device and already know how to interact with it. Furthermore we were interested in which locations and contexts potential users would interact with smart objects, and which interaction techniques they prefer. We utilised a three step process of evaluation. At the outset of our work we sought to get an initial unprejudiced user opinion via an online questionnaire which we then verified through the evaluation of our low and high fidelity prototypes. Thus the recognised weaknesses of users not being good at speculating about how they may or may not use systems was not a significant issue as the findings were tested via prototype evaluation.

Thus we conducted an initial web based questionnaire at the beginning of our work in November 2005. 134 people participated, 40% of the participants were female and 60% were male. The participants were between 17 and 59 years old with an average age of 28. 41% of the participants had a university degree and 95% of them owned a mobile phone.

At the beginning of the questionnaire we explained what intelligent environments were and solicited their opinions about various aspects of such environments. The findings revealed that the respondents had high expectations for the benefits such environment would bring to their life. For example, they described a smart environment as an interesting, practical and comfortable way to live, in particular they foresaw the possibility of saving time, energy and money. Many respondents mentioned benefits for older or handicapped people. In contrast some respondents were afraid of losing too much control. Many users mentioned a fear of a power blackout of the smart environment or were worried about the dependence on technology and a loss of human control.

We then asked about their general feeling regarding the usage of the mobile device for interacting with objects in smart environments. The corresponding feedback was positive. The respondents pointed out that mobile phones were widespread and familiar. They mentioned the benefit in interacting with their smart environment whilst away from home which provided a confident feeling of being able to regularly check the status of their home, whilst away. Additionally security issues were raised and it was apparent that there was no proper trust in the security of mobile phone technology.

The next section of the questionnaire presented three different application areas for mobile applications interaction with smart objects. The first one concerned getting information related to an object, such as getting online instructions for a device (e.g. washing machine), opening a web page related to a device (e.g. fridge), opening other websites related to the devices (e.g. recipes related to the microwave) or an online guide for the television or radio. The participants had mixed opinions about these application areas as one can see in the following Figure 1.

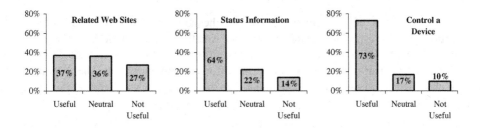

Fig. 1. Results of the online survey regarding the usefulness of predefined application areas for mobile interactions with objects in smart environments

37% saw retrieving information on related websites as a useful thing whilst 27% thought it was not useful. The next application area was about retrieving status information about physical appliances such as the status of the coffee machine (switched on/off) and the time a washing machine needs to complete a wash. Here 64% regarded such a service as useful. The last application was about controlling a device remotely such as the heating. Again this scored well with 73% of the participants considering such a service useful.

Subsequently the participants were asked when they would use the mobile phone for interactions with objects in smart environments. Figure 2 shows that most of the respondents (43%) would use such a system independently of their location. A third of the respondents (34%) would use it only remotely. 13% would use it only when at home. 10% of the respondent would refuse to use such a system at all.

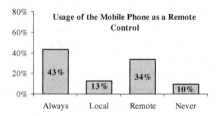

Fig. 2. Preferred location of the user when interacting via the mobile phone with smart objects

Next we explained the principle of the mobile interaction techniques and asked if they would use *scanning*, *pointing* or *touching* when interacting with smart objects in various contexts. Figure 3 and 4 summarise the overall findings and shows that, in general, users would prefer *pointing* and that they were almost equally split on the use of *scanning*, but they disliked *touching*. *Pointing* performs best because many participants saw it as an intuitive interaction technique with little physical effort. *Scanning* was preferred in situations in which a physical distance between the user and the target object existed. *Touching* proved unpopular because mostly respondents did not see any added value; rather it was seen to entail more unnecessary physical effort. The only reported merit was in situations where touching helped avoid ambiguity.

The advantages of *touching* were seen in the accuracy and uniqueness of the selection process especially when devices are small and close together. The most common complaint was the need for a physical closeness to the device which requires a high level of user motivation to make the effort of moving closer. The technique was classified as very intuitive and moreover the technique was seen as the most secure and trustworthy approach.

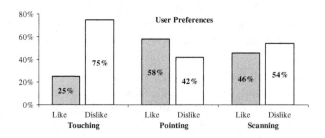

Fig. 3. Preferences (like, dislike) of the participants regarding the interaction techniques *touching*, *pointing* and *scanning* in general

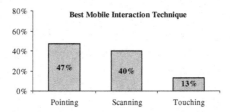

Fig. 4. Direct comparison of the three physical mobile interaction techniques touching, pointing and scanning

The benefits of *pointing* are seen as being natural, easy to use and quick for addressing the target device directly. In addition, the respondents mentioned that *pointing* avoids a complex user interface. However, ambiguities in the selection process were possible, especially if devices are close together or small.

A frequently mentioned benefit for *scanning* was that it operates at a distance and does not require proximity to the device and therefore requires less physical effort. Moreover the listing of all devices was seen as an advantage. Respondents mentioned that the mobile device becomes a mnemonic device for all available and usable smart objects. However, a drawback was that information must be displayed even when it is unimportant, although this is more an implementation issue.

Whilst this survey allowed us to scope the breadth of the issues to be investigated, by its nature there remained ambiguities that needed a more realistic context to resolve; thus we developed a low-fidelity and the high-fidelity prototype to refine our findings and to evaluate the interaction techniques in a more practical context.

4 Low-Fidelity Prototype

The second phase of the user centred design process was to create and evaluate a low fidelity paper prototype of the application. Figure 5 shows some examples of the paper prototype. The test was conducted by eight people whereby everybody performed both tasks described below to verify the assumptions of the analysis phase.

Before every test we explained how the interaction techniques work and how they could be used (taking into account it was a paper prototype).

In the first task the participants were asked to open a web page containing cooking recipes by selecting the fridge. In that situation the testers had line of sight to the fridge, but were too far away to perform *touching*. Six of the eight participants used *pointing* to select the fridge. They argued that, in the case of having a line of sight, *scanning* is too time-consuming. Furthermore, they were not motivated to move closer to perform *touching*. They mentioned they would use *touching* if they were already close enough to the smart object. Just two of the testers used *scanning* but they realized during the selection process that *scanning* was more time-consuming than using *pointing* or *touching*.

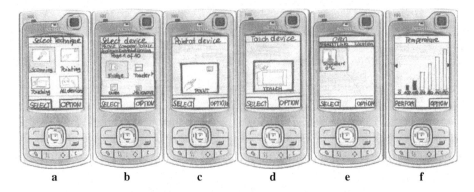

Fig. 5. Scans of the paper prototype: Selecting of a physical mobile interaction technique (a), interfaces after the selection of an interaction technique (b – d), selected smart object (e) and usage of a service provided by the smart object (f)

In the second task the users were asked to set the timer of the microwave to 5 minutes. In this case several devices were close together and a selection via pointing could be ambiguous. Seven of the test people used *pointing*; as long as *pointing* was in any way possible they preferred it. They mentioned that if there was no line of-sight and *pointing* was impossible they would switch to *scanning*. *Touching* was only an option if they were already close enough to the device.

Subsequently, we asked the participants which physical mobile interaction technique they would use if the smart object was in another room. All of them responded that they would use *scanning*. They did not show any motivation to move closer to perform *pointing* or *touching*.

Finally the users were asked which techniques they associate with the following features or attributes:

A. **Security:** All eight users mentioned *touching*. They trusted this technique because they subconsciously think it is the most secure one. They would use this technique if the smart object had some critical role in their life (e.g. a security observation camera or oven).

B. **Intuitive:** Four test people mentioned *pointing* because they compared it to the TV remote control metaphor. The four other mentioned *touching* because they liked the easy selection process.

C. **Speed:** Five of the participants mentioned *touching* because of the unambiguousness of the selection process. They thought that *pointing* needed more time because of the danger of selecting a wrong device and because of the pointing activity itself. The other three mentioned *pointing* because of the fact that they do not lose time while getting closer. Furthermore, they all mentioned that the process of *scanning* for and selecting one device takes more time than touching.

D. **Least error-prone:** All mentioned *touching* because they associated this interaction technique with attributes like error resistance and security.

E. **Highest cognitive effort:** Six participants mentioned *scanning* because they saw a high cognitive effort in finding the device and performing a mapping from name of the device to the device itself. Two mentioned *pointing* because they saw a cognitive effort in hitting the target.

F. **Highest physical effort:** All users mentioned *touching* because it requires more physical effort than the other interaction techniques.

5 High-Fidelity Prototype

After the analysis, the development of the low fidelity prototype and its evaluation, we started to implement a high-fidelity prototype to evaluate our previous findings in a more practical context. For this we used a previously existing smart environment which is a domestic apartment that includes a range of smart objects which can be addressed via UPnP to receive and perform services.

Such a practical evaluation is very important for the analysis of these interaction techniques because several physical or technical constraints could be not simulated with a paper prototype or in an online questionnaire. Examples include the time needed for a scanning process, the time needed until the mobile device points exactly on an object or the correct touching of a smart object.

5.1 Architecture

Figure 6 gives an overview of the architecture of our high-fidelity prototype which consists of the following five components: The smart objects in the previously existing smart environment, the mobile phone, a web server, a pointing recognition server and an UPnP server.

The smart objects and the services they offer can be accessed via Universal Plug and Play (UPnP). A heating system for instance could offer a service called *temperature*. Every service has a certain status which can be retrieved and changed via UPnP. Through this the mobile device is able to read the status of a smart object and to use a service provided by it. To identify an element in an UPnP network a Unique Device Name (UDN) number is required which is needed for addressing the devices in such a network. The physical mobile interaction techniques *touching*, *pointing* and *scanning* are used to select one of the UDNs through which a specific smart object is selected. For *pointing,* every smart object is augmented with a light sensor, which recognizes when the laser pointer attached to the mobile phone is pointing at it. For the implementation of *touching* we used Near Field Communication (NFC) [9] technology whereby the smart objects are augmented by Mifare NFC tags which can be sensed by the mobile phone. The physical mobile interaction technique *scanning* is implemented by using Bluetooth access points which provide information about nearby smart objects. Thus, for every object to be identifiable by all three interaction techniques, it must be an element of the UPnP network, be represented by at least one Bluetooth access point and be augmented with a solar cell and an NFC tag.

The mobile phone application which we call *Mobile Interaction Application* (MobileIA) is implemented using the Java 2 Micro Edition (J2ME) and communicates via a web server running on top of an UPnP framework to retrieve information and to perform services in the smart environment. MobileIA uses the Nokia NFC & RFID

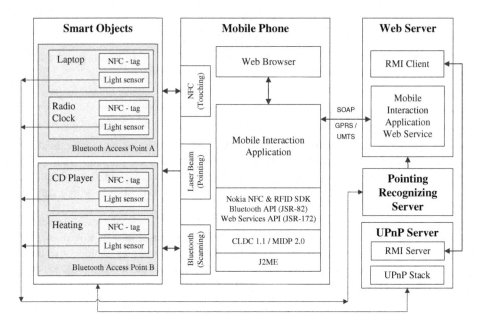

Fig. 6. Architecture of the high-fidelity prototype including smart objects, mobile phone, web server, pointing recognizing server and UPnP server

SDK 1.0 [18], the Bluetooth API (JSR 82) and the Web Services API (JSR 172); and is based on CLDC 1.1 and MIDP 2.0. MobileIA provides support for the interaction techniques *touching*, *pointing* and *scanning*. Whenever there is a need for information, requests are sent to the *Mobile Interaction Application Web Service* (MobileIA Web Service). The MobileIA Web Service offers a WSDL interface to the mobile phone clients. The MobileIA uses the Web Services API to send a Remote Procedure Call (RPC) to the web server. The messages are sent using the SOAP protocol.

After the identifier of the smart object is known, the mobile phone client requests its description. This description includes all services provided by the object and the current state of the smart object with respect to those services. From this, the mobile phone client generates a representation of the object. A user interface is generated that lists all available services, shows a graphical representation of the state and provides the means to invoke the service with parameters that can be specified. When the user changes the status of a device service, i.e. invokes the appropriate service, a request containing all relevant information is sent to the web server.

The web server gets the request and forwards it to the UPnP server. Since the web server and the UPnP server are separated, they communicate using Remote Method Invocation (RMI) from the RMI client (web server) to the RMI server (UPnP server). This RMI interface includes three operations. It allows a request to be sent to all available devices. Thus, the web server can continuously update its list of available devices providing immediate feedback if devices fall out. Moreover it allows a request to perform an action. The third method can be used to check if the status of a device has been changed.

The UPnP server can then execute the service passed from the web server. The result of this service call can then be transferred back to the web server which can communicate it back to the mobile phone. The UPnP service execution can be quite time consuming. To avoid a time-out in the communication between the mobile phone and the web server, the communication is closed after the service has been invoked. The result is stored in the database and can be queried by the mobile phone through the web server. This communication path can be used to send arbitrary results from the service back to the phone.

The following subsections discuss the implementation of *touching*, *pointing* and *scanning* in detail.

5.2 Touching

Touching is realized with Near Field Communication (NFC) technology [9]. The technology is based on RFID but combines it with chip card technology so there is no difference between readers and tag anymore. For our prototype we used a Nokia 3220 with an attached Nokia NFC shell [19] and Mifare NFC tags. If users want to use the *touching* technique, they first initiate the corresponding interaction mode. The NFC reader then starts looking for available tags in its reach. When the mobile phone is in the proximity of the smart object the NFC shell establishes an electromagnetic field to create a radio frequency connection. Thus, it can read data from the tag. A UDN identifier can be extracted form these packets.

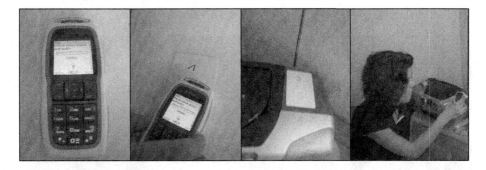

Fig. 7. The Nokia 3220 with integrated NFC chip, usage of the NFC phone for reading a Mifare NFC tag, a Mifare NFC tag attached to an smart object and a user who is using the NFC phone to touch the NFC tag

Communication between our Nokia 3220 and a tag is only possible in a range of 0 - 3 centimetres whereby just one tag can be read at the same time. To get the device identifier (UDN) from the Mifare NFC tag, the MobileIA uses the Nokia NFC & RFID SDK 1.0 [18]. Once the user has moved the mobile phone close enough to the Mifare NFC tag, the SDK triggers an event and notifies the MobileIA of the data packet. The UDN stored in the packet can then be read. As described above, the device description is retrieved through the infrastructure and can be used by the application running on the phone.

5.3 Pointing

Pointing is realized by a light beam from a laser pointer attached to a Nokia N70 that is sensed by light sensors on the smart object. This is equipped with a micro-controller on which a recognition algorithm is implemented. As the micro-controller we chose the Particle Computer platform [20]. Particle Computers are small wireless sensor nodes. The node's hardware comprises a microcontroller, a radio transceiver (125 kbit/s, with a range of up to 50 meters), a real-time clock, additional Flash memory and LEDs and a speaker for basic notification functionality. It can be powered using a single 1.2V battery and consumes on average 40mA. The particle computer can easily be extended by additional boards. For our prototype we added off-the-shelf light sensors (FW 300) with an active area of about 0.77 square centimetres. Each pointing sensor for the pointing action consists of three such light sensors to achieve a larger active area (about 2.3 square centimetres). A small LED is added to provide basic feedback if the pointing action was successful. This setting is enough to detect whether or not a light source like a laser pointer is aimed at such a sensor. However, a change in the ambient light can give exactly the same result, especially if the surroundings are rather dim and the main light is switched on. There is no way to distinguish these two cases by merely looking at the magnitude of the signal change. Therefore we added a chip to make the pointer pulse in a specific frequency. Using hardware, or (as in this prototype) software analysis directly on the Particle computer, it is possible to determine whether changes in the sensor values are caused by a pointer or just from changes in ambient light. This technique was also applied in [21] where the authors showed that it is even possible to transmit an ID through the laser beam.

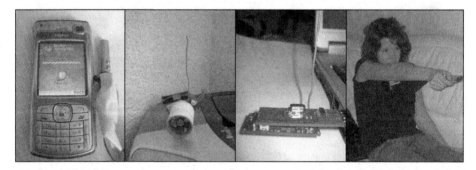

Fig. 8. Nokia N70 with attached laser pointer, smart object with attached light sensor connected to a particle, particle message receiver attached to a USB port and usage of the interaction technique pointing

After the Particle computer has detected that the laser pointer points to one of its sensors, a message is sent to a receiver connected to a USB port of the pointing recognizer server. This communication is performed using its radio frequency communication facility. On the pointing recognizer server side, the UDN sent with the message is retrieved. Upon reception of such a message, the UDN is passed to a Java Servlet on the web server where it is stored in a database together with time information.

The moment the user starts the pointing technique mode on the mobile phone, it periodically sends requests to the web server. Whenever there is an UDN available in the database that is not older than a specified time, this UDN is returned to the phone. As described in the previous section, the device description is then requested.

5.4 Scanning

Scanning is realized using Bluetooth access points which provide information about smart objects in its proximity. To implement this technique, we used the Nokia N70 phone since it provides Bluetooth support. The mobile phone user first chooses the scanning mode on the mobile phone. Then, the user explicitly starts a Bluetooth scan for all available Bluetooth enabled devices that can connect to the phone and selects one. This includes all access points in the user's proximity. The list of found access points can be used to get an approximation of the location of the user which could potentially be used to reduce the number of devices close to the user. The mobile phone sends the list of access points to the web server. There is a description in the infrastructure that maps each access point to devices that are located close to it. From that description the web server retrieves all available devices. The UDN and a human-readable name of each of the devices are sent back to the phone. The mobile phone application generates an appropriate graphical representation (for unknown devices, a standard representation including the name) for each of the devices and displays it. Now the user can select one of the smart objects from the list and its device description is retrieved in the same way as with the other two techniques.

5.5 User Study

The experiment based on the prototype previously described was conducted with 20 participants. The users were aged 9 to 52 with an average age of 28 years. 35% of the participants were male and 70% had an academic education. 55% of the participants did not have a technical background in their job or field of study. In the first part of the experiment the users had to perform different tasks using the high-fidelity prototype. The tasks had to be performed under different context of location and activity. In all of the following scenarios the participants were located in a living room. All scenarios were subdivided into the three activities sitting, lying and standing to cover most casual activities. We assumed that lying is related to activities like relaxing or laziness, sitting is related to talking or writing, and standing is related to working and hurry. All participants performed all tasks of the four scenarios while sitting. Afterwards we asked them about their behaviour and preferences when lying or standing.

In the first scenario the participants had to select a CD player and then had to turn it on. There was a distance of three meters between the participant and the device. The users had a line of sight to the smart object. 95% of all participants used pointing to select the CD player. This decision was independent of their activity. Just 5% of the participants used scanning.

In the second scenario the participants had to open a website related to a radio show. This link was available through the radio which was close to the participant.

All participants used touching in that situation. The decision was independent of the activity. The users mentioned that in that situation touching is the best and fastest technique because they do not need to spend physical effort because they were already in touching range.

In the third scenario of the experiment the participants had to select the heating of the bathroom, switch it on and set on 25 degrees. 100% of the participants used scanning to select the smart object. There were no differences when lying, sitting or standing. No participant was motivated to move to the other room and to use pointing or touching.

In the last scenario the participants had to select the laptop to access a Wikipedia link which was stored on it. The testers were not able to point on the laptop because there was no line of sight to it at the given position. The users had to move one meter for pointing and about four meters for touching. Unlike the first three scenarios, the activity of the user (sitting, lying or standing) in this scenario was an important factor for the selection of an interaction technique. When the users were lying or sitting, all participants used scanning to select the smart device. In contrast to that, in the case where the users were standing just 5% of the participants used scanning, 25% pointing and 65% touching. They refused to use *scanning* since this interaction technique takes more time than the other two. The reason for the high acceptance of touching was that the participants thought that if they are already standing they could move the short distance to the touching range as well.

6   Findings and Guidelines

This section summarises the results of the analysis phase described in section 3, the evaluation of the low-fidelity prototype described in section 4 and the practical evaluation of the high-fidelity prototype described in section 5.5. Based on these we discuss guidelines which should help application developers when designing systems that take physical mobile interaction techniques into account.

6.1   Advantages and Disadvantages of *Touching*, *Pointing* and *Scanning*

One general result from our observations was that *touching* and *pointing* are the preferred techniques if the user has line of sight to or is close to the device. The reason for this is that these techniques are based on our everyday interactions. For instance, we often point with our index finger at products in a shop to indicate what we want to buy or we touch things to feel their surface. *Scanning* is seen as a very technical interaction technique which is more complex to use because of its indirectness. Older users in particular prefer direct mobile interaction techniques because they want to avoid as much input on the mobile device as possible. *Touching* is regarded as an error resistant, very secure, very quick, intuitive and non-ambiguous selection process which can require physical effort. It is typically preferred when the smart device is in reach of the user. *Touching* often requires the users' motivation to approach the smart device. This motivation increases if the benefits of *touching* outweigh the necessary physical effort. *Pointing* is seen as an intuitive and quick technique but requires some cognitive effort to point at the smart device and needs line of sight. It is typically used when the smart device and its tag are in the line of sight of the user and the smart device cannot be grasped directly by the user. In the users' minds *pointing* makes most sense because it combines intuitive interaction with less physical effort.

The indirect mobile interaction technique *scanning* is avoided as much as possible. If there is a line of sight, the user normally switches to a direct mobile interaction technique such as *touching* or *pointing*. Indirect interaction is mainly used to bridge a physical distance and to avoid physical effort. Scanning is seen as the technique with the least physical effort. A disadvantage is that the user has to select the intended device after scanning; this process is more time-consuming than directly interacting when standing close to a smart object. Furthermore the cognitive effort is higher compared to *pointing* or *touching*. It is typically used when the smart device and its tag can not be seen by the user and when the smart device is in scanning range. Generally, if a movement is necessary the user tends to switch to scanning.

Table 1 summarizes the findings described in this subsection.

Table 1. Comparison of properties of the physical mobile interaction techniques

	Touching	Pointing	Scanning
Natural Interaction, Intuitiveness	Good	Good	Average
Felt error resistance, non-ambiguous	Good	Average	Bad
Performance (within interaction distance)	Good	Average	Bad
Cognitive Load	Low	Medium	High
Physical Effort (outside interaction distance)	High	Medium	Low

6.2   Which Interaction Technique in Which Context?

Based on our research as described in the previous sections we formulated the following basic guidelines:

1. Users tend to switch to a specific physical mobile interaction technique dependent on **location**, **activity** and **motivation**.
2. The **current location** of the user is the most important criterion for the selection of a physical mobile interaction technique.
3. The user's motivation to make any **physical effort** is generally low.

Next, the most important factors for the selection of an interaction technique will be discussed.

Location: In general the following three different situations exist.

A. The smart object is within the reach of the user. In this case, users prefer *touching* because in this context it is more intuitive and faster than the others techniques.

B. The smart object and its tags can be seen by the user but it is not in close reach. In this situation users mostly prefer *pointing* because they have to expend physical effort to use of *touching*. In addition, they avoid *scanning* because it is more time consuming and complex.

C. The smart object is in *scanning* and *pointing* range, but there is no line of sight between the user and the smart object. In this situation users mostly prefer *scanning* because they have to spend physical effort to use *touching* and *pointing*.

Activity: Besides the location, activity is another factor in the selection of a physical mobile interaction technique. In our research we considered three different activities *lie*, *sit* and *stand*. The results of the user tests showed that in the context of lying or sitting, the location context is much more important than the activity context. The situation when the user is standing is completely different. In this situation the motivation to move and to use *touching* or *pointing* is much higher. Another aspect of activity is the kind of occupation. If the user wants to relax, she does not want to make any physical effort, whereas she is more motivated to move when she is busy.

Motivation: Basically, the user is not willing to make any physical effort and chooses the physical mobile interaction technique mostly according to the location and activity context. Nevertheless, the motivation to approach a smart device can be increased. In particular the following aspects increase the motivation to move:

A. Security Issues: Users are willing to make a physical effort when they are highly motivated, e.g. when the smart device plays some critical role in their life. In these cases, the testers are prepared to get closer to perform a selection via *touching*. Examples include interaction with the security system of a smart environment or the oven. The reason is that users are convinced that this interaction technique is most secure. They think that because of the short distance between the mobile device and the smart object it is not possible to interrupt or eavesdrop on the connection, or to manipulate the transferred information. Furthermore, they think that the risk of selecting the wrong device is very low.

B. Speed: In some cases, the selection process must be performed very quickly. Here, the motivation is increased to move closer to use a fast direct interaction technique. An example for this is the control of the lights in the room. In this case the users are not willing to use a time-consuming scanning procedure, they prefer to point to or touch the object to quickly switch it on or off.

C. Intuitiveness: The intuitiveness of the direct interaction techniques can increase the motivation to approach an object for interaction. Older people in particular who are not used to mobile phones are more motivated to make a physical effort to prevent a more complex and time consuming indirect selection technique.

D. Maximum Physical Effort: The previously mentioned aspects to increase the motivation are only appropriate if the required physical effort is not too high, e.g. implies movement of up to 10 meters. The further the smart devices are away the less important are the motivation aspects.

These guidelines could help application designers in the future when developing systems that take physical mobile interaction into account. When looking on the results it must be considered that we did not run a long term study within the people's home environment. Based on these results we hope developers can better decide which interaction techniques should be provided in which context.

7 Conclusion

In this paper we have presented a comprehensive analysis of the physical mobile interaction techniques *touching*, *pointing* and *scanning*. First we conducted an online questionnaire asking the participants about their opinion with regard to mobile interactions in smart environments in general, and in particular which services they would use. Additionally, we asked them about their preferences regarding the three interaction techniques. Following this, we developed and evaluated a low-fidelity and a high-fidelity prototype which supported *touching*, *pointing* and *scanning*. Finally, we summarised all these findings and defined guidelines for which context a particular interaction technique is preferred or should be supported.

We analyzed the influence of the user's location, her activity and her motivation on the preference for a physical mobile interaction technique. We observed that location is by far the most important factor for the selection of *touching*, *pointing* or *scanning* within a given context. In addition to this, we analyzed how the activity of the user (standing, sitting, lying) related to the same decision. Generally it can be said that if the user is sitting or lying, she prefers an interaction technique which is possible without changing the location, even if the interaction might take more time. Furthermore, we deduced that factors such as security issues, speed and intuitiveness can also influence the preference for an interaction technique within a given context.

In short; people prefer to touch things that are near. If they're not near, and there's a clean line of sight, they prefer pointing. Only if all else fails they prefer scanning

In our future work, we will investigate further physical mobile interaction techniques in our smart environment. We also plan to conduct long term studies with residential users in the environment to learn more about the interplay between location, activity and motivation in relation to the choice of selection technology. In particular, for pointing we plan to investigate alternative implementation options based on cameras built into the phone.

Acknowledgement

This work was performed in the context the research project Embedded Interaction which is founded by the DFG and the PERCI (PERvasive ServiCe Interaction) project which is funded by NTT DoCoMo Euro-Labs.

References

1. Kindberg, T., Barton, J., Morgan, J., Becker, G., Caswell, D., Debaty, P., Gopal, G., Frid, M., Krishnan, V., Morris, H., Schettino, J., Serra, B., Spasojevic, M.: People, places, things: web presence for the real world. In: Mobile Networks and Applications, 7 (5). 2002.

2. Abramson, D., Lowe, G., Atkinson, P.: Are you interested in Computers and Electronics? In: Proceedings of the ACE 2000, Melbourne, Australia, 2000.
3. EURESCOM: Strategic Study Project P946-GI. When Things Start to Think? http://www.eurescom.de/~pub-deliverables/P900-series/P946/D1/p946d1.pdf. 2000.
4. Tarrini, L., Bandinelli, Rolando B., Miori, V., Bestini, G.: Remote Control of Home Automation Systems with Mobile Devices. In: Mobile HCI 2002. Pisa, Italy, 2002.
5. Meyers, Brad A., Nichols J., Wobbrock, Jacob O., Miller, Robert C.: Taking Handheld Devices to the Next Level. In: IEEE Computer Society, 36(12), 36-43, 2004.
6. Ballagas, R., Rohs, M., Sheridan, J., Borchers, J.: The Smart Phone: A Ubiquitous Input Device. In: IEEE Pervasive Computing, 5 (1), 70-77, 2006.
7. Want, R., Fishkin, K.P., Gujar, A., Harrison, B.L.: Bridging physical and virtual worlds with electronic tags. In: Proceedings of the SIGCHI conference on Human factors in computing systems: the CHI is the limit, ACM Press, Pittsburgh, Pennsylvania, United States, 1999.
8. Välkkynen, P., Tuomisto, T.: Physical Browsing Research. In: Workshop Pervasive Mobile Interaction Devices (PERMID 2005), Munich, Germany, 2005.
9. Near Field Communication (NFC), www.nfc-forum.org.
10. Fitzmaurice, G.W. Situated information spaces and spatially aware palmtop computers. In: Communications of the ACM, 36 (7), pp. 39-49. 1993.
11. Rekimoto, J., Nagao, K.: The World Through the Computer: Computer Augmented Interaction with Real World Environments. In: Proceedings of the 8th ACM Symposium on User Interface Software and Technology (UIST '95), (Pittsburgh, PA, USA, 1995), 29-36.
12. QR Code, http://www.qrcode.com/.
13. Semacode, www.semacode.org.
14. Rohs, M. and Gfeller, B.: Using Camera-Equipped Mobile Phones for Interacting with Real-World Objects. In: Advances in Pervasive Computing, Austrian Computer Society (OCG). 265-271, 2004.
15. Föckler, P., Zeidler, T., Brombach, B., Bruns, E., Bimber, O., PhoneGuide: Museum Guidance Supported by On-Device Object Recognition on Mobile Phones. In: International Conference on Mobile and Ubiquitous Computing (MUM'05), New Zealand, 2005.
16. Deutsche Post – Mobilepoint, http://www.mobilepoint.de/.
17. WikipediaTricorder, http://en.wikipedia.org/wiki/Tricorder.
18. Nokia NFC RFID SDK 1.0., http://europe.nokia.com/nokia/0,,76301,00.html.
19. Nokia NFC Shell, http://europe.nokia.com/nokia/0,,76314,00.html.
20. Decker, C., Krohn, A., Beigl, M., Zimmer, T.: The Particle Computer System. In: Proceedings of the 4th International Symposium on Information Processing in Sensor Networks (IPSN), Los Angeles, California, USA, 2005.
21. Ma, H. and Paradiso, J.A.: The FindIT Flashlight: Responsive Tagging Based on Optically Triggered Microprocessor Wakeup. In Proceedings of UbiComp 2002, Sweden, 2002.
22. Shafer, S., Brummit, B., Cadiz, J.: Interaction Issues in Context-Aware Intelligent Environments. In Human-Computer Interaction 16 (2, 3, 4), 363-378, 2001.

An Exploratory Study of How Older Women Use Mobile Phones

Sri Kurniawan

School of Informatics, The University of Manchester, PO Box 88, Manchester M60 1QD,
United Kingdom
s.kurniawan@manchester.ac.uk

Abstract. This paper reports on issues related to the use of mobile phones by women aged 60 years and over. The study started with a series of focus group discussions, which covered usage patterns, problems, benefits, ideal phone design, and desired and unwanted features. It then moved to an exploration of the group's cooperative learning process when encountering an unfamiliar mobile phone. The issues raised in the discussions were translated into an online questionnaire, which was responded to by 67 women aged 60 and over. This study makes two main contributions to the field. First, it is one of a very few studies that provides a diagrammatic representation of older mobile phone female users' cooperative learning process and strategies. Second, the study presents a combination of quantitative and qualitative data, which provides more nuanced interpretation and understanding of the use of mobile phones by older women.

Keywords: Elderly, mobile phone, older adults, focus group, questionnaire.

1   Introduction

Mobile phones are rapidly becoming a feature of today's society. A report published by Ofcom (the Office of Communications, the independent regulator and competition authority for the UK communications industries) in March 2006 stated that 82% of UK adults owned mobile phones. The ownership drops slightly for older people, with only 60% people aged 65-74 years old and 36% people aged 75 years old and over owning mobile phones [26]. People over the age of 60 use mobile phones for very limited purposes, such as for calling or texting in emergencies [6], on average making five calls and sending two text messages weekly [26]. Older people avoid using complex functions, caused by displays that are too small and difficult to see, buttons and characters that are too small causing them to push wrong numbers frequently, functions that are too many and too complex, non-user-friendly menu arrangement, unclear instruction on how to find and use some functions and services that are too expensive [25].

Mobile phones can potentially play an important role in helping older people in many ways if the problems related to the use of mobile phones can be solved (Help the Aged society identified that "mobile phone is not too complicated to use compared to the Internet and other modern technology that the younger generation is more

P. Dourish and A. Friday (Eds.): Ubicomp 2006, LNCS 4206, pp. 105–122, 2006.

used to using." [2]). They provide a sense of security for older people as they can be reached practically anytime and anywhere [25]. Some companies use mobile phones to provide emergency location reporting for older people who are lost or require emergency assistance [21], which is potentially useful for family members who are worried about the whereabouts of their older relatives. Another study suggests that the main functions of mobile technology are for maintaining and developing social relationships and providing health and security services. [20].

It is unfortunate that there have been few studies that involved older persons in the development phase of mobile phones (an exception is universal design activities reported by Fujitsu – although the oldest participant was 'only' 60 years old of age [10]). Past studies showed that when asked, older people were quite vocal in specifying the functions they would like to have in their mobile phones, e.g., health monitoring [1], or a simple, easy to use phone with speech-control [25]. Older persons were also able to come up with innovative and out-of-the-box ideas on futuristic use of mobile technology, such as one-stop help centre or security bracelet that can send calls for help (although most participants were only willing to pay €4-10 and most said that they preferred to start those innovative services "sometime in the future" [20]).

This paper reports on the issues related to the use of mobile phone by older women. This study focuses on women for several reasons. Firstly and most importantly, women perceived mobile phones as providing a sense of safety in emergencies much more strongly than men did [25]. Secondly, the same study also pointed out that mobile ownership in women in their sixties was much lower than that of men of similar age group (36% vs. 47%). Therefore, there is a need to ensure that older women can use their mobile phones when the need arises, through an investigation of their usage patterns, problems, perceived benefits, ideal phone design, and desired and unwanted features. In addition, an informal observation revealed that there are differences in men's and women's uses of mobile phones (e.g., men tend to keep their phones in their pockets while women keep their phones in their handbags – which might have some gender-specific design implications). The retirement age is used as the inclusion criterion, which is 60 years old for women in the UK.

2   Methods

This study combines quantitative and qualitative methods to explore issues related to the use of mobile phones by older women. Qualitatively, focus group discussions were used to extract the data. One session of the focus group discussions was used to reveal the group's learning process and strategies. Quantitatively, findings from the online questionnaire designed in collaboration with the focus group were explored. By combining the analysis of the survey, the learning process and the focus group discussions, the study aims to arrive at a more nuanced understanding of the nature of the use of mobile phone among older women to meet their needs. This combination is expected to be able to complement the pictures provided by individual methods.

2.1 Focus Group

Focus group discussions were used in this study because they have a long history in market and medical research and had been shown to be very effective in drawing upon respondents' attitudes, feelings, beliefs, experiences and reaction in a way that would not have been feasible using other methods [7]. The use of focus group is one method to get large amount of information in a short period and it is particularly useful to explore the degree of group consensus on a given topic [23]. Interaction is the key feature of focus groups as it highlights their view of the world, the language they use about an issue and their values and beliefs about a situation [14]. Moreover, focus groups enable us to find out why an issue is salient as well as what is salient about it [24] and the gap between what people say and what they do [16].

Focus group discussions had been used to investigate perceived context-related benefits of mobile phones for older persons. The focus group stated that the main benefits of mobile phones are to keep in touch with someone emotionally close who lives more than half an hour apart, to set time for a leisure activity with a friend, and to immediately share exciting good news [19].

The study follows the recommendation that the number of people per group should be between six and ten [18] and that the researchers met the same group several times [9]. We also arranged that each session lasted around two hours in a 'neutral' location, which was believed to be helpful for avoiding either negative or positive associations with a particular site or building [27]. Upon consultation with the focus group, it was decided to use the meeting room of the College of Third Age for the discussions.

The focus group moderators were carefully chosen to involve researchers from various backgrounds, i.e., two HCI researchers, one retired mobile phone company employee, and one social scientist (two doubled as note takers). It has been long known in the focus group tradition that the role of the moderators is very significant, as good levels of group leadership and interpersonal skill are required to moderate a group successfully [7]. These moderators extracted the information from a book on ethnographic study of mobile phone use in Norway [17] and other studies on the use of mobile phones by older persons (e.g., [20]) into six topics for the first focus group discussion session. These are: (1) usage pattern, (2) problems, (3) perceived benefits, (4) unwanted features, (5) desired features and (6) other concerns. A list of the subtopics that need to be covered in the discussions was drawn.

Initially, the topics were introduced in an open-ended fashion (e.g., "Describe the problems you experience using your mobile phone.") Occasionally, the moderators prompted the group on topics that they had not covered, such as "Are there any features that you wish to have but you don't currently have in your mobile phone?"

The second session was dedicated to brainstorming design features of the 'closest to ideal' commercially available mobile phone through a review of the brochures of 25 models. The models were carefully selected to ensure that they were carried by at least two mobile phone shops and were priced at £150 or less. The moderators then went to several mobile phone shops to find a commercial model that most closely matches the required criteria to allow the group to experience the look and feel of the phone. The last session aimed at exploring how older women learn to use a new mobile phone.

The participants of the focus group were recruited through flyers placed in super-markets and organisations for older persons such as the College of Third Age and Age Concern. In addition to their age and gender, the inclusion criteria required the participants to have some experience with mobile phone operation.

2.2 Cooperative Learning Observation

One obvious problem for anyone using a mobile phone is learning to use it. It has been widely accepted in HCI that observing how users learn to use a new system can have many theoretical and practical implications. To provide the learning context, some goal structures need to be established. There are three possible goal structures which can be implemented in a learning situation: competitive, cooperative and indi-vidualistic [11]. In a cooperative learning situation, when one learner achieves his or her goal, all of the other learners the learner is linked with also achieve their goals. In a competitive learning situation, when one learner achieves his or her goal, all of the other learners s/he is linked with fail to achieve their goals. In an individualistic learn-ing situation, learners' goal achievements are independent.

In this study, the cooperative structure was chosen because the focus group sug-gested that in reality, learning to use a mobile phone for older women is mostly a collaboration project between them and their offspring or friends. Therefore, the co-operative learning setting would be most appropriate in simulating real life situation.

It should be noted that a successful cooperative learning requires several specific criteria from the group [3]: positive dependence (members of the group depend on each other in a symbiotic manner), individual accountability (each person must con-tribute and learn), group processing (reflecting on how the group is working), good social skills (communication, leadership etc.), and healthy face-to-face interaction. Only after observing that the focus group members fulfilled those criteria, was the decision to adopt the cooperative learning in this study finalised.

Cooperative learning has been applied in different subject matter and a wide range of population. Cooperative learning has been used in studying the conceptual data modelling [29] and in a programming course [3]. In the later case, the cooperative learning exercises were designed to help students learn about the key mental model processes of programming and problem solving. No published literature was found on the application of cooperative learning in learning to use mobile phones. However, it appears that cooperative learning approach may be beneficial for women and mem-bers of underrepresented minority groups [30].

There are three major theoretical perspectives on cooperative learning and achievement [30]. *Motivational perspectives* focus primarily on the reward or goal structures under which learners operate. Under this perspective, cooperative incentive structures create a situation in which the only way group members can attain their own personal goals is if the group is successful. Not surprisingly, motivational theo-rists build group rewards into their cooperative learning methods.

In *social cohesion perspectives*, learners help one another learn because they care about one another and want one another to succeed. Social cohesion theorists tend to downplay or reject the group incentives and individual accountability held by motivationalist researchers to be essential.

The major alternative to the motivational and social cohesiveness perspectives, both of which focus primarily on group norms and interpersonal influence, are the *cognitive perspectives*, which hold that interactions among learners will increase learner's achievement for reasons, which have to do with mental processing of information rather than with motivations. The two major perspectives under this umbrella are the *developmental* and the *cognitive elaboration perspectives*.

The *developmental perspective* assumes that interaction among learners around appropriate tasks increases their mastery of critical concepts. One category of practical cooperative methods closely related to the developmental perspective is *group discovery methods*, where learners work in small groups to solve problems with relatively little guidance. Under the *cognitive elaboration perspective*, learners take roles as explainer and listener, with research finding that learners who gained the most from cooperative activities were those who provided elaborated explanations to others.

Those theoretical perspectives have well-established rationales, and most have supporting evidence. All apply in some circumstances, but none is probably both necessary and sufficient in all circumstances. Research in each tradition tends to establish setting conditions favourable to that perspective. For example, most research on cooperative learning from the motivational and social cohesiveness perspectives takes place over extended periods, as both extrinsic motivation and social cohesion may be assumed to take time to show their effects. In contrast, studies undertaken from the cognitive perspectives tend to be very short, making issues of motivation moot.

In this study, the cooperative learning of the focus group will be observed to investigate whether the pattern of learning matches any of the three major theoretical perspectives. It can be informally hypothesized that given the characteristics of these perspectives, it is more likely that the learning pattern would match the cognitive perspectives. It would be interesting, however, to investigate which perspective under the umbrella of cognitive perspectives would be more pronounced in the specific context of older women learning to use a new mobile phone.

3 The Focus Group Discussions

Seven older women participated in the focus group discussions (median age = 67.5 years old), four are diploma holders, three graduated from grammar schools. Six have been using mobile phones for several years; one started using it in the last 12 months.

Six did not use their mobile phones very often and therefore chose the pay-as-you-go (pre-pay) scheme with an average top-up frequency of once or twice a month. This finding repeats a study on consumer behaviour, which revealed that older people, who used a mobile phone only infrequently or for short calls in an emergency, generally liked to buy a certain amount of credit and then pay only for the calls they actually made. They believed their usage was not high enough to warrant paying a monthly fee [5]. The report also suggested that these people knew that choosing the pay-as-you-go was scheme costly in terms of price per call but found it was useful for controlling their usage and ensuring that they were on top of the costs.

They topped up in mobile phone shops or at supermarket tills. They (or their spouses) paid the bills. Half of them said that their phones were gifts from their children or grandchildren, a finding that is also reported in [5]. One participant stated that older women's phones would not usually be the newest model because most of them received their phones when their children or grandchildren upgraded their phones.

In general, the group quickly agreed on an opinion suggested by one group member. It was observed that sometimes the participants made contradictory statements between or within sessions. For example, while everybody agreed that *texting* had a bad influence on people's communication skill, they all agreed that Short Messaging Service (SMS) is one of the 'must have' features in a mobile phone.

The whole sessions were voice-recorded and videotaped using Sony digital camcorder for later review and analysis. The focus group records were analysed using content analysis. The first comment to note is that the participants preferred to be called 'mature women', which they argued would be the view shared by most women of their ages. However, as the term 'older' would be more familiar for the research community, this term will be used throughout the paper. The following sections describe the issues raised during the discussions.

3.1 Usage patterns

Older women most likely would only use mobile phones in unexpected situations such as when their trains were delayed; they did not use their mobile phones for casual conversations. The exception is when the persons they needed to call only own mobile phones as the cheapest way to contact them is by using a mobile phone.

The participants mostly called their family members, and very rarely their friends (whom they usually called using landline phones or met face to face). They rarely used SMS, as they believed that SMS ruined people's literacy. However, they understood most of the abbreviations in the SMS their grandchildren sent them (e.g., gr8 = great).

All participants reported that carrying mobile phones increased their feelings of safety and security but could not think of any other benefits of having a mobile phone.

3.2 Physical Design Related Issues

Physical design preferences were explored through a combination of open-ended and prompted discussions. To aid the prompted discussion, a series of brochures of commercial mobile phones were presented to the group. They were then given a printout with snapshots of various models that differ in one dimension to help them focus (see Figure 1 for an example) and asked to comment on those options and to suggest other preferred options if necessary.

The following design-related issues were raised:

- Display: not as important as text size (which has to be large enough to read comfortably).

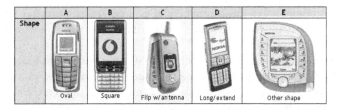

Fig. 1. An example of the snapshots of various shapes of mobile phones

- Size: 'bulky', can be grabbed and held comfortably.
- Shape: a flip phone with an antenna as the antenna is good for picking up the phone from a crowded handbag. A flip phone also allows easy phone call pickups and terminations.
- Colour: although the participants stated that colour was a priority when choosing a mobile phone, bold or silver coloured phone would be easier to spot in a crowded handbag. There were contradictory opinions among group members on this issue: the members who preferred silver were worried that bold-coloured phones were more prone to theft or mugging. In deed, mobile phone theft was one of the main public concerns in the UK [22].
- Buttons: square, raised, metallic buttons arranged similar to landline buttons' arrangement. A similar finding was reported in a study on mobile phone design for older persons performed by Fujitsu [10]. Small, rubbery buttons were disliked.
- Backlight: does not turn off too fast, as older users require longer time to think of what to type or to choose from many options.

Using the criteria proposed by the participants, a mobile phone which best fulfilled the requirements was purchased (an LG C3300 phone – see Figure 2). It is a flip phone, in silver and bold red colour, with metallic square raised buttons.

Fig. 2. The commercial model that is the closest to the ideal design specified by the group

3.2 Function-Related Issues

The participants raised concerns and preferences on the following functional issues:

- Memory aids: alarm, caller identification complemented with the picture of the caller, and multiple appointment reminders.

- Operational complexity: most commercial phones' menus are too many, often unnecessary, difficult to understand, complicated and thus impossible to recall, echoing the findings in [25].
- Layout: the home screen should only contain the most important functions, which are voice call, text, alarm and calendar. Textual menus arranged in a list are preferred to icon-based menus arranged in columns and rows. Frequently accessed functions should be grouped together and separated from others.
- Shortcuts: things such as a one button locking function to prevent accidental dialling, an easily accessible 'panic button' for emergencies, and a button to place a caller/number into a blacklist, should be provided.

3.3   Negative Effects

Finally, the following are what the participants consider as the negative effects of the use of mobile phones:

- Inadvertent listening: "ridiculous" choice and volume of ring tones, chatting loudly on stories listeners did not want to hear but forced to. Ling [17] reported that the latter case was the number one source of annoyance for people of all ages.
- Inappropriate use: using mobiles in prohibited places such as in restaurants, leisure places, public transportation, and cinemas (one participant said that "it glowed in the dark and the noise disturbed other viewers").
- Health scare: brain cancer and other health problem (e.g. RSI) in long term and heavy use. This brain cancer scare received such a high public airing that in 2002 the UK government launched a £7.4 million research programme to scientifically investigate this issue [22].
- Communication effect: it can reduce face-to-face interaction
- Negative effects on younger generation: texting is addictive, mobile phones impair their ability to plan, and some payment plans encourage excessive use without much consideration of the financial consequence (mostly for their parents).
- Unwanted functions: Camera and video phones were considered the 'most dangerous invention of the 21st century' as it encouraged bullying[1] and privacy violation, and therefore should be removed. Predictive texting should be easily disabled.

4   Exploration of the Group's Cooperative Learning

The last session was dedicated to the group's learning process exploration. For this purpose, the participants were handed the new phone in its original box and were asked to pretend they just received a new phone from their grandchildren. No task was assigned to allow the group to explore functions that were salient and attractive to them. No specific role was assigned to each individual, either, as one of the aims of this observation was to determine which theoretical cooperative learning

---

[1] A craze called 'happy slapping' in which an unsuspecting victim is attacked while an accomplice records the assault (commonly with a camera/video phone) had worryingly become a nationwide phenomenon in 2005, despite police effort to combat it [9].

perspective(s) emerged. Following studies on how to induce cooperative learning (e.g. [12]), the group was instructed to work together to master the use of the new phone. The group discussion and interaction were transcribed in real time as well as through later review of the video tapes.

It became obvious that most group members took turn in becoming the central point (the person holding the phone) and the support persons (the person reading the manual and the ones offering their opinions and suggestions on what to do when the phone holder seemed to be having problems) in the learning process.

Three phases of learning were observed: exploration, action and configuration. In the exploration phase, the group first explored the phone's physical design before moving on to feature/function exploration. Physical design is the tangible attributes of the device, which include the overall aesthetic (colour, button design, and overall design), weight, thickness, handiness, screen size, keypad layout etc.

When the group encountered a new feature, they entered a loop of exploring and trying out, utilizing help either from the manual or from the researchers (external factor) or through an association with their existing mental model (internal factor) to understand how the function works. In this discovery process, the existing model was sometimes used to acquire further knowledge about the feature. Some new features were selected for further exploration, which caused the mental model to be updated.

In the next phase, which was the action phase, the group created another loop of planning how to interact with the various functions and executing tasks. When the plan failed to achieve the result they desired, they changed strategy. The last phase was the configuration phase, which the users only performed after they were comfort-able with the more basic functions such as making and receiving voice calls. In this phase they changed the original setting of the phone, such as the time and date and the alarm. Figure 3 depicts a visual representation of these phases. This diagram is a re-sult of a brainstorming exercise of the focus group moderators and was later verified by the focus group (after some explanation of what a mental model is).

4.1 Exploration of Physical Design

Even though the group was instructed to work together, it was observed that there were traces of individualistic learning in this phase. One participant was excited and immediately reached out and opened the box. She picked out, closely observed, and removed the plastic wrappings of the items in the box. She was helped by the partici-pants sitting on her immediate left and right. She asked the moderators whether the phone had airtime and power. Another refused to touch the phone when another par-ticipant handed her the box. She commented that she would go "blank" because she was always nervous of trying new technology, or encountering an unfamiliar device in general. One took out her mobile phone and started exploring the new phone by comparing it to her current phone.

However, there were some similarities in this exploration phase, as well. In gen-eral, the sequence performed by the participants was:

1. Inspecting and picking out items in the box.
2. Flipping the phone open and close to get a feel of its stiffness (some commented that the phone was too stiff).

3. Closely examining what happened when the phone was flipped open.
4. Inspecting various physical designs: its design (weight and size – the participants used their palms to gauge the weight of the phone), colour, size of button, characters on the button, and button assignment (camera, volume, clear and OK). All of them agreed that the tested phone was "nicer" than their own phones. The most common comments referring to the characters on the keypad were "I cannot see [them] without my lenses."

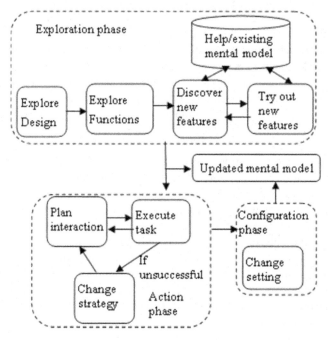

Fig. 3. The group's learning process when interacting with a new mobile phone

4.2 Exploration of Functions

While the exploration of physical design tended to be an individual activity, the exploration of functions tended to be collaborative learning. When the phone holder found a new function or feature, she demonstrated and explained this function to everybody. The participant naturally passed the phone to the next person when she finished one activity. The activities that this group performed in this process were:

1. Making and receiving voice calls.
2. Taking, sending and deleting photograph. The participants had some difficulties due to lack of feedback of whether a photograph was successfully taken/sent.
3. Sending and receiving text messages. The participants commented that they hated the text prediction feature and had problems disabling this feature.
4. Setting alarm after asking the moderators how to find this function.
5. Changing time and date.

These five functions can be argued to be the most salient features, at least in the tested phone. Upon closer observation, only the first three functions were either on the home screen or 'hardwired' to one of the control buttons. It seemed that the feature exploration process was influenced more by their needs than by the interface design, i.e. the features explored were not necessarily the most accessible ones. This was verified by the fact that when the participants were unable to find the alarm, they asked for help rather than abandoning the exploration of this function and trying another function.

4.3 Cooperative Learning Strategies

In general, the participants adopted four main learning strategies to help them learn to operate the new phone:

1. Transferring their existing knowledge/experience of operating their own phone (e.g., "I switched off and on my phone when I had problem. Let's try that").The participants were generally quite successful in transferring their knowledge. For example, the participant who used her phone as an alarm clock was able to set up the alarm clock of the tested phone even though the procedure was slightly different from that of her own phone.
2. Performing trial and error (e.g., "Let's see what this icon does").
3. Reading the manual and following the instructions systematically. The participants complained about the jargons used in the manual, highlighting the need to consider who the prospective users are when designing user manuals.
4. Requesting opinion and help from the researchers.

The third strategy was the most used strategy, and was usually performed when strategy 1 or 2 did not work. The fourth strategy was performed only when everything else failed. The decision to change strategies usually happened very quickly. The participants did not give up easily and were always confident that they could complete the tasks if they were given sufficient time. The group did not ask for any help from the researcher except for finding the location of the alarm function.

4.4 The Group's Mental Model on Mobile Phone Operation

During the learning process, some interesting mental models related to mobile phone operation emerged. One instance concerns the group's understanding on how mobile phone networks work. When the participants experimented with the texting feature of the new phone, there was a noticeable delay in receiving a text message. The group concluded that the delay was due to "different networks sending and receiving the message." This discussion extended to the differences between European and American networks and the limited coverage of British network as evidenced by the fact that one participant's phone did not work in the Lake district. (note: the Lake district is one of the major tourist destinations in the Northwest of England). This example was interesting because it showed that the participants were aware of the existence and [in]compatibility of different networks (within the country and between countries), something that can be considered as quite advanced knowledge about mobile phone operation.

5   Analysis of Questionnaire Data

Based on the transcript from the focus group sessions, a set of questions for a larger survey was developed. These questions were then discussed with the focus group during a lunch where a £50 participation reward was handed to each participant. The discussion with the focus group highlighted several issues that would not otherwise have been captured. For example, the focus group suggested that rather than asking for exact age (which many older women would not be willing to reveal), a range of ages should be used as options (e.g., 70-75 years old). Similarly, asking about income was deemed unnecessary and might be offending for some respondents as many retired women do not have any income or are on small pension.

The questionnaire was placed in a website dedicated for surveys, hosted by the University of Manchester. Invitations were mailed to organisations for older persons, mailing lists and personal email addresses (with the owners' permission). There were two inclusion criteria for participating in the survey: the respondents must be 60 years and over and have used a mobile phone before. To encourage participation, the purchased phone was given away through a lucky draw after the survey ended.

Sixty-seven women respondents participated in the survey, the majority (77.6%) of which were 60-65 years old and had used mobile phones for more than two years (62.7%). Half of them used mobile phones every day, and only 9% used mobile phones less than once a month. The respondents were split almost equally on the pay scheme (prepay vs. pay monthly). Their spending pattern was more varied: 38.8% paid more than £20, 25.4% paid £10-20 and the rest paid less than £10. The top three most called persons were partners, children and friends (a similar pattern was reported in a study of 300 older Japanese mobile phone users [25]).

The most used function other than voice call was changing the ringing setting, i.e., to silent, vibrate or loud (68.7%). The least used was video call (2 respondents). Around a third of the respondents frequently used 4-5 functions out of the eleven functions listed. The first two reasons for using a mobile phone were for emergency (59 respondents) and to let people know they were going to be late (54 respondents).

The respondents' experience with various aspects of their mobile phones (e.g. physical dimensions, navigation, learning to use, etc) was captured when they rated each feature from 'not a problem' to 'stressful'. They were instructed to select 'don't know' if they never used a certain feature. Around one third of respondents marked 'not a problem' for almost all features and around a fifth checked 'tolerable'. Very few respondents considered using any feature as 'stressful'. The number of functions was the feature that receives the most number of 'annoying' and 'stressful' ratings (34.3%). Very few marked 'don't know' (1-5%).

The respondents were also asked to rate, in a 5-point Likert-like scales from 'strongly disagree' to 'strongly agree' the various roles of mobile phones in their lives (as suggested by the focus group). These are:

1. It is cheaper to use mobile phone than to use landline phone.
2. I have more friends after having a mobile phone.
3. I feel more confident to go out by myself after having a mobile phone.
4. I am not afraid of getting lost after having a mobile phone.

5. I know I can always call somebody on my mobile phone when I am in trouble.
6. I feel safer to be alone because of my mobile phone
7. It is fun to use mobile phone

Figure 4 illustrates the distribution of ratings. As Figure 4 depicts, the most positively responded statement was one that suggests that mobile phones allow older women to call somebody when they were in trouble. The most negatively responded was that they had more friends after having mobile phones. There was almost an equal split of respondents agreeing and disagreeing that using mobile phones was fun.

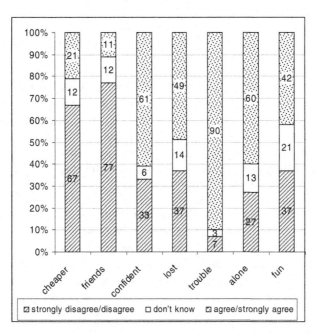

Fig. 4. Respondents' opinions on the roles of mobile phone use in their lives

Finally, to understand older women's opinions on less common functions, a list proposed by the focus group was created, with the options of 'must be removed', 'good if removed', 'can live without', 'good to have' and 'must have'. The respondents tended not to choose the 'must be removed' option. The majority checked 'can live without' or 'good to have'. The top three must have functions were music player, diary and map. Around one third of the respondents thought that the camera function must be removed or good if removed.

6 Discussion and Conclusions

People often underestimate the interest of older women on mobile technology. It is undeniable that ageing-related functional decline has some impact on their use of mobile phones. In addition, the lack of exposure to more advanced features, even if it is merely due to their decision not to upgrade their mobile phones, means that they are less up-to-date with the ever-changing mobile technology. However, this study shows that older women are keen to understand, enthusiastic to learn, and are quite well informed about some advanced features of mobile phones such as MMS (multimedia messaging services). Terms such as network provider, roaming, and satellite communication were discussed, and the participants showed evidence of some degree of understanding of these terms, either through their interaction with the younger generation (mostly grandchildren) or their own experience (e.g. holidaying abroad).

6.1 Patterns of Use

This study is an exploratory study of the use of mobile phone by older women. However, it presents very rich data gathered through a combination of several methods. As a research method, focus group discussions have been proven in this research to be quite successful in gaining an understanding of how some older women used mobile phone. Although focus group in HCI is less commonly used than other inquiry methods (e.g., contextual inquiry and interview), the focus group discussions were able to capture basic requirements of a mobile phone preferred by older women, prior to design. Studies suggested that when a focus group was involved in the decision making process, the participants felt that they benefited from being valued as experts, and being given the chance to work collaboratively with researchers [8]. When asked to comment on this statement, the focus group participants stated that the experience was empowering and "fun" and that they hoped they could see the fruit of their work in the form of an "older-women-friendly" mobile phone design.

The follow-up survey was intended to gain a balanced view of older women users with different expertise and patterns of use. Unfortunately, the data suggest that most respondents were frequent users, had used mobile phones for an extended period, and were familiar with some advanced functions. Undoubtedly, this was partly because the survey was online only. This, however, allows a peek into patterns of use and opinions of older women users at the high end of expertise level.

The survey data confirm the view of the focus group that mobile phones are for emergency rather than for casual conversation, and that it makes older women feel safer, especially when they are in trouble. The data also confirm the opinions of the focus group that camera and video features are deemed unnecessary, and that having too many functions makes mobile phone operation an unfavourable experience (i.e., annoying or downright stressful).

There are small differences in preferences of the survey respondents and those of the focus group participants. While text messaging featured high in the focus group discussions, it was not the most favoured nor used feature by the survey respondents (who chose music, map and diary). It is possible, however, that this is merely due to the way the options were presented. In the survey, the respondents were offered eight features while in the focus group discussions it was an open-ended topic with no options – and therefore, the suggested 'must have' features were highly dependent on the focus group's experience. However, considering that the options in the survey were suggested by the focus group, we can perhaps safely argue that the focus group was aware of these options.

In summary, these two data gathering methods have produced some expected findings and some surprises. These can be categorised into:

Design. Features that mediate ageing-related functional impairments appeared frequently (e.g. larger device, button and character sizes, simpler menus and manuals, memory aids, etc). Practicalities seemed to override aesthetics (e.g. bold colour was preferred for easy spotting, flip phone for easy call pickup, etc). This is perhaps the biggest difference between design preferences of older people and of their younger counterparts, which considered mobile phones as fashion statements [13].

Usage. As expected, mobile phones were not the main communication choice for older women, and the payment plan choice, spending patterns, features used and so on reflect this fact. The interesting thing is to observe that this choice was not based on inability to cope with the technology itself. Very few online respondents considered any feature as stressful to use or were not familiar with even advanced functions. This opens an avenue of investigation of what really causes older women to hesitate to use mobile phones. It is also expected that the main roles of mobile phones were to provide a sense of security and safety when older women were alone (inside and outside the house) or in trouble.

Roles within broader communication patterns. From the discussions (and later verified by a larger survey) it was apparent that mobile phones were viewed as supplement of other communication means such as face to face meetings, letters or landline phones. Only when other communication means fail or are less practical (such as when on the move or when calling somebody on their mobile phones), would mobile phones be the communication media choice. The issue of where mobile phones are situated within broader patterns of communication is an interesting one. Wellman, for example, noticed that community relations are no longer forged by door-to-door contact but rather place-to-place contact online or by phone and that mobile phones have shifted the emphasis from place-to-place to person-to-person communities [31]. In a cross-national (UK, Spain, Finland, and Estonia) study of grandparents-grandchildren communications, face-to-face contact remained the most frequent mean, followed closely by landline telephone; there was moderate use of mobile phones, and many used letters/cards occasionally; and a minority used SMS and e-mails [28]. The question that needs further investigation is, what factors influence the choice of communication means? For example, would geographical distance, the choice of technology used by their offspring, or communication costs affect this choice? This also opens another avenue for further study.

6.2 Cooperative Learning Observation

This study examined the cooperative learning process when the group interacted with a new mobile phone. The informal hypothesis that given the setting of the study, it would be more likely that the learning process would match the cognitive perspectives, was supported. A combination of the *developmental perspective* and the *cognitive elaboration perspective* were observed. The interaction among learners around some tasks did seem to increase the group's mastery of critical concepts related to the operation of an unfamiliar mobile phone. The group members took turn to be the explainer and listener. However, in this study, the knowledge gain was not measured, and therefore, which of the two gained the most from cooperative activities could not be verified. It should be noted that although the instruction was to work together as a group, unavoidably there were traces of individualistic learning, especially during the early physical design exploration. It can be argued this was caused by the individual difference in physical design preference (e.g. for some the buttons' layout was more important than the size of the phone).

Ideally, the study should compare the outcomes of competitive, cooperative and individualistic learning. However, with only seven participants in the focus group, it was impossible to split them into three groups. The cooperative learning was shown to successfully help them learn to use the new phone, arguably more than individualistic learning (as observed from the effect of the support provided by the persons sitting on the left and right of the phone holder). But until a comparative study is conducted, this should be treated as speculative argument.

The learning process was translated into a diagrammatic representation in Figure 3. A similar structure was observed in two quite different domains: older mobile phone users' menu navigation [32, 33] and the learning process of individual blind users when interacting with a new Windows environment [15]. This may indicate that there exists a basic structure of user's learning process of a new interactive system. The diagram indicates that older persons have a structured strategy of interacting with mobile phones. They first explored the physical design, and then started performing basic activities, where they could transfer their existing mental model to, before moving to new features. When exploring new features, they adopted several strategies, i.e., a combination of trial and error, relying on peer support for help (for advice or to find the information in the manual), and seeking expert help.

6.3 Limitations and Further Work

There are some limitations of the current study. The focus group participants are quite homogeneous: highly educated women, middle to upper class, and able-bodied. Although the use of mobile phones, to a certain extent, requires a certain economic and cognitive status, it would be interesting to conduct focus group discussions of older women from other socio-economic background, even if they are only exposed to mobile phones as the 'victims' of other people's inconsiderate use of mobile phones (e.g., loudly talking fellow train passengers). Another natural extension of this study is to replicate the study with older men to highlight gender-related differences in opinions, patterns of use and design choices. Although the online questionnaire was useful to capture quantitative data from a larger pool of older users, it largely failed to attract respondents who were novice mobile phone users. A study with paper-based survey will perhaps be more successful in capturing users with different characteristics.

This study visualises the learning process of a group of older women using a new mobile phone in a snapshot study. It would be more meaningful for mobile phone developers to understand the learning curve of this group, which will require a longitudinal study. As stated earlier, it would also be fruitful to compare the outcomes of various learning approaches.

This study has shown the importance of looking at under-represented population, at real-world practice. The knowledge gained can easily be translated into the development of mobile phones that would be usable and useful for older women. This study also shows that the methods used are have been successfully applied to, and can easily be adapted for requirement gathering exercises of future ubiquitous devices for this user population.

References

1. BBC News: Mobile users want cheaper calls (2004). http://news.bbc.co.uk/1/hi/ technolo gy/3656112.stm
2. BBC Wales News: Mobile use rise for over-65s (2003). http://news.bbc.co.uk/1/hi/wales/ 2802299.stm.
3. Beck, L.L., Chizhik, A.W., McElroy, A.C.: Cooperative Learning Techniques in CS1: Design and Experimental Evaluation. In: SIGSE, St Louis, Missouri (2005) pp. 470-474. New York: ACM Press
4. Bergel, M., Chadwick-Dias, A., Tullis, T.: Leveraging universal design in a financial services company. Accessibility and Computing 82 (2005), 18-24
5. Bonsall, P., Stone, V., Stewart, J., Dix, M.: Consumer Behaviour and Pricing Structures: Final Report on Qualitative Research.
6. Coates, H.: Mobile Phone Users: A Small-Scale Observational Study (2001). http://www.aber.ac.uk/media/Students/hec9901.html
7. Gibbs, A.: Focus Groups. Social Research Update 19. Department of Sociology, University of Surrey, Surrey, UK (1997). http://www.soc.surrey.ac.uk/sru/ SRU19.html
8. Goss J.D., Leinbach T.R.: Focus groups as alternative research practice. Area 28, 2 (1996), 115-123
9. Honigsbaum, M. Concern over rise of 'happy slapping' craze. The Guardian, April 26, 2005. http://www.guardian.co.uk/mobile/article/0,2763,1470214,00.html
10. Irie, T., Matsunaga, K., Nagano, Y.: Universal Design Activities for Mobile Phone: Raku Raku PHONE. Fujitsu Scientific and Technical Journal 41(1), Special Issue on Universal Design (2005), 78-85
11. Johnson, D.W., Johnson, R.T.: Instructional Goal Structure: Cooperative, Competitive, or Individualistic. Review of Educational Research, 44, 2. (Spring, 1974), 213-240
12. Johnson, R.T., Johnson, D.W., Stanne, M.: Comparison of Computer-Assisted Cooperative, Competitive and Individualistic Learning. American Educational Research Journal 23, 1, (1986), 382-392
13. Katz, J.E., Sukiyama, S. Mobile phones as fashion statements: evidence from student surveys in the US and Japan. New Media & Society, 8, 2 (2006), 321-337
14. Kitzinger J.: Introducing focus groups. British Medical Journal 311 (1995), 299-302
15. Kurniawan, S.H., Sutcliffe, A.G. & Blenkhon, P.L.: How Blind Users Mental Models Affect Their Perceived Usability of an Unfamiliar Screen Reader. Proc. Interact, IOS Press (2003), 631-638
16. Lankshear A.J.: The use of focus groups in a study of attitudes to student nurse assessment. Journal of Advanced Nursing 18 (1993), 1986-89
17. Ling, R.: The Mobile Connection: the Cell Phones Impact on Society. San Francisco, USA, Morgan Kaufmann (2004)
18. MacIntosh J.: Focus groups in distance nursing education. Journal of Advanced Nursing 18 (1981), 1981-1985

19. Melenhorst, A., Rogers, W.A., Caylor, E.C.: The Use of Communication Technologies by Older Adults: Exploring the Benefits from the Users Perspective. In: Proc. HFES 46th Annual Meeting, HFES Press (2001), 221-225

20. Mikkonen, M., Väyrynen, S., Ikonen, V., Heikkila, M.O.: User and Concept Studies as Tools in Developing Mobile Communication Services for the Elderly. Personal and Ubiquitous Computing 6 (2002), 113-124

21. Mobile Media: Secufone keeps an eye on elderly. http://www.mobiledia.com/forum/topic16830.html

22. Mobile UK: Mobile Phone and Everyday Life. http://www.theworkfoundation.com/re-search/isociety/MobileUK_main.jsp

23. Morgan D.L., Kreuger R.A.: When to use focus groups and why in Morgan D.L. (Ed.) Successful Focus Groups. London: Sage (1993)

24. Morgan D.L.: Focus groups as qualitative research. London: Sage (1988)

25. NTT DoCoMo: Mobile phones increasingly popular among the elderly. Press Release 34(11). http://www.nttdocomo.com/files/presscenter/34_No11_Doc.pdf

26. Ofcom: Media Literacy Audit: Report on media literacy amongst older people. Ofcom's Media Literacy Publications and Research, March 2006. http://www.ofcom.org.uk/ad-vice/media_literacy/medlitpub/medlitpubrss/older/older.pdf

27. Powell R.A., Single H.M.: Focus groups. International Journal of Quality in Health Care 8, 5 (1996), 499-504

28. Quadrello, T., Hurme, H., Menzinger, J., Smith, P.K., Veisson, M. Vidal, S., Westerback, S.: Grandparents use of new communication technologies in an European perspective. European Journal of Ageing (2005). Online, DOI: 10.1007/s10433-005-0004-y

29. Ryan, S.D., Bordoloi, B., Harrison, D.A.: Acquiring Conceptual Data Modeling Skills: The Effect of Cooperative Leaning and Self-Efficacy on Learning Outcomes. The DATA BASE for Advances in Information Systems, 31,4 (2000), 9-24

30. Slavin, R.E.: Cooperative Learning: Theory, Research and Practice (2nd Edition), Prentice Hall, 1995

31. Wellman, B.: Physical Place and CyberPlace: The rise of personalised Networking. International Journal of Urban and Regional Research, 25 (2001), 227-252

32. Ziefle, M., Bay, S.: How older adults meet complexity: aging effects on the usability of different mobile phones. Behaviour & Information Technology 24,5 (2005), 375-389

33. Ziefle, M., Bay, S.: Mental models of a cellular phone menu. Comparing older and younger novice users. In: S. Brewster & M. Dunlop (Eds), Mobile Human-Computer-Interaction. Springer, Berlin, Germany (2004), 25-37

Farther Than You May Think:
An Empirical Investigation of the Proximity of Users to Their Mobile Phones

Shwetak N. Patel, Julie A. Kientz, Gillian R. Hayes, Sooraj Bhat,
and Gregory D. Abowd

College of Computing & GVU Center
Georgia Institute of Technology
801 Atlantic Drive, Atlanta GA 30332-0280 USA
{shwetak, julie, gillian, sooraj, abowd}@cc.gatech.edu

Abstract. Implicit in much research and application development for mobile phones is the assumption that the mobile phone is a suitable proxy for its owner's location. We report an in-depth empirical investigation of this assumption in which we measured proximity of the phone to its owner over several weeks of continual observation. Our findings, summarizing results over 16 different subjects of a variety of ages and occupations, establish baseline statistics for the proximity relationship in a typical US metropolitan market. Supplemental interviews help us to establish reasons why the phone and owner are separated, leading to guidelines for developing mobile phone applications that can be smart with respect to the proximity assumption. We show it is possible to predict the proximity relationship with 86% confidence using simple parameters of the phone, such as current cell ID, current date and time, signal status, charger status and ring/vibrate mode.

1 Introduction and Motivation

Mobile computing systems have been one of the fastest evolving and growing technologies of the last decade. Simple mobile phones and pagers have given way to simultaneously complex and small computing artifacts that provide a myriad of services and can often even interact with each other. The increasing power and ubiquity of these mobile technologies make it possible to realize many of the early visions of ubiquitous computing. Many argue that the mobile phone, with its expanded capabilities, can be the platform of choice for applications that once required customized mobile hardware [23]. Examples of research focused on these expanded uses include memory aids [7], augmented cognition [8, 25], location-based services [12], medical data collection [27], authentication mechanisms [3, 20], and personal information stores [28].

The topic of location has been a common discussion point in ubiquitous computing with researchers making the mobile phone the platform of choice for location-aware computing. The PlaceLab effort at Intel Research and other location systems (see

P. Dourish and A. Friday (Eds.): Ubicomp 2006, LNCS 4206, pp. 123–140, 2006.

Hightower & Borriello [9] for a survey) have demonstrated that ubiquitous location-awareness can be delivered on commodity hardware, most interestingly mobile phones [12, 16]. This advance creates many opportunities for developing knowledge on the mobile phone of where a person has been and what they have been doing. However, this approach assumes that the mobile phone is an accurate proxy for the location of its owner. Intuitively and anecdotally, we know that people do in fact carry their mobile phones with them *much* of the time, but these same phones are not physically on their bodies nor within arm's reach at *all* times.

Many researchers and application designers make the implicit assumption that people are likely to have their mobile phones with them and available most of the time. However, little empirical evidence on the actual proximity relationship between a mobile phone and its owner exists. The results presented in this paper provide in-depth empirical results uncovering the habits of a small set of representative users in a major metropolitan US city (Atlanta, Georgia). This work not only tests the hypothesis that a user's phone is available to her most of the time but also provides an exploration of the situations in which the proximity assumption is broken and attempts to select the factors that best predict the proximity relationship. Through this evidence, we create concrete design advice for mobile phone applications that require knowledge about the proximity of the user to her phone. We also define for the first time a way to predict proximity using standard features of the phone, such as current cell tower, time, charger status, or ring profile. With an accurate predictor, an important piece of context, namely, how near the owner is, can inform context-aware behaviors on the mobile phone.

This paper provides four contributions. First, we present the design and creation of a proximity-sensing technique and the design of an empirical proximity study that can be replicated by others. Second, we present empirical evidence directly testing the strength of the assumption that the mobile phone is a good proxy for its owner's location. Third, we present a classification of situations that break the proximity assumption, information that can be interpreted as design advice for mobile phone applications. Fourth, we present a decision tree method for predicting proximity to mobile phones based on readily accessible features on the phone itself.

2   Related Work

The mobile phone, initially a device simply for strategic communications, has gone through a long evolutionary process. Originally designed primarily for durability, they were not particularly usable and certainly not stylish. In the 1980's, this trend shifted, and they moved into the consumer product space, complete with the power and status of a high-end watch or automobile. Now, they come in a wide variety of form factors with numerous possible combinations of services. During this evolution, people have been studying mobile phone usage patterns. Marketing firms and mobile phone manufacturers study a variety of user needs, from the calling plans that are most appealing to certain demographics to the usability of the handset itself.

Much of this research has focused on the design of new handsets and/or new services. For example, in 1998, Vaananen-Vainio-Mattila and Ruuska presented an ethnographic study of mobile phone users conducted at Nokia [26]. In this study, the authors used contextual inquiry to uncover both the sociological and cultural considerations affecting mobile phone usage and the design challenges and some potential basic solutions for the handset itself. Palen *et al.* took a slightly different approach, focusing on the use of the mobile phone *system*, including everything from the sales people to the phone itself to the service contacts [19]. Schlosser investigated the ways in which mobile phones are appropriated into organizations and daily activities [24]. She used interviews to uncover both these details and, in turn, how those individuals, organizations, and activities change based on this use.

This related research shows the power and the limitations of these types of studies with real mobile phone users. Palen and Salzman [18] note that although direct naturalistic observation can help investigators to understand interactions as they "really happen... tracking particular participants requires getting access to the many places participants spend their time while also involving a large time commitment for all parties." Thus, they chose to supplement interviews not with observation but with voice mail diary entries, in which mobile phone users called a voice mailbox daily to report their interactions and troubles. McGuigan explores how social science methods can and should be used to study mobile phone usage, describing in depth the strengths and weaknesses of four different sociological methods: social demography; political economy; conversation, discourse, and text analysis; and ethnography [14].

Automatic logging, in which software automatically records the user's actions for later analysis, provides many of the benefits of observation methods without some of the problems. Researchers can gather data across all times, locations and activities without being excessively intrusive to the participant. For example, Demumieux and Losquin developed a tool that collects logs of applications used on mobile devices, including both mobile phones and PDAs [5]. MIT's Reality Mining Project has used Bluetooth proximity and phone context to predict things such as daily routine, but has not yet explored proximity to mobile devices [6]. The ContextPhone system [22] also logs a variety of information on phone use both for research purposes and for context-aware applications. Similarly, the Mobile Media Metadata system leverages such context information to assist users in annotating images on their camera-phones (digital camera equipped mobile phones) [4], whereas other systems use cellular identification to predict user routes and location [11] and develop context-aware contact lists [17]. We are interested in inferring user proximity from contextual information already available on the mobile phone with minimal additional sensors.

3 Experimental Design

This paper presents a mixed-method approach, in which we use both interviews and automatic logging to develop a full picture of user practices. We collected data about the phone and about its owner to help understand and potentially predict the proximity relationship between owner and phone. These data, initially collected automatically, are verified using self-report. In this section, we describe the study design and participants and elaborate on the technology for automatic collection of data.

3.1 Study Method and Participants

A primary goal of this work includes gathering information about users and their mobile phones *all* day *every* day for some extended period introducing minimal burden and without relying on self-report. Due to the increased capabilities of mobile phones, we were able to gather much of the data using software custom-developed for this purpose and running on the phone itself. Recording the user's physical relationship to the phone, however, requires a reliable proxy for the user. We used small, plastic beacons that users wore on lanyards around their necks nearly all the time (shown in Figure 1). We were thus able to measure the phone's distance from the tag and assume this roughly equated to the phone's distance from the individual.

The tags measure 40 mm by 25 mm by 5 mm, approximately the size of an automobile keyless entry remote control. Each weighs approximately 20 grams, including the battery, and can be worn around the neck as a pendant. The tag is also weatherproof, shockproof, and hypoallergenic. The tag emits a Bluetooth signal detected by a custom-built application on the user's Bluetooth-enabled phone. The application on the phone pings the tag every 60 seconds and approximates the distance based on the strength of the signal received. This method allows for the determination of three levels of proximity: within arm's reach (strong signal); in the same room (signal is weak or varied); or unavailable (signal could not be detected). A separate application on the user's phone records contextual information, including signal strength, battery level, charge status, current running application, cell tower ID, area ID, ring volume, ring type, and vibration status. A third application inherent to most mobile phones logs incoming, outgoing, and missed calls and data usage.

Sixteen individuals participated for at least three weeks each. All of the subjects lived in the greater metropolitan area of Atlanta, Georgia, USA and were recruited via word of mouth and Internet classified advertisements. We compensated participants with $200 for completing the entire three-week study and returning the equipment. Participants ranged in age from 21 to 66 and included 9 males and 7 females. Self-reported phone plans ranged from a 5000 minute per month contract to a prepaid, "emergencies only" service plan. Participants also had a wide variety of professions and income levels (see Table 1 for details on each participant). Each participant completed a background interview to provide basic demographic information and data on perceptions of individual phone usage patterns. These questions included those about current phone-charging patterns, applications used on the phone, service plan information, and the perceived phone proximity throughout the day.

After the initial interview, we replaced the participant's phone with one of several form factors all capable of running the logging software, accomplished by a simple swap of SIM cards. We copied all contact list information to the new phone by using the SIM card's memory or, in rare situations, manually entering the information. We provided phones in a similar form factor and with similar software and menu structures to the phones already in use by the participants. Thus, we believe that the phones had minimal impact on the practices of the participants. Participants received a beacon pendant and instructions about charging the phone and the tag. We instructed them to use their phones as normal and to wear the tag at all times. Notable exceptions included while showering or swimming. Most subjects wore the tag while sleeping, but others preferred to place it next them while sleeping. If they removed the tag, we asked them to note the time and duration and keep the tag as near as possible.

During the three weeks of participation, the individuals met with us once per week when we downloaded the logging data from the phone and interviewed them about their usage patterns for the week. At the beginning of each interview, the participant completed a detailed diary of the previous 24-hour period, as suggested by the Day Reconstruction Method [10], breaking the day into episodes described by activities, locations, and the phone's location during these times. During these interviews, participants self-reported reasons they did or did not have their phones for various episodes reported on the diary. Together with the participant, we then compared this diary to the data recorded by the logging application (showing them visualizations of phone proximity similar to that in Figure 1) and asked clarifying questions for any inconsistencies. The diary and visualization could disagree for three reasons:

(1) The participant may have an error in recollection.
(2) The logging application and/or the hardware itself could produce an error.
(3) The tag was not an appropriate proxy (*e.g.* the user was not wearing it).

The interview closed with general questions about the remaining days from the preceding week, such as whether it was a normal workday or a day off, but did not include any specific details about the days that were further in the past. On the third and final interview for each participant, equipment was returned and replaced with the participant's original phone.

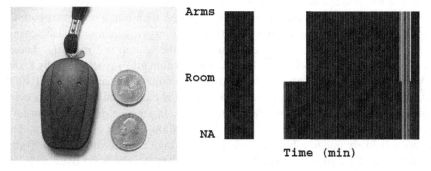

Fig. 1. The left image is a picture the Bluetooth tag. The right shows sample minute by minute proximity data from laboratory tests of the Bluetooth tag and mobile phone application. The full solid lines indicate the tag is within arms reach, the white indicates that it is not available and halfway between or oscillating indicates the tag is room level.

3.2 Phone Proximity Hardware Implementation Details

Although many other contextual indicators of phone usage could be gathered automatically using simply the mobile phone, detection of the user's proximity was more complicated and required development of a proxy for the user. The chosen embodiment of a proxy for the user was a Bluetooth tag from Bluelon Inc. using modified radio parameters, partially inspired by the SPECs project at HP Labs [13]. An application running on the mobile phone continuously records signal values from associated tags. The tag includes a low-power CSR BlueCore-02 Class 2 Bluetooth

RF module with an integrated antenna and a 3.7 V 345 mAh lithium ion battery (see Figure 1). The tag can signal every minute for approximately five days with a single two-hour charge. A buzzer and LED on the tag indicate when the battery is low.

The tag uses a Class 2 Bluetooth module with a 10 meter range, which is sufficient for registering the levels of proximity of interest to the study and uses much less power than the longer range Class 1 modules. The Bluetooth stack implements the Serial Port Profile (SPP) running over L2CAP and RFCOMM for firmware programming. The Bluetooth radio in the user's beacon was reduced to -22 dB to extend battery life and limit the maximum range at which the mobile phone can detect the tag to around 5 to 6 meters. The design of the radio output and subsequent distance analysis assumes a tag placed around the neck of an average adult. Thus, we assume a 5 dB signal loss from the human body due to absorption, with one tag reconfigured to account for a participant of larger size.

Rather than use a Received Signal Strength Indicator (RSSI), which is implemented inconsistently across mobile phones if at all, we implemented our own simpler signal strength indicator for proximity detection. In this solution, the round trip time of the Service Discovery Protocol (SDP) packets are used to estimate the distance between the tag and the mobile phone. As the distance increases between the mobile phone and the tag, the link quality should degrade. The lower link quality then increases the bit error rate and thus the number of packet retransmissions. The retransmits in turn increase the service discovery time. Despite the simplicity of this approach, it was more than sufficient for the level of granularity desired for this study.

By reducing the radio output of the tag, we can specify a rough range at which the bit error rates increase by a set amount. After some experimentation in lab settings with humans of average size, we determined that the appropriate range for human body signal absorption is around ten feet. A phone within arm's reach typically shows a service discovery time of about 2000-4000 ms, room level distance of about 4000-7000, and no returned service discovery information is interpreted as the phone being out of range or further than room level (5-6 meters). In practice, physical room level distance can result in fluctuating values between 4000 ms and no discovery. This fluctuation is likely due to a bit error rate that is so high the Bluetooth module times out and does not report a successful service discovery. One serious issue with this phenomenon is the difficulty that results in determining whether the phone is transitioning from "room level" and truly out of range or whether the phone is consistently at room level with the erroneous fluctuation described. Thus, if we observed high rates of fluctuation (*e.g.* alternating with every reading) over extended periods of time (more than five minutes), we classified the reading as room level.

We developed two applications for gathering the empirical evidence of users' relationships to their mobile phones. The Bluetooth distance logging application was written in Java 2, Micro Edition (J2ME) using the MIDP 2.0 and JSR-82 Bluetooth specification. This application, designed for the Nokia Series 60 platform, also works with other mobile phones that feature the Symbian 7.0 or higher operating system. The application used to log other contextual information, such as cell tower ID and battery status, was written in Symbian using C. Both applications log pertinent information to the removable memory card once per minute and run constantly in the background with minimal interference on other phone functionality. A watchdog application automatically restarts both logging applications in the event of a restart.

4   Results

All participants successfully completed the study for at least three weeks. In every case, at least one of these weeks represented what they considered "typical" patterns, and in many cases, all three weeks were "typical." Participants reported the tag was comfortable to wear and did not interfere with their day-to-day lives. In some instances, participants reported forgetting to put on the tag first thing in the morning after leaving it off for sleeping. We adjusted to account for these errors. In this section, we present the results from both the automatically-collected proximity and phone context data and the self-reported results from the interviews.

4.1   Proximity Levels

As described in Section 3.2, three levels of proximity between the user and the phone can be determined using the Bluetooth tag and application scheme. These are:

- Within arm's reach (within 1-2 meters of the tag)
- Within the same room (within 5-6 meters of the tag)
- Unavailable (beyond 6 meters from the tag)

From the minute-by-minute readings taken each day during the three-week study, we obtained between 6190 and 35791 proximity measurements, with an average of 1175 readings per day per person. When a phone is turned off, no proximity ratings can be logged, but the very nature of the phone being off indicates it is unavailable. Given the large quantities of data, we were able to analyze different scenarios which may or may not affect proximity. In this section, we report those scenarios that showed the most significant trends:

- In and out of the home (determined by cell ID)
- Waking vs. sleeping hours (determined by hours reported during interviews)
- Weekend vs. weekday (weekend being 12 AM Saturday to 12 AM Monday)

Overall, participants varied in their proximity levels, ranging from 17% of the time within arm's reach to 85% of the time, with an average of 58% of the time within arm's reach (see Figure 2). All but two users kept the phones on more than 85% of the time. Participant 7 had a prepaid plan and only had her phone on 21% of the time to conserve minutes, and Participant 14 turned his phone off almost every night while sleeping reportedly to avoid being disturbed.

Interestingly, participants showed a significant increase in the average percentage of time the phone was within arm's reach during times they were away from home (p < 0.0001; see Figure 2). Users were more likely to keep the phone at room level or even further while at home. In fact, two participants with the lowest overall proximity data (2 and 13) were "stay at home" mothers who spent a significant time at home.

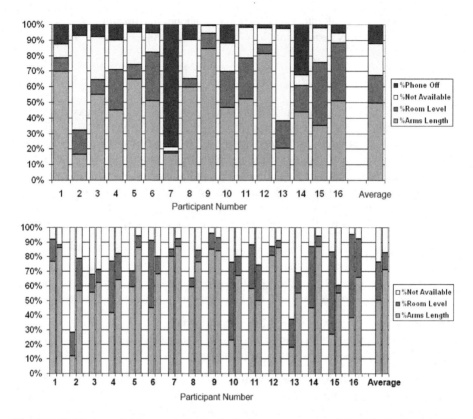

Fig. 2. Individuals varied in proximity levels, but on average people kept their phone within arm's reach half the time (Top). Most users carried the phone close to them at all times when away from home if the phones were turned on (Bottom: Left bar is at home, Right is away).

We compared proximity trends for individual users for times they were sleeping versus times they were awake. Participants had their phones within arm's reach more often while awake than they did while they were asleep (61% while awake, 52% while sleeping). Also, participants tended to keep their phones within arm's reach slightly more often on weekdays (59%) as opposed to weekends (53%). Although these values showed interesting trends, they did not demonstrate statistical significance.

The phone was within arm's reach and turned on, thus highly available, 50% of the time ($\sigma = 20.4$). Thus, we categorized users further than one standard deviation below the average (29.6%) as "Low" availability; users within one standard deviation as "Medium"; and users above one standard deviation (70.4%) as "High." Table 1 lists the proximity category. Contrary to our initial hypothesis, the number of minutes used per month on the phone does not correlate to the proximity relationship throughout the day. For example, the person with the highest number of minutes used per month, Participant 3, fits the Medium availability category. On the other hand, Participant 12 was highly available to the phone, but used it infrequently to make or to receive calls.

Table 1. Demographic information, basic data logged during study, and proximity levels

Participant	Gender	Age	Profession	Minutes Per Month	# Cell towers logged	% Phone off	%Arm's Reach	Proximity Category
1	M	24	Graduate Student	645	168	13	70	High
2	F	36	Homemaker	253	130	7	17	Low
3	M	46	Sales Rep.	4402	696	8	54	Med.
4	F	50	Graduate Student	344	253	10	45	Med.
5	M	41	Software Sales	1068	258	5	65	Med.
6	M	40	Mail Carrier	2905	269	6	51	Med.
7	F	47	Dry Cleaner	25	52	79	17	Low
8	F	23	Admin. Asst.	468	204	10	60	Med.
9	M	25	Consultant	559	139	1	84	High
10	M	61	Lecturer	384	414	12	47	Med.
11	F	21	Childcare Provider	1394	227	2	52	Med.
12	M	33	Project Manager	189	198	2	81	High
13	F	35	Homemaker	148	133	2	20	Low
14	M	32	Sales/Marketing	1769	900	32	44	Med.
15	M	66	Retired	984	227	2	35	Med.
16	F	24	Financial Associate	2075	254	5	51	Med.

4.2 Factors Affecting the Proximity of Mobile Phones to Users

The weekly participant interviews served two purposes. First, during these interviews, participants described their own recollections of proximity to the phone. At times, their recollections and the automatically gathered data, visualized as in Figure 1, appeared to disagree. The interviews provided a time to discuss these discrepancies. Occasionally, participants recalled more accurate information about daily activities after being prompted by the automatically collected data. The interviews also provided an opportunity to note times that the tag was not an adequate proxy, typically because the participant could not wear the tag for some reason. For cases in which no resolution could be reached through the interview discussions, the discrepancy was attributed to technical error. These error cases always registered for only short time periods (a single data point) and occurred on average 3 times in a given day for a participant out of over 1200 data points each day.

Second, the interviews provided participants an opportunity to reflect on and explain activities grounded in the data, both automatically-collected and self-reported. These discussions resulted in better understanding of the factors that contributed to an individual's phone being near or not than would have been possible using solely the automatically-logged contextual information. These factors were determined in two ways: by examining the variables that most directly affected the learned model of the user, as described in Section 5, and by using affinity clustering [21] to group the self-reported reasons for the phone's proximity from the interview data.

Specifically, the affinity clustering results were produced by three researchers. The first recorded each participant's stated reasons for the phone's proximity and availability during the interviews. Two researchers then independently categorized these statements using affinity clustering to determine themes, producing 15 unique themes, 13 of which were shared. The two coders agreed on categorization of most of the cases (105 of 120), and after discussion, agreement was made to include all 15 unique themes. One of the original coders then re-categorized all of the statements while the third researcher categorized them independently using the 15 themes (see Table 2 for inter-coder reliability). The 15 emergent themes follow:

1. *Routine*: The phone's proximity is related to anything that is part of a common routine for the individual, particularly those things that might help them to remember the phone's location or be within range of its use. Example: User always leaves phone on kitchen counter while at home.

2. *Environment*: The phone's proximity is related directly to the distance at which the user believes the phone should be due to the physical constraints of the space. Example: In a car, the phone is rarely out of arm's reach.

3. *Physicality of person/Activity*: The phone's proximity to the user is related directly to something physical about the person or the activity in which he/she is engaged. Example: Phone is awkward to carry while working out.

4. *Disruption to others*: User makes a choice about the phone's proximity and/or on/off status based on how that choice affects other people or the environment. Example: User turns off phone car during a client meeting.

5. *Disruption to self*: User makes a choice about the phone's proximity and/or on/off status based on that choice's effects on self. Example: User turns off phone at home after a long day of calls at work.

6. *Regulations*: Legal or other specific regulations prevent use, carrying, and/or powering of phone. Example: User has to turn off phone while in a hospital.

7. *Use of phone by self*: The phone's proximity is affected by the owner using it or anticipating use. Example: Phone is nearby while user is on a phone call.

8. *Need for use of phone by others*: The phone's proximity is affected by expectation that others may need to reach owner or otherwise make use of owner's phone. Example: Phone is nearby when the user is expecting a call.

9. *Need for use of phone both by self and by others*: The expectation of needing features for self as well as availability of self to others through the phone's features. Example: The user keeps the phone close while trying to coordinate a group of people at a social event.

10. *Use of handset by others*: Someone else is physically using the handset. Example: User loaned phone to spouse while she was out running errands.

11. *No need for use of phone*: Phone's availability directly affected by the belief that no use is imminent. Example: While at home, others can use a landline to reach the user.

12. *Technical resource issues*: The phone's availability and proximity are directly affected by technical considerations inherent to the phone or the network. Example: User moves close to a window to obtain a better signal or moves it to where the charger is located when the battery is low.

13. *Quick trips*: The timing (or expected timing) of an activity affects the user's choice about whether to explicitly consider/act on phone's proximity or not. Example: Phone is on the desk at work while taking a coffee break.

14. *Memory and forgetfulness*: Phone lost (at least temporarily) or unintentionally left behind due primarily to user's forgetfulness or memory error. Example: Phone is left behind while leaving the house.

15. *Protection of phone from others*: The user's choice about phone placement is directly related to protecting the physical handset or the resources that can be accessed through the phone from tampering or use by other people. Example: Phone on a high shelf out of the reach of children.

Table 2. Inter-coder reliability for each thematic cluster was determined using two measures: (1) Observed Agreement represents a measure of simple agreement between two coders for each theme and is measured by agreements divided by total number of statements coded; (2) Cohen's Kappa measures how much better than chance the agreement between the two coders is [1]. Both measure between 0 and 1 with 1 indicating perfect agreement between coders.

Cluster	1	2	3	4	5	6	7	8
Observed Agreement	.93	1	.99	.99	.98	1	.98	1
Cohen's Kappa (k)	.59	1	.83	.83	.81	1	.85	1

Cluster	9	10	11	12	13	14	15
Observed Agreement	.95	.99	.93	.99	.98	.99	.96
Cohen's Kappa (k)	.58	.91	.74	.75	.89	.95	.67

5 Predicting User's Proximity

The preceding section presents empirical findings on the proximity relationship as well as reasons for why a phone is not near its owner. An open question was whether this proximity relationship could be determined on the phone itself, without the aid of a proxy tag. We collected approximately 30,000 proximity readings per participant. In addition to proximity data, we also collected a variety of contextual data from the mobile phone. This information includes hour of day, day of week, cellular tower ID, cellular area ID, signal strength, battery level, charging status, ring volume, ring type or mode, vibration status, foreground application, idle status of the phone, missed calls, time and duration of incoming and outgoing calls, SMS messages, and GPRS data usage. We wanted to investigate whether the real proximity value could be deduced from some subset of those available data already on the phone and whether such a correlation was independent of the individual. If so, mobile phone application developers could create context-aware behaviors triggered by proximity.

The descriptive statistics and interviews summarized throughout this paper suggest that some features do have predictive power. For example, for participants with very structured work schedules, day and hour were effective features for predicting proximity to the phone. Cell tower IDs and charging status were two other contextual features that also showed promise. Many of our participants tended to have their phones on their bodies every time they were away from the cell towers near their homes. Some people only charged their phones while in the car, which made using the charger status (*i.e.,* whether or not connected to charger) one way of inferring that those users would be arms-length from their phones at those times. Figure 3 shows evidence of patterns existing between features and the user's proximity to their phone.

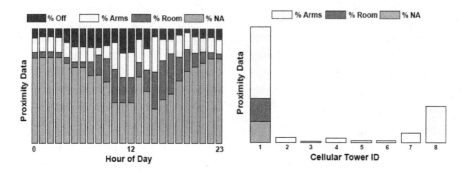

Fig. 3. Left: Proximity percentages for each hour of the day for Participant 2 (a homemaker). Right: Proximity percentage for each cellular tower ID, again for Participant 2. Cell ID #1 is the participant's home and is the only one that has variability on proximity level.

5.1 Proximity Classifier

From a machine learning perspective, the real question is whether the features that predict proximity were general across individuals. We created a model that could classify and predict the proximity of an owner to the mobile phone based on the logged contextual features. We employed a decision tree classifier using the ID3 algorithm [15]. Decision trees have several important advantages for our aim as compared with classifiers such as neural networks, support vector machines or boosting methods. First, they are lightweight yet effective predictors that can function on a mobile phone. Second, the internal representation of a decision tree is highly human-interpretable and thus can inform application design decisions. Furthermore, a decision tree built with the ID3 algorithm doubles as a feature selection mechanism. ID3 works by greedily applying an information gain criterion for selecting which features to use for prediction. Thus, the features near the root of the tree have high predictive power and can be thought of as the most important features. Therefore, the initial question of whether there are common features of significance across all individuals can be addressed by determining whether the root of the decision tree varies across users and, if so, how.

This challenge can be formulated as a supervised learning problem, in which the class labels are the three levels of proximity, and each instance is a feature vector encoding the logged contextual information. We first tested the performance of the decision trees by using all three weeks of data for each user. We used 10-fold cross-validation to ensure effective use of the entire data set without biasing the test phase. To ascertain how many weeks of training were actually necessary for high accuracies, we conducted tests using restricted training sets. In one test, we used the first two weeks of data for the training set and the third week for the test set. In the second, we used the first week of data for training and the other two weeks as the testing set.

Table 3. Classification accuracies in percentages. The test using 3 weeks of data was conducted using 10-fold cross-validation over the entire data set.

Participant	Majority Classifier	Tree: 3 wks training	Tree: 2 wks training	Tree: 1 wk training	Tree: cell id, hour, & day	Tree: the top 4 features
1	77.0	90.1	89.2	87.7	85.0	88.1
2	53.6	88.9	87.2	85.8	80.2	86.5
3	59.4	93.1	88.0	85.8	78.4	85.4
4	49.8	86.1	85.1	84.0	85.8	86.0
5	68.3	85.0	83.7	82.9	73.5	82.5
6	53.8	86.3	85.9	85.1	79.2	84.0
7	81.5	90.1	90.0	88.2	90.0	90.0
8	65.9	88.7	87.9	86.5	82.1	85.3
9	84.6	91.0	90.8	89.4	88.1	88.9
10	52.4	90.1	89.2	88.3	86.6	88.5
11	52.8	84.1	82.6	80.9	82.4	83.9
12	83.1	89.6	86.8	84.4	84.8	87.4
13	60.5	85.6	84.3	84.2	75.2	82.8
14	64.7	87.4	85.2	84.8	84.0	85.6
15	40.7	87.3	86.9	85.3	83.8	86.1
16	53.6	90.1	89.4	89.0	84.4	87.5
Averages	62.61	88.34	87.01	85.77	82.72	86.16

As a baseline, we compared decision trees against a majority classifier to demonstrate how much additional predictive power a decision tree actually provides (see Table 3). On average, the decision tree classifier ranged in accuracy from 85-90%. The subjects with high majority classification accuracies tended to be arms-length from their phones for significant periods; however, the prediction accuracy still improved when using decision trees. For subjects with an even distribution among the three proximity levels, the majority classifier performed poorly, as expected, and the decision trees dramatically increased the accuracy. Reducing the training set down to one week still provided classification accuracies between 84-88%, suggesting that one week of training is sufficient to provide near-optimal prediction accuracies.

5.2 Analyzing the Decision Trees

We analyzed the decision tree for each of the 16 participants and determined the most important features for classification (see Table 4). For every subject, either cell tower ID, hour of the day, or day of the week was the root node (*i.e.,* the most predictive feature). These three features also appeared in the top four contributing features for each subject. Depending on the user, the remaining best feature was one of signal strength, charger status, or ring/vibrate status. To test the power of these top features, we calculated the decision tree accuracies for each subject using only their top four features (see Table 3). Restricting the feature set to only the top four features does not result in a large decrease in accuracy. We also computed the classification accuracies using only the cell tower ID, hour, and day features for each subject and observed an average accuracy of 83% (an average accuracy loss of 5%). Thus, comparable classification accuracies can be obtained with a common set of minimal features, meaning we do not even need to have a training phase in practice.

Table 4. This table shows that three groups of users emerged based on their top four features. Note that we present the features in no particular order of predictive power.

% of Participants	Feature 1	Feature 2	Feature 3	Feature 4
19	Cell ID	Hour	Day	Ring/Vibrate
50	Cell ID	Hour	Day	Charger
31	Cell ID	Hour	Day	Signal

Time and location are major factors for predicting user proximity to a mobile phone. Participants with hour or day as their top feature typically had structured workdays in which they interacted with the phones in a consistent pattern. For some users, the ring or vibrate status was a good indicator for proximity to the phone. The phone being within arm's reach often correlated to the acts of disabling the ring volume and activating the vibrator. On the other hand, a high ring volume often correlated to the phone being distant from the user. Many users typically carried the phone very close to them when they were away from home, as determined by cell tower IDs. Charger status and signal strength may have provided some subtle location information as well. For example, participants that only charged the phone in the car were very likely to be within arm's reach of the phone during charging. Users that only charged at home tended to be further away from the phones during charging. Often, the signal strength branched from cell tower IDs in the decision trees, indicating that the signal strength was playing a disambiguating role in those cases.

6 Discussion

6.1 Potential Alternative Data Gathering Methods

We considered several different methods of data collection when designing this experiment. In addition to the constant logging method, we considered conducting an experience sampling method (ESM), such as that used by Consolvo and Walker [2], or using solely self-reported data via a diary study, surveys, or interviews. We did not believe that self-report would give us the fine-grained, accurate information we needed, and when conducting the actual study, we observed that individuals often could not even accurately report where the phone was in the past day, even though they could remember the episodes of the day clearly.

Diary studies would likely have required too much work from the participants to get a broad range of samples. ESM, on the other hand, might have been appropriate, but we were concerned that random sampling would not uncover the subtle details inherent to user habits with mobile phones. To test this hypothesis, we randomly selected 16 data points per day (1 per hour) from each participant (one probe per waking hour) and calculated the average proximity level for each participant. We calculated this average for 100 random samplings and an overall average was calculated (see Table 5). The simulation assumed participants would be willing and

Table 5. Comparison of empirical proximity data to percentages from a simulated ESM study

Level	Overall Empirical	Overall ESM	Weekend Empirical	Weekend ESM	Weekday Empirical	Weekday ESM
Arms	58	61	53	55	59	64
Room	20	14	18	13	20	15
NA	23	24	28	32	21	21

able to respond to 16 queries per day for a three-week period. The percentages provided by the simulations were close to the actual data for most participants, despite only having 16 samples per day, compared to 1440 per day for our empirical study.

Although the overall percentages were similar, the ESM data would not include some of the more fine-grained details we were able to harvest from the high resolution, automatically-collected data, including times when the user was away from their phone for a short period. For example, we calculated the number of times per day each person was away from his or her phone for a short amount of time (2-20 minutes), *i.e.*, a "quick trip" as defined above. The participants each reported from 1 to 20 of these quick trips away from the phone per day. This information could be crucial to applications on a phone that assume the user is nearby all the time, such as reminder systems or constant health monitoring. Furthermore, with a sampling method, overall trends in some of the other features, such as phone call usage and number of cell towers detected by the phones would likely be missed. Lastly, and possibly most importantly, the empirical study did not require users to be conscious of their phone's location at all times, thus allowing us to capture a more realistic data set.

6.2 Design Considerations for Mobile Applications

The empirical results presented in this paper begin to uncover some interesting insights for mobile phone application designers to consider.

- Mobile phones may not be as good of a location proxy as many people believe. The participant with the closest overall proximity level was within arm's reach of his phone 85% of the time, despite his strong intuition that he carried the phone nearly 100% of the time.
- Certain features, such as the number of minutes of "talk time" are not as good predictors as intuition might have us believe.
- When considering a particular group of users, designers can leverage simple information available on the phone itself (time and location) to infer a user's proximity to the mobile phone.
- When away from home, the phone is more likely to be with the individual. Thus, designing applications for use in home would need to make different assumptions about a mobile phone's proximity than those for outside the home.
- The effect of physical activity on participant choices about phone proximity is an indicator that those potential applications that focus on monitoring of

physical fitness activities should consider the physical reasons users might avoid carrying a phone during these periods in designing their form factors.

- As expected, users keep their phones near in the presence of perceived needs. Thus, one solution for applications that require the user and phone being close most of the time is to build in functionality that the users may need regularly.
- Control over disruptions is important to users. Thus, any applications relying on interruptions must consider social, regulatory, and personal reasons for minimizing disruptions.

6.3 The Value of Proximity Modeling

A small number of features can predict the likelihood of proximity with fairly high confidence. Some of these features are the same across all participants, such as cell tower ID, hour and day, and together yield 83% predictive power. The ease of sensing these features on a mobile phone and the availability of lightweight machine learning techniques suggest that it is possible to build a context-aware mobile phone that can predict relatively easily the user's proximity to the phone. Such a system is valuable for applications that rely on the mobile phone as a proxy for a user, because it would allow for appropriate adaptation to situations in which proximity is a concern.

Central to the development of such a system is the model of the individual user. A simple tagging scheme, such as the one used for this study, can result in an accurate model with one week of "typical" use. However, this tagging method may not be practical for everyone. Thus, creating predefined or easy to construct models *a priori* for particular types of mobile phone users is an important consideration for effective adoption of this kind of system. Having identified common features across users and categories of user with respect to these features, we believe it possible to devise a survey mechanism in which users answer high-level questions. The answers to these questions could then translate into low-level modeling information to form the basis of a proximity-aware mobile phone.

7 Conclusions and Future Work

We presented an empirical study of sixteen users and the proximity relationships to their phones over a three-week period. We demonstrated that people often have higher expectations of their own proximity and availability to their mobile phones than is accurate in reality. Furthermore, we catalogued those factors that may influence them to carry (or not) their phones with them. Based on this empirical evidence, we present information for application designers attempting to meet the needs of users with particular patterns, including providing an understanding of the likelihood of availability to the phone in general as well as ways to model the proximity relationship automatically to provide individualized services and preferences.

While this study provided insight into the proximity relationship between a diverse group of users and their phones and how this might be predicted, there is still more that needs to be done to obtain generalizable information. Participants were particular to one metropolitan area, and phone use is likely to differ substantially by geographical and cultural regions. Additionally, due to the narrow but deep nature of our investigation, generalization of results to the larger population, particularly across varied demographics is difficult. The promise of similar proximity results via our simulated ESM study, and the need for only one week's worth of data for our classifier suggest that a more large-scale investigation can be done across varied populations with a less involved experimental design. Furthermore, this same information may be useful in determining an appropriate set of simple questions to allow end users to "train" the phone without collecting a large number of samples.

The nature of this type of study allowed us to obtain realistic proximity data for users that may not have otherwise been obtained with more low fidelity studies. Although a sampling of data points obtained through ESM can come up with similar proximity relationships, it runs the risk of altering the user's proximity relationship to the phone by continually reminding users about their phones' whereabouts. We believe the type of study reported in this paper useful to obtain ground truth data about a user's proximity relationship to the phone. Perhaps more significantly, however, it can also result in baseline data to compare against similar proximity evidence that would result from the effects of new mobile phone applications, such as location-based services, continual health monitoring systems, or context-aware applications, will have on that proximity relationship. Finally, this same technique may be used to evaluate proximity relationships between collections of mobile phones and their owners as well as the proximity relationships between people and other technologies, mobile or stationary.

Acknowledgements

This work was sponsored by Intel Corporation and the National Science Foundation and is covered under IRB protocol H05205 at Georgia Tech. We also thank Nokia Research, and in particular Dana Pavel, for the donation of the mobile phones used in this study and the members of the Ubicomp Research Group at Georgia Tech.

References

1. Cohen, J., A Coefficient of Agreement for Nominal Scales. *Educational and Psychological Measurement*, 1960. **20**: p. 37-48.
2. Consolvo, S. and M. Walker, Using the experience sampling method to evelute ubicomp applications, in *IEEE Pervasive Computing*. 2003. p. 24-31.
3. Corner, M.D. and B.D. Noble. Zero-Interaction Authentication. in *Mobicom '02*. 2002. Atlanta, GA USA: ACM.
4. Davis, M., N. Good, and R. Sarvas. From Context to Content: Leveraging Context for Mobile Media Metadata. in *International Multimedia Conference: 12th annual ACM international conference on Multimedia*. 2004. New York, NY, USA.
5. Demumieux, R. and P. Losquin. Gather customer's real usage on mobile phones. in *Conference on Human Computer Interaction with Mobile Devices & Services*. 2005.
6. Eagle, N. and A. Pentland, Reality Mining: Sensing Complex Social Systems. *Personal and Ubiquitous Computing*, 2005. **10**(4): p. 255-268.
7. Hayes, G.R., S.N. Patel, K.N. Truong, G. Iachello, J.A. Kientz, R. Farmer, and G.D. Abowd. The Personal Audio Loop: Designing a Ubiquitous Audio-Based Memory Aid. in

Mobile HCI 2004: The 6th International Conference on Human Computer Interaction with Mobile Devices and Services. 2004. Glasgow, Scotland.

8. Helal, S., C. Giraldo, Y. Kaddoura, C. Lee, H.e. Zabadani, and W. Mann. Smart phone based cognitive assistant. in *UbiHealth 2003: The 2nd International Workshop on Ubiquitous Computing for Pervasive Healthcare Applications.* 2003. Seattle, Washington.

9. Hightower, J. and G. Borriello, A Survey and Taxonomy of Location Systems for Ubiquitous Computing. 2001, University of Washington.

10. Kahneman, D., A.B. Krueger, D.A. Schkade, N. Schwarz, and A.A. Stone, A Survey Method for Characterizing Daily Life Experience: The Day Reconstruction Method, in *Science.* 2004. p. 1776-1780.

11. Laasonen, K. Clustering and Prediction of Mobile User Routes from Cellular Data. in *PKDD 2005.* 2005: Springer Verlag.

12. LaMarca, A., et al. Place Lab: Device Positioning Using Radio Beacons in the Wild. in *Pervasive 2005.* 2005. Munich, Germany.

13. Lamming, M. SPECs: Another Approach to Human Context and Activity Sensing Research, Using Tiny Peer-to-Peer Wireless Computers. in *Ubicomp 2003.* 2003.

14. McGuigan, J., Towards a Sociology of the Mobile Phone. *Human Technology,* 2005.

15. Mitchell, T., *Machine Learning.* 1996, New York, US: McGraw Hill.

16. Otsason, V., A. Varshavsky, L. A., and E. de Lara. Accurate GSM Indoor Localization. in *The Seventh International Conference on Ubiquitous Computing (Ubi-Comp 2005).* 2005.

17. Oulasvirta, A., M. Raento, and S. Tiitta. ContextContacts: Re-Designing SmartPhone's Contact Book to Support Mobile Awareness and Collaboration. in *MobileHCI 2005.* 2005.

18. Palen, L. and M. Salzman, Beyond the handset: designing for wireless communications usability. *ACM Transactions on Computer-Human Interaction,* 2002. **9**(2): p. 125-151.

19. Palen, L., M. Salzman, and E. Youngs. Going Wireless: Behavior & Practice of New Mobile Phone Users. in *CSCW '00: Computer Supported Cooperative Work.* 2000.

20. Patel, S.N., J.S. Pierce, and G.D. Abowd. A gesture-based authentication scheme for untrusted public terminals in *17th annual ACM symposium on User interface software and technology* 2004. Santa Fe, NM, USA: ACM Press.

21. Preece, J., Y. Rogers, and H. Sharp, *Interaction design: beyond human-computer interaction.* 2002: John Wiley & Sons, Inc.

22. Raento, M., A. Oulasvirta, R. Petit, and H. Toivonen, ContextPhone - A prototyping platform for context-aware mobile applications, in *IEEE Pervasive Computing.* 2005.

23. Satyanarayanan, M., Swiss Army Knife or Wallet?, in *IEEE Pervasive Computing.* 2005.

24. 24. Schlosser, F.K., So, how do people really use their handheld devices? An interactive study of wireless technology use. *Journal of Organizational Behavior,* 2002. **23**(4): p. 401-423.

25. Sullivan, J. and G. Fischer. Mobile Architectures and Prototypes to Assist Persons with Cognitive Disabilities using Public Transportation. in *26th International Conference on Technology and Rehabilitation.* 2003. Atlanta GA, USA.

26. Vaananen-Vainio-Mattila, K. and S. Ruuska, User Needs for Mobile Communication Devices: Requirements Gathering and Analysis through Contextual Inquiry, in *First Workshop on HCI and Mobile Devices.* 1998.

27. Wang, X.H., R.S.H. Istepanian, and Y.H. Song, Mobile e-Health: The Unwired Evolution of Telemedicine. *Telemedicine Journal and e-Health,* 2003.

28. Want, R., T. Pering, G. Danneels, M. Kumar, M. Sundar, and J. Light. The Personal Server: Changing the Way We Think about Ubiquitous Computing. in *Ubicomp 2002.* 2002. Sweden: Springer-Verlag.

No More SMS from Jesus: Ubicomp, Religion and Techno-spiritual Practices

Genevieve Bell

Intel, 2111 NE 25th Avenue, Hillsboro, OR, 97124
genevieve.bell@intel.com

Abstract. Over the last decade, new information and communication technologies have lived a secret life. For individuals and institutions around the world, this constellation of mobile phones, personal computers, the internet, software, games, and other computing objects have supported a complex set of religious and spiritual needs. In this paper, I offer a survey of emerging and emergent techno-spiritual practices, and the anxieties surrounding their uptake. I am interested in particular in the ways in which religious uses of technology represent not only a critique of dominant visions of technology's futures, but also suggest a very different path(s) for ubiquitous computing's technology envisioning and development.

1 Introduction

In mid-January 2004, the Reuters news service flashed out the headline "No More Text Messages from Jesus" signaling the demise of a distinctive Finnish mobile service. According to the wire story, earlier that month, Ville Nurmi, the Ombudsman for Finland's mobile services and regulatory watchdog organization, shut down a mobile service provider that offered text messages from Jesus Christ. The company, which was not named in the proceedings, promised to answer people's prayer with a text message from Jesus [1]. This service, ruled spam through a complex set of maneuvers that included a determination that Jesus did not own a mobile phone, is but one manifestation of the increasing visible intersections of spiritual practice and technological development world wide. The Church of Jesus Christ of the Latter-day Saints runs the world's largest online genealogical service; religiously inspired web logs, portals, bulletin boards, dating sites and chat rooms are flourishing the world over; the Vatican has its own text message service and pod casts, and Pope Benedict XVI his own iPod. Christian gaming software is attracting a strong following, Hindi gods have their own websites, and there is an ongoing debate about the use of Cairo's nascent wireless cloud to broadcast a single call to prayer from the city's many minaret towers. And all around the world, technology manufacturers are increasingly catering to the ways in which computational devices might support religious practices, producing religion-specific technologies and experiences.

Given the ways in which religious practices are intimately woven into the fabric of daily life in most parts of the world, it is hardly far fetched to imagine that new information and communication technologies (ICTs) might support a range of existing religious and spiritual activities, as well as helping to create new ones. Here I

P. Dourish and A. Friday (Eds.): Ubicomp 2006, LNCS 4206, pp. 141–158, 2006.

am casting ICTs broadly to include personal computers, public computing sites (i.e.: cyber cafes, web-kiosks and gaming arcades), the Internet, software, games, accessories and gadgets (i.e.: USB flash keys, etc), mobile phones, other wireless devices and the various infrastructures that support them. And indeed recent surveys of internet habits, corporate marketing strategies, and new product developments, all point to the fact that there is a growing (perhaps already grown) segment of the population that uses technology to support religious practices, what I am calling "techno-spiritual practices". Some of these techno-spiritual re-purposings have been documented [2-8], some have been theorized [9-15], and some have been playfully and thoughtfully explored and elaborated [16-18], and there is certainly a growing literature about the impact of new technologies on Islamic practice [19-23], and well-rehearsed arguments on technological avoidances and resistances in certain religious communities [24-25]. For the most part, however, religious or spiritual relationships to, and usages of, ICTs seem to be marginalized to the realm of technological oddities, fodder for cheeky web logs and the occasional appearance in the pages of the New York Times or Wired, written off as just another trend.

However, it is my contention that these examples of the ways in which new technologies are delivering religious experiences represent the leading edge of a much larger re-purposing of the internet in particular, and of computational technologies more broadly, that has been underway for some time. Furthermore, as I have argued elsewhere [26] that ubicomp's frame of reference should extend to include any ICT that has a ubiquitous presence, this re-purposing could also be a subject of regular discussion or activities, developments and deployments in the ubiquitous computing (ubicomp) community. These techno-spiritual re-purposings are important for the ways in which they highlight alternate paradigms for technology creation, deployment, consumption and resistance, as well as pointing to different communities, practices and habits that could be supported. Furthermore, these re-purposings seems to be of critical importance as the realm of technological infrastructure extends progressively beyond the office, into the home, and many other points of social and cultural significance, including one presumes, places of worship, ritual and meditation. After all, life also happens in the sacred domain.

Between 2001 and 2004, I conducted a multi-sited ethnographic research project that sought critically interrogate the ways in which cultural practices were shaping people's relationships to new ICTs in urban Asia [27-28]. Informed by contemporary anthropological theory, the research followed a range of ICTs through seven different sites of production, consumption and resistance, encompassing urban life in India, China, Malaysia, Singapore, Korea, Indonesia and Australia. I relied on a range of ethnographic methods and methodologies, including participant observation, semi-structured interviews, 'deep hanging-out', and genealogies of ICTs to explore life in one hundred very different Asian households. Throughout the fieldwork process, and on many occasions since then, I have been stuck by the ways in which people's narratives of technology (and life) carried strong references to religious practices, spiritual life and ritual. However, whilst this paper is informed by that research, it does not represent a report on a bounded project that set out to investigate technology and religion at a set of specific sites; rather it is theoretical intervention into the ways in which we constitute ubiquitous computing and what we imagine to be its primary foci. As such, this paper is classic ethnographic intervention – it is descriptive and interpretative but not simply reportage, it is grounded in anthropological theory and praxis, and ultimately it is less concerned with "implications for design'" and more concerned with implications for theory [29]. Drawing on my fieldwork in Asia, as well as an ethnographically informed survey of religious expression and practice on new technologies (including the internet, mobile phones and computers), I articulate a relationship between religion and technology and explores the impact of such a relationship on ubiquitous computing.

In this paper, I argue that we need to design a ubiquitous computing not just for a secular life, but also for spiritual life, and we need to design it now! In no small part, this sense of urgency is informed by an awareness of the ways in which techno-spiritual practices are already unfolding; it is also informed by a clear sense that the ubicomp infrastructures we are building might actively preclude important spiritual practices and religious beliefs. A survey of these new technologies of enlightenment — that is ICTs being repurposed support a range of non-secular activities — reveals unexpected richness and complexity. Here I am interested in both excavating the ways in technology and religious practices have always been interpolated and also theorizing the impact of such an interpolation on ubiquitous computing; in particular the ways in which religious uses of technology represent not only a critique of dominant visions of technology's futures, but also suggest a very different path(s) for ubiquitous computing's technology envisioning and development. This paper is divided into three sections: (a) a theoretical framework within which to explore techno-spiritual practices; (b) a survey of the range of techno-spiritual practices with a focus on the mobile and internet spaces; and (c) finally a discussion of the impact of techno-spiritual on our imaginings and theorizing of ubiquitous computing.

2   A Theoretical Framework for Techno-spiritual Practices

Tirumal lives with his mother in the house in which he grew up in central India.[1] Every morning, before the rest of the household awakes, his mother paints *muggu* designs – white chalk outlines – on the concrete pavement outside of their gates to bring the house good fortune and prosperity as well as to protect her family from ill-health and ill-will. Most Telegu houses have such symbols painted at their doorways, as do many other Indian homes. To an untrained eye, these symbols appear to be little more than decoration. However, at a metaphoric level, this design and the practices it indexes suggest a very different conception of relationships between public and private spaces than found in many western homes. Furthermore, it alludes to a complex framing of danger and security that could imply new home networking, virus alerts and infrastructure securities solutions. What if protection is not about repelling attack, but courting good fortune? Might this inspire different design choices, different rhetorics, and even different technologies?

For Tirumal and his family, religion, and spiritual practices are seamless woven into day-to-day living. For others, it is about praying every day, or visiting the temple, or the mosque, or church, or consulting the *ngongli* [lunar almanac], or counting the

---

[1] In keeping with anthropological ethics, the names of people interviewed in the field have been changed throughout this paper protect confidentiality.

rosary. It might be individual activities, or those which connect an individual to a broader community of practice or perhaps a larger community undertaking. All of these practices are part of the fabric of daily life. In fact, in many cultures it is impossible to delineate between religious practices and beliefs and the larger structuring of society. In countless and not always subtle, ways religion shapes ideas about time, space and social relationships. Think, for instance, about the ways in which religion impacts the calendars; our distinctions between work days and rest days, holidays (i.e.: Christmas, Passover, Diwali), the reckoning of new years, even when the calendar commences are all products of various forms of religious thought. And this is as true for the major prophetic religions (i.e. Christianity, Buddhism, Hinduism, Islam and Judaism), as it is for more 'pre-axial' religions, including most First Nation religions. And while some nations might define themselves as secular, or endorse no state religion (the United States for instance), given than more than three-quarters of the world identifies itself as religious, religious identification seems a significant part of what it means to be human. There is some debate about the exact figures here, but there are approximately 2 billion Christians, 1.3 billion Muslims, 900 million Hindus, 360 million Buddhists and 225 million people practicing Chinese traditional religions. In addition there are an estimated 95 million practitioners of African religions; more than 150 million people glossed as 'indigenous' religions, 23 million Sikhs, 14 million Jews, and at least 1 million neo-pagans (including 70,000 individuals in New Zealand who declare themselves followers of the Jedi Faith). And of course there are many people who identify with two religious faiths – predominantly indigenous peoples. There are also estimate to approximately 15% of the world's population that is 'non-religious', secular, agnostic and atheist this includes many whose governments declare their populations 'agnostic.' There are few other practices or shaping narratives that impact so much of humanity.

2.1 Religion in Ubicomp and Beyond

Despite the almost fundamental nature of religion, the notion that computational technology might support religious or spiritual practice appears elusive in the broader HCI community. In 2000, in one of the first and only attempts I can find to include the spiritual in conversations about technology development, more than 50 people attended a special interest group session at the annual Computer Human Interaction Conference. The session framed around the question "Can We Have Spiritual Experiences online?" was apparently a lively one. In the paper that followed that session, participants wrote: "the dominant design rhetorics of design work in human-computer interactions (command-and-control; constant updates and interruptions of new information; fast-action games; denotative, explicit clarity rather than connotative, exploratory ambiguity) worked against what we called the "inner stillness" of spiritual life" [11: 82]. This opposition of HCI and a spiritual life reinforces the idea that technology and religion must exist in constant tension; each precluding a complete fulfillment of the other. In 2005, Joseph Jofish Kaye and I organized a workshop at the first Ethnographic Praxis in Industry conference, in which we sought to foreground and explore this tension [30].

It strikes me that this ideological and rhetorical separation of religion and technology informs an implicit understanding of the kinds of cultural work that technology should, does, and could perform. To date, these assumptions actively shape the narratives of ubicomp's future — in both the visionary talk of various technology gurus and in the specifics of technology design, manufacture, and deployment. Computational technology, within the ubicomp framework, supports work practices, mobility, urban sociality, leisure activities, health concerns and certain forms of social and institutional relationships – remote communication and monitoring in particular. There have also been attempts to expand the conversation to include notions of pleasure, affect, and intimacy [31-33]. But an ubicomp technology or design deployment for spiritual practice remains notably absent.

So how might we talk about the nascent techno-spiritual usages of ICTs? How might we celebrate these practices in our tales of cyberspace and technological utopias? To talk about religion is to traverse contested ground that is highly personal and emotional and increasingly politicized. In much of the western scientific tradition in which many of us were trained, religion is held as an opposition; in this framework, technology and computing embody rational thinking and logic, not religion, the spiritual, perhaps the mystical. This positioning is of course, deeply ironic, and oddly a-historical. After all, in the West, there is a long and complex relationship between technology and religion; religious institutions have been quick to adopt the advances that allowed them to operate with greater efficiencies and/or efficacies [34]. In his provocative book, The Religion of Technology [35], Noble advances this argument about the relationship between technology and religion one step further, claiming that technologies rapidly scaled only at the point that they were invested with spiritual significance.

2.2 An Approach Informed by Anthropology

So how might one approach the techno-spiritual? In this paper, I propose to rely on anthropological framings of both religion and technology as a way of unpacking the seeming contradictory nature of techno-spiritual practices. Throughout this paper, I am interested not only in the anthropology of religion per se, but in also in a wider set of disciplinary practices that include a grounded epistemological discourse, notions of cultural production, a focused attention on the particulars of place and location and critical reflexivity [29, 36-38].

Anthropologists have been interested in making sense of the function of religion within a society, as well as the details of particular religious practices. For anthropologists of religion, many activities can be of interest: specific activities carried out within and framed by a larger belief system (i.e.: rituals and practices [39]), the framing systems themselves (i.e.: theology, dogma, mythology [40-44]), the ways in which such framing systems are resisted or transformed (i.e.: syncretism [45-48). From the early work on "primitive religion" and comparative explorations of ritual and magic [49, 39], studies of religion within anthropology remain influenced by Durkheim, Weber, Marx and Freud, among others [50-52]. Weber's insistence on the common links between social and economic spheres of action seems to be a particular useful thread here in positing common links between religious and technical spheres of action.

In one of the definitive articles on the subject, Geertz defines religion as "a system of symbols which acts to establish powerful, pervasive and long-lasting moods and motivations in men [sic] by formulating conceptions of a general order of existence and clothing these conceptions with such an aura of factuality that the moods and motivations seem uniquely realistic" [39:90]. In other words, religions are a form of cultural logic or patterning that makes unique and distinct sense within a particular cultural context; religions are also an expression of those cultural contexts. It is this dialectic that is particularly important when thinking about the interplay of new technologies and religious practice. In this paper, I am interested in the larger formulations of religious practice as manifested by institutions (i.e.: formal religious structures and organizations) and also by individual practices – both religious and spiritual activities.

Today, in anthropology, we understand religion to be a sort of cultural script – a strong framing narrative for daily life in many parts of the world. Similarly, the very idea of technology has also always already been subject to ethnographic interpretation and scrutiny [53-54]. As such, it is easier to imagine the relationships between technology (and the theology of progress it encodes) and religions; after all within the ethnographic tradition both are sites for the production of cultural meaning, both are narratives. In as much as I am interested in thinking about religion as a cultural system or site of cultural production, I am also interested in scrutinizing technology through the same filters. It is certainly the case that new technologies do technical work, but they also do cultural work, and it is this latter work that is of particular interest in this paper.

This interpretation of technology owes much to the contemporary literature on consumption, consumer and material culture, in particular the work of Appadurai [55-56] and Miller [57] whose framing of objects and contexts of use help re-contextualize and locate technologies within particular cultural moments and practices. This attention to the cultural life of technology might help, in part, to explain why the tension between religion and technology is not felt so acutely in other parts of the world. In the western tradition, especially in this late capitalist, post-Enlightenment era, ICTs are linked to the cultural narratives of progress, change and even revolution. Without engaging in a kind of techno-orientalism, I think it is possible to argue that ICTs (and technology more broadly) map to alternate cultural discourses within Islam, Hinduism and Confucianism, just to name a few. This alternate mapping could produce different kinds of anxieties, adoption patterns and even framings of computational offerings. As such, throughout this paper, I will be cataloging techno-spiritual practices from a range of different religious and cultural traditions.

In addition to an anthropological framing of religion and technology, my treatment to techno-spiritual practices is shaped by the work of George Marcus, and his theorizing of multi-sited ethnography. Clearly, I am stitching together acts of many individuals and organizations in disparate locations and cultural contexts, sometimes sharing a common religious context. All the while, I am, to play on Marcus's words "tracing the circulation through different contexts of a manifestly material object of study (at least as initially conceived)" [58:91].

Elsewhere I have written about 'defamiliarization' – the act of making the familiar strange – as a methodology intervention that allows one to explore hither-to-fore implicit assumptions about domestic design [59]. In this paper, I propose to revisit the notion of defamiliarization as a way of unpacking and exposing our own assumptions about the kinds of work that technology could or should do. Here I am mindful of Marx's charge that religion sometimes functions as an opiate for the masses, and I am acutely aware of current geo-political sensitivities to issues of religion. One of the hallmarks of ethnographic epistemology is rigorous attention to and practice of critical reflexivity. By this I mean, that within ethnographic modes of inquiry and production, the subjectivity of the researcher is an important component – knowing who I am helps the reader situate my analysis and critique. As Ruth Frankenberg [60] has recently argued, in turning the ethnographic lens on contemporary religious practice, a nod towards reflexivity becomes more than just perfunctory. I am a cultural anthropologist with a primary concern in information technology as a site of cultural production and the consequences for technology innovation and diffusion. I am also the child of a symbolic anthropologist, and I grew up straddling multiple domains of religious signification in Australia – Catholicism and Catholic schooling; indigenous religious practices; a strongly agnostic home life; and close familial relationships with cultural and practicing Judaism. I am, as an Indian woman with whom I once worked described me, "a free thinker". As such, I find myself more interested in the study of religious practice than I am in endorsing a particular vein of religious dogma.

3 A Survey of Techno-spiritual Practices

In 2003, the Australia Bible Society began to offer the bible rendered in SMS or cell phone text message format on a single take-home CD-ROM. More than just a coding into short burst of text, the bible was also translated into the vernacular of SMS and of a certain imaging of youth discourses: the cover of the CD case proclaims – *for God so luvd da world*. The CD is designed to be loaded on a computer and Bluetoothed to a compatible cell phone and then broadcast out. This remarkable artifact, now augmented with a full website, was marketed as a tool to help pastors, youth group leaders, and other technology savvy Christians share the Bible with a wider range of their friends, acquaintances and parishioners.

This blending of ICTs and spiritual practices might seem surprising in a nation that casts itself as a secular one, without a state religion. However, such techno-spiritual practices seem to abound in both secular and religiously identified nations. Clearly, in some countries, governments do not have a role in the religious landscape; in others, endorsement or sometimes regulation of religious practice is not uncommon. Irrespective of government structure, scratch the surface of almost any nation, you will find an unexpectedly rich landscape of techno-spiritual practices. These practices operate through and with a range of ICTs and it is by making strange, or defamiliarizing, some of the most common of those – the cell phone and the internet – that such practices are revealed.

In American almost 70% of the population makes use of the internet regularly. The contours of American usage of the internet appear well documented: web-surfing, communication, data gathering, personal finances, e-commerce, gaming, pornography, gambling. Yet, according to a recent report by the Pew Internet and American Life Project, 64% of online Americans have also used the internet for religious or spiritual purposes [6] – this includes sending and receiving email and digital greeting cards with spiritual content, reading news accounts of religious events and affairs, and seeking information about religious holidays, services and events. These 128 million Americans utilizing the web for religious practices outnumber Americans gambling, using web auction sites, trading stock or doing online banking [6]. And whilst the slim majority of these users were female and little older, research at the University of North Carolina suggests that three times more teenagers access the web for religious purposes than for pornography [61]. This might suggest that younger Americans, often heralded as the internet generation take the religious aspects of the web as a given. American churches too have embraced ICTs deploying wireless networks, utilizing PowerPoint, websites and DVDs, as well as video-conferencing and email to connect with their parishioners – several interesting studies are underway to explore the impact of such deployments on church and spiritual life [62-64], and others are testing the relationship between religiosity and internet use in America [65]. And one can well imagine a series of projects exploring aspects of spiritual and religious practice as they related to ideas of community – and there is certainly much to suggest that ICTs can play a role in community building, as well as emotional and motivational support [11, 54, 66-68]. So if this is what is happening in the United States, an apparently well documented population when it comes to technology consumption, what might be happening elsewhere, slightly out of line of site? In the rest of this section, I provide a survey of techno-spiritual practices in both the mobile and internet spaces – in so doing, I hope to defamiliarize these seemingly familiar technologies and suggest alternate paradigms and patterns of use.

3.1 Mobile Techno-spiritual Practices

In Guangzhou, Gloria, a young woman in her late twenties, takes her mobile phone to a local Buddhist temple in the days before Chinese New Year. For a small 'ang pow' (red package) of money, a monk will bless it. When I ask what kinds of monks bless mobile phones, she tells me "well, old monks are best, but young monks are cheaper." Gloria also buys a jade amulet from the stalls outside the temple gates, and hangs it from her phone. For her, these acts and actions make the phone wearable; it can now rest around her neck, close to her body, closer to heart, without fear that it is causing her harm. Through this ritual of blessing, the phone is naturalized and incorporated safely into Gloria's daily life. Gloria is not alone in her ritual practices: many other young people through out China engage in similar activities in anticipation of the Chinese New Year.

The mobile telephony and communication space is clearly rich with spiritual possibilities, moral uplift and tools for devotion. Indeed, the intimate nature of mobile phones has lent themselves to all manner of inclusion within religious systems of practice [7]. Some practices extend an individual's spiritual capacity, allowing participation in events that would otherwise be geographic impossible. For instance, it is now possible to place a prayer at the Wailing Wall in Jerusalem via text-messages through a Russian mobile service provider. The text of the prayer is printed out and deposited at the Wall; the text also appears on a public display screen near the Wall [69]. This kind of remote participation extends into other domains of religious and spiritual activity too. Until March of 2003, in the Philippines, it was possible to send your confession and receive absolution via text message on a mobile phone; you could also confess via email or fax. This practice, which was obviously growing, came to light when a local Monsignor ruled that electronically mediated confessions were no longer acceptable, nor was granting absolution via the same mechanisms. Monsignor Cornel said "We have to protect that confidentiality and we insist on personal confession of the penitent to the priests" [70]. The security of the channel and the fidelity of the message seemed in question; according to one report, the Bishops were concerned about the confidentiality of confession and the sacrament. Whilst confession via SMS might represent a kind of rational efficiency, it thwarts much of the religious intent of confession as a semi-public act of contrition and subsequent state of grace which many would argue can only transpire inside a church. One suspects that providing greater levels of security provisions for electronically mediated communication is not the answer here.

Of course there are other instances of new technologies extending the reach of religious institutions without disrupting their core beliefs and practices. In Rome, the Vatican itself is embracing the potential of ICTs to reach a larger audience. Commencing in January of 2003, the Vatican in conjunction with Telecom Italia, Italy's largest mobile phone service provider, launched a daily text message service [71]. For US$0.15 per day, subscribers to the 'papa on' service were treated to thoughts and prayers from the Pope, including "as long as there is the spring of the spirit, good blooms" and "one should never stop praying for peace." There were more than 2 million subscribers to the service by the end of March 2003. In a time when church attendance was falling off in Italy; this represented an opportunity for unparalleled access. In May of 2004, three of the four major mobile services providers in the United States were quietly carrying this same service [72] – the implications here is even more interesting, given the doctrinal and ideological fissures between Rome and American Catholics. An in-depth analysis of the text of this service would be a fascinating study.

Mobile devices can also facilitate many daily religious rituals and practices. For devout Muslims, there is an expectation that one must pray at five particular times of the day, in a mosque if possible, but always facing Ka'bah in the city of Mecca. This direction is called *qiblah* or *qiblat*. In Malaysia, a self-styled 'modern' Muslim country, the latest generation of mobile phones allows users (through a simple software application) to find Mecca, via a 'm-qiblat' service. You can also download the Koran to your palm-pilot, and synchronize it to local prayer times for 1100 cities around the world. In 2003, Ilkone Mobile Telecommunications launched a new 3G cellular handset for the Middle East with the tagline: your phone, your life. This new handset explicitly caters to Islamic users. It has GPS-like functions which enable the handset to point its user to Mecca from any point on the globe and determine the appropriate local times to pray, polyphonic sound, Bluetooth capacities and the use of wireless networks can bring any user the call to prayer in the live voice; it calculates fasting times for Ramadan and has the entire of the Koran in Arabic and English stored on the handset. It also offers a mosque-function which disables the phone for a short period of time at *salat* so as not to inadvertently ring during prayer. This function can be read as a direct challenge to the notion of constant connectivity that periodically pervades ubicomp discourse. Here a technology is designed to be disconnected, rather than always-on. In thinking about designing for techno-spiritual practices, we might have to consider a different range of practices and priorities, and conceptualization of space and location that is driven by a broader set of use patterns. The Ilkone phone is a powerful reminder of the importance meditation, prayer or quiet time in sacred spaces is accorded in most religious systems.

There are now also various independent service and content providers the globe over offering forms of spiritual messaging on the mobile phone platform; Lent text messaging packages with Gospel verses every day at midday, religious ring-tones and hymns, the Rosary and Stations of the Cross in java applications, even Feng-Shui on your phone. Until February 2005, China Mobile and other mobile service providers have offered their customers the lunar almanac via text message. However, in a surprise move, coming immediately only a week before the Year of the Rooster began, the State Administration of Radio, Film and Television banned "any advertisements that harm young minds or violate regulations" through the promotion of superstition – this included 'birthday decoding', and 'new year fortune telling' text messages and phone services. Shares in China Mobile and Sina took an immediate beating on the market as it became clear that much of their revenue stream was derived from these very popular and culturally grounded services.

Elsewhere, in the Catholic world, there are concerns about the possibly negative impact of text messaging and mobile phones. During Lent, in 2002, the Archbishop of Salerno had proposed that Good Friday should be text-message free; "I'm asking this little sacrifice to my faithfuls to make clear the church's position," he said. "In a world dominated by the culture of possession, we should try to focus more on meditation, and leaving behind our mobile phones for a day will surely help" [73]. Other Catholic Churches in Europe, South America and Asia have commenced the installation of cell-site dampeners to preclude cell phone use during services. In one Seoul church I visited the sign in the vestibule read "turn off your cell phone and listen for the call of God." In several Muslim nations, debates are ongoing about the role of text-messaging in divorce proceedings and in India; several organizations are claiming a connection between the rise of text-messaging and a rise in divorce rates.

There are also ways in which new technologies are being naturalized, or incorporated into culture through religious systems at a symbolic level. In traditional Chinese culture, as part of funerary arrangements, people burn paper goods at the death of relatives. The fire transforms the paper into real artifacts in the world that the ancestors now inhabit. In addition to the funeral pyres, paper objects are also burnt at *QingMing*. Every year, Chinese people around the world visit the tombs of their ancestors to sweep the graves clean – this ritual time known as QingMing (or ChingMing) has been part of the Chinese calendar since the 700s. Traditionally, people burnt paper currency and also paper representations of common household good – clothes, furniture, food, and other luxury goods. Throughout the Chinese disaspora, a range of technologies have been added to the paper array burnt at funerals and QingMing, including televisions, fans, air-conditioners, mobile phones and computers including both laptops and PCs. In at least two Malaysian cities in which I conducted fieldwork, QingMing had been not only an occasion for tending ancestral tombs, but also for upgrading the mobile phones of the ancestors, as well as providing them with additional pre-paid phone cards. This tending of the ancestors' telecommunication needs was all done through the burning of paper representations. This techno-spiritual practice reflects not only the centrality of mobile phones in

Malaysian culture, but also the ways in which they have been seamlessly embedded in the daily life of the living and clearly that of the dead.

3.2 Techno-spiritual Practices Online

At 10AM on February 8, 1996, three Tibetan Buddhist monks in a monastery in Ithaca, New York blessed the internet. With a laptop loaded with an image of the Kalachakra Mandala, they prayed for half an hour, formal blessing of cyberspace: "We pray to reduce the negative things that may happen in cyberspace and to increase the positive things.... When we bless something, we are seeking to change its disposition – to eliminate negative things that come from that particular object – and we generate the motivation that the use of that object will be very positive and beneficial ...The person using the Internet has the choice. Whether the Internet becomes material for happiness or for suffering depends on your mind" [quoted in 13: 280]. This naturalization of cyber-space through prayer is but one indicator of the rich vein of techno-spiritual practices in and around the internet. These practices point to a wider ecology: religious expressions and rituals have found homes online in chat rooms, bulletin boards and religious portals, as well as in a range of services, content and applications and software. Sacred spaces have found web front-ends and religious communities have the potential to create new sacred spaces.

Some internet techno-spiritual practices are connected to larger religious agendas and organizations, and much like the mobile services described above, are intended to help extend the reach of a particular religious institution. For example, over the past three years, the Catholic Church has been conducting a search for a patron saint for the Internet; St. Isidore of Seville seems to be the most likely contender. In February of 2004, the Church of England launched a 'virtual parish' or i-church, "for people who travel a great deal or are unable to attend regularly, i-church can support them spiritually wherever they are in the world." The Church also announced it an opened a search for a pastor to oversee this new parish.

There are also other Christian websites, not linked to any specific churches or particular religious communities that are designed to support one's spiritual and moral development. There are discussion groups and chat rooms dedicated to religious topics, faith FAQs, and uplifting daily messages [74]. One such site provides a survey that helps users determine their best religious fit, another offers a count-down to Armageddon and the rapture. There are also websites with a moral edge: movies reviewed for their Christian content, online sport support sites with uplifting testimonials and a proliferation of "Christian-friendly" dating and social networking sites [75]. There are also a range of dating sites for other religious dominations and faiths, and arranged marriages organized over the web remain popular in India. In many ways, these religious sites are not that different from other interest-specific websites and services.

The technologizing of sacred spaces does offer a slightly different take on techno-spiritual practices. Whilst the monks who support the website 'nextscribe.org' believe that the internet as a network can be read as a sort of church, there are more instrumentalist uses of the internet already at work. Various sacred places and shrines in Asia (and the West) have their own websites, and new forms of virtual pilgrimages, digital relics and techno-spiritual practices are emerging [66]. For instance, a temple dedicated to the Hindu deity, Ganesh has its own website from which you can procure religious artifacts and makes acts of devotion. In neighboring Sri Lanka, one of the first local websites to go live offered virtual parrot auspice to Sri-Lankans all over the world. You can even add your own request for prayers at the website for the chapel of the Franciscan Sisters of Perpetual Adoration in Wisconsin, where the sisters have been praying continuously for 125 years. Avi Moskowitz has created a "Virtual Jerusalem" on line, among many other features; the site allows registered users to send prayer to the Wailing Wall.

In addition to all these online extensions of real places, are also a set of sites supporting familiar rituals in new ways. The Chinese government is actively supporting the creation of online memorial halls to facilitate the time honored filial practice of ancestor worship. In China, QingMing changed after the Revolution. While there is some burning of paper currency, there has been less elaboration of paper goods and rituals, especially during the early years of the Revolution. In recent years, the Chinese government has been attempting to "modernize" Chinese funerary practices. "The authorities argued that traditional forms of tribute waste money, cause fires and encourage superstition. According to ministry figures, Chinese people spent 16.2B Yuan (US$2B) a year on funerals and paying respect to the ancestors" [76].

In 2001, the Chinese government launched "Earth Village" – an online cemetery – and issued a notice to all local governments requiring that they promote the site [Bezlova 2002]. Earth Village is one of a growing number of Chinese-based online memorial halls; according to one source there are more than 100 such sites in operation [77]. At EarthVillage, you can choose from one of 12 e-tombstones, burn e-incense and leave e-flowers. "Netor", another funeral site, has more than 11,000 memorials to the dead at its portal; the company charges between 100-1000 Yuan (US$12-120) for a thirty day memorial site, ranging from a simple photo to streaming video [78]. In 2001, they estimated that they were receiving more than 600,000 hits per day [79]. "Wangtong", another of the funerary portals that operates locally in Shanghai, estimated that it has 20,000 such halls and as a result receives more than 10,000 daily visits and plans to start offering SMS memorial services [77]. There are several other QingMing portals that serve Chinese communities beyond China and their popularity continues to grow [80]: there were some reports of an upsurge in Singaporeans use of cyber QingMing services during April 2003 as a way of side-stepping SARs concerns and quarantines on the island-state.

New ICTs are also finding their way into the physical places in which people worship, meditate and pray. For example, worshippers in a Lutheran church in the small Swedish village of Norrfjaerden who can use their credit and debit cards to tithe [81]. Perhaps of greater interest, however, are also the ways in which new computational objects are making any space a sacred space. The availability of religious tracts and texts on various forms of media – god-casting [82], the BiblePlayer for iPod or on secure digital and other flash memory for PDAs – transforms ICTs into tools for religious and spiritual devotion. Building, one suspects, on the enduring popularity of Christian music (and other Christian themed content), there is a growing market of Christian gaming software [83-84], from Charlie Church Mouse Bible Adventures [83] to Catechumen in which a player goes through catacombs of Rome to free their mentor and fellow Christians, and convert demon possessed Roman soldiers. The 'ghost radar' – a ghost detector USB flash stick from

SolidAlliance which promises to illuminate the presence of ghosts; electronically augmented grave-stones, live-web cams at funerals and the practices of carrying death photos on cell-phones all point to another domain of the techno-spiritual.

Of course not all emergent practices are in support of established religious communities or practices. Members of Falun Gong, a religious community banned in China in the late 1990s, are hijacking new technologies to broadcast religious content, assertions of innocence and claims of harassment to Chinese citizens. As the official Chinese newspaper put it, "Although the cult has been banned in China, its leaders in foreign countries still the use the internet and other high technologies to control the followers to carry out destructive acts in China ...". Throughout 2002, Falun Gong hacked various Chinese television infrastructures, including local cable television and even SinoSat (one of Chinese national communication satellites), to send out messages about the group to the general public. Similarly, the group has found ways to take advantage of Chinese language chat rooms to spread their message; they have leafleted entire communities with video-discs, and they have used automated phone calling systems to call multiple numbers and play a recorded message. Here techno-spiritual practices focus on disrupting pre-established practices, challenging dominant discourses around religious identity.

4   Towards Spiritual Design?

In Mark Weiser's now famous future vision of ubiquitous computing, he wrote "we are trying to conceive a new way of thinking about computers in the world, one that takes into account the natural human environment and allows computers themselves to vanish into the background" [85: 94]. As one reflects on the range of spiritual and religious practices occasioned through and with new ICTs, one is stuck by the ways in which the religious and the spiritual are fore grounded. All kinds of different peoples and communities have already asserted the importance of their own cultural practices and co-opted ICTs accordingly. But what might it look like if we explicitly imagined religion and spirituality as part of Weiser's "natural human environment"? In his wonderfully textured story of Sal and her daily life, however, these are missing. Sal's life moves between two dominant sites of cultural production – the home and the office; it moves between two modes – leisure and work. Nowhere is there a sense of Sal's inner spiritual life – indeed, one might think she did not have one. As part of a corporate exercise to develop a future vision for user-centered computing in 2015, I wrote the two scenarios below [86]. I am choosing here to eschew the traditional section on 'implications for design' [29] and instead invite the reader to engage with me as a co-interlocutor, as we imagine a near-future in which computational technologies might actively and explicitly support techno-spiritual practices.

Li lives and works in upstate New York with her husband. She has family in Beijing and Hong Kong; they keep in touch through regular calls, emails and photos. Li's grandfather died in the fall after a long and prosperous life. After his cremation, the family added a new wing to their ancestor hall online. Different family members add photos, video, even long forgotten conversations. Li sends her own contributions – the smell of her grandfather's study with its cedar boxes of ancient calligraphy that her grandfather collected and preserved. Once the addition is complete, the family's various ancestral tablets are updated. Li's tablet resets itself and her grandfather's name joins the list of other names that can be seen in Li's hallway. The tablet emits the smell of burning incense to alert Li to the presence of her grandfather's name. At QingMing, families gather to 'sweep' clean their family tombs and feed, clothe and care for their ancestors. For Li's family, ancestral tablets around the world sound chimes to gather family members across different time zones. Li brings oranges and paper money to her hallway, the ancestral tablets glow more brightly as more and more family members stand before them in care of their ancestors.

Daniel lives with his parents in a satellite suburb of Chicago, he is eleven years old. Daniel has always lived in America, but he has cousins in Europe and the Middle East. In fact, his parents are the only ones who live in America. Still the whole family tries to gather once a year, usually for Passover. The adults like to spend time together talking about the happenings of the previous year, the ups and downs of business, family life, politics ... but for the kids, it is a chance to get together and play. This year, Daniel's parents won't be able to travel; there are just too many uncertainties and dangers, but they will still make it to the family Seder. In Europe, the extended family is taking advantage of their newly remodeled 'smart' home to create a 'digital'/real Seder. The kitchen is recorded and broadcasting the smell of brisket being prepared – in Daniel's kitchen he can smell faint hints of this traditional meal. It is also wafting to his cousin's house in Jordan. Later in the evening, the whole family will participate in the Haggadah – with the family taking it in turns to read. And because Daniel is the youngest, he will ask the Four Questions. Voices carry across thousands of miles – the traditional arguments and jokes. And the smell of food lingers. Aunty Rebecca has projected an orange onto everyone's Seder plate, again. And Daniel's grandparents have found a way to hide the afikomen (it's in Daniel's kitchen, projected onto the fridge). Seders in Daniel's family go on for hours. And this year, he is really missing his cousins at the kid's table, but his parents have created a virtual kid's table for him, and all the cousins are gathered there too. They joke around, reciting when they are called upon, and stealing food from their parent's plates.

So how might an understanding and awareness of the importance of religion impact the ways in which ubiquitous computing is developed and deployed? Clearly, as we move to the possibility of computing beyond the desktop and home office, to wireless hubs and hotspots, and from fixed devices to an array of mobile form factors, the need to account for the diversities of daily life starts to impose itself into the debate. In no small part, paying attention to religion and religious practices forces us to move beyond efficiency as a useful metric for measuring technology success. Similarly, the nature of certain kinds of religious practice and expression suggest that always-on connectivity and constant updating might not be desirable features of a computing system.

Clearly there have been some attempts to grapple with the complicated issues that arise when trying to account for a spiritual domain in technology design – there have been various strategies for thinking beyond the efficiency/leisure paradigm for computing. In collaboration with PARC's anthropologists, Mark Weiser and his team were made of aware of ways in which people's daily social practices impacted their consumption and understanding of computing; "In particular, how were computers embedded within the complex social framework of daily activity, and how did they interplay with the rest of our densely woven physical environment (also known as the "real world")?" [87: 693]. This consideration of social frameworks and physical environments led Weiser's team to propose calm computing as a way of managing the consequences of a ubiquitous computing environment. Weiser and Brown wrote, "if computers are everywhere they better stay out of the way, and that means designing them so that the people being shared by the computers remain serene and in control. Calmness is a new challenge that UC brings to computing ... Calmness is a fundamental challenge for all technology design of the next fifty years" [88]. Gaver and others have called for an interleaving of computational and everyday worlds through the trope of ambiguity – creating possibilities for other sorts of experiences and meaning making around technologies. Researchers at Georgia Tech have been exploring computer meditated religious communications and the role of technology in spiritual formations [64], while researchers at Cornell are experimenting with shyness and other forms of non-rational interaction.

Of course, it is also important to reflect upon why we have, thus far, tended to neglect spirituality and religion when we think of non-work usages and user models around technologies. We appear to be stubbornly secular in our imaginings of home and leisure contexts for computing. What we have to do is re-image the very contexts in which those technologies are conceived, created and consumed, making room not just for fun and enjoyment but also another fundamental set of cultural and human needs. If it is indeed the case, that religion is a primary framing narrative in most cultures, and then religion must also be one of the primary forces acting on people's relationships with and around new technologies – one could go as far as to suggest that there can be no real ubiquitous computing if it does not account for religion.

In this paper, I have provided examples of the many ways in which new technologies can and do deliver religious experiences; they are the leading edge of a much larger repurposing of computing and the Internet. Religion proves a useful vantage point from which to explore how much social and cultural institutions and practices are occasioned in and through technology. The re-purposing of ICTs for religious practices challenges some basic assumptions about what makes good technology; if not about efficiency and speed, then what? How might thinking about techno-spiritual practices inform ideas of privacy, identity, and security, for instance? Religious systems' cultural logic necessarily impact the very ways in which new technologies are created, consumed, and indeed rejected. Our desire to bring new technologies into our homes; the persistence of values such as simplicity, grace, humility, modesty, and purity; and ideas about modernity, subjectivity, and the self are all implicated in shaping the contexts for new technologies. And if we ignore them, we shortchange both our own experiences of the technology itself, as well as our understandings of what it could be for others.

Acknowledgements

I am extremely grateful for the interest showed in this project at Intel. I am also grateful for the insights of Diane Bell, Nina Wakeford, Paul Dourish, Adam Yeut Chau, Debashis Chaudhuri, Eunyun Park, Jofish Kaye, Dan Russell, Peter

Sheppard-Skaverd, Katrina Jungnickel, and Michael Erard. And I am also grateful to the anonymous reviewers who provided much useful feedback.

References

1. Anon.: No more text messages from Jesus. Reuters. 1/19 (2004), 10:50 AM EST.
2. Brasher, B.: Give me that online religion. Jossey-Bass, San Francisco (2001).
3. Beaudoin, T.: Virtual Faith: the irreverent spiritual quest of Generation X. Jossey-Bass Publishers (1998).
4. Cobb, J.: Cybergrace: the search for god in the digital world. Crown Pubs, (1998).
5. Ellwood-Clayton, B.: Texting & God: the Lord is my Textmate, Folk, Catholocism in the cyber-Philippines. In K. Nyiri (ed) A Sense of Place. Passagen Verlag (2005).
6. Hoover, S., Clark, L., & Rainie, L.: Faith Online. Pew Internet & Am. Life. (2004).
7. Katz, J.: Magic in the air: Spiritual & transcendental aspects of mobiles. Image, Understanding & Learning in the Mobile Age conference, Budapest, (2005).
8. Larsen, E.: Wired Churches, Wired Temples. Pew Report, (2000).
9. Bell, G.: The age of auspicious computing: ethnographic accounts of religion & new technology. ACM Interactions. Special Issue on Play. 11:5 (2004), 76-77.
10. Bell, G.: "Auspicous Computing?" IEEE Internet Comp, 8: 2, (2004).
11. Muller, M., Christiansen, E., Nardi, B. & Dray, S.: Spiritual Life & Information Technology. Comms of ACM, 44: 3, (2001), 82-83.
12. Swanson, D.: The Framing of Contemporary Christian Apostasy on the World Wide Web. Jrnl Media & Religion, 3:1, (2004), 1-20.
13. Zaleski, J.: The Soul of Cyber Space: how new technology is changing our spiritual lives. Harper Edge (1997).
14. Campbell, H.: Making Space for Religion in Internet Studies: Info Soc, 21: 4 (2005).
15. Davis, E.: Techgnosis: myth, magic + mysticism in the age of information. Three Rivers Press, California (1997).
16. Aloy, L.E.: Oh Maria Keep My Data Safe. The Show, Royal College of Art, 2005.
17. Hlubinka, M., Beaudin, J., Tapia, E.M., An, J.: AltarNation: interface design for meditative communities. In CHI '02. ACM Press, New York, NY, 612-613, (2002).
18. Ozenc, S.: Sajjadah 1426. St Martins College Art & Design, London (2005).
19. Anderson, J.: The Internet & Islam's new Interpreters. In: D. Eickelman, J. Anderson (eds). New Media in the Muslim World. Indiana Uni. (2003).
20. Blank, J.: Mullahs on the Mainframe: Islam & Modernity Among the Daudi Bohras. Uni of Chicago (2002).
21. Bunt, G.: Virtually Islamic: Computer-mediated communication & cyber-Islamic Environments. Uni. of Wales Press (2000).
22. Eickelman, D. & Anderson, J. (eds).: New Media in the Muslim World: The Emerging Public Sphere. Indiana Uni. Press (1999).
23. Lawrence, B.: Allah On-Line: The Practice of Global Islam in the Information Age. In S. Hoover, L.S. Clark (eds): Practicing Religion in the Age of the Media: Explorations in Media, Religion & Culture. Columbia Uni. Press (2002).
24. Reingold, H.: Look Who's Talking. Wired. 7: 1 (1999), January.
25. Erard, M.: The Geek Guide to Kosher Machines. Wired,12.11(2004), November.
26. Bell, G. & P. Dourish.: Yesterday's Tomorrows: Notes on Ubiquitous Computing's Vision. Personal & Ubiquitous Computing. In Press. (2006)

27. Bell, G.: The age of the thumb. In: P. Glotz, S. Bertschi & C. Locke (eds.): Thumb culture: Social trends & mobile phone use. Verlag, (2005): 67-88.
28. Bell, G.: Satu Keluarga, Satu Komputer: Cultural Accounts of ICTs in South & Southeast Asia. Design Issues, Vol 22:2. MIT Press (2006).
29. Dourish, P.: Implications for Design. Proc ACM Conf Human Factors in Computing System, CHI (2006), 541-550.
30. Bell, G. & J. Kaye.: Holy Hanging Out: Exploring Spirituality & Religion in the Corporate Environment. Ethnographic Praxis in Industry, November (2005).
31. Bell, G.: "Intimate Computing?" IEEE Internet Comp., 8:6, (2004).
32. Bell, G., T. Brooke, E. Churchill, & E. Paulos.: Intimate (Ubiquitous) Computing. Workshop, UBICOMP, Seattle, October (2003).
33. Brewer, J., Kaye, J., Williams, A., & Wyche, S.: Why we should talk about sex in HCI. Workshop. CHI (2006).
34. Lynch, C.: Selling Catholicism: Bishop Sheen & the power of television. Uni. of Kentucky Press (1998).
35. Noble, D.: The Religion of Technology. Apfred A Knopf (1997).
36. Clifford, J. & Marcus, GE.: Writing Culture: The Poetics & Politics of Ethnography. Berkeley: Uni of California Press (1986).
37. Holmes, D. & Marcus, G.E.: Refunctioning Ethnography within Cultures of Expertise. In: Yvonne Lincoln & Norm Denizen (eds.): Handbook of Qualitative Research. 3rd ed.. Thousand Oaks: Sage Publications (2005).
38. Geertz, C.: Local Knowledge. New York: Basic Books (1983).
39. Frazer, J. G. The Golden Bough: A Study in Magic & Religion. Macmillan, (1922).
40. Geertz, C. Religion as a cultural system. In: The Interpretation of Cultures. Basic Books (1973), 87-125.
41. Levis-Strauss, C.: The Raw and the Cooked. New York: Harper & Row (1969).
42. Weber, M.: The Protestant Ethic & Spirit of Capitalism. NY: Scribner's (1958).
43. Wallace, A. F.C.: Religion: An Anthropological View. NY: Random House. (1966).
44. Geertz, C.: The Religion of Java. Chicago : Uni of Chicago Press, (1976).
45. Brown, K.M.: Mama Lola. Berkeley: Uni of California Press (1991).
46. Gutierrez, R.: When Jesus Came, the Corn Mothers Went Away: Marriage, Sexuality & Power in New Mexico, 1500-1846. Stanford Uni Press (1991).
47. Ong, A.: Spirits of Resistance & Capitalist Discipline. SUNY Press (1987).
48. Taussig, M.: Shamanism, Colonialism, & the Wild Man: A Study in Terror and Healing. Uni of Chicago Press (1978).
49. Evans-Pritchard, E. E.: Theories of Primitive Religion. Oxford Uni Press, (1965).
50. Weber, M.: Sociology of Religion. Boston: Beacon Press, (1964).
51. Durkheim, E.: Elementary Forms of the Religious Life. Allen & Unwin, (1915).
52. Freud, S.: Totem and Taboo. J. Routledge & Kegan Paul. (1913).
53. Sharp, L. Steel Axes for Stone Age Australians. In E. H. Spicer (ed.): Human Problems in Technological Change, NY, Russell Sage Foundation, (1952), 69-72.
54. Pelto, PJ.: The Snowmobile Revolution: Technology & Social Change in the Arctic, Menlo Park, CA, (1973).
55. Appadurai, A. (ed): The Social Life of Things: Commodities in Cult. Perspective. Cambridge Uni. Press (1988).
56. Appadurai, A.: Globalization. NC: Duke Uni. Press (2001).
57. Miller, D.: Material Cultures: Why some things matter. IL: Uni of Chicago, (1998).
58. Marcus, G.: Ethnography in/of the World System: The Emergence of Multi-Sited Ethnography, Annual Review of Anthropology, 24 (1995), 95-117.

59. Bell, G., M. Blythe & P. Sengers.: Making by making strange: *defamiliarization* & the design of domestic technologies. Trans CHI–Social Issues, 12:2 (2005): 149-173.

60. Frankenberg, R.: Living Spirit, Living Practice. Duke Uni, (2004).

61. Williamson, D.: American teens so strong interest in using Internet for religious contacts. UNC News Service. 12/10 (2003), 638.

62. Fenimore, J.: High-Tech Worship: Media Technologies & Christian Liturgical Practice. PhD Project. RPI (2004).

63. Sturgill, A.: Scope and Purpose of Church Web Sites. Jrnl Media & Religion, 3: 3, (2004), 165-176.

64. Wyche, S.P., Hayes, G., Harvel, L., & Grinter, R.: Tech in Spiritual Formation: Exploratory Study of Computer Mediated Religious Communities. CSCW (2006).

65. Armfield, G., & Holbert, R.: The Relationship between Religiosity & Internet Use. Jrnl Media & Religion, 2:3 (2003), 129-144.

66. Campbell, H.: A New Forum for Religion: Spiritual Pilgrimage Online. The Bible in Transmission (2001), Summer.

67. Campbell, H.: Challenges Created by Online Religious Networks. Jrnl Media & Religion, 3: 2 (2004), 81-99.

68. Richardson, J.: Uses & Gratifications of Agnostic Refuge: Case Study of a Skeptical Online Congregation. Jrnl Media & Religion, 2:4, (2003) ,237-250.

69. Anon.: Russian Content Provider offers SMS Service to Wailing Wall in Jerusalem. Mosnews.com. 11/25 (2005).

70. Ananova.: Hi-tech Catholic confession banned. www.ananova.com. (2003).

71. Bruni, F.: Italians give thumbs up to wireless messages. NYTimes, 3/13 (2003).

72. Charny, B.: Pope to Ping the faithful. clnet. 4/7 (2004).

73. Anon.: Archbishop requests SMS-free Good Friday.Catholic Tele. News,3/22 (2002).

74. Leland, J.:Tucked behind the home page, a call to worship.NY Times, 1/31 (2004).

75. Scott, D.: Matchmaker, Matchmaker, Find Me a Match: A cultural examination of a Virtual Community of Single Mormons. Jrl Media & Religion, 1:4, (2002), 201-216.

76. Bezlova, A.: China: Battle with tradition spills into cyber-space – traditional funerals & the internet. Relgioscope, 4/9 (2002). www.religioscope.com

77. Anon.: Chinese Grieve Loved Ones at Cyber-memorials. China Daily, 4/5(2003).

78. Anon.: China Mourns Fighter Pilot in Online Memorial Hall. Reuters, 4/21 (2001).

79. Anon.: Online Tomb-sweeping debuts in China. China Daily, 4/5 (2001).

80. Tan, D.: Qingming goes online. Radio Singapore International. Broadcast 10 (2002).

81. Anon.: Reader in Collection Plate. Associated Press, 2/18 (2003).

82. Ralli, T.: Missed Church? Download It to your iPod. NY Times, 8/29 (2005).

83. Lin, Ed.: Spiritually Profitable Gaming. Forbes.com. 8/16 (2003).

84. Dee, J.: PlayStations of the Cross. NYTimes Magazine, 5/1 (2005).

85. Weiser, M.: The Computer for the 21st Century. Scientific Am., 265: 3 (1991), 94-10.

86. Sengupta, U. & Sherry, J.: Future Vision 2015. Tech@Intel Magazine, Sept (2004).

87. Weiser, M., Gold, R., Brown, J.S.: The Origins of ubiquitous computing research at PARC in the late 1980s. IBM Systems Journal, 38:4 (1999), 693-696.

88. Weiser, M. & Brown, J.S.: The Coming Age of Calm Technology. In P Denning & R Metcalfe (eds) Beyond Calculation: The Next Fifty Years of Computing, Spinger-Verlag, Inc. (1997).

Scribe4Me: Evaluating a Mobile
Sound Transcription Tool for the Deaf

Tara Matthews[1], Scott Carter[1], Carol Pai[2], Janette Fong[2], and Jennifer Mankoff[2]

[1] Berkeley Institute of Design, CS Division, University of California, Berkeley, CA, USA
{tmatthew, sacarter}@cs.berkeley.edu

[2] Human Computer Interaction Institute, Carnegie Mellon University, Pittsburgh, PA, USA
{magicpai, janette.fong}@gmail.com, jmankoff@cs.cmu.edu

Abstract. People who are deaf or hard-of-hearing may have challenges communicating with others *via* spoken words and may have challenges being aware of audio events in their environments. This is especially true in public places, which may not have accessible ways of communicating announcements and other audio events. In this paper, we present the design and evaluation of a mobile sound transcription tool for the deaf and hard-of-hearing. Our tool, Scribe4Me, is designed to improve awareness of sound-based information in any location. When a button is pushed on the tool, a transcription of the last 30 seconds of sound is given to the user in a text message. Transcriptions include dialog and descriptions of environmental sounds. We describe a 2-week field study of an exploratory prototype, which shows that our approach is feasible, highlights particular contexts in which it is useful, and provides information about what should be contained in transcriptions.

1 Introduction

"[I was] appreciative that [the tool] was available... to fill in the large gaping holes of conversation in a group I usually miss... I saw how [the translations] could create the gift of a conversation." –A study participant.

Sound plays an important role in communication and contextual awareness about interesting events and information. These sounds, and the information they convey, may not be easily available to people who are deaf or hard-of-hearing. The home environment can be controlled and augmented to support better awareness using alerting systems for things like phones, doorbells, alarms and a baby's crying (see [17] for a review of existing techniques and the sounds they support). However, other areas encountered in daily life (*e.g.*, public spaces, stores, restaurants, streets, airports, public transportation, and so on) do not always provide adequate support for communicating sound-based information to the deaf. For this reason, mobile support for better sound information awareness would be of great value to the deaf and hard-of-hearing.

We present the design and evaluation of a mobile sound transcription tool for the deaf and hard-of-hearing called Scribe4Me. When a user presses a button on her Scribe4Me PDA, the last 30 seconds of sound is uploaded, transcribed and sent back to her as a text message. Transcriptions include dialog and descriptions of environmental sounds. Scribe4Me is unique in providing support for both speech and

P. Dourish and A. Friday (Eds.): Ubicomp 2006, LNCS 4206, pp. 159–176, 2006.
© Springer-Verlag Berlin Heidelberg 2006

non-speech audio in mobile environments. It is also the only speech to text system for the deaf that is robust enough to be deployed in an unconstrained setting for two weeks.

Our main goal was to explore the potential uses of and issues surrounding a sound transcription tool. We conducted a 2-week field study of an exploratory prototype, gathering data about situations in which requests were made, transcriptions were sent, and gathering qualitative feedback from users (see Fig. 1). Results showed that despite issues such as a 3-5 minute delay, the prototype tool was useful in a variety of situations and most users were excited by it, especially for understanding conversations: "I don't really get all that much of the conversation and subside on a few words here and there. There were several times I used the tool… I was privy to the complete sentences, which was very nice. I very much enjoyed having it available…" Scribe4Me was useful to people with varying levels of hearing loss, from people who are profoundly deaf to those using cochlear implants and hearing aids.

Fig. 1. Field study users found the Scribe4Me tool valuable in many situations, including at grocery stores, in group conversations, in airports, and moving about the city

2   Related Work

Research for the deaf has often focused on communication support in both *mobile* and *non-mobile* settings. However, most commercial technologies focus on *non-speech audio* in *non-mobile* environments. This section provides an overview of research and products supporting transcription and review of speech and non-speech audio. We also discuss a related area that has received attention outside the assistive technology community: mobile tools for automatic storage and review of audio.

Mobile Communication: Communication options used by the deaf have changed radically since the introduction of mobile phones and PDAs. Text messaging is common among the deaf and has increased communication between the hearing and deaf [20]. WISDOM (Wireless Information Services for Deaf People on the Move) [8] was a collaborative effort between several research organizations and companies in Europe, focused on developing video sign language transmission on mobile devices (see [1] for a description of their vision-based sign language recognition system). No products exist as a result of this project. Another commercial software product, LipC-Cell [4], enables lip reading during mobile phone calls. The mobile phone connects to a PC, which converts the caller's voice into a 3D animated face with real-time lip movements (companies providing LipC-Cell are no longer in business and the software is not available). A number of wearable vibrotactile speech perception aids have been developed that extract voice fundamental frequency and deliver it *via* vibration. These systems improve speech perception for the deaf (see [2] for a survey). Impromptu is a mobile system for audio applications with speech interfaces, using speech recognition [21]. Though not intended for users who are deaf, Impromptu demonstrates mobile speech recognition. None of these tools can handle unconstrained audio recordings of varying quality and none include both speech and non-speech sounds.

Non-Mobile Communication: Assistive technology for the deaf used in static environments has also focused on communication. Common technologies include: assistive listening devices (improving the audibility of one sound source that is likely to be lost due to distance or background sounds such as a lecturer in an auditorium or a conversation in a loud restaurant); telecommunication devices (such as text telephones (TTDs), IP relay, and video relay services [6]); and close-captioning for TV and movies [7, 16]. Communication support in classrooms includes captioned dialogue with educational transcription services, computer-assisted note-taking, and, more recently, automatic speech recognition programs [9]. Research has also explored automatic sign language recognition. Edwards [10] summarizes work on developing techniques for capturing, segmenting (delimiting), and classifying sign language gestures. A number of systems have been developed to automatically translate English into American Sign Language (see [13] for a survey). Several other systems enable speech articulation practice. Sonido offers software that visualizes speech using spectrographs and allows users to practice speech articulation with recorded speech samples [22]. Ellsman and Maki study the effectiveness of spectrographs in speech training, suggesting that they can enable students to practice alone to a limited degree [11]. Finally, many systems translate speech between languages, *e.g.*, [3, 15, 19, 25].

Non-Mobile, Non-speech Audio: Other non-mobile systems enable non-speech sound awareness. Many commercial alerting systems can be installed in buildings and homes. These typically use flashing lights, vibration, or extra-loud sounds to provide awareness of alerting sounds (phones, doorbells, emergency alarms, and babies crying). However, alerting system are expensive, difficult to install, and non-mobile. In related past work on peripheral visualizations of non-speech sounds, we interviewed people who are deaf about sound awareness needs [17] (discussed in the next section).

Mobile Audio Buffer: Outside of assistive technology, researchers have explored mobile tools for recording sound for later review as a memory aid. For example, the Personal Audio Loop (PAL) [14] helps people avoid conversational break-downs that occur when a person forgets something that was said (*e.g., a conversation topic or a name*). PAL retains audio for about one hour, enabling users to replay conversations. Though not aimed at the deaf, PAL introduces privacy issues relevant to Scribe4Me. The unobtrusive nature of PAL makes it easy for the speech of people near the user to be recorded without their knowing or consenting. Use of Scribe4Me is hard to hide from conversation partners, can be hidden from passersby. In 38 of 50 states in the U.S., it is legal to record conversations to which you are a party without informing others [23]. PAL creators explored the ethics of this issue using an inquiry technique in which potential PAL users asked conversation partners to complete a survey after a conversation. The survey asked about privacy and consent preferences if the conversation had been recorded by PAL. Results showed that people wanted to be informed of and asked to give consent to audio recording and its replay to others *a priori*.

In summary, past research looks at mobile and non-mobile communication (*e.g.*, video relay on a PDA or PC), non-mobile sound awareness systems (*e.g.*, phone ring flashers), and privacy in recording audio. Notably missing from past work is a nuanced understanding of what *speech* and *non-speech sound* awareness is valued in *mobile* situations. Scribe4Me enables us to explore sound awareness user needs, which are further motivated in the next section.

3   Formative Work

In past work, we interviewed people who are deaf about sound awareness needs to inform peripheral, visual displays of non-speech sounds [17]. Participants emphasized the importance of sound-based awareness in *all locations*, something not adequately supported by existing technology. They listed many sounds of interest outside (*e.g.*, vehicles, people approaching, *etc.*), in the home (*e.g.*, appliances, knocking, TV, *etc.*), and in the office (*e.g.*, activities of coworkers, printers, phones, *etc.*). Participants sometimes relied on third party descriptions of sounds. One participant reported calling her hearing husband and putting the phone near the baby monitor when she was unsure about the sounds the baby was making.

Our formative interviews motivated the work described here. Based on those results [17], we decided to explore the idea of describing recent environmental sounds to people based on recordings made on a mobile tool. After feasibility testing to check that contextual audio recorded with a cellphone-quality microphone was understandable to a human (suggesting that transcription was at least possible), we conducted two Wizard-of-Oz pilot studies with four participants each. We followed participants and transcribed sounds by writing a description of them on paper when asked. We focused on testing feasibility, identifying situations in which the tool was useful and learning about what information to include in transcriptions.

The first pilot study included four hearing graduate students. One participant listened to music using ear-buds and the other three wore earplugs, to reduce hearing accuracy. We instructed participants to walk around the campus and surrounding city streets for 20 minutes, and did not assign a specific task. Participants were instructed to raise one hand to ask "what happened?" A researcher followed each participant and wrote a description of recent sounds on paper when a hand was raised, which was shown to the participant as soon as the transcription was complete. We transcribed a number of events onto paper, including short descriptions of ambient sounds ("two girls behind you are talking"), descriptions of speech ("a woman walked by said she parked at Dicks"), and no information ("not sure what happened"). Transcriptions did not include verbatim speech transcriptions, something participants suggested we add. Feedback from this pilot indicated that most participants did not find a compelling use for the tool. Thus, we conducted another pilot study with more representative users over a longer period of time.

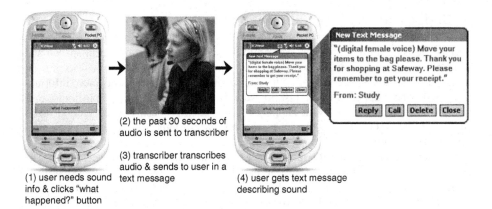

(2) the past 30 seconds of audio is sent to transcriber

(3) transcriber transcribes audio & sends to user in a text message

(1) user needs sound info & clicks "what happened?" button

(4) user gets text message describing sound

Fig. 2. System diagram showing the request process from left to right

In the second pilot study, which had similar goals to the first, we gathered feedback in more realistic situations. A researcher followed the user and transcribed audio on paper when a user pushed a portable, 1-button device (implemented using BOXES [12], a tool designed for early-stage prototyping of physically-based devices). Two people who are deaf participated while shopping at mall. Two people without hearing loss participated while grocery shopping. One also did a "staged" trip to a Greyhound bus station, in which she asked when the next bus was leaving. Study length varied from 40-90 minutes, depending on the activity.

All four participants found some compelling use for the tool. While grocery shopping, one participant used the tool because "I was anxious that the store was going to close soon because it's late, and I thought the announcement might have been asking us to check out." When at the Greyhound station, the same user used the tool because "I was trying to find out when the next bus was, and I thought there would be some kind of announcement, but I didn't hear anything. I was anxious that I missed it." In this particular instance, since there had been no distinguishable sounds, the tool had responded with, "Not sure what happened." The participant commented, "I liked that. It was comforting because it told me that I hadn't missed anything." A second participant was particularly interested in what others said, "…especially if they are talking about me. Don't be afraid to tell me bad things." Another participant didn't find a use for the tool in the mall, but thought the tool would be valuable in an airport or when "things didn't go according to plan." Suggested improvements centered on increasing the detail of transcriptions, especially including exactly what people nearby had said.

Overall, people in the *in situ* pilot found beneficial uses for the tool and speculated about others. In both pilot studies, the main feedback was that participants wanted the wizard to provide a complete transcript of the event instead of a summary (especially the exact dialog of others). Additionally, participants always asked for information about recent events, rather than events that had occurred some time ago. These results, along with strong user needs exposed in formative interviews, and gaps in existing technology, motivated the design, implementation, and field test of the mobile sound transcription tool discussed next.

4   Design and Implementation of Scribe4Me

Scribe4Me is a tool that provides descriptions and transcriptions of recent speech and sounds to users when they press a button. As illustrated in **Fig. 2**, Scribe4Me runs on a PDA and records 30 seconds of audio continuously. If the user wants more information about what happened in the last 30 seconds, she can *request* it by pushing a button on the screen labeled "what happened?" For each request, two 15 second audio files are sent *via* GPRS to a human transcriber, who sends back a text message describing the content of those files.

Our pilot studies helped to inform these design decisions. First, we learned that awareness of *recent* audio was useful to participants. Thus we designed Scribe4Me to buffer the last 30 seconds of audio. Second, participants wanted detailed information conveyed by both speech and non-speech sounds. To find out just how much detail is required, we designed Scribe4Me to include a human-in-the-loop to transcribe all possible sounds in detail. The field study would inform whether a human transcriber or automated sound recognition would be used in future iterations.

We implemented a functional prototype of Scribe4Me using Momento [5]. Momento is a tool designed to support rapid prototyping and situated evaluation of mobile Ubicomp applications. It has built-in support for long-term studies of `human-in-the-loop' systems, of the sort we were conducting. Momento was used to implement both the mobile interface and to support the transcription by the remote transcriber.

4.1 Mobile Client Implementation

The mobile part of the prototype was an alpha version of the Momento mobile client, configured to capture and transmit audio. The only additional coding needed was to create the UI screens shown in **Fig. 2**. While sending files, the "what happened?" button was disabled and progress messages were shown: "Sending file 1 of 3 of your request;" "Sending file 2 of 3. We've begun translation;" and "Sending file 3 of 3. You should receive a text message soon." The entire process from making a request to receiving a response took 3-5 minutes. This time was composed of GPRS transmission (2-4 minutes) and transcription time (about 1 minute). We used a Windows Mobile version of the Momento mobile client, rather than a J2ME version, because it was faster and less error prone on our deployment devices. Because Scribe4Me required a sensitive and accurate enough microphone to enable detailed transcriptions, we used Pocket PC devices (five Qtek 9090 PDA2Ks and one i-Mate PDA2K).

Our goal was to minimize transmission time and maximize audio quality. Both audio quality and transmission time increase with larger file sizes. Audio is recorded by the Momento client as WAV files at 11KHz in stereo. We customized Momento to slow the audio sampling rate to 8KHz mono (file sizes dropped from 320 kb to 115 kb). Testing showed that these files were as understandable to a human transcriber as at the default sample rate, although 8KHz is the minimum for speech recognition systems. It also resulted in a 2-4 minute drop in transmission time.

Because this was a rough prototype intended for evaluation, we had to make several design decisions that would be changed in a more polished tool. First, the "what happened?" button was implemented in software, requiring the user to press it with a stylus. This software button was implemented by customizing Momento's mobile interface to include a single button labeled "what happened?" Second, recording was paused while transmission was in progress due to limited device resources. Third, we asked users to take a photo with the PDA each time they pressed the "what happened?" button. The photo would not be part of a final tool but was important for providing the researchers and the participant with context about requests for later discussion in email journals and post-hoc interviews.

4.2 Remote Desktop Translation Implementation

The transcriber used the Momento tool to handle requests. Momento provided a generic interface for monitoring and responding to incoming multimedia data from mobile devices. When a request was made, Momento notified the transcriber with a sound. Using the Momento desktop interface, the transcriber listened to the incoming audio, typed a response, and sent it to the participant, who received it as a standard SMS (text) message. Longer transcriptions were split into multiple text messages due to software in the GSM network that imposes a 160 character size limit for SMS messages. The transcriber could begin translating the first audio file before other files finished transmitting.

The Momento desktop application coordinated communications with the PDAs. It provided a timeline visualization of all incoming and past requests. Furthermore, the application saved all communication logs in tab-separated files that could be imported into spreadsheet programs for later analysis.

5 User Study

We conducted a two-week field evaluation of a fully functional prototype with six participants who are deaf. The study helped us answer the following questions:

- Would Scribe4Me be useful for people with different levels of hearing loss?
- How would users decide when to use Scribe4Me?
- In what situations would Scribe4Me be useful?
- Would users value Scribe4Me enough to continue using it or to pay for it?
- What information is most useful to include in audio transcriptions? Are hard-to-transcribe details such as emotion valuable?
- What improvements could be made to Scribe4Me?
- How would others react to the participant using Scribe4Me?

5.1 Participants

We recruited 6 users living in two geographically distant, urban regions for the two week study: 2 profoundly deaf (hearing no sounds), 1 almost profoundly deaf (hearing only very loud sounds with little comprehension) and 3 hard-of-hearing with the help of hearing aids or cochlear implants (hearing level is highly variable; these participants all communicated verbally with others, but often missed sounds that were quiet, in noisy environments, or were not the focus of their attention). Four participants were female. Ages ranged from 25 to 51. Participants' occupations included a substitute teacher/student, an information services worker, a clerk, the CEO of a technology company, a marketing director, and a college student. Participants were volunteers recruited *via* an email sent to several distribution lists for the deaf and hard-of-hearing.

Participants were compensated based on their participation, with $155 (USD) as the maximum for 100% participation. All participants had 100% participation, except one who completed only 8 days of the field study (due to scheduling conflicts). Table 1 describes user hearing levels and participation results.

Table 1. Participation results per user

User	Days	Total requests	Avg. requests per day	Hearing / aids
1	7	47	6.7	minimal hearing, no aids
2	10	23	2.3	profoundly deaf
3	13	19	1.5	1 aid, 1 implant (recent)
4	14	14	1.0	profoundly deaf
5	15	13	0.9	1 aid, deaf in other ear
6	8	2	0.3	2 aids

5.2 Method

During the two week study, transcribers transcribed requests 7 days a week, 9 am to 9 pm for east coast participants, and 6 am to 6 pm for west coast participants (this accomplished the goal of having 9 am to 6 pm covered for all participants). Data collected from each participant included demographic information, a great deal of qualitative feedback during four interviews, audio and photos from requests, and tool usage descriptions and feedback included in a daily email journal.

The study began with a one-hour meeting in which the user was introduced to Scribe4Me and trained to use it. During the field study, users completed daily journals (see Figure 3 for an example). We also conducted two 30-minute interviews over the phone or Instant Messenger (IM) on days 4 and 8 of the study. We asked each participant if he or she were having any problems using Scribe4Me or the PDA, when it had been most useful, if he or she had hesitated to use it in any situations, how usage of the tool had changed since the beginning of the study, what issues had affected the usefulness of the tool, and how we could have improved the transcriptions. We finished the study with a one hour exit interview, in which we asked each participant about overall impressions of the tool, situations in which it was used, ways in which it could be improved, and whether he or she would continue using it for free and for a charge.

During the field study, we sent each user a daily summary of the photo and transcription associated with each request he or she had made. We asked the user to send us an email journal each day answering a series of questions about each request, such as why it was made and how useful it was. A sample email journal from the study is shown in Fig. 3. Users responded to email journals even when they made no requests that day (answering questions about what they did, why they did not need to use the tool that day, and if they thought about making any requests but did not).

Request 2: 11:55 am   *[No new picture.]*

Translation: "(male announcement) We are approaching <unclear>. <sound of a machine howling> <machine howling, digital beeps several times, muffled female and male voices in the background>"

- *Why did you ask "what happened?" in this situation? Please describe in as much detail as possible.* This one was hilarious… It's a pilot project of a crosswalk device that is beneficial to the blind pedestrian. I was very curious how it sounded. It helped me understand what blind people hear, and improved my ability to do my job on [a disability organization].

- *Where were you?* [named a landmark].

- *Was someone trying to communicate with you directly?* No.

- *How did you feel about using the tool in the environment you were in when you asked "what happened?"* Everybody is walking around with these types of devices these days, so I was one of the crowd.

- *How useful would you rate the response (1=not useful → 5=very useful)?* 5

- *If you rated the response 4 or 5: what made it useful?* Well, it helped me understand what blind people hear, and improved my ability to do my job on [a disability organization].

Looking back at the whole day, answer the following:

- *Of all the times you requested "what happened" today, which request was the most important to you? Why?* Hmmmm… Difficult question. Well, for novelty value, the howling crosswalk signal. But for information it would be talking about [a different request made that day about a conversation with a co-worker].

- *Where there any times that you thought about using the tool but decided not to or weren't able to? If so, (1) briefly describe the situation, and (2) why did you decide not to use the tool?* Oh, it's such a neat little device that I am enthused to use it anywhere and anytime.

  Please share any comments, suggestions, or stories related to your use of the tool today: It was fun!

Fig. 3. A participant's email journal with one request and one full-day summary. Text in *italics* are questions from researchers. Substitutes in brackets are for clarity or anonymization.

5.3 Data Collected

Three participants completed the full 2-week field study. One participant completed 8 days due to conflicts scheduling the training session. A second and third participant completed 10 and 7 days respectively due to technical issues with their PDAs: one had GPRS connectivity problems for 4 of 14 days and the other had battery power problems for 7 of 14 days. On these days, users were instructed to think about and report in the email journal when they would have used Scribe4Me that day and why.

For each request made during the study, we received two 15-second audio files and a photo taken by the user at the time of the request (43% of requests included photos; the rest were in similar situations or a photo was not practical). Occasionally, audio files from requests were not fully transmitted due to GPRS network connectivity issues, making it impossible to send a transcribed response. Momento did not support resending files lost in transmission because doing so would have increased response time to undesirable levels and compromised battery life. During the field study, both audio files from 16 (out of 118) requests were not transmitted, resulting in the response, "[Audio file not transmitted, possibly due to low connectivity. Please try again!]" One audio file from 36 additional requests was missing, indicated in the response by, "[1st/2nd audio file / 15 seconds missing]." Participants reported that even with only one of two audio files the responses were often useful. See Table 1 for a summary of each user's participation.

6 Results

Overall, participants were enthusiastic about Scribe4Me. All but one participant (#6 in Table 1) found at least one valuable use for the tool during the study. All participants said that they would continue to use Scribe4Me if they could install it on their mobile device. The major issue with Scribe4Me raised by all participants was the delay between requesting and receiving a transcription (which was 3-5 minutes). For 3 participants, this severely limited the scenarios in which Scribe4Me was useful, since they wanted a real-time aid for communicating with others. The other 3 participants found Scribe4Me to be valuable in a number of situations even with the delay: "It is a great idea. There are things that I'm curious about on a day to day basis. I don't mind waiting for the translation."

We next present results reflecting these user sentiments and showing the value of Scribe4Me to users with hearing loss. In particular, we describe differences in use between participants with different levels of hearing loss, situations in which Scribe4Me was useful, and users' thoughts on continued usage of Scribe4Me. Then we present results about those aspects of Scribe4Me that were successful and those that were less so in order to help improve similar tools in the future, including what information to include in transcriptions, technical limitations, user suggested improvements, and privacy issues.

6.1 When Was Scribe4Me Valuable?

Here we present the participants' experience with Scribe4Me during the 2-week field study. Feedback was largely positive and all participants wanted to continue using Scribe4Me in their daily lives. We include results about differences between users with different levels of hearing loss, especially what cues they used to decide when to use the tool. We then present situations in which the tool was valuable to users. Finally, we share participants' sentiments on continued use of Scribe4Me.

6.1.1 Equally Valuable for Users with Different Levels of Hearing Loss

Levels of hearing loss range roughly from profoundly deaf (no hearing) to moderately hard-of-hearing (hearing and comprehending most but not all sounds). Our study included participants from across this range and demonstrated the usefulness of the tool to people with diverse levels of hearing loss. There were no marked differences in how much participants with different levels of hearing loss valued using the tool or in how they used it. This was largely because all participants wanted to comprehend sounds better, which Scribe4Me helped them do. For example, one moderately hard-of-hearing participant who wore hearing aids said: "I don't think I have as good of comprehension [as the device]." Though cochlear implants and hearing aids amplify sound, they do not always improve comprehension, especially in noisy places.

The cues that prompted participants to use the tool differed between users with different levels of hearing loss. Users who are profoundly deaf often relied on a visual cue – either from the source of the sound itself or from others' reaction to it (*e.g.* "people turned their heads"). For the three hard-of-hearing participants, sounds that were audible but not comprehensible were often the cue for using the tool. Participants reported "hearing something" or missing parts of conversation and wanting a description of the sound or the missing words.

6.1.2 Valuable in Multiple Situations

Participants used the tool at home, work, restaurants, a drive-through, their own car, airports, business conferences, the grocery store, walking outside, riding public transportation, an animal shelter, church, group meetings, coffee shops, the post office, and other service-oriented businesses. All of the requests made are categorized in Table 2. Participants found the tool to be useful in a number of these situations, both for information awareness and for exploration:

Semi-public speech: Participants used Scribe4Me to learn about relevant conversations in which they were not obviously participating. "[The] meeting was over and various people were chatting. [The transcription was] useful after the fact, since this type of conversational situation is the most challenging for me. [I was] appreciative that [the tool] was available... to fill in the large gaping holes of conversation in a group I usually miss." Another participant said, "[I was in] the office. There was lots of stuff going on. Didn't know if there was a paging or just conversation. [The request was useful] because it seemed so loud." Another participant said, "It was during a break in the middle of an evening class and the professor started talking again just before the interpreter returned from her break. This is good for helping me to 'catch up' on the information prior to the interpreter's return."

Conversations in which the user was involved: Even though the delayed response made it difficult to use the tool in real-time conversation, one participant eloquently wrote about how the tool improved communication for her: "[The tool is most useful] conversation-wise. Usually I don't really get all that much of the conversation and subsist on a few words here and there. There were several times I used the tool and it may have taken a couple messages and a couple minutes but I was privy to the complete sentence, which was very nice. I think just having it as a tool... engages me into conversation which I would not normally have pursued. Even reading the responses after the fact and clarifying how the tool filled in what I did not lip read is encouraging. I very much enjoyed having it available and look forward to the day when programs such as this will provide the opportunity to further engage the deaf and hearing impaired into interaction with others."

Announcements in public places: "[I was in the] airport. There are many announcements in airports. [It is] hard to tell when something important is being announced or something relevant to your flight."

Using machines with voices: "[I was] at [the grocery store], in the self-check out aisle. I really like using the tool because the stupid machine doesn't use captions on its screens, and it's nice knowing what automated messages it spits out." Another participant said, "[This is a] request to hear that darn fax machine. Believe it or not this thing talks and does not text its voice." Another participant was listening to the radio: "[We were] in the car [and the] game was on. Trying to see if I could pick up key moments (when crowd noise occurred, *etc.*). [The] noise showed something important was happening – [I] wanted to get the synopsis."

Table 2. All situations in which Scribe4Me was used, categorized by type and whether or not the request raises privacy concerns. Out of 118 requests, 4 were put in multiple categories and 11 were not categorized because the user did not describe the request in an email journal.

Use Category	#Requests
privacy concern	46
public speech (others talking)	13
captured unintentionally	8
captured for curiosity, info gathering, or unknown intent	5
semi-public speech	33
class (teacher and student questions)	17
general workplace chatter	13
church	2
non-work meeting	1
no / limited privacy concern	65
conversation in which user was involved (hard to hide use of tool)	20
with friends / other people	10
with coworker or boss	5
with family, at home	3
strangers in stores / restaurants	2
announcements	14
airport announcements	9
BART train / bus digital announcements	3
announcements at restaurants / coffee shops	2
machine / electronic / TV / radio voice	16
TV	8
grocery store self-checkout machine	3
radio	3
calling card with digital voice prompts	1
fax with voice prompts	1
environmental sounds (no voices)	15
misc. environmental sounds	8
traffic / city street environmental sounds	4
environmental sounds at home	2
electronics / computers	1

Environmental sounds: "I must have been trekking home, which would be walking along [the street]. Just trying to get a gist of my audible surroundings." Another user said, "I was wondering if you could hear the [train] sounds (if it makes them)... The train was just arriving and I was curious if they had made an announcement about it (speaker) and if you could hear it. Wanting to know if [the train] makes noise isn't exactly useful to me (in that specific situation). It just satisfies my curiosity."

These examples show that the tool has great potential for improving situational awareness and communication abilities for the deaf.

6.1.3 Participants Want to Continue Using Scribe4Me

All users said they valued the tool enough to continue using it and to pay for it as part of a mobile service plan. Two users thought the tool would be useful on a frequent, ongoing basis. Four users said they would likely use the tool infrequently, but that it was useful to have. One of these participants said: "If it had the 1 min response time and background sounds were no longer an issue, I'd probably use it a couple of times a week. Maybe even daily if the results continued to come back accurate."

6.2 What Did We Learn About Scribe4Me's Design?

Participants valued Scribe4Me and wanted to continue using it, indicating that a wider deployment is worthwhile. The results presented next provide design implications for future iterations of the tool. In the next five subsections, we present results about what worked and what didn't to inform the design of similar tools in the future.

6.2.1 Participants Want Translations of All Types of Information

Participants wanted descriptions of environmental sounds in addition to speech. Of 102 total transcriptions, 75% included speech and other sounds, and 25% included only environmental sounds. One participant said he appreciated the non-speech transcriptions, "...and that's why a voice-recognition system would be more limited. It was good to know that a sound came from the TV, *etc.*" Another participant wanted a description of the crosswalk for the blind (see Fig. 3). She said, "It is interesting to me to reveal not only conversation but also certain sounds, like the howling crosswalk noise. I remember pressing that button before and noticing that people around me noticably raised their eyebrows, and I guess I would too if I had heard it howl!"

Also, participants wanted descriptions voices. For example, they wanted to know the gender of speakers: "Knowing the gender of people who were talking made it easier to understand." They also appreciated knowing when speakers were making an announcement or coming from a TV or radio (all of which human transcribers could usually determine). Participants also wanted to know the *mood* of speakers. A participant asked that moods be added to transcriptions mid-study: "[It would be nice] if you could add the emotion of the people talking. Not for all of them, but if the person were mad or teasing, it is good to have that information." Transcribers began including notable speaker emotions, resulting in positive user feedback.

6.2.2 Technical Issues Limited Communication

Two main problems reduced the effectiveness of the tool for all participants in face-to-face communication situations: the delay of 3-5 minutes between when a user made a request and received a transcription; and transcription errors. These problems were caused largely by limitations of current technology.

The delay made the tool less useful to participants, especially in situations where the participant was in a conversation or listening to a speaker because "language happens quickly." One participant summed up the issue well: "Three to five minutes [delay] leaves one as an observer rather than an active participant." All participants thought the value of the tool would be much higher if the delay was reduced.

The second major issue was with inaccurate transcriptions caused by less-than-perfect audio quality and/or lack of context. Though most transcriptions were accurate and detailed, there were times when background noise overwhelmed speakers (*e.g.,* at restaurants), speakers were too far away for all words to be audible (*e.g.,* when over-hearing conversations at work), and words were mistaken for others that sounded similar (*e.g.,* the word "terminations" was mistaken for "determination"). Lack of context made it hard to determine which sounds to transcribe and which to leave out. Due to these issues, participants felt the tool would not be useful in some critical situations, *e.g.,* "if there was a large group conversation."

6.2.3 Suggested Improvements: Less Delay, More Control

Based on issues encountered in the study, users suggested many improvements to the tool. Foremost was reducing the response delay. Participants also wanted the ability to choose the length of audio files and to send contextual information to transcribers (*e.g.,* which speaker to focus on among many). Participants thought long transcriptions sent in multiple messages were confusing, requesting that entire transcriptions be sent in one message. Finally, all participants wanted more accurate transcriptions and many suggested that the tool have an external microphone to better record audio. All of these suggestions are feasible to address in future iterations of the tool.

6.2.4 Privacy and Effects on Social Interactions

Because the Scribe4Me tool records the voices of people nearby, it introduces difficult privacy issues. Both privacy issues and the discomfort of using a device while interacting with someone, affected participants' use of the tool in social situations.

As discussed previously, the PAL memory aid system introduced similar privacy issues, recommending informed consent for recording peoples' voices and replaying them to third parties (*e.g.,* a transcriber). Arguably, a person who is deaf is not getting any information from Scribe4Me that a hearing person could not and so using the tool is socially justifiable. However, the transcriber certainly introduces privacy issues. We did not instruct participants to inform others of the tool, though most were very sensitive to the issue, informing conversation partners who were recorded or not making requests when they were unable to inform others. One participant said, "Everybody that I talked to, I showed it to them before I had to use it with them. I compare it to when you might ask someone if you might take their picture... In one sense, it makes others be more drawn into communicate, though there was still the hesitation of someone else hearing in on the conversation." Another said, "[When others saw me using the tool I felt the need to tell them about it] because otherwise it would feel like spying – even though I was getting information that would be readily available to a hearing person." Use of the Scribe4Me tool was somewhat discrete, but hard to hide in face-to-face conversation since users had to push a button and read the screen when a transcription arrived. This visible use may have encouraged participants to inform others, socially enforcing informed consent in conversational situations.

Table 2 categorizes all requests by whether or not they introduce privacy concerns. Consent is naturally enforced in face-to-face conversations and announcements are public, but other instances of speech are a privacy issue. To protect privacy, we need ways to prevent capture or enforce consent. By adding technology that detects speech client-side [21], we can put users in control of privacy decisions. For the deaf, we cannot indicate if the speech is an intended conversation partner or a nearby conversation. To be legally sound, the user would not make a request if the tool informs them speech is present and others are nearby. For other applications (*e.g.,* language translation) the tool could replay the audio so the user can tell if unintended speech was captured. Another possible solution is to change policy, enabling users who are deaf to use transcriptions tools and certifying transcribers.

Users also hesitated to use the device in some situations to avoid being rude. The most commonly avoided situation was interacting with others who did not know about the tool: "it is rude to check a phone when in the middle of a conversation." One hard-of-hearing participant felt uncomfortable using the tool in church, even though she thought it would be useful for catching parts of the sermon she missed: "In Church, we've been harped on about not using cell phones, people looked at me kind of sideways and I wanted to say, 'this is not a cell phone! I'm not talking to anybody!'"

Despite these awkward situations, people felt comfortable using the tool around people they could explain it to and in less participatory situations: "Everybody is walking around with these types of devices these days, so I was one of the crowd." One participant thought that the value added was worth some awkwardness: "I feel kind of awkward using the device in a public setting... With that said, if the device is truly helpful, it doesn't matter what the people think. So, if I were in a position to need your device, I would use it, regardless of what people around me think!"

6.2.5 Applying Lessons Learned to Other Ubicomp Applications

The Scribe4Me field study, though limited in size, may provide some guidance for similar applications that involve mobile sound recording and transcribing. In particular, the field study informs the sound information needed, situations of use, social implications, and the need for feasible human-in-the-loop systems.

People found the following information valuable in transcriptions: speech, descriptions of speaker voices (*e.g.,* gender, emotion), and environmental sounds. Other applications that transcribe sound will want to consider these pieces of information. An example application similar to Scribe4Me is a tool for travelers that translates speech into the user's language. Even though a user is primarily interested in speech, descriptions of speaker's voices and environmental sounds would be useful for placing the voices in context. Some situations in which users found Scribe4Me valuable may be useful for travelers: in conversations, using machines with voices, and announcements. Travelers may have addition needs, such as reading signs or notices that could be supported by translating text in photographs taken with the tool.

We learned about limitations of Scribe4Me that would likely be issues for similar applications. It is difficult to use in face-to-face conversations due to social expectations of eye contact and attention. Also, the most difficult situations for accurate transcriptions are loud environments (*e.g.,* restaurants) and situations with multiple conversations (*e.g.,* in a classroom). Difficulties were caused by background sounds drowning out more interesting sounds, not knowing which sounds were of interest to the user, and parsing sentences and conversations when multiple occurred at once.

Finally, results from our study provide motivation for exploring lower cost solutions to including humans in the system. While human are often included in telecommunication and video relay services for the deaf [6], these services are costly. Some projects have explored distributing work among many people on the Web [18, 24]. Scribe4Me or similar applications, could be powered by a huge pool of Internet users who share the transcribing load.

6.3 Summary

Results of the 2-week field study with 6 users showed that Scribe4Me had valued uses for both the deaf and hard-of-hearing. Though two weeks is not long enough to eliminate novelty effects, data gathered about when Scribe4Me is useful and how we can improve it are valuable. Participants acknowledged the affects of novelty on their usage but still considered the tool useful: "I could see a tool like this being a useful ongoing thing in my life… but I wouldn't use it that often as I did in the last couple of weeks in my daily life." Participants found it useful to "hear" people speaking, machines with voice prompts, announcements in public places, untranslated parts of lectures, the radio, and environmental sounds. The tool was often not useful in face-to-face communication due to the response delay and limited audio quality. Participants suggested several other improvements: that the length of captured audio could be chosen, an external microphone for better audio quality, a way to indicate which thing or person to focus on in transcriptions, and long transcription text in one message.

Recording others' voices introduced privacy issues to which participants were sensitive. Despite social issues, participants used the tool throughout the study and all predicted they would continue using it and would pay for it as part of a service plan.

7 Future Work and Conclusions

We presented the design and evaluation of Scribe4Me, a mobile sound transcription tool for the deaf and hard-of-hearing to improve awareness of sound information in any location. Results of a 2-week field study with 6 users showed many valuable uses. Technical hurdles for future iterations are to reduce the response delay and to improve the recorded audio quality. With these issues solved, users expected that it would be an even more powerful tool for communication and environmental awareness.

While it is possible to use humans for transcription in a full system, automated translation of non-speech audio may be an option in the future. We plan to address response time issues by adding support for a live (phone) connection in interactive settings, and by leveraging faster 4G networks or open WiFi networks when possible. Finally, future versions will encourage informed consent when audio recording other people, perhaps with a prompt to remind users.

Lastly, we are interested in using what we learned to explore new applications with remote transcription. For example, a similar tool could be used by travelers to translate different languages in settings where existing automated translation tools fail.

References

1. Akyol, S. and Alvarado, P.: Finding Relevant Image Content for Mobile Sign Language Recognition. In: Proc. of SPPRA. (2001) 48-52.
2. Auer, E.T., Bernstein, L.E. and Coulter, D.C.: Temporal and Spatio-Temporal Vibrotactile Displays for Voice Fundamental Frequency: An Initial Evaluation of a New Vibrotactile Speech Perception Aid with Normal-Hearing and Hearing-Impaired Individuals. J. of the Acoustical Society of America, 104, 4, (1998) 2477-2489.
3. Black, A.W., Brown, R.D., Frederking, R., K. Lenzo, J., Moody, A., Rudnicky, Singh, R. and Steinbrecher, E.: Rapid Development of Speech-to-Speech Translation Systems. In: Proc. of ICSLP. (2002) 1709-1712.
4. California Foundation for Independent Living Centers (2003), NorthView Wins Exclusive Rights to Market SpeechView's Solutions for Deaf. Assistive Technology Journal, 65, www.atnet.org/news/2003/jan03/011504.htm.
5. Carter, S. and Mankoff, J.: When Participants Do the Capturing: The Role of Media in Diary Studies. In: Proc. of CHI. (2005) 899 - 908.
6. Federal Communications Commission (2006), What You Need To Know About TRS. www.fcc.gov/cgb/dro/trs.html.
7. Cook, A.M. and Hussey, S.M.: Assistive Technologies: Principles and Practice. Mosby, Inc., St. Louis, (2002).
8. Deaf Studies Trust (2003), WISDOM: Wireless Information Services for Deaf people On the Move. www.deafstudiestrust.org.uk/research_projects/wisdom.htm.
9. Doyle, M. and Dye, L. Mainstreaming the Student Who is Deaf of Hard-of-Hearing, Alexander Graham Bell Association for the Deaf and Hard-of-Hearing, 2002.
10. Edwards, A.D.N.: Progress in Sign Language Recognition. In: Gesture and Sign-Language in Human-Computer Interaction. (1997) 13-21.
11. Elssmann, S.F. and Maki, J.E.: Speech Spectrographic Display: Use of Visual Feedback by Hearing-Impaired Adults During Independent Articulation Practice. American Annals of the Deaf, 132, 4, (1987) 276–279.
12. Hudson, S. and Mankoff, J.: Rapid Construction of Functioning Physical Interfaces from Cardboard, Thumbtacks and Masking Tape. In: Proc. of UIST. (2006) To Appear.
13. Huenerfauth, M. Survey and Critique of ASL Natural Language Generation and Machine Translation Systems Technical Report MS-CIS-03-32, University of Pennsylvania, 2003.
14. Iachello, G., Truong, K., Abowd, G., Hayes, G. and Stevens, M.: Event-Contingent Experience Sampling To Evaluate Ubicomp Technology In The Real World. In: Proc. of CHI. (2006) 1009-1018.
15. Liu, F.H., Gu, L., Gao, Y. and Picheny, M.: Use of Statistical N-Gram Models in Natural Language Generation for Machine Translation. In: Proc. of ICASSP. (2003) 636-639.
16. Mann, W.C. and Lane, J.P.: Assistive Technology for Persons with Disabilities. The American Occupational Therapy Association, Inc., Bethesda, MD, (1995).

17. Matthews, T., Fong, J., Ho-Ching, F.W. and Mankoff, J.: Evaluating Non-Speech Sound Visualizations for the Deaf. Behaviour & Information Technology, (2006) In Press.
18. Mycroft (2006). harbinger.sims.berkeley.edu/dmc/public/.
19. Pastor, M., Sanchis, A., Casacuberta, F. and Vidal, E.: EuTrans: a Speech-to-Speech Translator Prototype. In: Proc. of Eurospeech. (2001) 2385-2389.
20. Power, M.R. and Power, D.: Everyone here speaks TXT: Deaf People Using SMS in Australia and the Rest of the World. J. of Deaf Studies & Deaf Education, 9, 3, (2004) 350-360.
21. Schmandt, C., Lee, K., Kim, J. and Ackerman, M.: Impromptu: Managing Networked Audio Applications for Mobile Users. In: Proc. of MobiSys. (2004) 59 - 69.
22. Sonido Incorporated (2003), Auditory Visual Articulation Therapy Software. www.sonidoinc.com.
23. The Reporters Committee for Freedom of the Press (2003), The First Amendment Handbook. www.rcfp.org/handbook/c03p01.html.
24. von Ahn, L., Liu, R. and Blum, M.: Peekaboom: A Game for Locating Objects in Images. In: Proc. of CHI. (2006) 55-64.
25. Woszczyna, M., Coccaro, N., Eisele, A., Lavie, A., McNair, A., Polzin, T., Rogina, I., Rose, C.P., Sloboda, T., Tomita, M., Tsutsumi, J., Aoki-Waibel, N., Waibel, A. and Ward, W.: Recent Advances in JANUS: A Speech Translation System. In: Proc. of Eurospeech. (1993) 1295-1298.

SenseCam: A Retrospective Memory Aid

Steve Hodges, Lyndsay Williams, Emma Berry, Shahram Izadi,
James Srinivasan, Alex Butler, Gavin Smyth, Narinder Kapur[*], and Ken Wood

Microsoft Research, 7 JJ Thomson Avenue,
Cambridge, CB3 0FB, UK
{shodges, lyn, v-emmabe, shahrami, i-james, v-alexbu,
gavin.smyth, krw}@microsoft.com
http://research.microsoft.com/sendev/
* Cambridge Memory Clinic, R3 Neurosciences, Box 83,
Addenbrooke's Hospital, Cambridge, CB2 2QQ, UK
narinder.kapur@addenbrookes.nhs.uk

Abstract. This paper presents a novel ubiquitous computing device, the Sense-Cam, a sensor augmented wearable stills camera. SenseCam is designed to capture a digital record of the wearer's day, by recording a series of images and capturing a log of sensor data. We believe that reviewing this information will help the wearer recollect aspects of earlier experiences that have subsequently been forgotten, and thereby form a powerful retrospective memory aid. In this paper we review existing work on memory aids and conclude that there is scope for an improved device. We then report on the design of SenseCam in some detail for the first time. We explain the details of a first in-depth user study of this device, a 12-month clinical trial with a patient suffering from amnesia. The results of this initial evaluation are extremely promising; periodic review of images of events recorded by SenseCam results in significant recall of those events by the patient, which was previously impossible. We end the paper with a discussion of future work, including the application of SenseCam to a wider audience, such as those with neurodegenerative conditions such as Alzheimer's disease.

1 Introduction

Human memory is all too fallible – most of us frequently forget things that we have to do, and often find it hard to recall the details around what we have previously done. Of course, for those with clinically diagnosed memory disorders – which are by their nature more severe than those found in the average population – these issues are particularly troublesome. One example of such a diagnosis is acquired brain injury, which occurs either through a disease with lasting effect on brain tissue, or a traumatic incident like a car accident. Another example, perhaps of more significance in an aging population, is neurodegenerative disease – essentially an illness which damages the brain such that there is no possibility of recovery. The most prevalent neurodegenerative disease is Alzheimer's disease.

The effects of acquired brain injuries, neurodegenerative diseases and aging in general vary greatly from patient to patient. In a relatively moderate form, there may be

P. Dourish and A. Friday (Eds.): Ubicomp 2006, LNCS 4206, pp. 177–193, 2006.

little noticeable effect – perhaps a patient will be frustrated from time-to-time at their inability to organize themselves as well as they used to. At a more extreme level, a patient may suffer from a near complete inability to remember. Patients with moderate to severe memory problems may fail to remember future intentions, such as buying milk, or making and keeping appointments (*prospective memory*). Prospective memory problems clearly have a big impact on the ability of a patient to look after themselves on a day-to-day basis. A failure of past (*retrospective*) memory, however, and in particular *episodic* or *autobiographical* memory (i.e. the memory of things the patient has done, as opposed to their semantic memory for factual information) is actually critical for a patient to enjoy any real quality of life. This is firstly because nearly all future actions are based on past experiences, so practical day-to-day planning is very difficult when autobiographical memory is impaired. Secondly, and perhaps more importantly, a memory of past experiences is critical to a patient's 'self-concept'. For example, without a memory of shared experiences it is very hard to maintain any kind of relationship, whether it is professional, social or personal. This in turn frequently affects the patient's self-esteem, which can have significant knock-on effects on their well-being [13].

This paper presents a novel ubiquitous computing device, a wearable camera that keeps a digital record of the events that a person experiences. The nature of the device is to take these recordings automatically, without any user intervention and therefore without any conscious effort. We call the device SenseCam [4, 7] because two of the main components of its operation are **sens**ing its environment and using a built-in stills **cam**era to record images.[1] The rationale behind SenseCam is that having captured a digital record of an event, it can subsequently be reviewed by the wearer in order to stimulate their memory.

This paper describes the technology behind SenseCam in detail for the first time, presenting the design of our latest prototype (version 2.3) and discussing some of the issues that have come to light during its development. It also outlines a desktop application that has been developed in tandem with the hardware, to facilitate the viewing of data captured by SenseCam. The prototype hardware and software have been tested in an early clinical trial by a patient suffering from amnesia, and the promising results of this work are presented and discussed.

2   Related Work

The use of external memory aids to help people to compensate for their memory deficits is thought to be one of the most valuable and effective ways to aid rehabilitation (see [13] for a review). Most external memory aids serve to improve prospective memory; that is, they help people to remember to keep appointments, take medication and so forth. Many different types of device are available, including calendars, diaries, alarm watches, whiteboards, timers, post-it notes and more sophisticated tools, such as hand-held electronic schedulers. The combined use of these prospective aids has been effective in increasing independence in brain injured patients [13].

---

[1] "Cam" is also significant because the camera was conceived and built in Cambridge, UK.

In contrast, there are few external memory aids designed to improve the ability to remember past experiences. Perhaps the two most obvious examples of retrospective memory aids are cameras and diaries. Reviewing photographs and written diaries may stimulate memory for past events, e.g. photos of a family holiday ten years earlier or notes taken in a meeting two days previously [1, 13]. For example, in one study Bourgeois [1] used photographs to aid conversational skills in people with dementia. Not only did quality of conversation improve, but the memory aid appeared to prompt more general memories related to each item. Of course, in order to stimulate memory in this way, an investment of time and effort must be made *at the time of the original event* (or closely thereafter) in anticipation of a benefit many days or even many decades later. Unfortunately, experience shows that many people find it difficult to remember to take regular photos or keep diaries through their day (especially if they have a diagnosed memory disorder).

It is not surprising that photographs act as a memory stimulant – the importance of visual images in memory functioning is well established. Autobiographical memory is thought to be rich in visual imagery [2, 3]. Brewer [3] found that more than 80% of randomly sampled memories consisted of visual images. This emphasis on visual memory, and the successful role of photographs in memory recall, provides a strong indicator for the use of cameras as aids for autobiographical memory. However, traditional stills cameras have a number of drawbacks when used as a memory aid. Firstly, the patient has to remember to use the camera regularly, which is clearly a stumbling block. In addition, the act of stopping to take a photograph is very disruptive; it can break the patient's train of thought and it may be inappropriate from a social perspective. Finally, the resulting photographs may end up being quite staged rather than forming a simple record of events as they happened. It seems that some kind of 'wearable' camera which automatically captures images through the day might overcome some of these problems.

Wearable cameras have an established role in ubiquitous and wearable computing research and are now also appearing as consumer products [6, 18]. These devices are essentially manually-triggered cameras that can be worn. Mann [17] describes the implementation of WearCam, a wearable head mounted video camera, which can be user-triggered to take video of interesting events. HP's Casual Capture prototype [10] is an always-on wearable video camera. In order to manage the tremendous amount of data such a device captures, HP suggest the use of subsequent image processing to select 'interesting' images and short video clips.

Researchers have also begun to address the issue of automated capture control for wearable cameras. StartleCam [9] comprises of a wearable video camera, a computer (housed in a rucksack), and offboard skin conductance sensors. The system looks for patterns within the skin conductivity signal, which cause the camera to capture video, and optionally, download content to a webserver using onboard wireless communications. Hoisko [11] describes a wearable video camera, heads-up display and DAT recorder for capturing time triggered images and audio, and providing context triggered playback. IR beacons are deployed in the environment to associate a series of captured images and audio with a location. When the user is next in that particular location the appropriate recordings can be played back. Although a rudimentary prototype, the work is significant as it highlights the benefits that such captured data can provide in supporting recall of autobiographical memory.

In order to serve as a useful retrospective memory aid, a wearable camera needs to be very practical. Issues such as ease of use during capture and replay are paramount. The motivation for SenseCam is to extend and unify the body of work reviewed here to create a small, low power, easy to operate and carry, wearable camera, which can automatically capture images of a person's day using purely onboard sensing.

3 SenseCam

SenseCam is a small digital camera that is designed to take photographs automatically, without user intervention, whilst it is being worn (Figure 1). Unlike a regular digital camera or a cameraphone, it does not have a view finder or a display that can be used to frame photos. Instead, it is fitted with a wide-angle (fish-eye) lens that maximizes its field-of-view. This in turn means that nearly everything in view of the wearer is captured by the camera. Examples of the images taken by SenseCam are shown in Figure 2. In addition to the camera functionality, a number of different electronic sensors are built into SenseCam. These sensors are monitored by the camera's microprocessor, and certain changes in sensor readings can be used to automatically trigger a photograph to be taken. For example, a significant change in light level, or the detection of body heat in front of the camera can be used as triggers. Additionally, an internal timer may be used to trigger photograph capture, causing a photo to be taken automatically every 30 seconds, for example. SenseCam also has a manual

Fig. 1. The SenseCam v2.3 prototype shown standalone and as typically worn by a user. The model pictured here has a clear plastic case which reveals some of the internal components.

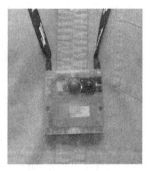

Fig. 2. Example images captured by SenseCam

trigger button that lets the wearer take pictures in the more traditional fashion and an on-off button which can be used to save the battery and prevent any sensor data logging/photograph capture. LEDs and an internal sounder are used to give the wearer feedback.

3.1 Design Requirements

Experience with early prototypes showed that the form factor of SenseCam is crucial. It must be convenient to put on and take off, and reasonably small and light so that it is comfortable whilst being worn. In trials to date, users have worn the camera on a lanyard around their neck, and this appears to meet these two criteria for most people, most types of clothing, and in most conditions. Our experience shows that ideally the camera should be worn reasonably high-up (towards the eye-line); this tends to generate more compelling images. In addition, the case of the SenseCam has been designed to allow the camera to stand freely on a flat surface. This allows the camera to be temporarily taken off and placed in an interesting vantage point – for example on a table or a shelf – thereby generating images from a third-person point of view. This is not practical for memory-loss patients (who might forget to put the camera back on), but gives flexibility as user trials are extended to a wider population.

In addition to the form factor of the device, other equally important practical issues include battery lifetime, storage capacity and ease of use. Experience with early SenseCam prototypes showed that it was critical for the device to operate for an entire day (i.e. 8-12 hours of continuous operation), and ideally for two to three days in case the patient forgets to recharge it or does not have a charger with them. A related requirement is enough storage for at least one day's worth of data, and ideally in excess of one week. This again means that if the patient forgets to upload data that the device can still be used the following day. With enough on-board storage, it would be possible to travel without needing a computer for data upload every evening. In this case, it is important that image upload time is not excessive.

3.2 SenseCam Hardware Design and Architecture

The SenseCam is built around a PIC 18F8722 6 MIPS microcontroller with 128KB of flash memory, 4KB RAM, copious general purpose I/O (GPIO) lines and several on-chip peripherals including PWM, UART, I^2C and SPI. Table 1 lists the major components in addition to the PIC along with their basic specifications and method of interface. Note that although a standard SD card is used, thereby supporting up to 2GB of flash memory in the camera, this card is not designed to be removed by the end user – it is hidden within the device. Instead, a high-speed mini-USB connection is used to copy data to and from the camera. This USB connectivity is achieved using a non-standard approach – the SD card is actually multiplexed between the PIC microcontroller (which is selected when the SenseCam is recording data) and an off-the-shelf USB-to-SD card interface chip (which is selected when a USB connection is detected). This allows us to support high speed USB 2.0 operation, which allows data to be transferred at approximately 4MB/s (around 175 images per second, or 10,000 per minute). Early experiments showed that without the speed of USB 2.0 transfer of large amounts of data (e.g. several days' worth) was unacceptably slow. Figure 3 shows the basic architecture of the SenseCam. Figure 4 depicts the front and the back of the SenseCam PCB, highlighting the main hardware components.

The VGA resolution images recorded by SenseCam are stored as compressed JPEG files on the internal SD memory card. The typical image size (around 30k bytes) allows for around 30 thousand images to be stored on a 1GB SD card. This clearly exceeds the design requirements for multi-day storage capacity. In addition to image data, the memory card is used to store a log file, which records the data from the sensors every few seconds in comma-separated variable format. The log file also records the reason for taking each photograph (e.g. manual shutter press, timed capture or significant change in sensor readings). The SenseCam has a built-in real time clock that ensures the timestamps of all files on the storage card are accurate. Timestamp information is also recorded in the log file along with each entry.

Table 1. The main peripherals (including all sensors) in the v2.3 SenseCam, with a summary of their specification and the method of interface to the PIC microcontroller

Component	Part number	Specification	Interface
Flash memory	Standard SD card	To 2GB (1GB standard)	SPI
Camera module	CoMedia C328-7640	VGA (onboard JPEG compression)	UART
Camera lens	Marshall Electronics V-4301.9-2.0FT-IRC	119º (diag) wide-angle lens w/ IR filter	n/a
Accelerometer	Kionix KXP84	Tri-axis	I²C
Temperature	Nat Semi LM75	Range -55 to +125ºC, ±2ºC	I²C
Real-time clock	Maxim/Dallas DS1340		I²C
Light level	TAOS TCS230	RGB intensity	PWM
Passive IR (PIR)	Seiko SKP-MS401	Miniature form factor	GPIO
Push buttons	Omron B3F-3150		GPIO
Sounder	Murata PKLCS1212		PWM
Audio recording[2]	Oki MS87V1021	2Mb DRAM for 60s audio at 8ksps	SPI
GPS[3]	n/a	External GPS unit	BT

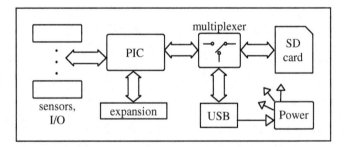

Fig. 3. The basic architecture of the SenseCam. A PIC microcontroller (6 MIPS, 128kB flash and 4kB RAM) interfaces with the major components. A digital multliplexer allows the SD card to be accessed by the PIC.

---

[2] Audio recording is still under development, and has not yet been tested in a user trial. Audio level (i.e. volume) sensing is present, however.

[3] GPS information from a standalone Bluetooth GPS receiver can be logged by the SenseCam using the Bluetooth plug-in unit (see Section 3.4). This has not yet been tested in a user trial.

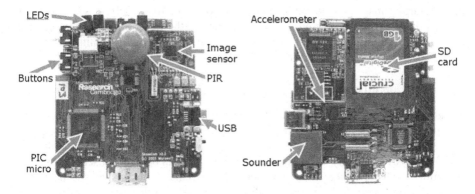

Fig. 4. The front and back of the SenseCam PCB (left and right respectively)

The SenseCam is powered from a built-in 980mAh 3.7V lithium ion rechargeable battery, from which 3.3V and 5V supplies are generated using a linear regulator and DC-DC converter respectively. The battery is recharged from a PC or from a mains power adapter over a USB connection. It takes around three hours to recharge using mains power, and ten hours to recharge whilst connected to a PC. In order to maintain the real-time clock and to detect the connection of a USB host when the SenseCam is not being used, there is no hard on-off switch. Instead, pressing the 'power' button causes the SenseCam to enter a very low power standby mode. The hardware is designed so that all peripherals which consume more than ~10uA in their lowest power state are subject to explicit power control by the microcontroller. This results in a total power consumption of 152uA in standby mode, which in turn means that the Sense-Cam will maintain its real-time clock for up to nine months without use.

The table shown in Figure 5 presents the power consumption of the SenseCam in its various operating modes. The most power is consumed when capturing images and saving them to flash memory. This means that battery lifetime depends on how frequently images are taken on average; the graph in Figure 5 shows this. Here we see

Mode	Description	Power consumption
Standby	Waiting for USB connection or power on, RTC running	152uA
Running	Microcontroller active but no sensing or logging	20.5mA
Sensor capture	Sensors being read and logged	35.0mA
Image capture	Image (or audio) being transferred to SD card	104mA

Fig. 5. The main operating modes of the SenseCam, and the associated current consumption for each of these (table left). Graph showing how battery life is affected by frequency of image capture (graph right).

that capturing images at the maximum rate of once approximately every 5 seconds yields a battery life just below 12 hours. Typically the SenseCam captures images every 30 seconds or so, yielding a battery life close to 24 hours of continuous operation. This meets the design requirement outlined in Section 3.1.

3.3 SenseCam Firmware

We employ a simple algorithm to trigger the camera based on data from the onboard sensors. The aim is to capture images of significant events, but without capturing excessive numbers of images. In theory, it would be possible for SenseCam to simply capture images as quickly as possible and then to select an optimal subset of these at a later time. However, there are a number of disadvantages to this approach from a practical point of view. In particular this would use significantly more power and memory which would likely violate our design requirements. Also, we felt that a wearable device that continuously captures images is more likely to arouse concern about privacy than something that takes a snapshot every thirty seconds or so.

The sensor-based algorithm used in the camera automatically triggers image capture if there is a significant change in light level, temperature or audio level. In addition, if the device is stationary (detected from accelerometer readings) and the PIR detects movement then image capture is also triggered. Finally, if no picture has been taken within a set timeframe (e.g. 30 seconds) then a picture is automatically taken. Sensors can be individually enabled or disabled at run time, through the use of a configuration file on the SD memory card. This file can be created or edited using a standard text editor while the SenseCam is connected to a PC over USB. When the SenseCam is then disconnected, the firmware updates the real-time clock if appropriate and reads in any new configuration settings.[4] Not only does this aid testing and development, but it makes it possible for patients themselves (or their carers) to tailor behaviour to suit particular requirements.

3.4 Developing and Extending SenseCam

From the outset it was clear that whatever selection of sensors was included in the SenseCam design, there would always be scenarios which warranted experimentation with additional types of sensors and hardware components. For this reason, the camera has an expansion port which exposes various electrical signals to facilitate the retro-fitting of additional functionality. The specific signals exposed (PIC in-circuit programming and debugging, power supply, general purpose I/O and communication buses) were chosen to provide the maximum flexibility for development, debugging and future expansion.

So far, we have built two different plug-in units. The first is a miniature 'external camera' that connects to the SenseCam via a flying lead. This can be used in place of the built-in camera – so that the SenseCam unit itself can be worn inside a pocket for example, to protect it from the rain. Alternatively, the external camera may be used as a second image capture device – to generate a larger field of view, or to take images in two different directions (e.g. facing forwards and backwards simultaneously). The

---

[4] To achieve the necessary PC compatibility, the SenseCam uses the FAT filesystem format. The associated firmware was developed from scratch in order to meet the PIC RAM limitations.

second plug-in device we have built for SenseCam is a Bluetooth adaptor, shown in Figure 6. This secures to the bottom of the main unit, making the camera body a little longer. A serial port profile connection may be established between the SenseCam and an external Bluetooth device to allow images to be sent wirelessly from the SenseCam to that device. For example, images sent to a Smartphone can be displayed on the phone or uploaded to a remote server over GPRS. It is also possible to use the Bluetooth plug-in to connect additional sensing devices. Examples which we are currently experimenting with include GPS and a heart-rate monitor.

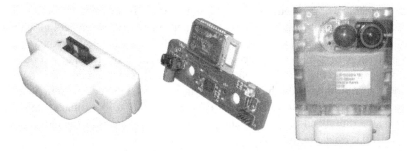

Fig. 6. The Bluetooth expansion adapter and the PCB shown on the left, and the assembled unit shown attached to a SenseCam on the right. It plugs directly into the SenseCam expansion connector and is secured from below with two M3 screws.

3.5 Replaying Captured Data

In addition to the SenseCam itself, we have also developed a PC-based viewer application (shown in Figure 7) that can be used to manage and replay image sequences and sensor data captured by the device at a later date.

Fig. 7. The SenseCam viewer application, allowing playback and review of SenseCam images and associated sensor readings

When the user attaches the SenseCam to a PC, the SenseCam Image Viewer software will automatically download the images and sensor data. The basis of the viewer, which is designed to be very straightforward to use, is a window in which images are displayed, and a simple VCR-type control which allows an image sequence to be played slowly (around 2 images/second), quickly (around 10 images/second), re-wound and paused. The fast-play option creates a kind of 'flip-book' movie effect – the entire event represented by he images is replayed as a time-compressed movie. It is possible to delete individual images from the sequence if they are badly framed or of poor quality. An additional option is provided to correct for the 'fish-eye' lens effect using an algorithm which applies an inverse model of the distortion. With long sequences of images, it can be useful to associate 'bookmarks' with certain images. A bookmark is created by pausing playback on the image in question, and then clicking on the 'Add' button at the bottom left of the screen. The bookmark will appear as a thumbnail on the left of the window, and a user can assign a name to it. Once created, bookmarks can be used to help navigate a long image sequence – clicking on the thumbnail of a bookmark automatically advances or rewinds playback to that particular image in the sequence.

There are several options for playback. It is possible to display an analogue clock face to the right of the image sequence during playback to indicate at what time of day the image currently displayed was originally taken. It is also possible to load and display the raw sensor data associated with an image sequence, although this feature was not used in our user study. An example is shown inset in Figure 7. One final option in the viewer software is to process the entire sequence of images to determine which images are most like each other, using an image similarity algorithm based on textons [12]. This effectively splits the image sequence into segments of related images, which may aid navigation of long sequences in particular.

4 Assessing SenseCam as a Retrospective Memory Aid

In order to test the hypothesis that SenseCam can be used as a retrospective memory aid, a preliminary study was conducted to evaluate its ability to improve recent autobiographical memory in a patient with amnesia. By capturing an event using SenseCam, and subsequently reviewing the captured data regularly, we hoped that the patient could use the SenseCam images as a pictorial diary to both cue and to consolidate autobiographical memories.

The patient for this study, referred to here as Mrs B, is a 63 year-old well educated woman, married to a retired businessman (Mr B). In March 2002, Mrs B was admitted to hospital with fever and confusion and was diagnosed with limbic encephalitis (inflammation of deep structures of the brain). Subsequent MRI scans revealed bilateral cell loss in the hippocampus, an important memory structure (see Figure 8). After her recovery from the physical illness, an assessment of Mrs B's cognitive functioning revealed that she had significant memory problems. Typically, Mrs B now only has partial recall of a significant event a couple of days after the event. After a week, she

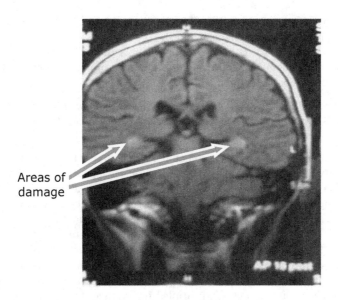

Areas of
damage

Fig. 8. Magnetic resonance (MRI) brain scan of Mrs B showing bilateral hippocampal lesions (the two brighter areas either side of the midline)

has no recall at all of the event.[5] Mrs B has tried to maintain and regularly review a written diary in order to improve this situation, but as is typical for people in her condition, she finds this a burden and it has little beneficial effect.

4.1   Evaluating the Effect of SenseCam on Short-Term Recall

Mrs B was given a SenseCam and asked, with the help of her husband, to wear it whenever she anticipated a 'significant event' – the sort of event that she would like to remember (i.e. not just something routine or mundane). After wearing SenseCam for the duration of such an event, Mr and Mrs B uploaded the SenseCam data to a laptop computer, but they *would not* review the data at all at this stage. The next day, Mr B asked his wife if she recalled the previous day's events. Mr B noted what Mrs B said about the events, and these responses were later graded. After noting her responses, Mr B immediately showed Mrs B the images from the SenseCam using the SenseCam image viewer software described in Section 3.5. Typically, they would run through the images one-at-a-time at first, and then review the entire sequence as a flip-book movie.[6] This was done up to three times, and Mr and Mrs B would talk about the images and the event as they did this. Two days later, Mr B again asked his wife what she remembered of the event that had occurred a few days previously. As before, he graded her responses and then showed her the SenseCam images. Two days later, the procedure was again repeated, and so on for a period of two weeks or more.

---

[5] Mrs B also has difficulty recollecting events from a 30 year period prior to her illness, but apart from these memory issues, her cognitive functioning is otherwise intact.

[6] Mr B usually reviewed the images himself before showing any to Mrs B, and he deleted any that he thought were not useful, for example if they were blurred or very badly framed.

Mr B kept a log of how many times Mrs B had viewed the images of an event, and her corresponding recall of that event each time.

At the time of each event Mr B documented a number of key points which he felt were important or memorable. The following is an example of the key points noted on a trip to Southampton General Hospital.

> *'Drive to East Cowes, walk to ferry, ferry to Southampton, taxi to hospital, taxi back to shopping centre, shopping, light lunch, walk to ferry, walk to car, drive home'.*

Other examples of important points to remember might be that they met up with friends (and if so which friends), if anything memorable happened whilst they were out and so on. The assessment of Mrs B's memory of an event was based on her ability to remember the associated key points. If Mr B recorded 10 key events and Mrs B subsequently remembered 7 of them when she was tested, she scored 70% recall.

Over the course of three months, Mrs B used the SenseCam to record nine different significant events. Some of these events were quite close in time to each other (i.e. the tests were not done in complete isolation from each other). The results were very encouraging; over the course of a two week period of testing and review of a given event, Mrs B's recall of that event nearly tripled on average, to a point where she could typically remember nearly everything about that event. This is compared to the situation with no SenseCam where Mrs. B would usually have forgotten the little that she could initially remember within just a few days.

4.2 Testing SenseCam as a Longer-Term Autobiographical Memory Aid

Given the success of the short-term memory testing with Mrs B, it was decided to carry out a longer-term assessment of her recall. Due to the limited availability of SenseCam prototypes, this longitudinal test with Mrs B was at the expense of additional short-term trials with new patients. However, we felt that it was equally important to see if the positive effects were longer-lived. Also, Mr and Mrs B found the SenseCam so beneficial that they did not want to give it back!

At the end of the three month period during which Mr and Mrs B regularly reviewed SenseCam images as part of the short-term recall experiment outlined above, there was a one month period during which they did not view or explicitly talk about the associated events at all. At the end of this one month period, Mr B tested his wife on her recall of all nine events. He once again graded her responses in the manner described previously.

Remarkably, despite the fact that Mrs B's memory had not been stimulated with images from the events for an entire month, she still showed significant recall when tested. This prompted two further similar tests, but for periods of two and three months. In each case, Mrs B initially reviewed images from all nine events, and at the end of the period (during which she did not see or discuss images from any of the events) she was tested. Mrs B showed a 76% average recall across all the events at the final test. Once again, this appears to be exceptional, bearing in mind that the original occurrence of some of the events and had been as much as 11 months earlier. Recall at this level of detail and after such a long period has not previously been reported in the literature.

4.3 Comparison with a Meticulous Written Diary

The results of the short- and longer-term studies described above are incredibly promising. They indicate that if Mrs B is exposed to a period of review of SenseCam images, this acts to consolidate her own memories of the event and this in turn aids their
subsequent recall. However, it is possible that any kind of rigorous review of an event
would have a similar effect – in which case there is nothing particularly special about
the use of SenseCam as a memory aid. For this reason, Mr and Mrs B took part in one
final experiment.

The method for this experiment was analogous to those described above, but instead of Mrs B recording an event using SenseCam, her husband instead kept a detailed written diary of it. Mrs B was tested in the same way as before, but after each
test Mr and Mrs B reviewed the written diary (rather than SenseCam images). This
was done for three different events across a one-month period. The results indicate
that periodic review of such detailed diaries acts to maintain Mrs B's memory of an
event, but that as soon as there is a significant gap those memories are completely
lost. This differs to the results when SenseCam is used, where Mrs B's memory actually improved during the periodic reviews, and was maintained across very significant
gaps.

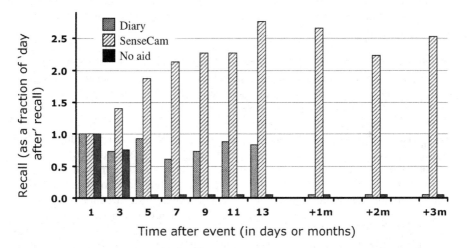

Fig. 9. Mrs B's recall of autobiographical events. Three conditions are plotted, namely recall
when no memory aid is used, the effect of reviewing a meticulous written diary, and what
happens when SenseCam is used.

4.4 Summary of Recall Testing

The results from all three experiments are brought together in Figure 9. Two events
were tested with no memory aid to demonstrate the baseline condition; in this case
Mrs B recalls nothing about an event that occurred just five days earlier, even if her
husband reminds her every couple of days. Three events were recorded with a meticulous written diary, and in this case Mrs B's memory can be maintained (more-or-less)
by way of periodic review. However, after a one month period of no review, this

memory is permanently lost. For the SenseCam study nine events were tested, and these clearly show two trends. Firstly, Mrs B's recall improves consistently ($X^2(1) = 62.59$, p<0.001) during the period of regular review, to the point where she can remember nearly three times as many details as she could before the first review. Secondly, in the SenseCam condition, Mrs B's ability to recall an event hardly reduces at all, even after a significant period during which that event has not even been mentioned. Such effects in an amnesic patient have never previously been reported.

5 Discussion

The study presented in the previous section demonstrates that through the use of SenseCam, a markedly amnesic patient was consistently able to remember aspects of several events. Recall was maintained almost a year after some of the events took place, and without any review of those events for up to three months. Since recall of a number of different events which occurred over a three month period was successfully demonstrated, it appears that there was little 'contamination' between the different events, which is clearly important. Equally significant is the anecdotal evidence reported by Mr and Mrs B during the period of the trial. Mrs B said that seeing the beginning of a clip brought memories *'flooding back'*. Her descriptions of events demonstrated that she remembered the events themselves, rather than the SenseCam pictures alone. For example, she would remark that someone had been rude to her on a particular day, or that the food hadn't tasted nice – clearly this information is being recalled from her own memory. Additionally, we observed that Mr. B. was always quick to point out when his wife was retelling facts or a narrative that she had learned rather than having a true recollective experience, suggesting that these would not be mistaken as false positives. These observations reflect very positively on the ability of SenseCam to act as a valuable, practical retrospective memory aid.

It is also worth noting that Mrs B's subjective levels of anxiety reduced when wearing SenseCam. Before she started using the device, she lacked confidence in company and was generally anxious in everyday life, which is common in patients with memory loss. However, when using SenseCam she felt more confident about her memory and she was more able to relax at social events instead of feeling anxious. When asked about the effectiveness of SenseCam as an aid to improve autobiographical memory Mrs B said *'I think it is a terrific help, I really and truly do'*. This was confirmed by Mr B, who said that SenseCam *'significantly helps her recall'* and expressed his *'sheer pleasure'* at being able to share experiences with his wife again.

The diary was not nearly so effective a memory aid as SenseCam. It is also important to note that maintaining such a written diary takes a lot of work, and reviewing it is much harder work and therefore less pleasant. In fact, the written diary study was limited to just three events because Mr and Mrs B found it very onerous. Although external memory aids are well recognized as an effective form of rehabilitation, the people who most need them – people with memory disorders – almost always have the most difficulty using them. This is not just because the patient has to remember to use them, but also because memory aids often require executive skills (the ability to plan, organize, problem-solve and think flexibly), which are often affected after brain injury. Moreover the use of memory aids may entail a great deal of motivation and effort. Health professionals have to weigh up the potential benefit of the memory aid with the motivation and the skills of the patient to use them.

SenseCam has the potential to form a more suitable tool for patients in this regard. Because it autonomously captures images, it has particular benefits for acquired and degenerative brain injured patients, enabling them to record their experiences without the need to keep operating equipment and without conscious thought. Because it allows a person to truly participate in an event without having to pause to capture the moment, the patient does not feel burdened. In our trial, no particular concerns over privacy were raised. Of course, many of the people who may have been captured by SenseCam were probably not aware of it, but we believe that the low resolution of the images coupled with the infrequency of capture (around one frame every 30 seconds) are important factors in alleviating privacy concerns. Nonetheless, part of our agenda of future work with respect to SenseCam is a more thorough investigation of the privacy issues raised.

It is not clear what neurological processes enhanced Mrs B's recall of events recorded by SenseCam (and to a lesser extent, those recorded in the written diary). However, it seems that regular review coupled with the process of talking through the events, facilitated consolidation and recall of autobiographical memories that had already been encoded. Similarly, intermittent review could be characterized as a form of spaced repetition, in which learning trials are distributed over a period of time, allowing for gradual consolidation and reconsolidation of memories. This form of spaced presentation is thought to be an effective way of improving learning [16]. As discussed earlier, there is strong evidence that visual imagery is important to the consolidation and retention of autobiographical memories [3, 8]. It is therefore likely that the SenseCam images provided a particularly powerful set of stimuli or triggers that cued recall of previously stored memories. Although these explanations may account in part for Mrs B's successful recall of events, they do not explain in full the significant retention of these memories many months after the event with no further SenseCam presentations.

6   Conclusions and Future Work

The results of this preliminary study using SenseCam as a retrospective memory aid for patients with memory loss are very promising. Mrs B, the patient who took part in the work reported here, showed a significantly improved recall of autobiographical memories which was maintained in the long-term. Reviewing SenseCam image sequences is clearly a powerful aid to recall, although it is not completely obvious why this effect is so marked. We are planning a series of further clinical studies using advanced brain activity imaging techniques such as functional magnetic resonance imaging (fMRI), with the aim of determining what effect viewing a SenseCam image sequence has on activity in different parts of the brain. It is hoped that this will further our understanding of the neurological processes associated with recall.

Although we are taking steps towards capturing additional data to draw more significant conclusions, one theory on the promising results from initial trials of SenseCam is that because the images are from the wearer's point of view, the sequences more closely mimic human autobiographical memories. Furthermore, human memory is thought to be split into short time slices, delimited by changes in intent. That is, episodic memories are formed at goal junctions of action sequences when there is major change in the predominating goal [5]. It is possible therefore that the detection of changes in the wearer's activity and in their environment through onboard sensors caused the SenseCam to trigger at junctions of goal processing. Therefore, for these reasons it could well be possible that SenseCam produces images that are close in nature to visual autobiographical memories, providing a strong stimulus for recall.

We are also planning another programme of clinical trials with a wider variety of memory-loss patients, including those with different types of acquired brain injuries (such as epilepsy, accident and stroke), and also those with degenerative brain pathology (e.g. Alzheimer's disease and Semantic dementia). It is hoped that SenseCam will prove useful in these more general cases, in which case it could be a powerful tool for combatting the early effects of such conditions.[7] We are building more SenseCams and working with a number of leading clinicians and academics to carry out these studies. Finally, we are starting a series of further trials with Mrs B, in order to answer questions such as: 'What is the optimum time between experiencing a significant event and viewing images, in terms of a patient retaining memories of that event?', 'How often and at what interval are patients required to view the images in order for the memories to become consolidated?' and 'For how long are memories retained?'.

In addition to these clinical trials we are also carrying out experiments with the onboard sensors to investigate and improve the triggering algorithm. Currently we make extensive use of PIR, light, audio level and accelerometer data, but we will be experimenting with audio capture, temperature and location information from GPS, and comparing these more sophisticated approaches with the simpler approach of purely timer-triggered capture. We seek to enhance the therapeutic effect of SenseCam by optimising the capture and replay of images.

References

1. Bourgeois, M.S.: Enhancing conversation skills in patients with Alzheimer's disease using a prosthetic memory aid. Journal of Applied Behavior Analysis, 23 (1990), 29-32.
2. Brewer, W. F.: What is autobiographical memory? In D. Rubin (Ed.), Autobiographical Memory (pp. 25-49). Cambridge: Cambridge University Press, 1986.
3. Brewer, W. F.: Qualitative analysis of the recalls of randomly sampled autobiographical events. In M. M. Gruneberg, P. E. Morris, & R. N. Sykes (Eds.), Practical Aspects of Memory: Current Research and Issues (Vol. 1, pp. 263-268). Chichester: Wiley, 1988.
4. Cherry, S.: Total Recall, IEEE Spectrum, November 2005, pp. 25-30.
5. Conway, M.A.: Memory and the self. Journal of Memory and Language, 53: 594-628 (2005).
6. DejaView: CamWear, http://www.mydejaview.com/, March 2006.
7. Gemmell, Jim, Williams, Lyndsay, Wood, Ken, Bell, Gordon and Lueder, Roger: Passive Capture and Ensuing Issues for a Personal Lifetime Store, Proceedings of The First ACM Workshop on Continuous Archival and Retrieval of Personal Experiences (CARPE '04), Oct. 15, 2004, New York, NY, USA, pp. 48-55.
8. Greenberg, D.L. & Rubin, D.C: Cortex, 39, 687-728 (2003).

---

[7] SenseCam is unlikely to be particularly useful in late-stage Alzheimer's disease, when memory loss is typically coupled with other cognitive impairments, such as executive dysfunction, attentional problems and visual perceptual difficulties.

9. Healey, J. and Picard, R. StartleCam: A Cybernetic Wearable Camera. Proceedings of the International Symposium on Wearable Computing, Pittsburgh, Pennsylvania, 19-20 October 1998, pp. 42-49.

10. HP Laboratories, The Casual Capture Prototype, http://www.hpl.hp.com/news/2004/jan-mar/casualcapture.html, March 2006.

11. Hoisko, J.: Context Triggered Visual Episodic Memory Prosthesis, Proceedings of the International Symposium on Wearable Computing, Washington, DC, October 2000, pp. 185.

12. Julesz, B.: Textons, the elements of texture perception, and their interactions. Nature, 290(5802):91–7, March 1981.

13. Kapur, N., Glisky, E.L. & Wilson, B.A.: External memory aids and computers in memory rehabilitation. In A.D. Baddeley, M.D. Kopelman & B.A. Wilson (Eds.), The Hand-book of Memory Disorders, Second Edition (pp. 757-784). Chichester, UK: John Wiley, 2002.

14. Kime, S.K., Lamb, D.G. & Wilson, M.B.: Use of a comprehensive programme of external cueing to enhance procedural memory in a patient with dense amnesia. Brain Injury, 10, (1), 17-25 (1996).

15. Lamming, M., Brown, P., Carter, K., Eldridge, M., Flynn, M., Louie, G., Robinson, P., & Sellen, AJ. (1994). The design of a human memory prosthesis. Computer Journal, 37(3), 153-163.

16. Landauer, T.K. & Bjork, R.A.: Optimum rehearsal patterns and name learning. In M. M. Gruneberg, P. E. Morris, & R. N. Sykes (Eds.), Practical Aspects of Memory (pp. 625-632). London: Academic Press, 1978.

17. Mann, S.: Wearcam (The Wearable Camera), Proceedings of the International Symposium on Wearable Computers, pages 124-131, 1998.

18. Minox: DD1 Camera, http://www.minox.com/, March 2006.

19. Ueoka, T., Kawamura, T., Baba, S. , Yoshimura, S., Kono, Y. and Kidode, M.: Wearable Camera Device for Supporting Object-Triggered Memory Augmentation, The 3rd CREST/ISWC Workshop on Advanced Computing and Communicating Techniques for Wearable Information Playing, Arlington, VA, October 2004.

20. Wilson, B.A., Evans, J.J., Emslie, H. & Malinek, V.: Evaluation of NeuroPage: a new memory aid. Journal of Neurology, Neurosurgery and Psychiatry, 63, 113-115 (1997).

21. Wilson, B.A., Emslie, H.C., Quirk, K. & Evans, J.J.: Reducing everyday memory and planning problems by means of a paging system: a randomised control crossover study. Journal of Neurology, Neurosurgery and Psychiatry, 70, 477 – 482 (2001).

22. Woods, B.: Reducing the impact of cognitive impairment in dementia. In A.D. Baddeley, M.D. Kopelman & B.A. Wilson (Eds.), The Handbook of Memory Disorders, Second Edition (pp. 757-784). Chichester, UK: John Wiley, 2002.

Development of a Privacy Addendum for Open Source Licenses: Value Sensitive Design in Industry

Batya Friedman[1], Ian Smith[2], Peter H. Kahn Jr.[3],
Sunny Consolvo[2], and Jaina Selawski[4]

[1] Information School
University of Washington, Seattle, WA, USA
batya@u.washington.edu
[2] Intel Research, Seattle, WA, USA
{ian.e.smith, sunny.consolvo}@intel.com
[3] Department Of Psychology
University of Washington, Seattle, WA, USA
pkahn@u.washington.edu
[4] Intel Corporation, Santa Clara, CA, USA
jaina.c.selawski@intel.com

Abstract. Drawing on Value Sensitive Design, we developed a workable privacy addendum for an open source software license that not only covers intellectual property rights while allowing software developers to modify the software (the usual scope of an open source license), but also addresses end-user privacy. One central innovation of our work entails the integration of an informed consent model and a threat model for developing privacy protections for ubiquitous location aware systems. We utilized technology that provided a device's location information in real-time: Intel's POLS, a "sister" system to Intel's Place Lab. In January 2006, POLS was released under a license combining the substantive terms of the Eclipse Public License together with this privacy addendum. In this paper, we describe how we developed the privacy addendum, present legal terms, and discuss characteristics of our design methods and results that have implications for protecting privacy in ubiquitous information systems released in open source.

1   Introduction

Within the fields of ubiquitous computing and human-computer interaction, there has been increasing attention to issues of privacy. One strand of research, for example, has investigated users' views, values, and experience of privacy with respect to novel ubiquitous technologies [5,6,14,22,24,28,31]. A second strand has investigated conceptual models for privacy management that, in turn, can be used to guide subsequent technical work [1,25,27,30]. A third strand has investigated privacy-sensitive technical solutions [3,4,7,11,16,20,21].

All three strands remain vitally important. At the same time, we sought to break some new ground – conceptually, technically, and with respect to social policy. Specifically, we asked ourselves: Is it possible to create a workable open source software license that addresses the privacy rights of end-users of software in addition

P. Dourish and A. Friday (Eds.): Ubicomp 2006, LNCS 4206, pp. 194–211, 2006.

to the usual provisions of such licenses (that seek to protect, for example, intellectual property rights and the ability of software developers to modify the source code)? If so, what would such privacy protections look like? Can these protections be translated into enforceable legal terms? Should the protections be defined specifically for location aware systems, or could the protections and corresponding terms be defined more generally for ubiquitous information systems overall? How would the privacy terms be shaped by the technology and, in turn, how might the terms impact the technology development, interaction design, and user experience?

To even begin to answer such difficult questions, we believed we needed two components. First, we needed an actual implementation of technology that created potential privacy implications to think with and act upon. Here we chose a system for providing a device's location information in real-time – Intel's POLS (the Privacy Observant Location System, a "sister" system to Intel's Place Lab [26]). Second, we needed a robust research and design methodology to help structure our analyses. Here we utilized Value Sensitive Design [9,12,13].

In this paper, we first provide a brief background on open source software licenses, POLS, and Value Sensitive Design. Next we report on one of our central innovations: the working out individually of an informed consent model and a threat model for a ubiquitous location aware system, and then integrating the results of both models in the development of the privacy addendum. Then we present the legal terms of the addendum itself, emphasizing the intellectual source of its various terms. Finally, we conclude with a statement of our contributions, and some open questions and reflection on the co-evolution of technology and policy.

2   Open Source Software

The subjects of "free software [http://en.wikipedia.org/wiki/Free_software]" and "open source software [http://en.wikipedia.org/wiki/Open_source]" are complex and interrelated; as such, a full discussion of would be well outside the scope of this paper. At the highest level, both free and open source software provide a means for software developers to examine other developers' code so as to understand how the code works as well as to utilize and improve techniques manifested in the code. For the purpose of simplicity, we will define "free software" as software that allows use[1] *without any restrictions*, whereas open source may bear restrictions. We have chosen this simplification because it makes the privacy addendum's difference most clear; certainly there are many arguments about which difference between the two types is the "most important." Throughout this paper we describe our work as an extension of the open source idea to emphasize our commitment to the idea that just because a piece of software can be studied, does not mean that it may be used in any way that a developer wishes.

The principal idea and ideals of open source – the ability to share techniques and to "see under the covers" – has had broad implications for the intellectual community. Extending beyond software, the intellectual property framework developed for open

---

[1] Typically the "four freedoms" of free software are the ability study the software, copy the software, redistribute the software, and use the software without restriction.

source software has been generalized to include creative works (http://creativecommons.org/), courseware (http://ocw.mit.edu), and genetic code (http://rsss.anu.edu.au/~janeth/home.html). To date, the open source concept has not been extended beyond ownership and licensing of intellectual property to include in its scope other central social values, such as that of privacy. Moreover, the terms of most open source and free software licenses expressly prohibit modifications or additions to the terms of the license.

Thus, from the perspective of open source what we propose here offers two innovations: First, we sought to extend the construct of making intellectual output widely available under specific conditions to address commitments to privacy along with intellectual property. Second, we sought to construct the parameters for a small, vetted set of modifications or addenda that could be appended to and not invalidate the underlying open source license.

3   Genesis of an Idea, POLS, and the Problem of Pre-existing Open Source Software Licenses

In early discussions, we asked the question: How might the designers of Place Lab (http://placelab.org/) ensure that those who built upon that technology would continue Place Lab's privacy-sensitive practices? An intriguing potential solution emerged: that Place Lab's license terms would address commitments to end-user privacy along with the license to intellectual property.

Thus, the early thinking about the privacy addendum took Place Lab as its starting point. However, Place Lab was built using open source code licensed in part under the GPL, and as a result, the Place Lab code would be deemed a "derivative" and therefore subject to the GPL. Part way into the project, it became apparent that a new code base, unfettered by the complications of a pre-existing license (i.e. the GPL), would be needed to move the project forward. Thus a distinct, new system, POLS, the Privacy Observant Location System (http://pols.sourceforge.net/), was built from scratch, to allow the designers to license the code subject to the "restrictions" implemented in the privacy addendum, which would not be permitted under the GPL.

That said, POLS resembles Place Lab in many key respects. Currently running on mobile phone platforms, POLS uses the location data of "nearby" radio transmitters, *beacons*, to determine the location of the device running the POLS software. The output from POLS is roughly the longitude and latitude of that device. In terms of privacy, POLS is implemented with an in-bound information only architecture. This type of architecture dictates that the device passively monitors the radio environment (the in-bound information) and then computes its location locally without communicating with the infrastructure. Systems that rely on some outside infrastructure to locate a user's device inherently compromise the user's privacy to some degree, since the owners and operators of the infrastructure portion of the system are at least somewhat aware of the user's location. POLS works quite differently: Each user's device carries a list of known positions of the environments' beacons and the phone's radio is monitored too see which beacons can be "heard" at the present time, allowing POLS to estimate the location based on the known position of the beacon.

4   Value Sensitive Design

This research was conceived within the framework of Value Sensitive Design, a theoretically grounded approach to the design of technology that accounts for human values in a principled and comprehensive manner throughout the design process [9, 12,13]. Central to this work is Value Sensitive Design's interactional stance that articulates mutual dependencies and interconnections both across levels within the technology as well as between the technology and the surrounding social systems. Thus, we expected the technical features of POLS (and location aware systems more generally) to shape the requirements for the privacy addendum. For example, the privacy addendum would need to address the ways in which access to real-time location information can put end-users at risk. In turn, as we developed the privacy addendum, we expected our analyses to push back on how the technology should function. For example, analyses that required certain end-user capabilities – that the end-user be able to give active consent, to revoke prior consent, to remove data from the system – would require corresponding technical implementations.

In addition, prior work in Value Sensitive Design alerted us to two practical challenges that we would likely encounter [9,11,12]. The first involves the balance between human values and usability. Here, we anticipated places in the privacy addendum where we would need to relax the required stringency of a privacy protection in order to allow for a workable level of usability. The second involves limitations in the state of professional knowledge. Here, we recognized that we might encounter places in our privacy analyses which would suggest technical requirements that as a field we do not yet know how to meet. Should that occur, we would need to carefully identify such areas and set them aside for the time being. Moreover, the identification of such areas could provide useful information for setting the direction for new technical work and moving the field forward. Such an approach parallels that in other fields such as medicine, where the state of standard professional practice co-evolves with the state of medical knowledge.

Methodologically, key to Value Sensitive Design's conceptual investigations are stakeholder analyses that identify relevant stakeholders by role and examine how those stakeholders might be impacted by the system under investigation. In the case of POLS (and other ubiquitous location aware systems), three stakeholder groups were identified that became the focus of this work: the *application developer* who would build upon the ubiquitous open source system, the *end-user* who would experience the system's privacy implications, and *third parties* – malicious or otherwise – who might exploit the system for their own purposes. Specifically, we sought to balance end-user privacy protections with realistic demands on the application developer, in light of a technology that may be vulnerable to attack from third parties. Toward that end, two conceptual investigations were undertaken. The first examined the behaviors we wished to require or, at a minimum, to recommend on the part of the application developer. We employed an informed consent model here. The second investigation examined end-user vulnerabilities and the corresponding behaviors we wished to prevent on the part of the application developer or a third party. We employed a threat model here. Results from the two models were then integrated.

5 Development of the Privacy Addendum

We report on our analyses, deliberations, and eventual design decisions that led to the privacy addendum.

5.1 Informed Consent Model

Informed consent provides a powerful construct for providing privacy protections by empowering the end-user with knowledge and choice about participation. In effect, when implemented well informed consent creates conditions by which end-users are positioned to protect themselves and their privacy as they want through selective participation. To develop initial parameters for the privacy addendum, we drew on an established model for informed consent for information systems, one that has been applied successfully in areas such as network security, cookies and web browsers, and web email [10,15].

The informed consent model is comprised of six components: *disclosure, comprehension, voluntariness, competence, agreement*, and *minimal distraction*. We systematically examined each component to identify design requirements. Our strategy was to require those that were reasonable given current technical knowledge and practices; others that we judged to be desirable but too difficult to implement or beyond the state of current knowledge, we would recommend or set aside completely. Throughout these deliberations, we used our experience with ubiquitous location aware systems in general, and POLS in particular, to ground our analyses in real features and consequences.

Table 1 summarizes the informed consent model and implications of our analyses for the privacy addendum. We describe each component in turn.

Disclosure
The act of informing entails disclosing appropriate and accurate information to the intended audience. In particular, end-users of ubiquitous location aware systems will likely want to know: (a) what information will be collected (e.g., my current location, including an association with a place name such as Seward Park); (b) who will have access to the information (e.g., my spouse and children); (c) how long the information will be archived (e.g., on the order of hours); (d) what the information will be used for (e.g., to coordinate family activities, such as soccer carpool); and (e) how the identity of the individual will be protected(e.g., not at all). With that information in hand, end-users are positioned to decide if they want to participate in use of the system for these purposes. As shown in Table 1, there is a close overlap between the type and level of specificity of information the informed consent model suggests be disclosed and that identified for the privacy addendum.

Comprehension
In order to truly inform, what is disclosed must be understood by the intended audience. Understanding is the crux of comprehension. While currently it is not possible to guarantee full end-user comprehension for all possible end-users, we can require that application developers disclose information to end-users in a manner reasonably designed to be understood and provide actual notice (e.g., using a "friend-finding" application to locate my sister will also reveal my location to my spouse as well as my friends Alice, Bob, and Chris).

Table 1. Summary of Informed Consent Analysis for Privacy Addendum

Component	Description	Implication for Privacy Addendum
DISCLOSURE	Refers to providing accurate information about the benefits and harms that might reasonably be expected from the action under consideration, including explicitly stating the purpose or reason for undertaking the action, and avoiding unnecessary technical detail. Moreover, if the action involves collecting information about an individual then the following should also be made explicit: (a) what information will be collected; (b) who will have access to the information; (c) how long the information will be archived; (d) what the information will be used for; and (e) how the identity of the individual will be protected.	• Disclose the following information: (a) what personal information will be collected; (b) how the personal information will be used; (c) who will have access to the information, including whether the recipient can transfer the information and, if so, if these principles continue to apply; (d) how long the personal information will be retained
COMPREHENSION	Refers to the individual's accurate interpretation of *what* is being disclosed.	• Effort should be made to disclose information to end-users in a manner reasonably designed to ensure the end-user's understanding – in effect, to provide actual notice
VOLUNTARINESS	Refers to ensuring that the individual's action is not coerced (e.g., controlled by compulsion, threat, or prevention) or overly manipulated (e.g., unduly altered or influenced by some means other than reason).	• Beyond the current state of knowledge in human-computer interaction
COMPETENCE	Refers to the individual possessing the mental, emotional and physical capabilities needed to give informed consent.	• Beyond the current state of knowledge in human-computer interaction
AGREEMENT	Refers to providing a reasonably clear opportunity for the individual to accept or decline to participate. Aspects to consider include: (1) Are opportunities to accept or decline visible, readily accessible, and on-going? (2) Is agreement by the participant on-going?	• Agreement must be obtained prior to any data collection • The opportunity to accept or decline must be visible and readily accessible • Where practicable, end-users should be able to revoke their prior consent and, if revoked, no further data collection should occur until a future agreement is made • Where practicable, opportunities for giving and/or withdrawing agreement should be on-going
MINIMAL DISTRACTION	Refers to meeting the above five components without overwhelming users with intolerable nuisance.	• Reasonably simple mechanisms should be used to disclose information and obtain agreement

Agreement

Once informed, the end-user then needs an opportunity to agree or decline to participate. That said, it was not entirely straightforward how to realize the component of *agreement* in the privacy addendum. The informed consent model presents a robust conception of agreement that includes not only visible active consent prior to data collection but also the on-going visible opportunity to revoke consent and potentially withdraw prior data. Here the privacy addendum is able to go some but not all of the distance. There have been disagreements among both the authors and those scholars that have reviewed the addendum about the degree to which active consent from the user should be required. . In part, there were concerns that passive consent might make sense for some applications (e.g., applications that run in the background should not be required to ask for user permission at every turn). Second, given limitations in technical know-how and interaction design the addendum stops short of requiring the opportunity to remove past data (because if the data has been aggregated with no links back to the end-user, then it may not be possible for past data to be removed) or to revoke agreement (because some viable applications may make it impossible to access the device at regular intervals and, thus, to change permissions).

Competence and Voluntariness
To fulfill the most robust conception of informed consent, the two components of *competence* and *voluntariness* all need to be addressed. Competence refers to the individual possessing the mental, emotional and physical capabilities needed to give informed consent, voluntariness to the ability to do so without coercion or undue manipulation. For remote interactions of the sort envisioned for ubiquitous applications, no one knows how to make these assessments. Thus, for purposes of the privacy addendum, we set them aside. As knowledge in the field develops, then one or both of these other two components may become relevant.

Minimal Distraction
Finally, usable informed consent requires a streamlined "informing" and "consenting" process that does not unduly distract end-users from their goals. While easier to state than implement, the requirement was integrated into the privacy addendum in phrases such as "provide an easy method by which an end user can ...."

5.2 Threat Model

The informed consent model provides protections for end-users by giving them control over their participation. By itself, it goes a good distance. With this research we sought to complement our informed consent analysis with an analysis of potential threats. In analyzing threats we consider both those that occur as "by-products" of the technical design without the intentional action of a third party, as well as those that result from the intentional and often malicious acts of others whom we shall refer to as "attackers."

Traditionally threat models have been employed within the field of security to systematically identify system vulnerabilities and potential harms to users. For example, Felten [8] writes: "[T]he first rule of security analysis is this: understand your threat model. Experience teaches that if you don't have a clear **threat model** – a clear idea of what you are trying to prevent and what technical capabilities your adversaries have – then you won't be able to think analytically about how to proceed." Such analyses have been used to assess the vulnerabilities of Internet protocols [2], web applications [29], and software-defined radio [19] to name but a few. While there are numerous variations in how threat models are conducted – what sorts of steps are taken and the order of those steps – the models share an emphasis on identifying what can be harmed (assets), who or what can cause those harms (threats), the ease with which those harms can be perpetrated (vulnerabilities), and means to address or mitigate the vulnerabilities (see, for example, [17,18,29].

For our purposes, we followed a process similar to that described by Goldberg [17] in which we (1) identified system assets, (2) identified system vulnerabilities, (3) classified potential attacker types, (4) identified potential entry points, and (5) constructed threat scenarios and mitigation plans. In conducting our threat analysis, we drew on potential harms and vulnerabilities identified in the literature, conceptually distinct categories of harms (e.g., physical, psychological, and financial), and our understanding of the technology. As with our analysis of informed consent, we considered location awareness systems as a touchstone to aid with identifying potential harms and vulnerabilities for the end-user.

Table 2 summarizes the four classes of threats that emerged from our analysis. We describe each class in turn.

Table 2. Summary of Threat Analysis for Privacy Addendum

Threat	Description	Implication for Privacy Addendum
I. DISCLOSURE TO UNAUTHORIZED PARTIES I.1 Reputation (Publicity) I.2 Solitude (To be "Left Alone")	Refers to threats to reputation and solitude that can occur when one person simply "knows" information about another person.	• Provide a general warning about malicious use • Provide a specific warning for vulnerable populations
II. UNAUTHORIZED USE OF INDIVIDUAL INFORMATION II.1 Attention II.2 Physical Welfare II.3 Data Privacy II.4 Property	Refers to threats to attention, physical welfare, data privacy, and property that can occur when information provided for one purpose is used without authorization for a second purpose,	• Same as for Threat I • Delete no longer needed identifiable information at reasonable intervals
III. UNAUTHORIZED USE OF AGGREGATED INFORMATION III.1 Attention III.2 Physical Welfare III.3 Data Privacy III.4 Property	Refers to threats to attention, physical welfare, data privacy, and property that can occur from the unauthorized use of aggregated information,	• Same as for Threat II • Delete no longer needed links between identifiable and aggregated information at reasonable intervals
IV. UNAUTHORIZED INFERENCE WITH UNEXPECTED EXTERNAL INFO.	Refers to threats that can occur from the unauthorized use of information when it is combined with other externally available information.	• Beyond the software developer's purview

Threat I. Disclosure to Unauthorized Parties
At times the simple act of one person knowing information about another person results in harm. In particular, unauthorized disclosure of information can affect someone's "reputation" (Threat I.1), at a minimum leading to embarrassment (e.g., a

system reveals to Alice's friend that she almost always spends Tuesday evening in close proximity to a building labeled as Alcoholics Anonymous). Unauthorized disclosure of information can also intrude on an individual's ability to be "left alone" (Threat I.2) (e.g., a location system that reveals an employee's location to an employer during the employee's vacation, "I saw you were back in the hotel so I decided to call and ask you about..."). Moreover, the concept of being "left-alone" has a strongly temporal element to it and, thus, links authorization with time and context (e.g., during work hours, an employee such as a traveling salesperson may be fine with an employer know his or her location but not so for non-work hours).

Threat II. Unauthorized Use of Individual Data

A second class of threats results when information provided for one purpose is used without authorization for a second purpose. While Threat I concerns *who* has access to the information, Threat II concerns *secondary uses* of the information.[2] At least four types of harms can be identified here: (1) Harm to "attention" (Threat II.1) can result when the unauthorized use requires a response from the user or otherwise places demands on the user's attention. (2) Unauthorized information use can also put users at risk for "physical welfare" (Threat II.2), either directly (e.g., when a system reveals that Chris's personal device is at particular location, say in a dark alleyway at 7 PM and can be mugged there) or through inference based on historical data about the individual (e.g., Chris usually travels home on weekdays at about 7 PM via this alley). Moreover, certain individuals due to their personal circumstances (e.g., prior victims of domestic violence) may be at greater risk than others. These populations may warrant special warnings and/or protections. (3) A third type of harm which we refer to as "data privacy" harm (Threat II.3) involves unauthorized use of one sort of information to "discover" other information about the user (e.g., since the locations where people spend most of their time is home and work, by analyzing location data an attacker could determine a user's home address). (4) Unauthorized use of information can also put the user's personal property at risk (Threat II.4). In the case of location information, the risk is typically for theft (the fact that a user is **not** at a given location can be used as a suggestion about when might be a good time to attempt a robbery).

Threat III. Unauthorized Use of Aggregated Data

While Threat II entails harms that result when information about a single individual is used for unauthorized purposes, the third class of threats entails harms that result from the unauthorized use of aggregated data. These attacks are more impersonal in the sense that an attacker does not identify a specific person to attack but rather a class of people. Each of the four types of harms – attention (Threat III.1), physical welfare (Threat III.2), data privacy (Threat III.3), and property (Threat III.4) – identified for Threat II are possible here, though cast in terms of aggregated data. For example, in terms of physical harm, rather than an attacker knowing that a particular person, say Chris, is walking down an alley at 7 PM and could be mugged, the attacker knows that most evenings at 7 PM at least one person walks alone down the alley and could

---

[2] When neither the party nor the use is authorized, then both Threat I (unauthorized disclosure) and Threat II (unauthorized use) are involved.

be mugged. Other threats based on unauthorized use of aggregated data arise when the aggregated data can be linked back to specific individuals. For example, if aggregated data suggests that a group of 102 people are currently at places labeled by the yellow pages as places of business, then an attacker could reasonably assume that a significant fraction of these individuals have empty houses right now. When possible, it is beneficial to design systems that do not maintain links from the aggregated data back to specific individuals.

Threat IV. Unauthorized Inference with Unexpected External Information
Threat IV represents a special case of Threat II, one in which the unauthorized use involves inference that combines information from even the best-designed, most privacy-sensitive system with other information externally available to the attacker. For example, Alice may choose to disclose to Bob her location at specific points through the day for a sensible set of reasons. However, Bob uses external knowledge—say of a city's demographic patterns—to conclude that Alice spends large amounts of her free time in an area that has a particular political affiliation. Alice intended to disclose one piece of information, but Bob used external knowledge to draw other conclusions that Alice never intended.

From the perspective of the privacy addendum class IV Threats, while a significant challenge to privacy are not tractable because they fall outside the purview of the application developer's control. That is, the application developer is not in a position to determine what other external information might be brought to bear and combined with the typical data of the software system.

Threats Beyond Privacy
In the process of conducting the threat analysis, we identified several additional threats that while legitimate, went beyond the scope of the privacy addendum. We mention them here both for completeness and to call attention to the ways in which privacy implicates other important human values such as *accessibility* and *credibility* (see [32] for a review; [14] and [33] for related discussion). These included threats to (a) the *quality of information* (e.g., due to limited precision, missing data, or other technical limitations the information system does not contain or produce wholly accurate or complete information), (b) *access to information* (e.g. due to technical limitations of the system or supporting infrastructure, the information system is not always available for use), and (c) *credibility of information* (e.g., due to malicious tampering of the system by a third party, the information system produces output that is intentionally misleading).

5.3   Integrating Results from the Informed Consent and Threat Models

Results from the informed consent analysis provided detailed insight into what information to disclose, how to disclose it, when and what type of agreement to obtain, and what assessments (e.g., of competence and voluntariness) would be reasonably beyond our reach. In contrast, results from the threat analysis pointed to vulnerabilities and means to remedy them. How then to bring the results of the two distinct models together to inform a single coherent set of legal of terms?

Our method proceeded as follows: We began with the key implications identified in the informed consent analysis (summarized in Table 1): namely, the comprehensible disclosure of information use prior to data collection and the on-going opportunity to provide agreement. This informed consent model provided a good deal of specificity and substantive direction. Where the state of knowledge was limited (e.g., the ability to remove data once it had been collected and aggregated), we correspondingly recommended but did not require action. Within the privacy addendum, this material formed the bulk of what became the Location Aware Privacy Principles (see Table 3, Addendum 2, Sections 1 and 2).

Next we examined implications identified by the threat analysis (summarized in Table 2); we acknowledged those that dovetailed with the informed consent model but focused our attention on unique aspects. One implication was the general adage to warn end-users of risk from third parties, if malicious software should access the system. This general warning overlapped with implications from the informed consent model and was incorporated into an "initial screen" warning (see Table 3, Addendum 1, Section II). A second implication entailed attention to the vulnerability of special populations, such as victims of domestic violence who can be placed at greater risk should their location be discovered. Thus, we added an additional requirement in the addendum for a special warning for these populations (see Table 3, Addendum 1, Section II). A third key implication entailed the recognition that deleting links or removing data could minimize the duration of time for which a threat was "active". Thus, in the Location Aware Privacy Principles we incorporated text to encourage safeguards against malicious software such as deleting personally identifiable information at reasonable intervals when it is no longer needed (see Table 3, Addendum 2, Sections 3 and 4).

We also considered interactions among results from the two models and corresponding design implications. For example, from the threat model we recognized that unauthorized disclosure depends not only to whom one discloses but also when and where that disclosure occurs. Thus, in order to provide meaningful informed consent, end-users may need to do so at a level of specificity that includes not only the recipient of the information but the context (e.g., location and time) as well. In turn, recognition of the dynamic nature of risk and consent, points to the need for ready-to-hand mechanisms that enable end-users to give and withdraw consent (e.g., to dynamically opt-in and opt-out of the location aware system).

Finally, we recognized that to be workable the privacy addendum would need to allow for legitimate circumstances in which application developers would need to access to personal information in order to provide the service, debug code, and otherwise maintain the system.

6 POL's Privacy Addendum

Based on our Value Sensitive Design analysis that integrated results from the informed consent and threat models, a premier legal team drafted the legal terms of the privacy addendum. The process used by that team is outside the scope of this paper. In this section we describe the structure of the privacy addendum in its current form. Table 3 contains the entire text of the addendum and section by section indicates the intellectual source (e.g. informed consent model, threat model, general Value Sensitive Design practices, general privacy addendum concept).

Table 3. Legal Text of POLS Privacy Addendum with Source

Privacy Addendum Legal Text	Source
Addendum 1: Privacy Addendum	
This addendum contains the additional terms applicable to development and distribution of a work (Work) containing all or a portion of the Program or that is otherwise derived from the Program.	PRIVACY ADDENDUM CONCEPT
I. You agree that: 1. Your compliance with this Addendum is a material condition of your license to the Program. 2. You will include in any follow-on licenses you make with other developers for building other applications or services for the Program and your Work the same terms and conditions as this license addendum provides (and you will bind any firm that acquires your firm to the same terms and conditions as this license provides). 3. Your development, use, and/or distribution of a Work constitutes an enforceable public commitment to comply with the provisions of this addendum. 4. Any collection, use, disclosure, and/or storage of personally identifiable location information about end-users will be undertaken in accordance with the Location Aware Privacy Principles (attached). 5. End users are entitled to enforce the terms of this Addendum and the Location Aware Privacy Principles as third party beneficiaries of the Agreement or as otherwise permitted under applicable law. 6. Any violation of the terms of this Addendum may constitute an unfair and/or deceptive trade practice in violation of state and federal consumer protection law.	
II. You further agree that all distributed Works will: Clearly, conspicuously, and verifiably (a) warn end users that the Work may disclose their physical location to third parties; and (b) obligate you to comply with the Location Aware Privacy Principles (set forth in Addendum 2, attached) by, without limitation, causing the following text (with sections in parentheses modified accordingly) to appear when the Work is first installed and at reasonable intervals thereafter: *When you use this application, (Software Name) (or other malicious software which takes advantage of (Software Name)) may cause your mobile device to communicate its physical location - and therefore your location - to application providers and/or third parties online*	INFORMED CONSENT MODEL • Disclosure • Comprehension
Please be aware of your circumstances and your safety and use appropriate caution when using (Software Name).	THREAT MODEL • Threat II
(Developer/Distributor) adheres to the Location Aware Computing Privacy Principles (attached). These principles require us to get your prior informed consent for any collection, use, disclosure and/or storage of your location information. Please review the (Software Name) privacy policy (include URL)	INFORMED CONSENT MODEL • Disclosure • Comprehension • Agreement
III. You also agree that to the extent practicable, your implementation of the Location Aware Privacy Principles will be consistent with the best practices set forth from time to time at the Intel Research/University of Washington Privacy Best Practices website.	GENERAL VALUE SENSITIVE DESIGN PRACTICE

Table 3. (*continued*)

Addendum 2: Location Aware Privacy Principles	

Addendum 2: Location Aware Privacy Principles
1.   End users will be informed, in a manner reasonably designed to provide actual notice and prior to any collection, use, retention, or disclosure of personally identifiable location information, of the following:
    a. What personal information will be collected;
    b. How that personal information will be used;
    c. To whom that personal information will be disclosed, how the recipient will be able to use the personal information, whether the recipient in turn will be able to transfer the information and whether the recipient is obligated to comply with these Principles.
    d. How long (or how often) the personal information will be disclosed (e.g. at the time of initial connection only, or periodically during the use of the software)
	INFORMED CONSENT MODEL
	• Disclosure
	• Comprehension

2. To the extent reasonably practicable under the circumstances, end users will be given conspicuous notice of the opportunity to prohibit the proposed collection, use, retention, and/or disclosure of their personally identifiable location information in whole or in part, and a reasonably simple mechanism for taking advantage of such opportunity. Where practicable, a Work will provide an easy method by which an end user can prohibit such collection, use, retention, and/or disclosure, on a case by case basis, at their discretion.	INFORMED CONSENT MODEL • Agreement • Minimal Distraction
3. Personally identifiable location information will be deleted regularly when it is no longer needed by the end-user or for the correct functioning of the Work.	THREAT MODEL • Threat III
4. Licensees will implement administrative, technical, and/or other safeguards appropriate in light of the sensitivity of the data to protect personally identifiable information from unauthorized access, use, disclosure, or damage.	THREAT MODEL • Threat I, II, III

6.1 The Legal Text

The text of the POLS Privacy Addendum is divided into two parts: Addendum 1 creates the general legal framework, and points to Addendum 2 for the particulars of location-aware systems. Addendum 2 is intended to provide guidelines specific to the problems of location-aware systems. This two part structure was devised by the team of legal scholars for two reasons. First, if the privacy addendum might someday be amended to open-source licenses of technology implicating other aspects of end-user privacy (say, genetic data in an open-source biology system) the general legal framework can still apply, when taken together with a new Addendum covering the specific implications of the specific technology and the types of data used by that technology. Second, to win industry and open-source community acceptance, it is necessary for the addendum to appeal to a broad spectrum of potential reviewers with many different points of view. The attempt to segregate the general legal framework from the specific issues would allow the overall scheme to move forward in cases where people agree with the general framework, but have a specific disagreement with the details of how location privacy should be handled, as the particulars of Addendum 2 may be debated. Similarly, the proposed best practices web site provides a way to assist application developers with potential solutions without burdening the legal document with specifics that could cause adoption problems.

A critical aspect of the addendum is Addendum 1, Sections 5 and 6, as they are designed to facilitate enforcement of the terms of the Privacy Addendum. The parties to the software license (which is a contract that includes the Privacy Addendum) are the technology developer and the application developer who wishes to incorporate and build on to the licensed technology. The end-user (whose privacy the addendum seeks to protect) is not a party to the agreement. Under contract law, normally only the parties to a contract have a right to enforce that contract. Section 5 is intended to convey a legal right to the non-party end-user, to enforce the terms of the privacy addendum if the terms are breached, because the non-party end-user is the one most likely to experience damages in case of breach of these terms. Similarly, Section 6 asks the software developer to agree that violating the terms of the Privacy Addendum may equate to a deceptive or unfair trade practice. In the United States, this could facilitate the process if the US Federal Trade Commission (FTC) or Department of Justice (DOJ) were to decide that encroachments on end-user privacy in breach of the terms of the Privacy Amendment should be handled as unfair or deceptive trade practice. When the developer has "acknowledged and agreed" that a violation may constitute an unfair trade practice, that element may then as a result be easier for the FTC or DOJ to prove in litigation.

6.2 Technical Implications

POLS' privacy addendum brings with it several design implications for application developers who build on POLS' infrastructure. These include: (1) First screen notifications about possible harms, vulnerable populations, and informed consent practices (Table 3, Addendum 1, Section II). (2) Interaction design and interface components for informing the end-user about the collection, use, retention and disclosure of personally identifiable information (Table 3, Addendum 2, Section 1). (3) Interaction design and interface components to provide end-users the opportunity for providing agreement and, if possible, also revoking agreement for participation (Table 3, Addendum 2, Section 2). (4) At reasonable intervals, deletion of personally identifiable information when it is no longer needed for the successful functioning of the application. (5) As feasible, other safeguards to protect personally identifiable information from unauthorized access, use, disclosure, or damage.

7   Contributions and Next Steps

POLS was released under a license combining the substantive terms of the Eclipse Public License together with this privacy addendum to the public in January 2006. As of this writing, the POLS system is being used by early university adopters from several academic institutions. As POLS application developers gain experience with the privacy addendum, we envision a best practices web site that would help to disseminate good design solutions as they are developed, and which would be a reference for developers implementing technology consistent with the principles outlined in Addendum 2. In this early phase of the privacy addendum's deployment, we are actively seeking input and commentary from the open source community.

The central contributions of this work are six-fold:

- Provides a "proof-of-concept" for what a privacy addendum might look like for a ubiquitous location aware system – that is, actual legal terms – and the release of a real system under those legal terms.
- Combines an informed consent and threat analysis to tackle the problem of privacy. Demonstrates that more comprehensive privacy solutions may be possible by combining approaches as compared with utilizing either approach alone.
- Demonstrates the co-evolution of policy and technology in the sense that (a) the legal terms were developed in response to current technical possibilities and limitations of ubiquitous location aware systems, and (b) the legal terms, in turn, are shaping and will continue to shape aspects of the interaction design and interface.
- Extends the scope of open source software licensing to commitments to end-user privacy as well as licenses to intellectual property. In so doing, we establish the possibility that open source licenses could embrace a range of other values.
- Extends the structure of open source licenses to consider accepting a small set of vetted addenda as a means to tailor these licenses to specific needs and desires on the part of the original developers.
- Demonstrates the success of using Value Sensitive Design theory and methods in an industry setting, namely within Intel Corporation. This effort represents one of the first industry applications of Value Sensitive Design.

As we move forward with the privacy addendum, a number of open questions remain. First and foremost: How can the privacy addendum be improved? As with any first effort, we expect there to be imperfections. For the addendum to succeed, it must strike the right balance between providing real protections for the end-user with reasonable constraints on the application developer. Is this version of the addendum too stringent, overly constraining application developers in some ways? We think not but are open to being shown otherwise. Is this version of the addendum not stringent enough in some aspects? Here we suspect so. In particular, there are differences of opinion about the need for a more active form of consent. Currently the addendum is United States centric, written in terms of US state and federal consumer protection law. How can the addendum be expanded to operate effectively in other jurisdictions? As applications developers gain experience working with the privacy addendum, other limitations of the addendum may be exposed. Thus, we expect to modify the addendum based on these experiences.

A second set of questions concerns how the privacy addendum will be integrated with existing open source software licenses. Virtually all open source licenses prohibit modification of the license terms. Such prohibitions protect against changes that could undermine the intention of the original license. Thus the privacy addendum cannot typically just be placed at the end of an existing open source license. Toward resolving this issue, we are currently beginning an engagement with the Open Source Initiative (OSI) the standards body that certifies open source licenses. Our hope is that OSI will certify the privacy addendum and allow the addendum to be added to existing certified open sources licenses without invalidating the prior certification. These discussions are beginning and will be on-going.

A third set of questions concern generalizing the privacy addendum. Beyond POLS, our hope is that the privacy addendum can evolve and generalize for use with other technology. It may be useful to begin with other location awareness systems or, at least, other ubiquitous computing systems. Over time, we hope to migrate the privacy addendum to a wide variety of information systems. The process of adapting the privacy addendum to a variety of technology areas would provide invaluable information and first hand experience with generalizing the privacy principles.

Acknowledgments

We would like to thank those who contributed in various ways to the project's success: Alan Borning, Dmitri Chmelev, Nathan G. Freier, Jeff Hughes, Dave Hoffman, Donald Horowitz, James Landay, Jessica Miller, Dierdre Mulligan, Fred Potter, Pamela Samuelson, Peter Seipel, and Jaina Selawski. This material is based, in part, upon work supported by the National Science Foundation under Grant No. 0325035. Any opinions, findings, and conclusions or recommendations expressed in this material are those of the authors and do not necessarily reflect the views of the National Science Foundation.

References

1. Ackerman, M., Darrell, T., Weitzner, D.J.: Privacy in context. Human-Computer Interaction, 16, (2001) 167-176
2. Atkins, D., Austein, R.: Threat Analysis of the Domain Name System (2004) Retrieved March 30, 2006 from http://www.ietf.org/rfc/rfc3833.txt?number=3833
3. Boyle, M., Edwards, C., Greenberg, S.: The effects of filtered video on awareness and privacy. Proceedings of CSCW '00 New York: ACM Press (2000) 1-10
4. Borriello, G., Brunette, W., Hall, M., Hartung, C., Tangney, C.: Reminding About Tagged Objects Using Passive RFIDs. Proceedings of UbiComp '04 (2004) 36-53
5. Consolvo, S., Roessler, P., Shelton, B. E.: The CareNet Display: Lessons Learned from an In Home Evaluation of an Ambient Display. Proceedings of UbiComp '04 (2004) 1-17
6. Consolvo, S., Smith, I. E., Matthews, T., LaMarca, A., Tabert, J., Powledge, P.: Location Disclosure to Social Relations: Why, When, & What People Want to Share. Proceedings of CHI 2005. ACM Press New York (2005) 81-90
7. Cranor, L.F., Garfinkel, S.: Security and usability: Designing secure systems that people can use. Cambridge, MA: O'Reilly (2005)
8. Felten, E.: DRM, and the First Rule of Security Analysis. Freedom to Tinker (2003) Retrieved March 30, 2006 from http://www.freedom-to-tinker.com/index.php?p=317
9. Friedman, B. (ed.): Human Values and the Design of Computer Technology. Cambridge University Press and CSLI New York Stanford University (1997)
10. Friedman, B., Felten, E., Millett, L. I.: Informed Consent Online: A Conceptual Model and Design Principles. CSE Technical Report 00-12-02. Department of Computer Science and Engineering, University of Washington, Seattle, Washington (2000)

11. Friedman, B., Howe, D.C., Felten, E.: Informed consent in the Mozilla browser: Implementing value-sensitive design. Proc of HICSS '02 Abstract, p. 247; CD-ROM of full-paper, OSPE101. Los Alamitos, CA: IEEE Computer Society (2002)

12. Friedman, B., Kahn, P.H., Jr.: Human values, ethics, & design. In Jacko, J., Sears, A. (Eds.): Handbook of human-computer interaction. Mahwah, NJ: Lawrence Erlbaum Associates (2003) 1177-1201

13. Friedman, B., Kahn, P.H., Jr., Borning, A.: Value Sensitive Design & information systems. In Zhang, P., Galletta, D. (Eds.): Human-computer interaction in management information systems: Foundations. Armonk, NY: M. E. Sharpe (in press)

14. Friedman, B., Kahn, P.H., Jr., Hagman, J., Severson, R.L., Gill, B.: The Watcher and The Watched: Social Judgments about Privacy in a Public Place. Human-Computer Interaction (in press)

15. Friedman, B., Lin, P., Miller, J.: Informed Consent by Design. In Cranor, L., Garfinkel, S. (eds.): Designing Secure Systems that People Can Use. O'Reilly & Associates, Cambridge, MA (2005) 495 – 521

16. Goecks, J., Mynatt, E. D.: Leveraging Social Networks for Information Sharing. Proceedings of CSCW '04 (2004) 328-331

17. Goldberg, Y. Practical Threat Analysis for the Software Industry. SecurityDocs.com. (2005) Retrieved March 30, 2006 from http://www.securitydocs.com/library/2848

18. Grinter, R.E., Smetters, D.K.: Three Challenges for Embedding Security into Applications HCISEC Workshop at CHI '03. Fort Lauderdale, Florida. (2003) Retrieved March 30, 2006 from http://www.andrewpatrick.ca/CHI2003/HCISEC/hcisec-workshop-grinter.pdf

19. Hill, R., Myagmar, S., Campbell, R.: Threat Analysis of GNU Software Radio. Proc. of WWC'05. Palo Alto, CA (2005)

20. Hudson, S.E., Smith, I.: Techniques for addressing fundamental privacy & disruption tradeoffs in awareness support systems. Proceedings of CSCW '96 (1996) 248-257

21. Hull, R., Kumar, B., Lieuwen, D., Patel-Schneider, P.F., Sahuguet, A., Varadarajan, S., Vyas, A., "Enabling Context-Aware and Privacy-Conscious User Data Sharing," Proceedings of MDM '04 (2004) 187-198

22. Iachello, G., Smith, I.E., Consolvo, S., Abowd, G.D., Hughes, J., Howard, J., Potter, F., Scott, J., Sohn, T., Hightower, J., LaMarca, A.: Control, Deception, and Communication: Evaluating the Deployment of a Location-Enhanced Messaging Service. Proceedings of UbiComp 2005 (2005) 213-231

23. Iachello, G., Smith, I.E., Consolvo, S., Chen, M., Abowd, G.D.: (2005). Developing Privacy Guidelines for Social Location Disclosure Applications and Services. Proceedings of SOUPS '05. ACM Press New York (2005) 65-76

24. Jancke, G., Venolia, G.D., Grudin, J., Cadiz, J.J., Gupta, A.: Linking Public Spaces: Technical & Social Issues. Proceedings of CHI '01. Seattle, WA (2001) 530-537

25. Jiang, X., Hong, J.I., Landay, J.A.: Approximate information flows: Socially-based modeling of privacy in ubiquitous computing. Proceedings of UbiComp '02 (2002) 176-93

26. LaMarca, A., Chawathe, Y., Consolvo, S., Hightower, J., Smith, I.E., Scott, J., Sohn, T., Howard, J., Hughes, J., Potter, F., Tabert, J., Powledge, P., Borriello, G., Schilit, B.: Place Lab: Device Positioning Using Radio Beacons in the Wild. Proceedings of Pervasive '05, Munich, Germany (2005) 116-133.

27. Langheinrich, M.: Privacy by design–Principles of privacy-aware ubiquitous systems. Proceedings of UbiComp '01. Berlin, Heidelberg (2001) 273-291

28. Lederer, S., Hong, J.I., Dey, A.K., Landay, J.A.: Personal Privacy through Understanding & Action: 5 Pitfalls for Designers. Personal & Ubiquitous Computing. 8(6) (2004) 440-54.

29. Meler, J.D., Mackman, A., Dunner, N., Vasireddy, S., Escamilla, R., Murukan, A.: Threat modeling. In Improving Web Application Security: Threats and Countermeasures (2003)
30. Palen, L., Dourish, P.: Unpacking "privacy" for a networked world. Proceedings of CHI '03 (2003) 129-136
31. Patil, S., Lai, J.: Who gets to know what when: configuring privacy permissions in an awareness application. Proceedings CHI '05, Portland, OR, USA (2005) 101-110
32. Schoeman, F. (ed): Philosophical Dimensions of Privacy: An Anthology. Cambridge, UK: Cambridge University Press (1984)
33. Warren, S.D., Brandeis, L.D.: The Right to Privacy. Harvard Law Review 4(5) (1890)

Mobility Detection Using Everyday GSM Traces

Timothy Sohn[1], Alex Varshavsky[2], Anthony LaMarca[3], Mike Y. Chen[3],
Tanzeem Choudhury[3], Ian Smith[3], Sunny Consolvo[3], Jeffrey Hightower[3],
William G. Griswold[1], and Eyal de Lara[2]

[1] Computer Science and Engineering
University of California, San Diego, La Jolla, CA, USA
{tsohn, wgg}@cs.ucsd.edu
[2] Computer Science, University of Toronto, Toronto, Canada
{walex, delara}@cs.toronto.edu
[3] Intel Research, Seattle, WA, USA
{anthony.lamarca, mike.y.chen, tanzeem.choudhury, ian.e.smith,
sunny.consolvo, jeffrey.r.hightower}@intel.com

Abstract. Recognition of everyday physical activities is difficult due to the challenges of building informative, yet unobtrusive sensors. The most widely deployed and used mobile computing device today is the mobile phone, which presents an obvious candidate for recognizing activities. This paper explores how coarse-grained GSM data from mobile phones can be used to recognize high-level properties of user mobility, and daily step count. We demonstrate that even without knowledge of observed cell tower locations, we can recognize mobility modes that are useful for several application domains. Our mobility detection system was evaluated with GSM traces from the everyday lives of three data collectors over a period of one month, yielding an overall average accuracy of 85%, and a daily step count number that reasonably approximates the numbers determined by several commercial pedometers.

1 Introduction

This paper introduces a technique for detecting a user's coarse-grained mobility using commodity cell phones. Pervasive computing applications have long made use of technologies for inferring a user's physical activities. Both coarse and fine-grained location systems have been used to perform location-driven activity inference [14, 34]. Smart spaces containing cameras, RFID tags, and the like, have been used to detect fine-grained user activities [3, 15, 25]. Unfortunately, the cost, complexity and maintenance overhead of such activity inference systems have hampered their mainstream adoption. Recent work has attempted to address some of these issues. An example is the belt-worn cluster of sensors developed by Lester et al. that can identify several physical activities including detecting subtle distinctions such as walking on level ground versus up stairs [19]. However, challenges in form factor and power usage still remain.

Fortunately, many applications do not require the detail and accuracy of the systems cited above. As an example, consider the domain of eldercare as depicted by Computer-Supported Coordinated Care (CSCC) [7]. CSCC describes the network of

P. Dourish and A. Friday (Eds.): Ubicomp 2006, LNCS 4206, pp. 212–224, 2006.
© Springer-Verlag Berlin Heidelberg 2006

people who help an elder *age in place* and seeks to improve the quality of her care while reducing the burden of providing care on the members of her network. Many of the elder's activities that are meaningful for her network members to know about involve high-level information about the elder such as whether or not she was up and about today, or if she had a sedentary day around the house.

The most widely deployed and used mobile computing device today is the mobile phone, which presents an obvious opportunity for high-level activity recognition such as that needed by CSCC applications. This paper investigates how without GPS, a commodity GSM phone could infer such high-level information without placing the types of additional burdens on the user that are typical of more heavyweight systems. Previous research has used GPS to detect the modes of transportation for an individual [23]. However, GPS positioning is available as little as 5% of a typical person's day [18], providing much lower coverage than we require. In contrast, cellular coverage is available throughout most, if not all, of a person's day and does not require line of sight to work [18]. Therefore, using a GSM sensor to detect high-level activities allows the sensing system to always be available, and allows users to continue to carry their mobile phones in their pockets, bags, etc.

The contribution of this paper is that, with unmodified GSM mobile phones and without relying on users to modify their behavior, we can recognize several high-level activities. Using statistical classification and boosting techniques, we successfully distinguished if a person is walking, driving, or remaining at one place with 85% accuracy. Additionally, we were able to build a GSM-based step count predictor that provides a reasonable approximation of the user's daily step count compared to several commercial pedometers. Our methods were tested with real-world data from three data collectors using the two major GSM networks in the United States (T-Mobile and Cingular). The data collectors gathered GSM network trace data over a period of one month, logging a total of 249 walking events and 171 driving events. Our methods show that GSM-based sensing from commodity devices may provide enough activity information for some applications, without the overhead of requiring additional sensors.

The remainder of this paper is organized as follows. Section 2 describes our algorithms to infer mobile activities and daily step counts. Our data collection, metrics, and evaluation results are presented in Section 3. Section 4 describes several application domains that could benefit from our mobility detection technique. Section 5 outlines related work, and we conclude in Section 6.

2 Mobility Detection with GSM

In this section, we offer a brief overview of the Global System for Mobile Communication (GSM) and describe algorithms that use traces of GSM signals to infer modes of mobility and to estimate daily step-count.

2.1 Global System for Mobile Communication (GSM)

GSM is the most widespread cellular telephony standard in the world, with deployments in more than 200 countries. As of September 2005, the GSM family of technologies has 1.5 billion subscribers and 78% of the world market [1]. A GSM base station is typically equipped with a number of directional antennas that define sectors of coverage, or cells. Each cell is allocated a number of physical channels based on the expected traffic load and the operator's requirements. Typically, the channels are allocated in a way that both increases coverage and reduces interference between cells.

We wrote a custom application for the Audiovox SMT 5600 mobile phone to measure and record the surrounding GSM radio environment. Each reading includes signal strength values, cell IDs and channel numbers of up to seven nearby cell towers. In addition, we extract channel numbers and associated signal strength values of up to 15 additional channels. Cell IDs are uniquely identified by the combination of Mobile Country Code (MCC), Mobile Network Code (MNC), Location Area Code (LAC), and cell id. Although other cell towers may be present in the area, our application only sees those associated with the phone's SIM card provider. We sampled our GSM radio environment with the mobile phone at a rate of one sample per second (1 Hz).

2.2 Inferring User Mobility Modes

Our method for detecting user mobility is based on the same principle as fingerprint-based location systems [5, 22]: namely that the radio signals observed from fixed sources are consistent in time, but variable in space. Thus, given a series of GSM observations with a stable set of towers and signal strengths, we conclude that the phone is not moving. Similarly, we interpret changes in the set of nearby towers and signal strengths as indicative of motion.

We conducted a simple controlled experiment to determine how the radio environment changes as a result of various movement activities. Fig. 1 shows the average Euclidean distance values between consecutive GSM measurements, as the data collectors stood still, walked and drove at different speeds. Conceptually, Euclidean distance captures the similarity between GSM measurements. The smaller the Euclidean distance between two measurements, the more similar these measurements are. For example, if measurement A has 3 cells/channels with signal strengths $\{R_1^A, R_2^A, R_3^A\}$ and measurement B has the same 3 cells/channels with signal strengths $\{R_1^B, R_2^B, R_3^B\}$, the Euclidean distance between measurements A and B will be calculated as:

$$\sqrt{(R_1^A - R_1^B)^2 + (R_2^A - R_2^B)^2 + (R_3^A - R_3^B)^2}$$

If a particular cell/channel is not present in one of the measurements, we substitute its signal strength with the minimal signal strength found in this measurement.

Figure 1 shows that the Euclidean distance between consecutive measurements is proportional with the speed of movement. During stationary periods, the distance values stay relatively small (< 5). The slow and fast walking periods show a distinct difference from the stationary period. The driving traces show the most rapid changes in the radio environment, greater than either walking or stationary. Fast walking and

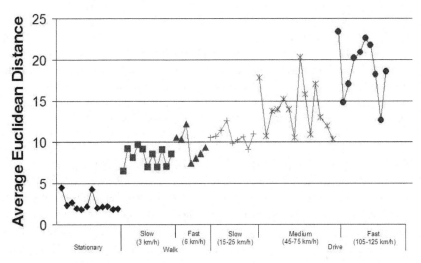

Fig. 1. Average Euclidean distance between consecutive measurements during a stationary period, slow/fast walking periods and slow/medium/fast driving periods

slow driving sometimes overlap in their range of Euclidean distance values, which may result in false recognition between the two states. For a given speed, the Euclidean distance values are not constant because changes in signal strengths are both a function of speed as well as the physical environment, such as buildings, people, or vehicles.

Based on these findings we extracted a set of seven different features to use in classifying a set of GSM measurements as either *stationary*, *walking*, or *driving*. Three features compare two consecutive measurements in time, while the other four features use a sliding window of measurements. We used window sizes of 10, 60, and 300 seconds. Our seven features are:

1. Euclidean distance between two consecutive measurements
2. Spearman rank correlation coefficient [36] between two consecutive measurements. (This number represents how closely the signal strengths from common cell towers were ranked. A more similar ranking indicates less movement.)
3. The number of common cell towers between two consecutive measurements.
4. Mean Euclidean distance over a window of measurements where the values are calculated between consecutive measurements and then averaged together.
5. Variance in Euclidean distance values over a window of measurements where the values are calculated between consecutive measurements.
6. The variance in signal strengths for each tower seen within a given window. (The variance values for each tower are averaged together to produce a single number representing the signal strength "spread" over the entire window.)
7. Euclidean distance value between the first and last measurement of a window.

We used these features to train a two-stage classification scheme. The first stage classified an instance as stationary or not. If the instance was classified as not stationary, a second classifier would determine if the instance was walking or driving. Both classifiers were trained using a boosted logistic regression technique [13] using decision stumps—a single node decision tree. All algorithms were provided by the Weka machine learning toolkit [37]. We chose to use boosting because it has been shown to work well in a variety of classification tasks [24, 27]. In our own experiments we compared boosted logistics regression with naïve Bayes, Support Vector Machines, AdaBoost [12], MultiBoost [35], and some heuristic-based methods; the boosted logistics classifier provided the best recognition rates. We also compared the two-stage classification approach to a single multi-class approach and found that the two-stage classifiers resulted in better accuracy. This is consistent with the findings of Viola and Jones [32], which showed that cascades of classifiers can achieve better recognition rates than single multi-class approaches in face detection tasks. The other advantage of the boosted logistic regression technique using decision stumps is that after the boosting process we have a ranking of features based on how useful they are during classification. Thus the system can be used to select features as well as learn classifiers simultaneously [19, 33]. Furthermore, using only a small subset of the most relevant features can provide computational savings, which is especially important when running inference on a mobile phone.

2.3 Estimating a User's Daily Step-Count

A nice feature of a mobile phone being able to determine periods when a user is walking is that it can be used to approximate how much a user walks, similar to the information provided by a pedometer. Pedometers are currently popular and are used worldwide as a tool to help people track the number of steps they take each day. The benefits of walking and the use of pedometers have been widely promoted by the healthcare community, and a popular suggestion is for people to walk at least 10,000 steps/day [32].

To provide a reasonable measurement of steps taken (or "step count"), a pedometer is clipped to the user's waistband, above the thigh's midline. This restriction may be problematic, as some users do not like the look of the pedometer, or may not have a place to clip it, for example, if the user is wearing a dress. The mobile phone does not have such a restriction, as it can be anywhere with the user, including in her bag. We do not expect a person to always have their phone on her, such as when she is at home. However, being able to provide pedometer-like functionality when outside the home can be useful to give a high-level report of a person's mobile activity for the day.

The GSM-based mobility recognition from the previous section allows us to add a pedometer-like capability to mobile phones. By totaling the number of walking periods and multiplying by an appropriate step rate, we can estimate the user's daily step count. Although this method of calculating step count may seem crude and prone to error, we show in Section 3.3 that our GSM-based step count estimates can approximate that of several commercially available pedometers.

3 Experimental Evaluation

In this section, we evaluate our mobility mode detection and step-count algorithms using data collected from three people to demonstrate the feasibility of using GSM traces to recognize high-level activities. We first describe our metrics and perform-ance for mobility detection. We then evaluate our ability to estimate a user's daily step count.

3.1 Data Trace Collection

Three members of our research team collected GSM network traces as they went about their daily lives for one month. Each data collector carried a commodity GSM phone, the Audiovox SMT 5600, running our software for recording readings from nearby cell towers. Two of the data collectors used Cingular, and one used T-Mobile, spanning the two major GSM network providers in the U.S.

Data collectors recorded their mobility activities using a custom diary application running on the phone that allowed them to indicate whether they were walking, driv-ing or in one place. Each collector also carried a paper notebook where he could re-cord any event that he forgot to indicate on the mobile phone. These paper logs were later transcribed and merged with the digital log for a complete self-reported ground truth. There were a total of 53 corrections (7% of all events) from the paper logs for all data collectors. To capture the ground truth for step counts, each data collector also wore a pedometer and manually recorded his daily step count in the paper notebook. Each collector's pedometer was calibrated with his stride length and weight to obtain the most accurate step-count estimates possible.

We chose to use members of our research team to serve as data collectors because ground-truth diary logging is a tedious, error-prone process that required significant technical expertise to trouble-shoot problems with prototype technology. Given this overhead, the lack of application value to offer data collectors, and the high reliability of data logging that we required to test our algorithms, we felt that this was a reason-able choice. Our data collectors went to common places one would expect any person to visit such as grocery stores, malls, parks, churches, and libraries.

In all, the sensor logs contained 249 walking events (avg. 9.1 min) and 171 driving events (avg. 18.5 min). Each of these mobility events provides a sequence of data points to test our algorithm because every second is one data point to test our classi-fier (the rate that the phone scanned the radio environment). In total we gathered 12 GB of GSM network traces, amounting to 78 days of sensor logs. Our data spans urban and suburban environments and three different metropolitan areas as the data collectors traveled during the collection period.

3.2 Inferring Mobility Modes

Our goal was to infer one of three mobility states: *stationary*, *walking*, or *driving*. Periods of walking and driving were identified in the data collector's diaries. We had initially hoped to use the remaining times, which data collectors marked as being at a "place", to identify periods of being stationary. Unfortunately being at a "place" can still involve a fair degree of mobility. In a grocery store, shoppers are in motion much of the time. Even reasonably sedentary activities such as watching TV include short periods of walking (to visit the refrigerator for example). This ambiguity prevents us from having the needed ground truth for training and testing our algorithm. To extract the most reliable ground truth from our data, we used the GSM trace data collected between 2am and 5am to represent periods of being stationary. During these times we used our data collectors' logs to verify that they were at home and sleeping, thus their phones would not be moving. Although this means dropping much of our collected trace data, it provides the best possible ground truth for determining how well our classifier can differentiate properties of mobility.

Using the labeled periods of activity, we trained our classifier and evaluated it using a 5-fold cross validation[1] method over the entire data set. This produced a single model that worked well across all three data collectors and both GSM network providers. Figure 2 shows the precision, (true positive/(true positive + false positive), and recall, (true positive/(true positive + false negative), percentages aggregated for all of our data collectors. The percentages along the diagonal indicate the classifiers' performance for predicting and matching the ground truth events. Precision is the percentage of predicted events that are correct. A low precision number indicates many false positives. Recall is the percentage of ground truth events that were correctly identified. A low recall number indicates that many ground truth events were missed. Accuracy represents the percentage of predictions that are correct. Our overall accuracy, ((true positive + true negative)/ (total number of samples)), is 85%.

Our classification scheme performs very well for stationary periods correctly detecting most periods of no movement (recall 92.5%) and not raising many spurious stationary events (precision 95.4%). Driving also performs quite well detecting most drives (recall 81.7%) and not raising many false positives (precision 84.3%). Walking activities were also detected with high percentage (recall 80%), but exhibited the most false positives out of the three classes (precision 70.2%). Within a driving activity, there are often times when a car is moving at slow speeds such as in traffic or roads with lower speed limits. In our controlled experiment, we saw that the changes in signal strengths for slow driving speeds are similar to fast walking speeds. Thus, one would expect the classifier to predict walking movement even though a segment was

Precision

		Predicted Movement		
		Stationary	Walking	Driving
Ground Truth	Stationary	95.4%	12.6%	6.9%
	Walking	2.5%	70.2%	8.8%
	Driving	2.1%	17.2%	84.3%

Recall

		Predicted Movement		
		Stationary	Walking	Driving
Ground Truth	Stationary	92.5%	4.5%	3.0%
	Walking	7.7%	80.0%	12.2%
	Driving	4.5%	13.8%	81.7%

Fig. 2. Precision and recall confusion matrices for all GSM network traces aggregated over all data collectors. Overall accuracy is 85%.

---

[1] In *k*-fold cross-validation, a data set is partitioned into *k*-folds, and *k* training and testing iterations are performed. On each iteration, *k-1* folds are used as a training set, and one fold is used as a testing set. The classification results from each iteration are averaged together to produce a final result.

marked as a driving activity. These types of misclassifications are reflected in the walking precision (17.2% driving) and driving recall (13.8% walking) numbers.

The results show that we are able to distinguish between different mobility states with high accuracy without having to instrument a person with any other additional sensors. The precision and recall numbers show that this type of scheme could be used in a person's daily life, to give an accurate diary of mobile activity. In Section 0 we will discuss several application domains where our techniques would be useful.

One question about our classification model is whether it is overfitted for our data set. As an external way to corroborate our classification model, we tested the model using the GSM traces gathered from our controlled experiment described in Section 0. These traces are independent of those used to build our model. The classifier achieved an overall accuracy of 90% on this controlled data set, with the only errors being that some portions of our slow walk were classified as stationary. Furthermore, boosting techniques have been shown to be robust to over fitting and generalizes well to unseen data [26].

3.3 Daily Step-Count Prediction for Data Collectors

To test the accuracy of a "virtual pedometer" capability, we asked our data collectors to wear an Omron Healthcare HJ-112 pedometer for a portion of the month during which they were collecting GSM data. We chose the Omron because it was rated as the overall best pedometer by Consumer Reports [9]. In all, we collected 50 days worth of daily step-count totals. In contrast to inferring mobility modes, for estimating step-count we want to be able to detect any walking activity throughout the day, even if it is for short periods of walking at a "place". The pedometer is always logging the steps a person takes, so our algorithm must also detect these periods of mobility. Thus, for step-count prediction we used all of the collected GSM trace data for each day.

We wanted our step-count predictor to work without any calibration for all users. This further allows us to promote ubiquitous mobility recognition with low setup costs. To predict a daily step count from our walking predictions, we used the following simple heuristic obtained by performing linear regression with a 5 fold cross validation on our data set:

daily step count = 25 · (minutes of walking)

For these 50 days of pedometer data, our heuristic predicted daily step counts ranging from 1500 to 12000 steps, with an average of 5000 steps. Comparing our estimates to the Omron step counts, we saw an average difference of 1400 steps per day (std. dev. 900 steps), with a minimum difference of 1 step and a maximum difference of 3500 steps. Our step count estimation worked uniformly well for all users: the correlation between measured and predicted step counts for the three data collectors were R=.71, .63, and .63. The error in our step count estimation is likely due more in part to errors in mobility estimation that to the user having different step rates.

To compare how well our step count predictions compared to other pedometers, we conducted a second experiment. We purchased four additional pedometers of varying brands, and collected seven more days of data for one data collector. For this experiment, he carried the GSM phone, while also wearing the Omron and the four other pedometers. Again, we used the Omron as ground truth in our evaluation. For these seven days, our GSM based predictions had an average difference of 1400 steps with a maximum difference of 2400. The average difference across the other pedometers varied between 500 and 900, with a maximum difference of 1500. These results show that while less accurate, our GSM-based step prediction approximates the results of off-the-shelf pedometers in predicting whether a person had a sedentary, moderately-active, or high-activity day.

4 Applications

Our mobility detection scheme provides a low-cost, ubiquitous method for high-level activity recognition. Since we use commodity GSM phones without any additional hardware, any owner of a GSM phone can use our mobility detection system. In this section, we describe two application domains where our mobility detection scheme would be useful.

4.1 Computer-Supported Coordinated Care (CSCC)

CSCC describes the network of people who help an elder *age in place*, *i.e.*, avoid the transition to a care facility, and seeks to improve the quality of her care while reducing the burden on the members of her care network, such as her family and friends [7]. The Digital Family Portrait [21] and CareNet Display [8] are two applications in the CSCC domain that aim to use sensor-driven activity inference to convey care and wellness information about an elder to members of her care network. The applications report information such as: Did the elder take her medication? Did she get out of bed? Did she have any visitors? Much research has focused on inferencing these types of in-home activities, but as the CareNet Display showed, an elder's care network is also concerned with activities that take place outside of the home, such as did the elder go to church on Sunday? Is she routinely late for her weekly doctor's appointment?

A recent report estimated that about 50% of Americans aged 65 to 74 are wireless customers and 30% of those aged 75 to 94 have mobile phones [2]. Given that so many elders already carry them, mobile phones present an interesting opportunity to provide detection of a range of activities that are meaningful to the elder's care network and can be detected today with a device that she already carries. With just a mobile phone, an elder would be able to relay information about her daily activity level, whether or not she was up and about today, or if she had a sedentary day around the house.

4.2 Social-Mobile Applications

Detecting mobility patterns is useful for applications that connect people with mobile devices together in their social environment--social mobile applications [28]. These applications-- if one includes voice calls and SMS --are key drivers of mobile phone usage today and are likely to continue as more and more of people's non-work lives revolve around mobile communications [16]. New applications are on the horizon that will help people communicate [30, 31] and coordinate [10, 29].

Mobility detection can provide context information to enhance these applications and provide a better experience for the user. For example, applications that prompt a user with information are competing for that person's attention and potentially interrupting an ongoing task. Our technique would be useful for example when driving, because the information might better serve the user if it is delayed. Mobility detection could be central to some applications such as one that computes estimated time of arrival for many people who want to rendezvous. In a scenario of this type, one user -- perhaps who is holding the movie tickets-- is very interested when the other 3 users will arrive. With mobility detection alone, the waiting user can discriminate that some others have parked already and are thus nearby and those who are still driving and thus distant; combining this with a location system provides an excellent tool for social coordination and obviates the need for many phone calls and SMS messages.

5 Related Work

The SHARP project aims to infer fine-grained activities by putting RFID tags on household objects and monitoring their usage with a wearable RFID reader [25]. Our approach complements the fine-grained activities SHARP can infer from instrumented objects, with high-level activities in the wider environment using low-resolution sensors.

GPS-based location sensing has been used for high-level activity recognition. Patterson et al. take a learning approach based on particle-filters to detect modes of transportation [23]. Similarly, Liao et al. extended Relational Markov Networks for learning models that, given a GPS location and the time, can differentiate among shopping, dining, visiting, at home, and at work [20]. GPS sensing today still often requires purchasing and carrying additional hardware. A recent study revealed that GPS positioning is available only about 5% of a typical person's day, as it needs a wide swath of clear sky to sense enough geostationary satellites [18]. In contrast, mobile phones provide ubiquitous coverage, and do not require any extra hardware from what people already carry. We have shown in this paper that similar recognition performance can be achieved observing changes in cell tower signal strengths, without the need for true location. This suggests that GPS should play an assistive role in everyday inference, rather than serving as the sole environmental sensor.

Two projects have looked at using radio signals for motion detection. LOCADIO used a Hidden Markov Model to infer motion of a device using 802.11 radio signals [17]. Anderson and Muller conducted a controlled, preliminary study with GSM mobile phones to detect motion of a device [4]. Similar to these two projects, our approach uses machine learning algorithms to infer motion. We have shown that motion detection using GSM is feasible for use outside the laboratory, and works well throughout people's daily lives.

A third approach to activity recognition is to use wearable sensors of a single modality [6] or multiple modalities [19]. Lester et al. use 7 different types of sensors, including light, audio, accelerometer, compass, temperature, humidity, and barometric pressure, to classify 10 activities such as sitting, standing, walking up stairs, and walking. The GSM radio can potentially be part of the sensor ensemble to improve recognition performance. Several commercial phones are now shipping with built-in accelerometers and compass, but, unfortunately, they do not expose the sensor readings to the application developers.

Finally, the Reality Mining project has used Bluetooth-capable GSM mobile phones to recognize social patterns in daily user activity, infer relationships, and model organizational rhythms [11]. It uses the single associated GSM cell tower, Bluetooth radio, application usage logs, and call logs to sense nearby Bluetooth phones and devices, time and duration of calls, caller ID, and so forth.

6   Conclusions and Future Work

We have demonstrated the feasibility of using an unmodified GSM phone, a coarse-grain but ubiquitous sensor with 1.5 billion subscribers worldwide [1], to recognize high-level properties of mobility that are valuable for application domains such as Computer-Supported Coordinated Care and social-mobile applications. To evaluate its effectiveness, we collected GSM traces and ground truth labels of walks and drives for a month from the everyday lives of three people, for a total of 78 days of GSM logs consisting of 249 walking events and 171 driving events. We have shown that we can recognize mobility modes among walking, driving, and stationary correctly 85% of the time, and estimate daily step counts that approximates commercial pedometers. Unlike other activity recognition systems that may require a person to wear a special device in a certain way, our approach lets users maintain their current mobile phone habits with no special requirements about where the phone is kept on their person. These results show that current mobile phones without extra sensors or devices can detect high-level activities, providing people with an estimate of their mobility patterns throughout the day.

Since our classification model was built mainly in one metropolitan area, we do not anticipate it working across different cell densities. However, building a model for our classifier with areas of different cell densities could enable our techniques to work in varying radio environments. Our future work involves exploring how our mobility detection technique and GSM-based step predictor would work in other parts of the country.

Acknowledgements

Thanks to Karen Tang who helped collect GSM network traces and provided feedback on several drafts of this paper. Susumu Harada, Dmitri Chmelev, and Fred Potter helped collect part of the data used for this research. Daniel Hsu explained many of the machine learning techniques used in this paper to us and gave several ideas on different methods to use. This research was supported in part by the UCSD FWGrid Project, NSF Research Infrastructure Grant EIA-0303622.

References

1. GSM Association Press Release, "Worldwide cellular connections exceeds 2 billion"
   http://www.gsmworld.com/news/press_2005/press05_21.shtml
2. Wireless Week, "Newer Phones, Older Users",
   http://www.wirelessweek.com/article/CA503601.html

3. Abowd, G. A. Bobick, I. Essa, E. Mynatt, and W. Rogers. The Aware Home: Developing Technologies for Successful Aging. In: Proceedings of AAAI Workshop and Automation as a Care Giver.

4. Anderson, I. and Muller, H. Context Awareness via GSM Signal Strength Fluctuation. In: Pervasive 2006, Late Breaking Results, pp. 27-31.

5. Bahl, P. and Padmanabhan, V. RADAR: An-In-Building RF-Based User Location and Tracking. In: Proceedings of IEEE Infocom 2000, pp. 775-784.

6. Bao, L. and Intille, S. S. Activity Recognition from User-Annotated Acceleration Data. In: Lecture Notes in Computer Science, Volume 3001, Jan 2004, Pages 1-17

7. Consolvo, S., Roessler, P., Shelton, B.E., LaMarca, A., Schilit, B., Bly, S. Technology for Care Networks of Elders. IEEE Pervasive Computing Mobile & Ubiquitous Systems: Successful Aging, Vol. 3, No. 2 (Apr-June 2004) pp. 22-29.

8. Consolvo, S., Roessler, P., and Shelton, B.E. The CareNet Display: Lessons Learned from an In Home Evaluation of an Ambient Display. In: Proceedings of UbiComp 2004, pp. 1-17.

9. Consumer Reports, "Pedometers: Walking by the numbers," Consumer Reports, 69(10), (2004), pp.30-2.

10. Dodgeball. http://www.dodgeball.com/

11. Eagle, N. and Pentland, A. Reality Mining: Sensing Complex Social Systems. Personal and Ubiquitous Computing (Jan 2006).

12. Freund, Y. and Schapire, R.E. Experiments with a new boosting algorithm. In: Proceedings of International Conference on Machine Learning, pp. 148-156, 1996.

13. Friedman, J.H., Hastie, T., Tibshirani, R. Additive logistic regression: A statistical view of boosting. Annals of Statistics (2000) 337--374

14. Hariharan, R., Krumm, J., Horvitz, E. Web-Enhanced GPS. In: Proceedings of the International Workshop on Location and Context Awareness (LoCA 2005), May 2005.

15. Intille, S. S., Larson, K., Beaudin, J. S., Nawyn, J., Tapia, E. M., and Kaushik, P. A living laboratory for the design and evaluation of ubiquitous computing technologies. In: CHI 2005 Extended Abstracts, pp. 1941-1944.

16. Ito, Mizuko, et. Al., eds. Personal, Portable, Pedestrian. Mobile Phones in Japanese Life. Cambridge, The MIT Press, 2005.

17. Krumm, J. and Horvitz, E. LOCADIO: Inferring Motion and Location from Wi-Fi Signal Strengths. In: Mobiquitous 2004, pp. 4-13.

18. LaMarca, A., Chawathe, Y., Consolvo, S., Hightower, J., Smith, I., Scott, J., Sohn, T., Howard, J., Hughes, J., Potter, F., Tabert, J., Powledge, P., Borriello, G., Schilit, B. Place Lab: Device Positioning Using Radio Beacons in the Wild. In: Pervasive 2005.

19. Lester, J., Choudhury, T., Kern, N., Borriello, G., and Hannaford, B. A Hybrid Discriminative-Generative Approach for Modeling Human Activities. In: Proceedings of International Joint Conference on Artificial Intelligence (IJCAI 2005).

20. Liao, L., Fox, D., Kautz, H. Location-Based Activity Recognition using Relational Markov Networks. In: Proceedings of the International Conference on Artificial Intelligence (IJCAI 2005).

21. Mynatt, E. D., Rowan, J., Craighill, S., and Jacobs. Digital family portraits: supporting peace of mind for extended family members. In: Proceedings of the CHI 2001, pp. 333-340.

22. Otsason, V., Varshavsky, A., LaMarca, A., and de Lara, E. Accurate GSM Indoor Localization. In: Ubicomp 2005.

23. Patterson, D.J., Liao, L., Fox, D., Kautz. Inferring High-Level Behavior from Low-Level Sensors. In: Ubicomp 2003.

24. Pavlovic, V., Garg, A., and Rehg, J.M. Multimodal speaker detection using error feedback dynamic bayesian networks. In: IEEE Conference on Computer Vision and Pattern Recognition 2000.

25. Philipose, M., Fishkin, K., Perkowitz, M., Patterson, D.J., Fox, D., Kautz, H., Hähnel, D., Inferring Activities from Interactions with Objects. In: IEEE Pervasive Computing, Oct 2004.

26. Schapire, R.E. The boosting approach to machine learning: An overview. In: D. D. Denison, M. H. Hansen, C. Holmes, B. Mallick, B. Yu, editors, Nonlinear Estimation and Classification. Springer, 2003

27. Schwenk, H. and Bengio, Y. Training methods for adaptive boosting of neural networks for character recognition. In: Proceedings of NIPS'98.

28. Smith, I. Social-Mobile Applications. IEEE Computer 38(4): 84-85 (2005)

29. Smith, I., Consolvo, S., Hightower, J., Hughes, J., Iachello, G., LaMarca, A., Scott, J., Sohn, T., Abowd, G. Social Disclosure of Place: From Location Technology to Communication Practice. In: Pervasive 2005.

30. Socialight. http://socialight.com

31. Textamerica. http://www.textamerica.com/

32. Tudor-Locke C, Bassett DR Jr., "How many steps/day are enough? Preliminary pedometer indices for public health," Sports Med., 34(1), (2004), pp.1-8.

33. Viola, P.A. and Jones, M.J. Robust real-time face detection. In: International Journal of Computer Vision, vol. 57, no. 2, pp. 137--154, 2004.

34. Ward, A.   Jones, A.   Hopper, A.   A new location technique for the active office. In: Personal Communications. Oct 1997.

35. Webb, G.I. MultiBoosting: A Technique for Combining Boosting and Wagging. Machine Learning, 40(2): 159-196, 2000.

36. Weisstein, E.W. "Spearman Rank Correlation Coefficient." http://mathworld.wolfram. com/SpearmanRankCorrelationCoefficient.html

37. Witten, I.H. and Frank, E. "Data Mining: Practical machine learning tools and techniques", 2nd Edition, Morgan Kaufmann, San Francisco, 2005.

Practical Metropolitan-Scale Positioning
for GSM Phones

Mike Y. Chen[1], Timothy Sohn[2], Dmitri Chmelev[3], Dirk Haehnel[1],
Jeffrey Hightower[1], Jeff Hughes[3], Anthony LaMarca[1], Fred Potter[3],
Ian Smith[1], and Alex Varshavsky[4]

[1] Intel Research Seattle, USA
[2] University of California at San Diego, USA
[3] University of Washington, USA
[4] University of Toronto, Canada

Abstract. This paper examines the positioning accuracy of a GSM beacon-based location system in a metropolitan environment. We explore five factors effecting positioning accuracy: location algorithm choice, scan set size, simultaneous use of cells from different providers, training and testing on different devices, and calibration data density. We collected a 208-hour, 4350Km driving trace of three different GSM networks covering the Seattle metropolitan area. We show a median error of 94m in downtown and 196m in residential areas using a single GSM network and the best algorithm for each area. Estimating location using multiple providers' cells reduces median error to 65-134 meters and 95% error to 163m in the downtown area, which meets the accuracy requirements for E911. We also show that a small 60-hour calibration drive is sufficient for enabling a metropolitan area similar to Seattle.

1 Introduction

While several research and commercial efforts now exist for WiFi beacon-location [6, 9, 25, 27], little research exists on how beacon-location extends to the most ubiquitous mobile computing platform today: the mobile phone. Mobile phones are an attractive platform for emerging location-aware applications [19, 20] with an estimated 2 billion subscribers world-wide as of 2005–about ten times as many as the total number of mobile PCs in-use [22, 24]. Specifically, the GSM family of technologies, which includes W-CDMA, has more than 1.5 billion subscribers, which is more than the total number of Internet users world-wide [23, 24]. In addition, mobile phones have long battery life, constant connectivity, and are usually at hand and powered on.

This paper examines the feasibility of a client-side, beacon-based GSM location system and whether the methods from the WiFi literature can be retargeted to GSM phones in a metropolitan setting. Our approach differs from operator-provided network-based GSM location solutions in that the phone can position itself in a *privacy-observant* manner and can use cell towers from *all network operators* to compute location without requiring assistance from the network operators. The approach also uses the *existing hardware* in mobile phones without requiring any additional hardware.

P. Dourish and A. Friday (Eds.): Ubicomp 2006, LNCS 4206, pp. 225–242, 2006.
© Springer-Verlag Berlin Heidelberg 2006

There are several important differences between WiFi and GSM. First, the range of a GSM cell can be up to 35Km, which is 70 times larger than WiFi's maximum range of around 500m. Second, the deployment of GSM networks is stable and planned compared to the more ad hoc deployment of WiFi access points. Third, GSM operates in a licensed frequency band and is thus less prone to interference caused by other electronic devices such as cordless phones and microwaves. To study the effect these differences have on accuracy, coverage, and calibration overhead, we collected an extensive 208-hour, 4350Km driving trace of three major GSM networks covering the Seattle metropolitan area: AT&T, Cingular, and T-Mobile.[1] Collecting such a large trace was necessary to assess the algorithms' accuracies without introducing significant experimental error, as we will describe in Section 0. For each GSM network, we sampled the radio environment at 1Hz throughout our drive. Each sample from each device on each network contained up to 7 different cell IDs with their associated signal strengths, network provider ID, and area ID.

Our contributions are the following:

- We characterize the accuracy of three published positioning algorithms: a simple centroid algorithm that does not model radio propagation, fingerprinting, and Monte Carlo localization with a Gaussian Processes signal propagation model. Our experiments show that we can achieve a median accuracy of 94m in downtown and 196m in residential areas. For GSM, choosing a good algorithm can result in up to 388% improvement in position accuracy, which is in stark contrast to past wide-area analyses of WiFi positioning algorithms where the choice of algorithm was comparatively irrelevant since accuracy only varied 20% across different algorithms [4].
- We show that using *cross-provider* GSM beacons can significantly improve positioning accuracy compared to only using cells from a single provider, achieving median accuracy of 65-134 meters. In the downtown Seattle area, this technique meets the E911 positioning requirements for network-based solutions.
- We show that *cross-device* operation is possible with only 6-8% degradation in accuracy for the centroid algorithm and 57%-63% for Gaussian Processes on devices with completely different radios and antennas.
- We also show that a small 60-hour calibration drive is sufficient for enabling a metropolitan area similar to Seattle.
- We have publicly released our GSM positioning toolkit [13] with the algorithmic implementations described in the paper along with tower location traces, allowing researchers at other institutions to experiment with new positioning algorithms. This data contains information about all three major GSM providers in the USA as well as WiFi scans over the 208 hours of data collection.

The rest of the paper is organized as follows: Section 2 presents our data collection methodology and the positioning algorithms, Section 3 characterizes the accuracy of the algorithms under various conditions, Section 4 discusses the implications of our findings, Section 5 presents related work, and Section 6 discusses future work and concludes.

---

[1] Cingular recently acquired AT&T Wireless, but many AT&T-identified towers still existed at the time of this study.

2 Methodology

This section describes our data collection methodology, the trace characteristics, and the positioning algorithms.

2.1 Data Collection

Our data collection hardware consisted of an IBM Thinkpad T30 laptop with a WiFi card, two GPS units, three Sony Ericsson GM28 GSM modems and three Audiovox SMT5600 phones (also known as the HTC Typhoon phones), shown in Figure 1. The GSM phones and GSM modems were fitted with SIM cards from each of the three GSM network providers in the area: AT&T, Cingular, and T-Mobile. A second, identical setup provides redundancy in the event of equipment failure. In all, we used 12 GSM devices to collect GSM traces and 4 redundant GPS units to provide ground truth for location.

Our data collection software is implemented in C#. It records the attached cell ID as well as observed signal strength in dBm for up to 7 GSM cells for each of the modems and the phones, independently once every second for the phones and the maximum scan rate of once every three seconds for the modems. Readings from each GPS unit are recorded once a second. For ground truth of location, we use the latitude and longitude values from the readings that meet the following criteria: valid GPS lock with 5 or more satellite and a low horizontal dilution of precision (HDOP).

A dense calibration trace allows us to characterize the best-case positioning accuracy of a GSM-based location system and perform sensitivity analyses. To collect such a trace, we put our data collection setup in a car and drove every publicly accessible street in the Seattle metropolitan area as shown in Figure 2. External antennas for the GSM modems and GPS units were placed on the car roof to improve signal reception. We drove over 208hrs, or 4350Km, and collected over 24GB of traces over a period of three months. The complete trace contains 6756 unique cells across the three network providers. During this effort, we had one laptop failure due to rain and one car accident.

Fig. 1. Our GSM/WiFi data collection device: one WiFi card, two GPS units (left), and three Sony Ericsson GM28 GSM modems (center) are connected to an IBM Thinkpad T30 laptop. The modems require external antennas (bottom) and we have modified them to be powered via USB hubs. Three Audiovox SMT5600 phones, one for each network provider, are shown on the right.

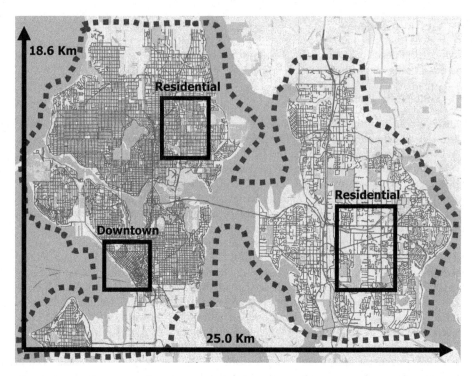

Fig. 2. Dotted-line area and street highlights show the roads driven during our GSM trace collection spanning an 18Km x 25Km region of the Seattle metropolitan area. The three solid rectangles outline the test areas: Downtown with high cell tower density and Residential, two neighborhoods with lower cell density.

The calibration trace is used to train the three positioning algorithms. To measure the accuracy of these algorithms, we selected three test neighborhoods and collected a second complete test trace in each neighborhood two weeks after the training trace was collected. Downtown Seattle was chosen as one test neighborhood as it had the highest tower density at 66 cells/Km^2. In addition, we selected two residential neighborhoods with lower cell tower densities. On average, these neighborhoods had 26 cells/Km^2 or 39% of Downtown's cell density. In our results, the data for the two low-density neighborhoods have been combined. Table 1 summarizes the properties of the training and the test traces.

Table 1. Properties of the collected training trace and two testing traces

	Training Trace	*Testing Traces*	
		Downtown	**Residential**
Name			
Duration	208hr	70min	169min
Distance	4350Km	24Km	89Km
Dimension	25.0 x 18.6Km	2.7 x 2.3Km	2.6 x 4.1Km + 4.6 x 5.5Km
Area	Greater Seattle	Downtown Seattle	Ravenna + East Bellevue
Avg. Cell Density	28 cells/Km^2	66 cells/Km^2	26 cells/Km^2

2.2 Training Area Size

A valid question to ask is why the algorithmic evaluation requires collecting training traces from a much larger area than the regions tested. The answer is that the training data must be large enough to cover the complete cells of all towers seen in the testing traces. If the training data does not meet this constraint then we risk artificially inflating the measured accuracy of the algorithms by not letting them make mistakes they might otherwise make. For example, an algorithm sensing a tower located on the border of the testing area should be allowed to err by estimating the phone's position to be in the part of that tower's cell that is outside the testing area. Indeed, by shrinking the training area to match the size of the testing area we found that we could artificially inflate the accuracy up to 41% for some algorithms. Therefore, we were careful to collect a wide-scale training trace of the entire greater Seattle area extending well beyond the boundaries of all our testing areas.

2.3 Positioning Algorithms

In this paper, we measure the performance of three positioning algorithms from the research literature: a centroid algorithm that does not model radio propagation [9], a radio fingerprinting algorithm [3], and Monte Carlo localization with a learned Gaussian Processes signal propagation model [5, 14]. While a wide variety of radio-based location algorithms have been published, we chose these three as they are representative of the spectrum of positioning algorithms and vary in complexity and expected accuracy.

All our algorithms have been implements in a C# location toolkit that runs on Microsoft Windows Mobile Smartphones, PDAs, and PCs running Windows. On an HTC Typhoon phone, our toolkit can poll GSM readings and calculate its location four times per second using the centroid algorithm and the cell tower maps size for the 6756 cells we observed in Seattle occupy only 44KB of compressed data.

There are two phases to analyzing the positioning accuracy of an algorithm. First, a training trace containing time-stamped GSM and GPS measurements is used to build a model that is specific to that algorithm. In the second phase, the algorithm uses the GSM measurements in an independent testing trace to estimate its position, and outputs latitude/longitude values in its position estimate. Positioning error is computed by calculating the distance between the positions estimated by the algorithm and the ground truth positions provided by GPS. We used the Haversine Formula of distance between two points over the earth as the distance metric [21].

2.3.1 Centroid Family

The centroid algorithm [9] is very fast to compute and, in its basic form, does not employ a radio propagation model. Given a lookup table of <Cell ID, Latitude, Longitude> entries, the centroid algorithm estimates the phone's position to be the geometric center of all the cells that are seen in a measurement. Weighting by the received signal strength observed in the scans is an extension that can offer a small improvement in accuracy. Our experiments used the centroid algorithm in its basic form without any modeling of radio propagation.

Downtown	Residential (cropped)

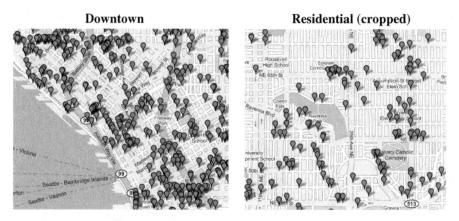

Fig. 3. Cell location map for the three network providers; each dot represents the estimated location of a cell. The left map shows Downtown with an average density of 66 cells/Km². The right map shows a cropped Residential region with an average cell density of 26 cells/Km².

Centroid is the only algorithm we consider that depends on having an estimate of the true tower positions. Because the true cell tower positions are not publicly available in the USA, the training phase estimates tower positions by averaging the places where the highest signal strengths in each cell was observed. Figure 3 shows map of the estimated tower positions for two of our test areas. To evaluate our tower placement accuracy, we randomly selected six cell towers and physically visited these towers to precisely verify their true location. In this test, we found an average error of 56m and a maximum error of 76m. These values are reasonable estimated lower bounds for position error in the centroid algorithm.

2.3.2 Fingerprinting

Radio fingerprinting is a positioning method that assumes the radio beacons and associated signal strengths observed at a particular location is stable over time. The training phase constructs a search index mapping radio fingerprints to locations. In testing, upon seeing a similar radio fingerprint the algorithm can use the index to deduce the phone's position. The RADAR system [3] is an example of this technique applied to WiFi positioning in laptops. Fingerprinting has also more recently been used with GSM radio signatures for server-side, wide-area positioning [10, 28] and indoor location and floor estimation [12].

The fingerprinting algorithm does not create a map of estimated tower positions nor does it model radio propagation. Instead, it creates a search index of radio fingerprints to latitude/longitude coordinates. To position a device, the algorithm uses the constructed index and calculates the Euclidean distance in signal strength space between the current fingerprint and all available fingerprints in the index [4]. It then selects k fingerprints with the smallest Euclidean distance as potential indicators of the current location. The location of the device is estimated as an average of the latitude and longitude coordinates of the best k matches. The accuracy of the location estimate is highly dependent on the density of the set of collected fingerprints. The indoor WiFi and GSM localization papers cited above collected fingerprints at a density of around one fingerprint per square meter. This paper investigates how well fingerprinting works with sparser calibration and less uniformly distributed set of GSM fingerprints at a metropolitan scale. We also characterize the effects of several practical factors on positioning accuracy.

2.3.3 Monte Carlo Localization with Gaussian Processes Signal Models

Gaussian Processes-based Monte Carlo localization uses a radio propagation model and Markov localization to predict the phone's position. The idea is to build a sensor model to predict the signal strength at each location and then use this information to compute the likelihood of measurements. The phone's position is estimated using a Bayesian particle filter.

This approach is like fingerprinting, except it uses an abstract parametric model of the signal environment instead of building a direct search index of the calibration data itself as is done with fingerprinting. To model the signal propagation, we use Gaussian Processes, which are nonparametric models that estimate Gaussian distributions over functions based on the training data [14]. In order to achieve fast execution we pre-process the signal propagation function to a grid with 15m grid-cells. The computation of the signal propagation can then be implemented simply by a look-up function in the maps of the cell towers. With the predicted signal strength, we can compute the likelihood of an observation given the phone is at a particular location.

To represent the posterior probability distribution about the position of the phone, we apply standard Monte-Carlo localization called particle filtering [5]. In Monte-Carlo localization, the belief about the phone's position is represented by a set of random samples. Each sample consists of a state vector of the underlying system, which is the position of the mobile phone, and a weighting factor. The weight is the likelihood of the measurement at the particle's location. The posterior is represented by the distribution of the samples and their importance factors. This particle filter algorithm used by our system is also known as sequential importance sampling [1].

3   Results

This section presents analyses that explore the effects of five factors on positioning accuracy: algorithm selection, scan set size, simultaneous use of cells from different providers, training and testing on different devices, and calibration drive density. Because our goal is to characterize the positioning accuracy of GSM, we have anonymized the names of the three network providers and we will refer to them as Provider A, B, and C. For single-provider results, we report the median values among the three providers.

3.1 Effect of Algorithm Selection on Positioning Accuracy

We evaluated the positioning error for each of the three algorithms described in Section 0 using the test traces collected from the test areas. Table 2 shows the median and 90th percentile error for each algorithm grouped by the test areas. All three algorithms performed better in the higher tower density area, Downtown, than the lower tower density area, with the median error ranging from 94-232 meters compared to 196-760 meters.

Table 2. Median and 90th-percentile positioning errors (in meters) for Centroid, Fingerprinting, and Gaussian Processes algorithms in the two test areas

	Downtown (higher density)		Residential (lower density)	
	50%	**90%**	**50%**	**90%**
Centroid	232	574	760	2479
Fingerprinting	94	291	277	984
Gaussian Processes	126	358	196	552

Since the centroid algorithm does not model signal strength and assigns equal weight to each cell, the position estimate can be greatly affected by the density and the placement of the cells resulting in the worst position estimates. The fingerprinting algorithm performs much better than centroid, achieving a 94m median error in Downtown and 277m in Residential. One reason for this decrease in error is that Downtown has more obstructions due to large buildings than the Residential area. These obstructions actually prove advantageous because they help form unique fingerprints to allow the algorithm to differentiate between nearby locations. The more open space coupled with the lower cell density in the Residential area results in less unique fingerprints, thereby increasing the positioning error.

The Gaussian Processes algorithm models signal strengths with continuous functions, and therefore is not able to capture the sharp changes in signal strengths due to obstructions as well as fingerprinting, resulting in slightly worse accuracy in Downtown. In the more open environments, however, it models the sparse training data sufficiently to produce the best accuracy in the residential areas.

Positioning error from WiFi localization techniques has been shown to be highly dependent on access point density. Moreover, the use of complex positioning algorithms only provide a 20% improvement in accuracy compared to the simple algorithms such as centroid [4]. With the much larger cell sizes of GSM, we found that algorithmic improvements can improve positioning accuracy by 247%- 388%.

3.2 Effects of Scan Set Size

At any given time, a GSM device may be within range of a large number of GSM cells. A client-side location system, however, may be limited in the number of nearby cells it can sense. For many models of mobile phones, normal user-level application are not allowed any information about which cell tower the phones are associated with or the observed signal strength. The Series 60 phones [26] (e.g. Nokia 6600 and N92) allow user programs to find out the ID and observed signal strength of the single cell with which the phone is currently associated. Other devices, such as the GSM modems and phones we used in our study, provide information about the cell the phone is associated with, as well as six other nearby cells (making a total of seven). In this experiment, we investigate what effect the size of this set has on position accuracy for all three algorithms. We vary the number of cells between one and seven by sorting the observed cells by signal strength and using only the n strongest.

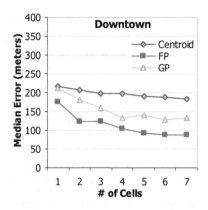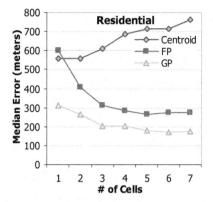

Fig. 4. Median positioning error as a function of the N cells with the strongest signal strengths for the Downtown and Residential test areas. FP stands for fingerprinting and GP stands for Gaussian Processes.

Figure 4 shows sensitivity analysis of positioning error versus the number of cells available for both Downtown and Residential. Both the fingerprinting and Gaussian Processes algorithms improve in accuracy as more cells are used for positioning, for a 50% and 37% improvement in Downtown, respectively. The additional cells, regardless of signals strengths, provide information that help differentiation among similar measurements and help improve the position estimates.

Centroid also exhibits the same trend in areas of high cell density, showing improved accuracy with more cells in Downtown. However, as cells become sparser and distant in the Residential area, the cells with weak signal strengths contribute to increased positioning error. This trend is evident in Figure 4, where surprisingly, using only 1-2 cells gives the best accuracy, and using 5 or more cells produce the worst positioning accuracy.

3.3 Effects of Using Towers from Multiple Providers

Once associated with a cell tower, GSM devices only monitor cells from that tower's network, even though cell towers from other providers may be closer and have stronger signals. Up to this point, all of the results have reflected this limitation: our AT&T phone estimates its location using the AT&T training data, the T-Mobile phone estimates its location using the T-Mobile data, etc. We now consider what would happen if a GSM phone could scan for cells from all available networks. Ideally, it would increase both the number of nearby observable cell towers and the number of strongly observable towers, thus providing an opportunity to improve positioning accuracy.

To evaluate its effectiveness, we simulate a cross-provider device by combining measurements from the three network providers: AT&T, Cingular, and T-Mobile that were collected within 5 seconds of each other, and use them to estimate location. Because each GSM device gets information for up to 7 nearby cells on its network, our simulated device will hear up to 21 nearby cells. This raised a concern that accuracy improvements may only be due to the magnitude of the scan set. To measure this effect, we first limit our simulated cross-provider device to only use the strongest 7 cells it hears across the three networks. We then evaluate the positioning accuracy when all available cells from all providers are used.

Table 3. Cross-provider median positioning error in meters when 1) using only cells from a single provider, 2) using the top 7 strongest cells across providers, and 3) using all available cells across providers

	Downtown			Residential		
	Single Provider (7)	Cross-Provider (7)	Cross-Provider (all)	Single Provider (7)	Cross-Provider (7)	Cross-Provider (all)
Centroid	187	166	170	647	456	574
Fingerprinting	94	153	245	277	313	297
Gaussian Processes	126	87	65	196	147	134

Table 3 shows the effect on positioning accuracy when each algorithm uses only cells from a single provider, the top 7 strongest cells across providers, and all possible cells. For Centroid, the increased ratio of nearby towers is the most significant with the strongest 7 cells, which shows an improvement of 11-30% compared to a single provider. Increasing the number of cells reduces the improvement.

Surprisingly, fingerprinting performs much worse when cells from multiple providers are used. A closer inspection shows that one of the network providers, Provider A, added new cells to the downtown area (or renamed existing cells) during our 3-month calibration drive. Because we drove the downtown area during the first month, we did not observe these new cells with strong signal strengths at their true location. Rather, we observed them with weak signal strengths kilometers away, resulting in skewed position estimates produced by fingerprinting and centroid. Gaussian Processes is more resistant to this effect because the models only contain information about these cells at weaks signal strengths, limiting their impact during the tests drive when these cells were observed at strong signal strengths.

For Gaussian Processes, using the strongest 7 cells across providers improves the median error by 27-40% compared to a single provider. Using all the available cells, it further improves the median error for a total improvement of 45-55%, achieving a median error of 65m for Downtown and 134m for Residential.

The cross-provider accuracy improvement is more significant towards the tail end of the distribution, as evident in the more vertical curves in the Cumulative Distribution Function (CDF) shown in Figure 5. When all available cells are being used, Gaussian Processes achieves 136m at the 90th percentile in Downtown compared to 308-907m for the three individual providers. Specifically, the 67th percentile error is 88m and the 95th percentile is 163m, which is within the E911 requirements of 100m and 300m, respectively, for network-based solutions.

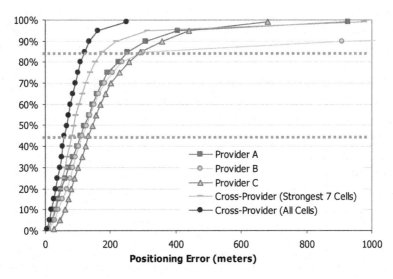

Fig. 5. CDF of positioning error for the Gaussian Processes algorithm in Downtown using 1) cells from a single provider, 2) the top 7 strongest cells across multiple network providers, and 3) all available cells from multiple network providers.

3.4 Effects of Training on One Device and Testing on Another

Our results thus far have all been presented based on a single GSM device: the HTC Typhoon phone. Moreover, we used the same device to gather data for both testing and training. A practical question is if other GSM devices, including another HTC Typhoon phone, can be used to achieve comparable positioning results using the same calibration data. For simple algorithms such as centroid, the only algorithmic requirement is that the device observes a similar set of cell towers as the HTC Typhoon. For other algorithms, the device must observe similar towers, and its signal strength values would have to correlate well with the HTC Typhoon. Given a strong correlation, a transformation function could convert the device's signal strength values to those reported by the HTC Typhoon.

We compared the common cells seen, and the signal strength values for those cells, among three GSM devices: a duplicate HTC Typhoon phone, a HTC Tornado phone, and a Sony Ericsson GM28 modem. These devices represent GSM units that have different radio and different antenna designs. All devices report a signal strength value with each observed cell.

Table 4 shows the average number of common towers seen per scan between each device and the reference device, and the Pearson correlation coefficient for the signal strength values of these common cells. Even though the HTC Tornado has a different antenna and the modem has both a different radio and antenna, all devices exhibit strong signal strength correlation that are statistically significant to the 0.001 level.

Given that a linear transformation function can map the signal strength from one device to another, we now explore the effect of training and testing on different devices. Because the handoff behavior are different on different GSM devices due to radio and antenna design, techniques such as fingerprinting that do exact pattern matching of signal strengths should see the most degradation.

Table 4. Similarity between different GSM devices and the reference HTC Typhoon phone, showing the number of cells that are the common when two different devices scan at the same time. Pearson correlation coefficient and significance are shown for the signal strengths of these common cells between each device and the reference phone.

Devices	Radio	Antenna	Average # of Common Cells	Signal Strength Correlation	Correlation Significance
HTC Typhoon (reference)	*Same*	*Same*	*7.000*	*1.000*	*.000*
HTC Typhoon (duplicate)	Same	Same	6.484	0.828	<.001
HTC Tornado	Same	Diff.	5.018	0.789	<.001
Sony Ericsson GM28 Modem	Diff.	Diff.	4.283	0.874	<.001

Table 5. Cross-device median positioning error and % change when training with the trace collected on one device (the HTC Typhoon phones) and testing on another device (the Sony Ericsson modems)

	Downtown		Residential	
	50% (meters)	**% change**	**50% (meters)**	**% change**
Centroid	245	5.6%	818	7.6%
Fingerprinting	366	289%	803	190%
Gaussian Processes	206	63%	307	57%

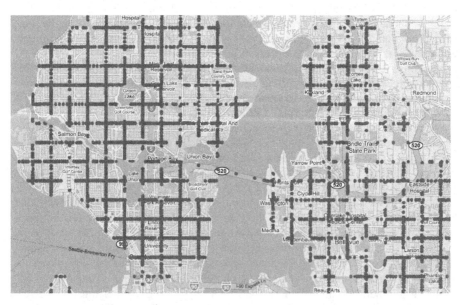

Fig. 6. Example of a generated, virtual street grid that simulates a drive density equivalent to 10% of the full training trace

Table 5 shows the median error when we train on the data from the HTC Typhoon phone and test on the GM28 modem after applying a linear transformation function for the observed signal strengths. These accuracy numbers are conservative because the phone and the modems had completely different radio and antenna designs, with the modems using roof-mounted antennas.

The Gaussian Processes algorithm had the best accuracy in both Downtown and Residential, with median accuracy of 206m and 307m, and degradation of 63% and 57%, respectively. Fingerprinting performed the worst in Downtown at 366m, and has the largest increase in error in both Downtown and Residential compared to training and testing on the same device. This is likely due to the modems switching over to different cells at slightly different times than the phones when they moved across cell boundaries. Centroid was the most robust with the least degradation at 6-8%.

3.5 Effects of Reducing Calibration Drive Density

We characterized the tradeoff between calibration drive density and positioning error by simulating a sparser driving pattern from our comprehensive data set. In contrast to prior experiments on WiFi density that effectively simulate devices with slower scanning rates [4], we are interested in spatial thinning that simulates the effect of driving fewer streets. Understanding this effect is useful to estimate the resource and cost necessary to calibrate a GSM-based positioning system to support accuracy requirements of the intended applications. Simple algorithms that do not model signal propagation characteristics only require the location of the cell towers, which can potentially be supplied by the GSM network providers. More sophisticated algorithms, however, rely on calibration data to improve positioning accuracy, but it is unclear how much calibration is necessary.

To simulate these sparse drives, we super-impose a virtual street grid pattern on our dense calibration trace and filter measurements that do not fall on the virtual street grid. By varying the width between the virtual streets, varying levels of driving density can be simulated. In order to reduce systematic error due to the interaction of the virtual and real grids, we use five random offsets for each grid width. We then average them for each width to estimate the positioning error given the level of density being simulated.

Figure 7 shows the median error versus the percentage of data dropped using our simulated street grids for Downtown. With centroid, using only 20% of the density produces statistically equivalent positioning accuracy as our full drive density. Both fingerprinting and Gaussian Proccesses algorithms show slight, but gradual degradation as the amount of data decreases, because the quality of the radio models degrades with less calibration. All three algorithms had median positioning error above 200m when only 10% of the density is used. Although a comprehensive drive still produces the best positioning error, less dense drives can still produce similar accuracy without the added expense. For the Seattle metropolitan area, 30%, or 60 hours of driving is sufficient to calibrate a GSM-based positioning system without a significant loss in accuracy. More sophisticated street selection can further reduce the amount of calibration required.

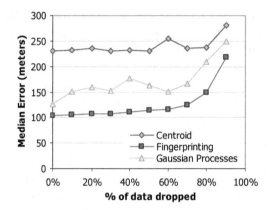

Fig. 7. Median positioning error as a function of the calibration drive density, simulating the effect of driving fewer streets. Dropping 70% of the data still provides comparable median error to the full calibration drive.

4 Discussion

We have presented a variety of results to show how three location estimation algorithms performed using GSM traces from three neighborhoods. By using data from different devices and by simulating varying scan-set sizes and training trace densities, we modeled the algorithms performance in a variety of situations. Table 6 show a high-level summary of these results. From this table, we can draw a number of conclusions about when and where these algorithms are the most appropriate.

A number of mobile phones, including the popular Series 60 phones [26], only provide information about a single tower at a time. For these devices, as well as phones with constrained storage and computation capability, the best algorithm is the centroid. The centroid algorithm uses very few resources, and is extremely robust to the quality of the training set. Our data showed the centroid to be the most resistant to sparse training data as well as training data collected on a different device. This simplicity comes at the cost of being the least accurate in areas with both high and low tower densities.

Table 6. Summary of the characteristics of the three positioning algorithms

	Storage Required (for Seattle, compressed)	CPU Usage	Accuracy (Dense Towers)	Accuracy (Sparse Towers)	Required Density of Training Data	Requires Same-Device Training Set	Benefits from Cross-Provider Scanning	Tolerant of Phones Exposing Single Cell
Centroid	Low (44KB)	Low	232m	760m	Low	No	Yes	Yes
Finger-printing	High (188MB)	Med.	94m	277m	High	Yes	No	No
Gaussian Processes	Med. (80MB)	High	126m	196m	Med.	No	Yes	Yes

For mobile phones with more storage and processing power and the ability to scan for multiple cell towers at a time, the Monte Carlo localization with Gaussian Processes model probably offers the best overall mix of accuracy and practicality. It was the most accurate in the residential neighborhoods and was close to the best algorithm in downtown. It was also robust to single cells positioning as well as cross-device training data.

Fingerprinting was the most accurate in the high-density urban area and performed well in the low-density area as well. The fingerprint training sets consume large amounts of storage, but with optimized indexing the relevant fingerprints can be accessed quickly. However, fingerprinting was the most fragile of the algorithms, requiring dense training data collected on similar, if not identical, mobile phones. It was also the most fragile to the addition of new cells during the calibration drive.

The most worrisome results in this study are the sensitivities we measured to cross-device accuracy degradation. Although we tested a particularly dramatic cross-device scenario (phone versus modem) with completely different antenna configuration (internal versus vehicle roof-mounted), the error increase was higher than we would like to see. We believe more research, both at the hardware and algorithmic levels is warranted to understand and mitigate the errors in this area.

Our data also shows that if future mobile phones support the ability to scan for towers across service providers, the Gaussian Process algorithm becomes the clear winner. While the Centroid and Fingerprinting showed no benefit from additional tower data, the Gaussian Process algorithm saw up to a 50% reduction in median error. Perhaps more importantly, the 95th-percentile error showed an even more pronounced drop, improving by over 70% in our downtown test area.

5 Related Work

The most common location technology today is the Global Positioning System (GPS). Although GPS is effective in open environments, it does not work well when the GPS receiver is indoors or in dense urban areas. The research community generally agrees that many location-enhanced mobile applications require another technology to augment or replace GPS to meet coverage and accuracy needs. GSM and WiFi-based location techniques are common ways to overcome the shortcomings in GPS.

The four papers most related to this work are follows: LaMarca et al [9] presents an overview of Place Lab, with experiments that are appropriate to study WiFi positioning accuracy, but not sufficient for characterizing GSM. Trevisani and Vitaletti [15] studies single cell-ID location in mobile phone networks that compares the accuracy and coverage of operators' location systems in different cities, Laitinen et al [10] analyzes the positioning accuracy of a server-side fingerprinting approach in both urban and suburban environments. Otsason et al [12] explores client-side indoor GSM location and floor differentiation. Our work characterizes the wide-area positioning accuracy for three classes of algorithms and investigates the effects of several practical issues such as cross-device positioning and calibration drive density. We also present a novel cross-provider positioning technique that significantly improves positioning accuracy.

The E911/E112 initiatives in the US and Europe specify requirements on localization accuracy for mobile phones placing emergency calls. These initiatives have catalyzed a market for network operator-provided location capabilities and services like AT&T Wireless' friend-finder and Sprint-NexTel's fleet management tools. Operators calculate mobile phone positions using hybrid network-client techniques like Assisted GPS (AGPS) where the network data links provide aiding information to a limited in-phone GPS chip, or network-only techniques like enhanced observed time difference (EOTD), angle of arrival (AOA), and time difference of arrival (TDOA) [15]. AGPS is more accurate than network-only techniques and extends the coverage of standalone GPS to operate in areas with limited GPS reception, such as urban canyons and some indoor environments.

Beacon-based location with WiFi positioning is also a well-studied problem by the Place Lab project and other researchers [4, 6, 9, 10, 11] and has been commercialized by Microsoft Virtual Earth [25] and SkyHook Wireless [28]. They have demonstrated that the WiFi beacon approach is viable and can result in a good indoor-outdoor location system with high coverage and sufficient accuracy for many mobile applications. Metrics including coverage, accuracy, beacon density, mapping and calibration drive overhead, and performance have all been evaluated. Median accuracy of the approach is 15m-60m with nearly 100% coverage in urban areas. Wide-area beacon-based approaches complement the many indoor positioning systems that provide high precision in indoor environments but require specialized hardware or have high installation costs. Examples of these systems include Cricket [15], Active Badge [16], and Active Floor [17].

A related but distinct class of research to the work in this paper is the problem of learning places using mobile devices carried by the user. These place-learning systems do not provide real-time navigation or fulfill the "dot-on-a-map" application scenarios. Instead, they provide the ability to recognize previously visited destinations by using metrics like GPS dropout [2], cell handoff patterns [8], or radio signatures [7] to match previously learned places.

6 Conclusions

This paper examined the positioning accuracy and the practical challenges in deploying a GSM beacon-based location system in a metropolitan environment. To do this, we collected data over a larger area than past WiFi beacon-based location projects because the range of GSM cells are up to 70 times larger than WiFi access points. We collected an extensive 208hr, 4350Km trace covering the Seattle metropolitan area.

Our results show that existing GSM devices can achieve a positioning accuracy with a median error of 94-196 meters using cells from a single provider. We have observed that the positioning accuracy varies significantly across algorithms, by a factor of almost 4x, compared to past characterizations for WiFi that have a maximum variation of 20%.

Our analysis on calibration drive density suggests that 30% of our dataset was sufficient to provide comparable positioning accuracy – suggesting that 60hrs of driving can cover a metropolitan area similar to the size of Seattle. Our results show that cross-device positioning is possible with only 6-8% degradation in accuracy for the centroid algorithm and 57%-63% for Gaussian Processes on devices with completely different radios and antennas. We believe more research, both at the hardware and algorithmic levels is warranted to understand and mitigate the errors in this area.

Finally, we have identified an opportunity to significantly improve accuracy by scanning cells across all available providers, for a median error of 65-134m, which is a factor of 3-4x of the published accuracy for WiFi.

Acknowledgements

We thank James Howard for developing the data logging software and David Sherrick for collecting the GSM traces. We also thank the anonymous reviewers for their comments.

References

1. S. Arulampalam, S. Maskell, N. Gordon, and T. Clapp, "A Tutorial on Particle Filters for Online Non-Linear/Non-Gaussian Bayesian Tracking", *IEEE Transactions on Signal Processing*, 50(2):174–188, 2002.
2. D. Ashbrook, T. Starner, "Using GPS to Learn Significant Locations and Predict Movement across Multiple Users", *Personal and Ubiquitous Computing* 7 (2003) 275–286
3. P. Bahl and V. N. Padmanabhan, "RADAR: An In-Building RF-Based User Location and Tracking System", in *Proceedings of IEEE INFOCOM* 2000, Vol. 2: 775-784
4. Y. Cheng, Y. Chawathe, A. LaMarca and J. Krumm, "Accuracy Characterization for Metropolitan-scale WiFi Localization", in *Proceedings of Mobisys* 2005.
5. D. Fox, W. Burgard, F. Dellaert, and S. Thrun, "Monte Carlo localization: Efficient Position Estimation for Mobile Robots", in *Proceedings of AAAI*, 1999.
6. A. Haeberlen, E. Flannery, A. M. Ladd, A. Rudys, D. S. Wallach, and L. E. Kavraki, "Practical Robust Localization over Large-scale 802.11 Wireless Networks," in *Proceedings of Mobicom*, 2004.
7. J. Hightower, et al, "Learning and Recognizing the Places We Go", in *Proceedings of Ubicomp*, pp. 159-176, Sep. 2005.
8. K. Laasonen, M. Raento, and H. Toivonen. "Adaptive On-device Location Recognition", in *Proceedings of the Second International Conference on Pervasive Computing*. Volume 3001 of Lecture Notes in Computer Science., Springer-Verlag (2004) 287–304
9. A. LaMarca, et al, "Place Lab: Device Positioning Using Radio Beacons in the Wild," in *Proceedings of the Third International Conference on Pervasive Computing*, May 2005.
10. H. Laitinen, J. Lahteenmaki, T. Nordstrom, "Database correlation method for GSM location", *IEEE 53rd Vehicular Technology Conference*, 2001.
11. J. Letchner, D. Fox, and A. LaMarca, "Large-Scale Localization from Wireless Signal Strength", In *Proceedings of the National Conference on Artificial Intelligence (AAAI-05)*.
12. V. Otsason, A. Varshavsky, A. LaMarca, E. de Lara: "Accurate GSM Indoor Localization," in *Proceedings of Ubicomp 2005*: 141-158.
13. Privacy-Observant Location System, http://pols.sourceforge.net/
14. A. Schwaighofer, M. Grigoras, V. Tresp, and C. Hoffmann. "GPPS: A Gaussian Process Positioning System for Cellular Networks", in *Proceedings of NIPS 2003*.
15. E. Trevisani and A. Vitaletti. "Cell-ID Location Technique, Limits and Benefits: An Experimental Study." In *Proceedings of WMCSA 2004*. 51—60.
16. N. B. Priyantha, A. Chakraborty, H. Balakrishnan. "The cricket location-support system." In *Proceedings of Mobicom 2000*, pp. 32-43

17. R. Want, A. Hopper, V. Falco, J. Gibbons. "The Active Badge Location System." *ACM Transactions on Information Systems* 10, 1 (1992), 91-102

18. M. D. Addlesee, A. Jones, F. Livesey, and F. Samaria. "The ORL Active Floor." *IEEE Personal Communications* 4, 5 (1997), 35-41.

19. T. Sohn, et al, "Place-Its: A Study of Location-Based Reminders on Mobile Phones." In *Proceedings of Ubicomp 2005*.

20. I. Smith, et al, "Social Disclosure of Place: From Location Technology to Communication Practice." In *Proceedings of Pervasive 2005*.

21. R.W. Sinnott, "Virtues of the Haversine", Sky and Telescope, vol. 68, no. 2, 1984, p. 159

22. Computer Industry Almanac Press Release. "Mobile PCs In-Use Surpass 200M." June, 2005. http://www.c-i-a.com/pr0605.htm

23. Computer Industry Almanac Press Release. "Worldwide Internet Users will Top 1 Billion in 2005." Sept 2004. http://www.c-i-a.com/pr0904.htm

24. GSM Association Press Release. "Worldwide cellular connections exceeds 2 billion." Sept 2005. http://www.gsmworld.com/news/press_2005/press05_21.shtml

25. Microsoft Virtual Earth. http://virtualearth.msn.com

26. Series 60 Phone Platform. http://s60.com

27. Skyhook Wireless. http://www.skyhookwireless.com

28. US Wireless. http://web.archive.org/web/20031124182802/http://uswcorp.com

Predestination:
Inferring Destinations from Partial Trajectories

John Krumm and Eric Horvitz

Microsoft Research
Microsoft Corporation
One Microsoft Way
Redmond, WA USA 98052
{jckrumm, horvitz}@microsoft.com

Abstract. We describe a method called *Predestination* that uses a history of a driver's destinations, along with data about driving behaviors, to predict where a driver is going as a trip progresses. Driving behaviors include types of destinations, driving efficiency, and trip times. Beyond considering previously visited destinations, Predestination leverages an *open-world* modeling methodology that considers the likelihood of users visiting previously unobserved locations based on trends in the data and on the background properties of locations. This allows our algorithm to smoothly transition between "out of the box" with no training data to more fully trained with increasing numbers of observations. Multiple components of the analysis are fused via Bayesian inference to produce a probabilistic map of destinations. Our algorithm was trained and tested on hold-out data drawn from a database of GPS driving data gathered from 169 different subjects who drove 7,335 different trips.

1 Introduction

Location has played a central role in ubiquitous computing research. Information about the location of users can enable numerous compelling location-based services. For example, location can be used to fetch relevant information such as nearby points of interest and available services. Beyond current location, services can be developed around predictions about future locations. For example, a driver may want to know about restaurants or traffic problems before encountering them to give time to prepare and make decisions. Location-based services could present their availability in anticipation of a user's arrival. In another application, a prediction of a person's destination can be helpful in deciding if the person is deviating from an intended route [2]. Cheng *et al.*[3] even speculate that destination prediction could be used to catch automobile thieves.

We present a methodology named *Predestination* that is aimed at predicting a driver's destination as a trip progresses. The probabilistic prediction is based on several sources of data, including the driver's history of destinations and an ensemble of trips from a group of drivers. We demonstrate how to combine these data sources in a

P. Dourish and A. Friday (Eds.): Ubicomp 2006, LNCS 4206, pp. 243–260, 2006.

principled way to reason about drivers' ultimate destinations, resulting in inferred probability distributions over a geographic region. We trained and tested our algorithm on GPS data from 169 different drivers who participated in a data-collection effort that we call the *Microsoft Multiperson Location Survey* (MSMLS)[4].

2   Related Research

Previous work in predicting users' locations includes an application designed for a pool of shared vehicles. Karbassi and Barth[5] process historical GPS data from the vehicles to extract the most common routes between five pre-designated locations. Given the destination, their goal is to predict the route in order to estimate arrival times. In contrast, Predestination is designed to predict the destination, not necessarily the route. And, our algorithm works on a fully tiled geographic region, not just a handful of discrete locations.

Systems for predicting locations can be used to make smooth handoffs between wireless communication cells, like Wi-Fi and cellular telephones. Cheng *et al.*[3] review the work in this area. The defining characteristics are that locations are represented as antenna cells and that prediction is based on past behavior.

Like ours, much of the previous work on destination prediction is based on GPS sensing. In their *comMotion* work, Marmasse and Schmandt[6] predict a person's destination from a list of previously visited destinations using a Bayes classifier, histogram matching, and an HMM. Ashbrook and Starner[7] find potential destinations by clustering GPS data, then predict destinations from these candidates based on Markov models trained to find the next most likely destination based on the one(s) that were recently visited. In Project Lachesis, Hariharan and Toyama[8] present a location clustering algorithm that is sensitive to scale in both space and time. They model transitions between clustered locations with a Markov model. Liao *et al.*[9] present a hierarchical dynamic Bayesian network to predict destinations, which is shown to outperform a 2nd-order Markov model. Using a dynamic network model, Gogate *et al.*[10] incorporate time-of-day and day-of-week evidence to predict a driver's route and destination. All of this work shares the trait that candidate destinations are extracted from GPS histories, *i.e.* places that subjects have actually visited.

Although previously visited locations are one component of our prediction algorithm as in the work above, we also predict destinations that the user has not necessarily ever visited before. We do this with an examination of ground cover (*e.g.* middles of lakes are unpopular driving destinations), the fact that drivers attempt to take efficient routes, and a distribution of likely trip times. In Predestination, all this information is combined with Bayes formula to give a probability distribution of destinations over a geographic area. We also introduce the concept of an *open-world* model that addresses the incompleteness of our models in an explicit manner. With the open-world method, we acknowledge and model the possibility that behaviors observed in the future may not be represented in the current dataset. In the case of Predestination, drivers may go to destinations that have not been previously recorded in the training data. The open-world model allows us to reason about new destinations seen as training progresses so as to capture a user's general patterns of trips and destinations, as well for capturing the ongoing background exploration of new locations that people may perform on an ongoing basis.

3 MSMLS: Multiperson Location Survey

We trained and tested our destination prediction algorithm on driving trip data gathered from 169 subjects[4]. These subjects volunteered to place one of our 55 GPS receivers in their car for two weeks (and occasionally longer) as they drove normally. Nearly all the subjects live in the Seattle, WA USA area, and they include employees of our institution and their family members. The GPS receivers were Geko 201 models, capable of recording up to 10,000 time-stamped (latitude, longitude) coordinates. Each subject was given a cable to supply GPS power from the car's cigarette lighter. Using a simple hardware modification, we altered the GPS receivers so they would automatically turn on whenever power was supplied. This meant that the drivers did not have to remember to turn the receivers on or off, and could instead just set the receiver on the dashboard and neglect it for the entire two weeks. Because some cars' cigarette lighters are powered even when the car is off, we used a mode on the GPS receivers that only recorded points when the receiver is in motion, eliminating the accumulation of points when the cars were parked.

We gathered a total of 1,228,237 (latitude, longitude) points for an average of 6,267 points per person. The points were separated by a median distance of 63 meters and 6 seconds. We also gathered demographic data from each subject: 75% were male, 71% had a domestic partner, 48% had children, and the average age of drivers was 36.

As the goal of this research is to predict destinations, we segmented our GPS data into discrete trips. We identified trips by looking for places in the sequence that met either of the following criteria:

- Gap of at least five minutes: A five-minute gap indicates that the GPS was not moving and, because of its adaptive recording mode, not recording new points. Such a gap can also come from vehicles where power to the device turns off with the car.
- At least five minutes of speeds below two miles per hour: Identifying such a period of low speed accounts for the fact that, even when parked, GPS noise can make it appear that the vehicle is moving slightly. We took measures of five minutes or more of extremely slow apparent motion to be a split between trips.

We deleted discrete trips whose maximum speed did not exceed 25 miles per hour in an effort to eliminate pedestrian and bicycle trips, because some of our study participants took their devices out of their cars. We also eliminated trips of less than one kilometer or with less than 10 GPS points. After this segmentation and culling, we had 7,335 discrete trips. We found that the average length of these trips is 14.4 minutes, and that subjects took an average of 3.3 trips per day.

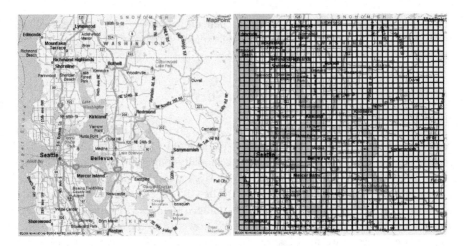

Fig. 1. We used a grid over the Seattle, WA area as the basis for modeling driver behavior and destination predictions. The left map shows the area without the grid. The cells are squares, one square kilometer in size.

4   Destination Probabilities

This section explains the probabilistic analysis of drivers' destinations. We first describe the spatial representation and the underlying probabilistic model for the Pre-destination method. Then we describe the four constituent components of the probabilistic analysis. Finally, we describe the probabilistic integration of the sources of information to produce a posterior probability distribution over destinations.

4.1   Probabilistic Grid on Map

We represent space as a 40x40, two-dimensional grid of square cells, each cell 1 kilometer on a side, as shown in Figure 1. Each cell represents one discrete location. Our destination prediction is aimed at picking the cell in which a driver will conclude his or her trip based on which cells the driver has already traversed and on the characteristics of each cell. This particular discretization of space is a heuristic choice, and we could have chosen a different tiling, size, and number of discrete cells. Each of the $N = 1600$ cells is given an index $i = 1,2,3, \ldots, N$.

Because our methods are probabilistic, we ultimately compute the probability of each cell being the destination, *i.e.* $P(D = i | \mathbf{X} = \mathbf{x})$, where D is a random variable representing the destination, and $\mathbf{X}$ is a random variable representing the vector of observed features from the trip so far. While we shall focus on trajectory-centric observations, other factors can be included in $\mathbf{X}$, such as time of day and day of week.

We decompose the inference about location into the prior probability and the likelihood of seeing data given that each cell is the destination. Appling Bayes rule gives

$$P(D = i|\mathbf{X} = \mathbf{x}) = \frac{P(\mathbf{X} = \mathbf{x}|D = i)P(D = i)}{\sum_{j=1}^{N} P(\mathbf{X} = \mathbf{x}|D = j)P(D = j)} \tag{1}$$

Here $P(D = i)$ is the prior probability of the destination being cell i. We shall compute the prior with two sources of map information, detailed in Sections 4.2 and 4.3. $P(\mathbf{X} = \mathbf{x}|D = i)$ is the likelihood of cell i being the destination based on the observed measurements $\mathbf{X}$. We compute this with two other sources of map information, detailed in Sections 4.4 and 4.5 below. The denominator is a normalization factor computed from the collected data.

4.2 Ground Cover Prior

We can use ground cover information as one source of information about the probability of destinations. For example, we can assert that the middles of lakes and oceans are unlikely destinations for drivers, and that commercial areas are more attractive destinations than places that are perennially covered with ice and snow. In order to verify these suspicions and use them for destination prediction, we characterized each cell in our grid based on a United States Geological Survey (USGS) ground cover map, available for free download [11]. These maps categorize each 30m x 30m square of the U.S. into 1 of 21 different types of ground cover whose types are given in Figure 2.

By looking at the (latitude, longitude) of each trip destination in our dataset, we created a normalized histogram over the 21 ground cover types, shown in Figure 2. As expected, water is an unpopular destination, although still more popular than some other categories, and commercial areas are more attractive than those covered with ice and snow The two most popular destinations are "commercial" and "low intensity residential", which the USGS describes as:

- Commercial/Industrial/Transportation – "Includes infrastructure (*e.g.* roads, railroads, etc.) and all highly developed areas not classified as High Intensity Residential."[12]
- Low Intensity Residential – "Includes areas with a mixture of constructed materials and vegetation. Constructed materials account for 30-80 percent of the cover. Vegetation may account for 20 to 70 percent of the cover. These areas most commonly include single-family housing units. Population densities will be lower than in high intensity residential areas."[12]

The "water" category was nonzero likely because a 30m x 30m USGS square is categorized as water even if it is up to 25% dry land, which could include beaches and waterfront property depending on how the squares are placed. We expect this distribution to be not generally applicable outside the immediate area of our testing, because different regions will have different mixes of ground cover and its people will have possibly different behaviors.

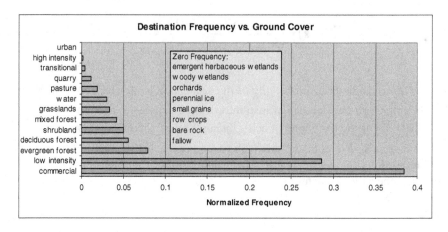

Fig. 2. Destination probabilities vary with the type of ground cover at the destination

The normalized histogram in Figure 2 represents $P(D = i | G = j)$, which gives the probability of a destination cell if it were completely covered by ground cover type j for $j = 1,2,3, ... ,21$. In reality, our 1 km x 1 km cells each contain about 1,111 30m x 30m ground cover labels, and they are usually not completely covered by the same type. To account for this, we compute the distribution of ground cover types for each cell, calling it $P_i(G = j)$. We compute the probability of each cell being a destination, based only on the ground cover information, by marginalizing the ground cover types in the cell:

$$P_G(D = i) = \sum_{j=1}^{21} P(D = i, G = j) = \sum_{j=1}^{21} P(D = i | G = j) P_i(G = j) \qquad (2)$$

$P_G(D = i)$ is the probability of a destination cell based on ground cover. A plot of this likelihood on a map is shown in Figure 3(a), which shows that water and more rural areas are lower-probability destinations.

4.3 Personal Destinations and Open World Modeling

We now turn to the incorporation of more informative probabilistic information based on the prior history of driver's destinations. We build on the intuition that drivers often go to places they have been before, and that such places should be given a higher destination probability. This is the main principle behind much previous work in pervasive computing on modeling and predicting transportation routines. For instance, Murmasse and Schmandt[6] used the loss of a GPS signal to indicate that a user had entered a building. If the user enters the same building a number of times, that location is marked as candidate destination for future prediction. Ashbrook and Starner[7] cluster GPS-measured locations where a user spent more than 10 minutes to extract likely destinations. In their work on learning and modeling transportation routines, Liao *et al.*[9] extracted destinations by clustering locations of long stays. In Project Lachesis, Hariharan and Toyama[8] infer potential destinations in a similar way, but explicitly account for variations in scale of a destination's size and duration of stay.

We model personal destinations as the grid cells containing endpoints of segmented trips. As such, the spatial scale of a candidate destination is the same as a cell's size, and the required stay time to be considered a destination is determined by our trip segmentation parameter, which is currently five minutes.

4.3.1 Closed-World Assumption

We first consider the case where drivers only visit destinations that they have been observed to visit in the past. We refer to this assumption as the *closed-world* assumption, and to corresponding analyses as closed-world analyses. Much of the prior research on predicting a person's location based on GPS data, including that described above, centers on closed-world analyses.

Making a closed-world assumption, we examine all the points at which the driver's trip concluded and make a histogram over the N cells. Normalizing gives a probability mass function $P_{closed}(D=i), i=1,2,3,\ldots,N$, where the "*closed*" subscript indicates that this probability is based on personal destinations. Figure 3(b) shows the cells with nonzero $P_{closed}(D=i)$ for one driver in our study. If a user has never visited a cell, the personal destinations probability for that cell will be zero. This is because, as explained in Section 4.6, this probability will be multiplied by other probabilities over the N cells in the Bayesian calculation to compute the posterior destination probability for each cell. If any cell has a zero prior, that cell will not survive as a possible destination.

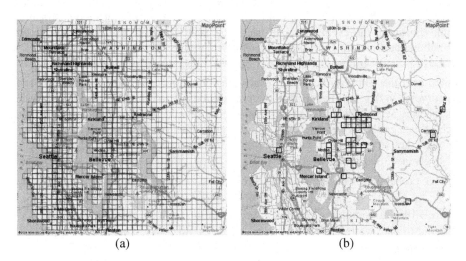

(a)   (b)

Fig. 3. (a) Probabilities based solely on ground cover information, with darker outlines showing cells of higher probability of being destinations. Water and rural regions are less probable destinations. (b) The destination cells recorded for one driver in the MSMLS study.

4.3.2 Open-World Analysis

The closed-world assumption is naïve in that people actually can visit locations they have never been observed to visit. This is the case in general, but such observations of new destinations are especially salient in the early phases of observing a driver. On the latter, "new" locations include places a driver has visited before, but had not been observed to visit during the course of a study, as well as genuinely new destinations for that driver. Thus, a more accurate approach to inferring the probability of a driver's destinations would consider the likelihood of seeing destinations that had not been seen before, thus leveraging an "open-world" model. If we can correctly model this effect, we can transform a closed-world probability mass function taken at an early point in the survey into an approximation of the steady state probability that we would have observed at the end of the survey and beyond. This open world model then replaces $P_{closed}(D=i)$, and we have a more accurate model of the places a subject tends to visit.

Focusing on open-world modeling, we model unvisited locations in two ways. The first is based on our observation that destinations tend to cluster, as seen in the example in Figure 3(b). Our intuition is that drivers tend to go to places near each other to save time, or to overall regions they are familiar with, *e.g.* drivers might chose gas stations and grocery stores that are near their place of work. We modeled this effect as a discretized probability distribution over the distance from previously visited points. This distribution has the overall shape of a tiered "wedding cake" as in Figure 4(a). Each tier gives the probabilities of new destinations around previously visited ones. Each tier of the wedding cake is a concentric ring of constant probability at some radius from center, and it is intended to model the eventual clustering of destinations in the steady state.

We measured this clustering tendency by looking at the normalized histograms of destinations on our grid over the days of each subject's GPS survey. For each destination on a given day, we computed the probability that an as-yet-unvisited destination would appear in the eventual steady state for each ring of a 10-tier wedding cake around that destination. Each tier is a ring of width one kilometer and a center radius of $r = \{1, 2, ..., 10\}$ kilometers, and the steady state was taken from all the destinations visited over the whole survey. The results are shown in Figure 4(b) for days 1-14 of the survey. On day 1 of the survey, the probabilities of finding unvisited steady-state destinations near already-visited destinations are relatively high. As the days go on, each subject gradually visits most of their usual destinations, so the probabilities drop. For each day, tiers near the center are higher than near the outer edge. Operationally, for a given closed-world probability $P_{closed}(D=i)$ from a given day, we compute another probability with the unvisited neighbors of each nonzero $P_{closed}(D=i)$ replaced by a wedding cake with probability values for the appropriate day taken from Figure 4(b). This simulates the spread we expect to see in the steady state. After normalizing to one, we refer to the wedding cakes as $W(D=i)$. This is done separately for each subject

Although the steady state destinations tend to cluster, isolated destinations also occur. We characterized this effect by computing the probability that a steady state destination would *not* be covered by a 10-tier wedding cake around a destination visited

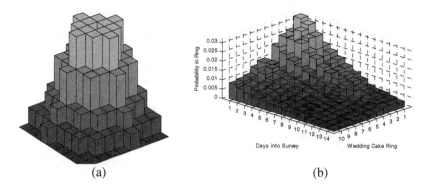

Fig. 4. (a) A 4-tier probability distribution, showing the discretization over four threshold radii from a previously visited location. We used a 10-tier version to model the clustering of destinations. (b) Probability distribution showing allocation of probability to each tier with each passing day. These probabilities were computed from our GPS data.

before steady state. This probability is shown as β in Figure 5(a). As expected, the probability of new, isolated destinations drops with time. One way to model this background probability is with a uniform distribution over all grid cells. However, this would have the undesirable effect of contributing probability to places where no one goes, like middles of lakes. Instead of a uniform distribution, we take the background as $P_G(D = i)$, which is the ground cover prior as described previously in Section 4.2.

We combine these effects to compute a probability distribution of destinations that more accurately models the steady-state probability. The three components are the closed-world prior $P_{closed}(D = i)$, the parameterized spread as represented by the wedding-cake shaped distributions $W(D = i)$ described above, and the background probability $P_G(D = i)$ to model isolated destinations. We apportion a fraction α of the total probability to $W(D = i)$, where α is the sum of the tiers from Figure 4(b) for the appropriate day, shown in Figure 5(a). A learned fraction β of the probability, capturing the probability that users will travel to places beyond the tiered distributions is allocated to the background, with β also shown in Figure 5(a). The open-world version for the probability of a driver's destinations, which we shall take as a prior probability for our analysis, is then computed as

$$P_{open}(D = i) = (1 - \alpha - \beta)P_{closed}(D = i) + \alpha W(D = i) + \beta P_G(D = i) \tag{3}$$

We refer to this as the *open-world prior probability distribution*.

Figure 5(a) shows the behavior of α, β, and $1 - \alpha - \beta$ with time. As time goes on, α and β tend to decrease, deemphasizing the adjustment for clustering and

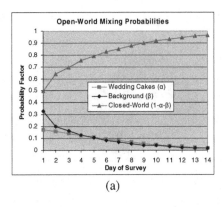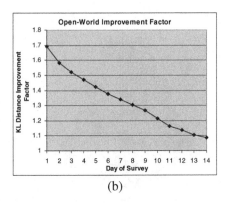

(a)   (b)

Fig. 5. (a) The mixing of probabilities for computing the open-world prior. As time goes on, the prior emphasizes the subject's previous destinations more strongly. (b) The multiplicative improvement in KL distance between the closed-world and open-world priors when compared to the true steady state.

background probability in favor of each subject's actual learned destinations. This represents the richness of an open-world model that takes into appropriate consideration the fact that people can visit new locations, especially early on in the observation period, but also in the long run.

The open-world prior probability distribution, $P_{open}(D = i)$, is designed to approximate a subject's steady state distribution of destinations better than the naïve, closed-world prior $P_{closed}(D = i)$. To test this, we computed the Kullback Leibler (KL) distance[1] between both of these models and the actual steady state prior for each subject. The steady state prior is simply the closed-world prior computed with each subject's entire survey data. Figure 5(b) shows the improvement factor as a function of days into the survey. At day one, the KL distance between the naïve, closed-world prior and the actual steady state is about 1.7 times as great as the distance between the open-world prior and the steady state. This factor decreases with time as the naïve prior approaches the steady state prior. The advantage of the open-world prior is that the system works with a prior much closer to the actual steady state than with the closed-world model.

Equation (**3**) is the prior probability that we use in Bayes formula in Equation (**1**). The next two subsections discuss the two likelihoods of the form $P(\mathbf{X} = \mathbf{x}|D = i)$, where $\mathbf{x}$ is some measured feature of the current drive, that we use to model other sources of information for destination prediction.

---

[1] The KL distance between a true distribution $p(x)$ and an approximate distribution $q(x)$ is $\sum p(x)\log_2[p(x)/q(x)]$. If the approximate distribution is zero anywhere, this results in a division by zero. The closed-world prior often has zeros, which we accounted for by modifying it in the standard way: $q'(x) = (1 - \lambda)q(x) + \lambda/N$ with $\lambda = 0.01$.

4.4 Efficient Driving Likelihood

Drivers tend to take purposeful and somewhat efficient routes to their destinations[13]. Intuitively, if a driver appears to be taking a very inefficient route to a candidate destination, then we can reason that that destination is unlikely. The efficient driving parameter is intended to capture this behavior in order to help narrow the set of likely destinations. We developed a different destination prediction algorithm using only efficient driving in [14].

We quantify efficiency using the driving time between points on the driver's path and candidate destinations. Thus, for each pair of cells (i, j) in our grid, we estimate the driving time $T_{i,j}$ between them. A first approximation to the driving time could come from a simple Euclidian distance and speed approximation between each pair of cells. Instead, we used Microsoft MapPoint desktop mapping software to plan a driving route that MapPoint considers to be ideal between the center (latitude, longitude) points of all pairs of cells. MapPoint provides a programmatic interface that returns the estimated driving time of planned routes. Using a driving route planner takes into account the road network and speed limits between cells, giving a more accurate driving time estimate.

For N cells, there are $N(N-1)$ different ordered pairs, not including pairs of identical cells. Our route planning software plans routes at the rate of about four per second on a 2.8 GHz PC, meaning it would take about 7.4 days to plan routes for all $N(N-1) \approx 2.6 \times 10^6$ pairs. We cut this time in half by assuming that the travel time from cell i to j is the same as from cell j to i, i.e. $T_{i,j} = T_{j,i}$. The computation time for route planning was the main barrier to increasing the resolution of our grid. Fortunately, this computation must be done only once for the grid.

We measure efficiency based on the trip's starting cell s and a candidate destination cell i. If the driver's route is efficient, then the total time required to go between these two cell should be about $T_{s,i}$. If the driver is currently at cell j, then the time to reach the candidate destination i should be about $T_{j,i}$. If i really is the destination, and if the driver is following an efficient route, then the driver should have taken a time of $T_{s,i} - T_{j,i}$ to reach the current cell j. We know that the driver's actual trip time to this point is Δt, which will be longer than $T_{s,i} - T_{j,i}$ if the driver is taking an inefficient route. Thus our measure of efficiency is the ratio of how much time the driver should have spent moving toward the candidate destination divided by how much time has actually transpired:

$$e_i = \frac{T_{s,i} - T_{j,i}}{\Delta t} \tag{4}$$

We expect this to be about one for an efficient trip between s and i. Using our GPS survey data, we computed the distributions of efficiency values based on known trips and their corresponding destinations. The efficiency likelihood $P_E(E = e | D = i)$

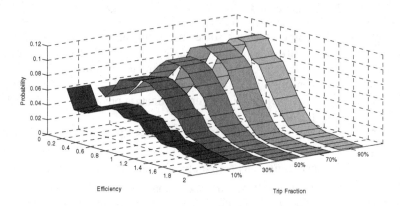

Fig. 6. These curves show the measured distributions of driving efficiency, which vary with the amount of the trip completed

represents the efficiency that drivers actually produce on their way to a destination. If a candidate destination results in a low-likelihood efficiency, its posterior probability will be corresponding low when $P_E(E = e|D = i)$ is incorporated in Bayes rule. As a function of the fraction of the trip, the efficiency likelihood is shown in Figure 6. The distribution near the beginning of the trip is unrealistic likely due to MapPoint's inability to give accurate travel times for short trips. For all trip fractions, some drivers are able to boost their efficiency beyond 1.0, either due to speeding or mistakes in the ideal trip time estimates from MapPoint. The effect of using this likelihood for destination prediction is that if a driver appears to be driving away from a candidate destination, that destination's probability will be lowered.

4.5   Trip Time Distribution

The final component we use for destination prediction is a distribution of trip times. Intuitively, we know that most car trips are measured in minutes, not hours, which limits the range of likely destinations. To quantify this intuition, we used data from the U.S. 2001 National Household Transportation Survey (NHTS)[1]. The NHTS collected data on daily and longer-distance travel from approximately 66,000 U.S. households based on travel diaries kept by participants. The survey results are available via a Web interface[15], from which we created a histogram of trip times, a normalized version of which is shown in Figure 7.[2]

The likelihood governing trip times is $P_{\Delta T}(\Delta T = \Delta t|D = i)$, where ΔT is the random variable representing the trip time so far. For use of this likelihood, we quantize our trip times according to the bins in Figure 7. Figure 7 actually represents the

---

[2] Specifically, from https://nhts.ornl.gov/2001/Login.do, we created a table whose analysis variable was "Annual vehicle trips (VT)" and whose row variable was "Calculated Time to complete trip (min.) (TRVLCMIN)".

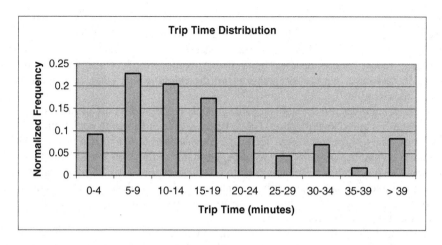

Fig. 7. This is a distribution of trip times taken from the 2001 U.S. National Household Transportation Survey[1].

distribution of destination times before a trip has started, *i.e.* $P(T_D = t_D)$, where T_D represents the total trip time. Once some time has passed on a trip, the probability of times passed drops to zero, so we renormalize to get

$$P_{\Delta T}(\Delta T = \Delta t | D = i) = \begin{cases} 0 \text{ if } t_D < \Delta t \\ P(T_D = t_D) \Big/ \sum_{t_D \geq t_S} p(T_D = t_D) \text{ if } t_D \geq \Delta t \end{cases} \tag{5}$$

To compute the likelihood for a candidate destination, we take Δt as the length of the trip so far and t_D as the estimated time to the candidate destination from the current cell, based on the $T_{i,j}$ estimated trip times explained in Section 4.4.

4.6 Inferring Posteriors Over Destinations

In Section 4.3, we described the generation of a prior probability distribution via the combination of visited locations and geographic data, combined with an open-world approach. Sections 4.4 and 4.5 introduced two likelihoods of seeing data given the truth of target destinations.

If we assume independence of the driving efficiency and the trip duration likelihoods given the destinations, we can combine these two elements and the prior into a single posterior probability for each destination using Bayes rule from Equation **(1)**, giving the destination probability as

$$P(D = i | E = e, \Delta T = \Delta t) = \frac{P_E(E = e | D = i) P_{\Delta T}(\Delta T = \Delta t | D = i) P_{open}(D = i)}{\sum_{j=1}^{N} P_E(E = e | D = j) P_{\Delta T}(\Delta T = \Delta t | D = j) P_{open}(D = j)} \tag{6}$$

Considering such independencies is referred to as the naïve Bayes formulation of Bayesian updating. Relaxing the independence assumptions to allow richer probabilistic dependencies would likely enhance the accuracy of the predictions because introducing realistic dependencies minimizes "overcounting" of probabilistic influences. In this case, we are not considering the relationships between driving efficiency and duration.

In the general case, more sophisticated models come at the cost of more complex representations and data collection. Naïve Bayes has been shown to perform relatively well in a variety of domains (e.g., see [16]). Angermann et al.[17] used a similar technique for combining probabilistic location estimates defined on a grid. Elfes[18] introduced the probabilistic grid approach to robotics for sensor-based mapping. Practically, we implement this equation by computing a grid of scalars for each of the probabilistic components, multiplying the scalars in corresponding cells, and normalizing to make the sum of the products one.

The probabilistic formulation of destination prediction means that uncertainties about the driver's true destination are represented in a coherent manner. This means that applications built on a system like ours can account for the inevitable uncertainty in a driver's destination. For instance, an application that shows restaurants or gas stations near a driver's destination could progressively show more detail and less area as the destination becomes more certain. Warnings about traffic problems could be held until the certainty of encountering them exceeds a certain threshold. Cognitively impaired people deviating from their intended destination could be warned only when the deviation becomes nearly certain.

5   Results

We tested our Predestination algorithm on trips from our database of GPS traces. We split the data into two halves, using one half for training the efficiency distributions $P_E(E = e|D = i)$ as explained in Section 4.4. Testing on the remaining half of the data (3667 trips), we iterated through each trip of each subject. For each trip, we trained the closed world prior $P_{closed}(D = i)$ on that subject's trips, omitting the one we were testing, resulting in a leave-one-out testing strategy. We tested the algorithm in three different modes:

- Simple closed-world model – This model uses only a closed-world prior based on survey data from days before the test day. It does not use the efficient driving likelihood nor the trip time likelihood, only a simple prior. This naïve model represents a first order attempt at predicting destinations based only on where a subject has gone in the past.
- Open-world model – This uses Equation (6) and the open-world prior from Equation (3). For training the $P_{closed}(D = i)$ part of the prior, it uses only survey data from days before the test day. This represents a realistic scenario of user starting with no training data.
- Complete data model – This uses a closed-world prior, but it is based on *all* the survey data (except the holdout trip), including survey data taken after the test

day. We expect this model to perform best since it has the benefit of using the steady state destination prior. This is how the system would work after it has been trained sufficiently to have seen nearly all the subject's destinations.

The result of computing a destination prediction from Equation (6) is a probability mass function over all the cells. Sorting the cells by this probability gives a ranking, from highest to lowest, of the posterior probability of each cell being the actual destination. It is this sorted list that Predestination would return to an application that needed to take an action as a function of the user's destination. Predestination makes such a prediction at every point along the trip. A simple way to examine the result is to consider the maximum *a posteriori* (MAP) estimate, which is the cell with the maximum probability. Figure 8 shows the median error between the MAP estimate and the actual destination as a function of the fraction of the trip completed. The complete data model has a median error of two kilometers at the halfway point, while the open-world model has an error of three kilometers at the same point. The simple open-world model gives an error that is consistently higher, around five kilometers. This result shows that our open-world model approaches the accuracy of the complete data model, and that the simple closed-world model is noticeably worse.

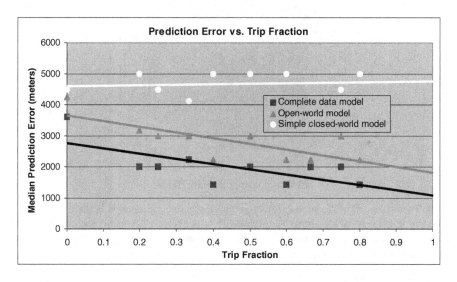

Fig. 8. The median prediction error using the MAP estimate drops with the fraction of the trip completed. At the halfway point of the trip, the complete data model's error is two kilometers. The open-world model comes within about one kilometer of the accuracy of the complete data model. The simple closed-world model is consistently poor.

In some instances, an application could make use of a list of highly probable destinations rather than just the single MAP estimate. For instance, in giving anticipatory point-of-interest data, a user might be willing to pick from a list of the top several likely destinations. In this case, Predestination would return a list of destination

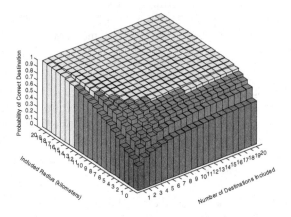

(a) Using open-world model

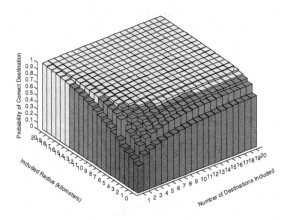

(b) Using complete data model

Fig. 9. These plots show the probability of getting the correct destination at the halfway point of the trip. Each vertical bar shows the probability of the correct destination being somewhere in the sorted list of the given number of destinations included and within the given radius of the computed destination(s). The light-colored bars show probabilities ≥ 0.9.

predictions sorted by probability. Figure 9 shows how the probability of finding the correct destination cell changes with the length of the sorted list and the distance tolerance for both the open-world model and the complete data models at the halfway point of the trip. Specifically, each bar in these figures shows the probability of the correct destination being both:

- Somewhere in the list of the most probable computed destinations, as a function of the length of the list, and
- Somewhere within a radius of the most probable computed destinations, as a function of radius.

As either the length of the list or the radius is increased, the probability of finding the correct destination goes up. The light gray bars show which probabilities are at least 0.9. Figure 9(a) shows the probabilities using the open-world model, where training on trips after the day in question was disallowed. Figure 9(b) shows the probabilities using a complete data distribution. The open-world model achieves nearly the same level of performance as the complete data model, validating our attempt to model the steady state in the early days of the GPS survey.

6 Conclusions

"Predestination" predicts a driver's destination as the trip progresses. In the approach described here, we considered four different probabilistic cues, and we combined the cues in a mathematically principled way to create a probability grid of likely destinations. The best performance on 3667 different driving trips gave a median error of two kilometers at the trip's halfway point. We introduced an open-world model of destinations that helps the algorithm work well in spite of a paucity of training data at the beginning of the training period. Applications of Predestination include proactively delivering information about upcoming points of interest and traffic problems. This could reduce cognitive load on the driver by eliminating information about places that he or she is unlikely to encounter. Destination prediction can also be used to detect if a user is deviating from the route to an expected location.

Future work in this area includes exploring the value of relaxing assumptions of probabilistic independence and incorporation of additional prediction features. As examples of the latter, the structure of the road network and locations of specific points of interest could be considered. In addition to absolute destinations, destination classes such as coffee shops, dinner spots, and antique stores could be learned for individual users. Destinations also likely show temporal dependence, so we expect that inclusion of variables representing time of day, day of week, month of year, and a user's calendar data would enhance predictive accuracy, especially with increasing amounts of data, providing representative coverage for different periods of time .

Acknowledgments

We thank Kelli McGee for assisting with the administration of the MSMLS study.

References

1. Hu, P.S. and T.R. Reuscher, *Summary of Travel Trends, 2001 National Household Travel Survey*. 2004, U. S. Department of Transportation, U.S. Federal Highway Administration. p. 135.
2. Patterson, D.J., et al. *Opportunity Knocks: A System to Provide Cognitive Assistance with Transportation Services*. in *UbiComp 2004: Ubiquitous Computing*. 2004. Nottingham, UK: Springer.
3. Cheng, C., R. Jain, and E.v.d. Berg, *Location Prediction Algorithms for Mobile Wireless Systems*, in *Wireless Internet Handbook: Technologies, Standards, and Application*. 2003, CRC Press: Boca Raton, FL, USA. p. 245 - 263.

4. Krumm, J. and E. Horvitz, *The Microsoft Multiperson Location Survey*. 2005, Microsoft Research (MSR-TR-2005-103): Redmond, WA USA.
5. Karbassi, A. and M. Barth. *Vehicle Route Prediction and Time of Arrival Estimation Techniques for Improved Transportation System Management*. in *Proceedings of the Intelligent Vehicles Symposium*. 2003.
6. Marmasse, N. and C. Schmandt, *A User-Centered Location Model*. Personal and Ubiquitous Computing, 2002(6): p. 318-321.
7. Ashbrook, D. and T. Starner, *Using GPS To Learn Significant Locations and Predict Movement Across Multiple Users*. Personal and Ubiquitous Computing, 2003. **7**(5): p. 275-286.
8. Hariharan, R. and K. Toyama. *Project Lachesis: Parsing and Modeling Location Histories*. in *Geographic Information Science: Third International Conference, GIScience 2004*. 2004. Adelphi, MD, USA: Springer-Verlag GmbH.
9. Liao, L., D. Fox, and H. Kautz. *Learning and Inferring Transportation Routines*. in *Proceedings of the 19th National Conference on Artificial Intelligence (AAAI 2004)*. 2004. San Jose, CA, USA.
10. Gogate, V., et al. *Modeling Transportation Routines using Hybrid Dynamic Mixed Networks*. in *Uncertainty in Artificial Intelligence (UAI 2005)*. 2005.
11. http://landcover.usgs.gov/ftpdownload.asp.
12. http://landcover.usgs.gov/classes.asp.
13. Letchner, J., J. Krumm, and E. Horvitz. *Trip Router with Individualized Preferences (TRIP): Incorporating Personalization into Route Planning*. in *Eighteenth Conference on Innovative Applications of Artificial Intelligence*. 2006. Boston.
14. Krumm, J. *Real Time Destination Prediction Based on Efficient Routes*. in *Society of Automotive Engineers (SAE) 2006 World Congress*. 2006. Detroit.
15. https://nhts.ornl.gov/2001/Login.do.
16. Rish, I. *An Empirical Study of the Naive Bayes Classifier*. in *IJCAI-01 Workshop on Empirical Methods in AI*. 2001.
17. Angermann, M., et al. *Software Representation for Heterogeneous Location Data Sources Using Probability Density Functions*. in *International Symposium on Location Based Services for Cellular Users (LOCELLUS 2001)*. 2001. Munich.
18. Elfes, A., *Using Occupancy Grids for Mobile Robot Perception and Navigation*. IEEE Computer, 1989. **22**(6): p. 46-57.

Fish'n'Steps: Encouraging Physical Activity with an Interactive Computer Game

James J. Lin, Lena Mamykina, Silvia Lindtner, Gregory Delajoux,
and Henry B. Strub

Siemens Corporate Research,
755 College Road East, Princeton, NJ 08540 USA
{jameslin, lena.mamykina, silvia.lindtner.ext, hank.strub}
@siemens.com, gregory.delajoux@gmail.com
http://www.scr.siemens.com

Abstract. A sedentary lifestyle is a contributing factor to chronic diseases, and it is often correlated with obesity. To promote an increase in physical activity, we created a social computer game, Fish'n'Steps, which links a player's daily foot step count to the growth and activity of an animated virtual character, a fish in a fish tank. As further encouragement, some of the players' fish tanks included other players' fish, thereby creating an environment of both cooperation and competition. In a fourteen-week study with nineteen participants, the game served as a catalyst for promoting exercise and for improving game players' attitudes towards physical activity. Furthermore, although most player's enthusiasm in the game decreased after the game's first two weeks, analyzing the results using Prochaska's Transtheoretical Model of Behavioral Change suggests that individuals had, by that time, established new routines that led to healthier patterns of physical activity in their daily lives. Lessons learned from this study underscore the value of such games to encourage rather than provide negative reinforcement, especially when individuals are not meeting their own expectations, to foster long-term behavioral change.

1 Introduction

In recent decades, obesity has become a problem on the scale of a world-wide epidemic. The 1999 National Health and Nutrition survey (NHANES) estimated that 61% of US adults are either overweight or obese. These people suffer from both deleterious health consequences and the corresponding psychological stigma [1] . Epidemiologic studies have identified several environmental factors that contribute to this continual gain of weight over recent decades. Lifestyles have become increasingly *sedentary* (e.g. less physical activity, commonly combined with more time spent watching television) and *energy-dense foods* (high-fat, concentrated-sugar, low-fiber) have become the common components of individuals' diets [2] .

The most effective approaches to treating people for being overweight or obese are similar to those for other chronic diseases. They begin with lifestyle improvements, and continue to more invasive treatments such as pharmaceuticals and even surgery.

P. Dourish and A. Friday (Eds.): Ubicomp 2006, LNCS 4206, pp. 261 – 278, 2006.
© Springer-Verlag Berlin Heidelberg 2006

Lifestyle improvements to control weight include exercise, diets that restrict calories, fat or carbohydrates, or a combination of both exercise and diets. Unfortunately, there is limited evidence of successful weight management through lifestyle alterations. "Studies paint a grim picture: those who complete weight-loss programs lose approximately 10% of their body weight, only to regain two-thirds of it back within a year and almost all of it back within 5 years" [3] . One of the main reasons for such a high relapse rate is that individuals have difficulty maintaining the necessary lifestyle improvements.

Many factors contribute to the challenges of maintaining lifestyle improvements. Some are economic, such as the availability and cost of healthy foods or the cost of joining a health club and the time required to regularly exercise. Others are psychological, for example depression and a lack of motivation to follow a healthy lifestyle every day when the improvements are only slowly noticeable. Even others are social, including the desire to fit in with one's existing social circles who engage in their own unhealthy behaviors [1] [4] . However, the desired changes can be achieved without a significant disruption of one's current lifestyle. For example, studies have demonstrated that individuals who walked at least 10,000 steps a day were more likely to maintain their desired weight [5] and [24] .

Individual behavior change has been a subject of active investigation in the areas of cognitive and clinical psychology. One of the most widely accepted theoretical models is the *Transtheoretical Model* (TTM), introduced by James Prochaska [6] . TTM argues that individuals change their behavior gradually, by advancing along a series of steps. These steps vary from pre-contemplation in which individuals have not realized the need for change, to termination in which the new behavior has become so habitual that there is no longer any danger of relapse. TTM has been successfully used to design interventions for such undesirable behaviors as alcoholism, smoking and domestic violence [6] [7] [8] and to motivate increase in exercise and other types of physical activity [9] [10] [11] . However, traditional techniques inspired by TTM rely on significant clinical resources for the individuals who seek the change. There is a need to develop more innovative and cost-effective intervention programs that supplement or replace meetings with a therapist [11] .

In the recent years a number of innovative programs introduced novel technologies to reduce the cost of continuous involvement of clinical personnel. Many of these techniques transform physical exercise into engaging individual or social games that often mix real and virtual environments [12] [13] [14] . In an alternative approach, pedometers, small electronic devices that monitor individual step counts have been used as a ubiquitous and unobtrusive motivational technique available anytime and anywhere [5] [15] [16] .

In this paper we describe Fish'n'Steps, an application that combines ubiquity and simplicity of pedometers with the engagement of social computing games (Fig. 1). Individuals enrolled in the game were provided with pedometers to measure their daily step count. The number of steps taken each day was then mapped to the growth and emotional state of a virtual pet that was "given" to each individual: a fish in a fish-tank. Additional incentives were designed to incorporate social dynamics, such as competition between teams of players.

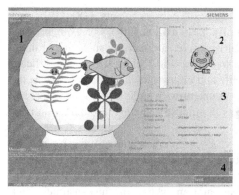

Fig. 1. *One participant's display after approximately two weeks into the trial in the Fish'n'Steps team-condition, also the public kiosk and pedometer platform, which rotated through each of the team fish-tanks.* The components of the personal display include: 1) Fish Tank - The fish tank contains the virtual pets belong to the participant and his/her team members, 2) Virtual Pet – The participant's own fish in a frontal view on the right side next to the fish tank, 3) Calculations and feedback - improvement, burned calories, progress bar, personal and team ranking, etc., 4) Chat window for communicating with team members.

To evaluate the effect of Fish'n'Steps, we recruited 19 participants from the staff of Siemens Corporate Research to participate in a 14-week study. Two experimental conditions were designed to separately assess the impact of the virtual pet and the social influences. Application of the TTM to assess behavior that changed during the study demonstrated that Fish'n'Steps was a catalyst of a positive change for 14 out of 19 participants. This effect was evident in either an increase in their daily step count (for 4 participants), a change in their attitudes towards physical activity (for 3 participants) or a combination of the two (for 7 participants). The greatest change in daily number of steps was by the participants who were at the TTM's intermediate levels of the behavior change. For these participants the game provided just enough motivation to translate mental readiness into action.

While the overall findings were encouraging, there are a number of possibilities for future investigations. For example, selecting participants from our own research organization limited representativeness of the sample to highly educated individuals relatively open to adopting new technologies. In addition, the game highlighted the importance of careful selection of incentives: unachievable or not challenging goals can fail to inspire the desired change.

2 Interventions for Behavior Change

There are a variety of techniques developed over the years to motivate behavior change. Traditional techniques are usually delivered by a trained specialist in either individual or group settings. Examples of these techniques include goal-setting, self-assessment, or monitoring of achieved progress [17] . Two particular approaches that influenced the current project include motivating behavior change by cultivating a strong internal locus of control through care of pets or plants [18] [19]   and incorporating social influences through family participation [20] . For example, in a classical study of elderly people living in an assistive care facility, such simple interventions as an opportunity to choose and then care for a plant led to a significant increase in the sense of control over one's life and improvement in health [18] . At the same time, engaging family members in a cooperative weight monitoring effort has been shown to lead to more enduring effects than those achieved through an individual's own motivation [20] .

New techniques developed in the recent years complement and at times replace the traditional physician involvement by introducing advanced computing technologies. These computerized interventions have a number of advantages. In addition to being cost-efficient, they can be delivered anytime and anywhere, or "just in time" for a decision – when they can have the highest potential impact. In studies conducted in public places, motivational messages delivered at the time of decision making inspired individuals to take simple steps to improving their health, such as choosing a staircase over the escalator [21] . At the same time, sensor technologies can be used to make these messages highly personalized. For example, artistic sculptures resembling human figures were used to enhance individuals' awareness of their posture [22] . Often, these techniques incorporate the emotional aspects, or persuasive computing techniques [23] . For example, an attachment to virtual creatures, such as Tamagotchi, inspired technological health interventions for children with chronic diseases [19] . In these games, strong and attractive animated characters have the same diseases as children who play the game, for example asthma or diabetes, thus providing positive role-models and reducing the stigma associated with the child's disease.

There are a number of applications that motivate increase in physical activity in a fun way through engaging individuals in games that mix real and computing worlds. These games became known as Serious Games or Exergames. For example, "Tagaboo", a collaborative children's game, focuses on developing coordination through playful interaction [24] . Exercise Bicycles enriches the experience of an indoor exercise bicycle in engaging users in a Virtual Environment single-player game [13] .Yet another, and perhaps the most researched Serious Game, Dance Dance Revolution connects a sensor-enabled dance floor with a video interface and provides stimulating exercise as a social activity – dance competition [12] .

An alternative approach to motivating physical activity that became popular in the resent years utilizes pedometers, small battery operated devices that count how many steps individuals' take each day [5] [15] . Usage of pedometers helps individuals realize their current level of activity, set achievable goals and monitor their progress towards the goals, either individually or in a social setting. For example, in a study by Consolvo et al [16] , groups of friends wearing pedometers could share each others' goals and progress via mobile phones. In addition, devices like Body-Bugg by BodyMedia can provide such measurements as consumed or burned calories.

While challenging and exciting, games like Tagaboo, Dance Dance Revolution and the Exercise Bicycle require focused engagement and are constrained in time and location. In our work, we looked for less focused and more ubiquitous ways to promote physical activity. At the same time, utilizing pedometers achieves the desired ubiquity but could benefit from providing additional motivation and incentives. Fish'n'Steps, described in this paper attempts to combine both, ubiquity and unobtrusiveness of pedometers, with engaging gaming approach of Serious Games.

3 Fish'n'Steps

3.1 Step Capture

"Fish'n'Steps" was built as a distributed software application that included several functioning components as well as some "Wizard of Oz" components. Simple commercially available pedometers, Sportline 330, were used to measure the step count of individual participants. The main considerations for selection of this model were its low price, large display with overall small size, and the cumulative step count display, rather than daily step count with overnight reset, which simplified the automated upload. However, the cumulative step count display, while increasing the value of the interventions in the game, reduced the overall benefit of the pedometers, To collect data from pedometers, individuals placed their pedometer on a platform at a public kiosk (Fig. 1), and took a picture of their pedometer screen, including the unique pedometer ID. The picture was captured and sent to a member of the research team who entered the appropriate data into a database. Due to the competitive nature of the game, such automated upload was essential to prevent tampering with the game and adjusting numbers to help one's team win. This daily upload could neither measure nor prevent tampering through shaking the pedometer while sitting to increase step count or giving the pedometer to somebody else to wear. While it was hard to avoid these more involved types of tampering, automated upload at least prevented false reports. In addition, kiosk upload combined with a public display was meant to simplify the upload procedures, and to foster individuals' interest in the game.

3.2 Establishing Daily Goals

Once an individual's daily step number was uploaded into the database, the application calculated the incremental daily increase and compared it with a personal goal that had been established for each individual during the pre-study phase. After reviewing previous pedometer studies [5] [15] , 3 heuristics were used to calculate custom goals for each participant:

Each participant should have a reasonable target over the 6 week intervention period. In previous studies, the average increase in step count was 2-3000 steps [15] [25] ;
The increase would be negatively correlated with participants' baseline step count;
An upper bound was set at 12,000 steps per day, since participants in previous studies tended to reach a plateau of 10-12,000 steps.

For example, a participant with a baseline of 3000 daily steps had an overall goal of 5250 steps, while a participant with a baseline of 11,000 daily steps had an overall goal of 11,630 steps. Although these goals may not seem ambitious, the study's incentive structure depended on participants receiving positive feedback to help guide them through daily encouragement.

These specific 6-week goals were calculated using an exponential function to set a goal for each week. Daily progress was sufficient when individuals reached their daily goal (1/5 of their weekly goal), nearly sufficient when they reached half of their daily goal, and insufficient when they did not reach even half of their daily goal. Subjects whose improvement exceeded their weekly goal were given a new goal based on an adjustment of their baseline.

3.3 Developing Incentives

Individuals' daily progress towards their goals was mapped to the development of the fish in two different ways. The daily step count for each participant contributed to the growth of his or her fish in a step-wise fashion. As soon as the total number of steps exceeded a predefined target, the fish's appearance changed to the next growth level (Fig. 2). If the fish's upper appearance level was reached, an additional ("baby") fish was attached to the fish tank, which grew according to the further increase of the user's step count. At the same time, success in reaching a participant's daily goal affected the facial expression of his or her fish—making it happy (in case of sufficient progress), angry (in case of nearly sufficient progress), or sad (insufficient progress) (Fig. 2).

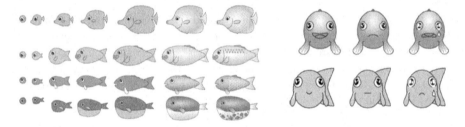

Fig. 2. *Seven growth levels (left panel) and examples of three types of facial expressions (right panel) of the virtual characters*

Two different versions of the game interface were used to create two experimental conditions. In one version, each participant's fish had its own fish tank and hence was not involved in a competition process. In the second version, each fish-tank was shared by four participants' fish. In this condition, the progress of each fish affected the entire fish tank: each "insufficient" day for any team member resulted in the tank's water getting darker, as well as the gradual removal of the fish-tank's decorations (plants, small animals, such as snails, etc.). Individuals within teams saw each others' progress, and could converse over an anonymous chat application.

Two displays were designed for the application. The public display was placed next to the upload kiosk and rotated through each group's fish-tank (Fig. 1), recognizable through the team's number. The public display was designed to promote a daily competition between teams for the "healthiest" fish tank. At the same time, individuals of both conditions could log in on their own computer to monitor the progress of their own fish, as well as other fish in their group's fish-tank.

The game application was realized as a web interface created with Macromedia Flash. The *Flash Interface* combined the game logic with input from a *mySql* database (daily number of steps, group and individual ranking, user properties). PHP language was used for communication between the Flash client and the *Apache* server.

4 Study Description

4.1 Participants

To assess the effectiveness of Fish'n'Steps, 19 participants (11 females and 8 males, aged from 23 to 63) were recruited among the staff of Siemens Corporate Research, Inc, The participants of the study were a relatively homogeneous group in terms of education (graduate degree), working environment, and even living environments (suburban New Jersey). However, as is discussed below, there were fairly large individual variations in their lifestyles and attitudes towards physical exercise. These span from individuals never having, nor wishing for an exercise routine, to individuals who exercised rigorously and regularly. The average daily step count collected during the pre-study reflected these differences, with numbers ranging from 3,700 to over 11,000. The participants were compensated $25 for enrolling in the 14 weeks study.

The selection of participants in this study received a lot of consideration. The research team was looking for participants with sedentary jobs that did not require physical activity. However, the need for automated step capture suggested recruitment of co-located participants. At the time of the study, the only pedometer that allowed upload to a PC via serial cable was not available in the US market. As a result, we developed an upload kiosk and invited fellow employees from Siemens Corporate Research (SCR) to volunteer for the study. This decision had limited the participant sample to highly educated individuals, who were moreover relatively technologically savvy and open to adopting new technologies. However, a number of measures were taken to preserve validity of the findings to the degree possible. The volunteers were selected from a relatively large pool of over 300 employees, including students and administrative personnel. None of the participants had any prior knowledge of or experience with the related research. Any employees in the organization working for the same department as the members of the research team were excluded from the participants' pool. The research team kept each participant's identification anonymous from all the others in the organization.

4.2 Procedure

The study consisted of 3 phases, as illustrated in Fig. 3.

Pre-intervention (4 weeks): During the pre-intervention phase, the participants were given a pedometer. The researchers suggested that participants wear their pedometers as much as possible but did not set any goals, and encouraged participants to maintain their regular lifestyles. At the end of this phase, the cumulative reading of each pedometer was used to establish individual baselines, and to set goals for the study's second phase.

Intervention (6 weeks): During the second, experimental phase, the participants were randomly assigned to one of the two experimental conditions. During this phase, the participants were encouraged to increase their daily step count to achieve their individual goals either during their work hours or during their leisure time. The participants were asked to make a daily stop at the public kiosk to update their pedometer number. Otherwise, the participants were free to engage with the game as little or as much as they wished; no additional interaction was required.

Post-intervention (4 weeks): At the end of the 6 weeks of the intervention phase, the game ended. However, participants were encouraged to continue wearing their pedometers for an additional 4 weeks. The final number captured by the pedometer at the end of the post-study phase allowed the researchers to observe any persistent effects of the game.

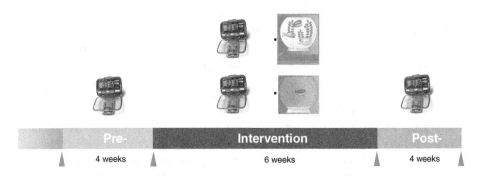

Fig. 3. *Study overview.* Qualitative interviews (4 total, indicated by triangles) were conducted between each of the phases in the study.

The mix-design of the study in two experimental conditions (team condition vs. single condition) allowed separate assessment of emotional attachment to the virtual pet, and the second condition that combined attachment to the virtual pet with social dynamics.

At the beginning and at the end of each intervention phase, each participant was interviewed for about 30 minutes to discuss their experiences. Researchers used handwritten notes to summarize interviews 1 and 2. Interviews 3 and 4 were video and audio-taped, and then transcribed. All the interview transcripts were coded according to categories that emerged during the study's analysis. The results were analyzed based on the data collected from the 19 participants who completed the entire 14-week study. Among these 19 participants, 6 were in the single-player condition and 13 were in the multi-player condition.

The research team chose not to use a control group who wore pedometers but had no other incentives. Many previous pedometer studies, including Tudor-Locke [5] and Chan [15], reported a plateau in their participants' daily step count after the studies' first 4 weeks of pedometer use. Following this pedometer "adoption" phase, the participants did not increase their daily step totals. For this study, we expected that effects due to the pedometers themselves would have been demonstrated in the first 4-week pre-study phase. Therefore, increases in daily step counts observed during the game were likely reflecting the additional incentives introduced by the game.

5 Findings

To assess the achieved advancement along the steps of behavior change suggested by the Transtheoretical Model, the research team applied the following methodology. Each pre-study interview was analyzed for evidence of the participants' current position within the stages of the Transtheoretical Model: 1) Pre-contemplation – individuals have no recognition of the need to change and, consequently, no intention to take action; 2) Contemplation – intention to take action within foreseeable future (next six months); 3) Preparation – intention to take action within immediate future (next 30 days and having taken initial preparatory steps); 4) Action – practicing new behavior for 3 to 6 months; 5) Maintenance – continuing commitment to sustaining behavior; 6) Termination – overt behavior will never return, and there is complete confidence that one can cope without fear of relapse. For exercise programs, termination means that the behavior is so ingrained that external reinforcements are no longer necessary.

Similar analysis was applied to the post-intervention interviews, in order to determine whether there were indications of progression towards more advanced stages of behavior change. The number of steps recorded by the pedometer was the primary indicator of each participant's behavior change. In addition, the interviews provided another way to measure attitude changes.

To complement these quantitative findings, grounded theory analysis was used to identify recurrent patterns of attitudes towards the game through analysis of each round of interviews. All the interview transcripts were coded according to categories that emerged during the analysis.

5.1 Initial Attitudes – Fish Buzz

The rumors about the game started spreading through the building several months prior to the study, and led to a general feeling of anticipation and excitement. Pictures of the study's fish, while still a work in progress, were shared among the extended intern community at Siemens Corporate Research, and were observed throughout the building – attached to name tags, next to office cubicles, or attached to windows.

Not surprisingly, many of the recruited participants had noticed the pictures of the fish and were intrigued by them. In addition, many of the participants had been dissatisfied with their own level of physical activity, and welcomed an opportunity to address the issue. This was not surprising given the general work style at Siemens Corporate Research: sitting in front of one's computer all day long, as well as the "drive everywhere" culture of suburban living for many participants. Thus, the average level of daily steps determined during the pre-study phase was under 7,000 – quite a bit lower than the recommended 10,000 steps per day.

5.2 Observable Behavior Change

According to the level definitions in the TTM, the following criteria were used to place participants in particular levels:

Table 1. TTM assessment results – pre-study

Level	Definition	Example evidence
1	No intention to take action in the next 6 months	"I had a membership at a gym last year, but dropped out. I don't have time anymore because of the baby." "I don't have an exercise routine or goal. I am not member of a gym. Doctor suggested me to do more exercising, but I didn't follow that advice."
2	Intention to take action within the next 6 months	"I am member of a gym, but I have never been there. I am thinking about going there."
3	Intention to take action within the next 30 days and some initial steps towards that action	"I don't have an exercise routine. But I want to develop one now and hope that this study helps me. I have never been in a gym. My exercise goal is to start exercising now."
4-5	Change in behavior occurred at some point in the past, but have not developed into habit	"I have a routine: 3 days a week squash and weights, 45 min total. I am member of a gym and usually exercise there."
6	Overt behavior will never return, and there is complete confidence in coping without tear of relapse.	"I have had the same morning routine for 11 years now; it includes a jog and an hour of yoga and then my coffee and a newspaper"

As a result of this assessment, the following pattern emerged:

- **Level 1:** 4 participants. These individuals had not established exercise routines, nor had any intension of establishing them in a foreseeable future.
- **Level 2:** 1 participant. This individual had no established routine, but had recognized this as a limitation and was developing plans for changing the situation. However, no action has been taken to realize the plans.
- **Level 3:** 6 participants. Individuals in this category were actively forming exercise plans when they joined the game. Some of them have joined gyms, but have not started exercising yet, or had previously attempted exercise but did not succeed at sustaining it.
- **Level 4-5:** 4 participants. Individuals in this category had an established exercise routine, but they did not form a habit yet. Because it was not always possible to determine the exact time when the routine was formed (less than 6 months ago or over 6 months ago), we have combined levels 4 and 5 into one level.
- **Level 6:** 4 participants. These individuals have followed established and rigorous exercise routines for many years and had indicated strong habits.

A similar analysis of post-game interviews, including interviews 3 and 4, produced the following results (Table 2):

Table 2. Cumulative TTM assessment results – pre-study and post-study. Gray rows indicate participants who achieved positive change in their daily steps.

#	Pre-study level	Pre-study steps	Post-study level	Post-study steps	Change
1	1	5,175	4	7,000	1,825
2	1	6,214	4	4,572	-1,642
3	1	7,140	2	6,676	-464
4	1	5,880	2	1,800	-4,080
5	2	4,904	2	3,742	-1,162
6	3	3,868	4	7,596	3,728
7	3	7,610	3	6,880	-730
8	3	5,849	4	8,832	2,983
9	3	1,884	3	1,920	36
10	3	5,104	4	9,494	4,390
11	3	6,546	4	11,725	5,179
12	4-5	3,705	4-5	6,016	2,311
13	4-5	7,756	5	10,616	2,860
14	4-5	11,667	5	15,012	3,345
15	4-5	6,666	4-5	7,026	360
16	6	9,378	6	9,187	-191
17	6	10,284	6	16,496	6,212
18	6	11,639	6	10,021	-1,618
19	6	7,171	6	8,123	952

Level 1, Pre-contemplation: All four individuals in Level 1 clearly indicated increased awareness of the low levels of their activity:

"It made me conscious, conscious that I need to exercise more..."

At the same time, this newly gained awareness rarely led to any significant change in either their exercise routines, or the level of daily steps. In fact, for most of them the number dropped below the pre-study baseline:

"The game and fish made me realize that I am walking so little. It made me conscious. But I was very busy and didn't have time for exercising. The consciousness overall increased. But I didn't change my exercise goals or routines. I will continue wearing the pedometer. I think if I start with the game now again, it would have impact."

Two of the participants in this group took immediate action; however, only one of their reports was supported by an actual increase in the number of steps (from 5,000 to 7,000 daily):

"It motivated me to start exercising. Before I wasn't doing any kind of jogging. The game made me realize that I need to exercise more. My goals have now increased. I try to jog now on a daily basis for 5-10 min.. I am planning to do more; I try to walk and exercise more in general."

Level 2, Contemplation: The only participant in this category did not demonstrate any engagement in the game, found wearing the pedometer inconvenient and uncomfortable and participating in the study unjustifiably effortful. This participant did not demonstrate any increase in the number of daily steps; on the contrary, the number decreased by over 1000 steps:

"It was too much effort to log in each day and I didn't have information about my team members. I didn't like to wear the pedometer. It's inconvenient."

Level 3, Preparation: The six participants in this category were already actively preparing for increasing their physical activity. For three of them, the game seems to have provided just the kind of additional motivation that was wanted. For another participant, the game coincided with the diagnosis of asthma and a doctor's recommendation to increase daily exercise. All of these participants increased the number of steps to varying degrees (from 36 steps to over 5,000 steps daily). Even more importantly, many of them indicated their commitment to sustaining their increases even after the game:

"The game had impact on my activity. I did more walking outside and inside; went on the treadmill - to walk away my pounds. I curtailed my appetite at lunch; that was good. I am walking everyday now; this game gave me more incentive to walk more each day, because I wanted to be competitive. I walked for about 45 minutes each day. I am at the point now where I will just walk anyways; I don't need the contest anymore. It motivated me to continue with this speed."

The two participants who did not demonstrate improvement attributed it to unusually heavy workload throughout the game:

"It makes me aware of exercising. I am very busy right now because of [heavy workload], so I didn't spend much time for exercising. It had impact on the weekends: I tried to walk around more, do a few more exercise, or take the stairs instead of the elevator. It helped me to stay interested in activity."

Level 4-5, Action and maintenance: As was expected, individuals on higher levels of TTM, who already took an action to establish an exercise routine, did not report significant changes in their exercise habits. However, even for these individuals the game presented a new concrete challenge and a target to strive for: a number of daily steps. All participants in this category increased their steps by 2,000 – 3,000 steps a day:

"I got up more in the evenings. I tried to reserve time from 8pm to 10pm for exercising. I developed a concrete goal: at least 10,000 each day, but that was very ambitious. So I made the goal smaller and could keep it every day then. Part of the goal was to increase speed."

Level 6, Termination: Similar to the Level 4-5 participants, the changes in attitudes were not as drastic as for those on the lower levels. All of these participants continued to maintain their well-established exercise routines; however, several of them became more mindful about their walking habits:

"I was already very active before. I enjoyed the graphical representation about my activity level. In addition to my exercise routine I walked more in the office and parked far away or used the stairs instead of the elevator."

In summary, application of the Transtheoretical Model for assessment of behavior change achieved in the course of the study demonstrated that Fish'n'Steps had a positive impact on 14 out of 19 participants as evident in either increase of their daily steps (for 4 participants), or advancements in TTM levels (for 3 participants) or both (for 7 participants).

The pattern of change across different levels very clearly indicated that individuals on the lowest (pre-contemplation) and highest (termination) levels were the least likely to achieve a significant change in their daily walking routines. The model provides a convincing explanation for this pattern: individuals in the pre-contemplation phase need to achieve a significant shift in attitude before demonstrating any observable change in behavior. At the same time, for individuals with well-defined exercise routines, the game did not generate any new awareness or motivation; these individuals could engage with the game for fun, but did not have a need to draw incentives from it.

Difference between conditions. Application of TTM analysis demonstrated no apparent differences in the achieved behavior change between the two experimental conditions as reflected by either the increase in the number of steps, or in the advancement in the TTM levels (see Table 3).

Table 3. Difference in achieved behavior change between the two experimental conditions

Type of improvement	Group condition	Individual condition
Average advancement in TTM levels	1,076	1
Average increase in number of steps	1,186	1,478

5.3 Reflecting on Intervention Design

In general, the game served its purpose: it created initial excitement, increased participants' awareness of their levels of physical activity and it provided motivation to increase their activity in a fun and engaging way. At the same time, the study allowed the research team to reflect on the design of this type of intervention.

Positive and negative incentives

A significant number of study participants (14 out of 19) developed a certain emotional attachment to their virtual pet: they mentioned feelings of guilt or happiness associated with their fish being sad or happy.

> *"I was really happy when I saw my fish grow. I tried to motivate myself to walk more to make it grow. I have even increased my regular walking activities; when I saw that the fish had grown I felt very happy."*
> *"The fish is part of me now. It was very good to have it as a motivation in the beginning. I miss the fish now."*

Most of these participants realized and appreciated the little extra motivation the fish was providing:

> *"It is much more friendly than an excel spreadsheet, it would help keep an interest in exercising because one of the problems of exercises it to be a boring routine."*

Unfortunately, this emotional attachment could at times backfire: when their fish did not grow, or had sad emotions, some of the participants chose to not look at their fish at all, rather than watch their unhappy fish.

"I didn't want to check on it, because I knew it was going to be sad."

Based on the classification of the participants according the levels of the Transtheoretical Model, the participants on both, the lowest and the highest levels were less likely to engage with the game and develop a sense of attachment to their virtual pet. Those on the lowest levels often were often discouraged by the overly negative state of their fish; those on the highest levels had no perceived need for additional motivation. However, participants classified on levels 3 to 5 demonstrated the highest general level of engagement with the game and with their virtual characters.

Cooperation and competition

The two experimental conditions were created to assess separately the effect of the virtual character, the fish, and the effect of the engagement in a social game. The application provided a number of mechanisms to facilitate such social engagement: participants were split into teams of four and provided with access to each others' progress and opportunity to communicate via chat. In addition, both individual and public displays highlighted the team with the highest daily achievement to facilitate bonding between members of each team and promote team spirit.

The competitive aspect of the game elicited mixed reactions in the participants. For some of them competitiveness was a more enduring motivation than the virtual character:

"It was cool for the first one or two weeks, but then as you are in the first place you think the fish can jump out of the bowl and I don't care; the fact that I was in the first place it's all I need; it means that I was competitive so the fish didn't have much of an effect."

At the same time, some felt competitiveness to be unnecessary and incompatible with the spirit of the game:

"There is enough competition in real life; I didn't really need more."

However, for a majority of the participants, having other fish presented a stimulating challenge and a benchmarking mechanism. Many of them compared their own virtual character's states, moods and sizes to those of their team members and were aware of their comparative performance.

"I was wondering who the other people behind the fishes were, the other fishes in my team were always crying, so I was wondering if my team members were working on it.", "...one fish in my team was really small the whole time, the others also got pretty big in the end. I was wondering, why the person with the small fish was not working."

At the same time, as discussed above, application of TTM to the two conditions separately did not demonstrate any difference in achievement between the two conditions.

In addition, providing mechanisms for anonymous team cooperation did not produce significant results. The majority of the participants felt awkward about contacting their team members without knowing who they were. The few that tried (3 out of 19) were quickly discouraged by the lack of response. Instead, because all of the participants were physically collocated and many knew each other well in person, the game was discussed actively over lunches, during coffee breaks, or other informal moments of face-to-face contact. On occasion, and especially at the beginning of the game, the participants were logging on to the same PC to compare their characters' moods and sizes.

Sustainability of the intervention
Despite the initial excitement about the game, the virtual characters and team competition, the game was perceived as increasingly repetitive as the study continued. While many of the participants (10 of 19) continued to have daily interactions, others limited their interaction to a few times a week. In addition, the inexpensive pedometers used for the study were meant to be worn on a belt, which was inconvenient for the female participants. All these aspects challenged continuous sustainability of the game.

"It was exciting at the beginning but then it turned into a nuisance; you would forget to put it on, or you would forget to log it in and stuff like that... I have to remember a lot of things during the day and that is on top of that..."

However, the game was not intended as a sustainable intervention, but as a temporary means of assisting the participants in advancing along the steps of behavioral change as proposed in the TTM.

6 Conclusions

Fish'n'Steps application was designed to provide multiple levels of incentives for increase in physical activity, which could be measured by a pedometer. These incentives included, on an individual level, the growth and emotional state of the individuals' virtual pets – fish in a fish-tank. Additional motivation was provided for participants in a team condition and included competition between teams with announcements of winning teams, and comparison between the states of the fish belonging to different members of the same team. To assess the potential of Fish'n'Steps to promote increase in individuals' activity levels, a 14-week study included 4 weeks of pre-study phase, in which individuals wore pedometers to establish their daily averages as a baseline; 6 weeks of participation in the game; and 4 weeks of post-study phase in which the game was terminated, but individuals continued to wear pedometers to assess sustainability of the potential change in their activity levels. As a result, 14 out of the 19 participants who completed the study demonstrated either advancement in the levels of Transtheoretical Model, or increase in the number of daily steps, or, and most commonly, both.

In general, the game seems to have served its purpose: created initial excitement, increased participants' awareness of their levels of physical activity and provided motivation to increase the activity level in a fun and engaging way. Although the initial fascination with the game subsided after the first couple of weeks, it nonetheless generated sustainable change in behavior and made continuing the game unnecessary.

It also became evident that participants' ability to take advantage of the game depended to a large degree on their current level of physical activity, their satisfaction with it, their desire to change it, and consequently their position within the TTM levels. Participants in pre-contemplation level (1) were most likely to change their attitude, but less likely to produce visible increase in the number of steps, as compared to other levels. Participants in termination level (6) were less likely to change either their attitude or the number of steps, as compared to other levels. And participants in the intermediate levels, preparation, action and maintenance, were most likely to change both, their attitude and their actual behavior.

The study also allowed researchers to reflect upon the design of the interventions. For example, the virtual pet character was designed to provide positive reinforcement to the desired behavior (happy growing fish) and negative reinforcement to the lack of the desired behavior (crying, not growing fish). While many participants felt certain level of responsibility for their character and tried to prevent it from crying, some reduced interactions with the game to avoid encounters with a crying fish.

To promote cooperation between the team members in a team condition, the application provided a possibility of chat communication. In addition, in order to preserve participants' privacy, they were encouraged to pick screen names. This combination created a surprising effect: instead of using chat for communication, participants tried to find each other and discuss the game during lunches, coffee breaks, or other informal face-to-face encounters. Many participants felt awkward contacting their team members without knowing who they really were. This approach of anonymous virtual communication might be more appropriate for distributed community in which members do not know each other.

One of the limitations of the game that prevented participants from engaging with it was intrusiveness of devices and procedures. The participants patiently followed the procedures of the study to assist researchers, however, most commented on the inconvenience of wearing the pedometer and uploading the data in the public kiosk. Less obtrusive uploading mechanisms might contribute to sustainability of the game.

References

[1] Orzano, A. J., Scott, J. G. (2004). Diagnosis and Treatment of Obesity in Adults: An Applied Evidence-Based Review. J Am Board Fam Med 17: 359-369.
[2] Purnell, J.Q., Knopp, R.H., Brunzell, J.D., Diatary fat and obesity, American Journal of Clinical Nutrition, 1999, pp.70-108.
[3] Bacon, L., Keim, N.L., Van Loan, M.D., Derricte, M., Gale, B., Kazaks, A., Stern, J.S., Evaluating a 'non-diet' wellness intervention for improvement of metabolic fitness, psychological well-being and eating and activity behaviors, International Journal of Obesity (2002) 26, 854-865.
[4] Bissell, P., Compliance, Concordance and Respect for the Patient's Agenda, The Pharmaceutical Journal, vol. 271, October 2003, pp.498-500.
[5] Tudor-Locke, C.E., Myers, A.M., Bell, R.C., Harris, S.B., Rodger, N.W., Preliminary Outcome Evaluation of the First Step Program: a daily physical activity intervention for individuals with type 2 diabetes, Patient Education and Counseling, 47 (2002) pp.23-28.

[6] Grimley, D., Prochaska, J.O., Velicer, W.F., Vlais, L.M., and DiClemente, C.C., 1994.
     The transtheoretical model of change. In T.M. Brinthaupt & R.P. Lipka, Changing the
     self: Philosophies, techniques, and experiences. SUNY series, studying the self (p. 201 –
     227). Albany, NY: State University of New York Press.

[7] Bandura, A., 1982. Self-efficacy mechanism in human agency. American Psychologist,
     37 (2), 122 – 147.

[8] DiClemente, C.C., Prochaska, J.O., Fairhurst, S.K., Veliceer, W.F., Velasquez, M.M,
     and Rossi, J.S., 1991, The process of smoking cessation: An analysis of precontempla-
     tion, contemplation, and preparation stages of change. Journal of Consulting and Clinical
     Psychology, 59, 295 – 304.

[9] Dallow CB, Anderson J. (2003).Using self-efficacy and a transtheoretical model to de-
     velop a physical activity intervention for obese women. American Journal of Health Pro-
     motion, 17, 373– 81.

[10] Marshall S., Biddle S. (2001). The transtheoretical model of behavior change: a meta-
     analysis of applications to physical activity and exercise. Annals of Behavioral Medi-
     cine, 23, 229– 46.

[11] Riebe D., Blissmer B., Greene G., Caldwell, M., Ruggiero, L., Stillwell, K., Nigg, C.
     (2005). Long-term maintenance of exercise and healthy eating behaviors in overweight
     adults, Preventive Medicine, 40, 769–778.

[12] Lieberman, D.: Dance Dance Revolution: The Most Researched Serious Game Ever.
     Why, and What Have We Learned?.
     https://www.cmpevents.com/GDsg05/a.asp?option=C&V=11&SessID=1075, Serious
     Games Summit DC 2005 Sessions.

[13] Mokka, S., Väätänen, A., Heinilä, J., Välkkynen, P., Fitness computer game with a bod-
     ily user interface, Proc ICEC '03, pp.1-3.

[14] Björk, St., Holopainen, J., Ljungstrand, P., Akesson, K.P., Designing Ubiquitous Com-
     puting Games – A Report from a Workshop Exploring Ubiquitous Computing Enter-
     tainment, Personal and Ubiquitous Computing (2002), pp.443-458.

[15] Chan, C., Ryan, D., Tudor-Locke C. (2004). Health benefits of a pedometer-based physi-
     cal activity intervention in sedentary workers, Preventive Medicine, 39, 1215–1222.

[16] Consolvo, S., Everitt, K., Smith, I., Landay, J.A., Design requirements for technologies
     that encourage physical activity. Proceedings of the SIGCHI conference on Human Fac-
     tors in computing systems, 2006, pp.457-466.

[17] Hardeman, W., Griffin, S., Johnston, M., Kinmonth, A.L., Wareham., N.J., Interventions
     to prevent weight gain: a systematic review of psychological models and behaviour
     change methods, International Journal of Obesity (2000) 24, 131-143.

[18] Langer, E.J., Rodin, J., 1976, The Effects of Choice and Enhanced Personal Responsibil-
     ity for the Aged: A Field Experiment in an Institutional Setting, Journal of Personality
     and Social Psychology 34: 191-198.

[19] Lieberman, D., Interactive Video Games for Health Promotion: Effects on Knowledge,
     Self-Efficacy, Social Support, and Health, Health Promotion and Interactive Technol-
     ogy: Theoretical Applications and Future Directions, 1997, Mahwah, NJ: Lawrence Erl-
     baum Associates.

[20] McLean, N., Griffin S., Toney, K., and Hardeman, W., Family involvement in weight
     control, weight maintenance and weight-loss interventions: a systematic review of ran-
     domized trials, International Journal of Obesity (2003) 27, 987-1005.

[21] Intille, S. S. (2003). Ubiquitous Computing Technology for Just-in-Time Motivation of
     Behavior Change (Position Paper), in Proceedings of the UbiHealth Workshop' 2003.

[22] Jafarinaimi, N., Forlizzi, J., Hurst, A., and Zimmerman, J. (2005). Breakaway: an ambient display designed to change human behavior. In CHI '05 Extended Abstracts on Human Factors in Computing Systems (Portland, OR, USA, April 02 - 07, 2005), 1945-1948.

[23] Fogg, B.J., Persuasive Technology : Using Computers to Change What We Think and Do, Morgan Kaufmann (December 2002).

[24] Konkel, M., Leung, V., Ullmer, B., Hu, C., Tagaboo. (2004). A collaborative children's game based upon wearable RFID technology, Pers Ubiquit Comput, pp.382-384.

[25] Croteau, K. (2004). A preliminary study on the impact of a pedometer-based intervention on daily steps, American Journal of Health Promotion, 18, 217-220.

Hitchers: Designing for Cellular Positioning

Adam Drozd[1], Steve Benford[1], Nick Tandavanitj[2], Michael Wright[1],
and Alan Chamberlain[1]

[1] The Mixed Reality Laboratory, University of Nottingham, Nottingham, NG8 1BB, UK
{asd, sdb, maw, azc}@cs.nott.ac.uk
[2] Blast Theory, Unit 4, Level 5 South, New England House, New England Street, Brighton,
BN1 4GH, UK
nick@blasttheory.co.uk

Abstract. Hitchers is a game for mobile phones that exploits cellular position-ing to support location-based play. Players create digital hitch hikers, giving them names, destinations and questions to ask other players, and then drop them into their current phone cell. Players then search their current cell for hitchers, pick them up, answer their questions, carry them to new locations and drop them again, providing location-labels as hint to where they can be found. In this way, hitchers pass from player to player, phone to phone and cell to cell, gather-ing information and encouraging players to label cells with meaningful place names. A formative study of Hitchers played by 47 players over 4 months shows how the seams in cellular positioning, including varying cell size, density and overlap, affected the experience. Building on previous discussions of de-signing for uncertainty and seamful design, we consider five ways of dealing with these seams: removing, hiding, managing, revealing and exploiting them. This leads us to propose the mechanism of a dynamic search focus, to explore new visualization tools for cellular data, and to reconsider the general relation-ship between 'virtual' and 'physical' worlds in location-based games.

Keywords: Mobile games, cellular positioning, ubiquitous computing, seamful design.

1 Introduction

Location-based games in which game-play responds to a player's location represent one of the most promising commercial applications of ubiquitous computing. Previ-ous location-based gaming projects have translated existing online computer games to a physical setting (e.g., *AR Quake* [13] and *Human Pacman* [7]); have used digital technologies to enhance or coordinate physical challenges (e.g., *The Go Game* [12] and *Mogi Mogi* [10]); have demonstrated new forms of collaboration across physical and virtual spaces (e.g., *Can You See Me Now?* [5] and *Uncle Roy All Around You* [3]); and have enabled players to explore and exploit the usually invisible seams in the ubiquitous infrastructure (e.g., *Treasure* [1] and *Feeding Yoshii* [2]). From a re-search perspective, games such as these provide an ideal way of engaging users in trials of emerging technologies and studying how they experience different aspects of ubiquitous computing when deployed 'in the wild', leading to new design sensitivi-ties, guidelines and technical innovations.

P. Dourish and A. Friday (Eds.): Ubicomp 2006, LNCS 4206, pp. 279–296, 2006.
© Springer-Verlag Berlin Heidelberg 2006

In this paper, we introduce a location-based game called *Hitchers* that is targeted at mobile phones and that is intended to provide experience with the use of cellular positioning (especially approaches where phones look up their own current mobile phone cell-ID) to create location based experiences. We present a formative study of Hitchers that shows how the seams in cellular positioning and communications affected the experience, leading us to propose new mechanisms, tools and approaches for designing location-based games for mobile phones.

2   Cellular Positioning for Mobile Phones

While the Global Positioning System (GPS) has been a popular positioning technology for supporting early location-based games for PDAs, it is currently not widely available on mobile phones in some countries. Rather, mobile phones come with their own positioning system, that of cellular positioning, in which a phone can be positioned relative to one or more mobile phone masts. There are two general approaches to cellular positioning. The first relies on operator or aggregator services that use information available from the operators' networks to estimate the location of a phone which is then reported back to an application as a georeferenced location; in most cases the latitude and longitude of the mobile device along with an associated estimate of error. The second is for the phone itself to look up and use its own current cell-ID, the identifier of the mast/antenna to which it is currently connected, which is currently possible on some handsets (most notably on Nokia Series 60).

There are advantages and disadvantages to each approach. Operator and aggregator services potentially offer a greater degree of precision and accuracy as operators can triangulate relative signal strengths across multiple masts for which they know precise geographical locations. Conversely, while looking up one's own mobile phone cell-ID may deliver less precise information (as it only uses information about one mast) and may even not even deliver a geo-referenced position (unless someone has found out and published the location of the mast), it does confer some potentially useful advantages. It is free to look up your own cell-ID, whereas operators and aggregators charge for each look up which can become expensive in an ongoing mobile game. Furthermore, the look up occurs on the player's own phone, not in the network, and so it is possible to control how location information is released to other players and game servers, with implications for maintaining privacy. A more detailed account of the potential benefits and limitations of using cell-ID for location can be found in [16].

In this paper, we focus on the second approach, a phone looking up its own cell-ID, introducing a game that exploits this without the need for georeferenced locations.

3   Introducing Hitchers

Hitchers is a location-based game for mobile phones that utilises GPRS networking and positioning using the cell-IDs from the players' phones to create an experience based around the metaphor of digital hitch-hiking.

In Hitchers, initially the world is empty but as the game is played the streets fill with characters who are trying to hitch-hike their way across the city or up and down the country. They have been created and released into the wild by their owners and are trying to find their way home, reach a specific destination, carry out a mission, or just share a journey with a stranger.

Players log into the game, giving their username and Personal Identification Number (PIN). They can then create new hitchers, giving each a name, a destination that it is trying to reach, and a question that it will ask each player it encounters (Figure 1).

Choose a name ...   destination ...   and question

Fig. 1. Creating a hitcher, giving it a name, destination and question

Once created, the player can 'drop off' their new hitcher, releasing it into the world to begin its journey. Metaphorically, the hitcher is now removed from their phone and waits in their current location for other players to come by and give it a ride.

Whenever a player drops a hitcher they are prompted with the question "Where are we now?" which encourages them to enter a text label describing their current location in the physical world, building on the interesting idea of encouraging players to label the places that they associate with cell-IDs as described in [14].

Players can search their current location for any hitchers that may want a ride, seeing two lists of available hitchers: new acquaintances that they have never met before and old friends who they have previously encountered (Figure 2). They can pick up a hitcher in which case it appears to jump onto their phone and will no longer be available to other players until they drop it off again. When a player picks up a hitcher they see its name, destination and question. They can choose to answer the question with a short text response. They can also drop off the hitcher again whenever they like, possibly after carrying it with them to a new location, perhaps one that it closer to its ultimate destination. In this way, hitchers make their way from phone to phone, player to player and place to place, trying to reach their destination and gathering answers to their question as they go. In the current version of the game, a hitcher can only ride with one player at a time and each player can only carry one hitcher at a time.

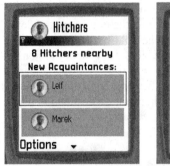

Search ...   pick up ...   ... answer

Fig. 2. Searching for, picking up and answering a hitcher

If there are no hitchers in their current location then the player may be told 'There are no hitchers here". However, sometimes the game is able to return a hint as to other nearby locations where they might be found in the form of "There are no hitchers here. Some were recently seen at <location-name>", encouraging the player to journey to another place in order to continue their search and find a hitcher that needs a ride.

Finally, the Hitchers website allows players to look up information about any hitcher that they have encountered and also the Hitchers they themselves have created and released. They can view where it has been, who it has met, the answers that it has collected, and can continue to follow its progress as the game continues. Figure 3 shows part of a webpage for a player who has encountered 177 hitchers thus far, listing the names of encountered hitchers on the left and the details (answers and places dropped) for the currently selected hitcher on the right. Thus, the website provides global information about the status and movement of Hitchers and the reward for picking up a Hitcher is to access both its past and future information.

3.1 Implementing Hitchers

Hitchers employs a standard client-server architecture (Figure 4). The client runs on a player's mobile phone, which is currently any of the Nokia Series 60 phones, and consists of two parts, the Place Lab cell-ID server that has supported a variety of context-aware projects for mobile phones, to enable the phone to report its current cell-ID [9] and a J2ME application that provides the client user interface, client side logic and the networking connection to the server. In Hitchers, the player's current location is therefore mapped onto the current cell-ID. The server component of the system runs on a standard web server with PHP and MySQL extensions. PHP is used to script the logic on the server with MySQL being used for persistent storage.

As most mobile phone networks do not provide mobile phones with routable IP addresses, all communications requests, which are in essence RPC calls, must be initiated from the client side. These RPC calls are sent from the client to the server over HTTP using POST requests, with the parameters being passed within the data of the POST request. The reply is then used to update the state of the client application

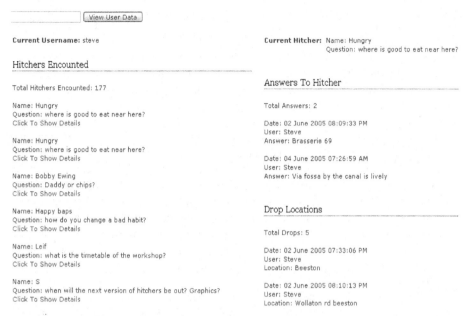

Fig. 3. Exploring Hitching history via the online web interface

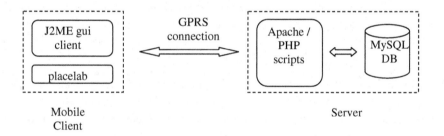

Mobile
Client

Server

Fig. 4. The Hitchers architecture

on the phone which persists between sessions, including when the phone is switched off and on again.

Consequently, the Hitchers client application only sends data to the server as a result of player initiated interactions (logging on and off, searching, creating, picking up, answering and dropping hitchers) and the server never initiates contact with the client. This also ensures that the player is directly in control of expenditure on GPRS data transfer at all times, which we believe to be a particularly important factor in mobile phone based games where players pay according to the volume of data transferred and where some players may have tightly restricted budgets (e.g., younger players who are often on 'pay as you go' contracts).

Information about Hitchers including their name, question, current location (cell-ID) and status (available to be picked up, or currently associated by a given player) is stored in the database along with the history of all previous answers and locations. Each player action results in a query to the database which is indexed by a combination of the player-ID, their current cell-ID and the hitcher-ID. The effects of these interactions are implemented by setting the values of the appropriate attributes for the row that represents this hitcher in the database. For example, dropping a hitcher involves changing its status attribute to be 'available' and updating its current cell-ID attribute.

In addition to the information that is directly required for the current operation, the client also uploads a list of the most recently observed cell-IDs for this player whenever they interact with the game. This chain of adjacent cell-IDs is then stored by the server which, over the course of the game, gradually builds up a connected graph of mapped cell-IDs. The nodes of this graph represent all of the cell-IDs that all players have collectively visited and its arcs show the direct transitions that were observed between them. By direct transitions we mean whenever a player's phone made a transition from one cell-ID to another without disconnecting in between. If a player leaves one cell-ID, either by quitting the game, switching off their phone, or losing network connectivity, to reappear at a new cell-ID sometime later, then no direct transition is recorded between the two cell-IDs.

This graph structure can be queried by the system to establish adjacency relationships between cell-IDs in order to generate 'hitcher hints'. Whenever a player searches for hitchers in their current location, the server sees if there are any in the database that are associated with their current cell-ID and whose status is 'available'. If so, it returns their details to the player. However, if there are no available hitchers in the player's current cell, the server uses the graph to identify any adjacent cells to the current cell that do contain available hitchers. It then chooses one of these (at random) and returns one of its location labels (also at random) to the user as a hint that tells them where they might go to find hitchers, using the phrase: "There are no Hitchers here. Some were recently seen at "<place label>" as noted previously. This phrasing carefully implies that the hitchers may no longer be at this location when the player reaches it We decided to initially opt for random choices so as to maximize player's knowledge of different locations and labels in the game.

3.2 Hitchers as a Framework for Different Games and as a Basis for Formative Study

Although we have described Hitchers as a game, it is currently more of a framework from which a variety of games might be created. As it stands, Hitchers currently has no specific goal, scoring mechanisms or game play beyond creating hitchers, moving them around the world and answering their questions. However, we envisage that it would be relatively straightforward to extend the rules of Hitchers to support a variety of games. Players might be rewarded for helping hitchers towards their destinations and answering their questions; they might be able to collect and carry multiple hitchers; hitchers might be given richer and more autonomous behaviors in terms of dialogue with users, the need for attention (perhaps requiring Tamagotchi style tending), deciding when to jump onto and off of players' phones, and even the ability to fight or breed among themselves. Such features could support a variety of games such as hitcher 'balloon races', missions, battling hitchers, territorial games, virus simulations and others.

This said, for the purposes of this paper, even this basic version of Hitchers is sufficient for us to be able to study the use cellular positioning to achieve location-specific play. We therefore now turn our attention to a formative study of Hitchers.

4   A Formative Study of Hitchers

Our formative study unfolded in two stages, an initial period of intense testing and software refinement over two months mostly involving members of the development team and other members of our research laboratory, followed by a broader deployment to players outside of our organization over about two months. This second main phase involved 47 players who were recruited from research teams across the UK and Sweden working in the area of ubiquitous computing, mobile games and also educational technologies, enabling us to draw on a strong base of expert opinion.

We begin with a discussion of how our initial period of intensive testing revealed key seams in the underlying cellular positioning system, before then turning our attention to how players experienced the game, including these seams.

4.1   Testing the Seams in Cellular Positioning

Throughout the trial, members of the development team played intensively at many different times and locations and on different forms of transportation with the specific intention of testing the potential impact of the underling cellular positioning mechanism on the game. Subsequent discussions of their experiences, backed up by inspection of system logs, raised a variety of issues concerning the use of cellular positioning, building on previous research in this area [11] [15].

Variable cell size and density – as one would expect, when compared to technologies such as GPS, positioning on raw cell-ID alone is relatively imprecise. From a player's point of view, cells appear to vary in size from a few hundred meters up to kilometers. While many factors might potentially affect apparent cell size, one highly significant factor is the density of mobile phone masts, which tend to be more densely distributed in urban environments and more sparsely distributed in rural ones. One implication of this observation is that successfully playing Hitchers requires significant mobility on behalf of players. As we shall see below, this is not a game that works well around a single building or campus, but rather requires movement across a city or better, between cities as this produces clearly noticeable differences in locations and hitchers. A second implication is that Hitchers themselves may behave in a more fine grained way (i.e., be associated with more specific locations) in built-up urban environments compared to rural ones.

Overlapping cells and cell flipping – mobile phone cells frequently overlap. It is often possible to see several cells from a given place and the system logs showed that a mobile phone would often rapidly flip back and forth between several different cells, sometimes as frequently as once every few seconds. This can occur for several reasons, including variations in signal strength due to interference, passing objects or subtle changes in the player's position as well as due to congestion in the network.

As we shall report below, cell flipping could have two noticeable effects on the experience. First, it could cause hitchers to mysteriously disappear and reappear again. A player might drop a hitcher in one cell, then flip to a nearby one (without changing location), search for it and not see it, then flip back, search again and now see it again, giving the impression that hitchers jump around of their own accord. Second, it could cause the hints mechanism to tell the player to try looking for hitchers in their current location. In this case, the player would drop the hitcher, giving a location label. They would then flip to an adjacent cell (without physically moving) and search for hitchers. If none were found, the hints mechanism would look in adjacent cells for labels to return as hints, and might possibly choose the player's previous cell and the label that they had just supplied – which would refer to where they were still standing.

Multiple networks and roaming – there may be multiple mobile phone networks available at a given location. Players playing on one network will see a quite different set of cell-IDs to players on another. Put another way, each physical location may be associated with a different set of cell IDs (and hence a different set of hitchers) for each network. However, hitchers may move between networks as players roam, either explicitly or automatically switching networks. One player reported an unexpected and involuntary case of roaming: their phone was out of coverage on their home network when they dropped a Hitcher. In the meantime it had connected to another network, even though the player had no contract to roam there, so that the player could access emergency services if needed (networks may have an agreement with regard to being able to access emergency services). Consequently, they dropped a hitcher on a 'foreign' network as a result of being out of coverage on their home network.

Network reconfiguration – the underlying infrastructure of mobile phone masts is itself not static. Masts may be added to the network, removed and their identifiers may be altered. One player reported playing Hitchers at a major music festival at which a temporary mobile phone mast had been erected. That cell ID – and presumably the hitchers that were left with it – has since disappeared, although perhaps it (and they) will reappear again elsewhere in the future, maybe even at the same festival next year.

Cell elasticity when playing at speed – testing also showed that the experience of Hitchers appears to vary according to the speed of the player. Quite often we have tried to drop Hitchers precisely at stations or junctions when moving through them on an outward journey. On the return journey however, they have not been found at the stations, but rather some distance beyond them (as seen from the return direction).

This effect makes sense if we consider the possible apparent elasticity of cells as illustrated by figure 5. Phones may tend to stay connected to their current cell until circumstances force them to disconnect. Imagine a station is overlapped by cells A and B. On the outward journey the train comes from cell A, is at cell A while passing the station when the player drops the Hitcher, then connects to cell B shortly afterwards. On the return journey they begin connected to B and remain in B as they pass through the station, only connecting to A – where they dropped the Hitcher – sometime afterwards.

Verifying the consistency and causes of this effect requires further experimentation. However, at a more general level, it is broadly consistent with experiences from other location-based games. For example, players of a WiFi-based game called Feeding Yoshi that involved connecting to different WiFi access points reported difficulties due to rapidly passing through WiFi zones when trying to play in cars [2]. At the other extreme, players of a pedestrian game called Savannah experienced difficulties when they would suddenly stop to access location-based content while using a positioning system that had been tuned to operate smoothly for moving objects (a GPS system employing dead-reckoning) [4]. From the point of view of Hitchers, it would appear that while transportation systems offer powerful opportunities pervasive games (as we see later), they may also introduce new challenges in terms of the relationship between rapid movement and the operation of positioning and communications systems. More generally, it would therefore appear that there are complex interactions between player speed and positioning systems that require further exploration.

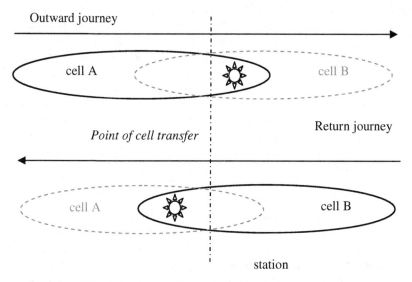

Fig. 5. Apparent cell elasticity when playing at speed

These various characteristics of cellular positioning in relation to coverage and how the mobile device establishes its connection to the network can be characterized as 'seams', the places in which technologies are stitched together to create an experience that are often intended to be transparent to the player, but that sometimes be revealed with unusual effects [6]. In this case, seams arise from the stitching together of multiple mobile phone cells to create multiple mobile phone networks. Ideally again from the our point of view of using cell-IDs for positioning, multiple cells and possibly even multiple networks would be seamlessly stitched together so that a mobile phone could roam between them, unaware of the underlying technical infrastructure. In practice, this is not always the case. Rather, mobile phone cells are not seamlessly stitched together, but instead overlap, vary in size and density, and on occasion leave gaps in coverage. This generally, except in the case of coverage does not affect the users when using the mobile as a phone, however when the cell-IDs are used directly as a positioning technology is does then affect users in the way the game behaves.

4.2 Feedback from Players

Our 47 players created 409 hitchers, gave 364 answers to questions, dropped hitchers with a corresponding location label 1211 times, and searched for hitchers 2623 times. They passed through 3119 unique cell-Ds spread over 6 countries, mostly in the UK (2,484 unique cell-IDs), followed by Sweden (475),Belgium (112), Germany (24), Italy (16) and France (8). 381 unique cells-IDs were labeled by 1211 supplied labels.

17 of our 47 players responded to a short email questionnaire that probed their opinions as to a range of issues, of which the relevant ones for this particular paper were: whether they had enjoyed hitchers and how they would improve it; where and when did they prefer to play; how did they chose to answer the question "where are we now?"; and did they notice anything strange about the behavior of hitchers.

Overall, players were evenly split between those who had enjoyed hitchers and those who had not. Those who enjoyed the experience appreciated the novelty of the idea, trying to associate hitchers with their owners, and seeing their own hitchers moved or answered. Those who did not enjoy it expressed frustrations that there were not enough players or hitchers in the areas in which they played, and that there were insufficient alerts to maintain their interest, suggesting that the game experience could become too sparse when only a few people were playing. Some players had experienced technical difficulties during the game (especially those who borrowed phones from us and so had to learn a new phone interface). Suggested improvements included being able to upload and download photographs (from several players), being able to carry several hitchers, having a rating system for hitchers, having 'rare' hitchers, and being able to add to hitcher stories.

In terms of preferred times and places for playing, work was mentioned frequently and home much less so. However, there were frequent references to railway stations, underground metro systems, buses and cars. Transportation systems appeared to be popular because there was often downtime when players were bored and looking for something to do. One observed: "usually at railway stations, or on trains, because I got fed up with whatever I was reading!" and another noted: "On trains and buses. While waiting for transport. Because I had slivers of down time." However, stations may also have been good destinations because they were obvious drop off and pick up points for hitchers. The Stockholm metro system was particularly notable as each underground station offered good connectivity and players would often commute back and forth. As one player noted: "there were trails of Hitchers in just about all subway stations I visited in Stockholm so it worked really well there."

On the whole, players did not greatly notice odd hitcher movements and behaviors with the exception of some who observed that they experienced difficulty with "finding hitchers again after they'd been put down" and several who did mention problems establishing connectivity. One player noted problems with the hints mechanism sometimes referring them to their current location as discussed above. One player observed that: "The accuracy of location was much too poor for the way everyone was trying to play (they were dropping a hitcher off at a location on campus and having it ask to be taken to different locations on campus). I imagine that given a bit of time, other players would have realised they could not play locally and would have sent hitchers on longer trips." We return to these issues in greater detail below.

Players adopted a range of strategies when answering the question "where are we now?" when dropping off a hitcher. The largest grouping claimed to give honest geographical descriptions of locations, for example: "I tried to give general descriptions of where I was", "nearest station", "I answered it as truthfully as I could (geographically)" and "honestly because I thought it would be interesting to other players". However, one player was more deliberately evasive for privacy reasons: "Not to give away directly where the location was. I just don't like people to know where I was exactly". A few players mixed strategies: "Mostly pragmatically, like at stations naming the station but sometimes atmospherically if I was in the mood or cryptically if I thought it would make it more intriguing for someone finding a specific Hitcher". Finally, one observed that it could be difficult to choose names when moving: "On the train I said 'on the train' as I had no idea where I was – that's a problem".

5 Designing for the Seams in Cellular Positioning

Within this paper we are regarding a seam as divergence within a system between the state of the system the players are meant to see and the state of the system in reality. These seams are caused by there being multiple parts to a system (the phone masts / mobile cells in this case) that are being experienced as a whole by the players. It should be noted that we are mainly looking at the seams generated when using these masts (and hence the cell-IDs) as the basis of a positioning system and not the mobile network as such, although as we will see the coverage of the mobile network does play a part in generating seams. The question then becomes how seams impact on the user's experience and what the designer or indeed the user can do about this? Previous research has suggested various strategies for dealing with the uncertainties caused by the seams in ubiquitous technologies [5]: *remove* them by improving or carefully deploying the technologies; *hide* them by designing experiences that are robust to the characteristics of seams; *manage* them by designing an experience that adapts to seams; *reveal* them to users and designers so that they are aware of the presence and effects of seams, enabling them to adapt their own behaviors; and finally, *exploit* them, requiring users to actively seek them out as part of the experience. We now consider each strategy in relation to the design of Hitchers and potentially other pervasive experiences.

5.1 Removing the Seams from Hitchers

It may be possible for operators to remove some of the seams from the cellular network, for example by providing greater network coverage; ever getting closer to 100%,and also by providing more consistent and accurate positioning services that draw on knowledge of a mobile phone's relationship to many masts, as indeed they already do to some extent in operator positioning services. However, operator positioning services do not currently fit the style of game play Hitchers is based upon, mainly due to the financial costs involved with operator services.   Cell handovers will however be an inevitable part of using cellular positioning in the way Hitchers does and this is discussed below in the section regarding managing seams.

5.2 Hiding the Seams in Hitchers

Although these various seams became apparent during our extensive testing of Hitchers, feedback from our players suggests that they often went unnoticed in the course of everyday play. We propose that this may be because the design of Hitchers is reasonably effective at hiding the worst effects of these seams. Users are on the whole, not exposed to location information (the cell-IDs in this case) other than through the sense of searching or dropping 'here' and through hints from the system that Hitchers may be at a nearby named place. In particular, there is no game map that tries to suggest to users where they are at any given moment in time. Even though hints do refer to places, they are careful to suggest only that Hitchers have recently been seen at this place – not that they would necessarily be found there now. Furthermore, there is the general idea in the concept of the game that Hitchers can move about, for example as other players pick them up, or possibly even of their own accord. Hitchers are therefore somewhat elusive and one would not always expect to find then where one left them, which may go some way to hiding seams such as variable sized and overlapping cells. In short, we suggest that Hitchers is reasonably – though not entirely – accommodating to the seams when using cell-ID positioning.

5.3 Managing the Seams in Hitchers

However, there are clearly times when seams do reveal themselves, including three of the effects that we described above: cell flipping causing hitchers to disappear and reappear; cell flipping causing the hints mechanism to return hints that refer to the player's current location; and problems caused by the apparently elastic effect of cell positioning when players are moving at speed.

We propose that a single mechanism – an *adaptive search focus* – could be introduced to help the game manage these effects. In the current game, the search focus is set to only look in the current cell. In contrast, in a very early test version we had experimented with a broader search focus that looked in the current cell, its immediate neighbours and their immediate neighbours (a search depth of 2 in the cell graph that is built up during the game). However, this had proved to be too broad in densely mapped areas leading to players seeing the same hitchers even after moving several kilometers. An adaptive search focus is then a mechanism that adapts the depth of searching to suit the player's current situation. For example:

- On detecting cell flipping (rapid oscillation between several cells) the search focus would extend to cover all of them (effectively treating them as a single cell while flipping continued). This might mitigate the problems with hitchers disappearing and reappearing and returning hints to the current location.
- On guessing that the player was moving at speed, for example by logging a continuous linear sequence of cells, the search focus might be extended to cover the current cell and its neighbors, potentially mitigating some of the effects of cell elasticity as noted previously.
- Extending and shrinking the search focus might also help manage the effects of sparse player density that frustrated some of our players. In an area shared

by many players the game would build up a dense map of local cells which would be highly interconnected. In this case, the search focus might be reduced to just the current cell providing maximum differentiation between different locations so that the game would respond to relatively small changes in position. In an area with few players, there would be a much less densely connected mapping of cells, in which case it might make sense to extend the search radius.

We propose that this mechanism of an adaptive search focus could provide a useful way of managing the effects of seams. However, it does require that the designer (for pre-programmed adaptation) or system (for automated and dynamic adaptation) can spot situations in which the focus needs to be adapted, i.e., when cell flipping is occurring, when players are moving rapidly or when players are in dense or sparse areas of the game. This brings us to the next strategy – revealing seams.

5.4 Revealing the Seams in Hitchers

Our fourth strategy involves revealing the seams in the underlying positioning infrastructure (the cell-IDs in this case) so that designers (and potentially players) can reason about their presence and effects and can adapt the experience accordingly. With this in mind, we have begun to develop new tools that help humans visualize the behavior of the cellular positioning system. The first of these is the tool shown in figure 6 that visualizes the cell data that is mapped and labeled by players. The visualization takes the form of a connected graph whose nodes represent unique cell-IDs and whose arcs represent direct transitions between pairs of cell-IDs that have been recorded by players during the game. This graph is visualized using a well known force-directed placement algorithm [8] that is implemented in the Java JGraph library [16]. Consequently, this is an abstract graph and the relative positions if the nodes bear no relation to geographical directions in the physical world.

Users can interact with this visualization in the following ways:

- Using the controls top-left, they can select the dataset to be visualized, filtering it by country and network.
- They can zoom in and out and pan across the visualization to inspect different patterns of cell trails, for example identifying tightly clustered areas.
- They can query individual cells in order to inspect their location labels.
- They can use the controls bottom-left to select all cells that have been labeled with a given text substring. These cells are then highlighted with a bold border and separate sub-graphs displaying only these cells and cells that connect them are displayed in the separate mini-visualization bottom-right.
- They can query the graph for information about Hitchers including showing the current location of a Hitcher as well as the Hitchers currently associated with a given cell. The size and shading of the nodes in the graph can also be dynamically configured using the controls middle-left to show the number of hitchers currently in a cell and the number dropped in this cell over time.

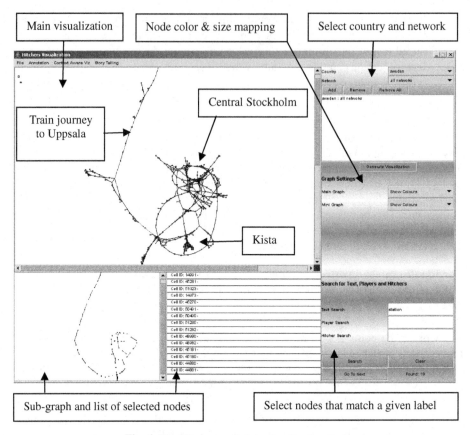

Fig. 6. The Hitchers cell-data visualization tool

We propose that visualizations such as this can help designers deal with the seams in cellular positioning as well as establish potential mappings between clusters of mapped cells and user-meaningful places and activities. For example, Figure 6 shows all data that was gathered from our trial by all players across all networks in Sweden. The figure reveals some distinctive dense clusters of cells as well as some long thin trials of cells that connect them. By inspecting the player-given labels for these cells, we have been able to assign likely physical locations to some of the key clusters (we have labeled two of the larger ones – the towns of Stockholm and Kista – in the figure). We have also been able to determine that the long trails of cells correspond to train and car journeys.

By filtering and zooming we are able to explore these further. For example, the bottom-right of figure 6 shows a sub-graph of all cells that have been labeled with the word 'station' along with intervening cells that connect these.

Figure 7 shows a series of views of a region of the graph that are highlighted according to three different location labels. The leftmost image highlights cells that have been labeled 'Kista' the middle image cells labeled 'SICS' (The Swedish Institute of Computer Science) and the right image cells labeled 'ICE' (Interactive Computing Environments lab), suggesting that ICE is a place within SICS which is a place within Kista. Images such as this may enable us to reason about the relationship between players' activities, places that are meaningful to them and potentially overlapping mobile phone cells. We anticipate that they could be especially useful to designers, as they can provide information about how to design a pervasive experience that adapts to the distinctive characteristics of cellular positioning. For example:

- We know from our player feedback, that transportation systems are good places to play. A tool such as this can help a designer identify which mobile phone cells are likely to be encountered on a journey via train, bus or car and to author specific hotspots or location triggers accordingly. For example, we can identify likely sequences of cells encountered when traveling on the Stockholm subway and author appropriate content for these.
- These visualizations also help designers identify clusters of cells that are associated with other kinds of player meaningful places (our data shows players labeling supermarkets, schools, places of work, their homes, restaurants and bars) which again can inform the design of hotspots and triggers.
- We have already proposed the idea of an adaptive search focus in the previous section. This visualization might help designers configure such a mechanism, for example, identifying sequences of cells that are associated with journeys (for which we want a wider focus) versus those that appear to be associated with more dense regions of play (for which we want a narrower focus).

Consequently, we suggest that visualizations such as might potentially form the basis of new design and authoring tools that reveal information captured from an experience so as to help designers refine that experience or potentially author new ones.

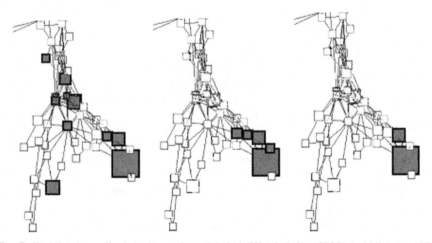

Fig. 7. Highlighting cells that players have labeled 'Kista' (left), 'SICS' (middle) and 'ICE' (right) by being shaded. Is ICE a place within SICS which in turn, is within Kista.

5.5 Exploiting Seams in Hitchers

Our final strategy focuses on how we might exploit these seams to create new kinds of experience. A distinctive and interesting feature Hitchers is the way in which it generates a virtual game board as it is played. At the beginning of a game, Hitchers has no knowledge of places that are meaningful to players or of how they map to mobile phone cells. However, as the game unfolds it constructs a continually changing map of interconnected cells and corresponding place labels. These can be thought of as a game board across which pieces – players and Hitchers in our case – can move. This perspective opens up intriguing new possibilities for designing games in which part of the experience is to map the infrastructure or perhaps to strategically change the map that has been generated thus far. For example, we could design games in which players acquire, defend, maintain or capture territory by mapping and labeling cells. Game mechanics might range from simply acquiring cells by being the first player to encounter them, through to more complex moves in which already mapped cells can be captured, for example by finding a new route through the physical world that encircles them or connects them in a new way.

This idea of being able to make new connections between new cells – forging shorter paths through the cell map by working out a new route through the physical world – could also offer players advantage in terms of transporting objects around the game board. For example, a skillful player would be able to reason about potential new connections between cells that appeared to be widely separated on the graph but perhaps shared some common or nearby place labels in the physical world. Perhaps this could be assisted by virtual maps based on the kinds of visualizations that we showed above? This kind of game mechanic would essentially be exploiting the imprecise nature of the mapping of places in the physical world to cells, encouraging players to reason about how different cells overlap with different places and potentially with each other. Skillful players might even be able to exploit deeper knowledge of the operation of mobile phone networks, for example realizing that at times of high congestion their phone may connect to more distant masts than usual, which might offer them a form of power-up – a virtual teleport – in a game.

At a more general level still, what we are proposing here is a reconsideration of the relationship between physical and virtual worlds in pervasive games. Most pervasive games to date have sought to establish a homogenous mapping between the physical environment of the players and virtual world of digital content, most often by directly overlapping the virtual on the physical so that movement in the latter drives movement in the former (e.g., Human Pacman [7], Can You See Me Now? [5], Savannah [4]), although often with only limited success due to the effects of underlying seams. Conversely, we are proposing designing for a much more 'slippery' and dynamic relationship between the physical and the virtual world in which a virtual game board is more loosely mapped to the physical world, and in which relationships between the two evolve and change according the behavior of underlying networks and positioning systems. We propose that such mappings, of which we see glimpses in our current visualizations, provide a further example of 'seamful design' in which experiences exploit the seams in the underlying technological infrastructure [6].

6 Summary

In summary, our study of Hitchers has revealed issues concerning the seams in cellular positioning on mobile phones. We have seen that cells vary in size and density, overlap, appear and disappear as the network evolves, and even behave elastically at speed. We have then discussed five different design strategies in relation to these seams: removing, hiding, managing, revealing and exploiting them. Player feedback suggests that the design of Hitchers is reasonably effective at hiding these seams for much of the time. That said, our discussions of other strategies have led us to propose three new techniques that might enable other experiences to adapt to seams, including employing an adaptive search focus; using visualization tools to understand the underlying seams and the relationship between mobile phone cells and meaningful places and activities; and finally, the idea of developing new kinds of games in which the goal is to map and explore a continually evolving virtual game board. Our future plans involve a more systematic and deeper meaning of these seams, in terms of their characteristics, impact on player experience, and approaches to design.

Acknowledgements

We gratefully acknowledge the support of IPerG, the European Project on Pervasive Gaming, project FP6-004457 under the European Commission's IST Programme (www.pervasive-gaming.org). We are also grateful for additional support from the Equator Interdisciplinary Research Collaboration which has been funded by the UK's Engineering and Physical Sciences Research Council (www.equator.ac.uk).

References

1. Barkhuus, L., Chalmers, M., Tennent, P., Hall, M., Bell, M., Sherwood, S. and Brown, B. (2005) "Picking pockets on the lawn". *UbiComp '05*, Tokyo: Springer.

2. Bell, M., Chalmers, M., Barkhuus, L., Hall, M., Sherwood, S., Brown, B., et al, Interweaving Mobile Games With Everyday Life, Proc CHI 2006, Montreal, Canada, April 2006, ACM.

3. Benford, S. et al. (2004) The error of our ways: the experience of self-reported position in a location-based game, *UbiComp '04*, pp. 70-87, Springer.

4. Benford, S. et al. (2005a) Life on the edge: supporting collaboration in location-based experiences, *Proceedings of ACM CHI '05*, pp. 721-730.

5. Benford, S. et al. (2006) Can You See Me Now?, *ACM Transactions on Computer-Human Interaction*, Vol. 13, No. 1, March 2006, Article 4.

6. Chalmers, M., And Galani, A., Seamful Interweaving: Heterogeneity in the Theory and Design of Interactive Systems, *ACM DIS 2004*, pp. 243-252, August 2004.

7. Cheok, A., Goh, K., Farbiz, F., Fong, S., Teo, S., Li, Y., Yang, X., Human Pacman: A Mobile, Wide-Area Entertainment System Based On Physical, Social And Ubiquitous Computing, *Personal And Ubiquitous Computing*, 8 (2), 71-81, May 2004, Springer-Verlag, ISSN 1617-4909.

8. Fruchterman, M. J. & Reingold, E.M., Graph Drawing by Force-directed Placement, Software - Practice and Experience. vol 21, number 11, 1129-1164,1991.

9. Hightower,   J.,   Consolvo,   S.,   LaMarca,   A.,   Smith,   I.,   & Hughes, J., Learning and Recognizing the Places We Go, *Ubicomp 2005*, Tokyo, Japan. September 2005.

10. Joffe, B. (2005) Mogi: Location and Presence in a Pervasive Community Game, Proc. Ubicomp Workshop on Ubiquitous Gaming and Entertainment.

11. Laasonen,   K.   Raento,   M.   Toivonen,   H.,   Adaptive   On-Device   Location Recognition, Lecture Notes in Computer Science, 3001, 287-304, 2004.

12. McGonigal, J., A Real Little Game: The Performance of Belief in Pervasive Play, Digital Games Research Associaton (DiGRA) "Level Up" Conference Proceedings. Utrecht, November 2003,.

13. Piekarski, W. And Thomas, B. 2002. ARQuake: The Outdoors Augmented Reality System. *Communications Of The ACM*, 45 (1), 36–38.

14. Smith, I., et al. *Social Disclosure of Place: From Location Technology to Communication Practices*. Pervasive Computing. 2005. Munich, Germany: Springer.

15. Trevisani E. & Vitaletti A (2004) Cell-id location technique, limits and benefits. *Proc. IEEE Workshop on Mobile Computing Systems and Applications.*

16. www.jgraph.com, Java JGraph Library (verified April 2006)

Embedding Behavior Modification Strategies into a Consumer Electronic Device: A Case Study

Jason Nawyn, Stephen S. Intille, and Kent Larson

Massachusetts Institute of Technology
77 Massachusetts Avenue, NE18-4FL
Cambridge, MA 02139
nawyn@alum.mit.edu, {intille, kll}@mit.edu

Abstract. Ubiquitous computing technologies create new opportunities for preventive healthcare researchers to deploy behavior modification strategies outside of clinical settings. In this paper, we describe how strategies for motivating behavior change might be embedded within usage patterns of a typical electronic device. This interaction model differs substantially from prior approaches to behavioral modification such as CD-ROMs: sensor-enabled technology can drive interventions that are timelier, tailored, subtle, and even fun. To explore these ideas, we developed a prototype system named *ViTo*. On one level, *ViTo* functions as a universal remote control for a home entertainment system. The interface of this device, however, is designed in such a way that it may unobtrusively promote a reduction in the user's television viewing while encouraging an increase in the frequency and quantity of non-sedentary activities. The design of *ViTo* demonstrates how a variety of behavioral science strategies for motivating behavior change can be carefully woven into the operation of a common consumer electronic device. Results of an exploratory evaluation of a single participant using the system in an instrumented home facility are presented.

1 Introduction

The average American watches over 4 hours of television each day [1]. As time spent in sedentary media consumption increases, the amount physical activity one incurs typically decreases. This is an unsettling fact of life for many Americans, 50% of whom feel they presently watch too much television and would like to reduce their viewing [2]. Meanwhile, rates of obesity have increased markedly in recent decades, and millions of Americans report engaging in weight-control efforts on a regular basis [3]. Few people, however, actually succeed in altering their long-term health outlook, in spite of accumulating evidence of the positive correlation between sedentary behavior and obesity [4] as well as lifestyle-related medical disorders such as Type 2 diabetes [5]. Similar trends are being reported in other industrialized countries.

Successfully reducing the time spent in television viewing over the long term could produce meaningful gains in an individual's overall health, especially if this activity is replaced with less sedentary alternatives. However, television habits are notoriously

P. Dourish and A. Friday (Eds.): Ubicomp 2006, LNCS 4206, pp. 297–314, 2006.

difficult to modify, often exhibiting the resilience of chemically based addictions [6]. The nature of the television viewing experience explains its addictive properties: the intrinsic rewards of watching television, such as relaxation and passivity are immediate and self-reinforcing. Unfortunately, these rewards diminish over time, and after periods of extended use, TV viewers often feel worse than before they started [7].

In contrast, the goal of increased physical activity is routinely impeded by the perceived high costs of entry into the pursuit. Engaging in exercise is typically thought to involve getting dressed, going to the gym, working out, showering, and then returning home. As a further impediment, the rewards of exercise—unlike television viewing—are not immediate, often to be noticed only months or years down the road. In fact, the main short-term effects of physical activity may be unpleasant ones, as captured by the common expression, "no pain, no gain."

The essential problem is that television viewing is instantaneously rewarding while exercise is instantaneously aversive. Intervention in this area has proved challenging in the past because successful behavior modification depends on delivery of motivational strategies at the precise place and time the behavior occurs. Advances in sensor-enabled mobile computing technologies will now facilitate the creation of applications that can intervene at critical moments throughout the day. As an exploration of how ubiquitous computing devices might enable novel approaches to improving lifestyle behaviors, we describe a case study with two interrelated objectives: (1) pilot the use of a novel technology to preempt or disrupt the stimulus-reward cycle of TV watching and (2) pilot the use of the same novel technology to decrease the costs of physical activity, while providing immediate positive reinforcement.

1.1 Technology-Enabled Behavioral Modification Strategies

This project builds upon prior work relevant to the motivation of lifestyle change. Knowledge campaigns (e.g. [8]) and clinical interventions (e.g. [9]) are the two most common approaches to the problem thus far. Other than websites and CD-ROMs, prior efforts at using technology to reduce television viewing have focused primarily on devices for children. The majority of these served as primitive electronic gatekeepers to limit a child's access to the TV. Specific examples include a key locking mechanism and a token access system [10]. These systems use forced rationing or punishment often imposed by the parents, and therefore they are less likely to be adopted by adults.

Several technology-related projects have attempted to simultaneously address the problems of television viewing and inactivity by creating exercise-contingent TV activation systems. One such system, *Telecycle* (see [11]), requires the user to pedal a stationary bicycle continuously in order to maintain a fully resolved television picture. While this approach is appealing in concept, it is designed to improve quality of exercise, not to reduce quantity of television viewing. Furthermore, the long-term effectiveness of any intervention that demands physical activity in exchange for television time should be suspect, since it obstructs a principle objective of television viewing – seeking relaxation.

Another recent attempt to address the problem of sedentary lifestyle and TV takes the form of a step-counting insole, *Square Eyes* [12], that allows a child to earn a daily television allowance based on their amount of walking. As in the case of the *Telecycle*, this approach effectively uses a short-term goal orientation to reward physical activity. However, as is the case for many existing television interventions, it does so by framing television as a conditional reward stimulus, opening up the possibility that it may ultimately increase the user's motivation to watch TV [13].

Research into the use of technology to increase physical activity independent of television viewing is more extensive. The most pervasive use of technologies is for measuring amount of ambulation and providing open-loop feedback (e.g. [14]). The current market proliferation of consumer-grade pedometers provides testament to the desire and willingness of individuals to adopt technologies that simply and non-intrusively assist in their quest to become more active. Preliminary research also suggests that more interactive just-in-time feedback such as that provided by the arcade game *Dance Dance Revolution* may be successful in producing short-term motivation for physical activity among otherwise sedentary children [15].

Another type of technology intervention proposes to motivate physical activity by mimicking the type of advice (and affect) used by a human personal trainer [16]. When delivered on a mobile computing device, such an interface may help users sustain an ongoing activity regimen. For individuals who do not already exercise regularly, new interventions might consider ways to lower the startup costs by focusing on small increases in physical activity that accumulate over time, rather than more intense and therefore intimidating regimens. Research suggests that simple body movements such as standing up, talking, and fidgeting—behaviors related to non-exercise activity thermogenesis (NEAT) [17]—may account for energy expenditures of over 300 kcal per day in obese individuals [18]. The intervention described in this paper builds on this finding by rewarding small activity increases in addition to intense or sustained exercise.

1.2 The Opportunity: Just-in-Time Interactions

The technological intervention we present relies on the same behavioral tendencies that have been proven effective in unmediated communication: that people respond best to information that is timely, tailored to their situation, often subtle, and easy to process [19]. Inexpensive sensors and mobile computing devices provide a platform that enables the achievement of these objectives through the design of an interface that draws upon behavioral science principles such as suggestion, goal setting, self-monitoring and conditioning. To provide further design insight into how these strategies might be embedded into consumer technologies, we have developed a prototype system to address the growing problem of television watching and physical inactivity.

1.3 Case Study Overview

The physical embodiment of this intervention is a multifunction handheld device called *ViTo*. This device, prototyped on a personal digital assistant (PDA) platform, is intended as a seamless replacement for the user's existing television remote control. It has been designed to provide value-adding features not presently available in commercial remote controls. These features, including a graphical interface, built-in program listings, access to a media library, integrated activity management, and interactive games, are used to entice users into adopting the persuasive remote control technology into their TV viewing routines.

Over time, the device deploys a series of behavior change strategies aimed at helping the user make more informed decisions about his or her viewing practices. It attempts to elicit the user's activity goals and suggest alternatives to TV watching in a timely manner. In conjunction with wearable acceleration sensors, it also functions as an electronic personal trainer, both prompting and rewarding physical activity.

A single-user exploratory case study evaluation was designed to test the viability of the device both as a research tool and as a technology for behavior change. This study will also be used to prepare for possible longitudinal testing of similar behavior change devices. The two-phase experimental design allowed assessment of user reaction to a non-persuasive PDA-based remote control as well as the complete *ViTo* system. The two main goals of this exercise were: (1) to demonstrate that ubiquitous computing technologies could measure changes in participant behavior between conditions and (2) to engage user feedback in evaluating the overall design of the device.

2   Challenges

The development of technologies that promote behavior change is inevitably subject to preconceptions of what a "persuasive" technology is and how it will behave. *ViTo* would be considered an *autogenous* technology, one that individuals might choose to adopt in an effort to change their own attitudes or behaviors [11]. Achieving this requires overcoming design challenges similar to those proposed for persuasive technologies to motivate healthy aging [19]: to provide a user experience that is rewarding enough for users to engage in regularly over an extended period of time. Toward this end, we sought to produce a prototype that shows how a consumer device might provide feedback that may motivate change while avoiding coercion and not relying on extrinsic justification.

2.1   Grabbing Attention Without Grabbing Time

Prior work on behavior change interventions reveals a tendency for these to be either (1) resource-intensive, often requiring extensive support staff, or (2) time-intensive, requiring the user to stop everyday activity to focus on relevant tasks. Most controlled clinical studies fall into the former category, and CD-ROM or web-based tools generally fall into the latter. For both approaches, the participant must stop what he or she would otherwise be doing to "receive" the intervention. The most promising CD-ROMs are engaging with game-like elements, but few are well suited for busy adults who find it difficult to repeatedly identify blocks of time during which they can focus on non-essential computer software.

The challenge of grabbing attention without grabbing time is addressed in the current project by embedding the intervention into an activity the target user population is certain to engage in: watching television. Although it may appear counterintuitive at first, the television remote control itself is an ideal platform upon which to develop this behavioral intervention. Ninety-four percent of all U.S. homes already contain at least one television with a remote control [10]. The remote control has become a central component of the TV viewing experience, and it is partly responsible for the increase in sedentary behavior associated with television viewing. The remote control has led to an increase in channel-surfing behavior, which frequently leads to extended and unplanned viewing [20].

ViTo is designed to modify the user's approach to program selection without interfering with the desire to do so remotely. A discussion of the techniques used to accomplish this objective is presented in Section 4. Additional strategies designed to promote physical activity are deployed not only during viewing, but whenever the user interacts with the device in other operational modes. Unlike interventions proposed in prior work, the device never requests exclusive interaction for more than a few seconds.

2.2 Sustaining the Interaction over Time

If a behavior change application is to have a meaningful impact, its outcome should be sustainable over the course of years. The design of *ViTo* as a multifunction device serves to add value that might encourage long-term adoption. With extended use, however, comes the risk of annoyance. To counter this possibility, content that may be viewed as paternalistic or authoritarian was rejected in favor of strategies that promote intrinsic motivation and self-reflection. Wherever possible, elements of fun, reward, and novelty are used to induce positive affect rather than feelings of guilt.

Overexposure to even the most innocuous of strategies creates further risk for discontinuation. Brevity of interaction sequences along with a time-out period between presentations serves to prevent excessive exposure to *ViTo*'s persuasive elements. Because natural usage patterns are likely to vary over time, the behavior change strategies use by *ViTo* are intended to be effective even if the user only occasionally interacts with the device.

2.3 Avoiding the Pitfall of Coercion

A review of websites, software, and technologies for behavior modification suggests a tendency for designers to succumb to the temptation of using coercion for motivation. In some cases, the result is a technology that prevents an activity such as watching television. In other examples, the user experience approximates the feeling of a medical professional mildly scolding the user for less-than-optimal compliance. More ominously, some systems use threats and fear appeals in an effort to motivate users to change lifestyle behaviors such as diet and exercise.

Particularly for preventive healthcare technologies aimed at users without immediate medical concerns, the likelihood that users with tolerate coercive devices for long is questionable. For this reason, the option to produce a device that nags, punishes, or otherwise inconveniences the user was expressly avoided in the design of *ViTo*.

2.4 Avoiding Reliance on Extrinsic Justification

The optimal outcome of any behavioral intervention is change that persists even if the technology is removed. Relying too heavily on extrinsic justification such as rewards and incentives may result in dependency that can lead to a falloff in progress if the incentives are removed. Although *ViTo* offers some rewards, this strategy is used in conjunction with many others to promote the more sustainable goal of increased self-awareness of activity patterns.

The use of an undesirable behavior as an incentive (e.g. rewarding exercise with access to television) is a particularly perilous form of extrinsic justification. Restricting the behavior and then framing it as a reward may increase the individual's motivation to engage in the activity, and will most likely lead to an increase in the behavior once the intervention is removed. Because of this possibility, *ViTo* is designed to reduce television viewing without restricting it or treating TV as a reward.

3 Case Study: *ViTo*

Our solution to the challenges of sustainable behavior modification is a device that exploits real-time feedback and game-style interaction to promote physical activity in a low cost, low impact manner. In this project, the intervention is conceived as a "universal" remote control that would seamlessly replace the user's existing devices. *ViTo*, shown in Figure 1, provides the basic functionality of a standard remote, but enhances it with a graphical user interface that supports additional capabilities such as digital audio control, activity management, and simple games.

The implementation of the *ViTo* prototype system is illustrated in Figure 2. The system was assembled primarily from readily available consumer hardware. Custom devices were used for infrared control of the home theatre system and for collection of bodily movement data [21]. A standard laptop computer was provided for management of a music library and a to-do task list. All other user interaction was conducted on the handheld PDA. Wireless communication between the PDA and a central server enabled seamless response from the system components.

All of the capabilities enabled by this device are accessed using a graphical user interface (GUI) on the PDA's touch-sensitive display (see Figure 1). The graphical elements have been designed to accommodate finger input; no stylus is necessary. Some standard remote control functions (e.g., power, volume up/down, and mute) have been assigned to hardware buttons on the PDA faceplate. Unlike most high-end screen-based remote controls, the goal is not to provide a touch screen surrogate for standard buttons, but to provide a content-based interface similar to that of a portable MP3 player.

The *Main Menu* selection grid featured in Figure 1 is the typical entry point of the user interface. Users can select among five main activities as indicated by labels (A)

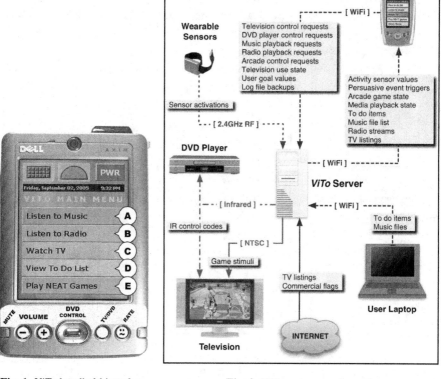

Fig. 1. *ViTo* handheld interface   **Fig. 2.** *ViTo* system configuration.

through (E). Each of these options initiates an interface sequence relevant to the selection. The principal display screens for these activities are shown in Figure 3, with corresponding labels (A) through (E). For media-related activities (A, B, C), the main interface screen features a selection grid representing all of the media content available at the current time. By default, content is sorted alphabetically by name, and two on-screen buttons allow the user to scroll through all of the pages in the list. When the user clicks on any of the available content, the *ViTo* server coordinates the appropriate response from the home theatre system. A separate display mode shown in Figure 3(F) allows control of a standard DVD video player.

Figure 3(D) shows a To-Do list screen that lets the user review a task list that is managed using a calendar-style application on a laptop computer. Figure 3(E) depicts the handheld interface that allows the user to start and stop "NEAT Games," a collection of simple puzzles that use physical activity as their input. Each puzzle begins with the presentation of provocative but incomplete information on the TV screen. As the user activates wearable movement sensors, he or she is rewarded with more information until a threshold is reached and the final answer is delivered. Sample game templates are shown in Figure 4.

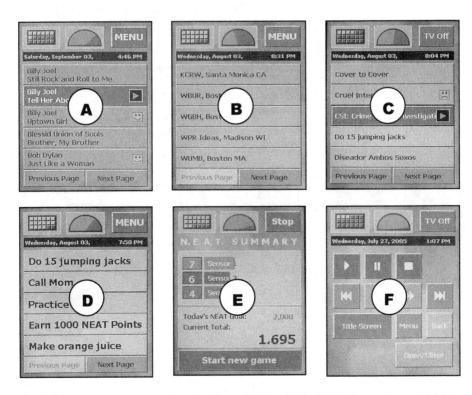

Fig. 3. Sample interface screens for activities enabled by *ViTo*: (A) Listen to Music, (B) Listen to Radio, (C) Watch TV, (D) View To Do List, (E) Play NEAT Games, and (F) Watch DVD

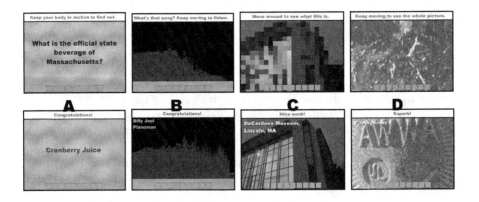

Fig. 4. NEAT Games stimuli as presented on the TV display. (A) Trivia Quiz, (B) Name That Song, (C) Pixellated Photos, and (D) Picture Zoom. As the user engages in physical activity, more information about the initial stimulus [top row] becomes available. The array of squares on each screen indicates progress toward final resolution [bottom row].

4   Behavior Modification Strategies

The *ViTo* case study was designed to investigate the viability of integrating behavior change strategies into everyday technologies like consumer electronics. Most of the strategies are derived from basic research on learning and decision-making. In the behavioral sciences, these phenomena (e.g. suggestibility, goal-setting, and operant conditioning) have been well studied and empirically supported. In creating *ViTo*, we sought to apply these same principles to the design of a motivational user interface. Similar interface elements could be adapted for use in other persuasive technologies.

Tables 1, 2, and 3 list the strategies employed with definitions relevant to technological intervention in the left-hand column. Where possible, the definitions used are similar to those in [11]. Specific examples of how the strategies were deployed in *ViTo* are listed in the right-hand column. Table 1 presents *user experience strategies* that are leveraged in an effort to create a satisfying and rewarding user experience, with the goal of promoting adoption and sustained use of the device. Table 2 shows a layer of persuasive content involving *activity transition strategies* designed to promote less sedentary alternatives to watching television. Table 3 presents a set of *proactive interface strategies* that encourage specific steps toward behavior change. These represent the most visible layer of persuasive elements.

Table 1. User experience strategies for behavior modification

Strategy	Example
Value integration. Delivering persuasive strategies within an application that otherwise provides value to the user increases the likelihood of adoption.	*ViTo* is a multifunction device that enables multimedia control of a home theatre system while delivering persuasive content in a way that is not disruptive to the other activities.
Reduction. Reducing the complexity of a task increases the likelihood that it will be performed.	(1) *ViTo* serves as a single alternative to multiple home theatre remote controls, likely increasing the chance that users with chose this device. (2) *ViTo* reduces the barriers to increased physical activity by encouraging small incremental changes rather than large lifestyle alterations.
Convenience. Small mobile devices can accompany the user throughout their day-to-day lives, increasing opportunities for delivery of behavior change strategies.	*ViTo* can be deployed on a handheld PDA or mobile phone, capitalizing on the fact that users are likely to already use such a devices on a regular basis.
Ease of use. Technologies that are easy to use are more likely to be adopted over a long term.	A participative design and testing process served to eliminate irritating behaviors that might otherwise prompt the user to discontinue using *ViTo*.
Intrinsic motivation. Incorporating elements of challenge, curiosity, and control into an activity can help sustain the user's interest [22].	*ViTo*'s NEAT Games were designed to reflect 5 features of intrinsically motivating activities: goals, uncertainty, feedback, self-esteem, and relevance. Other games more tailored to the user's interests could be substituted.

Table 2. Activity transition strategies for behavior modification

Strategy	Example
Suggestion. People can be biased toward a specific course of action through even very subtle prompts and cues.	*ViTo* extracts alternative activities from the Music, Radio, and To Do Menus, and systematically seeds these suggestions into the TV program listings.
Encouraging incompatible behavior. Engaging an individual in activities that inhibit an unwanted behavior can be effective in deterring the target behavior.	(1) *ViTo* gently promotes listening to music, playing games, and day-to-day chores as incompatible alternatives to sitting around and watching TV. (2) NEAT Games are started automatically when commercials begin in order to reduce exposure to program teasers and discourage channel surfing.
Disrupting habitual behavior. Bad habits can be eliminated if the conditions that enable them are removed or avoided.	(1) *ViTo* discourages habitual clicking on Watch TV by randomizing the order of Main Menu items. (2) *ViTo* disrupts habitual viewing practices such as channel surfing through the replacement of standard control buttons (i.e., channel-up and channel-down) with on-device program listings.

Table 3. Proactive interface strategies for behavior modification

Strategy	Example
Goal setting. Setting concrete, achievable goals promotes behavior change by orienting the individual toward a definable outcome.	*ViTo* prompts users to specify daily physical activity goals in terms of sensor movement counts called "NEAT Points" and daily TV viewing goals in terms of maximum minutes to watch. Timely reminders are used to encourage continual progress toward long-term improvements (Figure 5).
Self-monitoring. People who are motivated to change their behavior can do so more effectively when they are able to evaluate progress toward outcome goals.	*ViTo* features graphical meters that provide quick and easy feedback about the user's progress toward daily physical activity and TV viewing goals (Figure 6).
Proximal feedback. Feedback that occurs during or immediately after an activity has the greatest impact on behavior change.	*ViTo* provides real-time activity graphing to give users feedback about how many NEAT Points they are earning as they move around (Figure 7).
Operant conditioning. Desirable behaviors can be increased in frequency and intensity by pairing them with rewarding stimuli.	*ViTo* recognizes the user's progress toward his or her goals, and immediately rewards milestone achievements with congratulatory displays and reinforcing sounds (Figure 8).
Shaping. Conditioning can be used to transform a pre-existing behavior into a more desirable one by rewarding successive approximations of the end goal.	*ViTo* gradually increases its reinforcement thresholds over time. Users must work slightly harder each time they want to earn the next reward.
Consistency. The desire to demonstrate consistency between what we say and do is a basic trait that can be used to help people adhere to their stated goals.	*ViTo* prompts the user to specify how long he or she wants to watch prior to turning on the TV. After that duration expires, a second prompt reminds the user of the time, and asks whether he or she wishes to continue watching (Figure 9).

Fig. 5. Sample screen showing proactive elicitation of television viewing goals

Fig. 6. Graphical meters depict status of (A) NEAT goals and (B) TV goals

Fig. 7. Graphing bars show activity of 3 wearable motion sensors in real-time

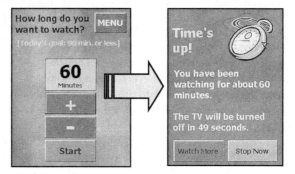

Fig. 8. Sample reward screen delivered for an extended period of movement

Fig. 9. Users are prompted to demonstrate consistency between how much TV they say they are going to watch, and how much they do

5   Exploratory Evaluation

For a device such as *ViTo* with clear outcome objectives, the overall effectiveness of the intervention—sustained change over time—would provide a valuable measure for evaluating the system's usefulness. Establishing the true ecological validity of this result, however, would require deployments in real homes for a period of years.

A long-term, wide-scale study is an ultimate goal of this work. Before such an effort can be justified, more evidence in support of project's viability is needed. To begin acquiring pilot data, an exploratory study of *ViTo* was conducted with four main objectives: (1) to stress-test the system in a live-in home setting for 1-2 weeks, (2) to collect a naturalistic dataset on which to conduct preliminary analyses, (3) to learn more about how a layperson—not a researcher—will react to the device, and (4) to determine what further study and improvements are warranted.

For this evaluation, a *ViTo* prototype system tailored for an individual who ordinarily lives and watches TV alone was deployed in a specially instrumented research apartment called the *PlaceLab*. This apartment is a live-in laboratory designed for the study of home-based activities located in a typical condominium in a residential neighborhood [23]. One participant, a 33-year-old male elementary school teacher who had responded to a recruitment flyer in an ice cream parlor, was selected to live in the *PlaceLab* for a total of 14 days. He was compensated $25 per day for his time according to the following schedule:

- 7 days in the *PlaceLab* for baseline data collection with a non-persuasive remote control
- 12 days at his permanent home while other work occurred at the *PlaceLab*
- 7 days in the *PlaceLab* for intervention data collection with the *ViTo* persuasive remote control

The participant was informed that he would be involved in research about everyday activities, and that data would be recorded from built-in and wearable sensors. A researcher explained that some technologies in the *PlaceLab* were experimental, including the remote control for the television and home theatre system. The device used during the baseline study was specifically designed to resemble *ViTo* but did not deploy persuasive strategies. For the intervention phase, the participant was issued the complete *ViTo* system, and was informed that the device had been improved during his absence. The participant was not instructed that this was a study of behavior changes related to television viewing and physical activity.

Although a technology like *ViTo* would ultimately be targeted at users with an expressed desire to change their lifestyle, this evaluation was intended to gauge the overall reaction of a user who was not intrinsically motivated to modify his behavior.

6   Results

Because each *PlaceLab* stay began and ended midday, the first and last half days of each study were excluded from the final analysis. Each experimental phase therefore yielded 6 days of data (Monday through Saturday). The content of this discussion is based on this dataset as well as *PlaceLab* audio/video recordings and an extensive post-study interview conducted by a researcher who was not a developer of *ViTo*. At the time of this interview, the participant had not yet been told the intent of the study. Because data were being collected for several other experiments, it would not necessarily have been obvious that the remote was the major focus of the study, a fact that was confirmed by the participant following the debriefing. The researcher who conducted the interview had previously interacted with the participant and summarized his temperament as "upbeat, high-energy, and accommodating [with a] strong affinity for new technologies." As is typical in the case of small-n research designs, individual personality traits of the participant and situational factors will limit the extent to which general conclusions can be drawn from this study.

Most of the discussion to follow pertains to the participant's use of the *ViTo* system during the intervention phase. The baseline stage was used to provide a point of comparison for interpretation of the participant's behaviors. During baseline, the participant watched an average of 133 minutes of television per day, a finding that was roughly consistent with his self-reported averages of 2 hours of television per day and 2-3 DVD movies per week. Use of the stereo system averaged 54 minutes per day, an amount that was consistent with self-reported averages of 1 hour per day at home.

Television use during the intervention phase was found to be significantly lower than baseline at an average of 41 minutes per day ($p < 0.05$; $F(1,11) = 8.79$). Use of the stereo system increased to 65 minutes per day, although this was not significant. Because there are many factors other than *ViTo* that may have influenced participant behavior, these statistical results should not be interpreted too strongly.

In sections 6.1, 6.2, and 6.3 we now discuss user reaction to the individual persuasive strategies described in Tables 1, 2, and 3 respectively. Where possible, feedback elicited during the post-study interview is used to help explain observed phenomena.

6.1 Reaction to User Experience Strategies

ViTo is intended first and foremost a tool that enables and simplifies certain daily activities in the home. This objective was serviced through the strategies in Table 1.

Value integration. Based on post-study interview responses, it appears the goal of providing a valuable convergent device was successful: "I just like the fact that it gives you the choice of what TV shows are on. And you can go right to a song that you like without having to swap CDs." The participant provided no indication that any of the persuasive content interfered with his enjoyment of the device.

Reduction. Although the participant was provided with the standard TV and home theatre remote controls to use if he found *ViTo* annoying or lacking control capabilities, he did not use these during the intervention phase. When prompted to explain, he responded, "I didn't use them ... I liked using the PDA ... I liked having the shows listed, plus the music and NEAT stuff."

Convenience. The participant did not currently own or use a mobile phone in his daily life, but reported finding potential in convergence of traditional mobile computing devices: "[*ViTo*] could maybe act as a portable phone, so if the phone rings you can use the PDA to pick up." During the intervention phase, he also expressed interest in using the device to track physical activity outside of the home.

Ease of use. To assess the learning curve for this device, a researcher observed the participant during a pre-study instruction session. The participant appeared very comfortable exploring the *ViTo* user interface, and had no questions about how to operate it. Only one unexpected behavior was noted – that the user misjudged how long to hold down the volume control buttons to reach the desired level.

Intrinsic motivation. The NEAT games were designed to appeal to a user's desire for a novel interactive experience. Over the course of his stay, the participant completed 27 puzzles, many of which he launched on demand using the *ViTo* Main Menu. Overall, the goal of producing an intrinsically motivating game experience appears to be supported. Video review revealed the participant frequently engaging in very rapid movements in an apparent effort to solve the puzzles quickly. This behavior suggests a desire for immediate gratification, a typical response to intrinsically motivating activities.

6.2 Reaction to Activity Transition Strategies

Engaging the user in activities other than watching television was a key objective in this work. The strategies in Table 2 were intended to address this challenge.

Suggestion. When interacting with *ViTo*, the participant was repeatedly exposed to activities as alternatives to watching TV. During the interview, he indicated there were two occasions when he had planned to watch TV but changed his mind: "So I decided, well, I don't want to watch anything ... I'll turn on some music instead or not turn on anything at all." While watching television, the participant also twice clicked on music tracks that were interspersed among TV program listings. After the selected songs ended, *ViTo* delivered a prompt asking if he would like to stop watching television and start listening to music. On one occasion he responded affirmatively and continued listening to music for about 14 minutes.

Encouraging incompatible behavior. Listening to music or radio is used as a distracter in part because it meets the user's motivation to watch TV—seeking relaxation—but is less likely to promote extended sedentary behavior because it is not linked to a single location. In fact, video review revealed that the participant would move around and occasionally "dance" while listening to music.

The just-in-time encouragement of alternative activities during commercial breaks responds to the fact that television programming is itself persuasively designed to engage the viewer for extended periods. To lesson the possibility that the viewer will be seduced into watching additional programs by network advertisements, *ViTo* can replace commercials with NEAT Games. A remotely operated "Wizard of Oz" simulation was used to flag the onset and offset of TV commercials. Due to practical challenges of remotely flagging these breaks, only five of the possible commercial segments were replaced with NEAT Games. On four of these occasions, the participant completed the games. Although it is not known whether this had an effect on the duration of viewing, it is clear that the games promoted physical activity that might not otherwise have occurred.

Interrupting habitual behavior. The first application of this principle, re-ordering main menu items, was assessed indirectly during the interview: when asked to recall the options in the list, he successfully named each one, but made no indication that he noticed the change in order.

The second interruption strategy was intended to discourage channel surfing. When asked whether he would rather use channel up/down buttons or program titles to select what to watch, the participant responded as follows: "I think it's a lot easier to use titles ... you know what's on without looking at all the channels." In contrast to on-TV program matrices, *ViTo* only lists content for the present time, thereby discouraging spontaneous decisions to watch more programming in the coming hour.

Based on data collected from the baseline and intervention phases of the case study, it appears that the effect for the reduction of channel surfing was robust. For this analysis, channel surfing is operationally defined as the number of TV channels displayed per minute of television watched. A significant ($p < 0.01$; $F(1,11) = 14.03$) difference in channel surfing was found between baseline (1.91 channels/min.) and intervention (0.29 channels/min.). Although this result should be viewed cautiously given a sample size of one, it does support the hypothesis that channel surfing behavior will be reduced through the use of content-based program selection.

6.3 Reaction to Proactive Interface Strategies

The target user population for a *ViTo*-like system is expected to be individuals with a preexisting desire to reduce their television viewing while increasing their physical activity. The strategies listed in Table 3 were selected with this population in mind.

Goal setting. During pre-study screening, the participant expressed interest in participating in exercise-related studies (as well as other study options). This inclination may explain his favorable response to the use of goal setting for physical activity. In *ViTo* the term "NEAT Point" was used as a unit of movement derived from simple accelerometer counts. Over the course of the study, the participant raised his daily NEAT Point goals from 8000 to 10000 per day, a 25% increase. When asked to discuss his use of NEAT goals, the participant explained, "That really encouraged me to go up to and to meet that goal. So when I sat down at the end of the night and I saw that I hadn't reached the goal, I would [start] waving my arms and legs, getting a little bit of exercise before I went up to the goal."

Perhaps because he did not have a preexisting desire to change his TV habits, the participant did not respond as strongly to goal setting for television viewing. When asked to describe his use of daily TV goals, the participant reported that he didn't set any: "I just didn't anticipate watching that much."

Self-monitoring. Consistent with the fact that he was not concerned about meeting his daily television goal, the participant indicated that he did not actively use the TV Meter (Figure 6(B)) to track his viewing duration. On the other hand, the participant reported that he used the NEAT Meter (Figure 6(A)) regularly to gauge his progress toward physical activity goals.

Proximal feedback. Clicking on the NEAT Meter from anywhere in the *ViTo* interface brings up a display offering real-time graphing of physical activity levels. Video review confirmed the participant's report that on several occasions he used the NEAT Meter to understand how his movement affected NEAT Point totals as he moved around the apartment engaging in different kinds of physical activity. In the post-study interview, the participant expressed a fair amount of enthusiasm for the use of technology to monitor physical activity. Although it is possible that the novelty of real-time feedback increased the use of this feature to levels that are not sustainable for the long term, the participant's response does support further investigation of how activity feedback might be used to promote healthier living.

Operant conditioning. Reinforcing desirable behaviors is another strategy that may prove viable for long-term motivation. During the course of the evaluation, the participant was rewarded six times for engaging in sustained or vigorous activity. Two of these were delivered during NEAT Games and another when the user was interacting with the real-time activity graph, further supporting the notion that computational feedback can effectively motivate meaningful changes in behavior.

Shaping. Gradually increasing the amount of physical activity necessary to earn rewards may lead to large changes over time. For the short duration of this case study, the effect of shaping was probably negligible, as reward thresholds were incremented only 1% for each delivery. For use of NEAT Games, however, the impact of incremental shaping was more apparent. At the start of the study, 72 NEAT Points were required to resolve each game. By the end of the study, that number had risen to 90. In spite of this 25% increase in difficulty, the participant revealed in the interview that he was unaware of the change.

Consistency. For television viewing, the participant encountered a commitment prompt sequence (Figure 9) eleven times. Again consistent with his lack of interest in tracking viewing time, the user did not appear to use this feature in a reflective manner. Nine of eleven times he responded that he would watch for 30 minutes. Four times he watched substantially less than this, four times he watched substantially more. On one occasion the commitment sequence ended with a prompt to turn off the television that coincided with the user's completion of his viewing session. The participant had left the room, so the device automatically turned off the television after a timeout period of 3 minutes. About this the participant reponded: "I had already finished watching and was doing something else, so I didn't bother turning it back on."

7   Conclusions

The results of this exploratory study may raise more questions than answers. There is clear evidence that the participant responded strongly and positively to certain aspects of the system design, such as value integration, ease of use, and reduction. His responses to specific persuasive elements related to physical activity—goal setting, self-monitoring, and proximal feedback—likewise show a willingness to tolerate or even value more proactive behavior change strategies.

Reaction to some of the more abstract strategies employed by *ViTo* (e.g. suggestion, intrinsic motivation, and consistency) cannot be easily measured using observational and self-report techniques. Where possible, evidence relevant to the participant's response to these strategies is presented, with the understanding that the evaluation described in this work only begins to address the myriad questions surrounding the design and use of persuasive technologies.

The study was undertaken with four goals. We successfully stress-tested the system in a real home setting for a week. We also collected a naturalistic dataset useful for preliminary analysis of the system, allowing evaluation of specific interactions in some depth. We gained additional insight into how a person might use a persuasive consumer electronic device. Finally, we used the experience to identify some issues that should be addressed before this system is tested longitudinally.

Among the most important design observations drawn from this work are the following: (1) Interventions based on consumer electronics may be particularly viable if the devices offer substantial improvement over competing technology—efforts focused on basic user experience will likely pay off in long-term adoption. (2) Designers should plan for long-term use and resist the temptation to impress users with an initial panoply of persuasive elements—strategies should be phased in over time so the user can react to them individually. (3) Most strategies will be initially received as novelty—user curiosity can be used to advantage by encouraging exploration of new features. (4) Not all users will react well to all strategies—interventions should adapt to the user's preferences; keep strategies that work, and phase out those that don't.

The case study evaluation featured in this research has inherent advantages as well as limitations. Although the small size and relatively short duration of this study will limit what conclusions can be drawn from the data, it is hoped that the results of the present study will provoke further interest in the deployment and evaluation of persuasive behavior change devices.

In combining aspects of ubiquitous computing, context-aware computing, and persuasive technology, this research undertakes a novel approach to the problem of lifestyle change. Successful demonstration of *ViTo* as a tool for behavior modification would have strong implications for the future of proactive healthcare.

The outcome measures from the case study evaluation described in this document are suggestive, lending support to the possibility that *ViTo* might succeed in helping individuals lead more active lives. It is hoped that researchers in the field of public health will find value in using a tool such as *ViTo* to study the wide scale deployment of proactive health technologies, and that researchers in ubiquitous computing and user interface design will begin to apply their expertise to create novel and high-impact behavior modification systems that are embedded into everyday life.

Acknowledgments

This work was supported, in part, by National Science Foundation ITR grant #0313065. The PlaceLab live-in laboratory is a joint initiative between the MIT House_n Consortium and TIAX, LLC. The authors would like to thank the research participant and gratefully acknowledge the help of J. S. Beaudin and S. J. Paterson.

References

1. Stanger, J.D. and N. Gridina: Media in the home 1999: The fourth annual survey of parents and children. Annenberg Public Policy Center, University of Pennsylvania (1999)
2. Fahey, V.: TV by the Numbers. Health. Vol. Dec/Jan: Issue (1992) 35
3. Hill, J.O.: Obesity treatment: does one size fit all? The American Journal of Clinical Nutrition. Vol. 81: 6 (2005) 1253-1254
4. Kaur, H., et al.: Duration of television watching is associated with increased body mass index. J Pediatr. Vol. 143: 4 (2003) 506-511
5. Redelmeier, D.A. and M.B. Stanbrook: Television viewing and risk of obesity. JAMA. Vol. 290: 3 (2003) 332 Author reply
6. Kubey, R. and M. Csikszentmihalyi: Television addiction is no mere metaphor. Scientific American: Issue (2002) 74-80
7. McIlwraith, R.D.: 'I'm addicted to television': The personality, imagination, and TV watching patterns of self-identified TV addicts. Journal of Broadcasting and Electronic Media. Vol. 42: 3 (1998) 371-386
8. http://www.tvturnoff.org. RealVision. [World Wide Web Site] [cited 03/31/2006]; An initiative to raise awareness about television's impact.

9. Epstein, L.H., et al.: Decreasing sedentary behaviors in treating pediatric obesity. Arch Pediatr Adolesc Med. Vol. 154: 3 (2000) 220-226

10. Jason, L.A. and L.K. Hanaway: Remote control: A sensible approach to kids, TV, and the new electronic media. Professional Resource Press / Professional Resource Exchange Inc, Sarasota, FL (1997)

11. Fogg, B.J.: Persuasive Technology: using computers to change what we think and do. Morgan Kaufmann Publishers, Boston (2003)

12. Bush, S.: Children earn television for exercise with Brunel project. In: Electronics Weekly, Sutton (2005) 8

13. Deci, E.L. and R.M. Ryan: Intrinsic motivation and self-determination in human behavior. Perspectives in Social Psychology. Plenum, New York (1985)

14. Roemmich, J.N., C.M. Gurgol, and L.H. Epstein: Open-loop feedback increases physical activity of youth. Med Sci Sports Exerc. Vol. 36: 4 (2004) 668-673

15. Barker, A.: Kids in study try to dance away weight. In: Associated Press. April 4, 2005

16. Bickmore, T., A. Gruber, and R.W. Picard: Establishing the Computer-patient Working Alliance in Automated Health Behavior Change Interventions. Patient Educational Counseling. Vol. 59: 1 (2005) 21-30

17. Levine, J.A., N.L. Eberhardt, and M.D. Jensen: Role of nonexercise activity thermogenesis in resistance to fat gain in humans. Science: Issue (1999) 212-214

18. Levine, J.A., et al.: Interindividual Variation in Posture Allocation: Possible Role in Human Obesity. Science. Vol. 307: Issue (2005) 584-586

19. Intille, S.S.: A new research challenge: persuasive technology to motivate healthy aging. IEEE Trans Inf Technol Biomed. Vol. 8: 3 (2004) 235-257

20. Kubey, R.W. and M. Csikszentmihalyi: Television and the quality of life : how viewing shapes everyday experience. L. Erlbaum Associates, Hillsdale, N.J. (1990)

21. Munguia Tapia, E., et al.: The design of a portable kit of wireless sensors for naturalistic data collection. In: Proceedings of PERVASIVE. Berlin Heidelberg: Springer-Verlag (2006)

22. Malone, T. and M. Lepper: Making learning fun: a taxonomy of intrinsic motivations in learning. In: Aptitude, Learning, and Instruction: Cognitive and Affective Process Analyses, R. Snow and M. Farr, Editors. Lawrence Erlbaum, Hillsdale, NJ (1987) 223-253

23. Intille, S.S., et al.: Using a live-in laboratory for ubiquitous computing research. In: Proceedings of PERVASIVE. Berlin Heidelberg, Springer-Verlag (2006)

Instrumenting the City: Developing Methods for Observing and Understanding the Digital Cityscape

Eamonn O'Neill[1], Vassilis Kostakos[1], Tim Kindberg[2], Ava Fatah gen. Schiek[3], Alan Penn[3], Danaë Stanton Fraser[4], and Tim Jones[4]

[1] Department of Computer Science, University of Bath, UK, BA2 7AY
{eamonn, vk}@cs.bath.ac.uk
http://www.cityware.org.uk
[2] Hewlett-Packard Laboratories, Bristol, UK, BS34 8QZ
timothy@hpl.hp.com
[3] The Bartlett, University College London, UK, WC1E 6BT
{ucftajf, a.penn}@ucl.ac.uk
[4] Department of Psychology, University of Bath, UK, BA2 7AY
{D.StantonFraser, t.jones}@bath.ac.uk

Abstract. We approach the design of ubiquitous computing systems in the urban environment as integral to urban design. To understand the city as a system encompassing physical and digital forms and their relationships with people's behaviours, we are developing, applying and refining methods of observing, recording, modelling and analysing the city, physically, digitally and socially. We draw on established methods used in the space syntax approach to urban design. Here we describe how we have combined scanning for discoverable Bluetooth devices with two such methods, gatecounts and static snapshots. We report our experiences in developing, field testing and refining these augmented methods. We present initial findings on the Bluetooth landscape in a city in terms of patterns of Bluetooth presence and Bluetooth naming practices.

1 Introduction

Building ubiquitous computing systems in our cities requires new ways of thinking about the design and use of technologies and how they interweave with the built environment. We propose a holistic approach to designing the urban environment as an integrated system of architecture and ubiquitous technologies. Our goal is to understand the city as a system, encompassing both its physical and its digital forms and their relationships with people's behaviours in the city. Achieving this goal will require the development, application and refinement of methods of observing, recording, modelling and analysing the city – physically, digitally and socially.

Researchers in the fields of ubiquitous and mobile computing have tended to investigate interventions or experiences in specific urban situations, rather than studying systemic properties of the city as a whole. For example, the Mobile Bristol project [Reid et al. 2005] created situated experiences, such as an "interactive play" in Bristol's Queen Square. The Equator Citywide project [Benford et al. 2003] developed games played in urban settings. The goal of those activities was to *overlay* an experience on city spaces, by giving mobile devices with GPS receivers to users, rather than

P. Dourish and A. Friday (Eds.): Ubicomp 2006, LNCS 4206, pp. 315–332, 2006.

by placing technology into the settings themselves – which is often not possible for practical or regulatory reasons. By contrast, several projects have *embedded* techno-logical artefacts into urban situations. For example, Urban Atmospheres' Jetsam project [Paulos & Jenkins 2005] augmented a city rubbish bin, so that it projects on to the pavement a representation of the activities in which it is involved, which are oth-erwise latent.

All of these projects are city probes: a technological perturbation of the city experi-ence made with the aim of understanding more about how to design experiences in the city. Other work has attempted to understand existing city behaviours, principally as a resource for designing new applications. Paulos and Goodman [2004] studied the phenomenon of familiar strangers – people we become accustomed to seeing in urban settings but do not communicate with – by asking subjects in Berkeley to record the people they recognised. This became the basis for tools designed, for example, to augment the user's sense of social relationship to different parts of a city. Others have looked principally at physical behaviours in cities, which themselves are often rooted in social behaviours. Höflich [2005] studied the movements and body lan-guage of people in the Piazza Matteotti in Udine as they made mobile telephone calls, relating them to the architectural features of that square and the different types of engagement people have with their interlocutors versus their surroundings. He identi-fied signature patterns and paths of movement, which the work of Mobile Bristol and Urban Atmospheres, cited above, also identified in their particular settings, reflecting a common interest in how technologies affect paths through space. But those patterns are informally described. Moreover, no attempt has been made to generalise them so that we could, for example, compare a class of behaviours in different settings. Mainwaring et al. [2005] studied "urbanites" in three major cities as somehow repre-sentative and thus a basis for comparing them. While this informal study gives a flavour of aspects of city life in different places, we aim to develop a basis for more systematic comparisons.

Space syntax [Hillier & Hanson, 1984; Hillier et al., 1993] provides us with a sys-temic approach to understanding and designing the city and a range of methods and modelling tools that have been extensively tried and tested in both analytical and de-sign practice [Stonor, 1997]. Our previous space syntax research has revealed how, through its structuring of space, urban design plays a critical role in the construction of society and social behaviours [Hillier et al., 1987]. In this paper we report our ongoing efforts to develop, apply and refine methods for understanding ubiquitous systems as an integral facet of the city. In section 2, we provide a brief introduction to space syn-tax, describing some of its main features and methods. In section 3, we describe how we are extending some of the methods used by space syntax to take account of the digital, as well as physical, form of the city. We illustrate this with examples from a study in the city of Bath, UK, in which we are developing and applying "digitally augmented" versions of two key space syntax observation methods: gatecounts and static snapshots. In section 4, we present some initial findings from our field trials with these methods, describing patterns of Bluetooth presence and Bluetooth naming prac-tices. We conclude by summarising our ongoing work on developing methods as part of a systemic approach and toolkit for analysing and understanding ubiquitous comput-ing systems as integral facets of the urban environment.

2   Space Syntax

Space syntax analyses cities as systems of space created by the physical artefacts of architecture and urban design in order to understand how the spatial structure of the city is related to aspects of its social function. Space syntax is distinct from other forms of spatial analysis in that it characterises spatial elements (rooms, street segments, squares etc) first and foremost in terms of their relations (e.g. their graph distance) to other elements in the system. The resulting patterns of values for elements have been shown to be related with many functional phenomena, such as pedestrian and vehicular movement and land use patterns. These findings suggest how it is that the city considered as a pattern of connected spaces takes on social meaning by constructing patterns of copresence between people in space. In the Cityware project this allows us to integrate a range of social, cultural and economic factors within a single study methodology.

A fundamental concept of space syntax is that a city can be represented as a graph of nodes and links. The graph is constructed from a map of the city by first making an "axial map" of the streets. In an axial map, the longest lines passing down streets are considered as nodes and their intersections as links in the graph. This graph can then be analysed in terms of its properties such as the depth between the nodes. This is characterised in space syntax as the level of integration of a node, i.e. the deepness or shallowness of a node in relation to the other nodes in the graph. Shallow streets are essentially fewer changes of direction from the other streets of a city, while deep streets are relatively isolated from other streets. Space syntax has found a consistent correlation between the shallowness of streets (in terms of integration) and pedestrian flows in the city.

The ability to interrogate the spatial structure of a city plan, and to investigate what factors lead to the presence or absence of people on the street is one of the central contributions of space syntax methodology. Designers can manipulate a city's map (e.g. when considering the construction of a new bridge), and can make predictions about the resulting impact on people's movements in the city. The first step in studies of this sort is to gain an understanding of how people use and move through urban space. Empirical observations record the fact of people's presence in the environment essentially *without* taking account of their intentions. If we ask an individual in the city about her pattern of movement, she is likely to respond in terms of purposes of journeys. However, the collective activity of a whole population gives rise to a pattern of use and movement that in itself forms an important aspect of the social context of the environment [Hillier & Hanson, 1984]. Through empirical observation, we can retrieve something of the objective properties of the built environment through its influence on people's behaviour at this aggregate level. Space syntax draws on an extensive range of empirical observation methods, many of them also used more widely in urban studies and ethnography. Here we note two of the methods most commonly used by space syntax: gatecounts and static snapshots.

2.1   Gatecounts

Gatecounts are used to establish the flows of people at sampled locations within the city over the course of a day. A gate is a conceptual line across a street, and gatecounts entail counting the number of people crossing that line. The observer stands on the street and counts the number of people crossing the gate in either direction. To demonstrate how gatecounts are traditionally performed, here we describe a set of observations in Bath. We established 96 gates throughout the city, and counted the number of people crossing them. Our observers took 5-minute samples from each gate in 5 cycles throughout the day, from 8:30am to 4:00pm over 2 days.

Observed flows of people ranged from high flows of 2750-4000 people per hour to low flows of 250 people per hour or less. The correlation between the predicted and actual flows of people is shown in Figure 1. In this figure we see a scattergram correlating the observed flows (vertical axis) with the integration value of the street (horizontal axis). The degree of correlation in Bath is low in comparison to that found in other cities. This indicates that patterns of movement are likely to be heavily influenced by a range of other factors – location of tourist "attractors" for example [Fatah gen Schieck et al., 2005; 2006].

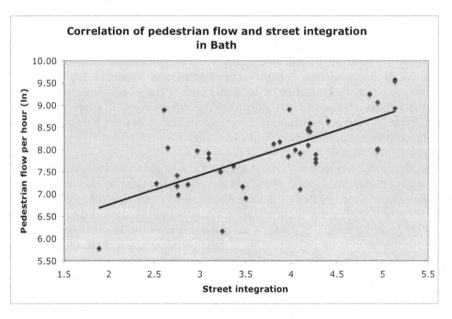

Fig. 1. Correlation between pedestrian movement (y-axis) and integration (x-axis) for 40 streets in the centre of Bath ($R^2 = 0.47$)

2.2 Static Snapshots

A second important method used by space syntax is *static snapshots*. Here, open spaces of the city are considered in detail. These spaces may be external, such as a plaza, or internal, such as a café. The method can be used for recording both stationary and moving activities, and is useful when a direct comparison is being made between the two types of space use. This method makes apparent the relationships between different types of space use in an urban area. For each open space under consideration, the observers record the movements in and out of the space, as well as the type of activity taking place in the space. This gives us an understanding of how people appropriate and make use of a particular space, and how these patterns of use bring people into contact with each other. For example, we may observe that a seating area in a park is actually not used for seating but for playing by children. A common observation is the use of certain spaces by people making calls on their mobile phones or using their laptop computers, and the way that these people then locate themselves with respect to the surrounding urban fabric and other people.

The space syntax methods described in this section provide a well established toolset for understanding the architectural landscape of a city, for considering design changes to be made (e.g. adding a new bridge, blocking a street), and for observing and evaluating the results of design decisions. In the next section we describe our first steps in incorporating space syntax methods into the understanding, design and evaluation of ubiquitous computing systems as integral facets of the urban landscape.

3 Studying Architectural Spaces and Interaction Spaces in the City

In previous work, we have compared architecturally defined spaces with the "interaction spaces" that are created by artefacts or devices such as computer displays [Kostakos, 2005]. These interaction spaces define the boundaries within which the artefact is usable [O'Neill et al., 1999]. An essential feature of interaction spaces is that they are defined both by the characteristics of the device and by the architectural space in which they are situated. For example, within a public architectural space, a large display can create a public interaction space. In addition to visual interaction spaces, interaction spaces may also be auditory. For example, open-air broadcast of audio content via loudspeakers can create a public interaction space while a headset can create a private interaction space that includes just the person wearing the headset [O'Neill et al., 2004].

Interaction spaces may also be wireless. For example, the wireless interaction spaces generated by 802.11, GPRS or 3G access points define spaces within which certain devices (such as phones and PDAs) and services (email, browsing etc) are usable. We differentiate between such fixed wireless interaction spaces and more mobile wireless interaction spaces. The former tend to be static in relation to the physical environment and their location within the city (although, for example, 3G cell coverage can expand and contract quite dramatically with network load). On the other hand, the wireless interaction spaces created by technologies such as Bluetooth are often mobile, and move around as users carry their devices through the city. As they move, they may come into contact with various other features of the digital landscape: services beaming out of an interactive poster, Bluetooth phones belonging to friends, colleagues and strangers, as well as various Bluetooth devices such as headsets, keyboards and mice.

Together, the concepts of architectural space and interaction space aid us in mapping from urban location to the technological artefacts that are available to us and the forms of interaction we wish to support. A challenge we face is recording, representing and understanding the patterns of presence and use of the diverse forms of interaction spaces that are emerging in our cities through the use of ubiquitous technologies.

In this section we report our first steps in adapting and extending space syntax methods to meet this challenge, extending space syntax's consideration of the architectural spaces created by the built environment to include the wireless interaction spaces created by Bluetooth devices.

Bluetooth technology has a characteristic that renders it appropriate for study by methods derived from those of space syntax. The vast majority of Bluetooth interaction spaces are created by small, personal devices such as mobile phones. Thus, in contrast to the interaction spaces created by typically static WiFi access points, the wireless interaction spaces created by Bluetooth devices map very closely to the movements of people around the city, which in turn are a primary concern of space syntax. In our work so far, we have extended both the gatecount and the static snapshot methods to include the observation and recording of Bluetooth interaction spaces and their relationship with people's movements in the city.

3.1 Extending the Gatecount Method to Include Bluetooth Interaction Spaces

Our basic extension to the gatecount method was to record the movement of discoverable Bluetooth devices past a gate. Even this simple extension allows us to correlate pedestrian movements with Bluetooth device movements, providing baseline data about the penetration of Bluetooth into city life. Beyond simply counting the appearance of Bluetooth devices, we have been using this method to uncover interesting data on patterns of presence of Bluetooth devices, and Bluetooth device names.

We face several technical challenges in developing a Bluetooth scanning method that will effectively augment the standard gatecount method. The main difficulty is that a space syntax gate is a distinct (conceptual) line across the street through which people are counted, whereas Bluetooth devices are counted when the wireless interaction space of the device intersects the wireless interaction space of our scanner. Even in a narrow street with no junctions, this intersection is not entirely predictable due to the variability in device characteristics and environmental influences on Bluetooth propagation. In our urban scans, we have the added complication of picking up devices moving along adjacent streets and in buildings.

A directional Bluetooth antenna pointing directly across the street from our scanner would seem to suggest itself as a means of creating a Bluetooth gate. However, the Bluetooth technology itself mitigates against this. Bluetooth discovery takes up to several seconds. Even with multiple-dongle scanning, described below, this would mean failing to record devices that moved through a narrow linear gate. Hence, we adopted the approach of recording with standard Bluetooth devices and performing post-analysis to identify the patterns in the data. We also used Bluetooth scanners with a range of only 10 metres to mitigate the effect of discovering distant devices.

3.1.1 Pilot Bluetooth Gatecounts

We ran a series of pilot Bluetooth gatecounts in various locations around the city, involving one of the authors standing on the side of a street with a notebook computer that performed Bluetooth scanning. Drawing on the results of the gatecounts reported in Section 2.1, we selected locations with low, medium and high pedestrian flows. Conventional space syntax gatecounts involve an observer standing at each gate for a relatively brief period (typically as little as 5 minutes) and iterating rapidly around multiple gates, repeating each gate several times. We could not predict in advance how many people would be carrying discoverable Bluetooth devices but expected it to be nowhere near every passer-by. Hence, one concern was that this conventional pattern of observation might under-record passing Bluetooth devices. We therefore varied the time period for these gatecounts in order to assess what would be a suitable period. In Table 1 we show the confidence intervals obtained by varying the period of scanning. From these trials we identified 30 minutes as a suitable period for Bluetooth gatecounts at both high and medium traffic locations, as this is enough to generate small errors ($\pm$ 3%). For low traffic locations a period of roughly 2 hours would achieve such small margins.

Table 1. Sample confidence intervals derived from varying the period of our mobile Bluetooth gatecounts (p=0.05) for locations with low, medium and high pedestrian flows

	Pedestrians	Bluetooth	%	Error
Location 1 (low traffic)				
10 Minutes	21	4	19%	$\pm$ 16.8%
20 Minutes	57	6	10.5%	$\pm$ 8%
30 Minutes	77	13	16.9%	$\pm$ 8.4%
Location 2 (medium traffic)				
10 Minutes	103	13	12.6%	$\pm$ 6.4%
20 Minutes	210	20	9.5%	$\pm$ 3.9%
30 Minutes	331	31	9.3%	$\pm$ 3.1%
Location 3 (high traffic)				
5 Minutes	384	39	10.2%	$\pm$ 3%
10 Minutes	746	69	9.2%	$\pm$ 2.1%

We learned several other lessons from these pilot trials and refined our techniques accordingly. First, a number of issues relating to the accuracy of Bluetooth scanning became apparent. We used a single Bluetooth dongle, which meant that if many Bluetooth devices passed the gate simultaneously, less information (or in some cases no information) was recorded. We found that if 20 people carrying discoverable Bluetooth devices crossed the gate simultaneously at walking pace, then approximately 60% of these devices would be recorded. This is due to the sequential nature of our scanning dongle's communication with the passing devices and the short time that they are in range. We subsequently mitigated this problem by using 3 dongles simultaneously. Because of the random frequency hopping employed by the Bluetooth discovery mechanism, using more dongles increases the chance of discovering a device as it moves past our scanner. 3 was the maximum number of dongles that our notebook computers could power for long enough.

We were also able to increase the discovery rate of our mobile Bluetooth scanning by reducing the amount of information we recorded for each device. By recording only the unique Bluetooth addresses of the discovered devices, we reduced the time our dongles spent communicating with each discovered device, allowing our dongles to contact more devices in a given period. The trade-off is that we lose much of the

richness of the recorded Bluetooth data, such as Bluetooth names and service identifiers, reducing the scan's value as an augmentation to the standard gatecount method.

3.1.2 Bluetooth-Augmented Space Syntax Gatecounts

In the next stage of our study we carried out 10 gatecounts throughout the city of
Bath. Once again, the locations were selected based on the results of the gatecounts
reported in Section 2.1 to cover low, medium and high pedestrian flows, but also to
cover various types of spaces from open spaces to long narrow streets with no nearby
junctions. These gatecounts closely resembled the conventional gatecount method but
involved a pair of observers working together at each gate. One observer performed
the manual pedestrian count while the other performed the Bluetooth count using our
mobile scanner. The observers iterated around the gates throughout the city, recording
the flow of people and Bluetooth activity at each gate over the course of two days.
We applied the lessons learned from our pilot trials. Here we used 3 dongles to perform Bluetooth scanning, we recorded for 30 minutes at each location, and we recorded only the unique Bluetooth addresses of the discovered devices.

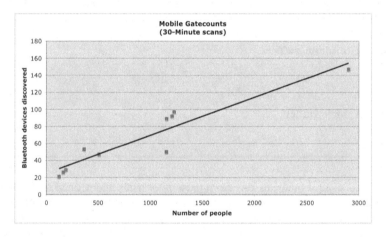

Fig. 2. Correlation between number of people (x-axis) and number of discoverable Bluetooth
devices (y-axis) across different locations in Bath (R^2 = 0.8855)

Figure 2 shows a high correlation between discovered Bluetooth devices and observed pedestrians. Overall, our scans suggested that 7% of observed pedestrians had
discoverable Bluetooth devices.

From our Bluetooth-augmented gatecounts we learned further lessons for the refinement of our methods. At some of our sites, adjacent offices had Bluetooth-enabled
computers, and these devices generated high Bluetooth activity. In this study, we were
not interested in total Bluetooth activity, but rather the presence of Bluetooth devices.
To measure this, we counted the number of distinct Bluetooth addresses in the recorded data as opposed to the raw Bluetooth activity. We also applied a filter to differentiate between persistent devices and those devices that appeared to be transient,
reflecting the distinction between static and mobile interaction spaces. From our gatecount data and experimentation with known static and transient devices, we

established empirically that a transient device typically appears for up to 90 seconds while it crosses a gate.

3.1.3 Fixed Long-Term Gatecounts

In addition to the Bluetooth-augmented gatecounts described above, we ran 2 fixed, long-term Bluetooth gatecounts: 1 at a site on the University of Bath campus (Figure 3), the other on a street in the centre of Bath. At these locations we installed scanners that continuously search for Bluetooth devices that are set to be discoverable. For each device we attempted to record the following data: unique Bluetooth address, Bluetooth name, date, time, class of device (e.g. phone, laptop), and the services offered by the device (e.g. OBEX push, modem, fax, etc).

Our Bluetooth scanner   A mobile phone generating a
                              wireless interaction space

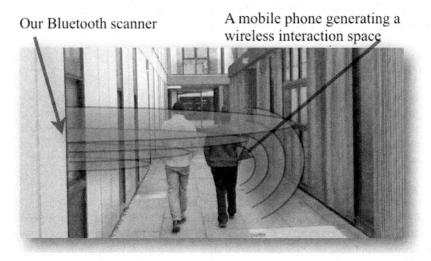

Fig. 3. A Bluetooth gate with a Bluetooth scanner placed on the inside of a window

Having the scanners continuously recording over a long period (at the time of writing, 3 months) avoids the problem that the conventional pattern of short observation periods at each gate might under-record passing Bluetooth devices. It also provides very clear data on the cyclical nature of passing Bluetooth traffic. This illustrates the new opportunities offered by our combined methods, providing continuity of data that is effectively impossible with human observers and can be complemented by manually collected data at desired intervals at the same gate.

3.2 Extending Static Snapshots to Include Bluetooth Interaction Spaces

We also extended the static snapshot method with Bluetooth scanning, drawing on the lessons learned in developing and refining our augmented gatecount method. To trial our Bluetooth-augmented static snapshot method, we installed a long-term scanner in a city centre pub, and another in a café. These scanners were technologically identical to the ones we used for our fixed long-term gatecounts. The difference was in the siting of the scanner. Both our fixed university gate and fixed city street gate employed scanners facing directly out a window. Although some Bluetooth activity was picked up from inside the building, devices crossing our gate generated most of the transient activity. In the pub we placed our scanner near the bar area, while in the café our scanner was placed near the seating area. In each case, we recorded Bluetooth activity generated mainly by devices in these areas.

In addition to the constant Bluetooth scanning, we carried out two 30-minute observation sessions in each of the two static snapshot locations. The purpose of these observations was to verify and correlate the recorded Bluetooth activity with the human activity in the area. Our human observers recorded people's positions, behaviours and movements through space, as well as the precise time of these activities. We subsequently compared these observations with the data recorded by our Bluetooth scanners, generating aggregate data, reported in Section 4.1, which was unavailable using conventional space syntax methods.

4 Field Trials of Our Augmented Methods

In this section we present our field trials using our newly developed methods. Although we are still refining our methods, these findings offer concrete examples of the results our methods can provide. We present our findings in terms of patterns of presence of Bluetooth activity in the city and an initial analysis of the Bluetooth names we recorded.

4.1 Patterns of Bluetooth Presence

Simply looking at the raw Bluetooth activity can be misleading. From Figure 4 it appears that the university gate was much busier than the city centre gate. However, filtering out multiple records per device and persistent devices (indicating nearby static Bluetooth devices), we can identify the transient Bluetooth devices, shown in Figure 5.

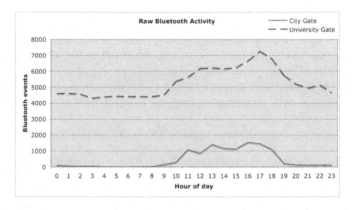

Fig. 4. Raw Bluetooth activity data for our campus and city centre fixed gates

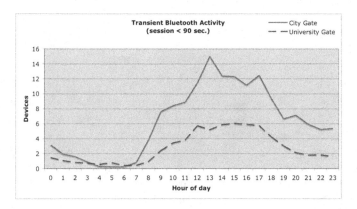

Fig. 5. Transient Bluetooth devices for our campus and city centre fixed gates

So, the city centre gate peaks at 15 unique transient devices per hour, while the campus gate peaks at 6 devices per hour. Intriguingly, the 2 graphs have a very similar profile despite recording Bluetooth traffic at very different sites. Another feature of note is the temporal pattern, with Bluetooth traffic at both sites peaking in mid-afternoon. The peak of 15 devices per hour for the city centre gate refers to the period 1pm to 2pm. This corresponds to 7.8% of the pedestrian traffic for that location, as recorded by our gatecount study reported in Section 2.1. This closely matches the 7% found in our Bluetooth-augmented gatecounts reported in Section 3.1.2, giving us a useful confidence check on our results.

The raw data recorded by our scanners are in the form of timestamped events. A single discovered device typically generates multiple events while it is within range of our scanners. In analysing the data, we developed a timeline visualisation, illustrated in Figure 6 where the top part of the figure is a magnified version of the area marked by the rectangle in the bottom part of the figure.

As a new device is discovered, we assign it to a new timeline. It then generates timestamps, indicated by circles on the timelines. In Figure 6, we see that device 12 was discovered at 15.5 minutes from the start of the observation, was visible for about 40 seconds, and was never seen again. Device 11, on the other hand was discovered at 14.5 minutes, and then again at 21.5 minutes. Devices 14 and 15 were discovered only once, which indicates that they may be at the periphery of our scanning range, and probably did not pass through our gate. As noted in Section 3.1.2, devices which pass through a gate are typically seen for up to 90 seconds. We use this 90-second period as a threshold for identifying highly transient devices.

Our timeline visualisation creates the cumulative effect of a diagonal line from bottom left to top right. Any activity recorded below this main diagonal is attributable to persistent devices. In Figure 7 we show data from 3 Bluetooth gatecounts which took place at different locations and reflect contrasting patterns of Bluetooth presence.

Gatecount 9 has a relatively high level of persistent devices, while gatecounts 5 and 10 recorded mostly transient devices. In gatecount 9, we can identify bursts of Bluetooth activity recorded at 0, 5, 13 and 23 minutes. Finally, in gatecount 5, we observe the continuous presence of a device for approximately 17 minutes.

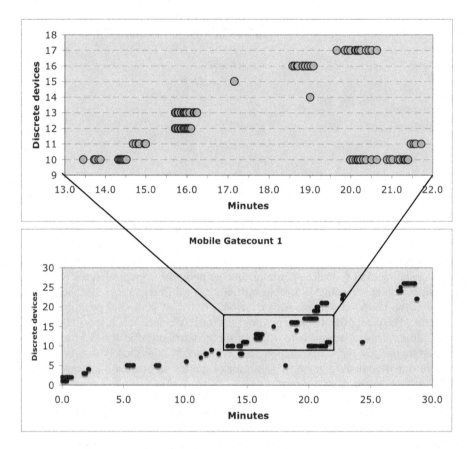

Fig. 6. A timeline visualization of our Bluetooth gatecounts. Each device is given its own timeline (dashed lines in top half) and each discovery event is plotted as a circle on the timeline.

We would expect major differences in the patterns of presence between our gatecount and static snapshot data, since one records primarily Bluetooth traffic passing along a street while the other records primarily the Bluetooth devices of people in a café or pub. Figure 8 shows the duration of Bluetooth sessions recorded at the university gate and the pub.

In Figure 8, the bars indicate frequency (measured on the left y-axis), while the line indicates cumulative percentage (measured on the right y-axis). The duration of the sessions is shown on the x-axis. The difference in patterns of presence between the two locations is clear. The university gate data showed 85% of sessions under 90 seconds, a threshold indicating highly transient devices. In the pub only 35% of sessions were below 90 seconds. The data from the pub also shows much more diversity in session length, with sessions recorded of up to 10 hours – generated by the pub manager's phone.

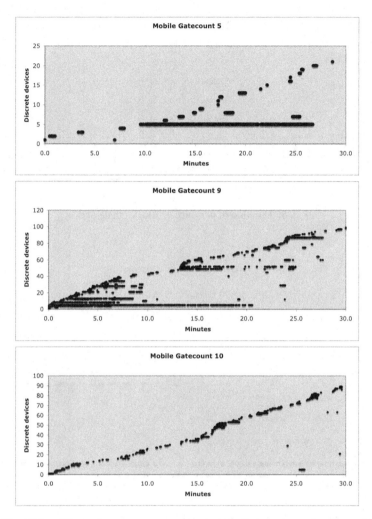

Fig. 7. Visualizing Bluetooth gatecount records. Activity below the main diagonal indicates persistent devices.

Our combination of conventional static snapshot recording by human observers and Bluetooth scanning enables further interpretation of our timeline visualizations. For example, Figure 9 presents the Bluetooth activity in the pub during one of our static snapshot observation sessions. Correlating these data with our observational data allowed us to identify devices 2 and 3 as belonging to members of staff. Device 7 disappeared when we observed two men leave the area after having lunch. Device 1 was our observer, who was carrying out Bluetooth discoveries with his phone. (During this operation, the Bluetooth device cannot itself be discovered.) When three women entered the area, devices 15, 16 and 17 appeared. These devices had feminine names: "Jen", "Cass" and "Han". Finally, we were able to attribute devices 9 and 10 to the same person. This person was briefly present in our observation area, and the

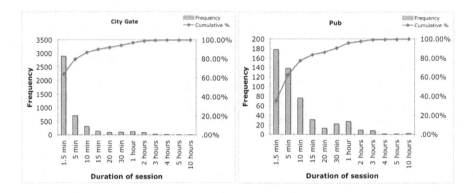

Fig. 8. Duration of presence of Bluetooth devices

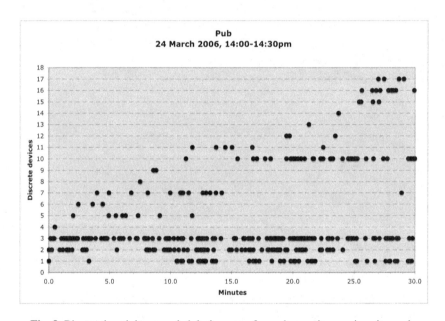

Fig. 9. Bluetooth activity recorded during one of our observation sessions in a pub

two devices were named "Sam K" and "Sam Karoot". In addition to patterns of Bluetooth presence, our methods are beginning to uncover patterns in user's Bluetooth naming practices. These are described in the next section.

4.2 Bluetooth Names

We collected Bluetooth name data at three of our scanning sites: the university campus, a street in the city centre, and inside a pub in the city centre. Discovering a device's Bluetooth name takes significantly longer than simply discovering its Bluetooth address, which meant that the names of many recorded transient devices went unrecorded. Nonetheless, we collected 1703 Bluetooth names: 771 from the city centre street, 307 from the pub and 625 from the campus. The great majority of these were names of mobile phones.

Devices are usually configured by default with names that state the make and model, such as "Nokia 6680" or "TomTom GO 300" (a satellite navigation unit). It is straightforward to distinguish variations from those defaults. Our logs revealed that 58% of discoverable devices had user-defined names in the city centre street; for the campus, the figure was 76%; and for the pub it was 88%. Interpreting these figures demands contextual data about user practices and intentions if we are to draw meaningful conclusions. But the figures are at least indicative of a thriving culture of Bluetooth naming. With factory default names, we simply cannot tell whether the user is unaware of the potential for setting – and making discoverable – a Bluetooth name, or if she is aware of Bluetooth and its properties and has chosen to retain the default name. However, from the user-defined names we may infer with some confidence that the user has an awareness of Bluetooth and its properties.

The choices of names themselves may suggest different forms of awareness of Bluetooth's properties, and variations in the degree and type of effect that users wanted to have upon other Bluetooth users when they were discovered. Some names show an acute awareness of Bluetooth and the possibility of being discovered: "Clear off!!", "Pick me pick me", "Send me porn", "U Found Meee...".

Being "Bluetooth aware" serves as a precondition for choosing names that may be characterised on a *self-others* spectrum, running from one extreme of simple presentation of self to another extreme of seeking an effect on other people. Many people chose simply to identify themselves. Some, such as "Nokia 6280 Wayne" did not remove the default name altogether, possibly because the type of phone had some significance. Others removed the default name entirely and provided a name in either a short ("Annie") or long ("John K. Taylor") form. Still others, such as "Snagglepuss" and "Crown Jools", gave themselves aliases. Here, we begin to see a movement along the spectrum from simply stating one's name to projecting an identity. This becomes even more apparent with others who identified themselves not so much by name as by what (or whom) they wished to associate themselves with. "Beer boy" is on the one hand an alias, but also associates this individual with drinking beer. "M.C.F.C OK!" refers to a football club; and "Pezza's girl" even associates herself with a (boy)friend. As we move towards the other extreme of this spectrum, the term *name* is less obviously apt for what people entered on their phones. Many provided texts that one might find in public places, such as graffiti and T-shirts: "4 a gay time call 077...", "$LiK JiM", "LesbiansAre4Girls", "Ima kettle".

Many accounts are possible of the foregoing examples. Our account here represents first thoughts on dimensions of variation in the data we are seeing. We are inferring patterns in what the names themselves suggest, rather than what the users intended. The latter requires further research and we are engaged in investigations to understand naming as a set of practices in particular contexts. A fuller understanding of the culture and practice of Bluetooth naming requires not just scanning passing devices but gathering data from users about their Bluetooth naming practices.

What these names substantiate, however, is that, for the majority of users who are Bluetooth aware, Bluetooth on mobile phones gives rise to a de facto rather than merely potential interaction space. There is little point in altering the device's name from the default unless there is an intention for either functional or social interaction (or both) through this new electronic medium. Through her choice of name, the user defines the "feel" of that interaction space. The fusion of such wireless interaction spaces with the spaces defined by the features of our built environment has the potential strongly to influence people's relationships with those urban spaces. For example, consider the different potential effects on your behaviour if you became aware that the café in which you had always felt most comfortable had amongst its customers a preponderance of discoverable Bluetooth names that you found either upsetting or reassuring.

5   Conclusions and Ongoing Work

Whilst we have already generated a large corpus of interesting data, the primary purpose of the work reported in this paper was to develop and refine the methods themselves, and we have made considerable progress in this respect. Our extended methods do not simply consist in our Bluetooth scanning. Rather, they consist in our Bluetooth scanning *in combination with* the conventional observational techniques.

Our data on the use of Bluetooth names suggests the appropriation of the technology to project identity and to engage with others whilst enjoying a cloak of relative anonymity. Other data shows people visiting a café for extended periods not to eat or drink, or even to engage socially with others in the café, but to use the WiFi service. Each of these examples was thrown up by our field studies but drew on only one side of our extended methods, conventional or electronic. The Bluetooth names were recorded by our electronic scanning and did not rely on the accompanying human observations, while the observations of non-eating, non-drinking WiFi users were made by standard static snapshot techniques and did not rely on the accompanying electronic scanning. These findings confirm the utility of our extended methods in capturing a wide range of data that neither approach alone would encompass.

In addition, our extended methods capture data that require the *combination* of both electronic and human observation. For example, a characteristic of conventional gatecounts and static snapshots that we are not able to reproduce with Bluetooth scans alone is the ability to classify pedestrian flow depending on people's characteristics, such as men, women, locals, tourists, children or adults. On the other hand, our Bluetooth scanning allows us to record and classify data that is simply not accessible to conventional gatecount and static snapshot methods, including characteristics of both the devices and the people carrying them. Thus, in addition to recording the presence and flows of Bluetooth interaction spaces, our extended methods gather data about the devices generating them, such as whether they are mobile phones or notebook computers, while our recording of Bluetooth names provides a rich dataset that allows us to classify people in terms other than the characteristics recorded by conventional observational methods.

We will continue to refine our methods, and indeed develop other methods, for both the capture and analysis of data. For example, we have not yet overcome the problem for Bluetooth-augmented gatecounts of discovering Bluetooth devices on adjacent streets or in adjacent buildings. We can in principle mitigate the adjacent streets problem by careful choice of scanner location. The ideal site for a gatecount scanner is on a long, narrow street with no nearby junctions, where we can be more confident that discovered devices have actually crossed our conceptual gate line. However, it is unlikely in general that sites where we can place fixed long-term scanners will coincide neatly with this ideal spatial morphology. We have much more freedom in choosing the location of our mobile scanners but this will not always help because our choice of site may be constrained by, for example, our research questions. Thus, we may be interested in studying Bluetooth flow in a particular urban space regardless of how well that space lends itself to our scanning.

The adjacent buildings problem is mitigated by our developing data analysis methods. While our analysis differentiates between static and transient Bluetooth devices, rather than between activity on the street and in buildings, we can usually infer location in a building for highly persistent devices. We have found empirically that fixed devices in buildings account for the majority of highly persistent devices recorded by gatecounts. While our analysis is less useful at distinguishing between less persistent devices in buildings and passing devices on the street, mobile devices within buildings are often more persistent than the transient devices of passers-by in the street.

We have demonstrated that augmenting established observational methods with Bluetooth scanning enables short-term capture of data that lends itself well to the study of wireless interaction spaces in the city. We hope to extend this approach to inspect changes in Bluetooth activities over longer time scales and thereby to monitor the patterned effects of our future technological interventions.

The field of ubiquitous computing in general lacks concrete methods grounded in the urban context. The methods we are exploring and extending, conventionally applied in analysing and understanding the traditional architectural features of the urban environment, can help us to analyse and understand ubiquitous computing features as integral aspects of that environment. Our ongoing research continues to develop and refine these and other methods, while gathering further interesting data as we progress towards our goal of understanding the city as a system encompassing both the built environment and ubiquitous technologies.

Acknowledgements

This research is funded by the UK Engineering and Physical Sciences Research Council grant EP/C547683/1 (Cityware: urban design and pervasive systems).

References

Benford, S., Anastasi, R., Flintham, M., Drozd, A., Crabtree, A., Greenhalgh, C., Tanda-Vanitj, N., Adams, M. and Row-Farr, J. (2003). Coping with uncertainty in a location-based game. IEEE Pervasive Computing, 2(3): 34-41.

Fatah gen. Schieck, A., Lopez de Vallejo, I. and Penn, A. (2005). Urban space and pervasive systems. In proceedings UbiComp 2005, Tokyo, Japan (poster).

Fatah gen. Schieck, Penn, A., Kostakos, V., O'Neill, E., Kindberg, T., Stanton Fraser, D. and Jones, T. (2006). Design tools for pervasive computing in urban environments. In proceedings 8th International Conference on Design & Decision Support Systems in Architecture and Urban Planning, Springer, in press.

Hillier, B., Penn, A., Hanson, J., Grajewski, T. and Xu, J. (1993). Natural movement; or, configuration and attraction in urban space use. Environment and Planning B, 1993.

Hillier, B. and Hanson, J. (1984). The social logic of space. Cambridge: Cambridge University Press.

Hillier, B., Burdett, R., Peponis J. and Penn, A. (1987). Creating life: or does architecture determine anything? Architecture and Behaviour, 3(3): 233-250.

Höflich, J. R. (2005). A certain sense of place. In K. Nyíri (ed.): A sense of place – the global and the local in mobile communication, Passagen Verlag, 159-168.

Kostakos, V. (2005). A design framework for pervasive computing systems. PhD Thesis, University of Bath, UK. Technical Report CSBU2005-02, ISSN 1740-9497.

Mainwaring, S.D., Anderson, K. and Chang, M.F. (2005). Living for the global city: mobile kits, urban interfaces, and ubicomp. In proceedings UbiComp 2005, Tokyo, Japan, 269-286.

O'Neill, E., Johnson, P., and Johnson, H. (1999). Representations and user-developer interaction in cooperative analysis and design. Human Computer Interaction, 14(1/2): 43-92.

O'Neill, E., Woodgate, D. and Kostakos, V. (2004). Easing the wait in the Emergency Room: building a theory of public information systems. In proceedings Designing Interactive Systems (DIS 2004), Cambridge, Massachusetts, 17-25.

Paulos, E. and Goodman, E. (2004). The familiar stranger: anxiety, comfort, and play in public places. In proceedings CHI 2004, ACM, 24-29.

Paulos, E. and Jenkins, T. (2005). Urban probes: encountering our emerging urban atmospheres. In proceedings CHI 2005, ACM, 341-350.

Reid, J., Hull, R., Cater, K. and Fleuriot, C. (2005). Magic moments in situated mediascapes. In proceedings ACM SIGCHI International Conference on Advances in Computer Entertainment Technology (ACE 2005), Spain, ACM.

Stonor, T. (1997). Making space: the use of space syntax in design. In proceedings First International Symposium on Space Syntax, 16-18 April 1997, UCL, London.

Voting with Your Feet:
An Investigative Study of the Relationship Between Place Visit Behavior and Preference*

Jon Froehlich[1], Mike Y. Chen[2], Ian E. Smith[2], and Fred Potter[1]

[1] Department of Computer Science and Engineering
University of Washington, Seattle, WA, USA
{jfroehli, fpotter}@cs.washington.edu
[2] Intel Research, Seattle, WA, USA
{mike.y.chen, ian.e.smith}@intel.com

Abstract. Real world recommendation systems, personalized mobile search, and online city guides could all benefit from data on personal place preferences. However, collecting explicit rating data of locations as users travel from place to place is impractical. This paper investigates the relationship between explicit place ratings and implicit aspects of travel behavior such as visit frequency and travel time. We conducted a four-week study with 16 participants using a novel sensor-based experience sampling tool, called My Experience (Me), which we developed for mobile phones. Over the course of the study Me was used to collect 3,458 in-situ questionnaires on 1,981 place visits. Our results show that, first, sensor-triggered experience sampling is a useful methodology for collecting targeted information in situ. Second, despite the complexities underlying travel routines and visit behavior, there exist positive correlations between place preference and automatically detectable features like visit frequency and travel time. And, third, we found that when combined, visit frequency and travel time result in stronger correlations with place rating than when measured individually. Finally, we found no significant difference in place ratings due to the presence of others.

1 Introduction

Why do we travel to some places but not others? What do these places say about our interests? Could a person's movements to and from places in the physical world be an implicit form of expressing preference? We studied the travel routines of 16 participants over the course of four-weeks to determine what factors of visit behaviors, if any, could be used to infer preference for places. Using GSM-based location sensing and experience sampling on mobile phones (a technique to capture self-report data from participants in situ), participants provided explicit ratings for the places they visited. We used these ratings to explore the correlation between place preference and two implicit aspects of place visit behavior, *visit frequency* and *travel distance*. In

---

* This work was approved by the University of Washington Human Subjects Division, application id: HSD# 05-6963-E/C 01.

P. Dourish and A. Friday (Eds.): Ubicomp 2006, LNCS 4206, pp. 333–350, 2006.

addition, we looked at the impact of social effects on place ratings in an attempt to discover whether the presence of others makes determining place preference more difficult.

Understanding individual user preferences for items is critical to many mainstream commercial online systems, but has been under-explored in physical world settings. Online applications like the Amazon.com® book recommender, the Last.fm® music-based social network, and the TiVo® personalized TV guide depend heavily on ob-serving human action to determine preference. Often, these inferences are augmented with explicit user ratings. With TiVo, for example, the only explicit feedback is the "thumbs-up/thumbs-down" button. However, when a user records a TV show, that show is automatically assigned a "thumbs-up" rating—thus, ordinary user activities are paired with explicit ratings to form a profile of likes and dislikes [1]. The benefit of explicit ratings is that they are precise and fairly well understood; however, they also interrupt the user experience and may not be consistently used across users [6]. Thus, recommenders and personalization engines typically rely on inferring prefer-ence from ordinary behaviors, as TiVo does when a user records a show, Last.fm does when a user listens to music and Amazon does when a user makes a purchase These implicit indicators remove the burden of explicitly having to rate an item. In addition, as [1, 6] point out, nearly every interaction with the system becomes a potential indi-cator of interest. In this paper we seek to determine if this type of implicit preference inferencing translates to behavior in the real world.

We explore how well *easily* detectable attributes of visit behavior correlate with explicit place ratings. If these attributes correlate positively, modern location sensing technologies (e.g., a mobile phone equipped with assisted GPS) could use inferred interests based on visit activity to build preference profiles of users. This has high value implications for a variety of mobile applications. Real world recommendation systems, online city guides, and personalized mobile search, could all potentially benefit from learning place preferences. For example, a recommendation system could be constructed to give personalized recommendations based on a user's move-ment—a tourist who makes frequent visits to Italian restaurants in his or her home-town is given a list of the top Italian restaurants on a mobile device when travling to a new city. These recommendations could even span the physical and virtual worlds. Frequent visits to a live jazz music club might indicate a musical preference that could be used by an online music store. Alternatively, user experience could be en-riched through an online city guide like Citysearch via personalized portal pages, event information and special discounts based on inferred interests. Finally, mobile search engines could return personalized local search results based not just on current location but also on previous visit behaviors and inferred interests.

One difficulty with using place visits for prediction is that people move around for a variety of reasons, not all of which can be predicted or modeled. For example, peo-ple often defer their tastes for the sake of convenience (e.g., I don't like fast food but was short on time) or the presence of others (e.g., all-day shoe shopping spree with spouse). To better understand these complexities and their impact on place ratings, two potential confounds are also investigated: social effects and the "convenience factor." In particular, we examined how place ratings changed when the participant was close to a location rather than far away. We also looked at how ratings differ when the participant was alone versus when they were with others.

In our analysis, we found that visit frequency and travel time as single factors were only slightly correlated with place ratings. However, when combined they became more effective predictors of preference. In addition, the results of social effects were mixed—in the general case, no significant difference was found for places visited alone versus with others. However, when with others, participants rated a place significantly higher if they chose to go to that place themselves (i.e., the decision of where to go was *not* made by someone else in the group). We also show through the perspective of a small case study how simple, pragmatic splits of data can result in much higher correlations between visit activity and explicit place ratings.

The rest of the paper is organized as follows: Section 2 provides background on our study techniques; Section 3 describes our study and participant background; Section 4 outlines some high level results including the number of ESM surveys and places captured; Section 5 analyzes the results from our field study; Section 6 discusses implications; Section 7 describes our related work; Section 8 discusses potential for future work and Section 9 presents our conclusions.

2 Background on User Study Techniques

Before describing the details of our study, we offer brief backgrounds on the primary user study techniques that we employed: experience sampling and web diaries.

2.1 Experience Sampling Background

In situ, self-report procedures such as the experience sampling method (ESM) have been used extensively in psychology and HCI to capture data on participants' thoughts, feelings, and behaviors as they are experienced [2, 8, 20]. Such procedures have a distinct methodological advantage over ex situ inquiries in that they do not rely on the reconstruction of information from memory, but rather involve reporting on experiences as they occur, thus minimizing recall bias. Traditionally this has been done with beepers and small booklets of paper-form questionnaires. The questionnaires would be carried and filled-out by participants when signaled by the beeper. This allowed researchers to get a sample of participants' experiences throughout the course of a study. Mobile computing has allowed this process to be computerized [2, 7]. One weakness of traditional ESM is that the beeper alerts may not always occur at relevant points of interest for the researchers.

In our study, we used a form of computerized ESM called "context-triggered sampling" to provide more targeted sampling of our participants. This technique, pioneered by MIT's Context-Aware Experience Sampling tool for the PDA [12], uses sensors to infer context to trigger a brief survey. It has several advantages when compared with traditional sampling methods, such as random or time-based triggering. For example, context-triggered surveys are much more likely to occur during events that are of interest to the researcher. This reduces disruption by decreasing the number of extraneous prompts on the participant. Additionally, context data can be continuously saved by the computer; allowing the researcher to cross-check answers with sensor data and perhaps uncover behavioral patterns not initially considered.

2.2 Web Diaries

Web diaries are often used in field studies [4, 21] to capture qualitative accounts of participants' thoughts and behaviors. Participants are asked to connect to a predetermined web site to fill out open-ended or semi-structured questionnaires at specific intervals. Sometimes the web site is used to upload pictures, recordings or other media captured by the participant [4]. We used web diaries in our study as a qualitative supplement to the quantitative data gathered through ESM (see Section 3.1).

3 Study Design

In our four-week, in situ study, we investigated the perceptions and feelings participants had about the places they visited. In this section, we describe our study design.

Our study consisted of three phases: Phase I: Participant backgrounds, Phase II: In situ experience sampling and Phase III: Study wrap-up. Phase I took place in our lab with one to five participants at a time and familiarized us with the participants' backgrounds and their general routines with respect to out-of-the-house activity. Participants were given an overview of the study and a training session on the technology they would use in Phase II. We administered two paper questionnaires: one to evaluate their visit behaviors and why they visited the places they did, and a second to determine their estimates of the number and variation of places they visited. Participants completed the second questionnaire (called the "My Places Questionnaire") on their own time and returned it at their second session in our lab.

In Phase II, sensor-triggered experience sampling was used to capture the places that the participants actually traveled and their subjective feelings for those places. Each participant was loaned an Audiovox® SMT 5600 mobile phone loaded with our novel sampling software, the My Experience (Me) Tool, which prompted participants to fill out a brief survey up to 11 times per day for four-weeks. In addition, participants kept a web diary to supplement the experience sampling surveys and validate features of our GSM place-tracking algorithm. Given the data input constraints of the mobile phone, we used web diaries to gather richer qualitative data on participants' places. At the midpoint of Phase II, participants returned to the lab for a one-on-one interview about their experiences using ESM so far.

In Phase III, participants returned to the lab for their final visit at the end of the four-week ESM period. A concluding interview was conducted that explored participants' attitudes and experiences with online web sites like Citysearch and Amazon and asked follow-up questions based on their ESM and web diary responses.

3.1 Experience Sampling and Web Diary Details

To implement experience sampling in our study, we built a generic, context-aware experience sampling tool called the "Me" (My Experience) Tool. This .NET based tool allows researchers to conduct in situ field studies using Windows Mobile® devices (e.g., PocketPC, SmartPhone, etc.). Similar to computerized sampling tools of the past   [2, 7, 12], Me allows non-technical researchers to build computerized self-report surveys simply by creating a textual input file. And, like CAES [12], Me supports context-triggered sampling. Unlike prior work, however, Me is the first tool to offer these capabilities on the mobile phone. Mobile phones are attractive data collection platforms for researchers because they offer real-time data connectivity, a small form factor, relatively long battery life, and an interaction paradigm familiar to most participants (e.g., keypad interactions). Of course, the mobile phone may not be suited for all studies as the small screens and buttons place certain physical demands on the participants. Me also runs on the PocketPC and PocketPC Phone platforms, which offer larger screens, higher resolutions, and touch panel interactions.

In our study, we built a software mobility sensor based on GSM signals received by the mobile phone [16]. ESM surveys were triggered by detecting when a participant's phone was stationary for a period of 10 minutes. Thus, once the phone shifted from "mobile" to "stationary" and remained in that state for the time threshold, a survey was triggered—see Fig. 1. If the phone remained stationary for longer than one hour, a random time-based survey would trigger. No two surveys were closer than 15 minutes apart. In addition to providing a fail safe against sensor failure, these time-based surveys allowed us to ensure that surveys were spaced throughout the day and that our quota of at least eight surveys per day was consistently met.

Fig. 1. Sample screenshots of the Me Tool on the Audiovox 5600 mobile phone used during the study

Our ESM surveys asked from one to twenty-three questions based on the participant's responses. A one-to-four question survey simply asked "Are you still at <last known place>?" If the participant responded "yes" that survey would end; if "no," at least three more questions were asked: "Place name," "Place category," and "Please rate how much you like this place." The rating scale was from 0.5 to 5 (5 is best), shown in Fig. 1 (right). To select a place name, participants could choose from previously entered names or enter a new one. This was the only ESM question that required text entry on the phone. The survey ended if the participant selected *Personal*, *Work*, or *Home*—all other responses would cause the survey to continue.

In addition to ESM surveys, participants were asked to fill out web diaries a few nights a week. These diaries were designed to capture information about place visits that were missed by the phone and augment the ESM responses with more qualitative data. Place visits were automatically uploaded to the website. Participants were then asked open-ended questions about a random subset of places marked as bars, cafes, restaurants or stores.

3.2 Participant Profiles and Compensation

We recruited 16 participants, 8 male/8 female, from the Seattle area through flyers posted at local restaurants, cafés, and apartment buildings, and through online postings on Craigslist.org. Participants were screened based on their mobile phone experience (e.g., that they could add a number to their phone's contact list) and out-of-house behavior (e.g. employed away from home, bar and restaurant visit frequency, etc.) and internet connectivity at home or work. Ages ranged from 22-56 (median 29). Two participants were full-time students; the others included a furniture designer, political consultant, bookseller, translator, grant manager, artist, etc. Six were in a serious relationship; one had children.

Each participant was supplied with an Audiovox SMT 5600 SmartPhone, wall-charger and car charger. The phones were preconfigured to run the Me Tool at startup. Other SmartPhone programs and menu items were removed to simplify interaction with the phone. Participants were asked to carry the phone with them at all times; the study phones were used only for experience sampling, and were not used, for example, to make calls or replace the participants' personal phones.

Participants were compensated based on their level of participation. Participants could complete up to 11 ESM surveys a day, at $1 USD per survey, regardless of their movement or place visit activity. This scheme was established to promote survey completion without artificially motivating behavior. The incentive was contingent on the participant regularly logging into the website and filling out the web diary—at a minimum of 3-4 times per week. Participants were also remunerated for their two interviews, paper questionnaires, and travel time to and from our lab. Participation was strictly voluntary and prorated compensation would be made if a participant dropped out prematurely.

4   High Level Results

On average, participants carried a study mobile phone for 28 days each[1] (median 29). The length of the study varied slightly per participant because of scheduling. The average completion rate for the ESM surveys was 80.5%. A total of 4,295 ESM surveys were administered, 3,458 were completed at a rate of 216 surveys per participant (median 211). A total of 19,865 questions were answered. The survey completion time ranged from 20 seconds to five minutes (1.5 minute average). Despite early technical issues with the web diary server, 368 web diary sessions were completed, averaging 23 per participant.

---

[1] We lost two weeks of data for one participant due to a multiple drive failure in a RAID5 storage system.

1,981 individual place visits were logged via ESM surveys. Of these, 862 were to a public place at a rate of 1.9 public place visits per day. The public place visits ranged from the usual—the grocery store, local park, Starbucks—to the rather unusual, an outdoor sausage festival, a wedding chapel and the state fair. Table 1 shows a breakdown of the types of places visited, the number of participants who logged at least one visit to that place, and its mean preference rating. The "Other" category is an amalgamation of 21 place categories including: Gas Stations, Shopping Malls, Movie Theatres, and Parks.

Table 1. Captured Places

Public and Private Places			
Place Category	# of Visits	# of Part.	Mean Place Rating (SD)
PUBLIC			
Bar	39	10	3.8 (0.76)
Café	122	15	3.8 (0.63)
Restaurant	251	16	3.8 (0.80)
Store	186	16	3.7 (0.91)
Other	266	16	3.6 (1.2)
PRIVATE			
Home	450	16	4.6 (0.85)
In Transit	354	16	2.9 (1.4)
Personal	253	16	4.4 (0.83)
Work	416	16	3.6 (0.99)

4.1 ESM Effectiveness

Given that we were interested in visit behaviors and travel routines, it was important to capture data about as many places as possible. We used context-triggered ESM to maximize the number of places surveyed and minimize participant disruption.

A majority of the 1,981 place visits were captured as a result of the mobility detection algorithm triggering a sensor-based survey. Fig. 2 reveals the effectiveness of the sensor-triggered ESM surveys in capturing public place visits versus private place visits. The graph is organized from left-to-right based on the percentage of sensor- versus time-triggered surveys completed at each place category. For example, over 80% of completed ESM surveys tagged as "at a store" were sensor-triggered vs. fewer than 40% for "at home." The three right most place categories are all "private places" and received the greatest percentage of time-triggered surveys. This is to be expected if the mobility detection algorithm was behaving appropriately: each of those place categories (work, personal, and home) are characterized by long periods of sedentary activity. The ESM survey system would only invoke a time-triggered survey after failing to sense mobility for one hour. The algorithm was not perfect—it suffered from both false positives (i.e., detecting a phone was stationary when mobile) and false negatives (i.e., detecting a phone was mobile when stationary). However, it was quite successful in capturing ESM data as participants traveled from place to place.

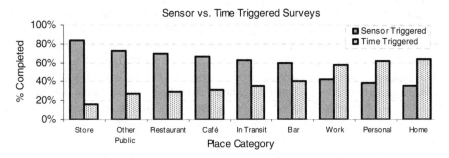

Fig. 2. The sensor-triggered surveys captured a majority of public place visits

4.2 The "My Places" Paper Questionnaire

The "My Places" questionnaire, administered at the beginning of the study, was an initial investigation into the complexities of visit behaviors. The purpose of this questionnaire was to establish a comparative point for the ESM data. It asked about travel routines to public places that are frequented two or more times a year. For each place the participant listed, the questionnaire asked for an explicit place rating, an approximate location, an approximate visit frequency per year, typical travel time, and their primary reasons for visiting that place. Place ratings were on a scale of 0.5 – to 5, where halves were allowed. A rating of 5 implied a strong liking for the place. The same scale was used in the ESM surveys.

The total number of places listed was 634—roughly 40 per participant. The average place rating was 3.8 (SD=0.79). While on the surface, the visit behaviors seemed routine (e.g. grocery shopping, eating out, going to the park) participants included stories that conveyed underlying complexities. One participant visited a particular coffee shop once a day "for the caffeine" despite conflicting feelings about the company's economic and political policies: the "Coffee is OK but they are too corporate and they give to democrats." Another participant patronized a restaurant 12 times a year, yet he rated it 2/5 stars because he "didn't like the food"—"[I go there] because my friends like it." Most often, proximity played a critical role—either because a service or item was only available in a certain area ("[this grocery store has] good selection—some foods I cannot get anywhere else") or because of sheer convenience ("It's nearby but the food is bad—it's cheap and easy").

5 Analysis

We present statistical analyses exploring the relationship between place visit behavior and a person's explicit place rating. The focus is on exploring factors that could be automatically detected by emerging location technologies, for example, with assisted GPS or beacon based location [14]. We explore two implicit factors in detail: *visit frequency* and *travel effort*. We hypothesize that the number of visits a person makes to a place and the required travel time to get there reflects a corresponding interest. We also investigate social effects to determine whether place ratings differ for those visited alone versus with others.

In the analysis below, Likert-scale responses are often categorized in two or three nominal groups (e.g. a "disagree" group and an "agree" group) to partition data for significance tests—in these cases we will use non-parametric tests for frequency distributions and t-tests to compare equality of means. For correlative analysis we will be using Spearman's correlation coefficient analysis (abbreviated ρ)[2]. Significance will be denoted by one star (*) for P<0.05 and two stars (**) for P<0.01.

Place ratings were on a scale of 0.5 to 5, where halves were allowed, resulting in ten discrete rating points. To better understand the rating variable as an expression of preference, we occasionally asked one or two additional follow-up "rating" questions during the course of an ESM survey: "I really like this place" and "This place is

---

[2] ρ measures association between ordinal data without making assumptions about the frequency distribution of the variables.

important to me." Each had answer choices on a 5-point Likert scale. As one would hope, both were positively correlated with rating. "I really like this place" was found to be highly correlated with the explicit place rating (ρ=0.68**). The second question, which inquired about importance rather than preference, resulted in a lower correlation, though still positive (ρ=0.47**).

5.1   Visit Frequency vs. Explicit Rating

Our first hypothesis is that the number of visits a person has to a place is a strong indicator of their preference for that place. We will investigate this in two ways: first, by examining participant responses to a paper questionnaire about place routines and, second, by looking at the participants' in situ, self-reported visit frequency to places as answered on ESM surveys.

My Places Questionnaires. For each place listed in the "My Places" paper questionnaire (see Section 0), the participant was asked to list their estimated visit frequency to that place. Using this data, we found a positive correlation between a person's preference for a place and their respective visit frequency (ρ=0.20**). When broken down into subcategories as shown in Fig. 3, only bar ratings and visit frequency are significantly correlated (ρ=0.29**). The correlation is weaker than we expected due to the unequal distribution of highly rated places amongst the visit frequency categories. That is, there is a distribution of places that people really like but only visit a few times a year. We note this occurrence in our ESM data as well.

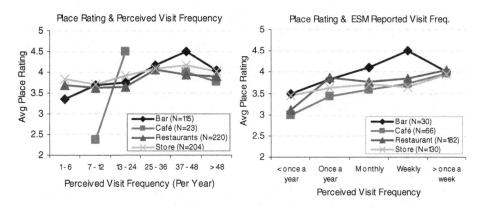

Fig. 3. "My Places" Questionnaire. Shows a correlation between bar ratings and visit frequency (ρ=0.29**). Other categories show similar trend but failed significance.

Fig. 4. ESM Data. Though all show a positive trend, only café and bar ratings were correlated with visit frequency (ρ=0.39* & ρ=0.27*).

Self-reported ESM Visit Frequency. Each "public place" ESM survey asked "How often do you go to this place?" with six answer choices, which ranged from "This is my first time" to "More than once a week." The purpose of this question was to collect visit frequency data in the event that the study was not long enough to capture a sufficient amount of *observed* repeat visits for statistical testing. We found a slight positive correlation (ρ=0.14**) between ESM reported visit frequency[3] and explicit place ratings. This is similar to what we found with the paper questionnaire. When divided into the categories shown in Fig. 4, we found that visit frequency is a modest indicator of preference for bars (ρ=0.39*) and cafes (ρ=0.27*) but not for restaurants and stores. We will discuss possible reasons for this in the next section.

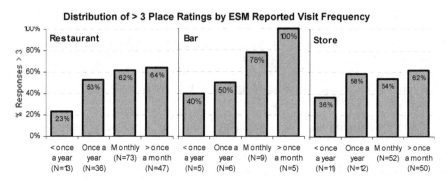

Fig. 5. Restaurant and bar visits show a clear monotonically increasing trend between visit frequency and preference. This trend is not evident in store visits.

To better understand the distribution of places that are liked, but only visited a few times a year, place rating data was split into two nominal groups: those places rated as less than or equal to 3 ("<= 3") and those places rated as greater than 3 ("> 3"). For restaurants, bars, and cafes the visit frequency distributions for the two categories were shown to be significantly different. For example, over 64% of the restaurants visited more than once a month were rated positively (> 3) while only 23.1% of the restaurants visited less than once a year were rated positively. A similar monotonic upward trend occurred for bars but not for stores—see Fig. 5.

Finally, looking at the ESM question "I plan on returning to this place" we see additional evidence that repeated place visits implies preference. This question uses a 5-point Likert-scale from "Strongly Disagree" to "Strongly Agree." We found a positive correlation between these responses and explicit place ratings (0.31**). When broken into sub-categories, the correlation for bars increases to ρ=0.91*—the other place types do not change significantly from 0.31**. The key takeaway here is that planned returned visits seem to indicate preference for a place. These correlations, although a bit stronger, are consistent with the correlations between ESM reported visit frequency and place ratings explained above.

We conclude that visit frequency is a modest indicator of preference for bars and cafes but not for restaurants and stores. We will explore how combining visit frequency with other factors can boost these correlation coefficients later in Section 0 by reducing "noise" in the data.

---

[3] The correlations were run on five answer choices instead of six. As we were only interested in judging visit frequency, "This is my first time" was removed, leaving the ordinal scale: "less than once a year" to "more once a week" as shown in Fig. 4.

5.2   Travel Effort and Explicit User Ratings

Our second hypothesis is that the amount of effort one must expend to get to a place reflects a corresponding interest in that place. We explore this in two ways. First, we examine our participants' responses regarding travel time on the "My Places" paper questionnaire and, second, we compare travel time to the explicit ratings as indicated by our participants via ESM.

My Places Questionnaire. In addition to approximate visit frequencies, participants were also asked to list "typical travel times" to each place. We found a positive correlation between explicit place ratings and typical travel times ($\rho=0.21^{**}$) listed on the paper questionnaire. The average rating of a place with travel time marked between "1 – 5 minutes" was 3.6 versus 4.0 for places "more than 20 minutes" away (both SD=0.8, P<0.001). Broken down by category, both restaurant and store ratings resulted in a positive correlation with travel time ($\rho=0.25^{**}$ and $\rho=0.28^{**}$ respectively); bars and cafes were insignificant—see Fig. 6.

Self-Reported ESM Travel Times. In each ESM survey, we asked our participants "How long did it take you to get here?" The answer choices ranged from "0 – 5 minutes" to "Over an hour." Similar to the paper questionnaire, we found that public place ratings and reported travel time share a positive correlation ($\rho=0.11^{**}$). Broken into bar, café, restaurant and store visits, each show a positive upward correlation with travel time—see Fig. 7. However, all failed the test for significance. A correlative analysis for travel time may be ill-suited here; there are likely a set of places that people like close by as well as far away, creating "noise" in the data. Plotting a histogram of ratings split by <= 3 and > 3 for all bar, café, restaurant and store visits shows that 68.2% of the visits made within 0-5 minutes travel time are

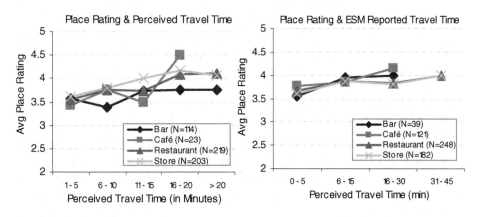

Fig. 6. "My Places" Questionnaire. A slight upward trend between place ratings and travel time is evident. Only restaurants and stores showed a positive correlation that was significant ($\rho=0.25^{**}$).

Fig. 7. ESM Data. Despite visual trend, all individual categories of place failed significance tests for correlation between place rating and travel time.

rated positively while 76.6% of the visits made over 15 minutes away are rated positively (P<0.04 for chi-square).

We conclude that travel time alone is a weak indicator of preference.

5.3 Combining Visit Frequency and Travel Effort

To examine whether visit frequency and travel time perform better together,, we split all place visits into two nominal groups: places marked "0 – 5 minutes" and "over 5 minutes." We would expect that filtering out visits to places within 0 – 5 minutes would reduce the amount of noise in the data by removing those trips highly motivated by convenience.

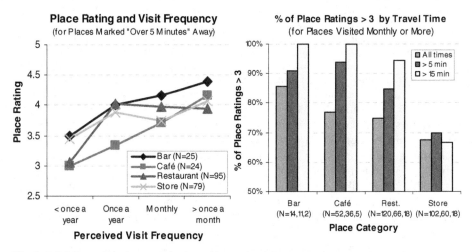

Fig. 8. ESM Data. A stronger upward trend is evident once removing "0-5 min" trips. Café ratings correlation w/visit frequency increases to $\rho=0.56^{**}$.

Fig. 9. ESM Data. The % of bars, cafes, and restaurants rated >3 increases steadily with travel time

Running correlative analysis between place ratings and visit frequency with the "over 5 minutes" group increased the previously calculated correlation $\rho=0.14^{**}$ to $\rho=0.21^{**}$ (see Fig. 8). The correlation increased significantly for cafes to $\rho=0.56^{**}$. Splitting at "0 – 15 minutes" and "over 15 minutes" instead results in even stronger correlations—$\rho=0.37^{**}$ for the "public place" general case and $\rho=0.38^{*}$ for restaurants. In addition, for places visited monthly or more, the percentage of places that are liked (>3) goes up significantly for bars, cafes, and restaurants as their travel time increases—see Fig. 10.

As a result, we conclude that combining visit frequency and travel effort result in better indicators of preference than treating each factor separately.

5.4 Exploring the Social Effect

The places we go are often affected by the presence of others. This is true both at the macro level as one must deal with commuter traffic, long lines at the supermarket, or a crowded public square during lunch as well as at the micro level as we are obliged to run errands for others, occasionally defer our tastes to those of our partners, or forgo our typical preferences for a special social event. We were interested in studying the more micro social effects to try and determine their impact on place ratings.

Of our 16 participants, 10 were single and 6 were involved in steady romantic relationships. Most of our participants lived with others (Median=1 housemate, SD=1.14) though three of our participants lived alone. A majority of the 862 public place visits logged by our participants were with others (62.2%); however, different levels of social activity exist between place categories. Bars, for example, were the most "social" place—nearly 90% of those visits were with a group of one or more. In contrast, café visits were split nearly 50/50 as participants would often pick up coffee on their route to work in the morning or, conversely, with co-workers during afternoon break. If there is a significant difference in place ratings when a participant is alone versus when they are with others, this may make it more difficult to infer a person's place preference based on their visit behavior as it is difficult to automatically sense when people are with others (though perhaps [15, 19] is a start).

Each ESM survey administered for a public place included the question "How many people are you with?" We used participant responses to this question to divide visits into two categories: those that occurred while alone and those that occurred while with others. We found no significant difference in mean ratings for public places as an aggregate variable when alone versus with others. When broken down by category, only restaurants had a significant difference. This was surprising; we expected a much larger disparity. However, the correlation between visit frequency and explicit rating did change slightly when a participant was with others versus when they were alone ($\rho=0.14**$ vs. $\rho=0.22**$). Similar results were found for travel time and place rating. In the general case, it does not appear that the presence of others serves as a strong confounding variable.

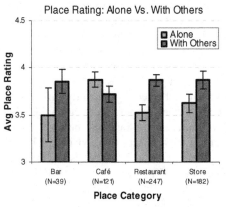

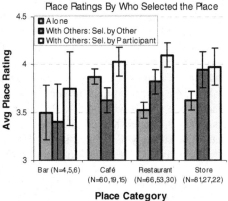

Fig. 10. ESM Data. Bars, restaurants and stores visited with others were rated higher than if alone. However, only restaurants pass significance tests.

Fig. 11. ESM Data. Exploring how the selection of place changes ratings.

To explore social effects in more detail, we asked follow-up 5-point Likert-scale questions after the participant indicated that they were with others. We explore two of these follow-up questions here: "I would not have gone here if it wasn't for the group" and "Someone in the group besides me selected this place." The responses were broken up into three categories: "Disagree," "Undecided," and "Agree." Average place ratings were then compared for the "Disagree" and "Agree" groups using t-tests for equality of means. For the first question, "I would not have gone here if it wasn't for the group," participants agreed 51.6% of the time. We would expect a place rating to be higher when the participant disagreed—meaning that they would go to that place regardless of the group. Our results concur with these expectations. Places were rated higher if the participant disagreed, but only slightly (4.0 versus 3.7, SD=0.9, 0.9** t-test). For the second question, "Someone in the group besides me selected this place," participants felt as though they selected the place a minority of the time (46.4%). We would expect a higher place rating when the participant themselves selected the place. A statistically significant increase was found, from 3.8 to 4.1 (SD=0.9, 0.8* t-test)—see Fig. 11.

We conclude that the presence of others in itself does not significantly change the explicit place ratings. It is the decision process that matters—that is, who selected the place, but even then the difference in rating is minimal.

6 Discussion

Based on our findings, we believe that creating a place-based preference inferencer is possible but not straightforward. Visit frequency and travel time treated separately were positively correlated with place ratings in our data. However, the magnitude of these correlations were far below our expectations ($\rho=0.14**$ and $\rho=0.11**$ respectively). Pairing these implicit factors together lead to better results. For example, places visited more than once a month and over five minutes away were rated significantly higher on average than places in general. This suggests that combinations of implicit factors will likely be the best indicator of preference. However, it's still unclear whether these correlation coefficients are strong enough to generalize a rule. A real application could also use the hybrid approach by combining both implicit and explicit ratings to correct and augment the inferred preferences.

We were surprised that, in general, places were not rated significantly differently when alone versus with others. However, the trend does suggest that when with others, a place is rated higher—particularly for restaurants and bars. We believe this is due to the strongly associated social component of those places (e.g., visiting a bar is a social activity). The question of alone versus others was found to be less significant than the question of who actually selected the place. When in a group, participants tended to rate a place higher if they themselves selected it rather than someone else in the group. Automatically detecting such nuances is probably not realistic. An opportunity for future research is whether such an effect is detrimental to actually determining preference.

We believe that a real system will likely need to control for noise in the data. The following describes a brief case study of restaurants to demonstrate how simple data filters can be applied to increase correlations.

6.1 A Case Study: Restaurants

This section offers insight into how multiple factors can be combined to increase the correlation between visit frequency and explicit place ratings. We believe that designers of location-aware applications could make certain adjustments for each place type based on expectations of travel behavior and a few basic intuitions. We will explore restaurants as an example.

As noted in Section 0, visit frequency and restaurant ratings failed the significance test for rank correlation. Given our suspicion that convenience would be a confounding variable in detecting place preference relationships, our first insight was to split restaurants into two groups, fast food and non-fast food. As a result of this split, the non-fast food group resulted in a slight, but statistically significant correlation between visit frequency and rating (ρ=0.24**). If we split the non-fast food group further into two groups based on travel time "0 – 15 minutes" and "over 15 minutes" the correlation coefficient increases to ρ=0.52 for the "over 15 minutes" group. So, simply by filtering restaurant visit behavior by fast food and distance, our correlation coefficient increases from ρ=0.14 (not significant) to ρ=0.52**. Similar steps could be taken with other place types to improve the correlations between visit behaviors and explicit place rating.

If we divide our data further along social lines, we see a very high correlation (ρ=0.84**) between visit frequency and place rating when our participants were alone, the restaurant was non-fast food and over 5 minutes away—see Fig. 12. This last analysis should be taken with caution due to the relatively small sample size.

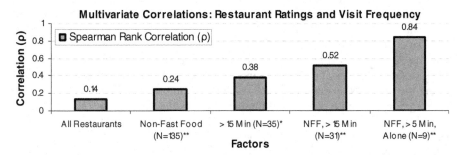

Fig. 12. Using intuitive splits in the data, correlation coefficients can be increased for specific place types. Here, splitting data across fast food and travel time result in an increase correlation between visit frequency and place rating for restaurants. Bars with stars are statistically significant. NFF=non-fast food.

7 Related Work

The study of human spatial and temporal behavior in the environment is a subset of human geography [9], which intersects with research in tourism, urban and transportation planning, and the study of travel behavior. Low-level research of individual travel patterns has historically been rare in these fields as past techniques such as paper diaries or direct observation were costly and required high personnel resources

[17, 18]. Quite recently, however, advances in location-sensing technology have begun to dramatically change the methodology employed in these areas [17, 18]. Schönfelder, for example, recently looked at the relationship between routines and variety seeking with respect to the characteristics of location choice in daily travel by studying GPS data streams. He found that location choice is strongly routinized (e.g. the top four "leisure" locations received 40-50% of all visits). Our study also found a high level of repeat visits (e.g., 40% of restaurant visits and 80% of café visits). Other researchers in this area have studied the spatial distribution of places that individuals come into contact with in their daily living [10]. Called "activity spaces," their size and structure depends on three factors: the individual's location of home (and duration of residence), their regular activities (e.g. work, school, working out at the gym) and the travel between and around these "place anchors." This has practical implications for customizing algorithms per individual based on their activity space—e.g. variety of places visited, typical travel time, etc.

The use of implicit features or "implicit interest indicators" [6] to infer preference is also an active research area, though to our knowledge we are the first to actively study it with respect to real world behaviors like visit patterns. One of the original systems, called GroupLens [13], studied the correlation between time spent reading an article and explicit user ratings. Mainstream commercial systems such as Last.fm, Amazon.com, and TiVo have successfully employed implicit interest indicators to make recommendations, improve the user experience through personalization and build stronger online community. Moving from the virtual to the real world, Chen [5] proposes a context-aware collaborative filtering system for the ubicomp environment to recommend activities based on what others have done in similar contexts (e.g., based on location, weather, group proximity, etc.) but did not investigate how well those context features could perform.

Brown et al. [3] describe a mobile system for sharing data amongst tourists. A collaborative filtering algorithm was used to recommend photos, web pages, and places to visit based on historical data (including GPS traces). Their focus was not on investigating the relationship between place preferences and visit behaviors but rather on exploring how a visit to a city could be shared across the Internet and, crucially, how physical and online visitors to an area could interact (e.g., an online visitor could "piggyback" on the experiences of a physical visitor). In this way, they did not evaluate the effectiveness of their recommender algorithm nor provide details on its function. However, they do show how the physical and virtual space can rather seamlessly converge in a location-aware mobile application as well as the potential of mobile recommenders for filtering and suggesting content.

Others have explored the detectability of place [11, 14, 22]. Zhou et al., for example, looked at the relationship between place discovery and importance and found that those places judged meaningful by the subject were much easier to detect. In our work, we found that 43.7% of all logged place visits were to home and work—places reasonably inferred to be "meaningful" by our participants. Given the large number of these visits compared with other locations, we would expect place discovery algorithms to do much better discovering them (particularly when tied to temporal patterns, e.g., work during day, home during night). Participants in our study were also asked about the meaningfulness of places via ESM surveys. We found evidence that an explicit judgment of preference for a place is correlated positively with an explicit judgment of meaningfulness ($\rho=0.47^{**}$). Future place discovery systems may want to investigate both.

8 Future Work

This paper presents the first investigation of implicit interest indicators derived from visit behaviors and explicit place ratings gathered in the field. As such, there are many opportunities for future work. First, this work only considered two implicit features of place visit behavior, visit frequency and travel time. We believe that other factors such as dwell time (e.g., how long one spends in a place), temporal patterns (e.g., weekday vs. weekend, lunch vs. dinner, season) and mode of transportation may also contribute to inferring preference. In addition, we did not look at negative interest indicators—those features that would correlate negatively with rating. For example, a restaurant that is across the street from work but never visited might indicate negative interest. As our GSM-based sensors did not provide us with high-resolution location data, an interesting follow-up study could correlate actual location data streams (e.g., assisted GPS) with explicit place ratings. A longitudinal study (i.e., 6-12 months) could be used to further investigate visit behaviors as well as to look at long-term temporal patterns and their relationship to preference. Future work could also explore the potential of generalizing place preferences to general interests. For example, frequent visits to a snowboarding shop may indicate a general interest in downhill snow sports.

We are currently in the process of collaborating with the Department of Statistics at the University of Washington regarding a more sophisticated analysis of this data. A linear mixed effects model has been created to take into account the variation between subjects and within subjects. Preliminary results from this analysis are in accordance with the findings above. For example, a slight, but statistically significant correlation was found between visit frequency and preference. When visit frequency and travel time were combined, the positive correlation strengthens.

9 Conclusion

This paper examines to what degree do automatically detectable visit behaviors indicate preference for a place. We explored two implicit factors in particular, visit frequency and travel time. We found that both features have a slight, but statistically significant positive correlation with explicit place ratings. When combined, however, they become better measures of preference. In general, we found that splitting public place visits into sub-categories based on place type resulted in significantly higher correlations, particularly for bars, cafes, and restaurants. This finding implies that studying travel routines at an aggregate level split simply between "private" and "public" is only somewhat effective at determining preference—there may be too many differing motivations for visiting a place at this resolution. Further, we found that the presence of others itself is not a confounding variable. Finally, our four-week study is the first to explore the use of context-triggered ESM on mobile phones. We believe that the Me Tool is a promising technology for studying human behavior on mobile platforms as well as for validating ubicomp technology in the field.

References

1. Ali, K. and van Stam, W. (2004), TiVo: Making Show Recommendations Using a Distributed Collaborative Filtering Architecture. In *Proc of KDD'04*. Aug 22-25. Seattle, WA.
2. Barrett, L.F. and Barrett, D.J. (2001), An Introduction to Computerized Experience Sampling in Psychology. *Social Science Computer Review.*, V. 19, No. 2, S01, pp. 175-185.
3. Brown B., M. Chalmers, M. Bell, I. et al. (2005) Sharing the square: collaborative leisure in the city streets. Proceedings of ECSCW 2005, Paris, France. pp. 427-429.
4. Carter, S., Mankoff, J. (2005). When Participants do the Capturing: The Role of Media in Diary Studies. In *Proc of CHI'05*. April 2- 7, Portland, OR.
5. Chen, A. (2005), Context-Aware Collaborative Filtering System: Predicting the User's Preferences in the Ubiquitous Computing Environment. In *Proc of CHI '05*.
6. Claypool, M., Phong, L., Waseda, M., Brown, D. (2001), Implicit Interest Indicators. In *Proceedings of Intelligent User Interfaces '01*, Jan 14-17 '01, Santa Fe, NM, pp 33-40.
7. Consolvo, S., Walker, M. (2003). Using the Experience Sampling Method to Evaluate Ubicomp Applications. *IEEE Pervasive: The Human Experience*, pp. 24-31.
8. Consolvo, S., Smith, I., Matthews, T., et al. (2005). Location Disclosure to Social Relations: Why, When & What People Want to Share. In *Proc of CHI'05*. Portland, OR.
9. Fellman, J.D., Getis, A & Getis, J (1999) Human Geography, WCB/McGraw-Hill, Boston.
10. Golledge, R.G. & Stimson, R.J. (1997) Spatial Behavior, Guilford Press, New York.
11. Hightower, J., Consolvo, S., LaMarca, A., Smith. I., and Hughes, J. (2005) Learning and Recognizing the Places We Go. *In Proc. Ubicomp 2005*. Tokyo, Japan.
12. Intille, S. S., Rondoni, J., Kukla, C., Anacona, I., and Bao, L. (2003), A context-aware experience sampling tool. In *Proc of CHI '03* NY, NY: ACM Press, 2003, pp. 972-973.
13. Konstan, J., Miller, B., Maltz, D., Herlocker, J., et al. (1997), GroupLens: Applying Collaborative Filtering to Usenet News. *Communications of the ACM*, 40(3):77-87, 1997.
14. LaMarca A., Chawathe Y., Consolvo S., et al. (2005). Place Lab: Device Positioning Using Radio Beacons in the Wild. *In Proc Pervasive'05*, Munich, Germany.
15. Paulos, E., Goodman, E. (2004) The Familiar Stranger: Anxiety, Comfort, and Play in Public Places. In *Proc of CHI'04*. April 24-29, Vienna, Austria
16. Smith, I., Chen, M., Varshavsky, A., Sohn, T., and Tang, K. (2005), Algorithms for Detecting Motion of a GSM Mobile Phone. In *ECSCW 2005*, Workshop Paper.
17. Schönfelder, S. (2003), Between routines and variety seeking: The characteristics of locational choice in daily travel. In *10th Intl Conf on Travel Behaviour*, Lucerne, Aug. '03.
18. Shoval, N., Isaacson, M. (2006). Tracking Tourists in the Digital Age. In *The Annals of Tourism Research*.
19. Terry, M., Mynatt, E. D., et al. (2002) Social Net: Using Patterns of Physical Proximity Over Time to Infer Shared Interests. In *Proc. CHI 2002*, Short Paper. pp., 816-817.
20. Wheeler, L., & Reis, H. (1991), "Self-recording of Everyday Life Events: Origins, Types, and Uses," *Journal of Personality*, 59, pp. 339-354.
21. Zhang, D. and Adipat, B (2005). Challenges, methodologies, and issues in the usability testing of mobile applications. *International Journal of HCI*. v18.3, pp. 293-308.
22. Zhou, C., Ludford, P., Frankowski, D., and Terveen, L. (2005) An Experiment in Discovering Personally Meaningful Places from Location Data. *In Proc. CHI 2005*.

Lo-Fi Matchmaking: A Study of Social Pairing for Backpackers

Jeff Axup, Stephen Viller, Ian MacColl, and Roslyn Cooper

Information Environments Program, University of Queensland, Australia
and
Australasian Cooperative Research Centre for Interaction Design (ACID)
axup@userdesign.com, viller@acm.org, ianm@itee.uq.edu.au,
roslyn.cooper@uq.edu.au

Abstract. It is technically feasible for mobile social software such as pairing or 'matchmaking' systems to introduce people to others and assist information exchange. However, little is known about the social structure of many mobile communities or why they would want such pairing systems. While engaged in other work determining requirements for a mobile travel assistant we saw a potentially useful application for a pairing system to facilitate the exchange of travel information between backpackers. To explore this area, we designed two studies involving usage of a low-fidelity role prototype of a social pairing system for backpackers. Backpackers rated the utility of different pairing types, and provided feedback on the social implications of being paired based on travel histories. Practical usage of the social network pairing activity and the implications of broader societal usage are discussed.

1   Introduction

The field of ubiquitous computing has typically progressed via the development of technologies that are ultimately evaluated through deployment in the field or in some more constrained situation. A user-centered perspective on design is often maintained through ethnographic studies of particular settings in order to inform the design of a technology to be introduced there, or in order to evaluate a new Ubicomp technology in situ once it has been deployed. In this paper, we propose low fidelity prototyping as an alternative, design-centered approach to bringing a people-centered focus to the design of Ubicomp systems The use of low fidelity prototypes is common in interaction design and participatory design where they allow design exploration for hardware and software interfaces [1-3], and have been found to be as effective as higher fidelity prototypes for identifying usability problems [4]. One of the chief advantages, other than cost, of a 'lo-fi' approach is that participants are more likely to engage creatively with the concepts underpinning the prototypes, rather than be distracted by the particulars of an interface.

In this paper we explore the concept of a pairing or matching system to support social contact and exchange of travel information between backpackers. Social software is being developed elsewhere that links people together as they move based on their pre-existing relationships, personal attributes, proximity and other variables.

P. Dourish and A. Friday (Eds.): Ubicomp 2006, LNCS 4206, pp. 351 – 368, 2006.

Many of these systems focus on traditional markets such as dating, and many do not have sufficient users to realize the full impact of proximity-based services. Clearly there is also an opportunity to explore different design concepts and other types of social interaction that could benefit from pairing services.

We are currently engaged in a number of projects developing requirements for a mobile travel assistant for backpackers[1]. This work has taken the form of contextual interviews, field trips, workshops, diary and postcard studies, and qualitative analysis of online travel diaries or travel blogs [5, 6]. In the course of this research we increasingly felt that social software functionality is likely to be useful to backpackers as they travel. As a result we thought it opportune to investigate how explicitly pairing backpackers based on travel itineraries would work in practice. For example, if one backpacker is traveling north and another is traveling south, then they might benefit from meeting in the middle and exchanging information about where they had just been. Several studies were conducted investigating mobile information sharing and social network formation amongst backpackers engaged in a typical tourist activity [7]. A social network pairing activity was run in conjunction with these studies and is the subject of this paper.

The paper is structured as follows. The literature review discusses backpackers, social networks and mobile social software. Then the social network pairing activity is presented, followed by study results, and resulting user and product requirements. Practical considerations and potential pitfalls for using this method and other user-centered approaches in this domain are presented, and potential solutions offered.

2 Literature Review

Research in ubiquitous computing and computer supported cooperative work (CSCW) is increasingly focusing on non-work activities, leisure, and play. Tourism is a key area in this with the development of tourist guides [8] and studies of tourist behavior [9] prominent in the literature. Elsewhere, studies of people on the move are also focusing on how people seek to remain in contact with the digital world when their physical surroundings are frequently changing [10]. Brown and Chalmers explore the design of mobile technology to support tourists' activities [9]. They focus on independent travelers, noting that backpackers form the majority of this population. They use ethnographic fieldwork to identify problems faced by tourists including: what to do (and how to do it), when to do it, way-finding, and sharing activities with others at home. They describe how tourists solve these problems—sharing visits with others, using guidebooks and maps, and engaging in pre- and post-visit activities— and they outline opportunities for mobile technologies to enhance these solutions. Among other things, they propose tourists use technology to share information on attractions and destinations, emphasizing the importance of interaction between tourists for both information-sharing and social purposes. In this paper we explore the value of and means for facilitating this interaction.

We have chosen to focus on backpackers who also represent a lifestyle that is constantly on the move, whilst they interact with people and locations that are not.

---

[1] http://www.itee.uq.edu.au/~backpack

One aspect of backpacker culture that is of particular interest to us is the way that their social networks of friends, fellow travelers, etc. are managed whilst they travel, and how they make use of available technologies to support this. Backpackers increasingly have access to mobile phones and other everyday examples of Ubicomp technologies which they use for these and other purposes during their travels.

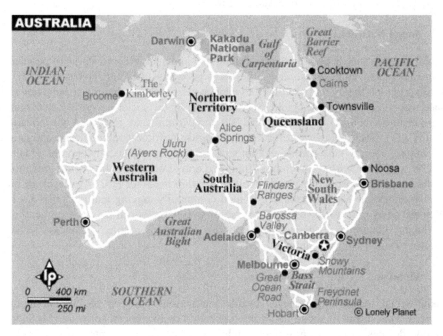

Fig. 1. Map of Australia showing major locations (from www.lonelyplanet.com). The backpackers in this study were mainly traveling between Cairns in the north of Queensland and Melbourne and Sydney in the south east.

2.1 Backpackers

Backpackers have been described as "travelers who exhibit a preference for budget accommodation; an emphasis on meeting other people (locals and travelers); an independently organized and flexible travel schedule; longer rather than brief holidays; and an emphasis on informal and participatory recreation activities." [11] Backpackers in Australia primarily flow in a bi-directional North-South current along the East coast where most of the tourist attractions and major conurbations are located [11]. (Fig. 1 presents a map of Australia showing major locations and attractions). It is easy to forget the huge scale involved when talking about travel in Australia: the island continent occupies a landmass which is comparable to the size of mainland USA, or continental Europe. Modes of transport used by backpackers include buses, car-pooling, combined coach and accommodation packages, and with the advent of discount air fares flights as well. Our own studies with backpackers in Brisbane have led to a more detailed understanding of their culture and activities which is presented elsewhere [6, 7]. Backpackers often take spontaneous side-trips away from this well-beaten track, or pause to rest with others in popular locations. They often wish to organize group activities, but have few options available for this kind of coordination. They regularly explore unfamiliar locations quickly, but have only basic resources to inform them about those places. Despite the desired collaboration, only limited communication is possible between them as they move. Many opportunities exist for the design of mobile devices to assist their travel.

2.2 Social Networks

Social network theory uses methods of depicting and analyzing networks of people to help understand and communicate the ways in which they are connected [12]. It draws on graph theory and sociology to understand group or community behavior and make social connections tangible. Software support for social network visualization (e.g. Netdraw, Pajek) has made analysis more rapid and increased visualization quality [13]. Social network research has recently become popular for investigating the impact of new networking technologies on community social relations [14]. In CSCW, social network research has often used e-mail or other online communications to discover relationships between people and group behavior [15, 16]. Research into tourist guides has also incorporated limited community tagging features [17]. Recent Web 2.0 developments have led to a surge of web-based social network applications, producing hundreds of networking services addressing dating, business, leisure, photos, pets and other common interests[2].

2.3 MoSoSo

Some social networking services enable interactions between people via mobile devices. This subset of social networking is called mobile social software (MoSoSo). Mobile devices operate in a diverse number of social environments and the services that can be created are still being explored by designers, users and the media [18]. A hoax in 2004 claimed that there was an active community of people using Bluetooth short-range wireless technology to arrange sexual encounters, and dubbed the phenomenon "toothing" (or bluetoothing)[3]. Regardless of the truth of the original report, Bluetooth does often permit exchange of messages between strangers. The Nokia Sensor[4] project has standardized many of the original intentions of toothing into an official product and protocol. Many products (e.g. Cellphedia, Crunkie, DodgeBall, Playtxt) are offering similar messaging services based around location, social network data and personal profiles. Some research has explored pairing systems for use in low-mobility situations such as conferences [19]. This study utilized high-fidelity prototypes and consequently received user feedback about interface issues and usability problems.

When they are introduced, mobile social software products merge with rich pre-existing social systems. Thus it is beneficial to use knowledge of the social reality to guide new technology designs. However, social network researchers indicate that moving and dynamic social networks are not yet well understood, and modelling them

---

[2] See listing at: http://socialsoftware.weblogsinc.com/entry/9817137581524458/

[3] http://www.wired.com/news/culture/0,1284,62687,00.html

[4] http://www.nokia.com/sensor/

remains a challenge [20]. Not only is understanding them difficult, but the practical utility, market perception, and social ramifications of using these systems remain unknown.

Given the lack of research into how MoSoSo should be structured and the availability of a highly mobile community with practical needs, we decided to explore the requirements for a social pairing system for use by backpackers.

3 Method

We conducted two workshops to investigate requirements for a social pairing system for backpackers. Both studies were similar in structure, but are presented separately to allow comparison and show iterative modifications to the research method. Rather than leap forward to developing functioning prototypes which run on existing technology platforms, with the associated problems already mentioned in terms of the type of feedback generated, we adopted an extremely low fidelity approach. Our approach to prototyping is akin to a 'contextual' walkthrough (c.f. contextual interviews [21]) or a *role prototype* [22]. One of our primary aims in planning these workshops was to take the concept of a design workshop out 'in the wild' and closer to the context where backpacker activities would normally take place—on the move, visiting somewhere new. One of the most common tourist destinations for people arriving in Brisbane is to go to the Lone Pine Koala Sanctuary[5]. We decided to arrange for our workshops to happen over a day from the hostel, to the koala sanctuary and back again, using a popular package trip on a river boat to travel between the locations. On each study, the backpacker participants were accompanied on their field trip by two or three researchers, who observed and recorded the study with video and/or still photographs, engaged in conversation with the participants at various points, and occasionally acted as sources of local information.

3.1 Social Pairing – Study 1

A large backpacker hostel in the centre of Brisbane assisted with recruiting volunteers for our studies. Out of the group of six backpackers recruited for the first study (see Fig. 2), four were female and two male. BP1 (Backpacker 1) and BP2 were married, from Ireland and Holland, and in their mid-thirties. They were traveling for 7 weeks with a moderate budget. BP3 & BP6 were friends from England in their late teens. They had recently spent a month in New Zealand and were spending several weeks in Australia on money borrowed from parents and credit cards. BP4 & BP5 were acquaintances from the day before. BP4 was from Holland and in her late teens, working while traveling, and on a very tight budget. BP5 was from Korea and in his early twenties and was traveling on a reasonable amount of savings.

While recruiting participants, hostel staff distributed a questionnaire concerning the participants' recent travel history, future travel plans and any travel-related questions they had. No attempt was made to restrict the participant demographic, other than to ensure they were traveling and not long-term residents. Backpackers typically stay

---

[5] http://www.koala.net/

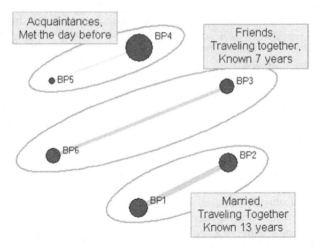

Fig. 2. Travel history of participants in Study 1. Line thickness indicates duration traveling with partners (line length has no meaning). Circle size indicates travel experience this trip for an individual, and the orange ellipses indicate the established groupings prior to the study.

two to three nights in Brisbane and most had arrived just prior to the study. Participants were compensated by receiving a combined boat cruise and trip to a local animal park for free.

Following their field trip to the animal park, the social pairing activity was conducted back at the hostel. It was intended to explore the utility of externally imposed social pairing systems for travel assistance. While the backpackers were away on the field trip, another researcher had paired backpackers in the group who had an affinity based on planned/visited locations. For example, BP5 had recently been surfing in Byron Bay and BP6 intended to travel there. Index cards were created

Fig. 3. Participants rating and discussing topics

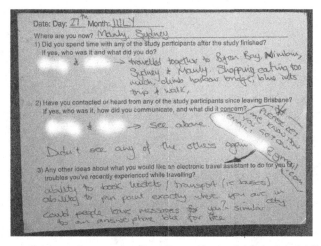

Fig. 4. A postcard returned a week after the study explaining longitudinal social tie development

for each participant, showing up to three people they should talk to and the compatible information they should talk about. Each backpacker was asked to spend roughly 5 minutes talking to each of the people they had been paired with (see Fig. 3). Following the pairing conversations, a researcher led a discussion of the utility of the automatic pairings between group members. This was followed by a short discussion about trust of travel information and possible uses for an information sharing system between backpackers.

To additionally explore how social networks change over time, backpackers were given a sealed envelope before leaving. It was requested that they wait a week to open it, and then complete and return the enclosed postcard (see Fig. 4). The postcard asked if group members took part in activities with each other after the study and whether they contacted each other after leaving the city.

3.2 Social Pairing – Study 2

It was intended that six backpackers be involved in the second study; however due to a miscommunication with the hostel recruiters, and participant characteristics, the study ended up with seven participants (see Fig. 5). Three English females (BP11, BP12 & BP13; all under 21 years) were old friends from school and were traveling together for a few weeks. Two of them (BP11 & BP12) had been traveling for 5 weeks, whereas the third (BP13) had been traveling for longer than the other two (5.5 months) and had just joined up with them. They had known each other for 8 years, were traveling south, and BP13 had recently been living in New Zealand. A Swedish male and female couple (BP9 & BP10; both in their late twenties) had known each other for 5 years. They had been traveling together for 8 weeks and were also traveling south. Two English males (BP7 & BP8; both under 21 years) had been friends for 11 years and were traveling north to Cairns. They had been traveling for 3 weeks.

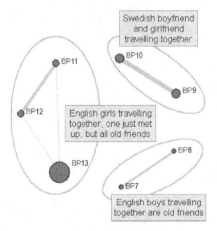

Fig. 5. Travel history of participants in Study 2. Line thickness indicates duration traveling with partners (line length has no meaning). Circle size indicates travel experience this trip for an individual, and the orange ellipses indicate the established groupings prior to the study.

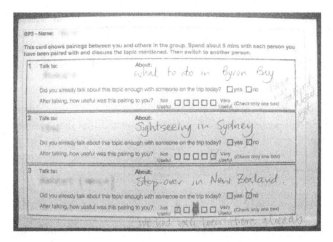

Fig. 6. A pairing card given to a backpacker and completed during discussions with other backpackers they were paired with

The structure of the second iteration of the study was similar to the first. Pre-arranged cards were distributed to backpackers with suggested discussion items. However, due to difficulties tracking the results of individual conversations in the first study, a simple rating system was introduced for each conversation (see Fig. 6). Participants were asked to rate how useful the conversation was on a scale of 1-5 (not useful—very useful) after completing it. They also recorded whether they had already discussed it earlier in the day. This allowed checking to see if conversations were not useful because they had already occurred, and allowed a measure of how commonly affinity information naturally arises during shared tourist activities. The [Future⇔Future] pairings (cases where both backpackers intended to travel to the same location, see also Table 1), were de-emphasized in this iteration to focus on other types of pairings which backpackers thought were more useful.

As with the first study, a group discussion followed the exercise. Backpackers used their cards to remember the conversations they had and explained their ratings along with other discussion topics. One of the observers was Marketing Manager for Lonely Planet and additional discussion topics concerning guidebooks were introduced at his request. Following the study, the backpackers were again given postcards to complete and return a week later.

4   Results of Artificially Pairing Backpackers

Both studies had similar findings which located pairing difficulties and indicated patterns of successful matching. Changes in the second study allowed the opinions of backpackers to be tracked more effectively and focused on the types of pairing participants found useful. The results are shown consecutively below.

4.1 Social Pairing – Study 1

While working with the data from the participant questionnaires it became apparent that at least three types of pairings are potentially of interest in the context of travel conversations amongst backpackers (see Table 1):

Table 1. Potential social pairings between backpackers

A.	Past⇔Past	Reliving old memories between people who have both been there or done that.
B.	Past⇨Future	Someone who has been to an intended destination giving advice to someone going there or doing that.
C.	Future⇔Future	People who both have plans to go to the same place or do the same thing there.

Pairing A [Past⇔Past] appears to be largely an entertainment association. Backpackers were able to discuss memorable things that had happened to them, but it didn't really help them in their future travels. Pair 1 (BP1 & BP2) asked about the past experiences of Pair 3 (BP3 & BP6) to determine if they had made the right decision in not visiting a location along a route. They confirmed that the location was not desirable and felt better about the decision. It is likely that sharing mutual past experiences increases initial bonding before longer-term relationships form. This could result in lasting friendships or finding compatible people to travel with.

Pairing B [Past⇨Future] is both very useful and potentially problematic because it is not reciprocal. Backpackers commonly offered advice based on past experience for the benefit of others. However, there is the potential for abuse if a well traveled person is used extensively for advice without receiving anything in return. There is, however, potential for indirect reciprocity [23], where a backpacker would receive advice from different backpackers to those they were giving it to. Experienced backpackers would still give more than they take, but they would get some information in return. It is possible that experienced travelers may not mind being used because they gain friendships and social status in return for the gift. This is likely to produce a fleeting form of social capital [24].

Pairing C [Future⇔⇒Future] does not involve much information exchange, but it does potentially enable backpackers to rendezvous in the future. Backpackers frequently have flexible schedules that allow them to join up with others if they wish. However, backpackers often already know if others they meet are going to the same place and may only have an interest in meeting up with certain people. This may not be as useful a pairing for these users.

Pairings between participants that were identified by researchers are shown in the chart (see Fig. 7). Some participants are hubs in the network (in particular see BP3 and BP5). BP3 is not giving any information away, but has a large potential to share many experiences with others in the future. BP5 has experience others want and is giving information away, but not receiving any in return.

The lack of functional prototypes did not hinder participants' ability to discuss or use the automated pairing system. The use of simple paper cards and the activity itself allowed participants to focus on the underlying reasons they were using the system, instead of the interface to the system. Backpackers were somewhat negative about the utility of the pairings that we arranged for them. However, both observing pairing discussions and backpacker responses have provided information about better ways to arrange pairings and where problems with the current prototype exist. Potential issues are as follows.

Some backpackers did not complete the whole questionnaire, resulting in less data. Also, some were traveling together, resulting in the same information for each person. The [Past⇔⇒Past] pairing worked well because backpackers could compare travel experiences and relive interesting moments. This was entertaining, but perhaps not very helpful for future travel. Few [Past⇒Future] pairings were possible, partially for the above reasons and because the group was small. The few pairings of this type were reported to be successful. For instance BP4 had spent time surfing in small towns around Byron Bay (200km south of Brisbane) and BP6 wanted to go surfing in the area and appreciated the advice (see Fig. 7). The [Future⇔⇒Future] pairings were the most common type arranged, and were a failure. Backpackers reported not having anything to talk about. We think this type of information could be useful for backpackers, but possibly not just after arriving in a city or while sitting in a research study. It also might be useful for occasional use when a backpacker meets someone particularly interesting or for people looking for travel partners. We concluded that the study should be run again, with increased detail of travel history, less emphasis on the [Future⇔⇒Future] pairings and more detailed tracking of opinions about individual pairings.

Three of the six postcards given to backpackers at the end of the study (see Fig. 4) were returned between 7-20 days following the study. BP5 had gone to a club with BP4 following the study and contacted her by mobile phone to see how she was doing after leaving the city. BP3 & BP1 hadn't contacted anyone other than their traveling partners. All three respondents were at different cities in Australia at the time of writing. Both of the traveling partners only submitted one card per pair and one single traveler (BP4) did not submit her card.

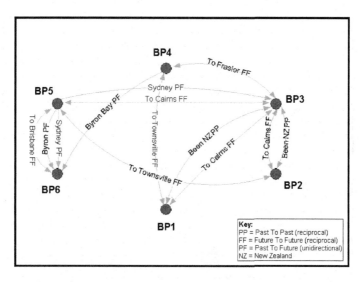

Fig. 7. Pairings selected for backpackers in study 1. Ties between traveling partners were not used in the study or shown above.

4.2 Social Pairing – Study 2

Analysis of the questionnaire data for the seven backpackers resulted in identification of 21 social pairings by researchers. Of these, 18 were actually discussed by participants due to time limitations or preference; 6 out of 18 of the pairings had already been discussed during the prior field trip, while the remaining 12 had not yet been discussed.

Both the previously discussed topics and the new topics had a wide range of ratings from useful to not useful. This indicates that being able to talk more about a topic that had already been discussed didn't necessarily change its perceived utility. BP7 & BP8 were the only backpackers traveling south to north, while the other five were headed south. This resulted in a bottleneck for pairing, with BP7 & BP8 as primary hubs in the network (see Fig. 8), since they had most of the travel information that others would want. Information flow in social networks is analogous to whirlpools and waterspouts in the ocean. BP12 & BP13 are primarily information-pools; they take in a lot of advice but give little back, which is a classic social dilemma [25, 26]. BP7 & BP8 are information-spouts; they receive some information, but push a lot of information out to other group members (see Fig. 8).

The twelve [Past⇨Future] pairings rated by participants received high usefulness ratings; they had an average of 3.75 and four of these were considered "highly useful". Three [Future⇦⇨Future] pairings were selected by experimenters and these again received very poor usefulness ratings from backpackers with an average of 1.3. The one [Past⇦⇨Past] pairing was rated as 1 (not-useful) and had a note scrawled next to it, "we had both been there already."

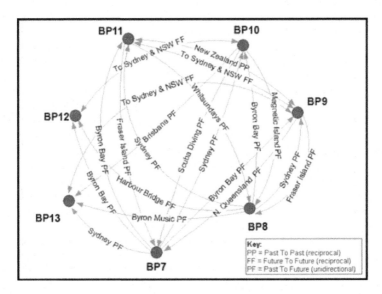

Fig. 8. Pairings selected for backpackers in study 2. Ties between traveling partners are not shown and not all ties made were discussed by backpackers.

Six bi-directional (reciprocal) [Past⇨Future] pairings were made (Fig. 8: BP7⇦⇨BP9, BP7⇦⇨BP11, BP7⇦⇨BP10, BP8⇦⇨BP9, BP8⇦⇨BP10, BP8⇦⇨BP11). This occurs where the uni-directional pairing happens both ways for different topics. For example, BP9 knew about tours on Fraser Island where BP8 was going, and BP8 knew about sightseeing in Sydney where BP9 was going. Of the 21 total pairings, 12 of the [Past⇨Future] pairings resulted in forming reciprocal relationships.

The construction of the social pairings was more complex to orchestrate than expected. It took two researchers who had been provided with a pairing process and supporting worksheets roughly two hours to complete. The seven backpackers had each listed five past locations, five future locations and five travel-related questions that they would like answers for. For the case of [Past⇨Future] pairings, any backpacker's five past locations could be associated with the other 60 future locations and travel questions of the other backpackers. This resulted in a theoretical upper bound of 300 bi-directional connections. There would be even more possibilities if directionality was considered, but an experimenter could easily spot connections in either direction. Practically speaking, many pairings were not close to being compatible, but still needed to be considered by the researcher. The pairing process first identified all past locations and allowed rapid scanning of matches from the future or question sections.

An added complication is that pairings contain cultural, geographical and semantic information. For instance, a researcher looking to make a pairing for a backpacker interested in scuba diving, would need to know which Australian coastal locations were near good dive sites. An additional variable was direction of travel. Backpackers who travel north on the east coast of Australia are more likely to have compatible pairings with those traveling south, and vice-versa. Furthermore the researcher had to be aware of who was traveling together. Everyone in a traveling group would already know similar information and there would be little utility in discussing the topic. Consequently promoting pairing with strangers would be likely to increase diversity of corresponding travel information and expected utility of pairings.

Locating enough [Past⇨Future] and [Past⇦⇨Past] pairings was difficult and three [Future⇦⇨Future] pairings had to be chosen. In some cases, there were no clear connections to be made and researchers had to guess at possible connections. Strategies for this included making connections at a higher level (e.g. a state instead of a city) or guessing at possible locations for activities (e.g. dive sites). One researcher commented that doing the pairing felt like an algorithmic process and that it should be automated.

Five of the seven postcards distributed at the end of the study were returned between 3-8 days following the activity. BP9 had briefly chatted with BP7 & BP8 in the kitchen of the hostel following the study and with her traveling partner BP10. BP10 indicated the same discussions on his card. BP12 had talked with her traveling partners BP11 & BP13. Coincidentally they had traveled the same route (Brisbane-Byron Bay-Sydney) as BP9 & BP10, but a week apart. BP11 & BP13s' cards confirmed BP12's account of the travels. The traveling pair BP7 & BP8 did not return their cards and were traveling in the opposite direction.

5 Discussion

Running the social pairing activities led us to draw a number of conclusions about where they are useful, how they should be structured, and what implications our experiences had for user-centered design practice for ubiquitous computing. These topics are discussed in the following sections.

5.1 Using Contextual Workshops to Simulate Pairing Systems

The pairing exercise is intended to probe the utility of automated matchmaking systems for mobile communities. We had the option of creating a high-fidelity prototype of a pairing system on mobile phones and testing it with backpackers. However, it would have introduced variables such as specific technologies used, ergonomics, and technical and usability problems. This would have changed the focus of backpacker input towards technology issues, which was not the focus of the investigation. Instead we used very low-fidelity methods.

Participants in the studies both used and enacted the low-fidelity prototype of the pairing system. In this case, the "system" was not computerized, nor did it have a physical interface. It was a conceptual design, which had certain rules for interaction with it (e.g. ask a travel question of your partner), and certain results as a consequence of using it (e.g. the advice received). When viewed from the perspective of ubiquitous computing, this is an interface-agnostic simulation. Participants spoke and used pieces of paper to interact with the system, which are so familiar as to be practically invisible for them. This meant that the users naturally focused on the underlying social issues and the utility of the information they were getting, instead of interface interaction issues. This is useful when attempting to determine what a product should do, before determining how it should be constructed to enable users to reach those ends.

A related issue is where participants (probable future users) can most effectively be involved during a development process. In this study participants did not design a physical interface; furthermore, we would not request that they do so, as they are not trained designers. However, the participants were able to provide excellent qualitative feedback on the design that they used. For example, during the discussion period following the pairings, one backpacker remarked that using the pairing system *"felt too formal"*. We as designers had built a logical pairing system with a fairly rigid structure without much thought as to what it would feel like to use. A backpacker trying a very simple version of our design had already found a serious design flaw relating to the social context in which it is used. In a similar fashion, all of the backpackers' participation was most useful for understanding user requirements for the system and evaluating design concepts. Thus, the backpackers beneficially participated in the larger design process (or development process) from within their own area of expertise: travel.

While designing the workshops, we were attempting to find a way to make them as in-situ as possible. The hostel was a typical environment, but we also wanted participants to be in a mobile context while they were considering the implications of mobility. It appeared impractical to actually hold the workshop while moving and the hostel represented a short pause in a larger pattern of regular movement. The activity itself also engaged backpackers in considering past and future movement and discussing this with others. Thus the design of the activity is perhaps not as contextually accurate as it could be, but is probably sufficient for the situation.

Most of the pairings made in the activity were based around location. This was primarily because of the correlation between past locations and travel knowledge, but it was also the primary focus of our questionnaires. Other types of pairings are possible. For instance, activity pairings may be as important as location pairings: if two backpackers both like scuba diving, then they may wish to compare notes on diving sites regardless of whether they have been, or intend to go to the same place.

Our studies did not address realistic conversational openings, or "breaking the ice" as it is more colloquially called. We simply requested that backpackers talk about a certain topic with others they had previously met. This is not representative of strangers needing an excuse to talk to someone without direction by an authority figure. It also ignored issues such as gender and cultural background which in many cases would clearly have an impact on one's choice to approach a stranger. It remains an area for future research to explore what pairings will actually convince people to chat with strangers, and in what circumstances. Physically locating paired strangers in different social environments is also an area of interest.

5.2 Toying with Travelers and Social Responsibility

The possible implications of wide-spread MoSoSo usage are significant. For example, consider a backpacker who gets recommendations on people (who to talk with, date, trust), places (which locations are safe, fun, cheap), things (which products are cheap, quality, effective) and broader social issues (political news, history, culture). This information is provided by a trusted system, which represents a trusted social network of other travelers in a similar social situation. What impact will design changes to such a tourist recommendation system have on the behavior of its users?

A recommendation promoting travel to a remote Asian country might corrupt native traditions when large numbers of tourists arrive. An effective service promoting dating might result in an increase in rates of sexually transmitted diseases. These high-tech quandaries are similar to those which guidebook manufacturers have long faced in a low-tech medium. However, if these systems are designed in a centralized manner, then someone (most likely a business) will be playing god with their users. Moral and ethical behavior will be greatly influenced by the system designers who will restrict and encourage those activities they wish to; this is already commonplace in web-based communities [27]. Thus, a challenge for those using user-centered methods to develop MoSoSo systems is to find a way for the community to set their own standards for the technologies they have helped design.

A key design challenge for backpacker MoSoSo relates to the need for a reputation system. Social capital forms very quickly amongst backpackers and often dissipates just as rapidly [6]. Hostels gain reputations since they stay in the same location and retain the same name; however backpackers move on and rarely gain reputations among others for long. This means that good reputations disappear just as rapidly as bad ones and give little incentive for good behavior (as defined by the larger community). It seems likely that a non-location-based reputation system would increase community awareness of model members. Resnick has discussed similar issues concerning impersonal sociotechnical capital [28].

The results section of Study 2 above also notes that there are design issues relating to distributing the responsibility of information exchange and dealing with information-pools. The backpacker social network has highly dynamic physical movement and information content.

To pose a hypothetical example: a backpacker traveling North⇨South might meet a group traveling South⇨North and be overwhelmed with questions, thus forming an information-spout in the network. One member of the South⇨North group may have only been traveling for a week and have very little to offer, forming an information-pool. However, this novice backpacker rapidly gains experience and information from others. In another week they may form an information-spout for other novice travelers. This results in the development of a social norm amongst a community with transitory membership. If a novice backpacker gets help from others when they are starting, they are likely to perpetuate this action to others. It is probable that this information-sharing system is already self-regulating in the offline medium; however it isn't clear how to transfer the natural physical and social boundaries regulating information flow into the online community space.

5.3 Summary of Requirements for Social Pairing Systems

The following requirements resulted from data analysis and experiences running the studies. It is likely that some of the requirements are peculiar to the needs of backpackers and may not be able to be generalized. However, it is likely that some requirements relate to common social norms and universal physical limitations which may be applicable in other situations. They have been developed from a small sample, but have been replicated and represent typical backpackers.

- Use pairings to help people achieve something. People are using the system for specific purposes. Theoretically accurate ties are not as important as those rated highly by those using the system.
- Support reciprocal [Past⇨Future] pairings where possible.
- Do not overload hubs. Some people will naturally have more useful information than others due to travel routes and duration of travel. Hubs will not be able to support all feasible ties to them unless automation is used.
- People may enjoy reliving mutual past travel experiences [Past⇦⇨Past]. Support users finding others whom they have shared past experiences with.
- Experienced travelers necessarily have more and better quality information to distribute. Social capital and reputation are currently gained for very short periods (a few days or less). Support methods of establishing lasting reputation between strangers so that appreciation expressed by one backpacker is not lost on others.
- [Future⇦⇨Future] pairings are not as useful to support unless users specifically desire to meet in the future.
- Include personality and behavioral traits in determining pairings. Informational affinities may not be rated as high by participants if they come from a person who doesn't value similar things or travel similarly.
- Expect short relationships most of the time. Returned postcards showed that few backpackers maintained contact with group members outside of their established traveling groups for long.

6 Conclusion

In this paper we have proposed that studies of in-situ use of low fidelity prototypes can be used to explore potential future applications of ubicomp technology. What we are suggesting is a methodological, rather than technological, intervention in order to learn more about the problem space and possible solutions from the perspective of the people who are target users of the technology.

Our subject matter, backpackers, present interesting challenges for many current methods due to their nomadic, transient existence in any particular location, combined with well established but dynamic social networks which may be influenced by direction of travel, chance encounters, shared interests, etc. Many backpackers already use mobile phones and other ubiquitous computing technologies in order to keep in touch with their extended social network as well as to plan their itinerary. Whilst everyday use of mobile phones may not often be the focus of ubicomp research, as a technology they are clearly ubiquitous in modern society, even amongst so-called budget travelers, and therefore warrant further study.

Finally, we believe that the approach we have taken here offers an alternative to complement the existing orthodoxy of conducting ubicomp research through technology development and ethnographic study. We have followed a design orientation to the problem, adapting participatory and user-centered techniques to the particular situation, probing and exploring potential solutions at the conceptual level in collaboration with people from the target audience for the technology. We believe this approach offers insights into what applications or future technologies could be developed for a particular setting or social group, which can build upon ethnographic studies, and provide vital clues for technology development at a very early stage in the design process.

In future work, we are interested in running larger social pairing activities with higher-fidelity prototypes, exploring social pairing in mobile environments, developing community reputation systems, and finding ways to break the ice for travelers.

Acknowledgments. We would like to thank to Dan Nicolau, Dave Nichols, Jason Shugg, Stacey Lamb of Palace Backpackers, Lone-Pine Koala Sanctuary and Mirimar Cruises for helping plan and conduct the studies, and to the volunteer backpackers for their participation. Use of the free NetDraw application was greatly appreciated (http://www.analytictech.com/downloadnd.htm). Also thanks to many other researchers who have provided discussion on the topics raised in this paper: Nicola J. Bidwell, Jacob Burr, Jared Donovan, Marcus Foth, and to Genevieve Bell for patient shepherding over the final hurdle. This research was partly conducted within the Australasian CRC for Interaction Design, which is established and supported under the Australian Government's Cooperative Research Centres Programme.

References

1. Ehn, P., Kyng, M.: Cardboard computers: mocking-it-up or hands-on the future. In: Greenbaum, J., Kyng, M. (eds.): *Design at Work: Cooperative Design of Computer Systems.* Lawrence Erlbaum, Hillsdale, NJ (1991) 169-195
2. Hanington, B.M.: Interface in form: paper and product prototyping for feedback and fun. *interactions* **13** (2006) 28-30
3. Rettig, M.: Prototyping for tiny fingers. *Communications of the ACM* **37** (1994) 21-27
4. Walker, M., Takayama, L., Landay, J.A.: High-fidelity or low-fidelity, paper or computer medium? : *Proceedings of HFES2002* (2002) 661-665
5. Axup, J., Viller, S.: Formative research methods for the extremely mobile: Supporting community interaction amongst backpackers. In: *Workshop on Appropriate Methods for Design in Complex and Sensitive Settings.* Dept. of Information Systems, Univ. of Melbourne, Australia (2005)
6. Axup, J., Viller, S.: Augmenting travel gossip: design for mobile communities. *Proceedings of OzCHI2005.* Computer-Human Interaction Special Interest Group (CHISIG) of Australia, Canberra, Australia (2005) 1-4
7. Axup, J., Viller, S.: *Conceptualizing New Mobile Devices By Observing Gossip and Social Network Formation Amongst the Extremely Mobile - Mobile Information Sharing 1 (MIS-1)*, ITEE Technical Report 459, University of Queensland, Brisbane, Australia (2005)
8. Cheverst, K., Davies, N., Mitchell, K., Friday, A., Efstratiou, C.: Developing a context-aware electronic tourist guide: some issues and experiences. *Proceedings of CHI'2000.* ACM Press, New York (2000) 17-24
9. Brown, B., Chalmers, M.: Tourism and mobile technology. In: Kuutti, K., Karsten, E.H. (eds.): *Proc. ECSCW 2003.* Kluwer Academic Press, Helsinki, Finland (2003) 335-355
10. Chang, M.: Play is hard work: Taking retirement on the road. *About, with & for: Advancing the practice of user-centered design research.* Institute of Design, Illinois Institute of Technology, Chicago, IL (2005)

11. Loker-Murphy, L., Pearce, P.L.: Young budget travelers: Backpackers in Australia. *Annals of Tourism Research* **22** (1995) 819-843
12. Wasserman, S., Faust, K.: *Social network analysis : methods and applications*. Cambridge University Press, Cambridge ; New York (1994)
13. Freeman, L.C.: Visualizing Social Networks. *Journal of Social Structure*, Vol. 1 (2000)
14. Hampton, K.N.: Living the Wired Life in the Wired Suburb: Netville, Glocalization and Civil Society. (2001)
15. Tyler, J.R., Wilkinson, D.M., Huberman, B.A.: Email as spectroscopy: automated discovery of community structure within organizations. *Communities and technologies*. Kluwer, B.V. (2003) 81-96
16. Carter, S., Mankoff, J., Goddi, P.: Building Connections among Loosely Coupled Groups: Hebb's Rule at Work. *Journal of CSCW*, Vol. 13. Kluwer Academic Publishers (2004) 305-327
17. Cheverst, K., Mitchell, K., Davies, N., Smith, G.: Exploiting context to support social awareness and social navigation. *SIGGROUP Bull.* **21** (2000) 43-48
18. Rheingold, H.: *Smart mobs: the next social revolution*. Perseus Pub, Cambridge, MA (2002)
19. Eagle, N., Pentland, A.: Social serendipity: mobilizing social software. *Pervasive Computing, IEEE* **4** (2005) 28-34
20. Gloor, P.A., Laubacher, R., Zhao, Y., Dynes, S.: Temporal Visualization and Analysis of Social Networks. (2004)
21. Beyer, H., Holtzblatt, K.: *Contextual Design: Defining Customer-Centered Systems*. Morgan Kaufmann, San Francisco, CA (1998)
22. Houde, S., Hill, C.: What Do Prototypes Prototype? In: Helander, M., Landauer, T., Prabhu, P. (eds.): *Handbook of Human-Computer Interaction* Elsevier Science B. V, Amsterdam, Holland (1997)
23. Mohtashemi, M., Mui, L.: Evolution of indirect reciprocity by social information: the role of trust and reputation in evolution of altruism. *Journal of Theoretical Biology*, Vol. 223. Elsevier (2003) 523-531
24. Wellman, B.: Computer Networks As Social Networks. *Science*, Vol. 293 (2001)
25. Axelrod, R.: *The complexity of cooperation : agent-based models of competition and collaboration*. Princeton University Press, Princeton, N.J. (1997)
26. Kollock, P.: Social Dilemmas: The Anatomy of Cooperation. *Annual Review Sociology* (1998) 183-214
27. Duff, A.S.: Social Engineering in the Information Age. *The Information Society*, Vol. 21 (2005) 67-71
28. Resnick, P.: Impersonal Sociotechnical Capital, ICTs, and Collective Action Among Strangers. *Transforming Enterprise* (2004)

Experiences from Real-World Deployment of Context-Aware Technologies in a Hospital Environment

Jakob E. Bardram, Thomas R. Hansen, Martin Mogensen, and Mads Soegaard

Centre for Pervasive Healthcare
Department of Computer Science, University of Aarhus
Aabogade 34, 8200 Aarhus N, Denmark
{bardram, thomasr, spider, madss}@daimi.au.dk

Abstract. Context-aware computing is a central concept in ubiquitous computing and many suggestions for context-aware technologies and applications have
been proposed. There is, however, little evidence on how these concepts and technologies play out in a real-world setting. In this paper we describe and discuss our
experiences from an ongoing deployment of a suite of context-aware technologies
and applications in a hospital environment, including a context-awareness infrastructure, a location tracking system, and two context-aware applications running
on interactive wall displays and mobile phones. Based on an analysis of the use
of these systems, we observe that many of the ideas behind context-aware computing are valid, and that the context-aware applications are useful for clinicians
in their work. By reflecting on the nature of the designed context-aware technologies, we present a model which states that the triggering of context-awareness
actions depend upon the accuracy of the sensed context information, the degree
to which you know which action to perform in a given situation, and the consequence of performing the action.

1 Introduction

The idea of *context-aware computing* was one of the early concepts introduced in some
of the pioneering work on ubiquitous computing research [23,16] and has been subject to extensive research since. 'Context' refers to the physical and social situation in
which computational devices are embedded. The goal of context-aware computing is
to acquire and utilize information about this context, to display relevant information,
or to provide services that are appropriate to this particular setting. For example, a cell
phone will always vibrate and never ring in a concert hall, if it somehow has knowledge about its current location and the activity going on (i.e. the concert) [19]. The core
premise of context-aware computing is to create more usable technology which adapt
to the user's context. Over the last decade, numerous context-aware applications have
been reported for use in e.g. hospitals [3,20], shops [1], museums [14,21], tourism [2,9],
zoological fieldwork [22], on universities [8,15], conferences [11,10], and offices [24].
Furthermore, numerous infrastructures and application frameworks have been proposed
to enable the easy development of context-aware applications, each having different
technological approaches and application focuses.

To our knowledge, however, only few of the proposed context-aware technologies
and applications have been deployed in a real use-setting outside the computer science

P. Dourish and A. Friday (Eds.): Ubicomp 2006, LNCS 4206, pp. 369–386, 2006.

lab for a longer period of time. Thus, despite the massive amount of research done within context-aware computing, little evidence actually exists of its utility. On a practical/empirical level, we therefore have little knowledge about how users perceive context-aware technologies, how they use them, what kind of automatic adaptation they find beneficial, and to what degree they find sensing technology privacy invading – just to name a few questions. Moreover, on a conceptual/theoretical level, we have a limited number of 'real-world' arguments for judging the scientific validity inherent to the notion of 'context-aware computing'. Recently, arguments have been aired that the current notion of 'context' and hence 'context-aware computing' builds on a positivist philosophical stance, where 'context' is stable, delineable, and sense able information separated from human activity. The argument is that the notion of 'context' – as referring to the 'usage context' for a specific person using some technology – cannot be separated from the human activity. 'Context' then becomes firmly tied to 'meaning' – i.e. that context cannot be seen (and much less sensed) as an objective entity in the world, but only exists in connection with subjective meaning in an activity [13]. But what does this argument implies when designing for real-world use of context-aware computing (or its like)?

In this paper we report from an ongoing deployment of a suite of context-awareness technologies and applications in an operating ward at a medium-size European hospital. The deployed systems consist of an indoor location tracking system; a context-awareness infrastructure for acquiring, managing, and distributing context information; a context-aware operation scheduling application; and a context-aware mobile phone application helping users to keep a social awareness on colleagues and the activities inside operating rooms. At the time of writing, the system has been deployed and used extensively for three month; is used by approximate 30 users each day; is handling thousands of context events for each user or place inside the hospital; and runs with very limited support from the developers. The system has been completely adopted by the users, and after one month of usage the context-aware scheduling application replaced the former paper-based operating schedules. Section 3 describe the deployed systems and section 4 describes the deployment at the operating ward.

The paper aims at two main contributions. First, we present 'real-world' evidence on the use of context-aware technologies in a non-trivial, hectic, life-critical work environment. Our findings indicate that the notion of context-aware computing is indeed useful for users and can be achieved on a large scale. Our study indicates that displaying (and distributing) context information was the most useful part of the gathered context information. Furthermore, the study revealed that privacy concerns regarding the display of personal context information (e.g. location, status, and activity) were fully acceptable and that the benefit outweighed privacy concerns. This contribution is based not only on the technology we built and deployed, but it is also based on several discussions with the users about a number of context-aware 'features' which we designed, but did not implement. It is interesting to note that most of the context information in the applications was used passively; i.e. primarily for displaying context information or displaying relevant clinical information in a specific usage context. Despite numerous attempts to build more active context-aware features into the systems, the clinicians rejected them all.

This leads to our second, more conceptual, contribution which is a thorough discussion of how to use context information. When is it beneficial to display context information? When would we like to find contextual 'relevant' material? When could we automatically execute an action or a service? We propose a simple general model for answering these questions, which takes into consideration issues like the accuracy of the sensed context information, the degree to which the system knows what the users wants in a specific 'context', and the consequences of displaying information or execution an action.

2   Related Work

Suggestions for context-aware infrastructures and applications are numerous in Pervasive and Ubiquitous Computing research, including suggestions for the use of context-aware technologies in a hospital setting. For example, the 'Intelligent Hospital' application [18] uses location awareness to enable video communication to follow clinicians around inside a hospital, and others have been adding context-awareness to the use of mobile technologies in hospitals [17,20] Far less research has, however, been done in the study of deployed context-aware infrastructures and applications – to date, most 'ubiquitous' computing experiments have been restricted to specific laboratories and buildings, or to specific research groups [6]. Consequently, little evidence exists on real-world usage of context-aware technologies. There are, however, a few notable exceptions.

Pascoe et al. [22] describe the design and deployment of a context-aware PDA application made to support ecologists in field studies in Africa. In the prototype, context awareness enables the mobile device to provide assistance based on knowledge of its environment in terms of time and position (using GPS). The paper gives few details on the lessons learned from the deployment, but in relation to this paper it is interesting to note that context information is only used passively, since the whole purpose of the application was to minimize user attention.

Active Campus, on the other hand is an example of a much larger deployment of location-based services [15]. The Active Campus Explorer application supports context-aware activities, such as instant messaging and location-aware maps annotated with dynamic hyperlinked information. Active Campus Explorer has been deployed for a year (2002–3) at the UC San Diego campus, encompassing hundreds of users. The study showed that students are willing to share location with buddies and even non-buddies for location-aware social computing; they are more likely to message each other when they are in close proximity to one another; and that just one percent of the users changed their default privacy settings to hide location from buddies.

The GUIDE system provides city visitors with a hand-held context-aware tourist guide. The system has been successfully deployed in a tourist setting and used over a period of four weeks by 60 people [9]. The major conclusions from the study were that visitors found the location-aware navigation and information retrieval mechanisms both useful and reassuring; and that the majority of visitors appreciated that the system were aware of their location to within a certain area.

In general, it is interesting to note that all of these deployed context-aware applications only use context information in a 'passive' way, i.e. for tagging [22], for displaying context information, like location [15], or for displaying relevant information in a specific context [9]. There are no examples reported on the use of 'active' use of context information for automatically triggering actions or services. A second interesting observation is, that all of these systems use *location* as the only context information – hence, there seem to be no evidence for the usefulness of other kinds of context information in real world deployment.

3   Context-Awareness Technology in Hospitals

The context-aware technologies discussed in this paper address the inherent problem of coordination and collaboration between clinicians working distributed within a hospital. The systems use context awareness to facilitate information about the location, status, and current activity of clinicians and different core locations, including operating rooms. The research is rooted in a wide range of field studies (see e.g. [5]) and a user-centered design process involving a wide range of clinicians in the design, development, and evaluation of the systems. The deployed system consists of the following four main components, which are illustrated in figure 1:

- A *context-awareness infrastructure* responsible for the acquisition, distribution, and modeling of context-awareness information.
- A *location tracking system* responsible for tracking clinicians' and patients' location.
- The *AwareMedia* application which is a context-aware scheduling and awareness system running on large interactive displays at the operating ward and inside the operating rooms.
- The *AwarePhone* application running on mobile phones which facilitates social awareness amongst clinicians.

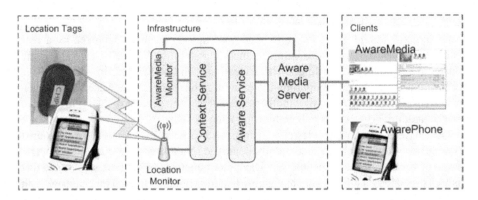

Fig. 1. The four main components deployed at the hospital: (i) location tracking (left); (ii) context-awareness infrastructure (middle); (iii) AwareMedia (top right); and (iv) AwarePhone (bottom right)

3.1 Context-Awareness Infrastructure

The context-awareness infrastructure is based on the Java Context-Awareness Framework (JCAF) [4]. In the deployment we are using JCAF for modeling entities and context information at the surgical ward, and for creating different types of context monitors. The context model includes entities like 'Personnel', 'Patient', and 'Operating Room'. The main context information modeled is 'location', 'status', and 'scheduled activity'; where status is self-reported status like 'operating' or 'ward round', and activity maps to the operation which the person is scheduled for.

The infrastructure is implemented following a three-tier architecture. First, a set of monitors are responsible for gathering location information from the location tracking system and activity information from the operating schedules. Second, the monitor layer forwards the information to a Context Service which is responsible for managing, storing and grouping context information. Third, an awareness layer (the Aware Service) is responsible for distributing relevant context information to clients subscribing to different kinds of context information. The awareness layer forwards information to the AwareMedia and AwarePhone applications used by the clinicians.

3.2 Location Tracking

In a large hospital, much time and effort is spent in order to locate staff, patients, and equipment. Hence, a hospital is a good candidate for indoor location-tracking technologies. In the hospital deployment we use a Bluetooth-based location-tracking system. Using Bluetooth has the benefits of being cheap and widely available in e.g. telephones, PDAs, and tablet PCs. A slightly modified USB stick deployed in stationary PCs is used to track mobile devices. The modification implies that its range is reduced to below 10 meters. The drawback of using Bluetooth is its low precision. But in most cases we were able to reveal which room the person was in, especially in operating rooms since such rooms have rather solid walls with X-ray shielding. Mobile phones are used to track surgeons, and clinicians. Persons who are not using a mobile phone are tracked via a small Bluetooth tag. Tags can be assigned and re-assigned to users via AwareMedia. Figure 2 (left) shows a technician with a Bluetooth tag.

3.3 AwareMedia

AwareMedia is a context-aware application running on larger interactive displays. It is designed to support coordination, the scheduling of surgeries, and social awareness amongst clinicians involved in surgeries. In AwareMedia, all clinicians are represented by an icon revealing a picture of the user, the user's location, self-reported status, and scheduled activity; all information coming from the context-awareness model in the infrastructure. Furthermore, AwareMedia has separate regions on the display representing different 'important' places in the hospital, like the different operating rooms, and the coordination central. The user's icon is located inside this region based on the location reported by the location system.

Similar to clinicians, each operating room is treated as a context entity and hence posses the context cues of 'location', 'status', and 'activity'. The location of an

Fig. 2. The deployed systems: AwareMedia deployed in the coordination center (left), an operating technician wearing a location tag (right, top), and the AwarePhone (right, bottom) showing a list of users, their location, status, and scheduled operation

operating room is clearly never used, but the status of the operation inside the rooms and the activity, i.e. the ongoing operation are important context information which are displayed at the AwareMedia and AwarePhone. Examples of status for an operations are 'patient arrived', 'patient anaesthetized', 'operation started', and 'patient left the operating room'. A message chat allows an unobtrusive and easy communication channel amongst clinicians involved in an operation. For example, the nurses at the patient ward can ask the surgeon to come to the ward to attend a patient, or the operating ward can broadcast a message about the last surgery being cancelled. A schedule on the interface shows planned and acute surgeries and changes made through an easy to use drag and drop interface are distributed to all clients. Figure 2 (left) shows AwareMedia deployed in the coordinating central.

3.4   AwarePhone

The AwarePhone system [5] runs on Symbian smart phones and provides an overview of the people at work, and the activity in each operating room. An interactive phone book displays each user's location, current activity (i.e. scheduled operation), and self-reported status. This implies that the user can see where specific colleagues are located, what they are scheduled to be doing, and what their status is – see figure 2. Similarly, the location, status, and activity (i.e. operation) is shown for each operating room. The phone book can be used to place a call to one of the listed persons. Or if the person appears to be occupied, a prioritized message can be sent. Because users and operating rooms are treated equally, messages can be received from, and sent to operating rooms, and calls can be made to the operating rooms directly, if needed.

4   Deployment

The AwareMedia and AwarePhone applications presented above have been designed, refined, and evaluated through a user-centered design process involving a wide range of clinicians. The next step in this line of research was to deploy these context-aware technologies in a real-world setting, more specifically at a surgical ward and some of the associated wards. The first parts of system were taken to the hospital in November 2005 and by early January 2006 the whole system went into daily use. At the time of writing it is still in use.

4.1   The Deployment Setting

The operating ward employs around 130 clinicians in total and there are 30-50 clinicians present during a normal workday. Some of the associated departments are the patient wards where the patients are hospitalized before and after a larger surgery, and the recovery ward where a patient is closely monitored while waking up from anesthesia.

The operating ward has in total ten operating rooms. AwareMedia was deployed in three of these rooms and in the coordination central. The coordination central is the coordination hub for all operations unfolding during the day and from this central, the head nurse closely follows the unfolding of the daily schedule, makes adjustments to the operation schedules, and ensures a smooth flow of work by coordinating all the involved clinicians. Inside the operating room, AwareMedia is deployed on an interactive display and in the coordination central, AwareMedia is deployed on two large interactive displays.

Ten Bluetooth tags are available at the entrance to the operating ward, and fifteen Nokia phones have been handed out to some of key surgeons and anesthetists, the head nurse, the coordinating nurse, and to some of the operation technicians. Figure 3 shows where the different departments are situated at the hospital and an overview of the surgery ward. The dots indicate deployed AwareMedia clients and the shaded areas shows the coverage of location tracking system.

4.2   Research Methods

The deployment of the system is motivated by the desire to investigate long term use and adaptation of advanced pervasive technology in a real world setting. Does ubiquitous computing technology provide a valuable tool or is the problem of managing complex technologies far greater than the benefits? How do you get an organization to incorporate advanced technology into its daily work practices? Are you able to improve the way work is done with context awareness technologies? To answer some of these questions we have used a wide variety of research approaches. Before, during, and after the deployment of the system we spent days performing field studies with the focus of analyzing work, identifying problems, and registering changes in work practices. Questionnaires have been used both before and after the deployment and a number of interviews have been performed with key personnel after the deployment, in order to identify the impact of the system on their daily work practices. The interviews were conducted in the clinicians' native language, but quotes from some of the interviews have been translated into English for this publication. In addition, the infrastructure

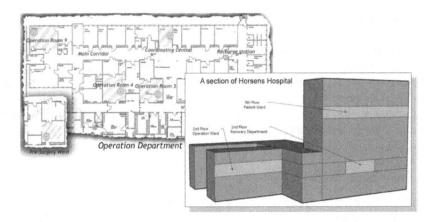

Fig. 3. The figure shows the parts of the hospital in which we installed the system and provide a detailed view of the operating ward

logs all interaction from AwareMedia clients and AwarePhones. The log files records 50.000+ entries a month; we have done 10 man-days of participant observations; and additional 12 semi-structured interviews with different types of clinicians working at the operating wards.

5   Context-Awareness in Use

The study has generated a large amount of data and we have hence chosen to discuss how context-awareness cues were used at the department in general, how context-awareness was used from the AwarePhones, and how privacy issues were conceived in the hospital since these issues illustrates central parts of the system usage. The discussion will be based on both logged data about the use of the system as well as data from the interviews.

5.1   Using Context-Awareness Cues

The top part of Figure 4 shows the number of discrete context-awareness events flowing through the system as a function of time and the bottom part of Figure 4 presents the number of unique persons, which has triggered events in the system as a function of time. Separate graphs for status, location, and scheduled activity events are shown in both figures.

There are several things that can be seen from the graphs:

– Usage is stable throughout the period. Overall we see the same usage pattern for all weeks in figure 4 except for the week following Feb. 11th, which is the general 'winter vacation' week. Since the number of 'activity' events correlates to the number of operations scheduled using AwareMedia, the patterns in Figure 4 imply first of all that the system has been used for all operations since it was deployed

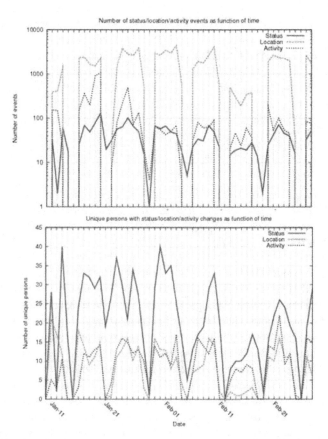

Fig. 4. Top: Number of unique context events pr. day. Bottom: Number of unique persons triggering a context event.

in January. It can be noted that interest is not fading as the technology moves from being 'new and exciting' to being adopted into the work at the department.

– On an average day we see 2,500 location events, 80 activity events, and 70 status events. Even though there is 30 times more location events, location events only relates to 12-13 unique 'entities' (i.e. persons), whereas about 25 unique 'entities' (i.e. persons and ORs) are using the status events. The fact that the 'status' context cue is the most frequently used, in terms of involved number of persons, is due to the system automatically setting the status in some situations, e.g. a person is put to be 'at work' when first located, but also manual reported status contributed to the overall number. Another reason for the relatively low number of unique persons located is the fact that we did not have enough Bluetooth chips and mobile devices to equip everyone with a chip; hence only selected persons are being tracked by the system in the pilot study.

These findings were consistent with our qualitative observations and interviews. Most significantly, during the second week of deployment, the head nurse told us that they had abandoned the use of their previous paper-based scheduling and awareness system and was entirely using AwareMedia, AwarePhone, and their underlying infrastructure. As she put it: *"[now] when we don't have the paper schedule anymore then we are feeling even more dependent on the system."* In our qualitative analysis, we were trying to understand how clinicians were using the context-awareness technology in general, and more specifically how the three context information about location, status, and activity was used by different types of clinicians in their work.

During our deployment we have found substantial evidence that providing location information to clinicians is indeed quite useful in a hospital setting. As stated by the head nurse:

> *It is something I can clearly use as the one responsible for the coordination. Especially the knowledge about where the replacements are located, because if they are carrying a chip or a phone it is really easy to get an overview about which rooms they are located in.*

As a manager responsible for the daily coordination of work at the operation ward, this nurse has started to use location information quite extensively. As she says, she has a much better overview of where people are especially the replacements and operating technicians who roam around and help out in different operating rooms when needed. Hence, if one room is calling for help, the head nurse would need to locate a replacement immediately, a task which clearly is significantly simplified by using location tracking technology. Looking at it from the operating technicians' point of view, they did not mind being tracked:

> *It is a way of using each other instead of saying "Where are you? What are you doing?" you can look at the display, [...] and then I don't have to let go of something to answer a phone and tell them where I am. You can really quickly get this information from the display and get an overview.*

Here the technician explains that because people calling him can see where he is, he would get less disruptive calls. There are actually two steps in his line of reasoning: first people can see where he is and then they can deduce the typical kind of activity he might be engaged in. For example, if the technician is inside an operating room, he is probably busy helping them. In this sense, location cues are not merely informative with respect to locating people, but are also an important source of information with respect to their current activity.

Revealing status information as a type of context information was also used in the coordination of work. When asking an operating nurse about the use of the status bar in the operating theatre and the relation to people at the recovery ward she says:

> *Interviewer: What about the collaboration or coordination with P5 [the patient ward] and the recovering department? Do you contact them from the ward or what happens? Operating nurse: No, it has more been the other way around. They have used us and asked questions such as how far we are with the surgery if we haven't moved the arrow [updated status], so they are using it.*

Hence, the operating staff inside the operating theatre – more or less to their own surprise – discovered that people outside the operating theatre and outside the department were actually relying on an updated status information in their own coordination of work. The realization of the benefit for others and the reduced number of misplaced and disruptive phone calls were some of the reasons the operating staff gave to explain why they kept the status bar up to date.

There were, however, also some challenging aspects to the use of context information. First of all, because not all persons had a personal location token, location tracking was not good enough. There was simply a too large overhead associated with picking up a tag and then going to the computer and associate this tag with a person. Furthermore, to our surprise, the doctors did not pick up on the use of the system. And finally, several complained that you had to set the status bar manually – they would prefer that it revealed some sensed real-world status, like when the patient enters the operating room, or when the cleaning is done.

5.2   AwarePhone Usage

Figure 5 shows the use of the fifteen AwarePhones and illustrates the number of distinct connection events of a phone and the number of unique phones connected to the Awareness Service during a day. Again we see a fairly stable usage pattern, except that the phones were not deployed during the first week, they were tested during the second week, and there is lower activity during the aforementioned winter vacation.

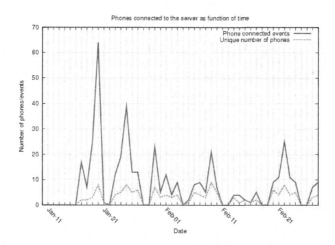

Fig. 5. The number of distinct connections from AwarePhones per day

In the original plan for deployment, the AwarePhone was targeted for the surgeons who typically roam around inside the hospital, and hence can be situated in many different places during a normal workday: the conference room, the bed ward, the operating ward, the operating room, in the recovery areas, and in their offices. Hence, mobile technology is particular well-suited for their type of work patterns and the AwarePhone could help them keep an awareness on the unfolding of work at the operating ward while roaming around. During the deployment study, however, we observed that the phones were gradually being taken over by the head nurse and by the operation techni-cians, as illustrated in the quotes above. In the deployment plan we had envisioned that technicians would carry passive location tags, which they also did in the beginning of the deployment period (figure 2). But it turned out that it was important for technicians to be able to monitor the status of the work as well, in order for them to align their own work accordingly. As one of the technicians explained:

> When I have the phone, I am updated on the program all the time. I don't need to go to the wall [referring to the screens in the coordinating central]. I can see how far the operating rooms are - if they are on the way out [if the patient is being moved out] or halfway. That, I think is really good for me when I am walking around out here - and the other way around ... when I am using the phone they also know where I am.

Here the technician explained how he was using the phone to maintain an awareness of the progress of the whole operating schedule while attending other duties inside the operating department. Moreover, what is interesting to note is that he is well aware that others can locate him, when he is using the AwarePhone – a fact that he (implicitly) see as a benefit, as illustrated in the quote from the technicians in the previous section.

5.3   Privacy in Context-Aware Technologies

In the design of the context-aware technologies, it was an open question whether clini-cians would accept that information about their location, status, and scheduled activity was sensed and broadcasted around for others to see. Most users, and especially the management of the ward, felt a need to openly discuss these aspects of the system. As the head nurse explained:

> It was important from the beginning that the people did not feel that the system was a surveillance system observing what they are doing. But it is a surveil-lance system because you track the surgeries and where people are located. It is just important to tell the people, that we watch the work processes and not the persons as such. We did a lot of considerations about the issue in the beginning, but I have not at any time heard about people feeling kept under surveillance.

In the design of the system we expected privacy issues to emerge, it was discussed during the design of the systems, and was also an issue in the beginning of the deploy-ment, as expressed by the head nurse above. However, in our observations and inter-views we have found no evidence that privacy is a major concern. The main argument is that the context information displayed (location, activity, and status) are no differ-ent from the information that all clinicians already try to obtain by other means. For example, by calling the coordinating nurse asking for status and activity reports, or by monitoring the work and whereabouts of others. Hence, in a professional setting like the hospital, displaying your current location, status, and activity did not cross any 'privacy border' in general. There are, however, some important deployment details to consider here. First, the clinicians did point out co-called 'non-tracking' zones, i.e. areas where they did not want to be tracked. Examples were the coffee room used during breaks, the staff canteen, and the toilets. Furthermore, the deployed JCAF context service did only display the current situation and it did not store context information. The 'history-less' nature of the context acquisition was understood by the clinicians and was hence seen as a guarantee that upper management would not use the data for analyzing the workflow inside the operating ward, and would not be able to see where people have been during the course of a day.

The patients overall were not involved with the use of the system since they were anaesthetized during most of their time at the operating ward. Some of the benefits for the patients were better information about when they were going to be operated and especially the relatives also appreciated to be able to get detailed information from the nurses about the progress of the surgery of their loved ones.

6   Discussion: A Model for Triggering Context-Aware Actions

At this point, we conclude that the users at the operating ward found the context-aware applications useful, and that context information was used quite extensively in the daily coordination of operations. It is, however, interesting to note that similar to other deployed context-aware applications (see section 2), we have designed applications which primarily employ a 'passive' approach to context-awareness. Despite the fact that we quite deliberately presented the clinicians with several suggestions for more 'active' context-aware features, they more or less rejected them all. Examples include automatically starting and stopping of video broadcasts from the operating rooms, based on the people present in it and their privacy preferences; and automatically changing the status of the operation based on people (including the patient) present in the room. The only example of a somewhat active use of context information is to change status for a clinician to 'at work', if they are located inside the hospital (i.e. their mobile phone can be seen by a location monitor). This feature can, however, lead to errors; it does happen that clinicians – especially surgeons – arrive at the hospital outside working shifts for doing administrative tasks or research. Hence, even though a surgeon is at the hospital, he may not actually be 'at work' with respect to the operating ward. The consequence of such a 'false positive' where a surgeon's status is set incorrectly was, however, deemed to be insignificant compared to the general benefit of the feature.

Observations like the ones above have lead us to consider a more general model, which can help designers of context-aware applications to establish which kind of actions to take based on context information. Basically, our model says that you should consider the following three factors in the design of context-aware computing systems:

– Accuracy of context information
– Confidence in the action to take
– The consequence of the action

The general design rule is that *the triggering of a context-awareness action depends upon the accuracy of the sensed context information, the degree to which you know what action to take in a certain situation, and the consequence of performing this action.*

6.1 Accuracy of Context Information

The basic premise in any context-aware system is that it makes decisions based on context information input – either raw sensed data, inferred data, or input from users. The core problem is, however, that this data will always be imperfect. A core challenge facing the development of realistic and deployable context-aware services, is therefore the ability to handle imperfect, or ambiguous, context – and yet this issue has often been ignored or glossed over [12]. It is hence important that context-awareness infrastructures which acquire, represent, and distribute raw sensed data and inferred data is also capable of handling imperfect data and can reveal some accuracy measurement for data. Data is always only valid within some level of accuracy. Given that data from a monitor is imperfect, it becomes essential to take the accuracy into account when deciding which actions to take. For example, the location system at the operating ward was accurate within rooms and could hence be used to display a user's icon in the room the person is located in on the AwareMedia interface. It could, however, not be used to automatically log in a person on a computer. Similarly, self-reported status was distributed to all clients since this was considered accurate (i.e. we trust people to set their status correctly).

6.2 Confidence in Action

Consider the situation where you are absolutely certain that the inferred 'context' is accurate, i.e. you have accurate data upon which you can base your decisions. Given this situation, is it then possible to decide with certainty which actions the user want to execute? We argue that this is only the case for very simple actions such as switching on a light or opening a door. But even these examples are not as simple as they seem. There may be exceptions to the normal rules. When I enter a room, it may be because I want to change the light bulb and it could be catastrophic if the context aware system were to switch on the electricity while I was doing that.

One may then ask the question, if it is not possible to sense that I am about to change the light bulb and adapt the actions accordingly? And yes, it may be, but it would always be possible to come up with another example which would ruin any decision making scheme. The reason, we argue, is that human context, defined in the subjective realm of the individual, is inaccessible to sensors and excessively complex. We may create a model representing context but we will never be able to get the *appropriate* information to consistently deduce the correct actions to execute.

The trouble is that we, in order to be aware of a context, must establish what that context *means*, i.e. what is the meaning of a person entering the room? This 'meaning' arises in the subjective realm of a person engaged in a meaningful activity, which makes it inaccessible to our sensors. It is not just a body passing through a doorframe. It is perhaps a person entering the room with the aim of doing maintenance, i.e. changing the light bulbs. Or a kid entering the room to play hide-and-seek, in which case an automatic light would ruin his hide-out. The person entering the room is in other words not just a human body, equipped with a visual system requiring light. In that case, our mapping would be a simple mapping from meaning (person entering) to action (turn on light). Instead, it is a person engaged in some meaningful activity, and that *meaning* exits in the subjective realm.

However, even though it is impossible to infer a person's intent from sensor data, it is still possible to make a qualified guess with some probability to what a person may need in the situation. For example, if a patient enters an operating room, there is a high probability that he or she is going to have a surgery, whereas a doctor can enter an operating room for wide variety of reasons. The point being that this difference in knowledge about what a person wants to achieve needs to be considered together with the quality of sensor data when building context awareness systems.

6.3 Consequence of Action

Independent of the accuracy of context data, and the confidence in a specific action, the actual triggering of this action still depends on the consequence of doing it. Some actions are less intrusive than others. For example, displaying the position of clinicians in AwareMedia, is far less intrusive than automatically ending anesthesia for a patient when the surgeon leaves the room, because in most cases the surgeon only leaves the room when the operation is finished. The same distinguishing goes for opening a door to the local supermarket, against opening the door to the local bank volt. In the former case it is desirable to open the door too often, whereas in the latter case the opposite is desirable.

It is therefore necessary to consider the consequences or intrusiveness of an action, when determining whether to execute a given action. The intrusiveness is tightly related to the *type of action*, but also to *the context* in which the action is executed. As we see it, there are four main types of actions:

Tagging actions focus on attaching meta-information to some data based on context information for later use. The user can then at a later point use this information to e.g. categorize captured images.
Displaying actions focus on organizing and displaying context awareness information to the user to enable decisions based on context aware information (context-mediated awareness)
Helping actions focus on preparing some actions that the computer thinks the user is going to need, but it is still the user who initialize the actions.
Executing actions focus on executing specific actions automatically without involving or asking the user in the process.

Overall the intrusiveness increase downwards in this list, but there are of course exceptions to this, which means that we also have to consider the context the action is executed in. Displaying a patient record in an operation room will seldom cause any harm, but displaying the same record in a public place can have serious privacy and legal consequences.

6.4 Using the Model

The model proposes that a successful context awareness system should execute actions based on knowledge about the accuracy of sensor data, about the confidence in the action to take, and about the consequence of performing the action. However, the model also propose that if sensor data is inaccurate, or if there is a high degree of uncertainty about which action to execute, this is not an argument for abandoning context aware-ness. Instead, the context aware system should then facilitate other types of action with less severe consequences, like tagging or displaying.

In retrospect, we would argue that in our design and deployment of context-aware technologies in the hospital, we had somewhat inaccurate sensor data, it was in some cases hard to decide what action to take based on the input, and the consequences of executing improper actions in a hospital might have been far-reaching. Therefore, we chose to let the system organize and display different views on the context aware in-formation to the users, which provided less intrusiveness than executing actions. More-over, we discovered that *juxtaposing* inaccurate and even conflicting sensor informa-tion to the user in many cases provided useful knowledge to the users. For example, a person may be scheduled for a surgery, his status is set to 'in surgery', but the loca-tion tracking system reports that he is in the outpatient clinic. This ambiguity in context would be hard to automatically deduce anything from, but the coordinating nurse would typically suspect that the operation has ended early or there might be a break in the surgery.

The main point being that there is a huge possibility for building context-awareness systems in the middle ground between automating actions and doing nothing at all, but a successful system needs to balance the action used with the sensor quality, the confidence in the action, and the action's consequences in a given context.

7   Conclusion

Based on an ongoing deployment of context-aware technologies in an operating ward we have found evidence for the usefulness of such technologies in this setting. The logs from the context-awareness infrastructure revealed that the use of these technolo-gies has been constant over a four months period. In our qualitative research, clinicians report on the benefit of having access to view context information on colleagues and op-erating rooms. The display of location, status, and current activity significantly helped them improve their coordination of work. Moreover, the study has shown that privacy concerns about revealing such context information was not a major issue.

The types of context-aware computing designed and deployed in the hospital ended up mainly displaying context information instead of performing automated action. Based on an analysis of the deployed technology, we propose a design rule which states that the design of a context-awareness actions depend upon the accuracy of the sensed context information, the degree to which you know which action to perform in a certain situation, and the consequence of performing this action. Given this model, we argue that actions should only be executed automatically in very limited and well-defined situations. Our experiences show that the mapping between context information and appropriate actions is highly challenging, both from a practical and empirical point of view, as well as from a more theoretical stance.

Acknowledgments

This research has been supported by the Competence Centre ISIS Katrinebjerg. We thank the surgical staff at Horsens Sygehus who enthusiastically participated in this project. Christian Jonikeit has implemented a substantial part of AwareMedia.

References

1. M. C. Abhaya Asthana and P. Krzyzanowski. An indoor wireless system for personalized shopping assistance. In *Proceedings of IEEE Workshop on Mobile Computing Systems and Applications*, pages 69–74. IEEE Computer Society Press, 1994.
2. G. D. Abowd, C. G. Atkeson, J. Hong, S. Long, R. Kooper, and M. Pinkerton. Cyberguide: a mobile context-aware tour guide. *Wirel. Netw.*, 3(5):421–433, 1997.
3. J. E. Bardram. Applications of ContextAware Computing in Hospital Work – Examples and Design Principles. In *Proceedings of the 2004 ACM Symposium on Applied Computing*, pages 1574–1579. ACM Press, 2004.
4. J. E. Bardram. The Java Context Awareness Framework (JCAF) – A Service Infrastructure and Programming Framework for Context-Aware Applications. In H. Gellersen, R. Want, and A. Schmidt, editors, *Proceedings of the 3rd International Conference on Pervasive Computing (Pervasive 2005)*, volume 3468 of *Lecture Notes in Computer Science*, pages 98–115, Munich, Germany, May 2005. Springer Verlag.
5. J. E. Bardram and T. R. Hansen. The AWARE architecture: supporting context-mediated social awareness in mobile cooperation. In *Proceedings of the 2004 ACM conference on Computer supported cooperative work*, pages 192–201. ACM Press, 2004.
6. L. Barkhuus and P. Dourish. Everyday encounters with context-aware computing in a campus environment. In *UbiComp 2004: Ubiquitous Computing: 6th International Conference*, pages 232–249, Berlin, 2004. Springer Verlag.
7. G. Borriello and L. Holmquist, editors. *Proceedings of UbiComp 2002: Ubiquitous Computing : 4th International Conference*, Göteborg, Sweden, Sept. 2002. Springer Verlag.
8. J. Burrell, G. K. Gay, K. Kubo, and N. Farina. Context-aware computing: A test case. In Borriello and Holmquist [7], pages 1–15.
9. K. Cheverst, N. Davies, K. Mitchell, and A. Friday. Experiences of developing and deploying a context-aware tourist guide: the guide project. In *MobiCom '00: Proceedings of the 6th annual international conference on Mobile computing and networking*, pages 20–31, New York, NY, USA, 2000. ACM Press.
10. A. Dey, G. D. Abowd, and D. Salber. A conceptual framework and a toolkit for supporting the rapid prototyping of context-aware applications. *Human-Computer Interaction*, 16:97–166, 2001.
11. A. K. Dey, M. Futakawa, D. Salber, and G. D. Abowd. The conference assistant: Combining context-awareness with wearable computing. In *Proceedings of the 3rd International Symposium on Wearable Computers (ISWC '99)*, pages 21–28. IEEE Computer Society Press, 1999.
12. A. K. Dey and J. Mankoff. Designing mediation for context-aware applications. *ACM Trans. Comput.-Hum. Interact.*, 12(1):53–80, 2005.
13. P. Dourish. What we talk about when we talk about context. *Personal and Ubiquitous Computing*, 8(1):19–30, 2004.
14. M. Fleck, M. Frid, T. Kindberg, E. O'Brien-Strain, R. Rajani, and M. Spasojevic. Rememberer: A tool for capturing museum visits. In Borriello and Holmquist [7], pages 48–55.

15. W. G. Griswold, P. Shanahan, S. W. Brown, R. Boyer, M. Ratto, R. B. Shapiro, and T. M. Truong. ActiveCampus: experiments in community-oriented ubiquitous computing. *IEEE Computer*, 37(10):73–81, 2004.

16. A. Harter, A. Hopper, P. Steggles, A. Ward, and P. Webster. The anatomy of a context-aware application. *Wireless Networks*, 8(2/3):187–197, 2002.

17. J. Kjeldskov and M. Skov. Supporting work activities in healthcare by mobile electronic patient records. In *Proceedings of the 6th Asia-Pacific Conference on Human-Computer Interaction, APCHI 2004*, 2004.

18. S. Mitchell, M. D. Spiteri, J. Bates, and G. Coulouris. Context-aware multimedia computing in the intelligent hospital. In *EW 9: Proceedings of the 9th workshop on ACM SIGOPS European workshop*, pages 13–18, New York, NY, USA, 2000. ACM Press.

19. T. Moran and P. Dourish. Introduction to this speical issue on context-aware computing. *Human-Computer Interaction*, 16:87–95, 2001.

20. M. Munoz, M. Rodriguez, J. Favela, A. Martinez-Garcia, and V. Gonzalez. Context-aware mobile communication in hospitals. *IEEE Computer*, 36(9):38–46, 2003.

21. R. Oppermann and M. Specht. A context-sensitive nomadic exhibition guide. In *Proceedings of Second International Symposium on Handheld and Ubiquitous Computing, HUC 2000*, pages 127–142, Berlin, 2000. Springer Verlag.

22. J. Pascoe, N. Ryan, and D. Morse. Using while moving: Hci issues in fieldwork environments. *ACM Trans. Comput.-Hum. Interact.*, 7(3):417–437, 2000.

23. R. Want, B. N. Schilit, N. I. Adams, R. Gold, K. Petersen, D. Goldberg, J. R. Ellis, and M. Weiser. An overview of the parctab ubiquitous computing environment. *IEEE Personal Communications*, 2(6):28–43, 1995.

24. H. Yan and T. Selker. Context-aware office assistant. In *IUI '00: Proceedings of the 5th international conference on Intelligent user interfaces*, pages 276–279, New York, NY, USA, 2000. ACM Press.

Doing Community: Co-construction of Meaning and Use with Interactive Information Kiosks

Tom Hope, Masahiro Hamasaki, Yutaka Matsuo, Yoshiyuki Nakamura,
Noriyuki Fujimura, and Takuichi Nishimura

Information Technology Research Institute,
National Institute of Advanced Industrial Science and Technology
2-41-6 Aomi, Koto-ku, Tokyo 135-0064, Japan
{tom-hope, masahiro.hamasaki, y.matsuo, nakamura-y,
nori.fujimura, takuichi.nishimura}@aist.go.jp
http://www.aist.go.jp/

Abstract. One of the challenges for ubiquitous computing is to design systems that can be both understood by their users and at the same time understand the users themselves. As information and its meaning becomes more associated with the communities that provide and use it, how will it be possible to build effective systems for these users? We have been examining these issues via ethnographic analysis of the information and community supporting system that we have developed and employed at conference events. This paper presents initial analysis and suggests greater focus on the interaction between members of micro-communities of users in future ubicomp research.

1 Introduction

As researchers and developers of ubiquitous computing, we continue to build on the notion of a world where computing systems 'disappear' into the background of social life, seamlessly providing greater abilities for their users to interact with the environment and each other [1,2]. This brings with it a responsibility for those involved in the development process to understand the contexts within which the technology is to be used, the users themselves, and, as such, requires knowledge of where similar technology is already in use. CSCW has produced research on computing in work settings, and it can be argued that ubiquitous computing is already a reality for many people in other environments. This is particularly the case in cities, where research is increasingly performed on the challenges of linking infrastructure to front-end sensors and devices, and their associated social systems [3,4]. From the perspective of industrial design, it seems difficult to suggest that ubiquitous technology as continued to be envisaged by many in the Ubicomp community can ever exist in the truly 'disappearing' sense. All technology is 'in the world' and humans interact with it as such. It has been suggested [5,6] that technology becomes ubiquitous not because it is physically unseen, but because it has been absorbed into social interaction sufficiently enough that it no longer stands out as being unusual, i.e. being invisible in use. Though

P. Dourish and A. Friday (Eds.): Ubicomp 2006, LNCS 4206, pp. 387–403, 2006.

clearly some infrastructure is largely hidden from view, when we interact with it via interfaces (whether in the form of devices or various sensors and their feedback effects), in other words, when it becomes an object or collection of objects, it becomes visible and exposed. Socially, infrastructure and its associated devices, as with any technology, must become incumbent with meaning when developed, designed and used [7]. A hope of Ubicomp must therefore be to work with these meanings and minimize discordant effects on users of the technology, while recognizing the influence of design processes. Consequently, viewed within a framework of social computing [8], we can assert that technologies can be considered to be ubiquitous when they provide useful functions and at the same time do not cause stoppage or unnecessary difficulties in the social interaction of their users. Using this definition as a basis, this paper presents some analysis of real-world usage of the conference-support system that we have developed. In the rest of this section, we introduce the background to the study and its relevance to ubiquitous computing research. Section 2 introduces some related work, followed by a description of our system, UbiCoAssist, in section 3. Section 4 presents the analysis of qualitative data of the system in use at two different events. In the light of the findings, we suggest some considerations for future development of Ubicomp at the end of the paper.

1.1   Community

In social research, notions of 'community' have always been central. Many of the early sociological studies examined the changing nature of society with reference to community, often mourning or celebrating the demise of a traditional communal way of life [9]. More recent work continues to emphasise the binding nature of community politically and socially, continuing in the same vein to discuss it in relation to its relative (in)stability and (im)permanence [10]. The impact of information and communication technologies, which reduce the need for face-to-face interaction, suggest that a sense of community can be gained in the virtual world [11], but space remains for further research into real-world community practices. This is evidenced by recent work on computer-supported cooperative work and ubiquitous computing systems. Many of these studies continue to deploy systems into pre-existant groups, grounded in physical space, and evaluate their designs based on the acceptance or rejection by those groups. Brignull et al, for example, introduced a shared interactive display into a community of high school students, noting both how the space affected use and suggesting that interactive applications should be designed so that "the community can adapt to their own activities" [12]. The sense appears to be that these communities or 'communities of practice' [13] can be designed for, and that by doing so, the technologies will disappear into everyday usage, thus becoming ubiquitous.

We began our own research aiming to support the communities that attend conferences and other similar events. UbiCoAssist therefore contains several concepts of community within its design. Firstly, there is the relatively abstract notion of a community of researchers, some of whom will attend the same events. This is concretised by perceiving of this community in terms of social networks, and then further solidified by the members physically attending conferences in the same locations. During the development and analysis of the system, we began to use the term 'micro-community' to denote the small groups of event participants who gather around the kiosks and use them to develop their social networks. The use of this term enables us, like the users, to focus on both the social network and the physical interaction simultaneously.

1.2   Ubiquitous Kiosks and IC Cards

While it is clear that multiple handheld technologies are integrated into everyday life for many–mobile phones, PDAs, wireless internet and are obvious examples– much of the ubiquitous computing presently in place outside of the laboratory remains geographically fixed. One such example of already existent ubiquitous technology is the information kiosk. In our research, we define such a kiosk as a terminal, located in public or semi-public space, from which users can gain information interactively. This information is often contextually oriented, based on the users identities and previous interactions with the system, and the location of the kiosk itself. Examples include museum information interfaces, interactive street maps, and shopping mall/airport guides. A defining feature of these kiosks is that they are accessible to more than one person. Though one user may control the interface itself, other individuals are able to view the information at the same time, forming groups around the kiosks. We can envisage that many of the functions of these kiosks will move onto mobile devices, but the social affordance of group viewing suggests that there will be a continued need for larger interfaces around which small groups of people can interact.

In addition to these kiosks, IC cards ('smart cards') continue to be taken up by multiple segments of society, as more and more devices and systems are being developed that utilize their relatively cheap and convenient properties. IC cards have recently become a popular alternative to travel fare systems [14] and electronic wallets. In a sense, we can see an IC card as a tangible bit [15], it is the tangible device–a card with information processing functions–of larger information systems. These are therefore tangible interfaces that are already well used in the real world. These cards have rules of use, in the sense that we generally use them in ways appropriate to their function, but this use may vary according to the place, including the country, where they are used. As kiosks, readers and cards become common ways of obtaining and providing information, it is important to understand the potential effects on social interaction. The intersection between these technologies, forms of which are already widely used, is therefore the foundation of our study. How will people understand and make use of interfaces, which directly aim to involve them in the sharing of relationship data?

2   Related Work

2.1   Kiosks, Tables and Public Displays

Development continues into making information kiosks more contextually sensitive. Intelligent kiosks [16], for example, aim to provide information in a way that is appropriate for the user. Work has been conducted on developing multimodal information kiosks that recognize who is speaking to it according to facial orientation and gaze [17,18]. These suggest that potential exists for extensions of our own work, into the information kiosk as a ubiquitous technology with continuing relevance. The emphasis on interface dynamics, such as in developments of information kiosks as embodied conversational agents [19], also influences the following paper. There is a continuing interest in developing multi-user displays and surfaces, which enable connection between users both publicly and in private [20]. The present work, therefore, lies at the intersection of ubiquitous computing, information design and research into conversation structure and sense-making [21,22] and on a broader level, what Dourish and Button [23] have called 'technomethodology'.

Essential to understanding our current research, is the fact that an information kiosk usually provides information specific to the area in which it is physically located. If it is a map, for example, it will show the location of the kiosk (often denoted as 'you are here'). As a kiosk it is therefore relatively immobile, thus users must themselves be located next to it in order to put it to use. Other potential interfaces have similar features. Tables, for example, arguably remain the most important collaborative spaces, and signify the physical meeting of individuals. This feature–the propensity for people to be physically present together at the object–provides unique opportunities for interaction, which may be lost should the interface be of a different type. In this vein, related work exists in tabletop interface research. One example is Ubitable [24], a system to facilitate collaboration on a tabletop interface. Ubitable enables users to choose where to sit and assigns that seat to them before engaging in interaction with the other user. In this case the space is organized prior to interaction due to the positioning that the interface affords. Where our research in this paper differs, is in the seemingly ad-hoc nature of arrangement around a kiosk-type interface and the possibilities that this brings to interaction with the system. A similar 'loose' arrangement was afforded by the study by Brignull already mentioned [25,12].

2.2   Conferences and Similar Spaces

Conference spaces are interesting for research in ubiquitous computing as they are bounded areas with events that occur in limited time periods. This, in combination with the desire to give and receive information, makes fertile ground for testing devices and systems in development. Related research in this field is work on augmenting spaces with various screens and displays. One such development is in proactive displays [26] that sense and react to nearby people. The work that most directly connects with our own is the installation of communityware at museums and conferences by Sumi and Mase [27]. In this, as with our own system, community awareness is central, providing opportunities for users to know of others with related interests and provide contextually relevant information. We have therefore also been interested and influenced by developments in mobile sensors [28] and possibilities for combining kiosks and wearable computing in event spaces [29], which may increase awareness.

3   System Design and Implementation

UbiCoAssist, forms part of a larger set of technologies developed to support users of conference spaces or other events. UbiCoAssist aims to give support by providing relevant information and allowing users to build and strengthen social relationships before, during and after the event. It consists of web-mining on top of which sits a social network and conference scheduling browser, and a kiosk-based interface. Using the system, a user can find research topics that another researcher is exploring or researchers with whom they are working. In the scheduling part, a user can register interesting presentations (papers, demonstrations and posters) and explore recommended presentations and other researchers.

Figure 1 presents a system overview of UbiCoAssist. Users can access it via PC or via one of the information kiosks at the conference site.

Figures 2 and 3 depict an information kiosk. We deployed several of these kiosks in the conference spaces, each with slightly differing designs. Some kiosks had larger screens than others (e.g. a plasma screen, a large projector screen and differing sizes of PC), but all included the same elements and all were positioned to enable the greatest visibility and access. Each information kiosk has two or three commercially available IC card readers [30] and one screen to view and interact with the application. When a single participant puts an IC card on the card reader, they can log in to the system directly. When two or more users log

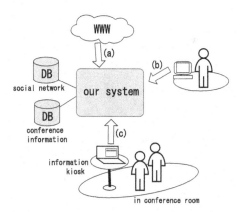

Fig. 1. (a) The system extracts social networks from the web. (b) Users use an online timetable and register their social networks. (c) They can view mutual social relationships. Information kiosks capture their interaction.

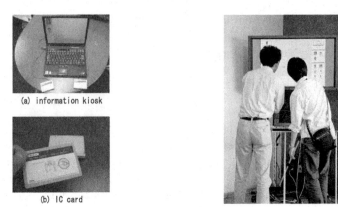

Fig. 2. Information Kiosk and IC Card   **Fig. 3.** Two Users at an Information Kiosk

in with their cards at the same kiosk, the action logs them in and presents them with a large social network diagram of their joint social network.

Figure 4 shows a screenshot of Mypage, the personal portal page of UbiCoAssist that users see when they log in. A personal acquaintance list is located in the middle of the left side. The right side consists of a list of authors and other users that have a strong edge-relationship in the social network. The individual user's surrounding social network is shown at the lower left of the page.

Three methods to Extract Social Networks. UbiCoAssist has three methods to extract social networks among participants. The first of these is based on a web mining technique. We call a link extracted by this method a 'Web Link'. The second is a 'Touch Link', which is based on real-world user interaction with the IC card. The last is 'Know Link', based on user interaction on the web system.

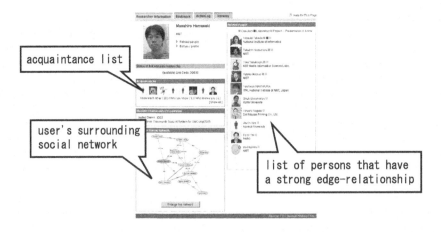

Fig. 4. Mypage

This latter method is similar to other Social Network Systems [31]. A 'Web-link is extracted from the Web using a web mining technique. We applied the web mining method based on method of Matsuo et al. [32] to extract a social network among all participants at each conference. Here we present a brief description of the method and its modifications for our system. The simplest approach is to measure the relevance of two nodes based on the number of retrieved results obtained by a search engine query. For example, assume we are to measure the relevance of two names: "Vannevar Bush" (denoted as X) and "Ted Nelson" (denoted as Y). We first address a query "X and Y" to a search engine and get documents including those words in the text. In addition, we make two queries "X" and "Y", and get b1 and b2 documents. The relevance of "Vannevar Bush" and "Ted Nelson"' is approximated as the Overlap coefficient [33]

$$rel(x, y) = Overlap(X, Y) = \frac{\sharp(X \cap Y)}{min(\sharp(X), \sharp(Y))}$$

For example, if a is divided by b, the rel(x,y) represents the relevance of nodes x and y.

More than one person can have the same family and given name. To alleviate this problem, one study suggested [32] adding affiliation to the query. However, our aim in developing this system is obtaining social networks in order to support the participants of particular events, to date, these being the community of users and researchers at conferences. Therefore, instead, we add to the query a keyword that is related to the specific community. We use the names of central figures with the above-mentioned method to select such keywords (which we term 'community keywords'). A keyword that is connected closely with central figures of a community and is relatively uncommon on the web serves well as a community keyword.

We discriminate between relationships by consulting retrieved page contents and applying classification rules [32], and define labels for each relationship as follows:

- Coauthor: Coauthors of a technical paper
- Lab: Members of the same laboratory or research institute
- Project: Members of the same project or committee
- Conf: Participants of the same conference or workshop

Using this method UbiCoAssist aims to build a foundation network that includes some information about types of relationships, which users can view and modify at the event with kiosks and their own computers.

A 'Touch-link is registered by users via an information kiosk. Users can see social networks among them when two or three participants use the information kiosk together. At this point, the social-tie "We meet and see our social network together" is added to UbiCoAssist automatically. These actions in the real world also create additions of a know-edge on the network.

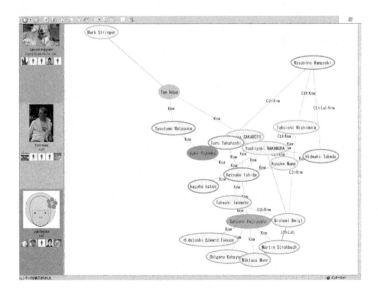

Fig. 5. Three users logged into a kiosk together can view their joint social network

Users on the web system can register a 'Know-link'. This creation of personal acquaintance lists ("I-know" and "I'm-known-by" lists) is a basic function of the system, providing power to the user to add others to their network via a PC. A user can make an addition to the "I-know" list when that user finds an acquaintance on paper or session pages, or from authors and other users listed in order of calculated weight. At that time, the acquaintance is also added to the acquaintances "I'm-known-by" list. These actions are also additions of a know-edge.

3.1   Applications with the Social Network

UbiCoAssist displays a social network among users when they use an information kiosk together (Figure 5). Colors around the users photographs to the left of the network diagram refer to the color of the IC card reader they used to log in. The network display is animated: users can drag nodes (names of individuals on their networks) around the screen, further modifying its appearance.

The system additionally has a person (authors and participants) page, session page, and a paper page. Each page shows a surrounding social network and users can view those associated persons. The person page shows a user-egocentric social network. The session page depicts a social network among authors whose papers are presented in a session. The paper page shows a social network among authors and users who are interested in that paper. There is also a paper search, which allows users to find the social network organization around inputted keywords.

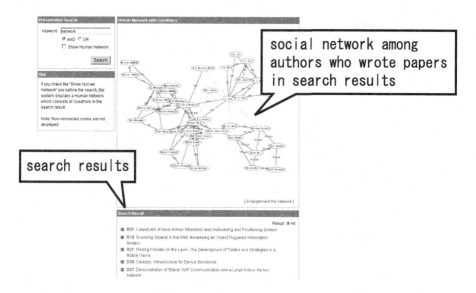

Fig. 6. Results of a paper search

4 User Study: Building Meaning in Social Network Relationships

We demonstrated and tested the current version of UbiCoAssist at two conferences in 2005: JSAI 2005[1] and UbiComp 2005. The conferences were in the research field of computing, but the participants of the first were mainly Japanese, with the second being an international conference. Both, however, were held inside Japan and so there were also many Japanese members at UbiComp 2005. At each conference several video cameras were arranged around one kiosk, deemed to be one of the most accessible in the space, while ethnographic observation [34] was done of users of all the kiosks.[2] Signs were displayed next to the kiosk to inform users that video was taken for use in developing the system and a privacy agreement explanation was in the system's accompanying leaflet. Additionally, some hand-held video data was collected along with many still photographs of use. Consequently data was gathered in the form of video, photographs and fieldnotes, along with informal on-site interviews. The use of strategically positioned video cameras and all-day recording to digital media allowed detailed post-event analysis to be done of users interaction with the system and with each other

---

[1] Japan Society for Artificial Intelligence Annual Conference.

[2] In much the same sense that 'community' has proved to be a difficult term to pin down, we adopt a broader understanding of ethnographic research than is often used in Ubicomp work. While traditionally, ethnography focusses on relatively long-term observation of members of a social group, here the formation of community in temporary spaces is the topic of study itself.

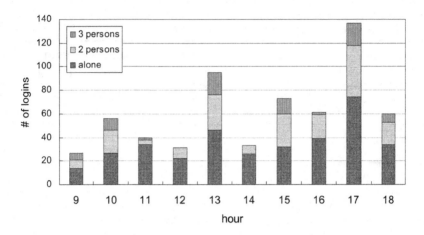

Fig. 7. Number of logins at the kiosk during one day of conference

in the conference space. The system also recorded an access log of users' kiosk usage. Figure 7 shows the kiosk usage in one hour blocks during September 13th at UbiComp 2005. We analyzed the recorded data using both video and access logs from each day.

All social interaction takes place within physical constraints and over definable periods of time. As an analytical strategy, we have found it beneficial to distinguish between the spatial and the temporal aspects to interaction, though in reality these are of course inseparable. Doing this is enabling us to get to grips with the usability issues, and interaction between members, and the methods of sense-making that users used in their interaction with UbiCoAssist.

4.1   Space and Access

At each conference, the web-based side of UbiCoAssist was set up online and was running prior to the actual event. Conference participants who registered with the system via their own PCs received passwords via email in order for them to be able to access the system and use its scheduling and network functions. These users were therefore familiar with the browser interface when they first encountered it at the events. However, initial reactions to the information kiosk system were unexpectedly troubled for many users. This was due to several reasons, all related to the physical space in which the kiosk and users were located, and the form of the kiosks themselves.

The first issue for users arose when they entered the conference building. A social event suggests expected behavior of participants, but there is also an assumed spatial arrangement, which can cause confusion if it does not fit with expectations. The conferences had registration desks where participants could collect their conference programs, proceedings and identification badges. At the first conference, each person was given an IC card at this desk and then they were directed to the location of the kiosks. The second conference, however, was arranged so that they could register their own (or supplied) IC card with UbiCoAssist at the kiosks themselves, thus allowing them to use any device with a unique ID (including, for example, some mobile phones containing smart chips) if they wished. However, users found it confusing why the kiosks were not located at the same point as the registration desk. The action of 'registering', whether for the conference or for UbiCoAssist, was expected to occur in one location.

It should not be surprising that users on their initial encounter with the system made sense of it according to prior understandings of conferences. UbiCoAssist is, after all, a system that supports conferences and similar events. But it also points to the fact that the space and its associated systems sensors (in this case card readers) are given meaning by the social context in which they are set. This denotes an important difference between space and place [8], and one that will affect the implementation of the system in other types of settings.

Once users were at a kiosk they were confronted with another problem, namely, how to use the IC cards. Users who had not yet registered the card to their identity in UbiCoAssist were required to do so at a kiosk. In order to do this, they needed to place a card onto the reader and leave it there. Removing the card would log them out of the system, partly as a security measure to avoid individuals leaving the kiosk while still logged in and thereby allowing their data to be modified by other participants. This action–placing the card on the reader and leaving it there–was frequently troublesome. Users would place the card and quickly remove it, looking at the screen only to discover that they were not logged in as they had expected. They would repeat the action and receive the same result. The problem was not rectified when more than one user logged in, as they would encounter the same. This can be explained by the affordances of IC cards.

Though not a sensor which requires no action on behalf of the user, IC cards are already a pervasive technology. Due to the limitations of card and sensor, they must be in the correct range of each other in order to function. There are many ways to use a card, and consequently to the user there is no use intrinsic to the object itself. Nevertheless, many of the conference participants use similar types of cards in their daily lives and, as was seen at the conference, this affected their use with the information kiosks. The cards that we use frequently, and that allow access to spaces, are usually used with a brief swiping motion. Keys, more often than not, are inserted upon entry and removed, as are credit cards and tickets. But not all cards are used like this, credit cards being a good example, so why did users, upon a first failure to log in, not switch to this other method of use?

The video data provided one explanation in the form of collaborative interaction, as users would negotiate with each other the meaning of the problem. Essentially, it emerged that the human error of not logging in correctly was often suggested to be a system error. As soon as one user stated this, the other user would soon agree and further attempts at using the system together would be abandoned. It may be that the members of the conferences, themselves being researchers and developers in computing, were expecting system errors. This may also have been the reason why some participants were unsure which other devices they could use to access UbiCoAssist. There were several occurrences of individuals asking how to access with their PDAs, mobile phones or indeed via the systems on display by other non-related demonstration teams in the conference space. Being somewhat contrary to the findings of Williams et al [35], who observed users seeking to understand their system, SignalPlay, in terms of individual components, these users of UbiCoAssist were attempting to understand the whole system and fit different devices into it.

The interface objects, then, and the space where they were used, did not in themselves inform users of the methods for their use. Clearly, there were expectations of how the system would behave, but when these were not fulfilled, users experienced difficulties.

4.2   Time and Identity

A significant characteristic of a conference or similar event is that it exists only for a specific time, and therefore systems of ubiquitous technology must deal with large aggregates of new users, who only have a relatively short time within which to develop appropriate practices. This time itself holds some order in the interaction of users. Failure to log in to the system the first time did not prevent the user from trying again. However, if the failure had been in a group, such as in the perceived system error described above, the user may attempt to access the system at a later time, individually. Conversely, we observed users who failed individually, trying again later, but this time in a group. The fact that these individuals are professional researchers of computing may have played no small part in the aversion to lose face [36], and a group could therefore provide, or not provide, mutual support. However, the fact that users could view the networks of others and see, therefore, if they had touch-links or not, may have served as a prompt.

We know from studies of conversation that interaction is ordered in a sequential manner [21]. This temporal order defines to some extent the meaning that is attributed to UbiCoAssist by its users. Figure 8 illustrates this with a transcribed excerpt from a conversation between two users of the system, A and B, who were viewing their joint social network. Both users had logged into the system before, using their IC cards, but this was the first time they had been at the same kiosk together.

As illustrated with the extract, the sequential order of interaction around the kiosk has possibilities to affect the understanding of the network. Some negotiation took place in the conversation, with neither party firmly stating the connection between them until the last line of the extract. The corresponding social network actually contained several linked people between them, so the negotiation may have been referring to who was thought to be the most direct, or influential link. In observing these and other users, it is apparent that the understanding of these links is very subjective. Figure 8 shows, therefore, how important the sequence of talk is to making sense of the visualized community. If either A or B had firmly claimed a relationship first, it could have changed the

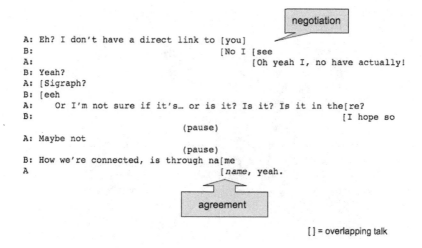

Fig. 8. Negotiating the network

course of the rest of the interaction, and therefore the sense of what relationships the social network was representing.

4.3   Doing Community

Information kiosks demand that users be standing near or next to them in order to be used. This requirement in and of itself provides a context in which groups can form with similar goals and interests. Much like a table or other communal object, there is the possibility for members of already existent communities to gather together, but we also found that small temporary communities can be created there. The physical gathering of users affords awareness [37] of the activities of others, which enables monitoring of their action with the system, and therefore can lead to mutual orientation to similar practices.

UbiCoAssist provides a visual diagram of a community of participants at an event, but, as powerful as the web-mining algorithm is, in itself it does not guarantee a perfectly correct representation. In fact, what we found was that its perceived imperfections created spaces for further interaction between users, as shown above in Figure 8. The perceived system errors described in section 4.1 occasionally did the same thing, but though we can attribute this as associated with the occupation of users, the former should feasibly be the case for any user at any event. Of course, users actions were not solely oral as suggested in this extract, but were wholly embodied, incorporating gesture, gaze, body-torque [38,39] and an understanding of social behavior (Figure 9). An example can be found in the relatively ordered manner in which some of the Japanese participants allowed particular members of their groups to access the interface before others. These members often held more influential positions on the social

Fig. 9. Gesturing to the Interface

network diagrams, but as this was not always the case, further study is required to fully grasp the role that it may play. The least we can say is that this form of granting access to other users was a negotiated action between several members of the groups at the kiosks.

Bodies hold very different meanings when in the setting of social networks and public displays. UbiCoAssist shares elements of both virtual and real-world communities and it was down to the users to negotiate the connections between these worlds at the time of the conferences. At the beginning of the events, the communities as envisaged by the developers of UbiCoAssist were principally virtual, diagrammatic ones, represented as social networks. During the actual events however, real-world communities soon formed. These may arguably be perceived as communities of practice [13], as they encompassed both knowledge of how to use UbiCoAssist, experience of its use, and an ongoing practice of using it in ways appropriate to each other, but seen in that frame it is remarkable how quickly the community formed and therefore perhaps this is not the appropriate definition. We have defined these small groups that form at the conferences around kiosks as 'micro-communities', denoting possibly transient interactions between people, but showing potential to become stronger connections in the social networks at future events.

5   Conclusions and Future Development

We have seen in this paper that it is not possible to rely purely on the physical form of interfaces and spaces in order to create smooth use of kiosk-based information and networking systems. In spite of advanced planning, usability issues quickly arise. Instead, if we are to produce technology that is invisible in use, it is essential to gain knowledge of the social understanding of the use and meaning of these systems. We saw that individuals when encountering the technology collaboratively work to understand its possible use and subsequently give it meaning in the way that they use it. With UbiCoAssist, this co-construction of social network, micro-community and the meaning of the system itself occurs in the temporally organized interaction around the kiosk. We can assert that other systems and settings where multiple users congregate will also be made sense of in a similar way, with the interaction between users again playing an important role. Though social expectations in some ways structured the access and use of the kiosks, it was negotiation between users at the time that gave meaning to its use.

It is clear that UbiCoAssist can be improved by addressing further the issues raised in this paper. While the system as it is does allow room for 'dissent'—i.e. users are able to modify their network if they disagree with it, or at least not take part in the system save for their name being used as a node on a social network—it may be possible to give an even greater sense of security to users developing ways to 'break' links or disassociate oneself from others. Nevertheless, the system as it is provides an effective platform for social engagement with others, within which negotiation can take place. The ability given to users to construct networks as they perceive them also negates to an extent some of the problems of building the initial social networks around community keywords (which some may disagree with). These keywords and the web-mining inherently structure the networks before the conferences and we are consequently continuing to explore these issues.

Many of us in the field of ubiquitous computing have an image in mind when we work on the development of our technologies. We conceive of products, and develop systems with ideas of an eventual end-user community. One of the dangers in this process is that it is easy to use the conception of community as a gloss—a categorization shorthand to describe what is actually a multitude of very different individuals. When faced with the task of understanding their own community, as was the case with the users of UbiCoAssist and its social network, it soon became clear that it was not as easy for them as one might have expected. There were times when, clearly, interaction with both the system and between users themselves was difficult, conversation became stilted and exasperation emerged. Yet, certain things did help combat these difficulties. Firstly, the ability to modify the social network in some way helped by giving control to the user to adjust the results of the web-mining. Secondly, the sequential manner of interaction enabled users to collaboratively construct a sense of what the network—and the individuals represented on it—meant to them. Thus, contextual information in the form of the social network became more accurate. This combination of automation and user control may improve the effectiveness of similar systems.

Community was, then, 'done' by the participants of the conference when they used UbiCoAssist, rather than simply existing before the event. This doing of community holds important ramifications for the development of ubiquitous computing that hopes to use contextual information about users identities or characteristics collected prior to use, as it suggests that real-time sensing of how micro-communities are forming and the practices they engage in will be a necessary addition.

Acknowledgements. This research has been supported by NEDO (New Energy and Industrial Technology Development Organization) as the project ID of 04A11502a.

References

1. Weiser, M.: The computer for the 21st century. Scientific American **265**(3) (1991) 66–75
2. Satyanarayanan, M.: Pervasive computing: Vision and challenges. IEEE Personal Communications (2001) 10–17
3. Mainwaring, S.D., Chang, M.F., Anderson, K.: Infrastructures and their discontents: Implications for ubicomp. In: Ubicomp 2004. (2004) 418–432
4. Star, S.L.: Infrastructure and ethnographic practice: working on the fringes. Scandinavian Journal of Information Systems **14**(2) (2002) 107–122
5. Kuniavsky, M.: What's invisible technology? no, really. Workshop on situated ubiquitous computing at Ubicomp 2005 (2005)
6. Heer, H., Khooshabeh, P.: Seeing the invisible. In: Workshop on Invisible and Transparent Interfaces at AVI 2004, ITI Workshop, part of AVI 2004 (Advanced Visual Interfaces) (2004)
7. Suchman, L.: Working relations of technology production and use. Computer-Supported Cooperative Work (CSCW) **2** (1994) 21–39
8. Dourish, P.: Where the action is: the foundations of embodied interaction. MIT Press, Cambridge, MA, USA (2001)
9. Tonnies, F.: Community and Civil Society. Cambridge University Press, Cambridge (2001)
10. Delanty, G.: Community. Routledge, London (2003)
11. Wellman, B.: The persistence and transformation of community: From neighborhood groups to social networks (2001)
12. Brignull, H., Izadi, S., Fitzpatrick, G., Rogers, Y., Rodden, T.: The introduction of a shared interactive surface into a communal space. In: CSCW '04: Proceedings of the 2004 ACM conference on Computer supported cooperative work, New York, NY, USA, ACM Press (2004) 49–58
13. Wenger, E.: Communities of practice: learning, meaning, and identity. Cambridge University Press, Cambridge, U.K. and New York, N.Y. (1998)
14. JR Suica: http://www.jreast.co.jp/suica/index.html (2006)
15. Ishii, H., Ullmer, B.: Tangible bits: towards seamless interfaces between people, bits and atoms. In: CHI '97: Proceedings of the SIGCHI conference on Human factors in computing systems, New York, NY, USA, ACM Press (1997) 234–241
16. Christian, A.D., Avery, B.L.: Speak out and annoy someone: experience with intelligent kiosks. In: CHI '00: Proceedings of the SIGCHI conference on Human factors in computing systems, New York, NY, USA, ACM Press (2000) 313–320
17. Bakx, I., van Turnhout, K., Terken, J.M.B.: Facial orientation during multi-party interaction with information kiosks. In: INTERACT. (2003)

18. Mäkinen, E., Patomäki, S., Raisamo, R.: Experiences on a multimodal information kiosk with an interactive agent. In: NordiCHI '02: Proceedings of the second Nordic conference on Human-computer interaction, New York, NY, USA, ACM Press (2002) 275–278

19. Cassell, J., Stocky, T., Bickmore, T., Gao, Y., Nakano, Y., Ryokai, K., Tversky, D., Vaucelle, C., Vilhjlmsson, H.: Mack: Media lab autonomous conversational kiosk. In: IMAGINA '02, Monte Carlo (2002)

20. Greenberg, S., Rounding, M.: The notification collage: posting information to public and personal displays. In: CHI '01: Proceedings of the SIGCHI conference on Human factors in computing systems, New York, NY, USA, ACM Press (2001) 514–521

21. Sacks, H.: Lectures on Conversation. Blackwell Publishers, Oxford (1995)

22. Garfinkel, H.: Studies in Ethnomethodology. Polity Press, Cambridge (1996)

23. Dourish, P., Button, G.: On "technomethodology": Foundational relationships between ethnomethodology and system design. Human-Computer Interaction 13(4) (1998) 395–432

24. Chia, S., Everitt, K.: Ubitable: Impromptu face-to-face collaboration on horizontal interactive surfaces. In: Proceedings of Ubicomp 2003, Ubicomp (2003)

25. Brignull, H., Rogers, Y.: Enticing people to interact with large public displays in public spaces. In: INTERACT. (2003)

26. McCarthy, J.F., Nguyen, D.H., Rashid, A.M., Soroczak, S.: Proactive displays and the experience ubicomp project. SIGGROUP Bull. 23(3) (2002) 38–41

27. Sumi, Y., Mase, K.: Supporting the awareness of shared interests and experiences in communities. International Journal of Human-Computer Studies 56(1) (2002) 127–146

28. Nakashima, H.: Cyber assist project for situated human support. In: Proceedings of the Eighth International Conference on Distributed Multimedia Systems. (2002) 1–3

29. Dey, A.K., Salber, D., Abowd, G.D., Futakawa, M.: The conference assistant: Combining context-awareness with wearable computing. In: ISWC '99: Proceedings of the 3rd IEEE International Symposium on Wearable Computers, Washington, DC, USA, IEEE Computer Society (1999) 21–28

30. Sony Corp., FeliCa: http://www.sony.net/Products/felica/index.html (2006)

31. Mixi: http://mixi.jp (2006)

32. Matsuo, Y., Tomobe, H., Hasida, K., Ishizuka, M.: Finding social network for trust calculation. In de Mántaras, R.L., Saitta, L., eds.: ECAI, IOS Press (2004) 510–514

33. Manning, C.D., Schütze, H.: Foundations of Statistical Natural Language Processing. The MIT Press, Cambridge, Massachusetts (1999)

34. Hammersley, M., Atkinson, P.: Ethnography: Principles in Practice. Routledge, London (1983)

35. Williams, A., Kabisch, E., Dourish, P.: From interaction to participation: Configuring space through embodied interaction. In: Ubicomp. (2005) 287–304

36. Goffman, E.: Interaction Ritual: Essays on Face-to-Face Behavior. Doubleday Anchor, New York, NY (1967)

37. Dourish, P., Bellotti, V.: Awareness and coordination in shared workspaces. In: Proceedings of the ACM Conference on Computer Supported Cooperative Work (CSCW'92), Toronto, Ontario, ACM Press (1992) 107–114

38. Lerner, G.: Selecting next speaker: The context-sensitive operation of a context-free organization. Language in Society 32 (2003) 177–201

39. Schegloff, E.A.: Body torque. Social Research 65 (1998) 535–86

Moving on from Weiser's Vision of Calm Computing: Engaging UbiComp Experiences

Yvonne Rogers

School of Informatics, Indiana University, 901 East 10th Street,
Bloomington, IN47408, USA
yrogers@indiana.edu

Abstract. A motivation behind much UbiComp research has been to make our lives convenient, comfortable and informed, following in the footsteps of Weiser's calm computing vision. Three themes that have dominated are context awareness, ambient intelligence and monitoring/tracking. While these avenues of research have been fruitful their accomplishments do not match up to anything like Weiser's world. This paper discusses why this is so and argues that is time for a change of direction in the field. An alternative agenda is outlined that focuses on engaging rather than calming people. Humans are very resourceful at exploiting their environments and extending their capabilities using existing strategies and tools. I describe how pervasive technologies can be added to the mix, outlining three areas of practice where there is much potential for professionals and laypeople alike to combine, adapt and use them in creative and constructive ways.

Keywords: calm computing, Weiser, user experiences, engaged living, UbiComp history, pervasive technologies, proactive computing.

1 Introduction

Mark Weiser's vision of ubiquitous computing has had an enormous impact on the directions that the nascent field of UbiComp has taken. A central thesis was that while "computers for personal use have focused on the excitement of interaction…the most potentially interesting, challenging and profound change implied by the ubiquitous computing era is a focus on calm." [46]. Given the likelihood that computers will be everywhere, in our environments and even embedded in our bodies, he argued that they better "stay out of the way" and not overburden us in our everyday lives. In contrast, his picture of calm technology portrayed a world of serenity, comfort and awareness, where we are kept perpetually informed of what is happening around us, what is going to happen and what has just happened. Information would appear in the center of our attention when needed and effortlessly disappear into the periphery of our attention when not.

Now regarded as the forefather of UbiComp, Weiser has inspired governments, researchers and developers across the globe. Most prominent was the European Community's Disappearing Computer initiative in the late 90s and early 2000s, that funded a large number of research projects to investigate how information technology could be diffused into everyday objects and settings and to see how this could lead to

P. Dourish and A. Friday (Eds.): Ubicomp 2006, LNCS 4206, pp. 404–421, 2006.

new ways of supporting and enhancing people's lives that went above and beyond what was possible using desktop machines. Other ambitious and far-reaching projects included MIT's Oxygen, HP's CoolTown, IBM's BlueEyes, Philips Vision of the Future and attempts by various telecom companies and academia to create the ultimate 'smart home', e.g., Orange-at-Home and Aware Home. A central aspiration running through these early efforts was that the environment, the home, and our possessions would be aware, adapt and respond to our varying comfort needs, individual moods and information requirements. We would only have to walk into a room, make a gesture or speak aloud and the environment would bend to our will and respond or react as deemed appropriate for that point in time.

Considerable effort has gone into realizing Weiser's vision in terms of developing frameworks, technologies and infrastructures. Proactive computing was put forward as an approach to determine how to program computers to take the initiative to act on people's behalf [43]. The environment has been augmented with various computational resources to provide information and services, when and where desired, with the implicit goal of "assisting everyday life and not overwhelming it" [1]. An assortment of sensors have been experimented with in our homes, hospitals, public buildings, physical environments and even our bodies to detect trends and anomalies, providing a dizzying array of data about our health, movements, changes in the environment and so on. Algorithms have been developed to analyze the data in order for inferences to be made about what actions to take for people. In addition, sensed data is increasingly being used to automate mundane operations and actions that we would have done in our everyday worlds using conventional knobs, buttons and other physical controls. For example, our favorite kind of music or TV show that we like to exercise to will automatically play as we enter a gym. Sensed data is also being used to remind us of things we often forget to do at salient times, such as detecting the absence of milk in the fridge and messaging us to buy a carton when passing the grocery store.

But, as advanced and impressive as these endeavors have been they still do not match up to anything like a world of calm computing. There is an enormous gap between the dream of comfortable, informed and effortless living and the accomplishments of UbiComp research. As pointed out by Greenfield [20] "we simply don't do 'smart' very well yet" because it involves solving very hard artificial intelligence problems that in many ways are more challenging than creating an artificial human [26]. A fundamental stumbling block has been harnessing the huge variability in what people do, their motives for doing it, when they do it and how they do it. Ethnographic studies of how people manage their lives – ranging from those suffering from Alzheimer's Disease to high-powered professionals – have revealed that the specifics of the context surrounding people's day-to-day living are much more subtle, fluid and idiosyncratic than theories of context have led us to believe [40]. This makes it difficult, if not impossible, to try to implement context in any practical sense and from which to make sensible predictions about what someone is feeling, wanting or needing at a given moment. Hence, while it has been possible to develop a range of simple UbiComp systems that can offer relevant information at opportune moments (e.g., reminding and recommending to us things that are considered useful and important) it is proving to be much more difficult to build truly smart systems that can understand or accurately model people's behaviors, moods and intentions.

The very idea of calm computing has also raised a number of ethical and social concerns. Even if it was possible for Weiser's dream to be fulfilled would we want to live in such a world? In particular, is it desirable to depend on computers to take on our day-to-day decision-making and planning activities? Will our abilities to learn, remember and think for ourselves suffer if we begin to rely increasingly on the environment to do them for us? Furthermore, how do designers decide which activities should be left for humans to control and which are acceptable and valuable for the environment to take over responsibility for?

In this paper I argue that progress in UbiComp research has been hampered by intractable computational and ethical problems and that we need to begin taking stock of both the dream and developments in the field. In particular, we need to rethink the value and role of calm and proactive computing as main driving forces. It is without question that Weiser's enormous legacy will (and should) continue to have an impact on UbiComp developments. However, sufficient time has passed since his untimely death and it should be possible now for researchers to take a critical stance. As part of this exercise, I propose that the field needs to broaden its scope, setting and addressing other goals that are more attainable and down-to-earth. New agendas need also to be outlined that can guide, stimulate and challenge UbiComp (and other) researchers and developers, building upon the growing body of research in the field.

To this end, I propose one such alternative agenda which focuses on designing UbiComp technologies for engaging user experiences. It argues for a significant shift from *proactive computing* to *proactive people*; where UbiComp technologies are designed not to do things for people but to engage them more actively in what they currently do. Rather than calm living it promotes engaged living, where technology is designed to *enable* people to do what they want, need or never even considered before by acting in and upon the environment. Instead of embedding pervasive computing everywhere in the environment it considers how UbiComp technologies can be created as ensembles or ecologies of resources, that can be mobile and/or fixed, to serve specific purposes and be situated in particular places. Furthermore, it argues that people rather than computers should take the initiative to be constructive, creative and, ultimately, in control of their interactions with the world – in novel and extensive ways.

While this agenda might appear to be a regressive step and even an anathema to some ardent followers of Weiser's vision, I argue that it (and other agendas) will turn out to be more beneficial for society than persisting with following an unrealistic goal. Current technological developments together with emerging findings from user studies, showing how human activities have been positively extended by 'bounded' (as opposed to pervasive) technologies, suggest that much can be gained from reconceptualizing UbiComp in terms of designing user experiences that creatively, excitedly, and constructively extend what people currently do. This does not mean that the main tenet of Weiser's vision be discarded (i.e., computers appearing when needed and disappearing when not) but rather we begin to entertain other possibilities – besides calmness – for steering UbiComp research. Examples include extending and supporting personal, cognitive and social processes such as habit-changing, problem-solving, creating, analyzing, learning or performing a skill. Ultimately, research and development should be driven by a better understanding of human activity rather than what has tended to happen, namely, "daring to intervene, clumsily, in situations that already work reasonably well" [20, p231].

In the remainder of this paper I offer a constructive critique of Weiser's vision and the subsequent research that has followed in its footsteps. I then outline an alternative agenda for UbiComp, highlighting pertinent questions, concerns and illustrative examples of how it can be achieved.

2 Weiser's Vision Revisited and Early Research

To illustrate how his early vision of ubiquitous computing could work, Weiser [47] presented a detailed scenario about a day in the life of Sal, an executive single mother. The scenario describes what Sal gets up to, as she moves from her domestic world to her work place, during which she is perpetually informed of the goings on of her family, neighbors, fellow citizens and work colleagues. With this knowledge she is able to keep up-to-date, avoid obstacles, make the most of her time and conduct her work – all in smooth and effective ways. The scenario emphasizes coziness, comfort and effortlessness:

"Sal awakens: she smells coffee. A few minutes ago her alarm clock, alerted by her restless rolling before waking, had quietly asked "coffee?", and she had mumbled "yes." "Yes" and "no" are the only words it knows.

Sal looks out her windows at her neighborhood. Sunlight and a fence are visible through one, but through others she sees electronic trails that have been kept for her of neighbors' coming and going during the early morning. Privacy conventions and practical data rates prevent displaying video footage, but time markers electronic tracks on the neighborhood map let Sal feel cozy in her street."

In this small excerpt we see how the world evolves around Sal's assumed needs, where computers, cameras and sensors are embedded into her world to make her life super efficient, smooth and calm. It is as if she glides through life, where everything is done or laid out for her and whenever there is potential for frustration, such as a traffic jam or parking problem, the invisible computers come to her rescue and gently inform her of what to do and where to go. It is worth drawing an analogy here with the world of the landed aristocracy in Victorian England who's day-to-day live was supported by a raft of servants that were deemed to be invisible to them. This scenario also highlights the ethical issues that such an informed world needs to address, namely the importance of establishing appropriate levels of privacy that are considered acceptable by a community (e.g., having abstract digital trails rather than video footage to ensure anonymity).

The core topics raised in Weiser's seminal papers have motivated much subsequent UbiComp research. Most prominent themes are context-aware computing, ambient/ubiquitous intelligence and recording/tracking and monitoring. (N.B. It should be noted that these are not mutually exclusive but overlap in the aims and methods used.)

2.1 Context-Aware Computing

Context-aware computing focuses on detecting, identifying and locating people's movements, routines or actions with a view to using this information to provide relevant information that may augment or assist a person or persons. Many projects have been conducted under this heading to the extent that it has been noted that ubiquitous computing is sometimes called context-aware computing [12]. In a nutshell, context is viewed as something that can be sensed and measured using location, time, person, activity type and other dimensions. An example of an early context-sensitive application was comMotion that used location information and a speech output system to inform people when they were driving or cycling past a store to buy the groceries they needed [30].

A motivation behind much context-aware computing is to find ways of compensating for limitations in human cognition, e.g., attention, memory, learning, comprehension, and decision-making, through the use of sensor-based and computational tools. For example, augmented cognition – originating in military research – seeks to develop methods "to open bottlenecks and address the biases and deficits in human cognition" by continually sensing the ongoing context and inferring what strategies to employ to help people in their tasks [5].

Key questions in context-aware computing concern what to sense, what form and what kind of information to represent to augment ongoing activities. A number of location and tagging technologies have been developed, such as RFID, satellite, GPS and ultrasonics, to enable certain categories of information to be tracked and detected. Many of these, however, have been beset with detection and precision limitations, sometimes resulting in unreliable and inaccurate data. Recent advances in cognitive radio technology that is software defined (SDR), promises to be more powerful; wireless systems will be able to locate and link to locally unused radio frequency, based on the ability to sense and remember various factors, such as human behavior, making them more dependable and more aware of their surroundings [4]. The advocates of this new technology portray its potential for highly complex settings, such as combat war zones to help commanders from different friendly forces stay appraised of the latest situation, through voice, data and video links, thereby reducing collateral damage [4].

While newer technological developments may enable more accurate data to be detected and collected it is questionable as to how effectively it can be used. It still involves Herculean efforts to understand, interpret and act upon in real-time and in meaningful ways. Context-aware systems that attempt to guide a person through certain activities require models of human behavior and intentionality that are based on rationality and predictability [40]. However, as already mentioned, people often behave in unpredictable and subtle ways in their day-to-day contexts. Therefore, it is likely that context-aware systems will only ever be successful in highly constrained settings.

2.2 Ambient and Ubiquitous Intelligence

Another dominant theme that has emerged in the field of UbiComp is ubiquitous or ambient intelligence, i.e., computational intelligence that is part of both the physical and the digital worlds. This approach follows on from work in artificial intelligence. The phrase 'right place/right time/right means' has been sloganized with visions of smart worlds and smart things, embedded with intelligence, that will predict people's needs and react accordingly [25]. Instead of reaching for the remote to change the TV channel the smart entertainment system will do it for us, instead of browsing the web the smart internet will find the information we need and so on. Just as it is becoming increasingly common place for supermarkets to automatically open their doors as we walk towards them, toilets to flush when we stand up and taps to release water as we wave our hands under them it is envisioned that information will appear on our TVs, watches, walls, and other displays as and when needed (e.g., children will be alerted of dangers and tourists will be informed of points of interest when walking through an unfamiliar city).

However, similar to context-aware computing, ambient intelligence is proving to be a hard nut to crack. While there have been significant advances in computer vision, speech recognition and gesture-based detection, the reality of multimodal interfaces – that can predict and deliver with accuracy and sensitivity what is assumed people want or need – is a long way off. One of the most well known attempts at implementing ambient intelligence was IBM's BlueEyes project, that sought to develop computers that could "see" and "feel" like humans. Sensing technology was used to identify a person's actions and to extract key information that was then analyzed to determine the person's physical, emotional, or informational state. This was intended to be used to help make people "more productive by performing expected actions or by providing expected information." The success of the BlueEyes project, however, was limited; an example of an achievement that is posted on its website is of a television that would turn itself on when a person in the room made eye contact with it. To turn it off, the person could 'tell' it to switch off.

Such meager accomplishments in both context-aware computing and ambient intelligence reflect just how difficult it can be to get a machine to behave like a human. But it is essential that such systems be accurate for them to be accepted by humans in their everyday context. Reading, interpreting and acting upon people's moods, intentions, desires, etc, at any given moment in an appropriate way is a highly developed human skill that when humans get it wrong can lead to misunderstanding. When a ubiquitous computing system gets it wrong – which is likely to be considerably more frequent – it is likely to be more frustrating and we are likely to be less forgiving. For example, when the system decides to switch on the TV because we happen momentarily to stare into space while reading a book, it is likely to be unnerving and extremely annoying, especially if 'it' persistently gets it wrong.

2.3 Recording, Tracking and Monitoring

The push towards developing assistive applications through sensing and alerting has been most marked for vulnerable people; a number of UbiComp systems have been built to constantly check up on the elderly, the physically and mentally disabled [34]. The movements, habits, health and mishaps of such people are recorded, tracked and presented via remote monitors to the families, carers and other people responsible for them, who can then use the information to make decisions about whether to intervene or administer alternative forms of medical care or help. In particular, there has been a move towards developing ubiquitous computing systems to aid elderly people, who need to be cared for, by helping them take their medicines regularly, checking up on their physical health, monitoring their whereabouts and detecting when they have fallen over [e.g., 13].

A number of assisted living applications and services has also been developed to help people with loss of vision or deteriorating memory to be more independent in their lives. For example, Cyber Crumbs was designed to help people with progressive vision loss find their way around a building using a reader badge system that reads out directions and warns of obstacles, such as fire hydrants [39]. Cook's Collage was developed as an aid for people with memory loss. It replays a series of digital still images in a comic strip reel format depicting people's cooking actions *in situ*, intended to help them remember if they have forgotten a step (e.g., adding a particular ingredient) after being distracted [45].

A reason for there being so much interest in helping the less able in UbiComp is that explicit needs and benefits can be readily identified for these user groups. Moreover, there is an assumption that pervasive technologies offer more flexibility and scope for providing solutions compared with other computing technologies since they can sense, monitor and detect people's movements, bodily functions, etc., in ways not possible before. There is a danger, however, that such techniques may probe too far into the lives of less able people resulting in – albeit unintentionally – 'extreme' forms of recording, tracking and monitoring that these people may have no control over. For example, consider the extent to which a group of researchers went to in order to help with the care of old people in a residential care home [6]. A variety of monitoring devices were installed in the home, including badges on the patients and the caregivers and switches on the room doors that detected when they were open or closed. Load sensors were also used to measure and monitor weight changes of people while in their beds; the primary aim was to track trends in weight gain or loss over time. But the sensors could also be used to infer how well someone was sleeping. If significant movement was detected during the night this could enable a caregiver to see whether the person was having trouble sleeping (and if there was a huge increase in weight this could be inferred as someone else getting in or on the bed).

Such panopticon developments elicit a knee-jerk reaction of horror in us. While the motives behind such projects are altruistic they can also be naïve, overlooking how vulnerable people's privacy and self-respect may be being violated. Not surprisingly, there has been enormous concern by the media and other social scientists about the social implications of recording, tracking and re-representing people's movements, conversations, actions and transactions. Inevitably, a focus has been on the negative aspects, namely a person's right to privacy being breached. Is it right to be videoing and sensing people when sleeping, eating, etc., especially when they are not at their best [2]? Is it right to be providing information to other family members about their granny's sleeping habits, especially if it can be inferred from the sensed data that she might have got into bed with another patient, which none of the vested parties might want to share or let the others know about.

While most projects are sensitive to the privacy and ethical problems surrounding the monitoring of people, they are not easy to solve and have ended up overwhelming UbiComp research. Indeed, much of the discussion about the human aspects in the field has been primarily about the trade-offs between security and privacy, convenience and privacy, and informedness and privacy. This focus has often been at the expense of other human concerns receiving less airing, such as how recording, tracking and re-representing movements and other information can be used to facilitate social and cognitive processes.

My intention here is not to diminish the importance of awareness, ambience and monitoring to detect and inform people in their everyday lives, together with the ethical and social issues they raise. Rather, my overview of the projects in these areas has revealed how difficult it is to build calm computing systems and yet the attempts have largely dominated the field of UbiComp. Those that have tried have fallen short, resulting in prototype systems that can sometimes appear to be trivial or demeaning. Conversely, there has been less focus on other areas of research that could prove to be easier to achieve and potentially of more benefit to society. The time is ripe for other directions to take center stage in UbiComp. One such avenue promoted here is to consider how humankind's evolved practices of science, learning, health, work and play can be enhanced. This involves thinking about UbiComp not in terms of embedding the environment with all manner of pervasive technologies but instead as bounded ensembles of entities (e.g., tools, surfaces and lenses) that can be mobile, collaborative or remote, through which information, other people and the environment are viewed and interacted with when needed. Importantly, it argues for rethinking the nature of our relationship with the computer.

3   A New Agenda for UbiComp: Engaging User Experiences

I suggest here that it is highly profitable to recast UbiComp research in the context of a central motivation that computers were originally designed for, namely, as tools, devices and systems that can extend and engage people in their activities and pursuits. My reason for proposing this is based on the success of researchers who have started to take this approach. In particular, a number of user studies, exploring how UbiComp technologies are being appropriated, are revealing how the 'excitement of interaction' can be brought back in innovative ways; that is not frustrating and which is quite different from that experienced with desktop applications. For example, various mixed reality, physical-digital spaces and sensor-rich physical environments have been developed to enable people to engage and use multiple dynamic representations in novel ways: in scientific and working practices and in collaborative learning and experimental games. More extensive inquiries and decisions have been enabled *in situ*, e.g., determining the effects of deforestation in different continents and working out when is the best time to spray or pick grapes in a vineyard.

Recently, world famous computer scientist John Seely Brown put forward his updated vision of UbiComp[1] in a keynote, outlining 'a common sense' model that emphasizes how UbiComp can help to catalyze creativity [41]. He proposed that creating and learning be seen as integral to our work and leisure that are formed through re-creation and appropriation activities. In a similar vein, I argue that it is timely to switch from a reactive view of people towards a more proactive one. Instead of augmenting the environment to reduce the need for humans to think for themselves about what to do, what to select, etc., and doing it for them, we should consider how UbiComp technologies can be designed to augment the human intellect so that people can perform ever greater feats, extending their ability to learn, make decisions, reason, create, solve complex problems and generate innovative ideas. Weiser's idea that

---

[1] John Seely Brown was a co-author of the paper written by Weiser on calm technology.

technologies be designed to be 'so embedded, so fitting and so natural' that we use them without thinking about them needs to be counter-balanced; we should also be designing them to be exciting, stimulating and even provocative – causing us to reflect upon and think about our interactions with them. While Weiser promoted the advantages of calm computing I advocate the benefits of engaging UbiComp experiences that provoke us to learn, understand and reflect more upon our interactions with technologies and each other.

A central concern of the engaging UbiComp experiences agenda is to fathom out how best to represent and present information that is accessible via different surfaces, devices and tools for the activity at hand. This requires determining how to make intelligible, usable and useful, the recordings of science, medicine, etc., that are streaming from an increasing array of sensors placed throughout the world. It also entails figuring out how to integrate and replay, in meaningful and powerful ways, the masses of digital recordings that are begin gathered and archived such that professionals and researchers can perform new forms of computation and problem-solving, leading to novel insights. In addition, it involves experimenting more with creative and constructive uses of UbiComp technologies and archived digital material that will excite and even make people feel uncomfortable.

In terms of who should benefit, it is useful to think of how UbiComp technologies can be developed not for the Sal's of the world, but for particular domains that can be set up and customized by an individual firm or organization, such as for agriculture production, environmental restoration or retailing. At a smaller scale, it is important to consider how suitable combinations of sensors, mobile devices, shared displays, and computational devices can be assembled by non-UbiComp experts (such as scientists, teachers, doctors) that they can learn, customize and 'mash' (i.e., combine together different components to create a new use). Such toolkits should not need an army of computer scientists to set up and maintain, rather the inhabitants of ubiquitous worlds should be able to take an active part in controlling their set up, evolution and destruction. Their benefits should be clear: enabling quite different forms of information flow (i.e., ways and means of accessing information) and information management (i.e., ways of storing, recording, and re-using information) from older technologies, making it possible for non-UbiCompers to begin to see how to and subsequently develop their own systems that can make a difference to their worlds. In so doing, there should be an emphasis on providing the means by which to augment and extend existing practices of working, learning and science.

As quoted by Bruner [10] "to assist the development of the powers of the mind is to provide amplification systems to which human beings, equipped with appropriate skills, can link themselves" (p.53). To enable this to happen requires a better understanding of existing human practices, be it learning, working, communicating, etc. Part of this reconceptualization should be to examine the interplay between technologies and their settings in terms of practice and appropriation [15]. "Practices develop around technologies, and technologies are adapted and incorporated into practices." (Dourish, 2001, p. 204). More studies are needed that examine what people do with their current tools and devices in their surrounding environments. In addition, more studies are needed of UbiComp technologies being used *in situ* or the wild – to help illuminate how people can construct, appropriate and use them [e.g., 16, 22, 23, 29].

With respect to interaction design issues, we need to consider how to represent and present data and information that will enable people to more extensively compute, analyze, integrate, inquire and make decisions; how to design appropriate kinds of interfaces and interaction styles for combinations of devices, displays and tools; and how to provide transparent systems that people can understand sufficiently to know how to control and interact with them. We also need to find ways of enabling professionals and laypeople alike to build, adapt and leverage UbiComp technologies in ways that extend and map onto their activities and identified needs.

A more engaging and bounded approach to UbiComp is beginning to happen but in a scattered way. Three of the most promising areas are described below: (i) playful and learning practices, (ii) scientific practices and (iii) persuasive practices. They show how UbiComp technologies can be developed to extend or change human activities together with the pertinent issues that need to be addressed. Quite different practices are covered, reflecting how the scope of UbiComp can be broad but at the same time targeted at specific users and uses.

3.1 Playful and Learning Practices

One promising approach is to develop small-scale toolkits and sandboxes, comprising interlinked tools, digital representations and physical artifacts that offer the means by which to facilitate creative authoring, designing, learning, thinking and playing. By a sandbox it is not meant the various senses it has been used in computing but more literally as a physical-digital place, kitted out with objects and tangibles to play and interact with. Importantly, these should allow different groups of people to participate in novel activities that will provoke and extend existing repertoires of technology-augmented learning, playing, improvising and creating. An example of a promising UbiComp technology toolkit is PicoCrickets, developed at MIT Media Lab, arising from the work of Mitch Resnick and his colleagues. The toolkit comprises sensors, motors, lights, microcomputers, and other physical and electrical devices that can be easily programmed and assembled to make them react, interact and communicate, enabling "musical sculptures, interactive jewelry, dancing creatures and other playful inventions" to be created by children and adults alike. An advantage of such lightweight, off-the-shelf tangible toolkits is that they offer many opportunities for different user groups (e.g., educators, consultants) to assemble and appropriate in a range of settings, such as schools, waiting rooms, playgrounds, national parks, and museums.

A nagging question, however, is how do the benefits of such UbiComp toolkits and sandboxes compare with those offered by more conventional ones – that are much cheaper and more practical to make? Is it not the case that children can be highly creative and imaginative when given simply a cardboard box to play with? If so, why go to such lengths to provide them with new tools? The debate is redolent of whether it is better for children to read a book or watch a 3D IMAX movie. One is not necessarily better than the other: the two provide quite different experiences, triggering different forms of imagination, enjoyment and reflection. Likewise, UbiComp and physical toys can both provoke and stimulate, but promote different kinds of learning and collaboration among children. However, a benefit of UbiComp toolkits over physical artifacts is that they offer new opportunities to combine physical interaction, through manipulation of objects or tools or through physical body postural movement and location, with new ways of interacting, through digital technology. In particular, they provide different ways of thinking about the world than interacting solely with digital representations or solely with the physical world. In turn, this can encourage or even enhance further exploration, discovery, reflection and collaboration [35].

Examples of projects that have pioneered the design of novel physical-digital spaces to facilitate creativity and reflection include the Hunting of the Snark [32], Ambient Wood [36], RoomQuake [33] Savannah [17], Environmental Detectives [27], Drift Table [19] and Feeding Yoshi [7]. Each of these have experimented with the use of mobile, sensor and fixed technologies in combination with wireless infrastructures to encourage exploration, invention, and out of the box thinking.

The Hunting of the Snark adventure game provoked young children into observing, wondering, understanding, and integrating their fragmented experiences of novel physical-digital spaces that subsequently they reflected upon and shared as a narrative with each other. A combination of sensor-based, tangible, handheld and wireless technologies was used to create the physical-digital spaces, where an imaginary virtual creature was purported to be roaming around in. The children had to work out how to entice the creature to appear in them and then gather evidence about its personality, moods, etc, by walking with it, feeding it and flying with it. Similarly, Savannah was designed as a physical-digital game to encourage the development of children's conceptual understanding of animal behavior and interactions in an imaginary virtual world. The project used GPS and handheld computers to digitally overlay a school playing field with a virtual plain. Children took on the roles of lions, had to hunt animals in the virtual savannah and capture them to maintain energy levels. After the game, the children reflected on their experiences by interacting with a visualization on a large interactive whiteboard, that showed the trails they made in the Savannah and the sounds and images that they encountered at specific place.

The Ambient Wood project used an assortment of UbiComp technologies to encourage more self-initiation in inquiry and reflective learning. Various wireless and sensor technologies, devices and representational media were combined, designed and choreographed to appear and be used in an 'ambient' woodland. Several handcrafted listening, recording and viewing devices were created to present certain kinds of digital augmentations, such as sounds of biological processes, images of organisms, and video clips of life cycles. Some of these were triggered by the children's exploratory movements, others were collected by the children, while still others were aggregated and represented as composite information visualizations of their exploratory behavior. RoomQuake was designed to encourage children to practice scientific investigatory practices: an earthquake was simulated in a classroom using a combination of interconnected ambient media, string and physical styrofoam balls. The ambient media provided dynamic readings of the simulated earthquakes, which students then re-represented as physical models using the physical artifacts. The combination of computer-based simulations and physical-based artifacts enabled the whole class to take part in the measuring, modeling, interpreting, sparking much debate and reflection among the children about the seismic events.

As part of the Equator collaboration, a number of innovative 'seamful games' have been developed. The inherent limitations of ubiquitous technologies have been deliberately exploited to provoke the players into thinking about and acting upon their significance to the ongoing activity. Two examples are Treasure in which players had to move in and out of a wireless network connectivity to collect and then deposit gold tokens and Feeding Yoshi where the players were required to feed virtual creatures scattered around a city with virtual fruits that popped up on their displays as a result of their location and activity therein.

Evaluations of this emerging genre of physical-digital spaces for learning and playing have been positive, highlighting enhanced understanding and an immense sense of engagement. Children and adults have been able to step back and think about what they are doing when taking part in the game or learning experience, examining the rationale behind their choices when acting out and interacting with the UbiComp-based technologies in the space. However, many of the pioneering projects were technology, resource and researcher intensive. While guidance is now beginning to appear to help those wanting to design UbiComp-based learning and playing experiences [e.g., 9, 36] we need also to strive towards creating the next generation of physical-digital spaces and toolkits that will be as easy, cheap and popular to construct as Lego kits once were.

3.2 Scientific Practices

Another area where UbiComp has great potential for augmenting human activities is the practice of scientific inquiry and research. Currently, the sciences are going through a major transformation in terms of how they are studied and the computational tools that are used and needed. Microsoft's 2020 Science report – a comprehensive vision of science for the next 14 years written by a group of internationally distinguished scientists – outlines this paradigm shift [31]. It points out how new conceptual and technological tools are needed that scientists from different fields can "understand and learn from each other's solutions, and ultimately for scientists to acquire a set of widely applicable complex problem solving capabilities". These include new programming, computational, analysis and publication tools. There is much scope, too, for utilizing UbiComp technologies to enhance computation thinking, through integrating sensor-based instrumentation in the medical, environmental and chemical sciences. The ability to deliver multiple streams of dynamic data to scientists, however, needs to be matched by powerful interfaces that allow them to manipulate and share them in new ways, from any location whether in the lab or in the field.

Areas where there is likely to be obvious benefits to scientists through the integration of UbiComp and computational tools are environmental science and climate change. These involve collaborative visualization of scientific data, mobile access to data and capture of data from sensors deployed in the physical world. Being able to gain a bigger, better and more accurate picture of the environmental processes may help scientists make more accurate predictions and anticipate more effectively natural disasters, such as tsunamis, volcanoes, earthquakes and flooding. However, it may not simply be a case of more is more. New ways of managing the burgeoning datasets needs to be developed, that can be largely automated, but which also allows scientists to have effective windows, lenses etc., into so that they can interpret and make intelligible inferences from them at relevant times.

The 2020 report notes how tomorrow's scientists will need to make sense of the masses of data by becoming more computationally literate – in the sense of knowing how to make inferences from the emerging patterns and anomalies that the new generation of software analysis tools provide. To this end, a quite different mindset is needed in schools for how science is taught. The design of new learning experiences that utilize UbiComp technologies, both indoors and outdoors, need to be developed to seed in young children the sense of what is involved in practicing new forms of complex, computational science. An example of how this can be achieved is the embedded phenomena approach; scientific phenomena are simulated using UbiComp technologies, for long periods of time, to create opportunities for groups of students to explore 'patient' science [32]. Essentially, this involves the accumulation, analysis and representation of data collected from multiple computational devices over extended periods of observation in the classroom or other sites. In so doing, it allows students to engage in the collaborative practice of scientific investigation that requires hard computational thinking but which is also exciting, creative and authentic. A core challenge, therefore, is to find ways of designing novel science learning experiences that capitalize on the benefits of combining UbiComp and PC technologies that can be used over extended periods.

3.3 Persuasive Practices

The third area where there is much potential for using UbiComp technologies to engage people is as part of self-monitoring and behavioral change programs. While a range of persuasive technologies (e.g., adverts, websites, posters) has already been developed to change people's attitudes and behaviors, based on models of social learning [18], UbiComp technologies provide opportunities for new techniques. Specifically, mobile devices, such as PDAs coupled with on-body sensors, can be designed to enable people to take control and change their habits or lifestyles to be healthier by taking account of and acting upon dynamically updated information provided by them. For example, Intille and his group are exploring how mobile computational tools for assessing behavioral change, based on social psychology models, can be developed to motivate physical activity and healthy eating.

A key question that needs to be addressed is whether UbiComp technologies are more (or less) effective compared with other technologies in changing behavior. A diversity of media-based techniques (e.g., pop-up warning messages, reminders, prompts, personalized messages) has been previously used to draw people's attention to certain kinds of information to change what they do or think at a given point. In terms of helping people give up habits (e.g., smoking, excessive eating) they have had mixed results since people often relapse. It is in the long-term context that UbiComp technologies may prove to be most effective, being able to monitor certain aspects of people's behavior and represent this information at critically weak moments in a cajoling way. A constant but gentle 'nagging' mechanism may also be effective at persuading people to do something they might not have otherwise done or to not to do something they are tempted to do. For example, a collaborative cell phone application integrated with a pedometer was used to encourage cliques of teenage girls to monitor their levels of exercise and learn more about nutrition in the context of their everyday activities [44]. The software was designed to present the monitored process (e.g., walking) in a way that made it easy for the girls to compute and make inferences of how well they were doing in terms of the number of steps taken relative to each other. A preliminary study showed that such a collaborative self-monitoring system was effective at increasing the girl's awareness of their diet, level of exercise and enabling them to understand the computations involved in burning food during different kinds of exercise. But most significantly, it enabled the girls to share and discuss this information with each other in their private clique, capitalizing on both the persuasive technology and peer pressure.

Incorporating fun into the interface can also be an effective strategy; for example, Nintendo's Pocket Pikachu with pedometer attached was designed to motivate children into being more physically active on a consistent basis. The owner of the digital pet that 'lives' in the device is required to walk, run or jump each day to keep it alive. If the owner does not exercise for a week the virtual pet becomes unhappy and eventually dies. This can be a powerful means of persuasion given that children often become emotionally attached to their virtual pets, especially when they start to care for them.

UbiComp technologies can also be used to reduce bad habits through explicitly providing dynamic information that someone would not have been aware of otherwise. In so doing, it can make them actively think about their behavior and modify it accordingly. The WaterBot system was developed using a special monitoring and feedback device to reduce householder's usage of water in their homes – based on the premise that many people are simply unaware of how wasteful they are [3]. A sensor-based system was developed that provided positive auditory messages and chimes when the tap was turned off. A central idea was to encourage members of the household to talk to one another about their relative levels of water usage provided by the display and to try to out do one another in the amount of water used.

But to what extent do UbiComp technologies, designed for persuasive uses, differ from the other forms of monitoring that were critiqued earlier in the paper? A main difference is that there is more active involvement of those being monitored in attaining their desired behavior change compared with those who were being monitored and assisted in care homes. The objective is to enable people, themselves, to engage with the collected information, by monitoring, understanding, interpreting and acting upon it – and not the environment or others to act upon their behalf. Much of the research to date in UbiComp and healthcare has focussed on automated bio-monitoring of physiological processes, such as EEGs and heart rate, which others, i.e., specialists, examine and use to monitor their patient's health. In contrast, persuasive technologies are intended to provide dynamic information about a behavioral process that will encourage people from doing or not doing something, by being alerted and/or made aware of the consequences of what they are about to do. Moreover, designing a device to be solely in the control of the users (and their social group) enables them to be the owners of the collected data. This circumvents the need to be centrally concerned with privacy issues, allowing the focus of the research to be more oriented towards considering how best to design dynamically updated information to support cognitive and social change. A challenge, however, in this area is for long term studies to be conducted that can convincingly show that it is the perpetual and time-sensitive nature of the sensed data and the type of feedback provided that contributes to behavioral modification.

4 Conclusions

Many of the research projects that have followed in the footsteps of Weiser's vision of calm computing have been disappointing; their achievements being limited by the extent to which they have been able to program computers to act on behalf of humans. Just as 'strong' AI failed to achieve its goals – where it was assumed that "the computer is not merely a tool in the study of the mind; rather, the appropriately programmed computer really is a mind" [41], it appears that 'strong' UbiComp is suffering from the same fate. And just as 'weak' AI² revived AI's fortunes, so, too, can 'weak' UbiComp bring success to the field. This will involve pursuing more practical goals and addressing less ambitious challenges; where ensembles of technologies are designed for specific activities to be used by people in bounded locations. To make this happen, however, requires moving from a mindset that wants to make the environment smart and proactive to one that enables people, themselves, to be smarter and proactive in their everyday and working practices. Three areas of research were suggested as to how this could be achieved; but, equally, there are others where there is much potential for enhancing and extending human activities (e.g., vineyard computing [11], firefighting [24] and sports). As part of the expansion of UbiComp, a wider range of human aspects should be considered, drawing upon alternative theory, guiding frameworks and metaphors [c.f. 8, 15]. To enable other human concerns to become more prominent, however, requires the hefty weight of privacy and other related ethical issues on UbiComp's shoulders to be lessoned.

The 'excitement of interaction' that Weiser suggested forsaking in the pursuit of a vision of calm living should be embraced again, enabling users, designers and researchers to participate in the creation of a new generation of user experiences that go beyond what is currently possible with our existing bricolage of tools and media. We should be provoking people in their scientific, learning, analytic, creative, playing and personal activities and pursuit. Finally, while we have been privileged to have had such a great visionary, whose legacy has done so much to help shape the field, it is timely for a new set of ideas, challenges and goals to come to the fore and open up the field.

Acknowledgements

Thanks to Tom Rodden for his suggestions on an earlier draft and the anonymous reviewers for their constructive comments.

References

1. Abowd, G.D., Mynatt. E.D.: Charting past, present, and future research in ubiquitous computing. ACM Transactions on Computer-Human Interaction, 7 (2000) 29-58
2. Anderson, K., Dourish, P.: Situated Privacies: Do you know where you mother [trucker] is? In Proceedings of the 11th International Conference on Human-Computer Interaction. Las Vegas. July 22-27, 2005

---

² Weak AI refers to the development of software programs to perform specific problem-solving or reasoning tasks that do not have to match the way humans do them.

3. Arroyo, E., Bonnanni, L., Selker, T.: WaterBot: exploring feedback and persuasive techniques at the sink. In CHI Proceedings, ACM, New York, 631-639, 2005

4. Ashley, S.: Cognitive Radio, Scientific American, (March 2006), 67-73

5. Augmented Cognition International Society. http://www.augmentedcognition.org/, Retrieved on 30/03/2006

6. Beckwith, R., Lederer, S.: Designing for one's dotage: UbiComp and Residential Care facilities. Conference on the Networked Home and the Home of the Future (HOIT 2003), Irvine, CA: April 2003

7. Bell, M., Chalmers, M., Barkhuus, L., Hall, M., Sherwood, S., Tennent, P., Brown. B., Rowland, D., Benford, S., Hampshire, A., Captra, M.: Interweaving mobile games with everyday life. In Proceedings of CHI'06, Conference on Human Factors in Computing. ACM Press, (2006) 417-426

8. Bellotti, V., Back, M., Edwards, K., Grinter, R., Henderson. A., Lopes, C.: Making sense of sensing systems: five questions for designers and researchers. In Proceedings of CHI'2002, ACM Press, (2002) 415-422

9. Benford, S., Schnädelbach, H., Koleva, B., Anastasi, R., Greenhalgh, C., Rodden, T., Green, J., Ghali, A., Pridmore, T., Gaver, B., Boucher, A., Walker, B., Pennington, S., Schmidt, A., Gellersen, H., Steed, A.: Expected, sensed, and desired: A framework for designing sensing-based interaction. ACM Trans. Comput.-Hum. Interact. 12 (2005) 3-30

10. Bruner, J.S. The Relevance of Education. Harmondsworth, Middlesex, UK. (1972)

11. Burrell, J., Brooke, T., Beckwith, R.: Vineyard Computing: Sensor Networks in agricultural production, Pervasive Computing, 3(1) (2004) 38-45

12. Chalmers, D., Chalmers, M., Crowcroft, J., Kwiatkowska, M., Milner, R., O'Neill, E., Rodden, T., Sassone, V., Sloman, M.: Ubiquitous Computing: Experience, design and science. Version 4. http://www-dse.doc.ic.ac.uk/Projects/UbiNet/GC/index.html Retrieved on 30/03/2006

13. Consolvo, S., Roessler, P., Shelton, B., LaMarca, A., Schilit, B., Bly, S.: Technology for care networks for elders. Pervasive Computing 3 (2004) 22-29

14. Digiens@U-City.:   Korea   moves   into   ubiquitous   mode. http://digiens.blogspot.com/2005/08/korea-moves-into-ubiquitous-mode.html.   Retrieved 30/03/2006

15. Dourish, P.: Where the action is: the foundation of embodied interaction. MIT, Cambridge, MA., (2001)

16. Dourish, P., Grinter, B., Delgado de la Flor, J., Joseph, M.: Security in the wild: user strategies for managing security as an everyday, practical problem. Personal and Ubiquitous Computing, 8 (6) (2004) 391-401

17. Facer, K., Joiner, R., Stanton, D., Reid, J., Hull, R., Kirk, D.: Savannah: mobile gaming and learning. Journal of Computer Assisted Learning, 20 (2004) 399-409

18. Fogg, B.J.: Persuasive Technology: Using Computers to change what we think and do. Morgan Kaufmann Publishers, San Fransisco. (2003)

19. Gaver, W. W., Bowers, J., Boucher, A., Gellersen, H., Pennington, S., Schmidt, A., Steed, A., Villars, N., Walker, B.: The drift table: designing for ludic engagement. In Proceedings of CHI Extended Abstracts (2004) 885-900.

20. Greenfield, A.: Everyware: The Dawning Age of Ubiquitous Computing. New Riders, Berkeley, CA. (2006)

21. Intel   Research   at   Intel: Research   Seattle. www.intel.com/research/network/seattle_collab.htm. Retrieved on 20/03/2006.

22. Intille, S., Larson, K., Beaudin, J., Nawyn, J., Munguia Tapia, E., Kaushik, P.: A living laboratory for the design and evaluation of ubiquitous computing technologies. In Proceedings of CHI Extended Abstracts (2005) 1941-1944

23. Intille, S.S., Bao, L., Munguia Tapia, E., Rondoni, J.: Acquiring in situ training data for context-aware ubiquitous computing applications. In Proceedings CHI (2004) 1-8

24. Jiang, X., Chen, N.Y., Hong, J.I., Wang, K., Takayama, L.A., Landay, J.A.: Siren: Context-aware Computing for Firefighting. In Proceedings of Second International Conference on Pervasive Computing. Lecture Notes in Computer Science, Springer Berlin Heidelberg 87-105 (2004)

25. Journal of Ubiquitous Computing and Intelligence. www.aspbs.com/juci.html Retrieved 20/03/2006/

26. Kindberg, T., Fox, A.: System Software for Ubiquitous Computing. IEEE Pervasive Computing, 1 (1) (2002) 70-81

27. Klopfer, E., K. Squire.: Environmental Detectives – The Development of an Augmented Reality Platform for Environmental Simulations. Educational Technology Research and Development. (2005)

28. Krikke, J.: T-Engine: Japan's Ubiquitous Computing Architecture is ready for prime time. Pervasive Computing (2005) 4-9

29. LaMarca, A., Chawathe, Y., Consolvo, S., Hightower, J., Smith, I., Scott, J., Sohn, T., Howard, J., Hughes, J., Potter, F., Tabert, J., Powledge, P., Borriello, G., Schilit. B.: Place Lab: Device Positioning Using Radio Beacons in the Wild, Intel Research, IRS-TR-04-016, (2004) http://placelab.org/publications/pubs/IRS-TR-04-016.pdf

30. Marmasse, N., Schmandt, C.: Location-aware information delivery with commotion, In HUC 2000 Proceedings, Springer-Verlag, (2000) 157-171

31. Microsoft 2020 Science.: http://research.microsoft.com/towards2020science/. Retrieved 30/03/2006

32. Moher, T.: Embedded Phenomena: Supporting science learning with classroom-sized-distribution simulations. In Proceedings of CHI 2006

33. Moher, T., Hussain, S., Halter, T., Kilb, D..: RoomQuake: embedding dynamic phenomena within the physical space of an elementary school classroom. Extended Abstracts, In Proceedings of CHI'05, Conference on Human Factors in Computing Systems. ACM Press (2005) 1655-1668

34. Mynatt, E., Melenhorst, A., Fisk, A.D., Rogers, W.: Aware technologies for aging in place: Understanding user needs and attitudes. Pervasive Computing (2004) 36-41

35. Price, S. Rogers, Y. Let's get physical: the learning benefits of interacting in digitally augmented physical spaces. Journal of Computers and Education, 43 (2004) 137-151

36. Rogers, Y., Muller, H.: A framework for designing sensor-based interactions to promote exploration and reflection. International Journal of Human-Computer Studies, 64 (1) (2005) 1-15

37. Rogers, Y., Price, S., Fitzpatrick, G., Fleck, R., Harris, E., Smith, H., Randell, C., Muller, H., O'Malley, C., Stanton, D., Thompson, M., Weal, M.: Ambient Wood: Designing new forms of digital augmentation for learning outdoors. In Proceedings of Interaction Design and Children, ACM (2004) 1-8

38. Rogers, Y., Scaife, M., Harris, E., Phelps, T., Price, S., Smith, H., Muller, H., Randall, C., Moss, A., Taylor, I., Stanton, D., O'Malley, C., Corke, G., Gabrielli, S.: Things aren't what they seem to be: innovation through technology inspiration. In Proceedings of DIS'2002 Designing Interactive Systems, ACM Press, (2002) 373-379

39. Ross, D.A.: Cyber Crumbs for successful aging with vision loss. Pervasive Computing, 3 (2004) 30-35

40. Salvador, T., Anderson, K. Practical Considerations of Context for Context Based Systems: An Example from an Ethnographic Case Study of a Man Diagnosed with Early Onset Alzheimer's Disease. In UbiComp'03 Proceedings, A.K. Dey et al. (Eds.), LNCS 2864, Springer-Verlag Berlin Heidelberg, 243-255, 2003

41. Seely Brown, J.: Ubiquitous Computing and beyond – an emerging new common sense model. www.johnseelybrown.com/JSB.pdf. Retrieved 20/03/2006

42. Stirling, B.: Without Vision, the People Perish. Speech Given at CRA Conference on Grand Research Challenges in Computer Science and Engineering. Airlie House, Warrenton, Virginia, June 23, 2002 www.cra.org/Activities/grand.challenges/sterling.html Retrieved 20/03/2006

43. Tennenhouse, D.L. "Proactive Computing," Communications of the ACM 43, No. 5, 43–50, 2000

44. Toscos, T., Faber, A., An, S., Gandhi, M.; Chick Clique: Persuasive Technology to Motivate Teenage Girls to Exercise. In CHI'06 Extended Abstracts on Human Factor in Computing Systems, ACM Press (2006) 1873-1878

45. Tran, Q., Calcaterra, G., Mynatt, E.: Cook's Collage: Deja Vu Display for a Home Kitchen. In Proceedings of HOIT 2005, 15-32

46. Weiser, M., Brown, J.S.: The coming age of calm technology. (1996) www.ubiq.com/hypertext/weiser/acmfuture2endnote.htm. Retrieved 20/03/2006/

47. Weiser, M.: The computer for the 21st century. Scientific American (1991) 94–104

Ferret: RFID Localization for Pervasive Multimedia

Xiaotao Liu, Mark D. Corner, and Prashant Shenoy

Department of Computer Science
University of Massachusetts, Amherst, MA
{xiaotaol, mcorner, shenoy}@cs.umass.edu

Abstract. The pervasive nature of multimedia recording devices enables novel pervasive multimedia applications with automatic, inexpensive, and ubiquitous identification and locationing abilities. We present
the design and implementation of Ferret, a scalable system for locating
nomadic objects augmented with RFID tags and displaying them to a
user in real-time. We present two alternative algorithms for refining a
postulation of an object's location using a stream of noisy readings from
an RFID reader: an online algorithm for real-time use on a mobile device,
and an offline algorithm for use in post-processing applications. We also
present methods for detecting when nomadic objects move and how to
reset the algorithms to restart the refinement process. An experimental
evaluation of the Ferret prototype shows that (i) Ferret can refine object
locations to only 1% of the reader's coverage region in less than 2 minutes with small error rate (2.22%); (ii) Ferret can detect nomadic objects
with 100% accuracy when the nomadic distances exceed 20cm; and (iii)
Ferret works with a variety of user mobility patterns.

1   Introduction

Advances in digital imaging technologies have led to a proliferation of consumer
devices with video capture capabilities. The pervasive nature of multimedia
recording devices such as cellphones, digital camcorders, PDAs and laptops,
has made it relatively simple to capture, transform, and share large volumes
of personal video and image content. A concurrent trend is the emergence of
low-cost identification technologies such as RFID tags, designed to replace barcodes [12]. Each tag contains a numeric code that uniquely identifies the object
and can be queried by a wireless reader. It is likely that in the near future many
personal objects (e.g., books, clothing, food items, furniture) will be equipped
with self-identifying RFID tags.

The confluence of these trends—the ubiquity of RFID tags and the pervasive
nature of multimedia recording devices—enables novel pervasive multimedia applications with automatic, inexpensive, and ubiquitous identification and location abilities. By equipping cameras with RFID readers, it is possible to record
images as well as the identities and locations of all RFID-tagged objects contained within each image. The captured video can then be queried in real-time
to display the location of a particular object.

P. Dourish and A. Friday (Eds.): Ubicomp 2006, LNCS 4206, pp. 422–440, 2006.

While the inexpensive nature of RFID tags eases large-scale deployment issues, their passive nature raises a number of hurdles. A key limitation is that passive RFID tags are *self-identifying* but not *self-locating* (i.e., upon being queried, a tag can report its identify but not its location). Consequently, if multiple objects are present in a captured image, it is not possible to distinguish between these objects or pinpoint their individual locations. Some of the applications (e.g., pinpointing a misplaced book on a bookshelf) require location information in addition to object identities. While numerous locationing technologies such as GPS and ultrasound [10,13,14] are available, it is not possible to equip passive RFID tags with these capabilities due to reasons of cost, form-factor and limited battery life. Instead, we require a locationing technology that does not depend on modifications to tags, is easily maintained, and scales to hundreds or thousands of tagged objects.

To address the above challenges, we have designed a system called *Ferret*. Ferret combines locationing technologies with pervasive multimedia applications. Ferret can locate objects using their RFID tags and displays their locations in real-time to a mobile user. As the positions of objects are uncertain, the system overlays the video display with an outline of where the object probably is. For instance, a user with a portable camera can ask the system to display the location of every new object in the room, and the display will show an outline of all of those locations. The display is constantly updated as the user moves using the continuous stream of tag readings to update locations.

Ferret uses the *location and directionality of RFID readers* to infer the locations of nearby *tags*. Ferret leverages the user's inherent mobility to produce readings of the tag from multiple vantage points. It does this through two novel algorithms that refine the locations of objects using a stream of noisy readings from RFID tags. One algorithm is designed for offline use, given a large amount of computational power, while the other is designed to operate in real-time on a mobile system. In the case of the offline algorithm, we also incorporate negative readings—when the reader *does not* see the object—this greatly reduces the object's possible locations.

We have implemented a prototype of Ferret and have used it to conduct a detailed performance evaluation. Our experiments pay specific attention to how fast Ferret can refine object locations, the error rate in locating objects, and how well it handles nomadic objects. Our results show that (i) Ferret can refine object locations to only 1% of the reader's coverage region in less than 2 minutes with small error rate (2.22%); (ii) The offline algorithm incorporates information about not seeing the object, outperforming the online algorithm by a factor of 13 or more; (iii) Ferret can detect nomadic objects with 100% accuracy when the moving distances exceed 20cm; and (iv) Ferret works with a wide variety of user mobility patterns.

Ferret provides systems support for a variety of new applications. For instance, users can locate a misplaced book on a bookshelf. Robots can use such devices to conduct real-time identification and search operations. Vision-based applications can use them to quickly learn the structure or organization of a

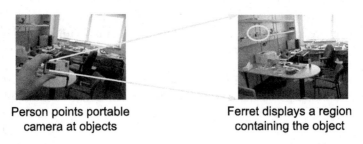

Person points portable   Ferret displays a region
camera at objects   containing the object

Fig. 1. Use of Ferret to discover the location of a soup can in an office

space. Inventory tracking applications can proactively generate missing object alerts upon detecting the absence of an object. We imagine that the ability to locate and identify thousands of objects in a space will enable new opportunities in vision and graphics, such as augmented reality and immersive systems.

2   Ferret Design

Ferret is designed to operate on a handheld video camera with a display. To use Ferret, the user selects some set of objects she would like to locate in the room and moves around the room with the camera. Using an RFID reader embedded in the video camera, Ferret samples for nearby tags, and in real-time updates the camera's display with an *outline* of the probable location of the objects she is searching for. Ferret's knowledge of object location can be imprecise, so rather than showing a single centroid point, Ferret displays the outline, leaving the interpretation of the precise location to the user's cognition. For instance, if Ferret can narrow the location of a book to a small region on a shelf, a user can quickly find the precise location. Figure 1 provides a pictorial representation of how the system would work. In this scenario the user is looking for a coffee cup in a messy office. After scanning the room using a Ferret-based camera, the system highlights a small region that contains the cup.

2.1   Nomadic Location with RFID

Many pervasive systems that rely on location are predicated on the assumption that the number of objects requiring location information is small and mobile. In contrast, we designed Ferret to support a massive number of mostly static, or nomadic objects—objects that change locations infrequently. As a fraction of all objects, nomadic and static ones are in the vast majority—in any given room it is likely that there are hundreds, or possibly thousands of nomadic and static objects, while there are only a few mobile ones.

The primary barrier to providing locationing information for such a large number of objects is the reliance on batteries—making objects self-locating requires the use of a battery-powered locationing hardware. Even though locationing systems such as ultrasound [10] and Ultra-Wide Band (UWB) are becoming more energy efficient, equipping hundreds of objects in a room with self-locating capabilities simply does not scale, since it will require changing an unmanageable number of batteries. In contrast, passive RFID provides a battery-free, inexpensive, distributed, and easily maintained method for identifying objects; Ferret adds locationing capabilities to such objects. Ferret leverages the fact that an increasing number of objects will be equipped with RFID tags as a replacement to barcodes. Further, RFID tags continue to drop in price, and one can imagine attaching tags to a large number of household or office objects.

As RFID tags are passive devices and have no notion of their own location, Ferret must continuously calculate and improve its own notion of the object locations. The system fuses a stream of noisy, and imprecise readings from an RFID reader to formulate a proposition of the object's location. The key insight in Ferret is to exploit the location of a camera/reader to infer the location of objects in its vicinity. In essence, any tag that can be read by a reader must be contained within its sensing range; by maintaining a history of tags read by the system, Ferret can progressively narrow the region containing the object. This is a simple yet elegant technique for inferring the location of passive RFID tags without expensive, battery-powered locationing capabilities.

2.2 Infrastructure Requirements

Strictly speaking, calculating and displaying object locations does not require any infrastructural support. Displaying a location on the video, as well as combining multiple readings of the object location, only requires *relative* locations, such as those from inertial navigation systems [1]. However, it is likely that knowledge of object locations in relation to a known coordinate system, such as GPS or a building map, will be useful for many applications. We assume that the camera/reader uses such a locationing system, such as ultrasound or UWB, to determine its own location and then uses it to infer the location of objects in its vicinity.

As Ferret uses a directional video camera and RFID reader, it also requires an orientation system that can measure the pan (also known as heading and yaw), tilt (also known as pitch), and roll of the system. While research has proposed orientation systems for ultrasound [10], we have chosen to a use commercially available digital compass. Similar to the locationing system, Ferret benefits from having absolute orientation, although it can operate with only a relative orientation.

2.3 Location Storage

For each object, Ferret must store a description of the object's location. Considering that some RFID tags are remotely rewritable, Ferret can store the location for an object directly on the tag itself. Other options are to store the locations locally in each Ferret reader, or in an online, external database. Each option provides different privacy, performance, and management tradeoffs. Storing locations locally on each reader means that each independent Ferret device must start finding objects with zero initial knowledge. As the device moves and senses the same object from different vantage points, it can use a sequence of readings to infer and refine the object location. The advantage of this method is that it works with read-only RFID tags and does not require any information sharing across devices. However, it prevents the device from exploiting history available from other readers that have seen the object in the recent past. In contrast, if location information can be remotely written to the RFID tags then other Ferret devices can start with better initial estimates of object location. However, this option requires writable tags and the small storage available on a tag limits the amount of history that can be maintained. In both of the above options, any device that has an RFID reader can determine object locations without needing the full complexity of the Ferret system.

A third option is to store the location information in a central database. This has the advantages of allowing offline querying and providing initial location estimates to mobile readers; further, since database storage is plentiful, the system can store long histories as well as past locations of nomadic objects. However, it requires readers to have connectivity to the database, the burden of management, and privacy controls on the database. Storing data on the tags also has implications for privacy control, however one must at least be proximate to the tag to query its location.

At the heart of Ferret is an RFID localization system that can infer the locations of individual passive RFID tagged objects. Ferret then uses this localization system to dynamically discover, update, store, and display object locations. The following section presents the design of our RFID localization technique.

3   RFID Locationing

Consider an RFID reader that queries all tags in its vicinity—the reader emits a signal and tags respond with their unique identifier. Given all responses to a query, the reader can produce positive or negative assertions whether a particular tag is present within its reading range. The reader can not directly determine the exact location of the tag in relation to the reader, or even a distance measurement. However, just one positive reading of a tag greatly reduces the possible locations for that particular object—a positive reading indicates that the object is contained in the volume defined by the read range of the reader (see Figure 2). Ferret leverages the user's mobility to produce a series of readings; the coverage region from each reading is intersected with all readings from the recent past, further reducing the possible locations for the object (see Figure 3). Using this method, Ferret can continually improve its postulation of the object location.

In addition to positive readings of an object's RFID tag, the reader implicitly indicates a negative reading whenever it fails to get a reading for a particular tag that it is looking for. Using a similar method to positive readings, Ferret subtracts the reader's coverage region from the postulation of the object's location. This also improves the postulation of the object's location. A third method to reduce the likely positions for the object is to modulate the power output of the reader. If a particular power output produces a positive reading, and a lower power produces a negative reading, the system has gained additional knowledge about the location of the object.

In general, whenever a tag is present in the read range, the reader is assumed to detect it with a certain probability—objects closer to the centroid of its read range are detected with higher probabilities, while objects at the boundary are detected with lower probabilities. Thus, each positive reading not only gives us a region that is likely to contain the object, it also associates probability values for each point within that region. This *coverage map* of a reader is shown in Figure 2. The map can be determined from the antenna data sheet, or by manually mapping the probability of detecting tags at different (x,y,z) offsets from the reader.

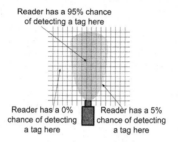

Fig. 2. Coverage region

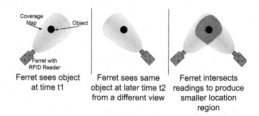

Fig. 3. Refining location estimates

Given a three dimensional grid of the environment and assuming no prior history, Ferret starts with an initial postulate that associates an unknown probability of finding the object at each coordinate within the grid. For each positive reading, the probability values of each grid point contained within the coverage range are refined (by intersecting the range with past history as shown in Figure 3). Similarly, for each negative reading, the the probability values of each grid point contained within the coverage range is decreased. This results in a three-dimensional map, $M(x, y, z)$, that contains the probability of seeing a tag at each data point in relation to the reader. Using multiple power outputs requires building a map for each power output level. Due to several constraints in our current prototype, Ferret currently does not use power modulation; however, adding this to the system will be trivial.

The amount of computation that the system can do drastically affects the location algorithm that performs intersections, the compensation for false negatives, and how it reflects the map to the user. Next we describe two alternative methods, one that is computationally intense and cannot be done in realtime on current mobile hardware. Such an offline technique is useful for describing an eventual goal for the system, or how to use the system for analyzing the data after it is collected. However, our goal is to implement Ferret on a mobile device so we also describe an online algorithm with drastically reduced computational cost.

3.1   Offline Locationing Algorithm

Formally, if we consider Ferret's readings as a series of readings, both positive and negative, as a series $D = \{D_1, D_2, D_3, ...D_n\}$, and we want to derive the probability of the object being at position X, given the readings from the RFID, or $P(X|D)$. If we assume that each reading of the RFID reader is an independent trial, we can compute the likelihood as:

$$P(X|D) = \frac{P(X|\{D_1, ...D_{n-1}\})P(D_n|X)}{P(\{D_1...D_N)\}} \frac{1}{Z}, \qquad (1)$$

where Z is a normalization factor. We omit the proof as it is a straight-forward application of conditional probability.

   If we first assume that the Ferret device (camera) is completely stationary, it operates as follows: i) once Ferret receives the first positive reading of a tag it initializes a three dimensional map, L, with the coverage map M, to track the probability that the object is at each of the coordinates in the map. ii) each successive reading multiplies each coordinate in L by $M(x, y, z)$ if the reading was positive, or $1 - M(x, y, z)$ if the reading was negative. This approach is derived from Elfes's work on occupancy grids for robotic navigation [3], and is equivalent to Hähnel's approach for using sensor readings to locate RFID tags [6].

3.2   Translation, Rotation and Projection

The basic algorithm described above assumes a stationary camera/reader; Ferret's notion of object location does not improve beyond a point, even with a large number of readings—most points in the reader's range (i.e., within the coverage map) will continue to have a high, and equally likely probability of detecting the tag. Subsequently, multiple readings produce a large map with equally likely probabilities of the object's location. Instead, Ferret depends on the user's *motion* to reduce the possibilities for the object location—as the user moves in the environment, the same object is observed by the camera from multiple vantage points and intersecting these ranges allows Ferret to narrow the region containing the object. Incorporating motion is straightforward; however, the coordinate system of the coverage map M must be reconciled with that of the map L before this can be done.

   The coverage map shown in Figure 3 is described in a three-dimensional coordinate system with the origin at the center of the reader's RFID antenna, which we refer to as the *reader coordinate system*. The camera, although attached to the RFID reader, is offset from the reader, and has a slightly different coordinate system. We refer to this as the *camera coordinate system* which has its origin at the center of the camera's CCD sensor. To combine multiple readings from the reader, and subsequently display them to the user, each map M must be transformed into a common coordinate system. We refer to this as the *world coordinate system*. The world can have its origin at any point in the space—with a locationing system we can use its origin, or with an inertial location system we can use the first location of the reader. Performing this transformation is possible using techniques from linear algebra and computer graphics [5]. Further details can be found in a technical report [15].

When computing the intersection of coverage maps, Ferret first transforms the coverage map, M into the world coordinate system, and computes the intersection according to the methods presented in Section 3.1 to produce a new map L containing the likelihood of an object's location.

Once Ferret produces a three dimensional map that it believes contains a particular object, it must overlay this region onto the video screen of the camera; doing so involves projecting a 3D map onto a two dimensional display. This is done in two steps: thresholding and projection. The threshold step places a minimum value for the likelihood on the map L— by using a small, but non-zero value for the threshold, Ferret reduces the volume that encompasses the likely position of the object. However, using a larger threshold may cause Ferret to shrink the volume excessively, thus missing the object. Currently this is a tunable parameter in Ferret—in the evaluation section we demonstrate how to choose a reasonable value.

Finally, Ferret projects the intersection map onto the image plane of the video display. Ferret must transform the intersection map from the world coordinate system into the camera coordinate system. Ferret performs this transformation using the camera's current position and orientation. Assuming that the z-axis of the camera coordinate system is co-linear with the camera's optical axis, projecting the image onto the image plane is straightforward.

For each reading the RFID reader produces, the location algorithm must perform $O(n^3)$ operations, for a three dimensional space that is $n \times n \times n$, in addition to translating and rotating the coverage map, and projecting the location map onto the display. If Ferret is searching for multiple objects, it must perform these operations for *each* individual object. In practice, we have found that each RFID reading consumes 0.7 seconds on a modern processor, while our RFID reader produces 4 readings per second. Given the speed at which a human may move the camera, this is not feasible to do in realtime, however it works well for an offline system that has less stringent latency requirements. An offline algorithm also has the opportunity to perform these operations for the whole video, and then use the smallest region that it computed to back-annotate the entire video stream with that region.

3.3   Online Locationing Algorithm

Given that the offline algorithm is too computationally intensive for a mobile device to operate in real-time, we describe a greatly simplified version of the locationing algorithm. The primary goal is to reduce the representation of the probability of where the object is. Instead of a full representation that describes the probability at each location, we reduce it to describing just the convex region where the object is with very high probability. Describing such a region is very compact, as we only need to track the points that describe the perimeter of the convex region. Intersecting two maps is very fast, as it is a series of line intersections.

Figure 4 shows this in detail for two dimensions, extending it to three dimensions is straightforward. The first half of the diagram shows sample points that describe the outside of the coverage map. Ferret rotates and translates the coverage map M as described in the previous section, and intersects it with the current map L. For each constant y value, the system finds the intersection of the two line segments and uses that as the description of the new map L. For instance in Figure 4, we choose a constant y value $y1$. After rotating and translating the map M to match to the reader's current position, the system intersects the two line segments, $(x1, y1) - (x3, y1)$ from the current map L, with $(x2, y1) - (x4, y1)$ from the new map M. The resulting intersection is the segment $(x2, y1) - (x3, y1)$, which describes the perimeter of the new location map L. Ferret repeats this process for all y values. Extending this to three dimensions is straightforward: intersect two line segments for each pair of constant y and z value. This means the complexity of the intersection is $O(n^2)$ rather than $O(n^3)$ as in the offline algorithm.

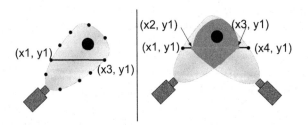

Fig. 4. Online location estimation

Also, instead of using a map of probabilities for the coverage map, we reduce it to the convex shape that describes the coverage region of the RFID reader than can read tags with some probability greater than 0. This virtually eliminates the possibility of false positives. Additionally, describing the perimeter only requires two x points for each pair of y and z values, thus the representation of the region is greatly reduced in size from $O(n^3)$ to $O(n^2)$. Using our prototype as an example, this reduces the storage requirement from 43.5M bytes to 178K bytes—each of these are highly compressible. This greatly aids Ferret's ability to store the regions directly on the storage-poor tags. The line segment representation does mean that the system cannot incorporate negative regions, as intersecting with a negative region can create a concave, rather than convex, region. A concave region would return the complexity of the representation and the intersection to $O(n^3)$. False negatives do not affect the system, as negative readings are not used at all.

3.4   Dealing with Nomadic Objects

We designed Ferret to deal with objects that move infrequently—commonly referred to as nomadic—as opposed to mobile objects that move frequently. When objects do move, Ferret should adjust to deal with this. In the online algorithm, this is straightforward. When the location algorithm performs an intersection of two maps, it may produce a region of zero volume. This indicates that the maps were disjoint, and the object could not possibly be within the previously postulated region. The system then reinitializes the location map, L, to the most current reading, which is M rotated and translated to the reader's current position.

However, the offline algorithm is more complicated as it produces a likelihood location map. One solution is applying a likelihood threshold to the likelihood location map and removing any location with a probability less than the threshold. If the resulting location map is empty, we will consider that the object has moved and reinitialize the location map, L, to the most current reading. Choosing an appropriate threshold is a critical factor in this approach. Using a larger threshold will increase the likelihood that the resulting location map is empty when the object actually did not move. In Section 5, we show how to choose an appropriate threshold.

4   Implementation Considerations

We have implemented a prototype Ferret system as shown in Figure 5. Although the prototype is quite large, this is due to the combination of many separate pieces of hardware—there is nothing that would preclude a much smaller commercial version. Our prototype is based on the following hardware:

A *ThingMagic Mercury4 RFID reader.* The output power of the reader is set to 30dBm (1Watt). This reader operates at the frequency range 909 – 928MHz, and supports RFID tags of EPC Class 0, EPC Class 1, and ISO 18000-6B. The reader is paired with a ThingMagic monostatic circular antenna that has a balloon shaped radiation pattern. An alternative is to a use a linear antenna that has a more focused radiation pattern and longer range; however, the narrower beam will produce fewer positive readings for each tag. The tradeoff in antenna choice and the possibility of future antennas with variable radiation patterns are interesting questions for future research. We used an orientation-insensitive, EPC Class 1, Alien Technology "M" RFID tag operating at 915MHz.

A *Sony Motion Eye web-camera* connected to a Sony Vaio laptop. This CMOS-based camera is set to a fixed focal length of 2.75mm, and uses a sensor size

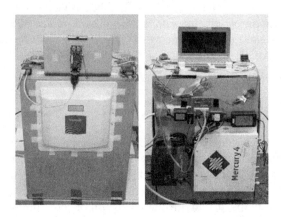

Fig. 5. Ferret Prototype System

of 2.4mm by 1.8mm. The camera provides uncompressed 320x240 video at 12 frames-per-second.

Cricket [10] ultrasound 3D locationing system to estimate the location of the camera and RFID reader. We deployed Cricket beacons on the ceiling, and attached a Cricket sensor to our prototype system. The Cricket sensor is offset from the camera and RFID reader and we correct for this translation in software.

A *Sparton SP3003D digital compass* to obtain the 3D orientations (pan, tilt, and roll) of the camera's lens and the reader's antenna. We mounted the compass, the camera's lens, and the reader's antenna with the same 3D orientation.

5 Experimental Evaluation

In this section, we evaluate Ferret by focusing on the performance of locationing and projection. In particular, we concentrate on how quickly Ferret can refine the location of an object for a user. We show how to tune the offline algorithm to trade the size of the location region and the overall error rate. We then show a comparison of the online and offline systems. We demonstrate that Ferret

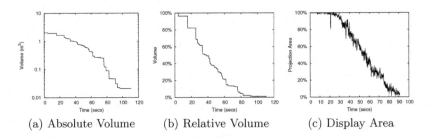

(a) Absolute Volume   (b) Relative Volume   (c) Display Area

Fig. 6. Online refinement of location

can detect objects that move within a room and we show the computation and storage costs of our system.

We measure Ferret's performance using two metrics: the size of the postulated location and the error rate. Ferret automatically provides the size, either the volume of the three-dimensional region, or the area of the two-dimensional projection on the video screen. The three-dimensional region is not spherical, but to interpret the results, a sphere with a volume of $0.01m^3$ has a diameter of $26.7cm$ and a volume of $0.1m^3$ has a diameter of $57.6cm$. Ferret's error rate is the number of objects that do not appear in the area projected onto the display. The error rate is determined through manual inspection of a video recording.

All of our experiments are conducted in a 4m x 10m x 3m room equipped with a Cricket ultrasound system. We used five beacons mounted on the ceiling which we manually calibrated. The origin of our world-coordinate system is a corner of the room. The camera records all video at 12 frames/second, and the RFID reader produces 4 readings per second. For the online system, we use a coverage map that includes all places where the tag has a non-zero probability of reading a tag. That region is an irregular shape that is 2.56m x 1.74m x 2.56m at the maximum and has a volume of approximately $2m^3$.

5.1   Online Refinement Performance

The primary goal of Ferret is to quickly locate, refine, and display an outline on the video display that contains a particular object. As this happens online, Ferret continuously collects readings and improves its postulation of the object's location—this is reflected as the volume of the region shrinking over time. To demonstrate this, we placed one tag in the room, and then walked "randomly" around the room with the prototype. We plot the volume of the location estimation versus time in Figure 6. The absolute volume tracks the total volume of the region, while the relative volume tracks the size of the region relative to the starting coverage region of the reader. In this case Ferret does not make any errors in locating the object. The time starts from the first positive reading of the tag and Ferret begins with no previous knowledge about object locations.

The results show that the volume size of the location estimation drops from $2m^3$ to $0.02m^3$ which is only 1% of the reader's coverage region in less than 2 minutes. The volume monotonically decreases, as intersecting positive readings only shrinks the area, while negative readings are ignored. Also, this is a pessimistic view of the refinement time—with prior knowledge, the process occurs much more rapidly. For instance, if the user switches to searching for another object in the same room, Ferret can take advantage of all of the previous readings. If a previous user has stored location information on the tag, this reader can also take advantage of that from the time of the first reading. Additionally, if some location information is stored in a centralized database, Ferret can immediately project an area onto the video without *any* positive readings.

In addition to the volume size of the location estimation, we also plot the projection area versus time in Figure 6(c) in which the projection areas are shown as a percentage of the image plane area. Our results show that the final projection area is only 3% of the whole image, or approximately a 54 pixel diameter circle on a 320 x 240 frame. However, the projection area does not monotonically decrease as the volume does. This is because the camera is constantly moving, thus the point-view constantly changes, and the same volume can project different areas from different orientations.

5.2 Offline Algorithm Performance

While the online algorithm is useful for current mobile devices, the offline algorithm uses more information, and a more precise representation of the object's location likelihood. To evaluate Ferret's precision in locating objects, we placed 30 tags in a 2.5m x 2.5m x 2m region, and we move the prototype around the room for 20 minutes. We repeat the experiment 3 times and record the volume of the postulated region, and manually verify how many objects are truly contained in the area projected onto the video plane. With 30 tags and 3 experiments, Ferret can make between 0 and 90 location errors.

Before evaluating the offline algorithm, we must set a threshold for the minimum likelihood for the object as described in Section 3. Recall that a larger threshold can reduce the volume encompassing the likely position of the object. However, a larger threshold will also increase the error rate of Ferret (the volume doesn't contain the object). In order to test the sensitivity of offline Ferret to the change of likelihood threshold, we varied the likelihood threshold from 0.00001 to 0.4, and ran the offline Ferret algorithm on the data we collected in the experiment. We show the results in Figure 7.

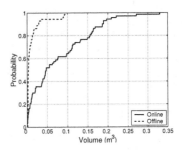

Threshold	Errors	Mean Volume
0.00001	5/90	$0.0117m^3$
0.0001	5/90	$0.0117m^3$
0.001	5/90	$0.0116m^3$
0.01	5/90	$0.0112m^3$
0.1	6/90	$0.0108m^3$
0.2	7/90	$0.0104m^3$
0.3	8/90	$0.0102m^3$
0.4	9/90	$0.0100m^3$

Fig. 7. Performance of offline Ferret under different likelihood thresholds

Fig. 8. CDF of locationing accuracy

The results show that: (i) the number of errors almost doubles from 5 to 9 as threshold increase from 0.00001 to 0.4 (ii) the mean volume of the location estimation is essentially constant; and (iii) for a threshold ≤ 0.01, the number of errors doesn't change. When using too high of a threshold Ferret incorrectly shrinks the volume, leaving out possible locations for the object. Considering the balance of error rate and mean volume, we choose a likelihood threshold of 0.01. Using this threshold, we run the offline algorithm and compare it to the performance of the online algorithm. In Figure 8, we plot the CDF of Ferret's location accuracy for both algorithms.

The results show that (i) The online algorithm can localize an object in $0.15m^3$ and $0.05m^3$ regions with 80% and 50% probability, respectively. The $0.15m^3$ and $0.05m^3$ regions are only 7.5% and 2.5% of the reader's coverage region which is $2m^3$; (ii) The offline algorithm outperforms the online algorithm by localizing an object in a $0.05m^3$ region with more then 90% probability and in a $0.1m^3$ region with 100% probability.

However, when we verify the online algorithm's error rate, it only makes 2 errors, as compared to the offline algorithm's 5 errors. We believe that the slightly greater number of errors in the offline algorithm is due to our incorporation of negative readings in the algorithm. In this experimental setup, the prototype system is constantly moving and the tags are in the coverage region of the RFID reader for a small portion of the total time (less than 5%). This scenario will generate 19 times the number of negative readings than positive readings, and negative readings are weighted as heavily as positive readings. Considering that we measured the performance of the reader under ideal conditions, we have overestimated the performance of the RFID reader. The online algorithm does not exhibit the same behavior as it does not ever use negative readings. As negative readings are correlated by orientation, and location, we believe that more accurate modeling of reader performance is an important direction for future research.

5.3 Mobility Effects

Ferret exploits the user's mobility to produce a series of readings from multiple positions, and further refine its location estimation via intersecting the coverage regions at these positions. The previous experiment showed the results of a human, yet uncontrolled, mobility pattern. In reality users move erratically; however, their motions are composed of smaller, discrete motion patterns. To study how individual patterns affect the performance of Ferret we placed a single tag in the room and evaluated Ferret with a small set of semi-repeatable motion patterns shown in Figure 9: (a) **straight line**, the prototype system moves in a straight line, tangential to the object, without changing the orientation of the camera lens and RFID reader; (b) **head-on**, the prototype moves straight at the object and stops when the reader reaches the object; (c) **z-Line**, the prototype system moves in a z-shaped line without changing its orientation; (d) **rotation**, the prototype system moves in an arc, while keeping the lens orientation radial to the path; (e) **circle**, the prototype system moves in a circle, while keeping the reader facing the object. Intuitively, the circular pattern may be the least likely of the mobility patterns, whereas the head-on is probably the most likely—once the user gets one positive reading, she will tend to head towards the object in a head-on pattern. We evaluated Ferret's performance using the volume of the resulting region. For each movement pattern we ran three experiments, averaged the results, and compared the smallest volume size of both online and offline Ferret. Our results are shown in Figure 11.

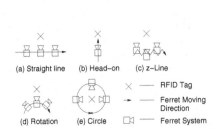

(a) Straight line   (b) Head–on   (c) z–Line

(d) Rotation   (e) Circle

× — RFID Tag

→ — Ferret Moving
        Direction

▭◁ — Ferret System

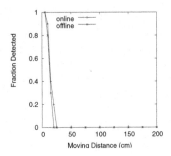

Fig. 9. Path of the Ferret device

Fig. 10. Detected object movements

	Straight line	Head-on	z-Line	Rotate	Circle
online Volume (m^3)	0.020	0.0042	0.023	0.026	0.032
offline Volume (m^3)	0.0015	0.0030	0.0017	0.0011	0.026
offline : online	13.33	1.40	13.52	23.63	1.23

Fig. 11. Performance of Ferret under various mobility patterns

The results show that Ferret performs similarly for each of the movement patterns; however the circular pattern performs the worst. The circular pattern always keeps the object in view and generally in the center of the reader's coverage region. This produces a set of readings that generally cover very similar regions. In each of the other cases, the mobility of the reader covers more disjoint spaces, and thus produces smaller volumes. This is true even of the head-on pattern as the first reading and the last reading have very little volume in common. Another result is that the offline algorithm widely outperforms the online algorithm, except in the case of the circular and head-on patterns, where the performance is similar. Much of the offline algorithm's performance advantage comes from incorporating negative readings to reduce the possible locations for the object. In the case of the circular and head-on patterns, the object is always in view, producing few negative readings, yielding similar performance to the online algorithm. Although non-intuitive, this means that *not* seeing the object is as important as seeing it to narrow its location.

5.4   Object Motion Detection

Ferret is designed to deal with objects that move infrequently, but when the object does move, Ferret should detect this and start its refinement process over. As discussed in Section 3, whenever Ferret encounters an empty location estimation, Ferret assumes that the corresponding object has moved. To evaluate Ferret's performance in detecting these nomadic objects we place a tag in the room and use Ferret to estimate its location. We then move the tag a distance between 5cm and 200cm and again use Ferret to estimate its location. We repeat the experiment ten times for each distance, and record the number of times that Ferret didn't detect a moved object. The results are shown in Figure 10.

The figure shows that the online and offline Ferret can detect 100% object movements when the moving distance exceeds 25cm and 20cm, respectively. This is consistent with our previous results that show that Ferret can localize an object to within an region with a volume of hundredths of a m^3—this gives a radius on the order of $20cm$, exactly how well Ferret can detect movement. As the object has not actually left the postulated area, Ferret is still correct about the object's location.

5.5 Spatial Requirements

The prototype has a non-zero probability of detecting tags in balloon-shaped region, with maximum dimensions of 2.56m x 2.56m x 1.74m—this shape has a volume of approximately $2m^3$. For the offline algorithm we sample this coverage region every centimeter. As discussed in Section 3, the offline algorithm requires every point in this space, while the online algorithm only requires a set of points that describe the exterior of the region. This reduced representation results in much smaller spatial requirements as compared to offline spatial requirements: (i) the offline algorithm uses a **float** of four bytes to describe the probability of a sample point, and the total space is $256 * 256 * 174 * 4 = 43.5M$ bytes using a three dimensional array to store the probabilities of all sample points, and (ii) the online algorithm uses a two dimensional array (the dimensions correspond to y and z) to represent the coverage region, and consequently, it only needs two bytes to track the x value of every outside sample point, thus the total space required is $256 * 174 * 2 = 178K$ bytes. Both the offline and online representations are highly compressible: the offline can be reduced to 250K bytes and the online representation to 5K bytes using the commonly available compression tool *gzip*. For the foreseeable future, RFID tags will not contain enough storage for the offline representation, while the online version is not unreasonable. If tags have more or less storage the number of sample points can be adjusted, although this will affect the precision of the system.

5.6 Computational Requirements

The computational requirements of the offline and online algorithms have a similar relationship. We measured the computational requirements of Ferret's locationing algorithm on an IBM X40 laptop equipped with a 1.5GHz Pentium-M processor: (i) the offline algorithm costs 749.32ms per reading for each object, and (ii) the online algorithm only costs 6ms per positive reading for each object, which is only 1/125 of the offline computational requirements. Our results show that the online algorithm incurs small overhead and will run online to track multiple tags simultaneously on relatively inexpensive hardware, while the offline algorithm incurs large overhead and can only run offline.

6 Related Work

Researchers have developed RFID-based indoor locationing systems [8,9] using active, battery powered, RFID tags. In SpotON [8], Hightower, et. al, use the radio signal attenuation to estimate tag's distance to the base stations, and triangulate the position of the tagged objects with the distance measurements to several base stations. LANDMARC [9] deploys multiple fixed RFID readers and reference tags as infrastructure, and measures the tracking tag's nearness to reference tags by the similarity of their signal received in multiple readers. LANDMARC uses the weighted sum (the weight is proportional to the nearness) of the positions of reference tags to determine the 2D position of the tag being tracked.

The above work use battery-powered sensors to identify and locate objects. These sensors are expensive (at least tens of dollars per sensor) and have limited lifetime (from several days to several years). These limitations prevent them from scaling to applications dealing with hundreds and thousands of objects. In contrast, passive RFID tags are inexpensive (less than a dollar per tag and falling) and do not require battery power source. These features make passive RFID technology ideal for such applications.

Fishkin, et.al, proposed a technique to detect human interactions with passive RFID tagged objects using static RFID readers in [4]. The proposed technique used the change of response rate of RFID tags to unobtrusively detect human activities on RFID tagged objects such as, rotating objects, moving objects, waving a hand in front of objects, and walking in front of objects. However, this doesn't consider the problem of estimating the locations of RFID tagged objects. Their experimental results show that their system could nearly always detect rotations, while the system performed poorly in detecting translation-only movement.

Hähnel, et.al proposed a navigation, mapping and localization approach using the combination of a laser-range scanner, a robot and RFID technology [6]. Their approach employed laser-based FastSLAM [7] and Monte Carlo localization [2] to generate offline maps of static RFID tags using mobile robots equipped with RFID readers and laser-range scanner. Through practical experiments they demonstrated that their system can build accurate 2D maps of RFID tags, and they further illustrated that resulting maps can be used to accurately localize the robot and moving tags. Ferret's offline algorithm uses the same underlying technique to map the detection probability and form a pose about the location of the tag. However, Ferret focuses on the novel problems posed by the integration of a handheld device and nomadic objects. In addition to the offline technique, Ferret also provides an online algorithm for real-time use on a mobile device—this technique greatly reduces complexity over the offline technique. Ferret also address the concerns of how to deal with nomadic objects, such as how to reset the locationing algorithm when objects move. Furthermore, Ferret incorporates a video display to show the tags' locations—the offline algorithm alone does not provide a method for displaying the uncertainty region to the user, something that Ferret adds. Our evaluation shows that Ferret can incorporate human movements, as opposed to robotic ones, demonstrating that these techniques will be useful for human-driven applications.

The 3D RFID system uses a robot-controlled uni-directional antenna, and the 3D tag consists of several combined tags [11]. Two kinds of 3D tags are developed: union tag and cubic tag. The proposed system can not only detect the existence of the 3D tag but also estimate the orientation and position of the object. However, they require specific orientation-sensitive 3D tags, custom-built from multiple tags. Furthermore, the system uses an expensive robot system to control the antenna's movement and then estimate the orientation and position of the object. In contrast, Ferret only needs one standard orientation-insensitive tag per object and the user's inherent mobility to estimate the object's location.

7   Conclusions

This paper presents the design and implementation of Ferret, a scalable system for locating nomadic objects augmented with RFID tags and displaying them to a user in real-time. We present two alternative algorithms for refining a postulation of an object's location using a stream of noisy readings from an RFID reader: an online algorithm for real-time use on a mobile device, and an offline algorithm for use in post-processing applications. We also present methods for detecting when nomadic objects move and how to reset the algorithms to restart the refinement process.

We present the results of experiments conducted using a fully working prototype. Our results show that (i) Ferret can refine object locations to only 1% of the reader's coverage region in less than 2 minutes with small error rate (2.22%); (ii) Ferret can detect nomadic objects with 100% accuracy when the moving distances exceed 20cm; and (iii) Ferret can use a variety of user mobility patterns.

References

1. B. Barshan and H. F. Durrant-Whyte. Inertial navigation systems for mobile robots. *IEEE Transactions on Robotics and Automation*, 11(3):328–342, June 1995.
2. F. Dellaert, D. Fox, W. Burgard, and S. Thrun. Monte carlo localization for mobile robots. In *Proceedings of the 1999 IEEE International Conference on Robotics and Automation (ICRA'99), Detroit, MI*, May 1999.
3. A. Elfes. Using occupancy grids for mobile robot perception and navigation. *IEEE Computer*, 22(6):46–57, June 1989.
4. K. Fishkin, B. Jiang, M. Philipose, and S. Roy. I sense a disturbance in the force: Long-range detection of interactions with rfid-tagged objects. In *Proceedings of UbiComp'04*, pages 268–282, September 2004.
5. J. D. Foley, A. V. Dam, S. K. Feiner, and J. F. Hughes. *Computer Graphics: Principles and Practice in C*. Addison-Wesley Professional, second edition, 1995.
6. D. Hähnel, W. Burgard, D. Fox, K. Fishkin, and M. Philipose. Mapping and localization with rfid technology. In *Proceedings of ICRA'05*, April 2004.
7. D. Hähnel, W. Burgard, D. Fox, and S. Thrun. An efficient fastslam algorithm for generating maps of large-scale cyclic environments from raw laser range measurements. In *Proceedings of IROS'03*, pages 206–211, October 2003.

8. J. Hightower, R. Want, and G. Borriello. Spoton: An indoor 3d location sensing technology based on rf signal strength. Technical Report 00-02-02, University of Washington, 2000.

9. L. M. Ni, Y. Liu, Y. C. Lau, and A. P. Patil. Landmarc: Indoor location sensing using active rfid. In *Proceedings of PerCom'03*, pages 407–417, March 2003.

10. N. B. Priyantha, A. Chakraborty, and H. Balakrishnan. The cricket location-support system. In *Proceedings of MobiCom'00, Boston, MA*, August 2000.

11. S. Roh, J. H. Park, Y. H. Lee, and H. R. Choi. Object recognition of robot using 3d rfid system. In *Proceedings of ICCAS'05*, June 2005.

12. R. Want. An introduction to rfid technology. *IEEE Pervasive Computing*, 5(1):25–33, January–March 2006.

13. R. Want, A. Hopper, V. Falcao, and J. Gibbons. The active badge location system. *ACM Transactions on Information Systems (TOIS)*, 10(1):91–102, January 1992.

14. A. Ward, A. Jones, and A. Hopper. A new location technique for the active office. *IEEE Personal Communications Magazine*, 4(5):42–47, October 1997.

15. X.Liu, M. Corner, and P. Shenoy. Ferret: Rfid localization for pervasive multimedia. Technical Report 06-22, University of Massachusets Amherst, 2006.

PowerLine Positioning: A Practical Sub-Room-Level Indoor Location System for Domestic Use

Shwetak N. Patel[1], Khai N. Truong[2], and Gregory D. Abowd[1]

[1] College of Computing & GVU Center
Georgia Institute of Technology
801 Atlantic Drive, Atlanta GA 30332-0280 USA
{shwetak, abowd}@cc.gatech.edu
[2] Department of Computer Science
University of Toronto
10 King's College Road, Toronto ON M5S 3G4 Canada
khai@cs.toronto.edu

Abstract. Using existing communications infrastructure, such as 802.11 and GSM, researchers have demonstrated effective indoor localization. Inspired by these previous approaches, and recognizing some limitations of relying on infrastructure users do not control, we present an indoor location system that uses an even more ubiquitous domestic infrastructure—the residential powerline. PowerLine Positioning (PLP) is an inexpensive technique that uses fingerprinting of multiple tones transmitted along the powerline to achieve sub-room-level localization. We describe the basics behind PLP and demonstrate how it compares favorably to other fingerprinting techniques.

1 Introduction

Recent advances in indoor location systems use existing wireless communication infrastructure (*e.g.*, 802.11 and GSM) to provide a value-added location service. The major advantage to these approaches is that a consumer does not have to purchase any specialized equipment and can still benefit from location-aware computing. Leveraging public infrastructure has many advantages, but one major drawback is that users have very little control of the infrastructure itself. Service providers adjust the operational parameters of WiFi access points and cellular towers with little warning. These changes require recalibration of the location system. An alternative is to introduce new infrastructure in the home by distributing many low-cost, short-range beacons. The time required for installation and the possible impact to home aesthetics, however, may limit adoption.

Inspired by this strategy of leveraging existing infrastructure, and recognizing that there are drawbacks to relying on infrastructure not controlled by an individual household, we were motivated to invent a solution for indoor localization that would work in nearly every household. This paper presents such a solution, with the significant insight being the use of the residential powerline as the signaling infrastructure. We describe the first example of an affordable, whole-house indoor localization system that works in the vast majority of households, scales cost-effectively to support the tracking

P. Dourish and A. Friday (Eds.): Ubicomp 2006, LNCS 4206, pp. 441–458, 2006.
© Springer-Verlag Berlin Heidelberg 2006

of multiple objects simultaneously, and does not require the installation of any new infrastructure. The solution requires the installation of two small plug-in modules at the extreme ends of the home. These modules inject a low frequency, attenuated signal throughout the electrical system of the home. Simple receivers, or positioning tags, listen for these signals and wirelessly transmit their positioning readings back to the environment. This solution, henceforth referred to as PowerLine Positioning, or PLP, provides sub-room-level positioning for multiple regions of a room and tracks multiple tags simultaneously. PLP has a localization accuracy of 87–95% for classifying regions at 3 meters and 67% at 1 meter resolution. We have installed and tested this system in a variety of homes and compare the performance against previous 802.11 and GSM solutions.

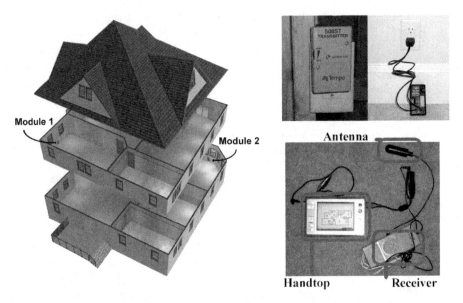

Fig. 1. Left: Placement of two signal-generating modules at extreme ends of a house. Right: The PLP system components. The top shows two examples of off-the-shelf, plug-in tone generator modules. The bottom shows a working prototype of the location tag, consisting of a receiver and antenna hooked to a handtop computer for analysis.

2 Related Work

Indoor positioning has been a very active research problem in the ubicomp community in the preceding half decade [5]. Several characteristics distinguish the different solutions, such as the underlying signaling technology (*e.g.*, IR, RF, load sensing, computer vision or audition), line-of-sight requirements, accuracy, and cost of scaling the solution over space and over number of items. Although we do not intend to provide a complete survey of this topic, we highlight projects with characteristics most relevant to the motivation for powerline positioning, namely the requirements for additional infrastructure and algorithmic approach.

The earliest indoor solutions introduced new infrastructure to support localization [1, 12, 14, 16]. Despite some success, as indicated by commercialized products [15], the cost and effort of installation is a major drawback to wide-scale deployment, particularly in domestic settings. Thus, new projects in location-based systems research reuse existing infrastructure to ease the burden of deployment and lower the cost. The earliest demonstrations use 802.11 access points [2, 3, 8], and more recent examples explore Bluetooth [9] and wireless telephony infrastructure, such as GSM [13] or FM transmission towers [7]. Concerns about system resolution eliminate the FM solution for domestic use. Another concern we highlighted in the introduction is that individuals and households may not be able to control the characteristics of these infrastructures, resulting in the need to recalibrate should parameters change. The desire to control the infrastructure and to scale inexpensively to track a large number of objects inspired the search for a solution like the powerline system presented here.

Traditional wireless signal triangulation, such as that using 802.11 access points, uses Received Signal Strength Indicator (RSSI) information to estimate distance and determine a location based on its geometric calculations Other techniques include the use of Time of Arrival, as in the case of ultrasound, or Angle of Arrival, such as with Ultra-wideband positioning [15]. Ultrasonic solutions, such as Cricket [14] and Active Bat [1], provide precise centimeter resolution, but require line-of-sight operation indoors and thus require considerable sensor installations for full coverage. Technologies, such as 802.11 triangulation, avoid issues of occlusion but suffer from multipath problems caused by reflections in the environment.

Fingerprinting of received signals can help overcome the multipath problem. Fingerprinting improves upon other means of estimation by taking into account the effects that buildings, solid objects, or people may have on a wireless or RF signal, such as reflection and attenuation. Fingerprinting works by recording the characteristics of wireless signals at a given position and later inferring that position when the same signature is seen again. A survey of signals over some space allow for the creation of a map that can be used to relate a signal fingerprint to a location.

Our location system relies on the space's powerline infrastructure. Powerlines are already in place in most homes and the power network reaches more homes than either cable systems or telephone lines. Thus, for many years, people have been using powerlines in homes to deliver more than just electricity. Several home technologies use the powerline for communications and control. The most popular example is the X10 control protocol for home automation, a standard that is more than 30 years old and is a very popular, low-cost solution for homeowners. Over the past decade, there have been a number of efforts to produce powerline communications capabilities, driven by industrial consortia like HomePlug Powerline Alliance [6] and efforts such as Broadband over Powerline (BPL).

3 System Overview

In this section, we present the theory behind the operation of PLP, discuss the two-phase localization algorithm based on signal fingerprinting, and describe the details of our prototype system that we used to evaluate the operation of PLP in real homes.

3.1 Theory of Operation

We developed the PLP system based on a popular wire-finding technique employed by many electricians and utility workers to locate or trace hidden wires behind a wall or underground. In this technique, an electrician connects an exposed end of the wire to a tone generator, which can range from 10–500 kHz, and locates the hidden wire using a handheld, inductive tone detector. Some detectors use LEDs to indicate the tone strength and others play an audible sound. In either case, the electrician scans the area for the loudest tone, indicating the approximate location of the wire. Following the presence of the tone reveals the path of the wire.

We use the following properties of the wire-finding technique to produce a viable solution for a location system:

- it is easy and inexpensive to propagate a signal or tone throughout the entire electrical system in a home without any electrical interference;
- it is possible to set the power of the tone so that it attenuates as it reaches the periphery of the home, and the electrical wiring appears in varying densities throughout the home, creating a time-independent spatial variation of the signal throughout the home; and
- the tone detectors or receivers are fairly simple, cheap to construct, and have low power requirements.

In the PLP system, we extend the wire-finding technique to include two plug-in signal generator modules. We connect the modules directly into electrical outlets, and their respective signals emanate from those outlets to the rest of the home. We install one of the two modules into an outlet close to the main electrical panel or circuit breaker and plug the other into an outlet that is located along the powerline infrastructure furthest from the first module (see Figure 1). In most cases, physical distance is a good estimate for electrical distance. In the case of a two-story house with a basement, for example, one module would be placed at the west end of the house in the basement (where the main panel is located) and the other in the east end on the second floor. Each module emits a different frequency tone throughout the powerline. As part of the installation, the signal strength must be adjusted such that significant attenuation occurs and the tone signal still reaches the opposite end of the home. Both modules continually emit their respective signals over the powerline and portable tags equipped with specially tuned tone detectors sense these signals in the home and relay them wirelessly to a receiver in the home. Depending on the location of the portable tag, the detected signal levels provide a distinctive signature, or fingerprint, resulting from the density of electrical wiring present at the given location. A receiving base station in the home (*e.g.*, a wireless receiver connected to a PC) analyzes the fingerprint and maps the signal signature to its associated location based on a site survey.

We currently focus on amplitude of the tones only, which has shown good results on its own. However, phase difference between tones is another feature characteristic that can further assist in localization and is the basis of some of our future work.

When the modules are active, the tone detector or receiver tag detects the presence and amplitude of the attenuated signals throughout the home. Because electrical wiring typically branches inside the walls, ceiling, and floors, signal will be present throughout much of the main living areas of the home. Some factors that contribute to the amplitude of the received signal at any given location:

- the distance between the receiver and electrical wiring,
- the density of electrical wiring in an area, and
- the length of electrical wiring from the modules to the receiver's location.

Figure 2 shows a signal map of a bedroom (left) and of a kitchen (right) from the same house. In the bedroom, the strength of both signals increases near the walls where there is the greatest concentration of electrical wiring and outlets. The strength of signal A (left value in each cell of Figure 2) is weaker than the strength of signal B (right value in each cell) in the kitchen, and the opposite is true for the bedroom. Because the two rooms are on different floors and at opposing ends of the house, each room is closer to a different module.

Fig. 2. Left: Signal map of a bedroom. In each 1 meter cell, the left-hand number corresponds to signal strength from one tone generator and the right-hand number corresponds to the signal strength of the other tone generator. Right: A similar signal map of the kitchen in the same house.

Most residential houses and apartments in North America and many parts of Asia have a single phase or a split single phase electrical system, which enables any signal generated on a given outlet to reach the entire electrical system. Larger buildings and even some homes in Europe have two and three phase electrical systems, in which the electrical system may split into separate legs for lower voltage applications. For multi-phase electrical systems, the signal can be coupled between the phases using a simple capacitor. In a home, this would typically be plugged-in in a 240 V outlet, such as that used for clothes dryer. We currently focus on common residential single or split single-phase electrical systems operating at 60 Hz. However, the system can be extended to accommodate other electrical systems.

3.2 PLP Localization Algorithm

The PLP system relies on a fingerprinting technique for localization. Although this technique often provides more detailed and reliable data, it requires the generation of a signal topology via a manual site survey. The granularity of the survey dictates the final accuracy of the positioning system. For PLP in the home, the site survey is a one-time task provided the modules stay fixed and the electrical characteristics of the home remain the same.

Effective application of fingerprinting requires the signals to have low temporal variations, but high spatial variation. As discussed above, the propagation of signals transmitted via the powerline exhibits both of these properties, because the detected signals vary little unless the modules have been moved or the electrical system has been significantly remodeled. The use of two different signals and the variability in the electrical wire density throughout the homes provides this spatial variation.

The localization algorithm used in PLP proceeds in two steps. The first step predicts the room, and the second predicts the sub-regions within that room. Both use k-Nearest Neighbor (KNN) classification.

3.2.1 k-Nearest Neighbor (KNN) Classification

The room and sub-room localizers use a k-Nearest Neighbor (KNN) [11] classification to determine the receiver's room location. KNN-is a memory-based model defined by a set of objects known as learned points, or samples, for which the outcomes are known. Each sample consists of a data case having a set of independent values labeled by a set of dependent outcomes. Given a new case of dependent values (the query point or unknown value), we estimate the outcome based on the KNN instances. KNN achieves this by finding k examples that are closest in distance to the query point. For KNN classification problems, as in our case, a majority vote determines the query point's class. For this task, given an unlabeled sample, χ, we find the k closest labeled room samples in our surveyed data and assign χ to the room that appears most frequently within the k-subset. For our distance measure d, we use the Euclidean distance,

$$d\ (x, y) = \sqrt{(\sum_{i=1}^{2} (x_i - y_i)^2)},$$

in which tuples x = <Signal A_{x1}, Signal B_{x2}> and y = <Signal A_{y1}, Signal B_{y2}>. The tuple x refers to the labeled signal point and tuple y refers to the unlabeled query point sensed by the receiver tag. For more modules, we increase the dimension to match the number of modules.

3.2.2 Room and Sub-room Localization

The key differences between the room and sub-room localizers are the labels assigned to the data points and the value for k used in the localization. For the room level classification, we assign room labels to samples from the site survey. In the sub-room classification, we further subdivide the same samples and assign sub-room labels to them. For each home, there is an optimal value of k for the room level localizer. Within the same home, there is an optimal value for the sub-room level localizer for each room. Thus, for localization, we first execute the KNN classification using the room labeled samples and its optimal k value. After determining the room, we execute KNN on the sub-room labeled samples from that room and its optimal k value to determine the sub-room.

3.2.3 Training the System and Determining k in KNN

The choice of k is essential in building the KNN model and strongly influences the quality of predictions, for both room-level and sub-room-level localization. For any given problem, a small value of k will lead to a large variance in predictions. Alternatively, setting k to a large value may lead to a skewed model. Thus, k should be set to a value large enough to minimize the probability of misclassification and small enough (with respect to the number of cases in the example sample) so that the k nearest points are close enough to the query point. Thus, an optimal value for k achieves the right balance between the bias and the variance of the model. KNN can provide an estimate of k using a cross-validation technique [11].

Splitting the localization into two steps can help control the cluster sizes. In localizing the room, we want to use a larger value of k so that we consider a larger region when trying to find where the unknown signal potentially maps. To localize within a room, we consider smaller values of k so that we match finer clusters and because of the smaller data sets within a room than the whole home.

The training interface allows end users to build a signal map of the home (see Figure 4). The user loads a pre-made or hand-drawn floor plan of the residence into the application. The interface displays the floor plan, and we physically travel to different locations in the home and choose the approximate location on the floor plan. When a location is selected, the application stores the fingerprint for that location, which is a one-second average of the two detected signals. The same process continues throughout different points in the home. Surveying at a granularity of approximately 2-3 meters in each room produces more than sufficient accuracy for the test cases presented in Section 4. The interface allows the user to assign meaningful labels to different room and sub-room areas, such as "kitchen" and "center of master bedroom."

For optimal performance in sub-room level localization, we typically segment each room into five regions: the center of the room and areas near the four walls of the room. The user is free to select the location granularity (assuming sufficient training sets) of their choice for important regions. However, the desired segmentation may not reflect the actual segmentation the underlying set of signals can provide. For example, a user may want to segment the middle part of a bedroom into four regions, but there might not be enough signal disparity among those regions for the KNN classifier to work well. We provide some assistance in overcoming those limitations by automatically clustering the room into potential sub-regions that are likely to be accurately classified based on the room's signal map. We employ a k-means clustering algorithm [4, 10, 11] to provide graphical suggestions on where to segment for a desired number of sub-regions.

After the signal map has been constructed and all data has been labeled, the algorithm cross-validates model data to find suitable k values for the room and sub-room classifiers. Cross-validation involves the division of the data samples into a number of v folds (randomly drawn, disjoint sub-samples or segments). For a fixed value of k, we apply the KNN model on each fold and evaluate the average error. The system repeats these steps for various k values. The system selects the value for k achieving the lowest error (or the highest classification accuracy) as the optimal value for k. This value for k depends on the home and the number of sample points. Generally, we see optimal k values near 10 for the room localizer and k values near 3-5 for the sub-room localizer.

3.3 Implementation Details

3.3.1 Module Design
For rapid development and investigation, we modified commercially available tone generators and tone detectors used by electricians for wire finding. We used the Textron Tempo 508S and the Pasar Amprobe 2000 tone generator modules. These modules produce a 447 kHz and 33 kHz tone, respectively, on an energized 120 V AC powerline without causing any interference to household appliances. Additionally, the modules are powerful enough to transmit a tone up to 500 meters over the electrical wire (both hot and ground) and can be adjusted to emit at a lower signal strength. For the PLP prototype in this paper, we manually adjusted the signal strength depending on the size of the residence. We collected samples with the receiver near the module and samples near the opposite side of the home where the second module is located. We then tuned the signal strength such that we produced a large signal difference between the two locations without turning it down so much that the tone did not reach the far end. It was important to turn down the output level and use the middle of the receiver's dynamic range, because very high signal strengths would overwhelm the receiver and would not produce as large of a signal difference. Although we manually performed the steps described above, it is possible to build the modules to self-calibrate its output level during the installation and surveying steps.

Based on the cost of the commercial wire-finder that inspired the PLP system, the cost for each module would be approximately US$50.

3.3.2 Tag Design
We modified a Textron Tempo 508R passive wideband tone detector to act as a prototype tag that would send sensed signals to a portable computer for analysis (see Figures 1 and 3). The toner has a built in frequency divider that maps a range of high frequency tones to audible sounds while still preserving the amplitude of the original signal. The receiver's internal frequency divider translated the 447 kHz signal to about 1000 Hz and 33 kHz signal to about 80 Hz. We altered the tone detector to interface with the audio line-in jack of a portable computer to capture the signals. The tone detector also has an integrated omnidirectional antenna. We found the antenna worked best when held vertically (perpendicular to the ground). When placed in this position, the azimuth orientation did not affect the received signal levels.

For experiments reported in this paper, we used a rather large tag prototype that was easier for us to build. There are a variety of ways to construct a small and inexpensive version of this tag. One way is to feed the radio transducer or antenna through a series of op-amps and into a DsPIC microcontroller. A low-power Ming or Linx RF transmitter would transmit the readings back to a receiving computer. Alternatively, we could bypass the need for a microcontroller by using multiple tone decoder ICs, similar to the NE567 IC, which supports signal power output. Powered by a small lithium cell, the tag could easily be the size of a small key fob and run for a significant period of time using a mechanical motion switch. We believe the tags could be constructed at US$20 each, based on current retail hobbyist prices.

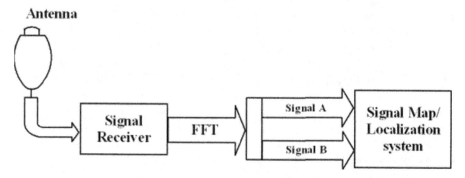

Fig. 3. Block diagram of the overall tagging system of the PLP System

3.3.3 Software

In our experimental set-up, we wrote an application in C++ to sample the signal from the sound card's line-in jack where the prototype receiver tag is connected. The application acquires 16-bit samples at a rate of up to 44 kHz and performs a Fast Fourier Transform (FFT) on the incoming signal to separate component frequencies for our analysis. The application performs this analysis in very close to real-time and makes the raw signal strengths for the two frequencies of interest (447 kHz and 33 kHz) available through a TCP connection for other parts of the PLP system to access (see Figure 3).

A second application, written in Java, performs the machine learning and provides the user interface for the system (see Figure 4). The Java application connects to the FFT application and reads the raw signal values. The application provides the user interface for surveying the home and an interface that shows the current location after it has been calibrated. The Weka toolkit [17] allows for real-time programmatic execution of KNN queries to our location model. We also use Weka for *post hoc* analysis, such as cross-validating the model when determining optimal k values and performance testing.

The experimental prototype used for empirical validation consisted of a Sony Vaio-U handheld computer with all software applications (signal receiver, learner, and the user interfaces) loaded and the receiver hardware connected (see Figures 1 and 4). Using this small but powerful device provided us with an easy method for surveying homes.

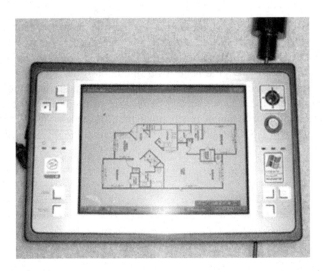

Fig. 4. User interface used for mapping and localizing the position of the connected receiver

4 Performance Evaluation

We evaluated the performance of the PLP system in 8 different homes of varying styles, age, sizes, and locations within the same metropolitan city. We evaluated new homes and older homes, both with and without remodeled and updated electrical systems (see Table 1 for specifications of the homes). In addition to evaluating our system, we simultaneously conducted infrastructure tests of WiFi and GSM availability to provide some comparison with other indoor localization results. The infrastructure tests only involved logging the availability of wireless 802.11 access points and multiple GSM towers in the home. A WiFi spotter application running on the Sony Vaio-U logged the wireless access points, and an application written on the Audiovox SMT-5600 GSM mobile phone the multiple cell towers.

In each home analyzed, we first installed the PLP system, calibrated the two tone modules, and created a signal map by surveying the whole home. When creating the signal map, we took at least two signal readings every 2-3 meters throughout the home to ensure we gathered enough training and test data (Table 2 shows the number of sample points for each home). Each reading was taken for 3 seconds with an individual holding the receiver in hand (about 1.5 meters from the ground). After creating the signal map, we used the interface on the handheld to assign the appropriate room and sub-room labels to the data.

We reported the classification accuracy of the room and sub-room predictors. The sub-room accuracy was calculated independent of the room-level predictor. We use 3 meter regions for the sub-room-level tests. To obtain room-level accuracy, we conducted a 10-fold cross-validation test on the room localizer using the collected data samples. We repeated this test for various k values to find the best accuracy measure, which also served as our reported accuracy value. To determine the sub-room level accuracy, we took the data samples for each room and performed a 10-fold cross-validation using the sub-room localizer, again for different values of k. Similar to the room-level tests, we looked for the k value that provided the highest accuracy for predicting regions in a room. After testing each room, we averaged all the sub-room localization accuracies to produce a single accuracy value for each home.

Table 1. Details of the homes where the PLP system was deployed and evaluated

Home	Year Built	Electrical Remodel Year	Floors/ Total Size (Sq Ft)/ (Sq M)	Style	Bedrooms/ Bathrooms/ Total Rms.	Population Density
1	2003	2003	3/4000/371	1 Family House	4/4/13	Suburb
2	2001	2001	3/5000/464	1 Family House	5/5/17	Suburb
3	1992	1992	1/1300/120	2 Bed Apartment	2/2/6	Downtown
4	2002	2002	3/2600/241	1 Family House	3/3/12	Suburb
5	1967	2001	2/2600/241	1 Family House	3/3/11	Suburb
6	1950	1970	1/1000/93	1 Family House	2/2/5	Suburb
7	1926	1990	1/800/74	1 Bed Loft	1/1/5	Downtown
8	1935	1991	1/1100/102	1 Family House	2/1/7	Suburb

4.1 PLP Accuracy

4.1.1 Between Homes Comparison

In Table 2, we report the results of the PLP room-level and sub-room level accuracies for various homes. Room accuracy ranged between 78–100% and sub-room accuracy ranged between 87–95%. The modern homes and the older homes with updated electrical infrastructure resulted in similar performance results. The updated electrical systems in these homes were accompanied with an overall remodel of the home, which tends to include the addition of electrical outlets and lighting. The single family home that exhibited a significantly lower accuracy (Home 8) was an older home with an updated electrical system. However, that home had a two-phase electrical system, which we only learned after installing the PLP system. Because it is a smaller house and Phase 1 drives a small number of outlets, we simply placed the modules on Phase 2 to produce acceptable (though not optimal) coverage throughout the house. However, installing a simple phase coupler would have improved its performance.

The condominium and apartment test cases also produced promising results. The condominium was converted from an office building, but the electrical system was completely remodeled to a residential style system. Although one wall of the condominium used a metal conduit to run its electrical wire, PLP still worked because the room with the conduit was small and the receiver was never too far from the wall. The apartment also featured a similar residential style electrical system. Because of the small size of the living spaces, we had to turn down the power of the modules significantly in the two cases, unlike the larger homes we tested.

The older homes without an updated electrical system exhibited lower results for two reasons. First, these homes lack a proper electrical ground, resulting in one less path for the signal to propagate, because we send the signal both on the hot and ground wires. Homes with an updated electrical system have an extra electrical ground wire running through the home, which is usually grounded to the copper water

Table 2. Accuracy results by home. For each home, we report the accuracy of room-level prediction and the average sub-room-level prediction across all rooms (Note the room-level and sub-room accuracy values are independent of each other). The sub-room-level regions were defined to be approximately a 3 meter square. The WiFi and GSM measurements indicate the maximum number of access points or towers seen at all times during the surveying and the total number of unique access points or towers seen during the whole surveying period.

Home	Size Sq Ft/ Sq M	Sample points	Rooms surveyed	Room Accuracy	Sub-Room Accuracy at 3 M	WiFi Always/ Max	GSM Always/ Max
1	4000/371	194	13	89%	92%	3/12	3/5
2	5000/464	206	15	95%	93%	1/3	2/4
3	1300/120	95	6	90%	90%	3/7	4/12
4	2600/241	183	11	88%	87%	1/3	3/5
5	2600/241	192	10	92%	93%	2/4	3/6
6	1000/93	76	5	100%	94%	0/2	4/6
7	800/74	65	5	93%	95%	2/11	3/9
8	1100/102	80	7	78%	88%	2/6	3/7

pipes. This grounding enables additional signal propagations to certain areas of the home. Second, these homes tended to have fewer electrical outlets than the modern or remodeled ones, resulting in poor detection in some areas.

4.1.2 Understanding Classification Errors

To understand the types of classification errors encountered by the PLP system, we analyzed the confusion matrices for each home. For some homes, most of the classification errors resulted from misclassifying rooms as one of the adjacent rooms. The adjacency errors appeared when trying to localize very near the boundary or the wall of a room. These errors were more prevalent in larger houses near common walls between two adjacent rooms of similar size. Open spaces that were divided into multiple rooms also resulted in errors. Other homes, however, exhibited more random

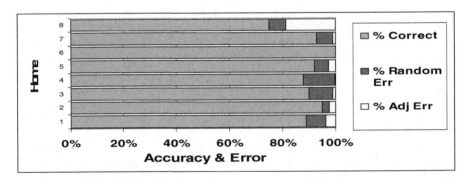

Fig. 5. The table shows the percentage of incorrect room predictions identifying a room that is adjacent to the correct room

classification errors possibly due to errors in the survey map, sparse sampling, or in error readings coming from the receiver at that time. One possible solution to guard against misclassifications is to use hysteresis to compare against certain classifications and see if those classifications follow a valid trail. Some homes could benefit from hysteresis, especially those with significant random error (see Figure 5).

4.2 Number of Modules and Performance

We conducted accuracy tests using a varying number of modules. Although our goal was to minimize the additional hardware the user must install in a home, there might be cases in which higher accuracy is more desirable. Adding additional modules is the main way to increase overall accuracy. Figure 6 shows both room-level and sub-room level accuracies for an increasing number of modules for a particular home as an example. Additional modules do increase the accuracy for both predictions, but there is a point of diminishing returns. For this home (Home 1), two or three modules are the best number. We observed similar trends in other homes we tested and generally, two modules were sufficient.

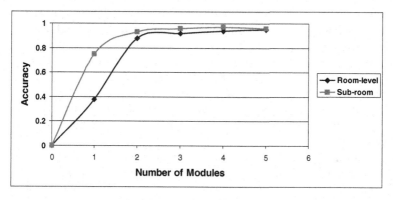

Fig. 6. The effect of number of modules on room-level and sub-room-level classification accuracies. Tests were conducted on Home 1.

4.3 Resolution

In our initial evaluation, we sub-divided rooms into approximately 3 meter regions. This resolution yielded high accuracies around 90%. Higher resolution, or smaller subdivisions of each room, is possible, but at the cost of accuracy. In addition, higher resolution also requires dense mapping of an area. To investigate the specific accuracy to resolution tradeoff, we performed a fine-grain survey (sampling down to every 0.5 meter for a total of 96 samples) of a room (6m X 6m) in Home 1. With our current implementation, the lowest obtainable practical resolution is 1 meter. The accuracy falls below 70% for 1 meter regions (see Table 3), because there is a theoretical limit to the detectable differences between small movements in the space and the signal amplitude. However, finer granularity may be possible by considering the phase difference between the two signals. From our observation, the maximum amplitude differential is about 20 units when moved 1 meter for a modern home.

Table 3. The sub-room-level accuracies for smaller sub-regions for a particular room in Home 1. A total of 96 points were surveyed.

Sub-room region size	4 m	3 m	2 m	1 m	0.5 m
% Accuracy	94%	91%	74%	67%	42%

4.4 Temporal Signal Stability

Fingerprinting works best with a signal that is time-independent but spatially diverse. The data presented so far only considered results over relatively short periods of time, usually around 1 hour worth of data collected at a particular home. To test the stability of the signals over time, we conducted two separate tests. First, in Home 1, we conducted separate surveys over the course of several weeks. We trained the system on data from one survey and checked its accuracy against data collected from different surveys. Room prediction was correct 88% of the time (compared with the value of 89% for Home 1 in Table 3) and sub-room level prediction was correct 89% of the time (compared with the value of 90% in Table 3). Second, in Home 2, we collected 45 hours of data over a three-day period (Saturday through Monday) in a single location (the kitchen). The kitchen was an interesting test because it contained a large number of features that could affect the tone signals (*e.g.,* plentiful overhead lighting, appliances being turned on and off throughout the day, talking on a cordless phone, people gathering around the tag). Figure 7 depicts the stability of the signal for four different 3-hour intervals. The results suggest there is deviation (17 units on average), but it is not significant enough over the full dynamic range to cause major classification errors.

Modifications to the electrical infrastructure can contribute to accuracy errors and require recalibration, which was a problem we noted for other infrastructure solutions (802.11 and GSM). However, most situations, such as turning on a light switch, only energize a portion of the electrical line and do not affect significantly the accuracy in our experience. More studies are needed to empirically study this. Construction of a "day" and "night" map using a richer data set can allay some of these concerns. The addition of an extension cord may impact the accuracy, depending on location and length. PLP could be designed to recognize potential changes in the infrastructure from past data to notify the user that re-surveying of a particular area is necessary.

Although we did not observe any problems with electrical interference with our continuous logging, during our site tests we did often observe electrical interference caused by home electronics and appliances, such as computers, televisions, and stereos. When we held the receiver next to some of these electronic devices, its broadband electrical noise often overwhelmed the receiver and caused spurious readings. This problem only existed when the receiver was very close (within a few centimeters) from such devices. To guard against learning or localizing incorrect fingerprints, one solution is to look for these signal interferences and filter out those readings, indicated by a clear broadband signature, before using the data in analysis.

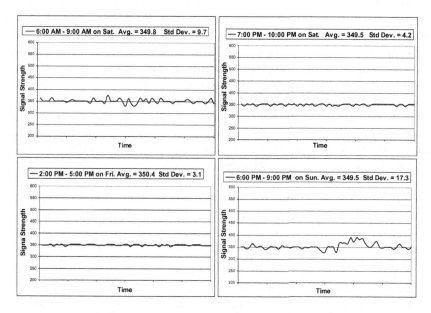

Fig. 7. Temporal signal stability in the kitchen area of Home 2. The graphs show the signal values for the two toner modules (combined using the Euclidean distance) over various intervals during four days of continuous recording. The average signal values and the standard deviations are shown above each graph. The full dynamic range of the vertical axis is 0-1000.

5 Discussion

PLP is very promising as an inexpensive and reliable sub-room-level indoor positioning service. In this section, we investigate the viability of this system and offer some comparison to previous solutions.

5.1 Infrastructure and Cost Comparison Against WiFi and GSM

The cost of infrastructure for WiFi is distributed across a community and assuming dense enough living conditions, it is a reasonable expectation that a single residence will be able to access other WiFi access points nearby. This is less likely in sparser housing, in which case users would be required to purchase multiple WiFi access points. Various cellular telephony service providers cover the cost of the infrastructure for GSM. The coverage is fairly dense in most metropolitan areas and will only get better over time. However, coverage is still fairly sparse in rural settings and many homes do not get very good cellular service in some rooms (see Table 2). Almost every home in the U.S. has electrical power, and it is an assumed cost of the homeowner to maintain this infrastructure over the lifetime of the home. Thus, the infrastructure is already available and usually well maintained.

One key advantage of leveraging the powerline infrastructure is user control of the infrastructure. Users have very little control of the parameters of GSM cellular towers or a neighbor's WiFi access point, thus changes can happen unexpectedly. In contrast, users have control of the powerline infrastructure. Furthermore, as we showed in Section 4.4, there is stability in signal propagation over this infrastructure.

The cost and power requirements of the location tags favor that of the PLP system because of its simple sensing requirements, as opposed to the more sophisticated chipset associated with GSM and WiFi reception. In addition, the cost of the tone generating modules would also be cheaper than buying additional access points if one were investing in a location system for the home.

5.2 The Powerline Infrastructure

In the United States, modern homes now follow a strict electrical code called the National Electronic Code (NEC). Electrical codes only became widely enforced in the 1980s, although many homes before that already followed similar guidelines. Although the specific regulations may change depending on state and city ordinances, each follows the same general requirements. These regulations ensure the electrical systems are consistent across homes of different sizes and styles. Specifically, the requirements outlined in the NEC favor the infrastructure requirements needed for the PLP system to work in modern homes. These requirements include regulations for certain "homerun" circuits through the house, a minimum number of outlets in a given space, and minimum lighting requirements throughout the house. Although PLP already performed reasonably well in older homes, it consistently achieved very good results in the new or remodeled homes that follow these requirements (see Table 3).

We specifically developed PLP to provide an affordable location system for home environments. However, commercial buildings must comply with strict electrical codes for which the PLP design must be altered to support. First, commercial wiring typically uses a two or three phase electrical system that prevents the signals from propagating throughout the entire electrical system. This problem is solved by installing an inexpensive phase coupler. Second, most commercial electrical wiring runs through a metal conduit, which blocks significant portions of the tone emanating from the wire (PVC conduits do not cause a problem). One solution to this problem is to increase greatly the signal strength and the other is to send the signal through both the electrical wiring and the metallic conduit itself. This problem also applies to homes that have been converted from commercial buildings without remodeling the electrical system.

5.3 General Comparison of PLP Against 802.11 and GSM

The significant advantage of PLP when compared against two popular fingerprinting techniques using WiFi/802.11 [2] and GSM [13] lies in the better resolution, control of the infrastructure, and power requirements (see Table 4).

Table 4. An overall comparison of PLP against two popular location systems that also use fingerprinting

	PLP	GSM	WiFi
Output Type	symbolic	symbolic	symbolic (geometric using triangulation)
Resolution and Accuracy	3 m – 90% 1 m – 67%	20 m – 90% 2-5 m – 50% [13]	6 m – 90% 2-3 m – 50 % [2]
Infrastructure Requirements.	2 plug-in signal modules	Located within GSM cellular service range	3 – 4 WiFi access points
Infrastructure Control	Full	None	Partial (dependent on ownership of access points)
Cost	US$20 for tag and US$50 per module	US$25 for tag	US$25 for tag and US$50 per access point
Spectral Requirements	10 kHz – 500 kHz	900 MHz and 1800 MHz	2.4 GHz
Update Rate	> 20 Hz	> 20 Hz	> 20 Hz
Tag power Req.	~50 mA (Pic + op-amp + antenna)	~200 mA (GSM receiver module)	~100 mA (microcontroller operated WiFi detector)
Simultaneous Tracking	Theoretically no limit	Theoretically no limit	Theoretically no limit

6 Conclusions and Future Work

PLP is a promising indoor positioning system for the home that uses its powerline infrastructure and requires only the addition of two plug-in modules to the home infrastructure and the use of simple location tags. The system is capable of localizing to sub-room level precision using a fingerprinting technique on the amplitude of tones produced by the two modules installed in extreme locations of the home. The density of electrical wiring at different locations throughout the home provides a time-independent spatial variation of signal propagation.

Our critical analysis of PLP, and the experimental validation in eight different homes, suggests the following advantages over current indoor location solutions:

- PLP leverages a truly ubiquitous resource, the powerline infrastructure, available in almost all homes.
- PLP requires very minimal addition to the infrastructure (two plug-in modules).
- PLP achieves superior sub-room-level classification, with an accuracy of 93% on average at a resolution of 3 meters.
- PLP does not detract from the appearance of the home.

Our next step is to build smaller, less expensive, and lower powered tags for practical deployments of PLP. In addition, we plan to incorporate other spatially varying signal features, such as phase differences between the tones in addition to the amplitude to increase the accuracy and resolution of PLP in the fingerprinting process. Further stability analysis is also planned to determine the full viability of PLP.

References

1. Active Bat. The BAT Ultrasonic Location System. http://www.uk.research.att.com/bat/.2006.
2. Bahl, P. and Padmanabhan, V. RADAR: An In-Building RF-Based User Location and Tracking System. In the proceedings of *IEEE Infocom*. Los Alamitos. pp. 775-784. 2000.
3. Castro, P., Chiu, P., Kremenek, T., and Muntz, R.R. A Probabilistic Room Location Service for Wireless Networked Environments. In proceedings of *Ubicomp* 2001. pp. 18-34. 2001.
4. Hamerly, G. and Elkan, C. Learning the k in k-means. In the proceedings of *The Seventeenth Annual Conference Neural Information Processing Systems (NIPS)*. 2003.
5. Hightower, J. and Borriello, G. A Survey and Taxonomy of Location Systems for Ubiquitous Computing, University of Washington Tech Report CSC-01-08-03. 2001.
6. HomePlug Powerline Alliance. http://www.homeplug.org. March 2006.
7. Krumm, J., Cermak, G., and Horvitz, E. RightSPOT: A Novel Sense of Location for a Smart Personal Object. In the proceedings of *Ubicomp 2003,* Seattle, WA, pp. 36-43. 2003.
8. LaMarca, A., Chawathe, Y., Consolvo, S., Hightower, J., Smith, I., Scott, I., Sohn, T., Howard, J., Hughes, J., Potter, F., Tabert, J., Powledge, R., Borriello, G., and Schilit, B. Place Lab: Device Positioning Using Radio Beacons in the Wild. In the proceedings of *Pervasive 2005*, Munich, Germany. pp. 116 – 133. 2005.
9. Madhavapeddy, A. and Tse, T. Study of Bluetooth Propagation Using Accurate Indoor Location Mapping. *The Seventh International Conference on Ubiquitous Computing (UbiComp 2005)*. Tokyo, Japan. pp 105-122. September 2005.
10. MacQueen, J.B. Some Methods for Classification and Analysis of Multivariate Observations. In the proceedings of *The Fifth Berkeley Symposium on Mathematical Statistics and Probability*. pp 281-297. 1967.
11. Mitchell, T. *Machine Learning*, McGraw Hill. ISBN 0070428077. 1997.
12. O'Connell, T., Jensen, P., Dey, A.K., and Abowd, G.D. Location in the Aware Home. Position paper for Workshop on Location Modeling for Ubiquitous Computing at Ubicomp 2001. September 30, Atlanta, GA. 2001.
13. Otsason, V., Varshavsky, A., LaMarca A., and de Lara, E. Accurate GSM Indoor Localization. In the proceedings of *The Seventh International Conference on Ubiquitous Computing (UbiComp 2005)*. Tokyo, Japan. September 2005.
14. Priyantha, N. B., Chakraborty, A., and Balakrishnan, H. The Cricket Location-Support System. In the proceedings of *The International Conference on Mobile Computing and Networking (Mobicom 2000)*. Boston, MA. August 2000.
15. Ubisense. http://www.ubisense.net. 2006.
16. Want, R., Hopper, A., Falcao, V., and Gibbons, J. The active badge location system. *ACM Transactions on Information Systems*. Volume 10. pp. 91-102. January 1992.
17. Weka 3: Data Mining Software in Java. http://www.cs.waikato.ac.nz/ml/weka/. March 2006.

UbiREAL: Realistic Smartspace Simulator for Systematic Testing

Hiroshi Nishikawa[1], Shinya Yamamoto[1], Morihiko Tamai[1], Kouji Nishigaki[1], Tomoya Kitani[1], Naoki Shibata[2], Keiichi Yasumoto[1], and Minoru Ito[1]

[1] Graduate School of Information Science, Nara Institute of Science and Technology
8916-5, Takayama, Ikoma, Nara 630-0192, Japan
{hirosh-n, shiny-ya, morihi-t, koji-ni,
t-kitani, yasumoto, ito}@is.naist.jp
[2] Department of Information Processing and Management, Shiga University
Hikone, Shiga 522-8522, Japan
shibata@biwako.shiga-u.ac.jp

Abstract. In this paper, we propose a simulator for facilitating reliable and inexpensive development of ubiquitous applications where each application software controls a lot of information appliances based on the state of external environment, user's contexts and preferences. The proposed simulator realistically reproduces behavior of application software on virtual devices in a virtual 3D space. For this purpose, the simulator provides functions to facilitate deployment of virtual devices in a 3D space, simulates communication among the devices from MAC level to application level, and reproduces the change of physical quantities (e.g., temperature) caused by devices (e.g., air conditioners). Also, we keep software portability between virtual devices and real devices. As the most prominent function of the simulator, we provide a systematic and visual testing method for testing whether a given application software satisfies specified requirements.

1 Introduction

It is one of the most important challenges to realize Smartspace environments which provide people useful services by making embedded devices cooperate based on contexts. In order to realize Smartspace, we need ubiquitous application softwares which control many information appliances based on contexts and user preferences. We also need ubiquitous sensor networks as infrastructure for these applications. There are many studies on realizing middleware for facilitating development of ubiquitous applications and testbeds for testing if those applications work expectedly [1,2,3,4].

Since applications running on Smartspace have influence on convenience and even safety of our daily life, those applications must be developed carefully so that they run expectedly and safely. However, it is difficult and expensive to test them thoroughly in real world environments, since test examiners have to assemble testbeds using various types of sensors and information appliances and generate a quite large number of contexts for tests where each context consists

P. Dourish and A. Friday (Eds.): Ubicomp 2006, LNCS 4206, pp. 459–476, 2006.

of user locations/behavior, time, and so on. Also, there are so many possible deployment patterns of sensors and appliances. In addition, users of Smartspace may want to know how devices work based on typical contexts and their preferences in advance and change deployment of devices, control policies (rules) and/or preferences to find the best configurations to fit their life styles. However, this kind of trial and error burdens users too much if it is conducted in real world environments.

For evaluating protocols in large scale wired and/or wireless networks, network simulators such as ns-2 and QualNet are widely used. Those network simulators can be used to evaluate only aspects of communication between devices of Smartspace. So, in order to cope with the above problems, we need a simulator for realistically simulating Smartspace environments. For this purpose, the following criteria should be satisfied with a Smartspace simulator: (1) *Support to design Smartspace* which allows test examiner to easily deploy networked devices in a freely designed 3D virtual space; (2) *Realistic context generation* which generates various contexts based on user behavior and device actions/communications in the virtual space; (3) *Graceful visualization* which intuitively informs test examiner of how devices work based on contexts through visual animations; (4) *Software compatibility* which allows software and protocols (such as device drivers) to run on the virtual space as well as in real world environments; and (5) *Systematic testing* which systematically generates possible contexts and checks whether the system runs expectedly.

There are several studies to realize a Smartspace simulator such as UBIWISE [5] and TATUS [6]. These existing simulators partly achieve the above criteria (1), (3) and (4). However, the important criteria (2) and (5) are not realized.

In this paper, we propose a Smartspace simulator called *UbiREAL* (Ubiquitous Application Simulator with REAListic Environments) which provides a virtual testbed for ubiquitous applications in a 3D space.

For the criteria (1)-(5), UbiREAL provides the following functions: (i) arrangement of devices in a 3D space by GUI; (ii) simulation of wired and wireless communication between devices (i.e., sensors and information appliances) from MAC layer to application layer; (iii) emulation of temporal transition of physical quantities in a space; (iv) visualization of device states by 3D animations; and (v) systematic tests for a given application under test and deployment of devices in a space. The above function (ii) realizes the software compatibility (criterion (4)), and (iii) realizes the realistic context generation (criterion (2)). These functions cooperate to achieve the systematic tests (criterion (5)).

The rest of the paper is composed as follows. Section 2 briefly describes the related work. In Section 3, we explain overall structure of UbiREAL. In Sections 4, 5, 6 and 7, we present the details of UbiREAL, that is, device arrangement and visualization in a virtual Smartspace, simulation of communication, simulation of physical quantities, and systematic tests, respectively. Experimental results for UbiREAL performance are shown in Section 8. Finally, Section 9 concludes the paper.

2   Related Work

There are many research efforts which aim to facilitate development of ubiquitous applications and/or improve reliability of those applications. The existing studies are largely classified to three groups treating middleware, testbeds and simulators.

Firstly, as middleware and/or framework for efficient development of ubiquitous applications, many studies such as Refs. [1,7,8] have been researched.

Biegel et al. have proposed middleware which controls sensors, actuators and application components in an event-driven manner, in order to facilitate development of mobile and context-aware applications [1]. Niemelä et al. addressed that it is important to achieve inter-operability, adaptability and scalability among components for agile pervasive computing, and they proposed an architecture achieving them [7]. Roman et al. have proposed middleware called "Gaia", which provides various services in Smartspace [8]. In addition, Chan et al. have proposed a J2ME-based middleware with micro-server proxy for thin clients to use services of Gaia [9]. Messer et al. have developed middleware which integrates different CE (Customer Edge) devices, where it allows users to only choose what they want to do through comprehensive pseudo-English interface when using the middleware [10]. Nishigaki et al. have proposed a language called "CADEL" which facilitates rule description by defining complex conditions/contexts as simple phrases in natural language and developed a framework for context-aware applications with information appliances which aim to allow ordinary home users to easily configure device controls [2]. These researches for middleware mainly focus on facilitating application development and increasing availability of various devices and usability of systems. Thus goals of these middleware overlap with our goal. Since these existing middleware can be applications of our UbiREAL simulator, we can say that the middleware researches and UbiREAL research are mutually complementary.

Secondly, there are several existing studies concerning testbeds of ubiquitous applications [11,12]. Consolvo et al. have evaluated advantages and drawbacks of existing methods by experiments designing a Smartspace called Labscape [11]. Nakata et al. have noticed that a simulation to make testbeds is very hard, and thus proposed a simulation method which virtually executes not only virtual devices but also real devices in the simulation [12].

These researches on testbeds are important for ubiquitous applications to be developed efficiently and improve reliability, but it would be hard and costly to construct various configurations of devices in a real environment for tests. For this problem, Ref. [12] adopts an approach similar to UbiREAL, that is, to execute real devices and virtual devices cooperatively with interactions. However, the project is in early phase, and the paper describes only rough ideas without detailed implementation or method.

Thirdly, as studies concerning simulations of ubiquitous environments, Refs. [5,6,13,14] have been proposed. Hewlett-Packard Laboratories have proposed a simulator called *UBIWISE* [5]. UBIWISE is designed for development of prototypes and for tests of new hardware device and its software in the virtual ubiquitous computing environment. UBIWISE consists of two simulators; UbiSim, which generates 3D virtual space, and WISE, which displays how devices are running through 2D visual graphics. In addition, the research team in Trinity College has proposed the simulator called *TATUS* [6]. TATUS can simulate a ubiquitous application in a 3D virtual space. TATUS has a wireless network simulator in it. However, TATUS is developed with 3D-game-engine, and so the tester has to operate and move a user-character in the virtual space or let multiple characters move based on simple AI. TATUS also simulates packet loss ratio in wireless communication when characters frequently cross line-of-sight between devices. However, it is not mentioned in detail how to simulate other physical quantities in a virtual space in response to human behavior and/or device states. Sanmugalingam et al. have proposed an event simulator which aims to visualize and test scalability of given location-aware applications developed based on the proposed event-driven middleware [13]. Roy et al. showed that it is very important to track location of inhabitants in order to generate various contexts in smarthome, but they also showed that an algorithm for tracking locations of several inhabitants in an optimal way is NP-hard [14]. As a result, they have proposed a framework which stochastically generates likely interaction patterns between the inhabitants based on the game theory.

Those existing simulators simulate only restricted cases of inhabitants' behavior because they achieve the behavior manually or based on simple automation. Thus, they are not enough to confirm that a given ubiquitous application program runs as expected for all possible context patterns. They neither simulate it accurately that inhabitant and device behavior changes physical quantities such as temperature in the target space. So, it would be hard to guarantee validity of the given application implementation.

3   UbiREAL Overview

In this section, we briefly outline overview of proposed UbiREAL simulator.

3.1   Objectives and Applications

We first describe a typical ubiquitous application example which automatically controls home appliances based on contexts. We assume a house consisting of a living room and several other rooms, where three inhabitants Alice and her parents are living. We also assume that lamps, TV, video recorder, stereo and air conditioner as well as various sensors are deployed in the living room, and they can be controlled through network installed at the house. We suppose to control those appliances as follows.

- When Alice enters living room, illumination of the room is turned down, and the stereo begins playing jazz music quietly. The air conditioner is automatically configured at 25 degrees Celsius of temperature and 50% of humidity.
- Then, her father and mother come into the room. This time, the illumination is set bright, and the air conditioner is configured at 27 degrees Celsius and 60% of humidity. The stereo begins playing classic music.

– When baseball broadcast begins, TV is automatically turned on with the baseball channel, if father is in the living room. If father is not present, the video recorder starts recording the program.

When home appliances are controlled in the way described above, we have to consider the cases where several inhabitants (application user) have different preferences of the settings of air conditioner, TV programs or so on. The sound produced by stereo and TV can conflict with each other. Lamps should not be controlled so that it continuously repeat turning on and off. Air conditioner and heater in a room should not be turned on simultaneously. Situations like these may occur unintentionally when brightness or temperature is within a specific range.

As seen above, we have to test if home appliances are controlled as application users intended. But, finding all possible glitches is difficult by only observing the application behavior for several patterns. Testing rules under many possible contexts using real appliances in a real house requires tremendous labor and time.

Our UbiREAL simulator has been designed and developed to simulate and test ubiquitous applications with various contexts. The objectives of developing UbiREAL include the followings in addition to resolving the problem described above.

(1) To offer a way to inhabitants (application users) to intuitively check how devices work

If home appliances are controlled by rules like the case described above, the rules are sometimes specified from the scratch and/or modified by application users themselves. In order to allow ordinary people to manipulate rules, the system should offer a 3D view of a virtual space with which users can check places and operations of virtual devices. When the system finds situations (contexts) that some rules do not work as expected, those situations and wrong operations should be shown to users through 3D view.

(2) To enable cooperation between virtual devices and real devices

Even if there is no software problem, devices can operate incorrectly due to hardware failures or other problems. In such a case, it would be convenient if parts of virtual devices are replaced with real devices. This function also allows users to perceive how the real devices work based on the context in accordance with the (virtual) surrounding environment. For example, by applying this function to air conditioners or lamps, users can perceive the effective temperature or brightness. It greatly helps users to specify rules so that services are given as expected.

(3) To make device drivers (software) for real devices executable as virtual devices without large modification

When devices are simulated on existing network simulators like ns-2, the device drivers have to be written in event-driven way, and thus drivers for real devices, which are usually written in flow-driven way, cannot be executed "as-is". Writing driver software for various virtual devices from scratch costs huge amount of labor. Moreover, since drivers for virtual devices and real devices are different, even if virtual devices are confirmed to work correctly, we cannot guarantee that real devices should also work correctly.

(4) To allow testers to systematically test the whole application system by automatically generating many possible contexts

Even using simulation, it would be hard task to generate many possible contexts by hand and check whether devices work as expected by simulating the given application for those contexts.

3.2   UbiREAL Structure

We compose UbiREAL simulator of the following four parts as shown in Fig.1: (1) Visualizer and GUI for designing virtual Smartspace; (2) Network simulator; (3) Simulators for physical quantities; and (4) Systematic tester.

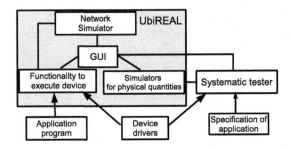

Fig. 1. UbiREAL Architecture

Basically, we allow UbiREAL to execute any device driver software [1] developed for real devices and application program developed for devices (or in a home server) to be executed as virtual devices without large modification. For this purpose, UbiREAL is designed so that general communication protocols and APIs for information appliances within UPnP framework such as SOAP and SSDP can be used on it. However, for visualization purpose, some devices have to send all states to the simulator when requested. So, software drivers for such devices have to be modified slightly. Devices with switches manually manipulated by users also have to send a signal to the simulator when states of these switches are changed. The states obtained from devices are used for visualization and tests.

Hereafter, we describe the four main functions of UbiREAL.

Visualizer and GUI for designing Smartspace This function helps user to create virtual home and rooms in which virtual devices are placed. Also, this function

---

[1] We suppose that the device driver software is executed at user mode of operating system. It commits to OS operations for controlling its locally attached actuators or obtaining values from its sensors using, e.g., UPnP library, and exchanges messages with the device driver software running on other devices.

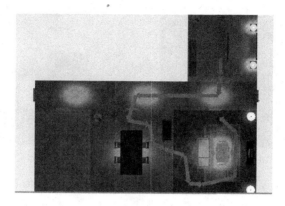

Fig. 2. Specifying Route of Avatar

helps designing routes which (virtual) application users and other movable devices trace. Details are described in Section 4.

Network simulator Network simulator simulates communication between virtual devices as well as between virtual and real devices, taking into account their positions and obstacles on their line-of-sights. Details are described in Section 5.

Simulators for physical quantities In order to reproduce temporal variation of physical quantities such as temperature, illumination and loudness in a specific region in the virtual Smartspace, a dedicated simulator is prepared for each physical quantity. Details are described in Section 6.

Systematic tester Systematic tester systematically generates many possible contexts and tests if given ubiquitous application operates as expected, in cooperation with simulators for physical quantities. Details are given in Section 7.

4   Visualizer and GUI for Designing Smartspace

UbiREAL has a GUI and a visualizer with which application users and/or test examiners (users, hereafter) can design Smartspace and observe how the Smartspace works depending on temporal variation of contexts. We call the software to realize this functionality simply GUI module, hereafter.

4.1   GUI for Designing Smartspace

GUI module allows users to place virtual devices in a 3D virtual space to compose Smartspace. Appearances of virtual devices can be designed using 3D modeling software on the market or can be substituted by 3D object data in VRML or other languages. 3D virtual space such as homes and rooms are constructed by 3-dimensionalizing a floor plan drawing using 3D modeling software. Users place various objects such as furniture (e.g., desk, chair, etc) and networked

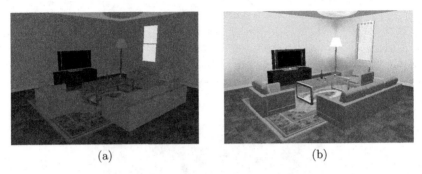

Fig. 3. Visualization of Illumination of Lamps: (a) off, (b) on

Fig. 4. Visualization of Heater's State: (a) off, (b) on

Fig. 5. Visualization of TV's State: (a) off, (b) on

appliances (e.g., TV, stereo, air conditioner and sensor) in the 3D space. Devices are classified into static objects and movable objects. Static objects are selected from a pull-down menu, and placed by drag-and-drop with a mouse. Movable objects like a virtual inhabitant is placed by specifying a route in the 3D space as shown in Fig. 2. Routes can be either specified manually or automatically by the systematic test function in Section 7. Each route of a movable device can include actions like pushing button or manipulating remote control, at specified coordinates. Each movable object which represents an inhabitant is called *avatar*.

4.2 Visualization of Smartspace

When a state of a virtual device changes (e.g., lamp is turned on) or physical environment changes (e.g. room darkens after sunset), these changes should be observed by users through visually changing appearances of the virtual devices or virtual space as shown in Fig. 3. UbiREAL visualizer allows users to choose one view among 2D bird-eye view, first person view from the avatar, and so on. If there are more than one avatar, view can be switched among those avatars.

Now, we give a simple example of how Smartspace behavior is visualized using a scenario where a virtual inhabitant with an RFID gets close to an RFID reader, and consequently air conditioner is turned on.

When the inhabitant gets close to the RFID reader, RFID tag device and reader device communicate with each other via our network simulator in Section 5. Wireless communication is simulated based on positions of the RFID and RFID reader and obstacles on line-of-sight between them. The RFID reader communicates with a home server to turn on an air conditioner. Then, device driver on the air conditioner updates its state to change direction of its louver. GUI module obtains the updated state of the air conditioner and changes appearance of the air conditioner appropriately. The simulators for temperature and humidity also obtain the updated state, and change those physical quantities in the room gradually as time passes.

UbiREAL has a function to output results of simulation as a log file. So, users can observe simulation results repeatedly from the log file.

We show snapshots of how Smartspace is visualized in Figures 3, 4 and 5, when an avatar approaches lamp, heater and TV devices by following the route in Fig. 2.

5 Network Simulator

In this section, we describe details of the network simulation module of UbiREAL. As explained before, it is important to allow driver programs implemented for real devices to be executed in a virtual space, in order to keep compatibility between virtual and real ones. So, first, we explain the difference between UbiREAL network simulator and existing network simulators. Then, we describe the architecture of our network simulator.

5.1 Simulation Using Driver Programs for Real Devices

Existing network simulators like ns-2 do not assume that programs for real devices are used in simulation. Instead, users of these existing network simulators have to write programs dedicated for virtual devices to be used in simulation. So, even when simulation was successful, programs must be re-written for real devices to execute the target application in a real world. In terms of development efficiency, it is desirable to reduce this labor. However, since many of existing network simulators require programs for devices to be written in event-driven manner, and thus it is difficult to use the programs for real devices for simulation, which are usually written in flow-driven manner.

In UbiREAL network simulator, programs written in flow-driven manner can be used in simulation. As we mentioned in Section 4, some devices require modifications of device driver programs in order to send the latest state of the device to GUI module of UbiREAL. By changing compile-time options, binary programs for real devices and virtual devices can be built from the same source program.

5.2 Architecture

For programmers of device drivers, UbiREAL network simulator can be accessed via ordinary service primitives of TCP/IP protocol stack. Protocols like UPnP can be used via existing libraries which run on TCP/IP. As for MAC layer, our network simulator supports IEEE802.11a/b/g, ZigBee and Bluetooth besides ordinary Ethernet (10/100/1000MBps). As for network layer, it supports AODV and DSR to simulate wireless ad hoc networks. The user can change simulation granularity of each layer by selecting one of supported simulation models. Network configurations of each device such as IP address and ESS ID are given via configuration files for each device. Physical network structures like subnet of Ethernet are simulated by virtual hub devices.

Positions of movable devices change as time passes. Conditions of communication between devices change accordingly, and this can be reproduced by simulation of physical layer. Physical layer simulation keeps track of the positions of movable devices, and when each device transmits, e.g., an Ethernet frame, it decides which devices can receive the frame taking into account positions of devices and obstacles. It also adds error to frames according to condition of communication. Queries of positions for each device are implemented as ordinary method invocations. When a device enters wave range of another device, these devices can hear beacons from each other, and thus these devices will be able to communicate with each other. When a device receives a frame, the frame is handed to upper layer protocol.

5.3 Communication Between Virtual Device and Real Device

UbiREAL network simulator allows virtual devices to communicate with real devices using TCP/IP protocol. With this feature, real devices can be used as the devices placed in the virtual Smartspace during tests. For example, when we need some of the virtual devices under test to behave especially correctly, real devices can be used for these virtual devices. This feature is also useful when we want to test some part of Smartspace through human perception.

By using operating systems like Linux, any form of Ethernet frames can be transmitted and received. Thus, it is possible to make a PC on which the simulator is running to be regarded as a router connected to the virtual network, and make real and virtual devices communicate with each other. Also, some network interface card can alter MAC addresses for every transmitted frame, and this makes virtual devices as if they are running on the same network as real devices.

6   Simulation of Physical Quantities

In order to know that a given ubiquitous application runs appropriately in a real world environment by simulation, we must be able to reproduce the temporal variation of physical quantities such as temperature and illumination in a virtual space considering effects of device and human behavior as well as characteristics of the target space.

Various simulators for real-time 3D environments have been researched and developed, and Ref.[15] surveys them. For example, Unreal Game Engine [16] uses a high performance physical engine and it calculates effects of light and sound. However, these existing simulators focus only on visible or audible physical phenomena. On the other hand, TATUS [6] simulates the effect of human behavior with respect to variation of packet loss ratio in a wireless LAN depending on how frequently human users cross the line-of-sight between devices. However, other invisible physical quantities are not simulated interactively with devices and human users.

UbiREAL simulates invisible physical quantities such as temperature, humidity, electricity and radio as well as visible (audible) quantities such as acoustic volume and illumination. In order to support any physical quantity, we adopted a publish-subscribe model for communication between virtual sensor devices and *physical quantity simulators*. Each physical quantity simulator is implemented based on appropriate formula in Physics for simulating a physical quantity. Each software driver of a sensor device concerning a physical quantity subscribes to the corresponding physical quantity simulator with parameter values necessary to update it. Each physical quantity simulator periodically calculates the latest value of the physical quantity and sends the value to subscribers if it has been changed. As necessary parameter values, each physical quantity simulator needs the previous quantity value, the characteristics such as size and capacity of the target room in the virtual space, device states, human behavior, other physical quantities and the time elapsed from the previous calculation.

For example, when we want to simulate temperature, the following formula in Physics is used as necessary parameters where C denotes heat capacity of the target room, and t, $\Delta T(t)$ and $Q(t)$ denote elapsed units of time, temperature difference and obtained heat quantity from previous evaluation, respectively.

$$\Delta T(t) = \frac{Q(t)}{C}$$

Each physical quantity simulator is implemented as a Plug-In program. Thus, it is easy to add new physical quantities and replace each Plug-In program by advanced one.

7   Systematic Testing

UbiREAL provides a function to systematically test the correctness of given application software in a given environment. For this purpose, we define a formal model to represent the service specification (i.e., service requirement) of ubiquitous applications. We also define the correctness of the application with respect to the service specification. Based on the formal model, we propose a method for systematically test the correctness of the application.

7.1   Formal Model for Service Specification

A Smartspace U is defined as a tuple $U = (R, D)$, where $R = \{r_1, ..., r_n\}$ denotes the set of rooms in U and $D = \{d_1, ..., d_m\}$ denotes the set of devices.

Each room $r_i \in R$ has the following attributes: *pos* representing the position of r_i in U; *base* representing the shape and size of r_i's base; *cap* representing the capacity of r_i; and physical quantities of r_i such as temperature *temp*, humidity *humid*, heat capacity *heatcap*, illumination *illum* and acoustic volume *vol* in r_i. Each attribute is denoted like $r_i.temp$.

We assume that initial values of physical quantities at each room are given in advance. If doors or windows are open in some rooms, we suppose that the physical quantities calculated for those situations are given as initial attribute values.

Each device $d_j \in D$ has the following attributes: r representing the room where d_j is deployed; *pos* representing $d'_j s$ position in r, and *state* representing the state of d_j. Each attribute is denoted e.g., by $d_j.state$.

Each device d_j may have sensors which can obtain physical quantities around the device as sensed values. Device d_j may have actuators which execute actions to change physical quantities such as cooling, dehumidifying and lighting. As a result of action, $d_j.state$ and some physical quantities of room $d_j.r$ may change.

We assume that each attribute of a room or a device can have a discrete value in a predefined range. We define the global state of Smartspace U as a tuple of values for attributes of all rooms and devices in U.

In the proposed test method, we assume that the service specification *Spec* is given as a set of rules $AP = \{l_1, .., l_h\}$ and a set of requisite propositions $P = \{p_1, ..., p_l\}$. Here, each rule $l_i = (c_i, a_i)$ is a tuple consisting of a condition c_i and an action a_i, representing that a_i is executed when c_i holds. Here, as condition c_i, only linear inequalities with constants and sensor variables can be specified. As a_i, an action to a device can be specified.

We assume that there are no conflicting rules which simultaneously execute different actions to a device[2].

We can specify each proposition $p_k \in P$ with temporal logic such as CTL [17]. In this paper, we restrict each proposition to be represented by the following style of CTL.

$$AG(\phi_1 \Rightarrow AF(\phi_2))$$

Here, ϕ_1 and ϕ_2 represent propositions and are defined to be *true* or *false* for each state of U. $AG(\phi)$ means that proposition ϕ is *true* for every state reachable

---

[2] Such conflicting rules can automatically be detected when specifying rules with the technique in [2].

from the current state, and $AF(\phi)$ means that ϕ will eventually be *true* in a state reachable from the current state.

As a result, the above example proposition means that if the system is in a state which makes ϕ_1 *true*, the system will eventually transit to a state which makes ϕ_2 *true*, and that this always happens.

Using temporal logic like CTL, we can intuitively specify a proposition such that "if User1 is in room A, then the temperature and the humidity of room A will eventually be regulated around 23C and 60%, respectively".

Currently, the proposed test function is mainly targeting rule-based applications since we can easily obtain the specification from the application scenario. In order to support applications which are not rule-based, we may need a tool to facilitate derivation of the set of rules from the application scenario. It is beyond the scope of this paper.

7.2   Correctness of Application and Testing Method

Given Smartspace U with initial attribute values, the service specification $Spec = (AP, P)$ and the service implementation I under test, we say I is correct with respect to $Spec$ iff the following conditions hold.

(1) For every rule $l = (c, a) \in AP$ and every state s of U, if condition c holds for state s, then action a is executed.
(2) Every proposition $p \in P$ holds.

In order to test condition (1), we must generate all possible states of sensor values for each rule of AP, and input each state to I and observe whether the expected action is executed. However, all possible states of sensor values would be numerous even when we restrict sensor values to be discrete. So, in the proposed method, for a predefined number C, if each rule fires for C sample states which approximately cover all possible states, we regard that the rule is correctly implemented in I. By using a large number for C, we can improve reliability of tests, whereas the cost of tests increases. So, appropriate number must be decided as C by test examiner considering tradeoff.

For example, for a condition of a rule "if temperature and humidity are more than 28C and 70%", we can generate sample states $(temp, humid)=\{(28,70), (28,80), (32,70), (32,80), (36,90)\}$ when $C = 5$, where other attribute values in states are omitted.

In order to test whether implementation I satisfies each requisite proposition, we must examine how the action executed by some rule influences the physical quantities of the room as time passes. In the proposed method, we use simulators for physical quantities to know the physical quantities at each time after some action is executed. By obtaining the latest values of physical quantities from the simulators periodically, we can test whether each proposition holds or not.

When multiple devices are running at the same time in a room, physical quantities may change in a different way compared with the case when a single device is running. For example, if an air conditioner is working at a specified power, how fast the temperature/humidity decreases/increases may be different among cases with or without other running devices such as TV and PC located in the same room. To cope with this problem, for a room with n devices, we test I for all possible combinations of those devices, that is, 2^n patterns (each device is working or not) as a total. If n is large, the patterns will be numerous. In that case, we can reduce the patterns by eliminating some patterns which unlikely happen.

7.3   Test Sequence Generation

In this section, we briefly explain how to generate test sequences using detailed examples. Suppose that the service specification $Spec = (AP, P)$ is given as follows.

$AP = \{(Exist(u_1, r_1) \land 28 \leq r_1.temp \land 70 \leq r_1.humid, Aircon_1.on(24, 60)),$

$(Exist(u_2, r_1) \land \neg Exist(u_1, r_1) \land 30 \leq r_1.temp \land 60 \leq r_1.humid, Aircon_1.on(28, 50)),$

$(Exist(u_1, r_2) \land Exist(u_2, r_2) \land Day = "Sun" \land Time = "6 : 30pm", TV_2.on("CNN")),$

$("11 : 00pm" < Time, Lamp_1.off), ...\}$

$P = \{AG(Exist(u_1, r_1) \Rightarrow AF(23 \leq r_1.temp \leq 25)),$
$AG("11 : 00pm" < Time \Rightarrow AF(r_1.illum \leq 10))\}$

The first rule in AP specifies that air conditioner $Aircon_1$ should be turned on with 24C of temperature setting and 60 % of humidity setting, if user u_1 is in room r_1 and room temperature and humidity are more than 28C and 70 %, respectively. The second rule similarly specifies the behavior of air conditioner based on user u_2's preference, but if users u_1 and u_2 are in room r_2 at the same time, this rule are not executed (i.e., the first rule for u_1 is executed prior to u_2's rule). The third rule specifies the control of television TV_2 so that it will be turned on with channel "CNN" if two users u_1 and u_2 are in room r_2, the day is Sunday and the time is 6:30PM. The last rule specifies lamp $Lamp_1$ to be turned off if the time is over 11:00PM.

The first proposition in P specifies that the room temperature of r_1 will eventually be regulated between 23C and 25C if user u_1 is in room r_1. The second proposition specifies that the illumination of room r_1 will eventually be regulated less than 10 lux if the time is over 11:00PM.

The above rules in AP, our proposed test method generates the test sequence as shown in Table 1.

In Table 1, $\leftarrow$ means the value assignment, $Check(a)$ represents a function which returns $true$ if action a has been executed, and parameters like $\%v11$ are assigned appropriate values which are generated every test sequence execution. During test sequence execution, if every $Check$ returns $true$, then we think that the test is successful, otherwise, the test fails.

For each proposition in P, our method generates the test sequence as shown in Table 2.

In Table 2, $CheckProp(\phi)$ represents a function which periodically checks if ϕ holds for the current state of U. It returns $true$ if ϕ holds, and returns $false$ if ϕ does not hold for a predefined time interval. Test sequence execution is conducted similarly to the test sequence for rules.

Table 1. Test Sequence for Rules

---

(1) $u_1.pos$ $\leftarrow$ $r_1.pos$ + $\%v11$; $r_1.temp$ $\leftarrow$ $\%v12$; $r_1.humid$ $\leftarrow$ $\%v13$; $Check(Aircon_1.on(24, 60))$

(2) $u_1.pos \leftarrow r_1.pos + \%v21$; $u_2.pos \leftarrow r_1.pos + \%v22$; $r_1.temp \leftarrow \%v23$; $r_1.humid \leftarrow \%v24$; $Check(Aircon_1.on(24, 60))$

(3) $u_2.pos$ $\leftarrow$ $r_1.pos + \%v31$; $u_2.pos$ $\leftarrow$ $r_3.pos$; $r_1.temp$ $\leftarrow$ $\%v32$; $r_1.humid$ $\leftarrow$ $\%v33$; $Check(Aircon_1.on(28, 50))$

(4) $u_1.pos \leftarrow r_1.pos + \%v41$; $u_2.pos \leftarrow r_1.pos + \%v42$; $Day \leftarrow$ "Sun"; $Time \leftarrow$ "$6 : 30pm$"; $Check(TV_2.on("CNN"))$

(5) $Time \leftarrow \%v51$; $Check(Lamp_1.off)$

Table 2. Test Sequence for Propositions

---

(1) $u_1.pos \leftarrow r_1.pos + \%v11$; $r_1.temp \leftarrow \%v12$; $r_1.humid \leftarrow \%v13$; $CheckProp(23 \leq r_1.temp \leq 25)$

(2) $Time \leftarrow \%v51$; $CheckProp(r_1.illum \leq 10)$

The test sequence is likely to be long. To shorten the length and reduce the time for testing, we can combine multiple test sequences and execute part of them simultaneously so that the common part is executed only once. Also if test examiner wants to execute test sequences with visual 3D animation in real-time, we can calculate the shortest route of a user to travel all devices in U. The positions of the calculated route are assigned to parameters such as $u_1.pos$ and $u_2.pos$ in the test sequence every execution of test sequence.

7.4   Inconsistency Detection

If some rules are inconsistent (e.g., in some contexts, cooling and heating devices run simultaneously at the same room), they should be detected. With UbiREAL simulator, basically users can detect such rules through graphical animation during simulation time.

There are other possibilities to realize inconsistency detection, although we do not go into detail. Some of them are shown below.

(1) Implement a tool to solve expressions consisting of logical product of conditions specified in rules which conflict with each other (e.g., simultaneously operate the same device) [2].

(2) Add a test sequence to detect, e.g., abnormal oscillation of some physical quantities.

8   Experiments

In this section, we describe the results of experiments to test performance of the proposed method. We used a PC with AMD Athlon 64×2 4200+ (CPU), ATI Radeon X1300Pro (graphics card), 2GB of memory on Windows XP Pro SP2 and Java JSE5.0 in the experiments.

8.1   Performance of Test Sequence Execution to Validate Rules

First, we conducted the following experiment in order to check simulation speed when testing if action a is correctly executed in each rule $l = (c, a) \in AP$, as described in Section 7.

We placed in a virtual space a temperature sensor device, an air conditioner device and a home server device with a rule l which is "If the temperature is higher than 26 degrees Celsius, turn on the air conditioner". We measured the time t_1 when temperature sensor detects temperature change and the time t_2 when the execution of the action to turn on the air conditioner completes, in order to know the response time defined by $t = t2 - t1$.

In the experiment, we assumed that all devices are connected to a network via an Ethernet hub, and devices communicate with each other by standard protocols in UPnP framework. In the experiment, the network simulator only emulates protocol layers above session layer, which includes the set of UPnP protocols. A home server device is developed based on CADEL framework [2] so that it evaluates condition c of rule l and sends a request to execute a to a target device if c holds.

By repeating the experiment more than 100 times, we found that it takes approximately 17.5ms to execute a test sequence for validating a rule. This suggests that supposing ordinary home environments, if there are 5 inhabitants, 100 devices, one rule is associated for each pair of a device and an inhabitant, and 100 tests are executed for each rule (i.e., $C = 100$), total time needed for the whole tests is about $5 \times 100 \times 100 \times 0.02s = 17$ minutes, and we believe that this would be practical enough. In reality, tests may take longer time since multiple devices are executed in parallel and conditions of all rules must be evaluated periodically in a PC executing simulation.

8.2   Performance of Simulation with Visualization

Next, we evaluated performance of the simulator when we use visualization function of UbiREAL. It is important to check if simulations can be performed in real time in order to allow users to intuitively observe how devices work as context changes through realtime 3D graphics. In the experiments, we let GUI module, network simulator module and a home server device developed based on CADEL framework run cooperatively, increasing the number of devices and rules. We measured framerate of 3D view when all rules are executed. We used 3 virtual rooms, and placed some objects in the rooms. The screen resolution of 3D view is 1600×1200 pixels, and the number of polygons drawn is 103,000 at maximum independently of the number of devices. We changed the number of devices from 0 to 25 and assigned two rules to each device, which means that the number of rules is changed between 0 and 50. The route of an avatar is set so that all rules are executed one by one. We measured framerate of visual simulation from avatar's view when the avatar moves following the route.

The experimental results are shown on Fig. 6. Fig. 6 shows that even when the numbers of devices and rules increase, there is only small influence to

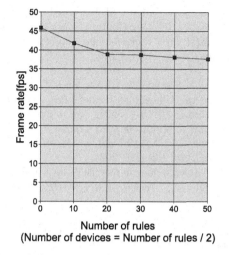

Fig. 6. Achieved Framerate vs. Number of Rules

framerate, and thus realtime simulation is feasible even with large number of devices and rules.

9   Conclusion

In this paper, we proposed a ubiquitous application simulator *UbiREAL*. The UbiREAL simulator can simulate Smartspace so that users can intuitively grasp how devices are controlled depending on temporal variation of contexts in a virtual space and systematically test the correctness of the given application implementation for a given environment.

Main contribution and novelty of UbiREAL are that it incorporates simulators for physical quantities and network simulator with a visualization mechanism which cooperate to achieve systematic tests for ubiquitous applications using software for real devices. Through experiments, we showed that the tests for validating rules can be conducted in practical time for realistic ubiquitous applications, although the tests for requisite propositions depend on how accurately simulating temporal variation of physical quantities. Part of our future work includes evaluation of systematic test performance for requisite propositions with accurate physical quantity simulations.

References

1. G. Biegel, and V. Cahill : "A Framework for Developing Mobile, Context-aware Applications", *Proc. of 2nd IEEE Int'l Conf. on Pervasive Computing and Communications (PerCom2004)*, pp. 361–365, 2004.

2. K. Nishigaki, K. Yasumoto, N. Shibata, M. Ito, and T. Higashino : "Framework and Rule-based Language for Facilitating Context-aware Computing using Information Appliances", *Proc. of 1st Int'l Workshop on Services and Infrastructure for the Ubiquitous and Mobile Internet (SIUMI'05) (ICDCS'05 Workshop)*, pp. 345–351, 2005.

3. T. Yamazaki, H. Ueda, A. Sawada, Y. Tajika, and M. Minoh : "Networked Appliances Collaboration on the Ubiquitous Home", *Proc. of 3rd Int'l Conf. on Smart homes and health Telematic (ICOST 2005)*, Vol. 15, pp. 135–142, 2005.

4. N. Kawaguchi : "Cogma: A Middleware for Cooperative Smart Appliances for Ad hoc Environment", *Proc. of 1st Int'l Conf. on Mobile Computing and Ubiquitous Networking(ICMU2004)*, pp. 146–151, 2004.

5. J.J. Barton, and V. Vijayaraghavan : "UBIWISE, A Simulator for Ubiquitous Computing Systems Design", *Technical Report HPL-2003-93*, HP Laboratories, Palo Alto, 2003.

6. E. O'Neill, M. Klepal, D. Lewis, T. O'Donnell, D. O'Sullivan, and D. Pesch : "A Testbed for Evaluating Human Interaction with Ubiquitous Computing Environments", *Proc. of 1st Int'l Conf. on Testbeds and Research Infrastructures for the Development of NeTworks and Communities*, pp. 60–69, 2005.

7. E. Niemelä, and T. Vaskivuo : "Agile Middleware of Pervasive Computing Environments", *Proc. of 2nd IEEE Annual Conf. on Pervasive Computing and Communications Workshops (PerCom 2004 Workshop)*, pp. 192–197, 2004.

8. M. Roman, C.K. Hess, R. Cerqueira, R.H. Campbell, and K. Narhstedt : "Gaia: A Middleware Infrastructure to Enable Active spaces", *IEEE Pervasive Computing Magazine*, Vol. 1, pp. 74–83, 2002.

9. E. Chan, J. Bresler, J. Al-Muhtadi, and R. Campbell : "Gaia Microserver: An Extendable Mobile Middleware Platform", *Proc. of 3rd IEEE Int'l Conf. on Pervasive Computing and Communications (PerCom2005)*, pp. 309–313, 2005.

10. A. Messer, A. Kunjithapatham, M. Sheshagiri, H. Song, P. Kumar, P. Nguyen, and K.H. Yi : "InterPlay: A Middleware for Seamless Device Integration and Task Orchestration in a Networked Home", *Proc. of 4th IEEE Int'l Conf. on Pervasive Computing and Communications (PerCom2006)*, 2006.

11. S. Consolvo, L. Arnstein, and B.R. Franza : "User Study Techniques in the Design and Evaluation of a Ubicomp Environment", *Proc. of 4th Int'l Conf. on Ubiquitous Computing (UbiComp2002)*, pp. 73–90, 2002.

12. J. Nakata, and Y. Tan : "The Design and Implementation of Large Scale Ubiquitous Network Testbed", *Proc. of Workshop on Smart Object Systems (SObS05) (UbiComp 2005 Workshop)*, 2005.

13. K. Sanmugalingam, and G. Coulouris : "A Generic Location Event Simulator", *Proc. of 4th Int'l Conf. on Ubiquitous Computing (UbiComp2002)*, pp. 308–315 , 2002.

14. N. Roy, A. Roy, and S.K. Das : "Context-Aware Resource Management in Multi-Inhabitant Smart Homes: A Nash H-Learning based Approach", *Proc. of 4th IEEE Int'l Conf. on Pervasive Computing and Communications (PerCom2006)*, 2006.

15. J.L. Asbahr : "Beyond: A Portable Virtual World Simulation Framework", *Proc. of 7th Int'l Python Conf.*, 1998.

16. Unreal Engine: http://www.unrealtechnology.com/

17. E.M. Clarke, E.A. Emerson, and A.P. Sistla : "Automatic verification of finite state concurrent systems using temporal logic specifications", *ACM Trans. on Program Languages and Semantics*, Vol. 8, No. 2, pp. 244–263, 1986.

Instant Matchmaking: Simple and Secure Integrated Ubiquitous Computing Environments

D.K. Smetters[1], Dirk Balfanz[1], Glenn Durfee[1],
Trevor F. Smith[1], and Kyung-Hee Lee[2]

[1] Palo Alto Research Center, 3333 Coyote Hill Road, Palo Alto, CA 94304, U.S.A.
[2] Samsung Advanced Institute of Technology, P.O. Box 111, Suwon 440-600, Korea
{smetters, balfanz, gdurfee, tfsmith}@parc.com, kyungheelee@samsung.com

Abstract. Effective ubiquitous computing applications need to integrate users' personal devices and data with the devices and resources
they encounter around them. Previous work addressed this problem by
simply enabling the user to take all of their data with them wherever
they go. In this paper, we present a more flexible approach: the "instant
matchmaker", a personal device that allows a user to seamlessly and securely connect his local computing environment with his other personal
resources, wherever they are. The matchmaker provides an intuitive user
experience, while simultaneously enabling extremely fine-grained control
over access to resources. We have implemented a cellphone-based matchmaker and explored its use in a secure media sharing application. The
matchmaker concept, however, is general, and can be used to enable a
range of appealing and secure ubicomp applications.

1 Introduction

Ubiquitous computing offers the promise that users will be able to take advantage of resources – devices, services, and data – embedded into the environment
around them. Those local resources are most useful when combined with the
user's own personal resources, which may reside elsewhere. This poses a challenge: building applications that seamlessly integrate a variety of devices and
resources – some local, some remote, some trusted, some untrusted, some sensitive, some not – in a way that is simultaneously easy to use and secure.

In this paper we introduce the *Instant Matchmaker*, a device which enables
users to easily and securely integrate local and remote computing resources
into seamless ubiquitous computing applications. The Instant Matchmaker functionality can be embodied in a cell phone, PDA or another commonly-carried
portable device. The Matchmaker supports a simple trust model for managing
access, namely that of *security by introduction*. A user uses their Instant Matchmaker to securely introduce a new, untrusted device they encounter in their
environment to a trusted personal resource. At the same time, the Matchmaker
takes care of the mechanics of helping these two devices find each other and
establish network connections, *etc.*

By capturing the user's intent at the level of application tasks, the Instant
Matchmaker then acts on the user's behalf to extend only the necessary *limited*

P. Dourish and A. Friday (Eds.): Ubicomp 2006, LNCS 4206, pp. 477–494, 2006.

trust to that new, untrusted device to accomplish the intended task and nothing else. For instance, if the user so requests, a local display should be able to access and display the feed from her home webcam. However, it shouldn't be able to access any of her other resources, and it should be able to access the selected resources only at her discretion – allowing it to access that content this one time should not grant it any access at any future time, and she should also be able to terminate even the current access at any point she desires.

The Instant Matchmaker reconciles ease of use with access control. It enables users to co-opt nearby devices to work with personal resources residing elsewhere, while limiting these co-opted devices to precisely the access needed to accomplish the requested task. The user doesn't even think about access control: limitations are automatically inferred and enforced based on the user's actions. We validate our model and design through a concrete implementation.

We begin in Section 2 by motivating the Instant Matchmaker approach and deriving requirements for any system providing ubiquitous access to personal resources. We evaluate previous work in Section 3. Section 4 presents our system design, and Section 5 provides details of our current implementation. Finally in Section 6, we discuss and generalize our current results, and present opportunities for future work.

2   Motivation

Consider the following scenarios:

- A traveler, Alice, wishes to use a large-screen TV in her hotel room to display the new home movie her partner has just placed on her home media server. She doesn't want that TV to access any other resources on her media server or home network, such as her personal photos or tax returns.
- Bob wishes to display a presentation on a projector in a meeting room, but the presentation is back on the computer in his office. He wants to enable the projector to retrieve it, but the administrator of his network wants to ensure that only legitimate users can grant such access, and then only to resources they really intend to share.
- Charlotte has purchased a new informative picture frame that shows her how well her mother in Germany is doing by monitoring activity sensors in her mother's house. Her mother doesn't want anyone else to be able to observe her activity.
- David gets a cell phone call with video from his girlfriend, and wishes to transfer it to the speakers and display in the room he is currently in. He doesn't want just any speakers he happens to pass by to hear his conversation, only those he specifically indicates.

These are all instances of a single, general pattern: a user wishes to access her personal content via a rendering (or other type of) device she encounters in her immediate vicinity. She would like to do so regardless of where the content is stored or originates from. And she would like the option to use any rendering

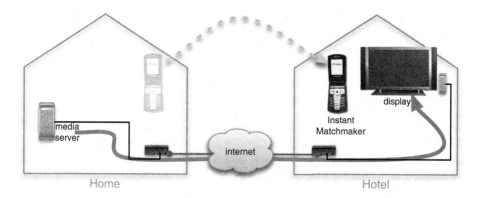

Fig. 1. Example scenario: secure remote access to personal resources

device she encounters – even a completely *untrusted* one with which she has no *a priori* relationship, and which may be also used by others who might be malicious, or managed by entities whom she cannot rely on to enforce security guarantees on her behalf (*e.g.,* to maintain anti-virus software to protect her from key-loggers, or to erase her stored state after she leaves).

We would like to design a general approach to providing secure, easy integration of local and remote ubiquitous computing resources. We briefly look at two popular approaches, before we identify a set of basic requirements that any such system must meet. We base those requirements on both analysis of the problem itself, and examination of the issues left unsolved by previous approaches.

2.1 Previous Approaches

There are two very commonly proposed approaches to this problem. We examine them here in some detail, as their shortcomings help to illustrate critical requirements any effective solution must address.

Dynamic Local Caching. One might obviate the requirement for secure remote access to resources and data by simply arranging to carry all of your data with you all of the time (*e.g.,* [1, 2]). This approach suffers from two critical problems: first, it simply may not be possible to ensure that you have with you all the content you will ever need. The content might be *new*, for example a movie of Alice's son taken after she left home, it might be *live*, as in the feed from a camera or other sensing device, or what you need access to might be a device or service that simply isn't "portable". Second, even for data that you do cache locally, say on a personal trusted device, you must address the problem of how to protect that data and usably limit access to only what you intend.

"Guest" Access. Consider the case of Alice, above. If her home network (where her media server is) is secure, any remote device wishing to access that network needs to be authorized. If Alice provides the hotel TV with a password that allows access to her home network, or plugs a smartcard into it containing her home network access credentials, the TV now has full access to her home network. This constitutes a significant security risk – remember that the TV is an *untrusted* device.

Alice could delegate more *limited* access to her home network to the hotel TV, by giving the TV a special "guest user" password or credential. The problem with such "guest" access is that the user who wishes to access his trusted resources remotely has a choice between insecurity – where a "guest" has full access to all of his protected resources – and inconvenience, where he has to correctly guess, and then specify, or re-specify, which of his personal resources an untrusted device such as a hotel TV should have permission to access – something users are unlikely to put up with.

2.2 System Requirements

We can now derive a set of design requirements that should be met by any system promising ubiquitous access to personal data and services.

Opportunistic access to encountered resources. Users should be able to take advantage of any resource they encounter around them. Those resources should not need to be "approved" in advance – *i.e.*, to hold a credential issued by a particular trusted party, to have access to or be listed in some database of authorized users and devices, or even share a particular password.[1]

Universal access to personal resources. Users should be able to access *any* of their personal resources on-the-fly, wherever and whenever they need them. This should include live, or continuously updated data, or new data created by others in their absence. This implies that we must enable the user to compose network access to those resources with the local resources in their environment, rather than expecting them to bring everything they might ever need with them. This is not to say that such caching is not valuable; in fact a system combining on-line access to resources with automatic caching of content for efficient local use is a direct, and very powerful, superset of a caching-only approach.

No need to specify an access policy a priori. Not only should the user not have to anticipate what data they will need to access, they should also not have to anticipate which devices they will need to access it from, or what sort of permissions they will need to grant those devices. Instead, they should be able to defer access control decisions until they face a particular device to which they would like to grant (limited) access in order to accomplish a particular task.

Least privilege access boundary. Any system providing ubiquitous access to personal resources should ideally make the following security guarantee: that the specific device that the user selects, *and only that device*, should be able to access

---

[1] This is not to say that we do not require such devices to run particular software or speak a particular protocol, but those requirements are common to all ubiquitous computing applications, secure or not.

the particular resources they indicate, *and nothing else*. This "and nothing else" approach to usable security design is actually quite general – it says simply that users are interested in performing a particular application task, and are willing to implicitly grant any rights necessary to allow that task to be completed. To be intuitive and secure, a system must often just transparently implement those grants, while preventing all other unspecified access. In other words, users are often willing to assume some risk in return for desired functionality – *e.g.,* they choose to display their home movie on a large display they encounter even though it may also maliciously stream it to the Internet; we aim to ensure they assume no more risk than is absolutely necessary to accomplish their goal.

Here this translates into the following concrete requirements:

- Access to resources must be limited to only those devices the user authorizes.
- All resource access must be *authenticated*, in order to be able to limit such access only to devices the user intends. Such authentication must be done in terms appropriate to the application context, *i.e.,* "this network connection really comes from the device I am standing in front of".
- Access by user-authorized devices must be limited to only those resources the user intends.
- Network communication between user-authorized devices must be secure – *i.e.,* protected from eavesdropping and modification by unauthorized entities on the network.

Minimize required user effort. The challenge in effecting such a least privilege access boundary is that it requires very fine-grained specification of access control policy, tightly coupled to the details of the user's current application task. Manually managing such a policy is cumbersome, outside of most users' domain of expertise, and peripheral to the application task the user is actually interested in.

We should minimize the amount of explicit management a user must do, instead letting them focus on their application task. One approach to this, termed *implicit security* [3] focuses on allowing the system to infer the user's access control requirements directly from their application-related decisions. This allows fine-grained control of access without directly involving the user.

In the first example scenario above, Alice should not have to decide which principal should have access to which resource in her home network separately from deciding which movie to watch. Doing the latter (*e.g.,* deciding to watch a movie) should *automatically* trigger the former (*e.g.,* opening up access to the movie for the device Alice chose to watch the movie on), as well as establishing any necessary network connections and so on. Ideally, users should not even be aware of the fact that they are making an *access control decision*. And if the system is forced to ask the user directly for guidance in a case where their intent is not clear, it should do so in terms of application-level events and concepts that are more accessible and intuitive than questions about the details of unfamiliar security mechanisms.

Reliable and secure indicators of user intent. Such a system must effectively capture and communicate user intent, for two reasons. First, if we are to minimize the work the user has to do to convey their desired access policy to the system, we must design the user interaction and user interface such that they give us reliable and clear indicators of user intent.

Second, for maximal security we must ensure that those indicators actually come from the user, and not, say, from the untrusted device she is targeting. For example, say that Alice uses the hotel TV remote and GUI to browse resources on her home network, and has the TV send a message to her home media server indicating which movie she wishes to play. If the TV were malicious, it could simply tell Alice that it has requested the specific movie she chose from her home media server, and display only that movie. However, under the covers, it could also tell her home network that Alice also wishes it to obtain a copy of all of her personal files. There is no way for Alice's trusted devices to distinguish between a legitimate request from Alice sent by the untrusted device, and an illegitimate request added by the device itself.

To mitigate the effects of such an attack, Alice could either limit the actions she herself can take on her trusted resources from a remote location, thus also limiting what a malicious intermediary can do. She could also carefully review the logs on her home network to detect such an attack after the fact. But to prevent such manipulation entirely, she must use a *trusted input path* to indicate her requests. In other words, indications of Alice's intent must come not from the untrusted device she is intending to access, but instead from a device trusted by Alice and her personal networked resources, such as her Instant Matchmaker.

3   Related Work

The idea of ubiquitous access to personal resources is not new. However, much previous work in this area either fails to meet important security or usability requirements, or is more narrowly targeted than that presented here.

Personal Server. The *Personal Server* [1,2] is a small, wireless personal storage platform that the user carries with them, and on which they store all of their personal data. The advantages of the Personal Server (PS) is that, in theory, that data is then immediately accessible to them wherever they are, in a form that is resilient to network problems and the availability of remote servers. This is a prototypical example of a dynamic caching system, and as such suffers from all of the limitations of such described in section 2.1.

This system also suffers from significant security problems. The initial design for use of the Personal Server has it make itself promiscuously available over a short-range wireless link to any device it encounters, without further user intervention [1]. This makes it vulnerable to any device within radio range.[2] Password protection mitigates some threats [2]; nevertheless, the user still has

---

[2] And inexpensive antennas can make even supposedly "short-range" radio systems such as BlueTooth accessible from miles away [4,5].

little or no indication of what data is being accessed by the interfacing devices. Furthermore, as this device carries all of a user's sensitive personal data, it is also extremely vulnerable in the case of loss or theft; mitigating that risk via strong encryption then adds its own usability burden.

Remote Media Access Services. Remote access to personal media is a compelling enough application in and of itself that a number of commercial services have sprung up to support it. Two of the most popular are Slingbox [6] and Orb Networks [7].

In Orb's system [7], each device on a user's home network runs a piece of software provided by Orb, which allows the user to access them from any web browser via the Orb Networks server. Slingbox [6] elegantly overcomes the constraints imposed by legacy devices by providing a media server box that the user connects to their home network and incoming cable or satellite feed. The Slingbox then provides network access to exactly the same set of media that the user would be able to access if they were at home.

While providing ubiquitous access to live data and services, they suffer from all the problems typical of such "guest access" systems (described in section 2.1). In both cases, access is protected by a static username and password; any device by which the user accesses their network learns that password, which allows it complete access to that network both now and in the future. Additionally, in Orb's system the Orb server has continuous access to all the devices in a user's home, and can monitor their behavior as well as access their data and resources. An attacker gaining access to that server immediately gets extensive access to the home networks of all Orb users.

PC-Based Remote Access Services. A wide variety of software provides remote access to networked computers. Some, such as *www.GoToMyPC.com* [8] use applet-based approaches to provide easy-to-use access to trusted resources from any untrusted host. Though communication to the target PC is secure, in the absence of a *trusted input path*, the user is still vulnerable to the host they choose to use for access, which may insert its own operations into the stream of commands it sends on behalf of the user (see section 2.2). A general solution to this problem was provided in [9], which used a trusted PDA as an input device to allow secure use of a protected computer from an untrusted kiosk. The work presented here builds on this idea of using a portable device as a trusted input path to enable secure access to protected resources from untrusted devices.

Device-Mediated Access. A variety of systems use a smart device in some fashion to aid users in gaining access to local resources, or controlling access to resources in general.

In Zero-Interaction Authentication [10], a device is only usable when it is in proximity to a trusted personal hardware token. In their system, the device in question is a trusted computer (*e.g.*, a laptop) that is to remain secure in the case of theft. They do not address access to untrusted resources, and as such also do not require that their token provide a trusted input path.

The Grey system [11, 12] allows users to delegate access to resources using a trusted cell phone as an intermediary. They focus on the support of a general-purpose access logic enabling the user to make arbitrary policy statements. In contrast, we focus on providing a seamless user experience; providing strong security without requiring the user to explicitly manage access policy.

Trust Management Systems. Trust-management systems (*e.g.,* [13, 14, 15, 16, 17, 18]) share our goal of enabling fine-grained access control to resources. They follow, however, a completely different approach: Usually, they provide a language in which to express complex conditions under which access should be granted (an *access control policy*). One of the requirements we have identified for integrated ubiquitous computing environments is to do without *without* an *a priori* access control policy. As a trade-off, we require the user to be available at the time of access and make ad-hoc access control decisions himself.

Proximity-Based Authentication of Arbitrary Devices. Stajano *et al.* [19] suggested the idea that security associations can be established among mobile devices through use of a trusted secondary authentication channel. This work was extended by Balfanz *et al.* [20] with concrete protocols using public key cryptography. This enables such authentication to occur over a wide range of secondary, *location-limited* channels such as infrared and audio. Further work [21, 22, 23, 24, 25] has extended this to yet other channel types, and incorporated it in a number of applications [26]. We use this approach here as a tool to enable secure on-the-fly authentication of and communication with any device a user might encounter.

4   System Overview

The operation of an Instant Matchmaker-based system is shown abstractly in Figure 2. The Instant Matchmaker (here implemented in a cell phone, center)

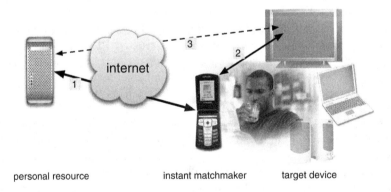

personal resource   instant matchmaker   target device

Fig. 2. The structure of an Instant Matchmaker-enabled integrated ubiquitous computing environment

acts on the user's behalf as a trusted proxy, enabling limited access to remote *personal resources*, shown at left, by a *target device* selected by the user (at right). The Matchmaker is used to select target devices, choose personal resources to share, and initiate and terminate transactions between these.

As a member of the user's home network, the Matchmaker is assumed to have a pre-existing trust relationship with the user's other personal resources (arrow 1). When the user uses the Matchmaker to select a local target device to which she will grant resource access, she establishes a limited, and selective trust association (arrow 2) with that particular device using proximity-based authentication. When the user indicates a resource she wishes to share, she does so using the Matchmaker as a *trusted input path*, securely capturing her intent. The Matchmaker then notifies the device hosting the personal resource of the grant of access (arrow 3), providing the identity of the target device and an identifier of the resource to which it should be allowed access.

Implementing an effective Instant Matchmaker-based system requires designing a user experience that allows a user to specify what resources she wants to share with which target device intuitively in the context of her application task (for a specific example, see Section 5). It also requires implementing appropriate protocols to allow the actual sharing of resources. The protocols necessary to implement the security model are largely independent of these details, and are described in the next section.

4.1   Operation and Protocol

The main message flows used in an Instant Matchmaker-based system are illustrated in Figure 3. This is a generic protocol framework, and though the details will vary slightly depending on the application implemented, we highlight common elements here. See Section 5 for an implementation.

Setup. All devices are configured initially with cryptographic key pairs consisting of a private key and a public key. These can be automatically generated when devices are first powered on; notably, no user (or administrator) need ever be aware of the presence of these keys. We assume that the Instant Matchmaker and the device hosting the personal resource already trust each other and know each others' public keys. This can be accomplished reliably, without requiring user involvement, as described in [27, 26].

Protocol: The steps in the protocol flow are as follows:

1. The user signals their intention to use a particular target device, for example by "pointing out" that device using an infrared or contact-based interface on their Instant Matchmaker. Via this interface, the Instant Matchmaker learns the public key and network address of the target device and vice versa.

2. As part of their ongoing task, the user identifies a personal resource they wish to use with the target device to the Instant Matchmaker, indicating implicitly that they would like all steps necessary to make that possible – grants of access, network connections, *etc.*, to take place as well. The Instant

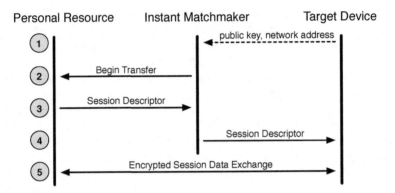

Fig. 3. The protocol flows for a transactions in an extended ubiquitous computing environment

Matchmaker then informs the personal resource about the transaction to occur (*e.g.*, the video that Alice has selected to play). As part of the message, the Instant Matchmaker also transmits the target device's public key. The device hosting the personal resource will "whitelist" this public key for one-time access to that particular resource, for that particular transaction.

3. The personal resource sets up a "session" and responds with information about this session, including an identifier, (*e.g.*, a URL), where the resource (in our case the video) will be available. If necessary, the personal resource also configures its network security environment (*e.g.*, firewall) to allow communication from the target device.

4. The Instant Matchmaker passes this information on to the target device, along with the public key of the personal resource. At this point, the target device and personal resource are both ready to conduct the transaction.

5. The target device connects to the personal resource to conduct the transaction. This connection is encrypted and authenticated using those devices' public keys.

4.2   Adequacy of Instant Matchmaker Design

Let's review the system requirements outlined in Section 2.2, and evaluate our design in terms of those requirements.

First, we note that the Instant Matchmaker learns the public key of a target device using a proximity-based exchange. Before that step, the target device need not participate in any common trust framework with the personal resource and the Instant Matchmaker; *i.e.*, they do not need to all belong to the same PKI, have keys signed by Verisign, or have any other pre-existing trust relationship. Consequently, we have achieved our first design goal, *opportunistic access to encountered resources*.

Our second design goal, *universal access to personal resources*, is achieved by mediating a *live* connection between a personal resource and the target device.

This is in contrast to designs like the Personal Server or iPod, which assume that resource needs will be anticipated by the user and cached in advance.

We also see that the user has *no need to specify an a priori access policy*. The user's specific action, at the moment, decides which resources are to be used by which devices in their environment. The user does not need to set up ahead of time which personal resources are to be shared, and to whom it can be shared.

Our fourth design goal, *least privilege*, is also satisfied. The personal resource makes only the minimal changes in security necessary to enable the user-requested action, and automatically returns the system to the most secure state possible as soon as the action completes.

The fifth design goal, *minimize required user effort*, is accomplished by hiding as much as possible the details of the security exchange from the user. Identification and public key exchange between the Instant Matchmaker and the target device is embedded in an Infrared exchange; the whitelisting of the target device by the personal resource occurs automatically in response to the requested user action. Encryption and integrity protection of communication is transparent to the user.

Finally, our sixth design goal is ensured: since the Instant Matchmaker and personal resource know each other's cryptographic public keys, they authenticate and encrypt all communication with each other, yielding a *trusted path* from the Instant Matchmaker to the personal resource that provides the resource with *reliable and secure indication of user intent*.

5   Implementation

In order to explore the practicality of our approach, we have implemented a system supporting the application scenario introduced in Section 2: secure remote access to personal media. This implementation consists of two parts: first, a system security layer implementing the basic Instant Matchmaker functionality, capable of supporting a variety of applications. Second, an application-specific user interface layer designed to make the particular application we have implemented as intuitive and easy for the end user as possible.

5.1   Remote Media Access Scenario: User Experience

We consider the concrete scenario shown in Figure 1; where a user, Alice, wishes to play videos stored on her home media server on the large-screen TV in her hotel room. In order to do so, she does the following:

1. Alice, in her hotel room, takes out her cell phone, and starts a "TV Remote Control" application (shown in Figure 4). Pointing the infrared port of her phone at the hotel TV, she turns it on by pressing the **Power** button on the remote control interface.

2. When the TV turns on, she sees a menu of available options displayed simultaneously on the TV and on her mobile phone. This menu includes both TV channels provided by the hotel and resources (only) available to Alice, such as the media repository on her home network.

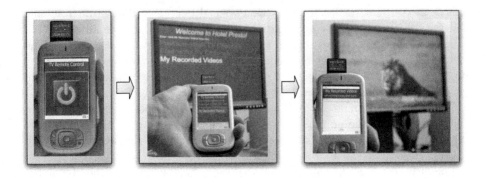

Fig. 4. Screen shots of our implementation. The left panel shows the remote control application of the Instant Matchmaker ready to turn on a TV through infrared. The center panel shows how the user interface of the Instant Matchmaker is mirrored on the TV while the user makes selections. The right panel shows the Instant Matchmaker and the TV while a selected movie is streamed from the user's home network.

3. Using the **Up** and **Down** buttons on her phone as a remote control, Alice finds the video she is interested in in her home media repository. She starts streaming that particular video by pressing the **Select** button on her phone. At this point, the TV (and only that hotel TV) becomes authorized to download that particular video once.
4. The video starts playing on the TV. On Alice's phone, there is now a GUI that shows the progress of the video, and provides buttons that allow her to control playback (*e.g.,* **Stop**, **Pause**, *etc.*).
5. If Alice presses the **Stop** button on her phone, the video stops and she sees the menu of available video sources again. At the same time, pressing the **Stop** button has revoked the TV's ability to access the remainder of the content it was previously authorized to download.
6. Alice can turn off the TV using her phone, or can resume watching a video. Again, as she selects a video to play, the TV is automatically authorized to access to stream that particular video from her home media server one time.

Alice's user experience is seamless, in that it is basically identical to how she would operate the hotel TV using its normal remote control (which we expect to still be present, for the benefit of users without an Instant Matchmaker). However, this system has added functionality – Alice's personal network resources, such videos stored on her home media server, are automatically made available to her in addition to any services provided by the hotel itself.

5.2 Setup

Alice's Personal Resources. In our implementation, Alice's home network consists of a media server and networked display connected via a wired Ethernet hub, which also serves as a home gateway connected to the Internet. The media server and networked display are both standard Mac computing platforms running Mac OS 10.4, Java, and our secure middleware layer (see Section 5.5). The home gateway additionally provides a firewall, NAT translation, and 802.11 wireless connectivity. The media server, networked display, Instant Matchmaker and home gateway all posses public-private key pairs and associated digital certificates issued by the home gateway, set up using the approach presented in [26] (this requires no user awareness of digital certificates or cryptographic keys). These devices use these credentials to secure their communications, from connecting to Alice's secure wireless network, to making a secure virtual private network (VPN) connection back inside Alice's home network from anywhere on the Internet, to authenticating and securing middleware connections as described in Section 5.5.

Alice's Instant Matchmaker is implemented on a PDA phone running Windows Mobile 2003, the CreMe Java VM, and a port of our secure middleware layer.

The Hotel Network. The hotel network consists of a wired LAN connecting a networked display ("hotel TV") to gateway/firewall device, which is in turn connected to both the Internet and a 802.11 wireless network available for guest access. The hotel TV is connected to a network proxy device which implements our secure middleware layer. We implement such a network proxy in the form of a Mac Mini running Mac OS 10.4, Java, and our secure middleware layer. The hotel TV's proxy has a public-private key pair that it uses to secure its communications. The first time it is turned on, it automatically generates this key pair and creates a certificate for it, which it signs itself without requiring any help from an administrator or certification authority.

5.3   Selecting Target Devices

Alice identifies the hotel TV she wishes to see her video on to the trusted devices on her home network by "pointing out" the TV using the infrared (IR) interface of her Instant Matchmaker. Using it literally as a remote control, she powers on the hotel TV. We also use that simple IR exchange to establish trust between Alice's Instant Matchmaker and the hotel TV. Using *proximity-based authentication* [20], each device sends the other the cryptographic digest of their public key over IR. Alice's Instant Matchmaker and the hotel TV can then secure all of their further communication using the TLS (SSL) protocol [28]; they authenticate each other by demonstrating that each possesses the private key corresponding to the public key the other received over the IR channel, or that simply they were the device that user wanted the other to talk to.

5.4   User Interface

At this point Alice's Instant Matchmaker makes a secure VPN connection to her home network using the Internet access provided by the hotel, and authenticated by the certificate it has that verifies it is indeed a member of her home network.

The Instant Matchmaker discovers content accessible to it both locally, *i.e.,* via the hotel TV and on the hotel's WLAN/LAN, as well as in Alice's home domain (to which it is connected via a VPN). It displays the available content on its screen to the user. At the same time, it sends a copy of this user interface to the hotel TV, making it easier for the user to navigate the available content. Because the Instant Matchmaker can authenticate the hotel TV, we can be sure that the UI (and later, the actual content) is displayed on the TV that Alice is standing in front of, and not, say, on the TV in the hotel room next door.

At this point, the hotel TV receives a user interface listing the available content[3] (including, for example, the names of the various home movies on Alice's home media server). It does not, however, have sufficient privileges to *access* the content. In order for it gain those privileges, the content has to be selected on the Instant Matchmaker explicitly by Alice. Although the hotel TV's UI can aid Alice in the process of content selection, Alice should glance at the UI on her Instant Matchmaker to confirm her choice before actually accessing the content, to thwart UI substitution attacks.[4]

5.5   Middleware for Secure Remote Resource Access

Now that Alice's Instant Matchmaker knows which resource she would like displayed on what particular target device, it must actually enable that device to access that piece of content. It must also enable Alice to control or terminate the ongoing playback if she so desires. At the same time, it must provide basic security guarantees appropriate to the application context.

We implement these remaining components of the system on top of a general middleware layer that enables easy remote access to arbitrary types of devices, services, and data, which we have extended to incorporate a general security framework allowing application developers to easily incorporate intuitive security policies into distributed applications. Developers can specify security policies in terms of the application tasks the users will understand, while the system takes care of implementing the underlying security mechanisms those developers may not be as familiar with.

As our underlying middleware layer, we use the Obje Interoperability Framework, a middleware framework designed for radical interoperability [29, 30, 31]. This framework encapsulates a wide variety of devices and services as *data sources* that send data or *data sinks* that receive and process it; automatically translating data formats as necessary to ensure interoperability. Obje is general enough to support anything from sending a document to a printer to sending a movie or webcam feed to a networked display; selection of which source to connect to which sink is done through a combination of application filtering (only some source and sink types may relevant to a particular application) and user input. In the current application, Obje handles all the details necessary to

---

[3] We note that if the content *list* is sensitive (and not just the content itself), the application should use only the Instant Matchmaker's UI, and not send a UI to the hotel TV.

[4] Note that if the TV does trick Alice into requesting a piece of content other than the one she intended, it will only get that other content. To hide the attack from Alice, it would also need to obtain the content she did request from another source.

actually deliver selected images, movies, video feeds or even documents to the display indicated by Alice.

The middleware security framework uses TLS [28] to secure all interactions between Obje components and hosts, and to exchange and verify credentials that are used to enable access control decisions to be made in these distributed applications. We use TLS in client-authentication mode, which means that two peers will mutually authenticate each other. In its default configuration, the middleware security framework will either use a "device certificate" available on the device (*e.g.*, one that has been issued by a certification authority) to authenticate itself to a remote peer, or – if not such certificate is present – create new key pair and self-signed certificate for future use.

To build a secured application, developers are required to implement only a small number of security-related security call-backs. These call-backs are invoked when one device attempts to access a resource held by another; we ensure that the application developer has access to all of the information necessary to respond to the call-back in an application-appropriate manner. For example, we implemented the call-backs for the remote media access application, achieving the following behavior:

- **The Home Media Server:** allows access by any other member device from Alice's home domain, including her Instant Matchmaker. It can recognize those devices as they all have certificates issued by the same entity [26]. It also allows any access requests from any other device that have been specifically allowed, or "whitelisted" by any home domain member device.
- **Alice's Instant Matchmaker:** allows access by any other member device from Alice's home domain. Also allows this device to control any target device whose public key it received over IR.
- **Hotel TV:** allows access and control by the last device whose public key it received over IR.

Our middleware automatically grants access according to these policies and revokes access as soon as an application transaction ends or is interrupted by the user.

6   Discussion and Future Work

We have demonstrated an approach for securely and easily integrating personal resources, wherever they might be located, into local ubiquitous computing environments and applications. Our approach relies on the use of a trusted device, the Instant Matchmaker, to securely introduce new, untrusted devices to the user's personal resources.

We have implemented an Instant Matchmaker in the form of a cell phone and demonstrated its use in a remote media access application. The inherent flexibility of the Obje Interoperability Framework, the middleware layer used in our implementation, allows even the simple application here to immediately support secure remote display of all sorts of personal media – *e.g.*, still images, movies, live camera feeds, *etc.* In order to maximize the intuitiveness of the Instant Matchmaker user interface used to securely capture user intent, we have tailored it to the application at hand – remote display of personal media – in the form of a familiar "remote control". Supporting other applications equally intuitively may require comparable interface tailoring, though it is also possible to allow more flexible and general use of a trusted input path at the cost of some usability (as in [9]). Though our current implementation relies on the Obje Interoperability Framework to handle many of the "messy details" of data exchange, the Instant Matchmaker approach can also be used with a wide variety of distributed systems and protocols.

One can also extend the applicability of the Instant Matchmaker approach beyond the class of applications considered here. Abstractly, the Matchmaker acts as a *trust bridge*, allowing transparent delegation of access between two mutually untrusting resources mediated in a user-friendly way by a device, the Matchmaker, trusted (to some degree) by both. Here we consider mediation between Alice's personal devices, with whom her Matchmaker has a long-term trust relationship, and a local device, with whom limited trust is established in a proximity-based fashion. However, many other combinations (and resulting applications) are possible.

In conclusion, this approach has a number of advantages. It enables secure universal access to all sorts of personal devices and services, not just static data. It provides a flexible mechanism for specifying and implementing access control policy on-the-fly, in response to user needs. User intent is captured as they interact with the application at hand, and the matchmaker translates that automatically into the implicitly requested modifications of security policy necessary to "make it so" without requiring any explicit security-related action on the part of the end user. Because these changes in access control policy are automatic, the matchmaker can implement extremely fine-grained access control without undue user burden, limiting access to only those specific resources the user intends. The Instant Matchmaker also provides a trusted input path to communicate those policy changes securely to the user's personal resources, and protect those resources even if the users selects a malicious device to access personal data. In essence, the Instant Matchmaker can be considered a key or porthole into trusted resources stored elsewhere.

In future work, we plan to perform usability tests to validate and improve the Instant Matchmaker user experience. We also plan to explore the use of this model in a number of additional applications. Finally, the Instant Matchmaker model serves in essence as a design pattern applicable to a range of ubiquitous computing applications. We are currently exploring other potential design patterns for usable secure ubiquitous computing applications.

Acknowledgments

We would like to thank Paul Stewart and Bum-Jin Im for their invaluable help, and the anonymous reviewers for their comments. Part of this work was supported by NIST contract 70NANB3H3052.

References

1. Want, R., Pering, T., Danneels, G., Kumar, M., Sundar, M., Light, J.: The personal server: Changing the way we think about ubiquitous computing. In: Ubicomp. (2002) 194–209
2. Pering, T., Nguyen, D.H., Light, J., Want, R.: Face-to-face media sharing using wireless mobile devices. In: Seventh IEEE International Symposium on Multimedia (ISM'05). (2005) 269–276
3. Smetters, D.K., Grinter, R.E.: Moving from the design of usable security technologies to the design of useful secure applications. In: New Security Paradigms Workshop '02, ACM (2002)
4. Cheung, H.:   How   To: Building   a   BlueSniper   rifle   -   Part   1. http://www.tomsnetworking.com/2005/03/08/how_to/ (2005)
5. The Trifinite Group: The car whisperer. http://trifinite.org/trifinite_stuff_carwhisperer.html(2005)
6. Slingbox. http://www.slingbox.com (2006)
7. Orb Networks. http://www.orb.com (2006)
8. GoToMyPC. http://www.gotomypc.com (2006)
9. Oprea, A., Balfanz, D., Durfee, G., Smetters, D.: Securing a remote terminal application with a mobile trusted device. In: Proceedings of the Annual Computer Security Applications Conference, Tucson, AZ (2004)
10. Corner, M.D., Noble, B.D.: Zero-interaction authentication. In: Proceedings of the eighth Annual International Conference on Mobile Computing and Networking (MOBICOM-02), New York, ACM Press (2002) 1–11
11. Bauer, L., Garriss, S., Reiter, M.K.: Distributed proving in access-control systems. In: IEEE Symposium on Security and Privacy. (2005) 81–95
12. Bauer, L., Garriss, S., McCune, J.M., Reiter, M.K., Rouse, J., Rutenbar, P.: Device-enabled authorization in the grey-system. In: ISC. (2005) 431–445
13. Balfanz, D., Dean, D., Spreitzer, M.: A security infrastructure for distributed Java applications. In: 21th IEEE Computer Society Symposium on Research in Security and Privacy, Oakland, CA (2000)
14. Blaze, M., Feigenbaum, J., Ioannidis, J., Keromytis, A.: The KeyNote Trust-Management System Version 2. IETF - Network Working Group, The Internet Society. (1999) RFC 2704.
15. DeTreville, J.: Binder, a logic-based security language. In: 2002 IEEE Symposium on Security and Privacy, Oakland, CA (2002)
16. Bauer, L., Schneider, M.A., Felten, E.W.: A general and flexible access-control system for the web. In: Proceedings of the 11th USENIX Security Symposium, San Francisco, CA (2002)
17. Abadi, M., Burrows, M., Lampson, B.: A calculus for access control in distributed systems. In Feigenbaum, J., ed.: "Proc. CRYPTO 91", Springer (1992) 1–23 Lecture Notes in Computer Science No. 576.
18. Halpern, J.Y., van der Meyden, R.: A logic for SDSI's linked local name spaces. In: Proceedings of the 12th IEEE Computer Security Foundations Workshop, Mordano, Italy (1999) 111–122
19. Stajano, F., Anderson, R.J.: The resurrecting duckling: Security issues for ad-hoc wireless networks. In: 7th Security Protocols Workshop. Volume 1796 of Lecture Notes in Computer Science., Cambridge, United Kingdom, Springer-Verlag, Berlin Germany (1999) 172–194

20. Balfanz, D., Smetters, D., Stewart, P., Wong, H.C.: Talking to strangers: Authentication in ad-hoc wireless networks. In: Proceedings of the 2002 Network and Distributed Systems Security Symposium (NDSS'02), San Diego, CA, The Internet Society (2002)
21. Rekimoto, J., Ayatsuka, Y., Kohno, M., Oba, H.: Proximal interactions: A direct manipulation technique for wireless networking. In: INTERACT 2003. (2003)
22. Kohno, M., Rekimoto, J.: New generation of ip-phone enabled mobile devices. In: Mobile HCI 2002. (2002) 319–323
23. Kindberg, T., Zhang, K.: Secure spontaneous device association. In: UbiComp 2003. (2003)
24. Kindberg, T., Zhang, K.: Validating and securing spontaneous associations between wireless devices. In: Proceedings of the 6th Information Security Conference (ISC03). (2003)
25. McCune, J.M., Perrig, A., Reiter, M.K.: Seeing-is-believing: Using camera phones for human-verifiable authentication. In: Proceedings of the IEEE Symposium on Security and Privacy. (2005)
26. Balfanz, D., Durfee, G., Grinter, R.E., Smetters, D., Stewart, P.: Network-in-a-box: How to set up a secure wireless network in under a minute. In: Proceedings of the 13th USENIX Security Symposium, San Diego, CA (2004)
27. Balfanz, D., Durfee, G., Smetters, D.: Making the impossible easy: Usable PKI. In Cranor, L.F., Garfinkel, S., eds.: Security and Usability – Designing Secure Systems that People Can Use. O'Reilly Media, Inc. (2005) 319–334
28. Dierks, T., Allen, C.: The TLS Protocol Version 1.0. IETF - Network Working Group, The Internet Society. (1999) RFC 2246.
29. Edwards, W.K., Newman, M.W., Sedivy, J.Z., Smith, T.F., Izadi, S.: Challenge: Recombinant computing and the Speakeasy approach. In: Proceedings of the The Eighth ACM International Conference on Mobile Computing and Networking (Mobicom 2002), Atlanta, GA (2002)
30. Newman, M.W., Sedivy, J.Z., Edwards, W.K., Smith, T.F., Marcelo, K., Neuwirth, C.M., Hong, J.I., Izadi, S.: Designing for serendipity: Supporting end-user configuration of ubiquitous computing environments. In: Proceedings of the Conference on Designing Interactive Systems (DIS '02), London, UK (2002)
31. Newman, M.W., Izadi, S., Edwards, W.K., Smith, T.F., Sedivy, J.Z.: User interfaces when and where they are needed: An infrastructure for recombinant computing. In: Proceedings of the Symposium on User Interface Software and Technology (UIST), Paris, France, ACM (2002)

A Wirelessly-Powered Platform for Sensing and Computation

Joshua R. Smith[1], Alanson P. Sample[2], Pauline S. Powledge[1],
Sumit Roy[2], and Alexander Mamishev[2]

[1] Intel Research Seattle
1100 NE 45th Street
Seattle, WA 98105
USA
[2] Department of Electrical Engineering,
Box 352500, University of Washington,
Seattle, WA 98195
USA

Joshua.r.smith@intel.com, alanson@u.washington.edu,
pauline.s.powledge@intel.com, {roy, mamishev}@ee.washington.edu

Abstract. We present WISP, a wireless, battery-free platform for sensing and computation that is powered and read by a standards compliant Ultra-High Frequency (UHF) RFID reader. To the reader, the WISP appears to be an ordinary RFID tag. The WISP platform includes a general-purpose programmable flash microcontroller and implements the bi-directional communication primitives required by the Electronic Product Code (EPC) RFID standard, which allows it to communicate arbitrary sensor data via an EPC RFID reader by dynamically changing the ID it presents to the reader. For each 64 bit "packet," the WISP's microcontroller dynamically computes the 16-bit CRC that the EPC standard requires of valid packets. Because the WISP device can control all bits of the presented ID, 64 bits of sensor data can be communicated with a single RFID read event. As an example of the system in operation, we present 13 hours of continuous-valued light-level data measured by the device. All the measurements were made using power harvested from the RFID reader. No battery, and no wired connections (for either power or data) were used. As far as we are aware, this paper reports the first fully programmable computing platform that can operate using power transmitted from a long-range (UHF) RFID reader and communicate arbitrary, multi-bit data in response to a single RFID reader poll event.

1 Introduction and Prior Work

This paper describes WISP, a wireless, battery-free platform for sensing and computation that is powered and read by a standards-compliant Ultra-High Frequency (UHF) RFID reader. The notable features of the device are a wireless power supply, low bit-rate UHF backscatter communication, and a fully programmable ultra-low-power 16-bit flash microcontroller. This particular point in the sensor platform design space

P. Dourish and A. Friday (Eds.): Ubicomp 2006, LNCS 4206, pp. 495–506, 2006.

offers some attractive features for ubiquitous computing, but has not yet been explored very thoroughly.

One approach to ubiquitous sensing is to use wired sensors. This approach is well-suited to creating purpose-built instrumented environments supporting long-term observation.[1] This approach has the advantage that there is no battery lifetime or battery size constraint. The drawback is the need for wires. In [1], the authors describe such a purpose-built living space, which includes custom cabinetry to house sensors as well as cables for both power and data. A second approach, favored by the Wireless Sensor Networks community, is to use battery-powered devices that communicate by ordinary radio communication, often in a peer-to-peer fashion.[2] One disadvantage of this approach is the size and lifetime constraints imposed by batteries. Because of the lifetime constraint, it would not be possible to permanently embed a battery-powered device in a building or civil structure such as a bridge. A third approach includes generating power from environmental sources[3], such as vibration, light, or human motion,[4] and then communicating the sensor data by ordinary RF transmission. The final class of approaches, within which this work fits, is to deliberately transmit power from a large source device to the sensor platforms, which then harvest this "planted" power, rather than relying on generation of electrical energy from naturally occurring or "wild" sources as in the third approach.

The space of wireless power/data transmission can be subdivided further. Chip-less approaches such as Theremin's cavity resonator microphone[5], as well as more recent examples such as [6] and [7], are based on an analog technique in which a quantity to be sensed modifies the frequency or quality factor of a resonant structure. Changes in the resonance can be detected by a "reader" device that is effectively supplying power and collecting analog sensor data. This analog approach is generally limited to a small number of sensors, since the devices cannot be given arbitrarily long unique IDs. Furthermore, these analog sensor devices are not capable of on-board computation, which means the system cannot benefit from channel sharing, error detection and correction, embedded compression and filtering, and other capabilities enabled by digital computation and communication.

RFID tags are wirelessly powered digital devices that include a conventional Integrated Circuit (IC).[8] Conventional RFID tags are fixed function devices that typically use a minimal, non-programmable state machine to report a hard-coded ID when energized by a reader. The Electronic Product Code (EPC) standard operates in the Ultra-High Frequency (UHF) band (915MHz in the U.S.), which has substantially improved the range and field-of-view for RFID reading over previous generations of RFID technology. The standard's broad adoption is enabling a new generation of applications and interoperable products. The "EPC Class 1 Generation 1" specification [9] ("Gen1") is the most widely deployed so far. Conventional RFID tags with a worn RFID reader have been used for activity monitoring in eldercare scenarios[15]; in this case, the RFID read event is in effect a reader-tag proximity sensor.

Integrating RFID tags with secondary sensors has been proposed [10] or implemented [11] in various contexts, and a small number of commercially available RFID sensors exist. In almost all cases, these devices are fixed-function, and simply report a unique ID and sensor data. Most of the commercially available products assume that the sensor platform is battery-powered, and use the RFID channel for communication but not power. Also, existing RFID-sensor devices are generally not programmable platforms supporting arbitrary computation. What may be the only commercially available fully programmable microcontroller with an RFID interface is described in [12]. However, this device can only transmit one bit of sensor data per read event, and, like [11], operates at 125kHz, which limits its range to inches, and thus substantially curtails its applicability for ubiquitous computing applications. The Near Field Communication (NFC) standard is also a relevant point of comparison[16]. NFC uses short-range RFID-style backscatter communication to link powered devices. It does not provide any power harvesting capability. In prior work [13], the WISP team described a microcontroller powered by a long-range EPC-compatible RFID reader, but this prior system used a very rudimentary communication mechanism: an RF semiconductor switch multiplexed two commercially manufactured RFID chips to one RFID antenna. This system, therefore, was capable of transmitting just one bit of sensor data per read event, which substantially limited its usefulness for ubiquitous sensing and computing applications. Further disadvantages of the earlier system were the requirement of two separate antennae (one for harvesting and one for communication), and the highly non-standard manual fabrication process required to connect the RF switch, the two RFID chips, and the RFID tag antenna. The device presented in the present paper uses a single antenna for power harvesting and communication, and (with the possible exception of the antenna) its printed circuit board can be assembled via standard automated equipment using conventional electronic components (i.e. it does not require any commercial RFID tags, which are generally proprietary, undocumented black boxes).

As far as we are aware, this paper reports the first fully programmable computing platform that can operate using power transmitted from a long-range (UHF) RFID reader and communicate arbitrary, multi-bit data in response to a single RFID reader poll event.

2 System Design

By encoding the sensor data in the field normally used for the EPC ID, we are able (in principle) to read our devices with any EPC-standard commercial RFID reader. This is attractive because it allows us to make use of the large installed base of EPC-standard readers, and leverage the RFID industry's significant past and future investments in reader technology development.

The EPC standard provides a mechanism that allows a single reader to communicate with multiple tags in its field of view [9]. The "singulation" mechanism that allows the tags to share the reader channel requires bi-directional communication between reader and tags. To sketch the protocol briefly, the reader polls the population of tags asking "which tag present has high bit 1?" If more than one tag replies by broadcasting their full IDs, the reader detects the collision and further sub-divides the tag population, by refining the query to ask for tags with high bits "11," and then (if necessary, depending on the results), "111," "110," "10," and so on. Once a tag's ID has been read without a collision, the reader causes it to go "quiet" until further notice, and not participate in the protocol until it is "awakened." This singulation procedure is sometimes referred to informally as "tree walking," because the reader explores the "tree" of IDs. Note that the depth of the tree is logarithmic in the number of IDs (and linear in the number of ID bits), so this procedure is efficient in a computational complexity sense.

The EPC standard provides multiple low-level query commands, and particular readers provide multiple modes that compose these commands in different fashions, to allow application developers to make different trade-offs among performance attributes such as read latency, read reliability, number of tags that can be acquired per read event, and so forth.

Because of the bi-directional communication requirements of the EPC standard, our device has to implement three distinct analog functions: power harvesting, reader-to-WISP communication, and WISP-to-reader communication.

We have taken a "software radio" approach to the timing and protocol logic: the analog hardware provides minimal physical layer (PHY) functionality, demodulating the 915MHz carrier and thresholding to extract raw amplitude levels (low or high) from the reader-to-WISP signal, and generating raw backscatter signals (low or high) for detection by the reader. All the timing and protocol logic is generated via software running on the microcontroller.

2.1 Hardware

Figure 1 shows a block diagram of the WISP platform. Figure 3 contains photos of a functional WISP unit. The WISP's computational capability is provided by the TI MSP-430F-1232 [14], a 16-bit, ultra-low-power flash microcontroller. This device provides 8 KBytes + 256 Bytes of Flash memory, 256 bytes of RAM, and a 10 bit, 200kilo-samples-per-second Analog to Digital Converter (ADC). The low power consumption features of this relatively new device family are a major part of the reason it has become possible to power a general purpose microcontroller using a long-range RFID reader.

The analog circuitry for power harvesting, reader-to-WISP communication, and WISP-to-reader communication is provided by a custom analog printed circuit board of our own design. The main WISP board has header connectors for a daughterboard to which sensors can be added, and which has a connector for programming and debugging via a JTAG interface.

2.1.1 Power Harvesting
The power harvester rectifies the 915MHz carrier generated by the RFID reader into a DC voltage that then powers the rest of the system. Our harvester is a multi-stage voltage multiplier, shown schematically in Figure 2. The power harvester functions in "half wave" rectifier mode: current is only passed to the next stage during the positive phase of the RF signal. Low threshold Schottky diodes are used to reduce losses and increase the maximum operating distance. Care must be taken to properly match the impedance of the antenna to that of the rest of the circuit. To design the impedance matching network for optimal power transfer (or alternatively maximum voltage output), we connected a network analyzer to the antenna ports of the WISP and adjusted a variable capacitor in the LC impedance-matching network. We adjusted

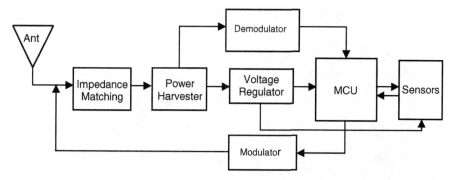

Fig. 1. WISP block diagram. Many of the same elements are found in conventional Wireless Sensor Network nodes. One key difference is that the WISP contains an RF power harvesting module instead of a battery. A second key difference is the box labeled "Modulator." In the WISP presented in this paper, the Modulator box contains just a single transistor, all that is required for WISP-to-reader communication. In a conventional WSN node, a radio frequency oscillator and other radio components are required to transmit data.

the value of this variable component to ensure that the impedance of the power harvesting circuit viewed from the antenna is purely real. Once an appropriate value has been discovered in this fashion, the design can be fixed, and non-variable components used.

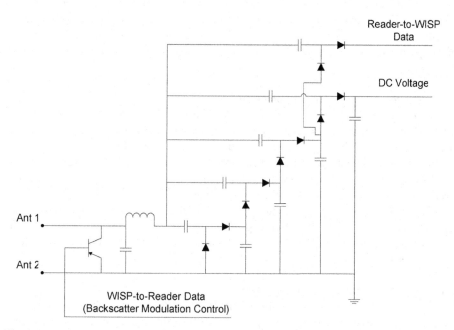

Fig. 2. WISP Analog Front End (AFE) schematic. The WISP AFE has connections for the two branches of a dipole antenna, an input for controlling the uplink (WISP-to-reader) modulation, an output for DC power, and an output for downlink (reader-to-WISP) data.

Fig. 3. Photographs of WISP. LEFT IMAGE: the microcontroller is the square black QFN package in the lower portion of the image. The two branches of the dipole antenna are visible at the top of the image. The two pins exiting the right side of the image are power output and ground. The microcontroller's pins are broken out to the small header pins surrounding the microcontroller. The large silver square is a reset switch. RIGHT IMAGE: WISP with sensor daughterboard attached. A light sensor and three tilt switches are mounted on the daughter-board. This image shows the size of the dipole antenna.

When implementing the software-radio functions our current design requires, the MSP430 microcontroller consumes more power than the harvester is typically able to supply. Thus the WISP microcontroller is duty-cycled so that the harvester has enough time to charge up storage capacitors which are then discharged when the MCU is active.

2.1.2 Reader to WISP Communication

To encode reader-to-tag data, the reader amplitude-modulates the 915MHz RF carrier wave it emits. Normally the carrier wave form remains at a constant amplitude; when bits are transmitted, the amplitude of the carrier drops to approximately ten percent of its normal value. The duration of the low indicates a logical "one" or a "zero." A short break indicates a "zero," and a long break indicates a "one." Before the signal can be decoded by the microcontroller it passes through an additional multiplier stage in parallel with the final voltage output stage. Unlike the ordinary multiplier stages, the decoder stage has no final buffer capacitor. The decoder produces a signal that matches the envelope of the carrier emitted by the reader. The MCU's software then decodes the duration of the lows into reader-to-tag bits.

2.1.3 WISP to Reader Communication

Unlike more conventional sensor nodes, RFID tags do not actively transmit radio signals. Instead they modulate the impedance of their antenna which causes a change in the amount of energy reflected back to the reader. This modulated reflection is typically referred to as backscatter radiation. In order to change the impendence of the antenna, a transistor is placed between the two branches of the dipole antenna. When the transistor is in conducting mode, it short circuits the two branches of the antenna together, changing the antenna impendence; in the non-conducting state, the transistor has no effect on the antenna, and the power harvesting and data downlink functions occur as if it were not present. The WISP-to-reader communication is currently implemented with a bipolar junction transistor rated for RF operation.

2.1.4 Communication Implementation; Verify ID

For our initial proof of concept, we have implemented just the simplest EPC read mode, Verify ID. This read command is ordinarily used to verify the ID of a tag whose ID has just been re-programmed. A timing diagram for Verify ID is shown in figure 4. This mode does not do any "tree walking" singulation, and is really suited for reading just one tag at a time. We believe that singulation protocols that provide for both sensing and ID functionality are a promising area for future research.

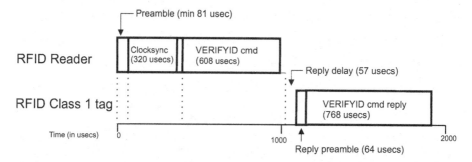

Fig. 4. Timing of EPC Verify ID transaction. The values shown are not the nominal timings provided in the EPC specification, but the (substantially different) actual values measured for an Alien Nanoscanner 915MHz RFID reader.

4 Experimental Results

As an end-to-end test of our system in operation, we built a sensor daughterboard with a light sensor and 5 one bit tilt sensors (mercury switches). The microcontroller has an integrated temperature sensor. The microcontroller was programmed to include, in each response packet, 10 bits of light-level data, 10 bits of temperature data, 5 bits of tilt-switch data, and 8 bits of configuration data. The configuration field can be thought of as a pointer to a configuration record that is intended to allow the application to learn what sensors are being reported.

Crucially, the WISP must also compute the CRC for the "live" sensor data to form a valid packet. (Older models of Alien RFID readers ignore the CRC in Verify mode, but newer models seem to filter out most Verify ID reads containing invalid CRCs.) Note that ordinary fixed-ID RFID tags have the CRC hard-coded; they do not need to dynamically compute it. We made use of the WISP's general-purpose computing capability to implement this dynamic CRC functionality.

Figure 5 shows the output voltage from the power harvester as a function of distance, under several different loads: no load, 100K, and 10K. The different load

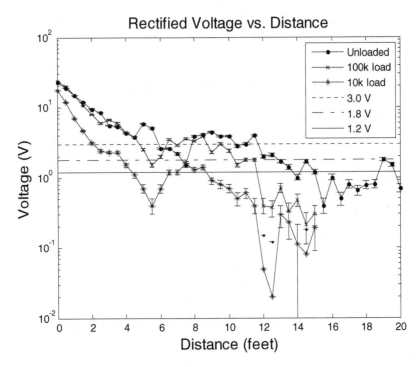

Fig. 5. Power harvesting performance of WISP under several loads. The WISP's power requirements, modeled by the load resistance in the figure, can be changed by adjusting the duty cycle at which it operates. The "no load" line can be thought of as the low duty-cycle limit. In addition to the power constraint, there is a voltage constraint: if the microcontroller is not supplied with sufficient voltage, it either will not be able to operate at all, or will not operate at the desired frequency. The figure shows three voltage thresholds: 3V, 1.8V, and 1.2V. Below the 3V threshold, the current WISP implementation cannot operate at the speed required to implement the EPC communication protocol. The microcontroller can also be run at 1.8V, but at slower clock speeds. We believe that incremental improvements to the system design may enable the device to run at these lower voltages. The thresholds help illustrate the range improvements that can be expected as operating voltage requirements are dropped.

resistors model different power consumption "workloads." As we will explain later, the 10K value corresponds most closely to our microcontroller running at full speed, though in fact the microcontroller consume more power than a 10K resistor.

When the WISP is running at full speed (i.e. running the EPC communication code), it consumes 900uA at 3V, which can be modeled by a load resistance of 3.3K. In sleep mode it consumes 5uA at 3V. The power harvesting performance plot of figure 5 shows that at 3 feet, the harvester outputs less than 3V with a 10K load; with a 100K load, the harvester outputs more than 3V.

Thus the harvester does not produce enough power to run the WISP continuously. By duty-cycling the device, we can reduce the net power consumption so that it can be run steady state. We programmed the WISP to collect a packet of sensor measurements, compute the CRC, and then transmit this data repeatedly when polled for

0.25s, and then sleep for 2s before resuming the cycle. This is a duty cycle of 1/9, which can be mapped into a load resistance of 9*3.3K = 30K. When the WISP is asleep, the harvester accumulates power.

To demonstrate steady-state operation for a long period of time, we mounted the WISP to an exterior window using a suction cup, and placed an Alien RFID reader about 3 ft away from the WISP. We collected data using the Verify ID command as fast as the system would allow (about 15 polls per second).

When the WISP is asleep, the reader returns "No tag detected." When the WISP is awake, the reader usually receives a burst of ID read packets. When a non-trivial packet is received, the time and the packet contents are logged to disk.

Later, for analysis, we loaded the read log data into Matlab and recomputed the CRCs. According to the CRC, the packet error rate is about 0.26: about one quarter of the packets are bad. So, just as in the ordinary EPC ID reading case, the CRC is a very convenient, practical, and reliable error detection mechanism.

The raw communication rate of the WISP device was about 15 packets per second, each packet containing 64 bits, resulting in 960 bits per second throughput (uncorrected). Future versions of the EPC specification (especially the Class 1 Gen 2 protocols) promise much higher data rates.

4.1 Light Level Measurement Experiment

The WISP was mounted by suction cup to the inside surface of an exterior window in an office environment, pictured in figure 6. The light sensor was oriented inward. Figure 7 shows the light level measured by the WISP over a 13 hour period. The measurement was begun at 5:20 pm, and the initial part of the measurement shows the light level dropping due to the sunset. After sunset, the light level remains constant for about three hours. We believe that all the interior lights were on during this period. Then, we believe that the interior lights nearest the WISP were extinguished, with lights further away remaining on, for about one hour. Then, the light level drops to a minimum when all the remaining interior lights were extinguished. This low light level persists until sunrise begins the next morning.

Fig. 6. WISP mounted by suction cup to interior window for light level measurement experiment

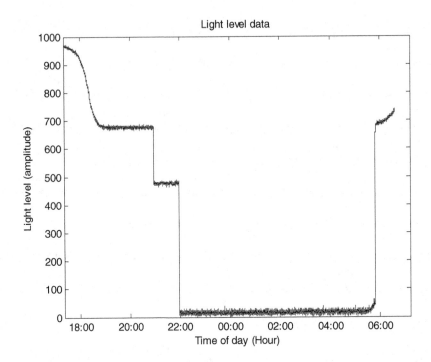

Fig. 7. Light level measured by WISP in a 13 hour period. The experiment began at about 5:40pm (17:40 hours). The first curve down is sunset. At around 9pm (21:00 hours), the measured light level drops substantially, probably because some lights in the laboratory were extinguished. At about 10pm (22:00 hours), the light level drops very low, probably because the remainder of the lights in the laboratory were extinguished. Just before 6am (06:00 hours), the beginning of sunrise is visible, and the laboratory lights turn on. The total number of measurement packets received was 115,413. Of these, 85,135 had valid CRCs. Only messages with valid CRCs are plotted above. This corresponds to a packet error rate of 0.26.

5   Discussion and Future Work

One of the primary challenges we are addressing next is improving the range of the WISP. There are two constraints that can prevent WISP operation: power and voltage. If either resource is insufficient, the WISP cannot function. As we have demonstrated with the duty cycling technique, the power constraint is relatively easy to work around: by dialing down the system's duty cycle, we can dial down the net power requirements as much as desired. It turns out that voltage is a harder constraint. If sufficient voltage is not available, the system cannot function at all, regardless of the duty cycle.

There are to basic ways to address the voltage constraint: lowering the voltage required by the microcontroller, and increasing the voltage delivered by the power harvester. We plan to make use of both approaches to improve read range.

To implement the EPC protocol in the "full software radio" fashion reported here, we had to run the microcontroller at 5MHz, which requires a 3V power supply. The microcontroller can also be run at 1.8V or 1.2V, at lower clock rates. By offloading into dedicated hardware key pieces of protocol logic that are now implemented in software (or possibly with improved firmware alone), we believe it will be possible to run the microcontroller at slower speeds. This should allow it to operate at 1.8V or 1.2V, which would increase our range substantially. Because the plot of voltage vs distance (figure 5) is relatively flat between 5 feet and 15 feet, we believe that small reductions in platform voltage requirements will deliver relatively large increases in range.

Improving the WISP antenna one obvious route for increasing the available voltage. In future work, we will investigate this and other approaches for increasing the voltage delivered by the power harvester, in order to improve the system's range.

Once the WISP hardware is more mature (for example offering better range), we believe that a range of interesting systems questions can be addressed. Using the WISP's on-board processing, data compression and streaming query functions can be implemented. Also, we believe that reader-WISP protocols that address identification and sensing jointly will be a rich area for future research. Current RFID protocols are designed to solve the problem of identification (i.e. singulation) only. The identification and sensing functions can be traded off in many different ways, and the desired trade off will be heavily application dependent. Thus the design of ID-sensing protocols, informed by application requirements, appears to be a promising area for future research.

6   Conclusion

We believe that the WISP platform represents an under-explored point in the sensor node design space with properties that differentiate it from other approaches. It requires no batteries, and no wires for power or data. The device appears to offer the promise of perpetual embedded wireless sensing, in appropriate usage model settings. A key constraint of the WISP system is the requirement of a reader. Nevertheless, we believe that many applications for this ubiquitous, battery-free sensing and computing platform exist. Since the constraints overlap substantially with those of conventional RFID, applications of conventional RFID are a natural place to begin seeking sensing applications of WISP.

Another category of applications we believe may be promising is hybridizing WISP with more conventional sensor nodes. WISP could be used in a battery-powered mode as a "backscatter modem" for a more conventional device. The power requirements of its backscatter radio are quite different than ordinary radios. Or, the power harvesting capability of WISP could be used to wake up more conventional and power hungry sensing and computing platforms.

As the WISP platform matures and its range increases, we are looking forward to exploring both "pure" perpetual sensing as well as "hybrid" applications of the WISP platform in future work.

References

1. S. S. Intille, K. Larson, E. Munguia Tapia, J.S. Beaudin, P. Kaushik, J. Nawyn, and R. Rockinson, "Using a live-in laboratory for ubiquitous computing research" in *Proceedings of PERVASIVE 2006*. Berlin Heidelberg: Springer-Verlag, 2006, to appear.
2. D.E. Culler and H. Mulder, "Smart Sensors to Network the World," Scientific American, June 2004, pp. 85–91.
3. S. Roundy et al., Energy Scavenging for Wireless Sensor Networks, Kluwer Academic Publishers, 2003.
4. J. Paradiso and M. Feldmeier, "A Compact, Wireless, Self-Powered Pushbutton Control-ler," Proc. 3rd Int'l Conf. Ubiquitous Computing (Ubicomp 2001), Springer-Verlag, 2001, pp. 299-304.
5. Webpages on the cavity resonator microphone can be found at http://www.nsa.gov/museum/museu00029.cfm and http://www.spybusters.com/Great_Seal_Bug.html.
6. R. Fletcher, Low-Cost Electromagnetic Tagging: Design and Implementation, PhD disser-tation, MIT, 2001.
7. J. Paradiso, K. Hsiao, and A. Benbasat, "Tangible Music Interfaces Using Passive Mag-netic Tags," Proc. ACM Conf. Human Factors in Computing Systems: Special Workshop on New Interfaces for Musical Expression (CHI 2001), ACM Press, 2001.
8. K. Finkenzeller, RFID Handbook, 2nd ed., John Wiley & Sons, 2003.
9. http://www.epcglobalinc.org/standards_technology/Secure/v1.0/UHF-class1.pdf
10. R. Want, "Enabling Ubiquitous Sensing with RFID." *Computer*, Vol. 37 No. 4, April 2004, pp. 84-86.
11. K. Opasjumruskit, T. Thanthipwan, O. Sathusen, P. Sirinamarattana, P. Gadmanee, E. Pootarapan, N. Wongkomet, A. Thanachayanont, M. Thamsirianunt, "Self-Powered Wire-less Temperature Sensors Exploit RFID Technology," *IEEE Pervasive Computing Maga-zine*, January-March 2006 (Vol. 5, No. 1) pp. 54-61.
12. http://www.datasheetcatalog.com/datasheets_pdf/M/C/R/F/MCRF202.shtml
13. J.R. Smith, K.P. Fishkin, B. Jiang, A. Mamishev, M. Philipose, A.D. Rea, S. Roy, K. Sundara-Rajan, "RFID-based Techniques for Human-Activity Detection," *Communica-tions of the ACM*, September 2005/Vol. 48, No. 9, pp. 39-44.
14. http://focus.ti.com/general/docs/lit/getliterature.tsp?genericPartNumber=msp430f1232
15. M. Philipose, K.P. Fishkin, M. Perkowitz, D.J. Patterson, D. Fox, H. Kautz, and D. Häh-nel, "Inferring Activities from Interactions with Objects," IEEE Pervasive Computing, vol. 3, no. 4, 2004, pp. 50–57.
16. http://www.nfc-forum.org/home

Automated Application-Specific Tuning of Parameterized Sensor-Based Embedded System Building Blocks

Susan Lysecky[1] and Frank Vahid[2,*]

[1] Department of Electrical and Computer Engineering
University of Arizona
Tucson, AZ 85721
slysecky@ece.arizona.edu

[2] Department of Computer Science and Engineering
University of California, Riverside
Riverside, CA 92521
vahid@cs.ucr.edu

Abstract. We previously developed building blocks to enable end-users to construct customized sensor-based embedded systems to help monitor and control a users' environment. Because design objectives, like battery lifetime, reliability, and responsiveness, vary across applications, these building blocks have software-configurable parameters that control features like operating voltage, frequency, and communication baud rate. The parameters enable the same blocks to be used in diverse applications, in turn enabling mass-produced and hence low-cost blocks. However, tuning block parameters to an application is hard. We thus present an automated approach, wherein an end-user simply defines objectives using an intuitive graphical method, and our tool automatically tunes the parameter values to those objectives. The automated tuning improved satisfaction of design objectives, compared to a default general-purpose block configuration, by 40% on average, and by as much as 80%. The tuning required only 10-20 minutes of end-user time for each application.

1 Introduction

Silicon technology continues to becomes cheaper, smaller, and consume less power, following Moore's Law. This trend has not only enabled new complex computing applications such as military surveillance, health monitoring, and industrial equipment monitoring using what is commonly referred to as sensor networks [16], but opens up numerous possibilities for lower complexity applications within the embedded system domain. Such applications in the home might include a system to monitor if any windows are left open at night, an indicator to alert a homeowner that mail is present in the mail box, or an alarm that detects if a child is sleepwalking at night. In the

---

* Also with the Center for Embedded Computer Systems at UC Irvine.

P. Dourish and A. Friday (Eds.): Ubicomp 2006, LNCS 4206, pp. 507–524, 2006.

office, employees may monitor which conference rooms are available, track temperatures at various locations within the building, or wirelessly alert a receptionist away from his/her desk. Furthermore, scientists may setup a system to activate a video camera at night when motion is detected near an animal watering hole, or to monitor weather conditions over several weeks. Numerous possible examples exist that span varied domains, professions, and age groups. In this paper, an end-user is an individual developing a sensor-based computing application, such as a homeowner, teacher, scientist, etc., who does not have programming or electronics expertise.

With so many application possibilities, why aren't these sensor-based systems more prevalent? The reason is that creating customized embedded systems today requires expertise in electronics and programming. For example, a homeowner may want to create a seemingly simple system to detect if the garage door is left open at night. He would first need to figure out how to detect nighttime and would thus need a light sensor. However, searching for "light sensor" in popular parts catalogs [4,9,15] will not yield the desired results. Instead, the homeowner would need a light dependent resistor or photoresistor, along with a handful of resistors, an opamp, and/or transistors, depending on the specific implementation. Figuring out how to connect these components will require reading a datasheets and schematics. Next, he would need a power supply, and must consider voltage levels, grounding principles, and electric current issues. The homeowner would also need to determine what type of sensor to use to detect if the garage door is open, to implement wireless communication (the homeowner probably doesn't want a wire running from the garage to an upstairs bedroom or kitchen), to program microprocessors to send packets to conserve power, and so on. The seemingly simple garage-open-at-night system actually requires much expertise to build. Alternatively, an engineer could be hired to build a custom system, but the cost is seldom justifiable. Off-the-shelf systems [8,18] provide another option, but highly specific systems tend to be expensive due to low volume. Also, if the desired functionality is not found (e.g., a a system for two garage doors), customizing the system can be difficult or impossible.

We aim to enable end-users with no engineering or programming experience to build customized sensor-based systems. Our approach is to incorporate a tiny cheap microprocessor with previously passive devices. We incorporate a microprocessor with buttons, beepers, LEDs (light emitting diodes), motion sensors, light sensors, sound sensors, etc., along with additional hardware, such that those devices can simply be connected with other devices using simple plugs. Interfacing to hardware and communication between blocks is already incorporated within each individual block. We refer to such devices as *eBlocks* – electronic blocks – which we developed in previous work [2,5]. eBlocks eliminate the electronics and programming experience previously required to build sensor-based systems. The user-created block connectivity determines the functionality of the system, as shown in Figure 1. Furthermore, because the same blocks can be used in a variety of applications, high volume manufacturing results in low block costs of a few dollars or less.

The variety of application possibilities results in a variety of application objectives. For example, one application may require high responsiveness and reliability, whereas another application may require long battery lifetime. One way to support the variety of objectives is to include software-configurable parameters in each eBlock. Thus, the same eBlock may operate at any of several voltage levels and frequencies,

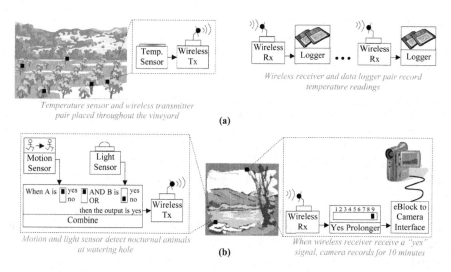

Fig. 1. Sample applications built with eBlocks, (a) vineyard weather tracker and (b) endangered species monitor

may communicate using any of several baud rates, may utilize any of several error detection/correction schemes, and so on, depending on the configuration settings in software. An end-user could then tune a block's parameter values to optimize for particular design objectives. Existing sensor-based block platforms contain many such parameters [3,7,20]. Some parameters correspond to hardware settings, others to low-level software settings (such as low-layer network settings, sleep-mode settings, etc.). Other parameters may involve higher-level software settings, such as algorithmic-level choices impacting compression schemes or data aggregation methods. In this paper, we focus on the hardware and low-level software parameters, as those parameters most directly enable mass-produced blocks.

However, tuning a block's parameter values to an application's design objectives is hard, beyond the expertise of most end-users. A block's parameter space may consist of billions of possible configurations, and those parameters are heavily interdependent. Yet careful tuning of those parameters can have a large impact on design objectives. Adlakha et al [1] showed the impact and relationship of the parameters of a block's shutdown scheme, network routing algorithms, and data compression schemes. Yuan and Qu [21] showed the relationship and impact of the parameters of processor type, encryption/decryption algorithms, and dynamic voltage scaling. Tilak et al [19] studied the impact of the parameters of sensor capability, number of sensors deployed, and deployment strategy (grid, random, and biased deployment) on design metrics of accuracy, latency, energy, throughput, and scalability. Heinzelman et al [6] showed the energy impacts of the parameters of different communication protocols, transmit/receive circuitry, message size, distance between blocks, and number of intermediate blocks. Martin et al [14] considers the effects of number of sensors and sampling rate on the accuracy and power consumption. Shih et al [17] examined the impact of different protocols and algorithms on energy consumption, including use of dynamic voltage scaling and sleep states. Some research on block synthesis [13] has appeared, emphasizing the different but possibly complementary problem of mapping an application's behavioral description onto a fixed or custom designed network of blocks.

Many of these previously researched parameters can be incorporated into a block as software-configurable parameters. Most previous works have only studied the parameters and then indicated the need for careful tuning. In this paper, we present a first approach to automating the support of such tuning. Essentially, our approach represents employment of established synthesis methodology to a problem until now investigated primarily as a networking problem. We refined the synthesis methods, especially that of objective function definition, to the problem. The contribution of the work is in enabling end-users, without engineering experience, to straightforwardly define design objectives, through our introduction of an intuitive graphical objective function definition approach for use by end-users, and our development of fast methods to automatically tune parameters according to those functions. The net result is that these block-based embedded computing systems can better satisfy end-user requirements on battery lifetime, reliability, and responsiveness.

We have also developed complementary computer-based tools that automatically generate an optimized physical implementation of an eBlock system derived from a virtual system function description [12]. End-users are able to specify optimization criteria and constraint libraries that guide the tool in generating a suitable physical implementation, without requiring the end-user to have prior programming or electronics experience. In contrast, this paper considers the resulting physical implementation and automatically tunes software parameters to meet high-level goals such as lifetime or reliability.

Section 2 of this paper provides an overview of our approach. Sections 3, 4 and 5 describe our approach's steps of block characterization, application characterization, and exploration/feedback. Section 6 highlights results of experiments using our prototype tool implementing the approach.

2 Approach Overview

Figure 2, provides an overview of our proposed approach for tuning a parameterized block to an application's design objectives. A block designer provides a block configuration tool, including pre-characterization of the block parameters, as a support tool to the end-user, along with other support tools like programming and debug environments (such as the TinyOS and NesC environments provided with a particular sensor block type [17]). An end-user characterizes application design objectives to the tool by modifying the default objectives, and then asks the tool to tune parameters to the objectives. The tool applies an exploration heuristic and finds parameter values best satisfying the objectives. Based on the values, the end-user may choose to modify the objectives – in case not all objectives could be met, the end-user may wish to modify the objectives – resulting in an iterative use of the tool. Once the end-user is satisfied, the tool outputs a set of parameter values (known as a configuration) for the blocks. The block support tools download those parameter

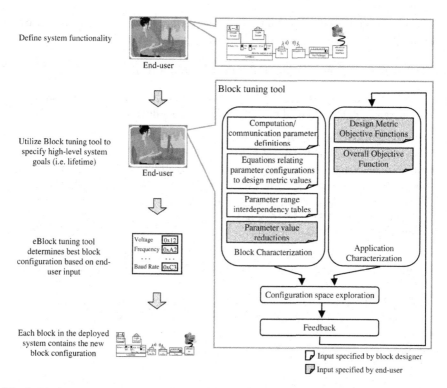

Fig. 2. Block tuning tool overview. A block designer performs block characterization once. An end-user performs application characterization by customizing objective functions, optionally refines the block characterization by reducing possible parameter values, and then executes the parameter space exploration heuristic. The tool provides feedback on objective function achievement, based on which the end-user may choose to refine objective functions and re-iterate. Once done, the tool incorporates the chosen parameter values into the block's startup/reset software.

values into the blocks, along with block programs and possible data, and those values configure the block's hardware and software components upon startup/reset of the block in a deployed network. Presently, all blocks would have the same configuration, but future directions may support different configurations for different blocks.

We now describe the approach's parts in more detail, and indicate how we addressed each part in our prototype tool. We developed the tool with eBlocks in mind, but the approach can be applied and/or generalized for other block types.

3 Block Characterization by the Block Designer

A block designer must characterize the block for the block-tuning tool. Such characterization consists of creating three items: computation/communication parameter definitions, equations relating parameter configurations to design metrics, and a parameter interdependency description. Note that these items are created by a block designer, who is an engineering expert, and *not* by end users.

3.1 Computation/Communication Parameter Definitions

The block designer must define the list of block parameters and the possible values for each parameter. The physical block we used supported the following parameters:

- Microcontroller Supply Voltage (V) = {3.0, 3.1, 3.2, 3.3, 3.4, 3.5, 3.6, 3.7, 3.8, 3.9, 4.0, 4.1, 4.2, 4.3, 4.4, 4.5, 4.6, 4.7, 4.8, 4.9, 5.0, 5.1, 5.2, 5.3, 5.4, 5.5}
- Microcontroller Clock Frequency (Hz) = {32k, 100k, 200k, 300k, 400k, 455k, 480k, 500k, 640k, 800k, 1M, 1.6M, 2M, 2.45M, 3M, 3.6M, 4M, 5.3M, 6M, 7.4M, 8M, 8.192M, 9M, 9.216M, 9.8304M, 10M, 10.4M, 11.06M, 12M, 13.5M, 14.74M, 16M, 16.384M, 16.6666MHz, 17.73M, 18M, 18.432M, 19.6608M, 20M}
- Communication Baud Rate (bps) = {1200, 2400, 4800, 9600, 14.4K, 28.8K}
- Data Packet Transmission Size = {4 bits, 1B, 2B, 4B}
- Data Timeout = {0.2s, 0.3s, 0.4s, 0.5s, 0.6s, 0.7s, 0.8s, 0.9s, 1s, 1.25s, 1.50s, 1.75s, 2s, 2.5s, 3s, 3.5s, 4s, 4.5s, 5s, 6s, 7s, 8s, 9s, 10s, 20s, 30s, 40s, 50s, 1m, 2m, 3m, 4m, 5m, 6m, 7m, 8m, 9m, 10m, 15m, 20m, 25m, 30m}
- Alive Timeout = {0.1s, 0.2s, 0.3s, 0.4s, 0.5s, 0.6s, 0.7s, 0.8s, 0.9s, 1s, 1.25s, 1.50s, 1.75s, 2s, 2.5s, 3s, 3.5s, 4s, 4.5s, 5s, 6s, 7s, 8s, 9s, 10s, 20s, 30s, 40s, 50s, 1m, 2m, 3m, 4m, 5m, 6m, 7m, 8m, 9m, 10m, 15m, 20m, 25m}
- Error Check/Correct (ECC) Strategy = {none, crc, parity, checksum1, checksum2, hamming1, hamming2}

The supply voltage, clock frequency, and baud rate possible values came from the databook of the physical block's microcontroller, in this case a PIC device, and were all software configurable in the physical block.

The data packet size, data timeout, alive timeout, and error check/correct strategies were all user-specified settings in the basic support software of the physical block. Data packet size is the number of bits in a data packet – in our block, the choice impacted the range of integers transmittable. Data timeout is the maximum time between successive data packets – shorter timeouts result in faster responsiveness as blocks are added/removed to/from a network. Alive timeout is the maximum time between short (and hence low power) "I'm alive" messages used by the blocks to indicate that the block is still functioning, again impacting responsiveness. The error checking/correcting (ECC) strategies are extra bits placed in data packets to detect or forward-error-correct incorrectly received bits. The *parity* strategy uses sends a single parity bit for every 8-bit data packet. The *crc* strategy transmits an extra packet containing the remainder of the data packets and a CRC-3 generating polynomial. The *checksum1* strategy transmits an extra packet consisting of the corresponding sum of the data packets. The *checksum2* ECC strategy negates the extra packet before transmission. The *hamming1* ECC strategy considers the data as a matrix and generates row and column parity error checking packets. The *hamming2* strategy embeds parity bits within the packets at every power of two-bit location (bit 1, 2, 4, etc.). All these methods are standard methods.

A set of values, one for each parameter, defines a block configuration. We presently require the block designer to explicitly list possible values for a parameter. A similar method would allow a block designer to specify the value range along with the step size between successive values for a parameter. However, a block designer must be careful to avoid introducing unnecessarily-fine granularity to a parameter's values, as such granularity increases the configuration space to be explored by the tool, and may increase the number of interdependency tables (discussed in the next section). For the same reasons, we require that the block designer explicitly quantize a parameter's possible values, rather than merely specifying the parameter's range.

3.2   Parameter Range Interdependency Tables

Not every parameter configuration is valid. For example, a particular voltage setting may limit the range of possible clock frequencies. Likewise, a particular frequency may limit the range of possible baud rates. A block designer indicates such interdependencies using tables. For a given parameter, the block designer may optionally create a table providing, for any parameter value, lower and upper bounds for any other parameter. The exploration tool will use these tables to exclude invalid configurations from consideration.

3.3   Equations Relating Parameter Configurations to Design Metric Values

The block configuration tool must map a given parameter configuration to specific values for each design metric supported by the tool. Our tool presently supports the design metrics of lifetime, reliability, block latency, connect responsiveness, and disconnect responsiveness, defined in Section 4.1. We derived equations from datasheet information, textbooks, and previous findings, and thus we do not claim those equations as a contribution of this work. Highly accurate equations can become rather complex if all parameter values are carefully considered. While verifying and improving the accuracy of those equations is an important direction of investigation, that direction is largely orthogonal to the development of our overall methodology.

3.4   Parameter Value Reductions

A block designer performs the three above-described block characterization subtasks only once, and then incorporates the characterizations into the tool. A fourth, optional, block characterization subtask may be performed by an end-user to reduce the number of possible configurations and hence speedup the exploration step. In this fourth task, the end-user reduces the number of possible values for a given parameter, either by restricting the parameter's range, or by reducing the granularity of steps between successive parameters. Our present tool allows the end-user to manually exclude particular parameter values from consideration. However, the tool does not allow the end-user to add new values, because such new values would require new range interdependency tables, and because the equations mapping configurations to design metric values might not be valid for new values outside the range defined by the block

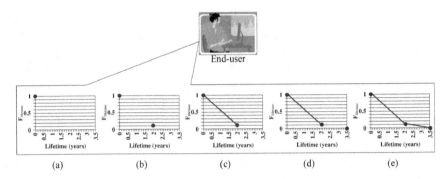

Fig. 3. End-user specifies the "goodness" of a lifetime value by assigning normalize values between 0 (best) and 1 (worst) to various lifetimes. (a) End-user determines a lifetime of 0 years is inadequate, sets goodness to 1, (b) lifetime of 2 years is adequate, sets goodness to 0.1, (c) intermediate goodness are automatically determined by the tool, (d) lifetime of 3.5 meets system requirements, sets goodness to 0, (e) intermediate goodness determined by tool.

designer. If an end-user deletes all but one possible value for a parameter (the tool requires that at least one value remain for each parameter), that parameter ceases to act as a parameter during exploration, being fixed at the chosen value.

4 Application Characterization by the End User

The previous section discussed block characterization, a job performed once by a block designer, and incorporated into the block configuration tool. Different end-users will then use this tool to tune the block to different applications. The end-user must characterize the application for the tool so that the tool can tune to that application. Thus, application characterization will be performed many times.

Application characterization consists of specifying the *design metric objective functions* and specifying the *overall objective function*. Our tool provides default functions targeted to general-purpose block use, so the end-user can merely customize particular functions that should deviate from the defaults.

4.1 Design Metric Objective Function

A design metric objective function maps a design metric's raw value to a normalized value between 0 and 1 representing the "goodness" of the value, with 1 being the worst and 0 being best. An end-user specifies a design metric objective function for each design metric by defining the range of the X-axis and then by drawing a plot that maps each X-axis value to a value between 0 and 1, as shown in Figure 3. Our present tool captures the function as a table rather than plot, but the concept is the same. The end-user currently captures "goodness" as a piecewise linear function, however, the end-user can ideally specify "goodness" in any format desired (e.g. linear, quadratic, exponential) limited only by the formats supported by the capture methodology.

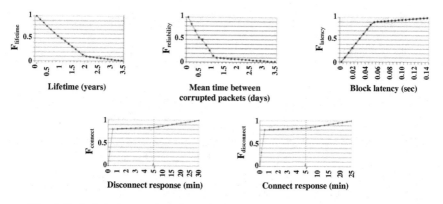

Fig. 4. Default design metric objective functions for general purpose block usage

Our tool presently supports capture of the following design metric objective functions:

- Lifetime – the number of days a block can run powered by the block's battery.
- Reliability – the mean time in days between undetected corrupt data packets.
- Block Latency – the time in seconds for a single block to process an input event and generate new output.
- Connect Response – the time for newly connected blocks to receive good input and behave properly.
- Disconnect Response – the time for newly disconnected blocks to behave as disconnected.

Initially, in developing eBlocks, the above design metrics were most relevant. However, more design metrics are certainly possible. An end-user developing systems intended to monitor a battlefield for troop movements would likely be interested a design metric describing security. Alternatively, an end-user developing systems intended to process video or audio data would likely be interested in a design metric describing throughput of the system. The end-user determines which designs metric are important for their particular application and chooses which design metrics they want to consider in determining a block configuration.

Figure 4. illustrates example definitions of objective functions for these design metrics. The functions correspond to the default functions that our tool provides, intended for a general application. For example, the function for lifetime indicates that a lifetime of 0 years is the worst possible and of 2 years is nearly the best possible, with linear improvement in between. Lifetime improvements from 2 years to 3.5 years are only slightly better than 2 years, and improvements beyond 3.5 years are not important according to the function. As another example, the function for mean time between corrupted packets indicates goodness improvement from 0 days to 1 day, with reduced improvement beyond 1 day. The function for block latency says that 0 second latency is the best, quickly degrading up to 0.06 seconds. Latencies beyond 0.06 seconds are very bad. Although all the functions shown are piecewise linear, the functions can also be non-linear.

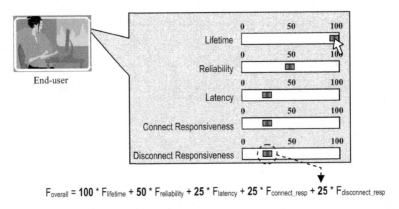

$$F_{overall} = 100 * F_{lifetime} + 50 * F_{reliability} + 25 * F_{latency} + 25 * F_{connect\_resp} + 25 * F_{disconnect\_resp}$$

Fig. 5. End-users utilize a web-based interface to specify the relative importance of each design metric. Individual weights are assigned by setting the corresponding slide switch to the desired position. Each design metric weight is then combined into an overall objective function.

Providing the ability to custom define each design metric's objective function is an important part of our approach. We observed that traditionally-used standard functions, such as those based on mean-square error, penalty, or barrier functions [11], do not readily capture the end-user's true intent – Figure 6, discussed later, illustrates this point.

Notice that the end-user need not know how those metrics are related to a block's parameters, and in fact need not even be aware of what block parameters exist. The end-user merely customizes the design metric objective functions.

4.2   Overall Objective Function

The end-user also configures an *overall objective function*, which captures the relative importance of the individual design metrics in a function that maps the individual metric values to a single value. We currently define the default overall objective function as a weighted sum of the individual design metric normalized values:

$$F_{overall} = (A * F_{lifetime}) + (B * F_{reliability}) + (C * F_{latency}) + (D * F_{connect\_resp.}) +$$
$$(E * F_{disconnect\_resp.})$$

The end-user customizes the values of the constants A, B, C, D and E to indicate the relative importance of the metrics, as shown in Figure 5. A more-advanced end-user can instead use a spreadsheet-like entry method to redefine the overall objective function as any linear or non-linear function of the design metric function values.

A key feature of our approach is the separation of defining design metric objective functions, and weighing those functions' importance in an overall objective function. This separation enables an end-user to focus first on what metric values are good or bad – e.g., a lifetime below 6 months is bad for one application, below 2 years for another application – and then separately to focus on the relative importance of those metrics – e.g., lifetime may be twice as important as latency in one application, but one third as important for another application. Hence, the orthogonality of the definition of metric values as good or bad, and of the relative importance of metrics, is supported by our approach.

5 Configuration Space Exploration and Feedback

Configuration space exploration searches the space of valid parameter values for a configuration that minimizes the value of the overall objective function. For each possible configuration, the exploration tool applies the block designer specified design metric evaluation equations to obtain raw values for each design metric, which the tool then inputs to the end-user specified design metric objective functions to obtain normalized values, and which the tool finally combines into a single value using the end-user specified overall objective function.

One search method is exhaustive search, which enumerates all possible parameter value configurations and chooses the configuration yielding the minimized objective function value. For the parameter ranges and values defined earlier in the paper, the search space (after pruning invalid configurations caused by parameter interdependencies) consists of over 100 million configurations. Searching that space exhaustively is feasible, requiring 3-4 minutes on a 3 GHz Pentium processor. However, for blocks with more parameters or more values, exhaustive search may be infeasible. We thus investigated faster methods.

As our parameter search problem resembles an integer linear program, we considered integer linear program solution methods (optimal or heuristic), but a problem is that such an approach limits the objective functions to linear functions. Instead, an end-user might desire a non-linear function, to greatly penalize values over a certain amount for squaring, for example.

We also considered greedy or constructive approaches that used some knowledge of the problem structure to efficiently traverse the search space. However, we sought to keep the exploration tool independent of the particular block parameters and objective functions. Greedy or constructive heuristics that don't consider problem structure may perform poorly. However, the block-designer-specified equations and parameter interdependency descriptions can improve the design of such heuristics. We leave this direction for future investigation.

Ultimately, we chose to use an iterative improvement approach, namely the simulated annealing heuristic [10]. The heuristic has the advantage of being independent of block parameters and objective functions. Furthermore, the heuristic provides a simple means for an end-user to tradeoff exploration time with optimization amount. The end-user can indicate allowable runtime, from which the tool can derive an appropriate annealing cooling schedule. We presently utilize a cooling schedule that executes for just a few seconds on a 3 GHz Pentium, while yielding near-optimal solutions. The time complexity of the simulated annealing heuristic is in general not known, depending heavily on the cooling schedule and problem features. Yet in practice, a specific cooling schedule yields roughly similar runtimes for the same general problem, as occurred in our case.

For the chosen best configuration, the tool provides feedback to the end-user in two forms. One form is the value of the overall objective function and the relative contribution of each design metric objective function value to the overall value end-user specified design metric objective function, for each design metric. Based on this information, the end-user may actually choose to refine his/her design metric or overall objective function definitions, iterating several times until finding a satisfactory configuration.

The block configuration tool converts the final configuration into software that appropriately fixes the sensor block parameters to the configuration's values. The tool achieves such fixing primarily by setting constant values for global variables uses by the microcontroller's startup/reset code. Many of those global variables actually correspond to special microcontroller or peripheral built-in registers, such a microcontroller registers that select clock frequency or baud rate, and a register in a digital voltage regular that controls supply voltage to the microcontroller. Other variables are used by software routines to choose among data structures and/or functions, such as for the error check/correct routine.

6 Experiments

We implemented our approach in a prototype tool, consisting of 8,000 lines of Java code, and interfacing with Excel spreadsheets to support equation capture and plot displays. We considered four different applications, all but the "Vineyard" example being derived from actual projects involving the physical blocks. Those applications' design metric objective functions appear in Figure 6.

The *Educational Science Kit* application utilizes eBlocks to introduce middle-school students to simple engineering concepts. Students combine and configure blocks to create customized sensor-based embedded systems in their classrooms. For the purposes of this paper, the students are *not* the end-users – rather, the end-user is the person putting eBlocks into the kit for student use. Acting as that end-user, we defined the design metric objective functions shown in Figure 6(a). The reliability function (mean time between corrupted packets) differs from its general case version in Figure 4, as reliability is less important because the systems being built in classrooms don't monitor or control important situations. In contrast, the block latency and connect response functions both demand higher performance than for the general case, as the students basic usage of the blocks will involve repeated adding/deleting of blocks, and students might be confused by long latencies or slow response. For the overall objective function, we weighed lifetime with 0.1 (unimportant), reliability with 0.5, throughput with 0.5, connect response with 1, and disconnect response with 1 (important).

The *Vineyard Weather Tracker* application is a long-life application deployed in a vineyard to track temperature, rainfall, and average hours of sunlight. Compared to the general case of Figure 4, Figure 6(b) shows that longer latency is acceptable because the items being monitored are not rapidly changing, and that slower

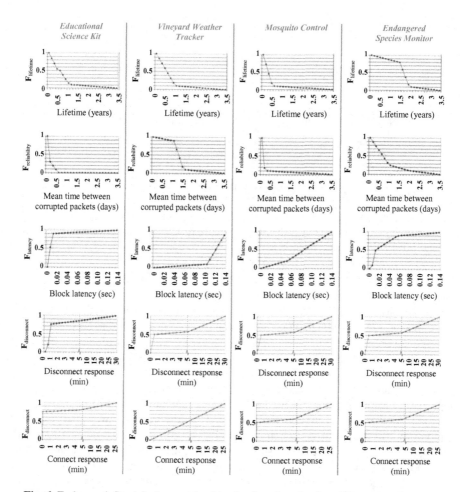

Fig. 6. End-user defined design metric objective functions for four different applications

disconnect and connect responses are also acceptable as blocks won't be disconnected/connected frequently. For the overall objective function, we weighed lifetime with 1 (important), reliability with 0.5, latency with 0.5, disconnect response with 0.1, and connect response with 0.1 (unimportant).

The *Mosquito Control* application reads data from a mosquito trap and meters out insecticide accordingly. Figure 6(c) shows that lifetime beyond 6 months is not necessary because the mosquito season lasts only 6 months, after which all blocks will be reclaimed and stored, with all batteries replaced the following season. We weighed lifetime with 0.5, reliability with 1, latency with 0.5, and disconnect/connect responses with 0.2. The weights indicate that reliability is most important, as improper output of insecticide should be avoided.

The *Endangered Species Monitoring* system detects motion near a feeding site and video-records the site for a specified duration, for later analysis by environmental

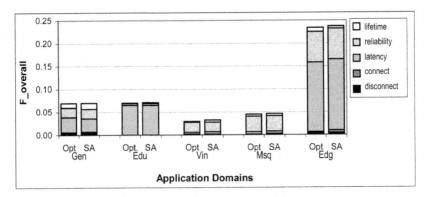

Fig. 7. Normalized overall objective function results comparing the various application configurations obtained utilizing exhaustive search (Opt) verses simulated annealing (SA): General (Gen), Educational Science Kit (Edu), Vineyard Weather Tracker (Vin), Mosquito Control (Msq), and Endangered Species Monitor (Edg).

scientists estimating the population of endangered species. Figure 4(d) shows that the key difference from the general case is that lifetime less than 1.5 years is unacceptable, as the feeding site is in a remote location that is hard to access, and thus batteries should not have to be replaced frequently. We assigned lifetime a weight of 1, reliability 0.8, latency 0.8, and disconnect/connect responses weights of 0.1 each.

Using our tools, characterized each applications requires only 10 minutes.

For each application, we executed our automated tuning tool, for both the end-user application characterizations in Figure 6, and the general case of Figure 4. To verify that the tool was effectively finding good configurations, we also executed exploration using exhaustive search. The tool's execution time averaged 10 seconds per application, while exhaustive search averaged over 3.5 minutes, both methodologies running on the same 3 GHz Pentium computer. Figure 7 summarizes results, showing that the tool's simulated annealing heuristic found near optimal results for all the applications. The figure also shows the relative contribution of each design metric objective function to the overall objective function, showing similar achievements between heuristic and exhaustive exploration. Table 1 shows the

Table 1. Configurations achieved by heuristic exploration for various applications. Numbers in parentheses indicate values obtained by exhaustive search, where those values differed from heuristically-obtained values.

	Applications				
	General	Vineyard Weather Tracker	Educational Science Kit	Mosquito Control	Endangered Species Monitoring
Voltage (V)	3.1 (3)	4.8 (3.0)	3.5 (3.0)	3.1 (3.0)	3.1 (3.0)
Frequency (MHz)	2.45	11.06 (9)	2 (1.6)	2 (0.64)	3 (2.45)
Baudrate	9600	14400	4800	9600	9600
Data Packet (bytes)	4 (2)	1	2	1	2 (4)
Data Timeout (sec)	1.25 (1)	0.2	20	1.75 (0.9)	7
Alive Timeout(sec)	0.3	0.1	2.5 (5)	0.1	0.7 (0.3)
ECC Strategy	crc	none	hamming1	none	hamming2

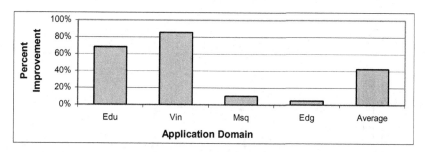

Fig. 8. Percent improvement in overall objective function utilizing customized block configuration verses general block configuration across various applications: Educational Science Kit (Edu), Vineyard Weather Tracker (Vin), Mosquito Control (Msq), and Endangered Species Monitor (Edg)

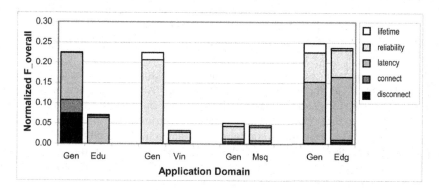

Fig. 9. Normalized overall objective function results comparing the general configuration (Gen) verses the application specific configuration across various applications: Educational Science Kit (Edu), Vineyard Weather Tracker (Vin), Mosquito Control (Msq), and Endangered Species Monitor (Edg)

specific configurations found by the heuristic and exhaustive exploration methods. The differing values obtained by the two methods show that different parameter configurations can yield similar overall objective function values.

Figure 8 shows the more important results that compare the use of the general block configuration to the configuration obtained through our tuning approach (using the heuristic exploration). The results show that the general block configuration works well for the latter two applications (Mosquito Control, and Endangered Species Monitor). However, the general configuration does not work well for the first two applications (Educational Science Kit, and Vineyard Weather Tracker) – tuning significantly improves the overall objective function value for those applications.

Figure 9 summarizes the percent improvement of overall objective function values for the tuned blocks compared to the generally configured blocks.

Figure 10 illustrates the type of feedback provided by the block-tuning tool to the end-user. Figure 10(a) provides the overall objective function value achieved by

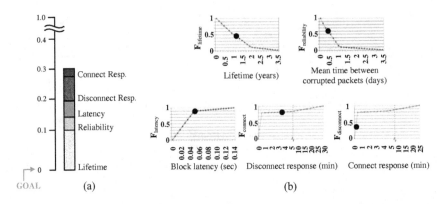

Fig. 10. Goal of the tool is to minimize the overall objective function value. Tool provides feedback of the tool to the end-user after exploration illustrating the configuration's (a) overall objective function value achieved along with the relative contribution of each design metric and (b) the raw values and their mapping to normalized values for each design metric.

exploration, along with the relative contribution of each design metric to that value. Further, Figure 10(b) shows the configuration's raw values and their mapping to normalized values for each design metric. Note that the overall objective function value is not just a sum of the normalized design metric values, because of weights assigned by the end-user in the overall objective function. Based on the feedback, the end-user may decide to refine a particular design metric objective function, perhaps deciding that tolerating poorer performance on one metric (e.g., connect response) is acceptable in the hopes of improving another metric (e.g., lifetime). Alternatively, the end-user might modify the weights in the overall objective function.

Notice that the end-user need not have any awareness of what parameters exist on the block (e.g., voltage, baud rate), nor of the values of those parameters for a particular configuration (e.g., 3 V, 2400 baud). The tuning approach instead presents the end-user with an abstraction that only deals with objective functions. Such abstraction enabled the end-user to perform all necessary tuning steps, including application characterization, exploration, and feedback analysis, in just 10 minutes.

7 Conclusions

We presented an approach that enables end-users to automatically tune parameterized building blocks to meet end-user defined application goals such as battery lifetime, reliability, responsiveness, and latency. The block tuning approach consisted of the key steps of block characterization by the block design, and then application characterization, exploration, and feedback involving the end user. Our approach provides an abstraction of the block to the end-user such that the end-user need only deal with characterizing the application through definition of intuitive graphical objective functions, requiring on the order of 10 minutes for a given application. The objective function definition approach separates definition of individual design metric objective values from definition of the relative importance among those metrics.

Furthermore, experiments show that our tool can tune blocks in just a few seconds to near-optimal values, and that the tuned blocks exhibit greatly superior performance for two of the four applications we examined, compared to a block configured for general-purpose use. Our work represents use of established synthesis methodology, with some refinement, to a problem considered primarily in the networking domain. The work's contribution is in enabling end-users with domain experience, but without engineering experience, to effectively utilize mass-produced computing blocks intended to monitor and control the user's environment.

Future work will involve expanding the parameters and design metrics supported by the tool, requiring careful attention to design of accurate evaluation equations. Another direction involves allowing an end-user to characterize the network structure and environment, in which case the tuning tool might determine different configurations for different blocks in the network. Future directions involve higher-level parameters relating to algorithmic and high-layer networking choices.

Acknowledgments

This work is supported in part by the National Science Foundation under grant CCR-0311026. Any opinions, findings, and conclusions or recommendations expressed in this material are those of the author(s) and do not necessarily reflect the views of the National Science Foundation.

References

1. Adlakha, S., S. Ganeriwal, C. Schurger, M. Srivastava. Density, Accuracy, Latency and Lifetime Tradeoffs in Wireless Sensor Networks – A Multidimensional Design Perspective. Embedded Network Sensor Systems, 2003.
2. Cotterell, S., F. Vahid. Usability of State Based Boolean eBlocks. International Conference on Human-Computer Interaction (HCII), July 2005.
3. Cotterell, S., F. Vahid, W. Najjar, H. Hsieh. First Results with eBlocks: Embedded Systems Building Blocks. CODES+ISSS Merged Conference, October 2003.
4. Digikey, http://www.digikey.com, 2006.
5. eBlocks: Embedded Systems Building Blocks. http://www.cs.ucr.edu/~eblock
6. Heinzelman, W., A. Chandrakasan, H. Balakrishnan. Energy-Efficient Communication Protocols for Wireless Microsensor Networks. Hawaii International Conference on System Sciences, 2000.
7. Hill, J., D. Culler. MICA: A Wireless Platform For Deeply Embedded Networks. IEEE Micro, Vol. 22. No. 6, November/December 2002.
8. Home Heartbeat, http://www.homeheartbeat.com, 2006.
9. Jameco, http://www.jameco.com, 2006.
10. Kirkpatrick, S., C. Gerlatt, M. Vecchi. Optimization by Simulated Annealing, Science 220, 671-680, 1983.
11. Lopez-Vallejo, M., J. Grajal, J. Lopez. Constraint-driven System Partitioning. Design Automation and Test in Europe, 2000.
12. Lysecky, S., F. Vahid. Automated Generation of Basic Custom Sensor-Based Embedded Computing Systems Guided by End-User Optimization Criteria. UbiComp, 2006.

13. Mannion, R., H. Hsieh, S. Cotterell, F. Vahid. System Synthesis for Networks of Programmable Blocks. Design Automation and Test in Europe, 2005.
14. Martin, T., M. Jones, J. Edmison, R. Shenoy. Towards a design framework for wearable electronic textiles. IEEE International Symposium on Wearable Computers, 2003.
15. Mouser, http://www.mouser.com, 2006.
16. National Research Council. Embedded, Everywhere: A Research Agenda for Networked Systems of Embedded Computers. National Academies Press, 2001.
17. Shih, E. S. Cho, N. Ickes, R. Min, A. Sinha, A. Wang, A. Chandrakasan. Physical Layer Driven Protocol and Algorithm Design for Energy-Efficient Wireless Sensor Networks. International Conference on Mobile Computing and Networking (MobiCom), 2001.
18. Smart Home, http://www.smarthome.com, 2006.
19. Tilak, S., N. Abu-Ghazaleh, W. Heinzelman. Infrastructure Tradeoffs for Sensor Networks. Int. Workshop on Wireless Sensor Networks and Applications, 2002.
20. Warneke, B., M. Last, B. Liebowitz, and K. Pister. Smart Dust: Communicating with a Cubic-Millimeter Computer. Computer Magazine, pg. 44-51, January 2001.
21. Yuan, L., G. Qu. Design Space Exploration for Energy-Efficient Secure Sensor Network. Conf. on Application-Specific Systems, Architectures, and Processors, 2002.

Author Index

Abowd, Gregory D.   123, 441
Aipperspach, Ryan   1
Axup, Jeff   351

Balfanz, Dirk   477
Bardram, Jakob E.   369
Bell, Genevieve   141
Benford, Steve   52, 279
Berry, Emma   177
Bhat, Sooraj   123
Broll, Gregor   52
Butler, Alex   177

Callaghan, Vic   87
Canny, John   1
Capra, Mauricio   52
Carter, Scott   159
Chamberlain, Alan   279
Chen, Mike Y.   212, 225, 333
Chin, Jeannette   87
Chmelev, Dmitri   225
Choudhury, Tanzeem   212
Consolvo, Sunny   194, 212
Cooper, Roslyn   351
Corner, Mark D.   422

Davidoff, Scott   19
Delajoux, Gregory   261
Dey, Anind K.   19
Drozd, Adam   279
Durfee, Glenn   477

Fong, Janette   159
Fraser, Danaë Stanton   315
Friedman, Batya   194
Froehlich, Jon   333
Fujimura, Noriyuki   387

Grinter, Rebecca E.   35
Griswold, William G.   212

Haehnel, Dirk   225
Hamasaki, Masahiro   387
Hansen, Thomas R.   369
Hayes, Gillian R.   123

Hightower, Jeffrey   212, 225
Hodges, Steve   177
Holleis, Paul   87
Hope, Tom   387
Horvitz, Eric   243
Hughes, Jeff   225

Intille, Stephen S.   297
Ito, Minoru   459
Izadi, Shahram   177

Jones, Tim   315

Kahn Jr., Peter H.   194
Kapur, Narinder   177
Kientz, Julie A.   123
Kindberg, Tim   315
Kitani, Tomoya   459
Kostakos, Vassilis   315
Krumm, John   243
Kurniawan, Sri   105

LaMarca, Anthony   212, 225
Lara, Eyal de   212
Larson, Kent   297
Lee, Kyung-Hee   477
Lee, Min Kyung   19
Leichtenstern, Karin   87
Lin, James J.   261
Lindtner, Silvia   261
Liu, Xiaotao   422
Lysecky, Susan   69, 507

MacColl, Ian   351
Mamishev, Alexander   495
Mamykina, Lena   261
Mankoff, Jennifer   159
Matsuo, Yutaka   387
Matthews, Tara   159
Mogensen, Martin   369

Nakamura, Yoshiyuki   387
Nawyn, Jason   297
Nishigaki, Kouji   459
Nishikawa, Hiroshi   459
Nishimura, Takuichi   387

O'Neill, Eamonn   315
Oppermann, Leif   52

Pai, Carol   159
Patel, Shwetak N.   123, 441
Penn, Alan   315
Potter, Fred   225, 333
Powledge, Pauline S.   495

Rattenbury, Tye   1
Rogers, Yvonne   404
Roy, Sumit   495
Rukzio, Enrico   87

Sample, Alanson P.   495
Schiek, Ava Fatah gen.   315
Schmidt, Albrecht   87
Selawski, Jaina   194
Sengers, Phoebe   35
Shenoy, Prashant   422
Shibata, Naoki   459
Smetters, D.K.   477
Smith, Ian   194, 212, 225
Smith, Ian E.   333
Smith, Joshua R.   495
Smith, Trevor F.   477

Smyth, Gavin   177
Soegaard, Mads   369
Sohn, Timothy   212, 225
Srinivasan, James   177
Strub, Henry B.   261

Tamai, Morihiko   459
Tandavanitj, Nick   279
Truong, Khai N.   441

Vahid, Frank   69, 507
Varshavsky, Alex   212, 225
Viller, Stephen   351

Williams, Lyndsay   177
Wood, Ken   177
Woodruff, Allison   1
Wright, Michael   279
Wyche, Susan   35

Yamamoto, Shinya   459
Yasumoto, Keiichi   459
Yiu, Charles   19

Zimmerman, John   19

Lecture Notes in Computer Science

For information about Vols. 1–4076

please contact your bookseller or Springer

Vol. 4206: P. Dourish, A. Friday (Eds.), UbiComp 2006: Ubiquitous Computing. XIX, 526 pages. 2006.

Vol. 4193: T.P. Runarsson, H.-G. Beyer, E. Burke, J.J. Merelo-Guervós, L. D. Whitley, X. Yao (Eds.), Parallel Problem Solving from Nature - PPSN IX. XIX, 1061 pages. 2006.

Vol. 4192: B. Mohr, J.L. Traeff, J. Worringen, J. Dongarra (Eds.), Recent Advances in Parallel Virtual Machine and Message Passing Interface. XVI, 414 pages. 2006.

Vol. 4188: P. Sojka, I. Kopeček, K. Pala (Eds.), Text, Speech and Dialogue. XIV, 721 pages. 2006. (Sublibrary LNAI).

Vol. 4186: C. Jesshope, C. Egan (Eds.), Advances in Computer Systems Architecture. XIV, 605 pages. 2006.

Vol. 4185: R. Mizoguchi, Z. Shi, F. Giunchiglia (Eds.), The Semantic Web – ASWC 2006. XX, 778 pages. 2006.

Vol. 4184: M. Bravetti, M. Nuñes, G. Zavattaro (Eds.), Web Services and Formal Methods. X, 289 pages. 2006.

Vol. 4180: M. Kohlhase, OMDoc – An Open Markup Format for Mathematical Documents [version 1.2]. XIX, 428 pages. 2006. (Sublibrary LNAI).

Vol. 4178: A. Corradini, H. Ehrig, U. Montanary, L. Ribeiro, G. Rozenberg (Eds.), Graph Transformations. XII, 473 pages. 2006.

Vol. 4176: S.K. Katsikas, J. Lopez, M. Backes, S. Gritzalis, B. Preneel (Eds.), Information Security. XIV, 548 pages. 2006.

Vol. 4169: H.L. Bodlaender, M.A. Langston (Eds.), Parameterized and Exact Computation. XI, 279 pages. 2006.

Vol. 4168: Y. Azar, T. Erlebach (Eds.), Algorithms – ESA 2006. XVIII, 843 pages. 2006.

Vol. 4165: W. Jonker, M. Petkovic (Eds.), Secure Data Management. X, 185 pages. 2006.

Vol. 4163: H. Bersini, J. Carneiro (Eds.), Artificial Immune Systems. XII, 460 pages. 2006.

Vol. 4162: R. Královič, P. Urzyczyn (Eds.), Mathematical Foundations of Computer Science 2006. XV, 814 pages. 2006.

Vol. 4159: J. Ma, H. Jin, L.T. Yang, J.J.-P. Tsai (Eds.), Ubiquitous Intelligence and Computing. XXII, 1190 pages. 2006.

Vol. 4158: L.T. Yang, H. Jin, J. Ma, T. Ungerer (Eds.), Autonomic and Trusted Computing. XIV, 613 pages. 2006.

Vol. 4156: S. Amer-Yahia, Z. Bellahsène, E. Hunt, R. Unland, J.X. Yu (Eds.), Database and XML Technologies. IX, 123 pages. 2006.

Vol. 4155: O. Stock, M. Schaerf (Eds.), Reasoning, Action and Interaction in AI Theories and Systems. XVIII, 343 pages. 2006. (Sublibrary LNAI).

Vol. 4153: N. Zheng, X. Jiang, X. Lan (Eds.), Advances in Machine Vision, Image Processing, and Pattern Analysis. XIII, 506 pages. 2006.

Vol. 4152: Y. Manolopoulos, J. Pokorný, T. Sellis (Eds.), Advances in Databases and Information Systems. XV, 448 pages. 2006.

Vol. 4151: A. Iglesias, N. Takayama (Eds.), Mathematical Software - ICMS 2006. XVII, 452 pages. 2006.

Vol. 4150: M. Dorigo, L.M. Gambardella, M. Birattari, A. Martinoli, R. Poli, T. Stützle (Eds.), Ant Colony Optimization and Swarm Intelligence. XVI, 526 pages. 2006.

Vol. 4149: M. Klusch, M. Rovatsos, T.R. Payne (Eds.), Cooperative Information Agents X. XII, 477 pages. 2006. (Sublibrary LNAI).

Vol. 4148: J. Vounckx, N. Azemard, P. Maurine (Eds.), Integrated Circuit and System Design. XVI, 677 pages. 2006.

Vol. 4146: J.C. Rajapakse, L. Wong, R. Acharya (Eds.), Pattern Recognition in Bioinformatics. XIV, 186 pages. 2006. (Sublibrary LNBI).

Vol. 4144: T. Ball, R.B. Jones (Eds.), Computer Aided Verification. XV, 564 pages. 2006.

Vol. 4139: T. Salakoski, F. Ginter, S. Pyysalo, T. Pahikkala, Advances in Natural Language Processing. XVI, 771 pages. 2006. (Sublibrary LNAI).

Vol. 4138: X. Cheng, W. Li, T. Znati (Eds.), Wireless Algorithms, Systems, and Applications. XVI, 709 pages. 2006.

Vol. 4137: C. Baier, H. Hermanns (Eds.), CONCUR 2006 – Concurrency Theory. XIII, 525 pages. 2006.

Vol. 4136: R.A. Schmidt (Ed.), Relations and Kleene Algebra in Computer Science. XI, 433 pages. 2006.

Vol. 4135: C.S. Calude, M.J. Dinneen, G. Păun, G. Rozenberg, S. Stepney (Eds.), Unconventional Computation. X, 267 pages. 2006.

Vol. 4134: K. Yi (Ed.), Static Analysis. XIII, 443 pages. 2006.

Vol. 4133: J. Gratch, M. Young, R. Aylett, D. Ballin, P. Olivier (Eds.), Intelligent Virtual Agents. XIV, 472 pages. 2006. (Sublibrary LNAI).

Vol. 4132: S. Kollias, A. Stafylopatis, W. Duch, E. Oja (Eds.), Artificial Neural Networks – ICANN 2006, Part II. XXXIV, 1028 pages. 2006.

Vol. 4131: S. Kollias, A. Stafylopatis, W. Duch, E. Oja (Eds.), Artificial Neural Networks – ICANN 2006, Part I. XXXIV, 1008 pages. 2006.

Vol. 4130: U. Furbach, N. Shankar (Eds.), Automated Reasoning. XV, 680 pages. 2006. (Sublibrary LNAI).

Vol. 4129: D. McGookin, S. Brewster (Eds.), Haptic and Audio Interaction Design. XII, 167 pages. 2006.

Vol. 4128: W.E. Nagel, W.V. Walter, W. Lehner (Eds.), Euro-Par 2006 Parallel Processing. XXXIII, 1221 pages. 2006.

Vol. 4127: E. Damiani, P. Liu (Eds.), Data and Applications Security XX. X, 319 pages. 2006.

Vol. 4126: P. Barahona, F. Bry, E. Franconi, N. Henze, U. Sattler, Reasoning Web. X, 269 pages. 2006.

Vol. 4124: H. de Meer, J.P. G. Sterbenz (Eds.), Self-Organizing Systems. XIV, 261 pages. 2006.

Vol. 4121: A. Biere, C.P. Gomes (Eds.), Theory and Applications of Satisfiability Testing - SAT 2006. XII, 438 pages. 2006.

Vol. 4119: C. Dony, J.L. Knudsen, A. Romanovsky, A. Tripathi (Eds.), Advanced Topics in Exception Handling Components. X, 302 pages. 2006.

Vol. 4117: C. Dwork (Ed.), Advances in Cryptology - CRYPTO 2006. XIII, 621 pages. 2006.

Vol. 4116: R. De Prisco, M. Yung (Eds.), Security and Cryptography for Networks. XI, 366 pages. 2006.

Vol. 4115: D.-S. Huang, K. Li, G.W. Irwin (Eds.), Computational Intelligence and Bioinformatics, Part III. XXI, 803 pages. 2006. (Sublibrary LNBI).

Vol. 4114: D.-S. Huang, K. Li, G.W. Irwin (Eds.), Computational Intelligence, Part II. XXVII, 1337 pages. 2006. (Sublibrary LNAI).

Vol. 4113: D.-S. Huang, K. Li, G.W. Irwin (Eds.), Intelligent Computing, Part I. XXVII, 1331 pages. 2006.

Vol. 4112: D.Z. Chen, D. T. Lee (Eds.), Computing and Combinatorics. XIV, 528 pages. 2006.

Vol. 4111: F.S. de Boer, M.M. Bonsangue, S. Graf, W.-P. de Roever (Eds.), Formal Methods for Components and Objects. VIII, 447 pages. 2006.

Vol. 4110: J. Díaz, K. Jansen, J.D.P. Rolim, U. Zwick (Eds.), Approximation, Randomization, and Combinatorial Optimization. XII, 522 pages. 2006.

Vol. 4109: D.-Y. Yeung, J.T. Kwok, A. Fred, F. Roli, D. de Ridder (Eds.), Structural, Syntactic, and Statistical Pattern Recognition. XXI, 939 pages. 2006.

Vol. 4108: J.M. Borwein, W.M. Farmer (Eds.), Mathematical Knowledge Management. VIII, 295 pages. 2006. (Sublibrary LNAI).

Vol. 4106: T.R. Roth-Berghofer, M.H. Göker, H. A. Güvenir (Eds.), Advances in Case-Based Reasoning. XIV, 566 pages. 2006. (Sublibrary LNAI).

Vol. 4105: B. Gunsel, A.K. Jain, A. M. Tekalp, B. Sankur (Eds.), Multimedia, Content Representation, Classification and Security. XIX, 804 pages. 2006.

Vol. 4104: T. Kunz, S.S. Ravi (Eds.), Ad-Hoc, Mobile, and Wireless Networks. XII, 474 pages. 2006.

Vol. 4103: J. Eder, S. Dustdar (Eds.), Business Process Management Workshops. XI, 508 pages. 2006.

Vol. 4102: S. Dustdar, J.L. Fiadeiro, A. Sheth (Eds.), Business Process Management. XV, 486 pages. 2006.

Vol. 4099: Q. Yang, G. Webb (Eds.), PRICAI 2006: Trends in Artificial Intelligence. XXVIII, 1263 pages. 2006. (Sublibrary LNAI).

Vol. 4098: F. Pfenning (Ed.), Term Rewriting and Applications. XIII, 415 pages. 2006.

Vol. 4097: X. Zhou, O. Sokolsky, L. Yan, E.-S. Jung, Z. Shao, Y. Mu, D.C. Lee, D. Kim, Y.-S. Jeong, C.-Z. Xu (Eds.), Emerging Directions in Embedded and Ubiquitous Computing. XXVII, 1034 pages. 2006.

Vol. 4096: E. Sha, S.-K. Han, C.-Z. Xu, M.H. Kim, L.T. Yang, B. Xiao (Eds.), Embedded and Ubiquitous Computing. XXIV, 1170 pages. 2006.

Vol. 4095: S. Nolfi, G. Baldassare, R. Calabretta, D. Marocco, D. Parisi, J.C. T. Hallam, O. Miglino, J.-A. Meyer (Eds.), From Animals to Animats 9. XV, 869 pages. 2006. (Sublibrary LNAI).

Vol. 4094: O. H. Ibarra, H.-C. Yen (Eds.), Implementation and Application of Automata. XIII, 291 pages. 2006.

Vol. 4093: X. Li, O.R. Zaïane, Z. Li (Eds.), Advanced Data Mining and Applications. XXI, 1110 pages. 2006. (Sublibrary LNAI).

Vol. 4092: J. Lang, F. Lin, J. Wang (Eds.), Knowledge Science, Engineering and Management. XV, 664 pages. 2006. (Sublibrary LNAI).

Vol. 4091: G.-Z. Yang, T. Jiang, D. Shen, L. Gu, J. Yang (Eds.), Medical Imaging and Augmented Reality. XIII, 399 pages. 2006.

Vol. 4090: S. Spaccapietra, K. Aberer, P. Cudré-Mauroux (Eds.), Journal on Data Semantics VI. XI, 211 pages. 2006.

Vol. 4089: W. Löwe, M. Südholt (Eds.), Software Composition. X, 339 pages. 2006.

Vol. 4088: Z.-Z. Shi, R. Sadananda (Eds.), Agent Computing and Multi-Agent Systems. XVII, 827 pages. 2006. (Sublibrary LNAI).

Vol. 4087: F. Schwenker, S. Marinai (Eds.), Artificial Neural Networks in Pattern Recognition. IX, 299 pages. 2006. (Sublibrary LNAI).

Vol. 4085: J. Misra, T. Nipkow, E. Sekerinski (Eds.), FM 2006: Formal Methods. XV, 620 pages. 2006.

Vol. 4084: M.A. Wimmer, H.J. Scholl, Å. Grönlund, K.V. Andersen (Eds.), Electronic Government. XV, 353 pages. 2006.

Vol. 4083: S. Fischer-Hübner, S. Furnell, C. Lambrinoudakis (Eds.), Trust and Privacy in Digital Business. XIII, 243 pages. 2006.

Vol. 4082: K. Bauknecht, B. Pröll, H. Werthner (Eds.), E-Commerce and Web Technologies. XIII, 243 pages. 2006.

Vol. 4081: A. M. Tjoa, J. Trujillo (Eds.), Data Warehousing and Knowledge Discovery. XVII, 578 pages. 2006.

Vol. 4080: S. Bressan, J. Küng, R. Wagner (Eds.), Database and Expert Systems Applications. XXI, 959 pages. 2006.

Vol. 4079: S. Etalle, M. Truszczyński (Eds.), Logic Programming. XIV, 474 pages. 2006.

Vol. 4077: M.-S. Kim, K. Shimada (Eds.), Geometric Modeling and Processing - GMP 2006. XVI, 696 pages. 2006.